PARAGON
ISSUES IN
PHILOSOPHY

PARAGON ISSUES IN PHILOSOPHY

FORTHCOMING TITLES

THE PARAGON ISSUES IN PHILOSOPHY SERIES

At colleges and universities, interest in the traditional areas of philosophy remains strong. Many new currents flow within them, too, but some of these—the rise of cognitive science, for example, or feminist philosophy—went largely unnoticed in undergraduate philosophy courses until the end of the 1980s. The Paragon Issues in Philosophy Series responds to both perennial and newly influential concerns by bringing together a team of able philosophers to address the fundamental issues in philosophy today and to outline the state of contemporary discussion about them.

More than twenty volumes are scheduled; they are organized into three major categories. The first covers the standard topics—metaphysics, theory of knowledge, ethics, and political philosophy—stressing innovative developments in those disciplines. The second focuses on more specialized but still vital concerns in the philosophies of science, religion, history, sport, and other areas. The third category explores new work that relates philosophy and fields such as feminist criticism, medicine, economics, technology, and literature.

The level of writing is aimed at undergraduate students who have little previous experience studying philosophy. The books provide brief but accurate introductions that appraise the state of the art in their fields and show how the history of thought about their topics developed. Each volume is complete in itself but also complements others in the series.

Traumatic change characterizes these last years of the twentieth century: all of it involves philosophical issues. The editorial staff at Paragon House has worked with us to develop this series. We hope it will encourage the understanding needed in our times, which are as complicated and problematic as they are promising.

John K. Roth
Claremont McKenna College

Frederick Sontag
Pomona College

CRITICAL THEORY: THE ESSENTIAL READINGS

ALSO BY DAVID INGRAM

EDITED BY

DAVID INGRAM
LOYOLA UNIVERSITY
CHICAGO, ILLINOIS

&

JULIA SIMON-INGRAM
WASHINGTON UNIVERSITY
ST. LOUIS, MISSOURI

CRITICAL THEORY
THE
ESSENTIAL READINGS

PARAGON HOUSE · NEW YORK

FIRST EDITION, 1992

PUBLISHED IN THE UNITED STATES BY PARAGON HOUSE

PARAGON HOUSE
90 FIFTH AVENUE
NEW YORK, NY 10011

COPYRIGHT © 1991 BY PARAGON HOUSE

SERIES DESIGN BY KATHY KIKKERT

LIBRARY OF CONGRESS CATALOGING-IN-PUBLICATION DATA

CRITICAL THEORY : THE ESSENTIAL READINGS / EDITED BY
    DAVID INGRAM AND JULIA SIMON-INGRAM. — 1ST ED.
        P.   CM. — (PARAGON ISSUES IN PHILOSOPHY)
    COMPANION VOLUME TO: CRITICAL THEORY AND PHILOSOPHY /
DAVID INGRAM. 1990.
    ISBN 1-55778-353-5 : $15.95
    1. CRITICAL THEORY. I. INGRAM, DAVID, 1952–   . II. SIMON-
INGRAM, JULIA, 1961–   III. INGRAM, DAVID, 1952–   .
CRITICAL THEORY AND PHILOSOPHY. IV. SERIES.
BD175.C75   1991
142—DC20   90-40648
                                                            CIP

MANUFACTURED IN THE UNITED STATES OF AMERICA
THE PAPER USED IN THIS PUBLICATION MEETS THE MINIMUM
REQUIREMENTS OF AMERICAN NATIONAL STANDARD FOR INFORMATION
SCIENCES—PERMANENCE OF PAPER FOR PRINTED LIBRARY
MATERIALS, ANSI Z39.48-1984.

10   9   8   7   6   5   4   3   2   1

CONTENTS

PREFACE

Critical Theory: The Essential Readings is designed to provide a survey of the most important writings by critical theorists and their critics. The selections have been chosen for their accessibility to undergraduate and graduate students who have had little or no exposure to critical theory. (In the case of Adorno, this consideration weighed against excerpting selections from his late masterpieces, *Negative Dialectics* and *Aesthetic Theory*.) The choice and sequence of subheadings have also been designed to facilitate accessibility. In general, more difficult topics of foundation and method follow those devoted to social analysis and ideology critique. This organization roughly corresponds to the chapter headings of the companion text, *Critical Theory and Philosophy*. Ideally, the selections in the anthology should be read in conjunction with the textbook, especially at the introductory undergraduate level. The introduction offers a sense of the continuity, breadth, and diversity of the selections presented.

For the sake of brevity, we focus primarily on what are unquestionably the four major representatives of critical theory: Theodor Adorno, Max Horkheimer, Herbert Marcuse, and Jürgen Habermas. As it turns out, they were also the ones who most devoted themselves to working out the philosophical justification of critical theory.

In some cases the original pieces were too long to be included in their entirety and were therefore excerpted. We have attempted to preserve maximum continuity in the overall flow of the argument.

David Ingram
Loyola University of Chicago

Julia Simon-Ingram
Washington University
June 1, 1990

ACKNOWLEDGMENTS

Preparing an anthology requires the assistance of many people. We would like to thank Loyola University of Chicago for research support for this project, and Betsy Wootten and Susan Nishiyama at Kresge College of the University of California, Santa Cruz, for their help in preparing the manuscript. Our thanks also go to Karen Bassi of UC/Santa Cruz for assisting in the Latin translations. Without the support of our authors, this task would have been much more difficult; we thank Seyla Benhabib, Nancy Fraser, and Jürgen Habermas for their assistance. We are also grateful to Shierry Nicholsen for her willingness to translate the Habermas essay on short notice. We would like to thank Don Fehr for providing help in the initial stages of the project. Finally, we are especially grateful to Jo Glorie at Paragon House for her assistance during difficult negotiations and her commitment to seeing this volume through to the end.

Acknowledgment is also made to other publishers of included materials:

Adorno, Theodor W., "How to Look at Television," copyright © 1954 by the Regents of the University of California. Reprinted from the *Quarterly of Film, Radio and Television*, Vol. 8, no. 3 (Spring 1954), 213–235, by permission of the University of California Press.

————, "Freudian Theory and the Pattern of Fascist Propaganda," reprinted from *Gesammelte Schriften*, Vol. 8, 408–433, by permission of Suhrkamp Verlag, Frankfurt am Main, Federal Republic of Germany.

————, "Society," reprinted by permission of Europäische Verlags-Anstalt.

————, "Why Philosophy?" reprinted from *Man and Philosophy* 4, 11–24, by permission of Max Hueber Verlag.

Adorno, Theodor W. and Horkheimer, Max, "The Concept of Enlightenment," reprinted from *Dialectic of Enlightenment*, 3–42, by permission of Continuum/Crossroads Publishing Company.

Benhabib, Seyla, "The Utopian Dimension of Communicative Ethics," reprinted from *New German Critique*, no. 35, 83–96, by permission of *New German Critique* and the author.

Foucault, Michel, "The Subject and Power," reprinted from *Michel Foucault: Beyond Hermeneutics and Structuralism*, 208–226, copyright © 1982, 1983 by the University of Chicago, by permission of the University of Chicago Press.

Fraser, Nancy, "What's Critical About Critical Theory? The Case of Habermas and Gender," reprinted from *Unruly Practices: Power, Discourse and Gender in Contemporary Social Theory*, copyright © 1989 by the Regents of the University of Minnesota. Originally appeared in *New German Critique*, no. 33. Reprinted by permission of the University of Minnesota Press.

Habermas, Jürgen, "An Alternative Way Out of the Philosophy of the Subject: Communicative Versus Subject-Centered Reason," reprinted from *The Philosophical Discourse of Modernity: Twelve Lectures*, trans. Frederick Lawrence, translation copyright © 1987 by the Massachusetts Institute of Technology. This work originally appeared in German under the title *Der Philosophische Diskurs der Moderne: Zwölf Vorlesungen*, copyright © 1985 Suhrkamp Verlag, Frankfurt am Main, Federal Republic of Germany. Reprinted by permission of the MIT Press.

————, "Knowledge and Human Interests: A General Perspective," reprinted from *Knowledge and Human Interests*, 301–317, by permission of Beacon Press.

————, "Modernity: An Unfinished Project," originally appeared under the title "Die Moderne—ein unvollendetes Projekt," translated and reprinted by permission of Suhrkamp Verlag, Frankfurt am Main, Federal Republic of Germany.

————, "The Relation of Practical Questions to Truth" and "The Model of the Suppression of Generalizable Interests," reprinted from *Legitimation Crisis*, 102–117, by permission of Beacon Press.

————, "What Does a Legitimation Crisis Mean Today? Legitimation Problems in Late Capitalism," reprinted from *Social Research* (Winter 1973) by permission of *Social Research*.

————, "Technology and Science as 'Ideology'," reprinted from *Toward a Rational Society*, 81–127, by permission of Beacon Press.

Horkheimer, Max, "Materialism and Morality," reprinted from *Telos*, Vol. 69 (Fall 1986), 85–118, by permission of Telos Press.

————, "Means and Ends," reprinted from *Eclipse of Reason*, 3–57, by permission of Continuum/Crossroads Publishing Company.

————, "Traditional and Critical Theory," reprinted from *Critical Theory: Selected Essays: Max Horkheimer*, 188–243, by permission of Continuum/Crossroads Publishing Company.

Lyotard, Jean-François, *The Postmodern Condition: A Report on Knowledge*, sections 4, 5, 10 and 14, trans. Geoff Bennington and Brian Massumi, translation copyright © 1984 by the Regents of the University of Minnesota. This work originally appeared under the title *La Condition postmoderne: rapport sur le savoir*, copyright © 1979 Les Editions de Minuit. Reprinted by permission of the University of Minnesota Press and Les Editions de Minuit.

Marcuse, Herbert, "The Catastrophe of Liberation," reprinted from *One-*

Dimensional Man: Studies in the Ideology of Advanced Industrial Society, 225–246, reprinted by permission of Beacon Press.

———, "Freedom and Freud's Theory of the Instincts," reprinted from *Five Lectures*, 1–27, by permission of Beacon Press.

———, "On Hedonism," reprinted from *Negations: Essays in Critical Theory*, 159–200, by permission of Beacon Press.

———, "Philosophy and Critical Theory," reprinted from *Negations: Essays in Critical Theory*, 134–158, by permission of Beacon Press.

INTRODUCTION

In 1937 the *Journal of the Institute for Social Research* published a programmatic essay by its chief editor and director, Max Horkheimer, entitled "Traditional and Critical Theory."[1] From that moment *critical theory* has designated a school of thought (known by many as simply the Frankfurt School) whose most prominent members include the writers represented in this volume: Theodor W. Adorno, Herbert Marcuse, Jürgen Habermas, and Max Horkheimer.[2]

Critical theory has been variously characterized as a radical social theory (or sociology), a sophisticated form of cultural criticism combining Freudian and Marxist ideas, and a utopian style of philosophical speculation deeply rooted in Jewish and German idealism. For their own part, critical theorists saw themselves as responding to the historical events of their day. The changing composition and direction of the European labor movement and the evolution of Soviet communism and Western capitalism attracted their attention initially. They later expanded their focus to include the decline of patriarchy in the nuclear family; the psychosocial dynamics underlying authoritarian, anti-Semitic, and fascist tendencies; and the rising potential for totalitarian mind control in the mass production and consumption of "culture."

In assembling this anthology we have organized these themes around seven topic headings. The initial sections deal with topics that are relatively concrete, followed by sections treating more abstract methodological issues.[3] Part I, on critical theory and philosophy, addresses the theory/practice problem. The second part follows with a discussion of the dialectic of enlightenment. The latter discussion further elaborates the theory/practice problem by showing how philosophy reflects the very contradictions—inherent in modern "rationalized" societies—it seeks to criticize. These contradictions are examined in greater detail in Part III. The essays in this section show how reason, which ostensibly emancipates and enlightens, issues in the dominance of technology and science, the fragmentation of masses susceptible to authoritarianism, and the "commodification" of culture.

The section on ethics that follows brings together some of the most important themes of Frankfurt School philosophy. The various critiques of modern morality offered here attempt to sketch out the social and political conditions requisite for achieving true freedom, justice, and happiness. They also raise questions regarding the foundations and methods of ethical reflection and social critique treated explicitly in Part V. The essays in Part VI, by Jürgen Habermas, reformulate these methodological questions in an attempt to provide a more analytically rigorous grounding of moral reason. His appeal to the communicative basis of moral reason in evaluating the dialectic of enlightenment (here reflected in essays dealing with legitimation crises and other forms of modern social disintegration) rounds out this anthology. Part VII concludes with critical appraisals of Habermas's work by poststructuralists, postmodernists, and feminists.

CRITICAL THEORY AND PHILOSOPHY

Unlike most contemporary theories of society, whose primary aim is to provide the best description and explanation of social phenomena, critical theories are chiefly concerned with evaluating the freedom, justice, and happiness of societies. In their concern with values they show themselves more akin to moral philosophy than to predictive science.

From its earliest inception in ancient Greece, philosophy designated *rational* inquiry into basic principles of reality that had hitherto been the exclusive province of myth, poetry, and religion. Writing about contemporary philosophy, Adorno points out ("Why Philosophy?") that the dual nature of classical philosophy—at once rational and ontological—has broken apart into two diametrically opposed tendencies: the one subservient to scientific specialization and analysis, the other (largely inspired by the existential phenomenology of such thinkers as Martin Heidegger) oriented toward a global, prerational, and poetic disclosure of Being in general. At the same time, he observes, these tendencies converge in their abandonment of critical thought. Anglo-American logical positivists criticize the existential philosophy of their Continental counterparts for being uncritical in its speculative reference to empirically unverifiable "essences." But logical positivists, Adorno argues, are just as uncritical in their assumption that true knowledge corresponds to conceptually unmediated facts. Thus, existential phenomenologists rightly debunk the artificiality of distinctions drawn by philosophical analysis. However, they too are uncritical in their acceptance of a true being whose original meaning somehow precedes conceptual articulation.

According to Adorno, neither adherence to the "facts" as they present themselves to scientific analysis nor poetic receptivity to a preordained and prediscursive horizon of meaning transcending human thought and volition (Being) realizes the rational (and critical) potential of philosophy. On the contrary, critical philosophy resists immediate identification with what exists. Thought and reality are mutually interdependent but irreducible terms. Hence, for Adorno, philosophy presupposes the *negative* "unity" of subject and object, conceptual thought and sensuous being, transcendent idea and mundane reality, universal essence and particular fact, "ought" and "is." This dialectical unity, he notes, was first articulated by German philosophy during the late eighteenth and early nineteenth centuries and enabled thinkers like Hegel and Marx to grasp existing social reality as a contradictory movement anticipating resolution in a free and just society. While philosophy can no longer guarantee this resolution, it can hope, Adorno believes, "for reconciliation with the nonidentical that is being degraded continuously by affirmative philosophies" (29).

Marcuse's essay "Philosophy and Critical Theory" helps situate Adorno's argument within the context of classical German philosophy. Following Kant and Hegel—the two great philosophers of German Idealism—he maintains that philosophy (theory) and social reform (practice) are inseparable. Construction of a free, just, and happy society must be guided by philosophical reflection, which emancipates us from ideology and dogma. Conversely, reason, understood as a collective enterprise of mutual critique, demands for its realization a society of free individuals; that is, individuals who are free from want and from the domination that comes with social inequality and injustice. In the words of Marcuse, "the philosophical construction of reason is replaced by the creation of a rational society. . . . The philosophical ideals of a better world and of true Being are incorporated into the practical aim of struggling mankind, where they take on a human form" (p. 9).

Yet, as Marcuse and Horkheimer remind us, critical theory must also criticize its own philosophical assumptions. It accomplishes this by using the method of historical materialism developed by Marx, which shows how the goals of political practice, far from representing ahistorical ideals, are generated within existing social reality as dialectical countertendencies. Most importantly, historical materialism shows how a one-sided reliance on philosophical idealism can become ideological. First, idealism tends to conceive its goals as if they were attainable by individuals in abstraction from social change. Freedom and happiness are reduced to "states of mind" divorced from material (economic, social, and political) constraints. To the extent that material reality is seen as a conditioning factor, its imperfect instantiation of freedom and happiness is never fully recognized. Second, by asserting that existing material conditions embody the ideal (a view more typical of Hegel than Kant) philosophical idealism ends up justifying the universal validity of practices and institutions that sustain historically contingent forms of class domination. Marcuse therefore agrees with Adorno that critical theory must be conceived as a dialectical movement within existing social reality. In the final analysis, the contradiction in which philosophy finds itself—between idealism and materialism—is but a reflection of a society "in crisis" torn between its transcendent ideals and its historical imperfections.

THE DIALECTIC OF ENLIGHTENMENT: REASON AS EMANCIPATION AND DOMINATION

Critical theorists maintain that the "crisis" of modern society is directly related to the rational social basis that forms the core of their own critical philosophy. As Horkheimer's essay "Means and Ends" makes clear, this crisis involves the degeneration of moral reflection regarding ultimate ends—the basic standards of right and wrong, good and bad, which are brought to bear in any critical evaluation. Growing out of religious and metaphysical concerns, philosophy from antiquity through the Middle Ages sought insight into the universal structures and ultimate ends implicit in objective nature. From a moral perspective, it was assumed that "laws of nature" reflected divine commands specifying "natural" rights and obligations. However, as philosophy emancipated itself from religious dogma, reason increasingly signified the subject's capacity to calculate the most efficient means for attaining any end whatsoever. Limited to instrumental calculation, reason retained its universal validity at the cost of abandoning its moral content. Persons who are rational in this sense take responsibility for the consequences of "freely" chosen actions by using formal procedures for calculating efficient means. So construed, reason becomes *subjective*. That is, it serves "the subject's interest in relation to self-preservation—be it that of the single individual, or of the community on whose maintenance that of the individual depends" (35).

There is profound irony in Horkheimer's account of the Enlightenment. Reason was supposed to secure the individual's subjective moral freedom with respect to religious dogma and fatalism. However, by criticizing metaphysical speculation on ultimate ends, reason undermines its own critical foundation. Freedom and justice are no longer valued for their own sake. At most, they are "means" that can be discarded whenever it is prudent to do so. But that is not the only paradox implicit in Horkheimer's account. As he and Adorno argue in "The Concept of Enlightenment," the reduction of reason to means–ends calculation has far-reaching consequences for the entire organization of society. The defenders of enlightenment in the eighteenth century thought that the dissemination of reason would encourage the establishment of institutions permitting a critical formation of public opinion, an idea that clearly has democratic overtones. Yet the dissemination of means–ends rationality, Adorno and Horkheimer contend, promoted the one-sided growth of modern science and technology in ways that were thoroughly undemocratic.

Much of what Adorno and Horkheimer say still rings true. Integrated into an emergent capitalist economy, the techniques of rational management and efficient administration required forms of hierarchy and segmentation that heightened domination. Governed by the fortuitous forces of the market (and reflecting the uncoordinated decisions of entrepreneurs "rationally" seeking to maximize profits), this economy produced unintended side effects—recessions, uneven development, uncontrolled growth and waste, and environmental pollution—which today confront us with a new form of unfreedom that may well be more insidious than that imposed by either religion or personal tyranny. Yet Adorno, Horkheimer, and Marcuse go well beyond this diagnosis in arguing that modern capitalism embodies a form of totalitarianism that is not, in their opinion, essentially different from that prevalent in bureaucratic socialist societies. For them, East and West converge in their conceptual reduction of nature and humanity to an objectified system of mathematical equivalences and functional exchange relationships susceptible to total prediction and control. Given this dismal diagnosis, it comes as no surprise that what they perceive to be the mythic origins of reason, understood as an instrument of classification and identification essential to the constitution of nature and self as unified identities, comes back to haunt rationalized society in the form of a new fatalism.

CULTURE AND TECHNOLOGY AS IDEOLOGY

Adorno's essay "Society" furnishes a summary account of the ways in which the social rationalization of modern society (Weber) have profoundly changed culture and technology. The technological division of labor into efficient units of production transforms modern society into a unified organism held together by functional interdependencies arranged hierarchically and controlled from the top (Durkheim). The most important interdependencies are exchange relations governed by the price system, which reduces all values—human and material—to quantifiable commodities. As the capitalist system extends its hegemony throughout the world it achieves ever higher levels of integration and adaptation—thanks in large part to the intervention of the state. The "culture industry" in turn provides the consumer goods that endow individuals with a false sense of happiness.

Adorno notes that from an external, or *objective*, point of view, modern society appears to be a seamless totality. However, from the internal standpoint of the *subjects* who experience life within the system, society still appears to be something alien and overwhelming—a kind of fate opposed to their desire for self-determination. Still, even Adorno acknowledges that the residual embers of class conflict and class consciousness are not wholly extinguished; in his opinion the cynical realism of workers and marginalized groups testifies to the continued existence of contradictions within the system itself.

According to Adorno, critical social theory must try to understand society the way it is understood by the subjects who live within it, while showing how this understanding both reflects and resists the totalitarian tendencies of social production. Critical theory, he insists, must penetrate the popular ideology of harmony and happiness that pervades average consumer consciousness. Adorno's description of the powerful effects of TV in shaping consumer consciousness ("How to Look at Television") exemplifies this form of critique. For Adorno, "the repetitiveness, the self-sameness, and the ubiquity of modern mass culture tend to make for automatized reactions and to weaken the forces of individual resistance" (p. 71). In this way the reduction of culture to popular consumer commodity reinforces authoritarian and conformist patterns of behavior. As Adorno rightly notes, resignation, avoidance of conflict, anti-intellectualism, and stereotyping are familiar messages of mass culture that lend themselves all too easily to political propaganda.

These psychological dynamics are developed further by Adorno in "Freudian Theory and the Pattern of Fascist Propaganda." In Adorno's opinion, the allure of fascist propaganda presupposes the transformation of autonomous individuals into a mass requiring organization by a leader. Appealing to Freud, Adorno argues that the basic mechanism for generating moral conscience in the individual—identification with the father—is perverted into an authoritarian identification with the leader. With the decreasing authority of the father as an autonomous figure, individuals narcissistically project their own self-image on a leader who is both like them—infantile, rebellious, ordinary, resentful—and "better" than them: the ideal extension of their own ego. In this way "the leader image gratifies the follower's twofold wish to submit to authority and to be authority himself" (p. 91). The sadomasochistic dynamics motivating this identification further explain the sort of negative integration achieved by the mass, which defines itself in opposition to out-groups (workers, socialists, Jews, homosexuals, gypsies, etc.) who, in comparison to the mass, are perceived to be inferior, superior, or both at once. Ultimately, fascist propaganda merely exploits the fragmentation and instinctual repression already present in modern society.

Given the pessimistic tone of Adorno's analysis of mass society, the question arises whether all critical theorists are as resigned to playing the role of detached skeptic as he was. That they are not is apparent from the selections by Marcuse and Habermas. Both of these philosophers pinpoint countervailing tendencies within the system which, they believe, might realize the emancipatory legacy of the Enlightenment. In "The Catastrophe of Liberation" Marcuse argues that technology and science—in short, social rationalization—need not issue in increased domination. The key to exploding the totalitarian shell of rationalized society resides in the emancipation of technology itself. Appealing to the archaic relationship between art, political praxis, and technique in classical philosophy, Marcuse suggests that, having once achieved the mechanization of all socially necessary but repressive labor, society could transform science and technology into a means for freeing and pacifying nature. This would involve a qualitative change in the very essence of technology and science: from an instrument of objectification and domination to a medium of receptivity.

Despite the obvious attraction of this "solution" to the dialectic of enlightenment, Habermas contends ("Technology and Science as 'Ideology' ") that a transformation of technology of the sort envisaged by Marcuse seems all but inconceivable. Arguing that the objectifying structure of science and technology is necessitated by the very nature of objective cognition and self-preservation, Habermas suggests that emancipation can only occur when the existence of a different kind of rationality is acknowledged—one that is necessitated by an equally fundamental interest in achieving an integrated identity through free, undistorted *communication*. Science and technology, he contends, do not essentially tend toward totalitarian domination, but they do function as "ideology" in a society that stresses economic growth to the detriment of democratic self-determination nurtured in free, open discussion among social and political equals. Consequently, he concludes, the search for emancipatory possibilities must begin with the democratization of society, support for which can be found in various resistance movements.

ETHICS AND CRITICAL THEORY

Critical theorists are fond of reminding us that rationalism begins by promising freedom, justice, and happiness but ends up legitimating domination. The essays included in Part IV address the source of this contradiction and suggest possibilities for developing a more enlightened ethics. Horkheimer's essay "Materialism and Morality" exemplifies the method of ideology critique in its multilevel examination of modern morality. On the one hand, it reveals contradictions internal to bourgeois moral ideals. On the other hand, it shows how these ideals reflect social relations peculiar to capitalist society. Using the method of historical materialism, Horkheimer argues that bourgeois morality, like the contradictory society it legitimates, antici-pates an emancipated life in which these contradictions are resolved.

The internal critique focuses on Kant's exemplary—and highly rationalistic—formulation of bourgeois morality. As described in Kant's writings, morality consists of acting in a good-intentioned manner that is rationally consistent or harmonious with the actions of all rationally like-minded persons. It requires that we refrain from violating the rights of others even when such violation is in our self-interest. And it admonishes us to treat others as possessing intrinsic dignity and worth. Above all, it enjoins us to follow the dictates of our own conscience without heeding the com-mands of external (religious, political, and social) authority.

Horkheimer finds much that is valuable in Kant's moral philosophy. He points out, however, that respect for individual freedom and dignity remains insufficiently thought out. Moreover, he observes that what duty commands ultimately means whatever individuals, relying on their own fallible opinions, happen to think it commands. Besides its lack of moral content, the main difficulty with Kant's moral theory, Horkheimer notes, consists in its opposing reason (duty) to happiness, univer-sal interest to particular interest, freedom to instinctual motivation, and individual to society. In Horkheimer's judgment, Kant's ethics makes happiness coincidental to the attainment of individual moral freedom, and both freedom and happiness remain coincidental to the attainment of a just society.

Horkheimer supplements this internal critique with a materialist analysis showing how the tensions implicit in Kant's idealistic philosophy mirror tensions within a capitalist society regulated by contractual agreements. Under capitalism individuals feel torn between the competing demands of self-interest and morality and continu-ally identify their own particular interests with the good of all. At the same time, however, they experience their freedom and individuality as something internal (private), as opposed to the unfreedom and uniformity of physical (working-day) existence. Although Kant's moral philosophy postulates the ideal harmony of inter-ests in a community of free, rational beings, it does so, Horkheimer believes, in a manner that can only be described as ideological. In Horkheimer's opinion, it either postulates reason and freedom as eternal facts of human nature or it regards these preconditions of moral life as goals capable of being satisfactorily secured in a republic based on bourgeois principles of private property.

Horkheimer concludes his essay by indicating how, for a materialist perspective, bourgeois moral idealism points beyond itself and the capitalist society it reflects. Historical materialism emphasizes the inextricable connection between private morality and public life. The universal goal that Kant postulates for the isolated individual—freedom and happiness—can only be secured in a just society. In such a society, Horkheimer claims, "the degree of inequality of the life-conditions of individuals [should be] at least no greater than that dictated by the maintenance of the total social supply of goods at the given level" (194). Under these conditions the opposition between *is* and *ought*, particular and universal interest, freedom and happiness would no longer be necessary. The opposition among freedom, happiness, and justice demanded by Kant's formalistic conception of moral rationality ceases to compel once we realize that true freedom presupposes the satisfaction of human needs (the development of human powers) under democratic conditions guaranteeing equality of power.

Marcuse's contribution to the problem ("On Hedonism") is chiefly devoted to resolving the contradiction between happiness and reason that arises in modern moral philosophy. Like Horkheimer, he affirms the essential connection between rational freedom and happiness. Under capitalism, he argues, reason and happiness are opposed to one another; the "freely willed" universal law of moral duty confronts pleasure as something utterly subjective, particularistic, and instinctual. Rational behavior—whether it involves acting morally or just efficiently—requires the repression of desire. However, when desire is permitted satisfaction, it always appears under the guise of an immediate, irrational impulse. Under the assumption that pleasures as such are neither objectively good (true) nor objectively bad (false), bourgeois society, Marcuse claims, encourages the untrammeled pursuit of illusory goods (especially forms of wasteful consumption and destructive production) that ends up perpetuating unfreedom and unhappiness for the broad mass of people.

Marcuse returns to the hedonistic philosophy of Epicurus to redeem the idea of a pleasure that is intrinsically rational. On this model "true" pleasures are those that allow for the complete (integral and harmonious) development of human faculties, both intellectual and sensual. Appealing to Plato and Aristotle, Marcuse argues that the precondition for such development is a just society. Indeed, he notes that the exact determination of which pleasures are "true" must await the establishment of a fully emancipated democratic society in which all persons can rationally agree on their common interests independently of internal ideological constraints and external (class) domination. Although the determination of true pleasures—like the determination of basic instincts and sensory organs—is relative to the level of enlightenment, Marcuse does not hesitate to condemn the current regime of social production based on profit and consumption as contrary to true freedom, justice, and happiness. He believes that capitalism generates emancipatory needs it cannot satisfy.

Habermas's analysis of political legitimation develops some of the themes discussed by Horkheimer and Adorno concerning the relationship between truth, justice, freedom, and happiness. Habermas argues against the position of Weber and others that political institutions and norms are legitimated solely by public recognition of their validity *regardless of how this recognition comes about*. Belief in the legitimacy of such institutions and norms, he reminds us, can be ideologically coerced. Yet, as he himself acknowledges, in order to defend the notion of ideology and, therewith, the notion of *ideology critique*, one must show that the distinction (denied by many) between true and false interests, valid and invalid norms, general and particular interests, makes sense.

Positivists assume that only statements of fact are susceptible of being proved true and that prescriptive statements regarding values, norms, and obligations, which cannot be deduced logically from statements of fact, are neither true nor false. Although positivists concede that values, norms, and obligations may be justified with reference to more general (basic) moral principles, they hold that these principles, being "basic" and "underived," can have no further justification. Hence they conclude that all prescriptive statements ultimately rest on arbitrary, subjective choices (decisionism).

Habermas points out that this skepticism with respect to the truth or falsity of prescriptive statements follows from two questionable assumptions: that *true* means "corresponds to observed facts" and that *rationally justified* means "deductively proven." Appealing to the pragmatist account of argumentation developed by Charles Peirce and Stephen Toulmin, Habermas argues that rational justification must be conceived as a dialogical process of reaching agreement on contested statements. What ultimately establishes the validity (or truth) of a statement or norm is not its correspondence with facts or its logical derivation from more basic principles. Statements of fact, he notes, are interpretations (or conceptual constructs) that cannot be said to "correspond" to a preinterpreted ("given") reality in any meaningful sense. Since descriptive and prescriptive statements are interpretations—either of reality or of basic human needs—their claim to validity resides solely in the fact that all persons would agree on them under egalitarian conditions permitting free and open discussion—what Habermas calls the "ideal speech situation."

Given this model of justification, Habermas maintains that a norm or institution would be legitimate only if all persons affected by it unanimously agreed, under the conditions of argumentation stipulated above, that it was in their common interest. Contrary to Kant, then, the question of rights and duties can no more be answered in abstraction from historical needs and interests than can the question of valid needs and interests be answered apart from critical discourses instantiating certain rights and duties.

The remainder of Habermas's essay is chiefly devoted to examining how Western democracies violate the presumption of rational accountability by suppressing discussion regarding common interests behind the façade of "pseudo-compromise." Parties of unequal bargaining strength negotiate compromises expressing a strategic weighing of particular interests without first bothering to determine whether such interests are rational, or "generalizable." In conclusion Habermas suggests several ways in which the model of ideal speech might be used to critically expose pseudo-compromises and ideologies based on the suppression of generalizable interests.

THE FOUNDATIONS AND METHODS OF CRITICAL THEORY

Two problems emerged in our discussion of the ethics of critical theory. The first concerns the normative foundations of a social theory cognizant of its own insertion in historical reality. The normative standards critical theory brings to bear in evaluating historical reality are seen as specifying possibilities, potentials, and goals already implicit in that reality. The question therefore arises: To what extent do these ideals represent features of social life that are invariant, transhistorical, and necessarily and universally implicated in the human condition as such? To what extent are they shaped and transformed by historical forces that endow them with a content and validity peculiar to specific types of human society?

The second problem concerns the methods by which critical theorists discover and apply their normative standards for purposes of ideology critique. Which methods should guide critical theory: those of psychology, economics, history, philosophy, or social science? And how should these methods be interpreted and applied?

Horkheimer's essay "Traditional and Critical Theory" represents the earliest programmatic statement of the foundations and methods of critical theory. Traditional theories, Horkheimer claims, consist of a system of logically interconnected principles—reducible to mathematical equations linking simple elements—from whose combination particular causal laws are derived and predictions and explanations proferred. Controlled experiments are supposed to provide an indubitable and wholly objective (that is, value-free and factual) verification of laws and the theories from which they are derived. Such laws can then be used for purposes of dominating nature and society.

Traditional scientific theories, Horkheimer claims, are ideological in two senses. First, they falsely assume that "facts" exist independently of theoretical concepts and that theoretical concept formation (or scientific thought) is detached from historical circumstances that condition it from without. Modern science, he argues, is a product of capitalist society; its "positivistic" belief in the independence of theoretical insight and the independence of "objective" reality vis-à-vis existing social norms reflects the abstract individualism and alienation of that society. Second, Horkheimer claims that traditional theories in social science are ideological in that they reduce society to a system of ahistorical, lawlike regularities resistant to freely willed change. Worse still, they lend themselves to forms of social engineering that enhance the power of those at the top—industrialists, government bureaucrats, and managers—who seek more efficient methods of controlling those at the bottom.

Critical theories, Horkheimer claims, embody a different rationale; they aim at emancipating their addressees from ideology. In order to achieve this goal they must combine, he argues, the objective, explanatory methods of traditional theory with an empathetic understanding of subjective attitudes and experiences of actual historical agents. For Horkheimer, capitalist society does indeed operate according to economic laws that escape the *conscious* control of the producers. Nevertheless, as Marx noted, these laws contain internal contradictions that are reflected in the alienation and discontent of workers. To understand the "truth" implicit in their "false" consciousness of capitalism's contradictions requires a deeper philosophical reflection on the totality of society itself. Above all, it involves reflecting on the very cultural ideals that legitimate existing domination in order to determine their potential for realization given existing levels of technological development. Once enlightened about their real interests and the prospects for satisfying them, people will be freed from the compulsion of social habits based on false consciousness.

Written in 1937, Horkheimer's essay evinced confidence in the notion of an interdisciplinary social theory combining philosophy and various other social sciences. In the years immediately following the publication of this essay he and Adorno would develop this line of research in a number of studies while at the same time problematizing the synthesis of science and philosophy in their theoretical writings.[4] In many respects their theoretical writing became more philosophical and less scientific.

This trend is also evident in Marcuse's contribution. "Freedom and Freud's Theory of Instincts" advances an openly speculative reading of Freud's theory of instincts— the biological foundation Marcuse believed to be essential for grasping humanity's emancipatory goals. In *Civilization and Its Discontents* (1930) Freud argued that civilization is the product of two contradictory instincts: a life instinct (*eros*), which desires bonding and community, and a death instinct (*thanatos*), which desires separation and dissolution. Civilization cannot exist without social bonds that extend beyond the isolated family; yet social bonds based on work and moral constraint require the repression of sexuality (*eros*) and the splitting of the self into a rational *ego*, an instinctual *id*, and an internalized source of social domination, the *superego*. Progress is therefore paradoxical, for in Freud's reading civilization is necessarily incompatible with pleasure, freedom, and happiness and, worst of all, continually threatens to destroy itself in increasing fits of aggression.

Marcuse argues that the conflict between life and death instincts is not as absolute as Freud thought. Under the imperatives of the performance principle civilization has indeed pursued the goal of higher productivity at the expense of freedom and happiness. However, current levels of technological development and affluence, he claims, make possible the elimination of repressive production or its reduction to a minimum. Indeed, he believes that technological rationality, which currently follows the destructive impulse of *thanatos*, might serve the erotic desire for a liberated sexuality—a sexuality not limited by the demands of reproduction but encompassing the individual's entire aesthetic sensibility. In the final analysis, Marcuse is convinced that the biological constitution of the species pushes toward a resolution of life-and-death instincts requiring the total emancipation of society.

Habermas's earliest reflections on the foundations and methods of critical theory attempt to forge a middle path between the biologism of Marcuse's theory of instincts and the historicism of Horkheimer's critique of culture.[5] Yet its indebtedness to both approaches is evident. "Knowledge and Human Interests: A General Perspective" attacks the false objectivism of traditional theory by defending the close link between knowledge and interest. At the same time, it draws close parallels between critical social science and Freudian psychoanalysis as exemplary models of reflection aimed at emancipating subjects from forms of mental and behavioral compulsion (neurotic delusion and ideological false consciousness) rooted in social repression (domination).[6]

Habermas advances the idea that there are three kinds of knowledge: empirical-analytic, historical-hermeneutic, and critical. Each kind, he argues, possesses a distinct structure and methodology that rationally articulates a particular type of action. In turn, each type of action can be understood as furthering a basic interest in self-preservation and, indirectly, self-determination. The *empirical-analytic* sciences incorporate an objectifying experimental method that constitutes nature as a lawful system of interconnected facts. This method refines a prescientific mode of instrumental activity necessitated by a *technical* interest in controlling nature. The *historical-hermeneutic* sciences incorporate an interpretative method that constitutes social reality as a symbolic text comprising meaningful actions, artifacts, and events. The method of subjective understanding refines a prescientific mode of communicative activity necessitated by a *practical* interest in coordinating action and establishing a common identity (or mutual understanding) between persons. Finally, the *critical social* sciences incorporate a reflective method that combines both objectifying (causal explanatory) and interpretative procedures in determining which social regularities are invariant and which are not. The critique of ideology refines a prescientific mode of critical self-examination necessitated by an *emancipatory* interest in achieving freedom from domination.

In Habermas's opinion, these modes of knowledge and their corresponding action/interest frameworks are not simply "necessary" for the self-preservation of the human species at a certain stage in its evolution. Since self-preservation has come to mean living a good life, and since a good life has come to mean a life of freedom and rationality, they also serve the goal of emancipation. However, only in critical reflection does knowledge have direct, emancipatory consequences. And it is only here that knowledge shows itself to be *necessarily* dependent on interests. Indeed, for Habermas knowledge as instrument of self-preservation is inconceivable apart from knowledge aimed at emancipation, for the validity of statements can only be determined in rational discussion free of ideological constraint. "To this extent," Habermas concludes, "the truth of statements is based on anticipating the realization of the good life" (p. 264). Self-preservation and happiness, knowledge and freedom are thus explicitly united in emancipatory reflection. Yet, while "standards of reflection"—autonomy and responsibility—are indubitably present in the linguistic conditions constitutive of our very identities, knowledge of true needs remains less certain, depending on the relative state of social emancipation and justice achieved at any given moment.

COMMUNICATION AND SOCIAL CRISIS: RECENT TRENDS IN CRITICAL THEORY

Recent trends in critical theory attempt to deal with the issues discussed above in ways that are less overtly dialectical and speculative than the approaches taken by Adorno, Horkheimer, and Marcuse. The latter were influenced by Heidegger's existential critique of science and technology and even came to regard poetry and art as the proper medium of critical "thought." Contemporary critical theorists, by contrast, have turned to Anglo-American philosophy (pragmatism, philosophy of language, and philosophy of science) to clarify in a more analytically rigorous manner the foundations and methods of critical theory.

The most important figure among the new wave of critical theorists is Jürgen Habermas. In his essay "An Alternative Way Out of the Philosophy of the Subject: Communicative Versus Subject-Centered Reason" he argues that his predecessors failed to grasp the true nature of reason and thus ended up identifying reason with domination. Their mistake, he claims, involved conceiving rationality as the conceptual unification and instrumental calculation of objective processes by a sovereign subject seeking self-preservation. Such "subject-centered" rationality, Habermas contends, is a partial form of reasoning derived from a more basic type of communicative rationality. Communicative rationality involves competencies for structuring an *intersubjective* relationship based on free consent among equals. Its ideal is not the scientific one of sovereign mastery over nature but the democratic formation of a common identity under conditions of perfect freedom and reciprocity.

Habermas also contends that his predecessors did not adequately ground critical reason in universal structures. Thus, much of his research consists of showing how communicative rationality is necessarily implicated in the structure of ordinary speech. Communication (speaking) is the primary vehicle by which personal and social identity is shaped and mutual understanding regarding a shared world is brought about. Language, Habermas argues, has evolved to the point where one can distinguish propositional (descriptive), interpersonal (prescriptive), and personal (expressive) uses. In everyday speech geared toward facilitating interaction—what Habermas, following John Austin and John Searle, calls *speech action*—all three uses are combined. For example, whenever I promise to do something I simultaneously assert (describe) something to be done, prescribe to myself an interpersonal obligation, and express a personal intention. Most important, what I say (describe, prescribe, and express) is tacitly accompanied by validity claims: to the truth of what I assert to be the case, the rightness of what I prescribe, and the sincerity of what I express. These universal claims, Habermas contends, require rational justification if challenged, but rational justification implies anticipating an ideal speech situation.

Hence, according to Habermas, the ideal freedom and reciprocity associated with communicative rationality is necessarily presupposed whenever we engage in speech action, no matter how distorted our communication may be.

The second focus of Habermas's research has been to show how the dialectic of enlightenment is not, contrary to the opinions of first-generation critical theorists, necessitated by rationality as such, but rather stems from its one-sided and distorted development under capitalism. Although communicative rationality consists only in formal procedures of free, reciprocal conversation, it nonetheless implies, Habermas claims, an *ideally* democratic and egalitarian community whose specific meaning must be continually and collectively reinterpreted. However, as he points out in "What Does a Legitimation Crisis Mean Today? Legitimation Problems in Late Capitalism," the dynamics of the social welfare state essentially oppose democratization. Late capitalist societies attempt to resolve chronic economic crises of overproduction characteristic of laissez-faire capitalism through state intervention in the economy. This burdens the state with a new contradiction. It must allocate scarce tax revenues requisite for sustaining economic growth while compensating the victims of such growth. In order to conceal this contradiction and thereby retain the broad loyalty of citizens who demand that their interests be served, the state, Habermas argues, must suppress debate regarding the foundations of the system: private property. The "depoliticization" of the public, which the political system encourages, should enable the state to plan the economy free of demands for public accountability. But this, Habermas notes, has not happened, since increased state intervention in education, health, and welfare tends to *re*politicize the public. In his opinion, the only thing standing in the way of a legitimation crisis is the continued efficacy of bourgeois ideologies revolving around competitive achievement, possessive individualism, familial privatism, and consumerism. However, he also observes that the requisite motivation for competing and consuming is continually threatened by the social welfare policies of the state, the deskilling of manual labor, the increasing desire for nonmonetary forms of compensation (leisure, benefits, job control, etc.), and most importantly, the emancipatory values gravitating around modern science, art, and morality.

CRITICAL THEORY AND ITS CRITICS

No discussion of critical theory would be complete without addressing three recent trends in social philosophy that at once complement and challenge its idealistic heritage. These trends are poststructuralism, postmodernism, and feminism. Together they comprise a formidable critique of existing forms of domination based on race, gender, class, and technical expertise. At the same time, they challenge critical theory's faith in the emancipatory potential of reason.

Poststructuralism and postmodernism designate distinct but overlapping tendencies. Both are critical of idealist philosophies that reduce the constitution of reality to the meaning-endowing achievements of a sovereign subject. Moreover, they also adopt a skeptical stance with respect to universal reason. To begin with, they argue that the basic rules, norms, and structures governing linguistic and cultural practices are not rigidly fixed but undergo constant mutation. Consequently, they emphasize the contextuality and relativity of all structures, including those governing "rational" behavior. However, like first-generation critical theory, these movements also adopt a skeptical stance with respect to the emancipatory achievements of reason. They too are opposed to the overextension of bureaucratic domination, the totalitarian subordination of dissident subcultures to the dominant culture, and the marginalization of the ethical and the aesthetic with respect to the scientific and technological—trends they blame on the rational demand for systematic unity, purity, and universality.

Among those social theorists who are typically considered to be poststructuralist in orientation, one in particular has come closest to articulating the concerns of critical theorists: Michel Foucault. His essay "The Subject and Power" summarizes the major themes of his research spanning several decades and relates them to the work of the Frankfurt School. To begin with, Foucault is deeply concerned with the ways in which human beings are constituted as autonomous subjects who are subjected to control by other persons and by themselves. Like Adorno and Horkheimer (following Hegel and Marx), he conceives this process as one of objectification, facilitated by human science, dividing and exclusionary practices, and internalization of sexuality and gender roles. Reason and power both play a part in this process, but Foucault eschews any global theory of social rationalization and domination of the sort advanced by Adorno and Horkheimer. Instead, he undertakes an empirical analysis of power struggles and power relations. These, he argues, cannot all be reduced to economic exploitation and political domination. Since the sixteenth century a new kind of relationship revolving around "pastoral" forms of power has emerged. Pastoral power originated in Christianity's organization of the means of salvation and became secularized in the modern state's concern with sustaining the social welfare of its citizenry. Most important, the human sciences that deploy pastoral power—medicine, economics, social statistics, administration, penology, psychiatry, and education—have the dual effect of "individualizing" subjects and integrating them into a "totalized" framework: the general population.

The ethical and political goal of today's struggles, Foucault claims, cannot be liberation from power per se but liberation from the peculiar type of power relationship associated with the individualizing/totalizing practices of the state. Since power relations are as diffuse as they are concentrated, liberation must assume the form of local struggles and strategies. Although Foucault thinks it important for purposes of analysis to distinguish, as Habermas does, power relations from communication and instrumental capacities, he insists that none of these essential aspects of social life exist apart from the other. In some areas of life communicative reciprocity and freedom may be more significant than the play of power relations, but there is no communication without some constraint. Habermas's "ideal speech situation" is therefore a rather empty and impractical goal in Foucault's reading. More fundamentally, in Foucault's opinion, power can only exist where there is freedom to resist. Power relationships are therefore not opposed to communicative relationships based on freedom and are not relationships to which ideal notions of free universal consent (legitimacy) meaningfully apply. Yet, despite the fact that there can be no rational moral foundation authorizing resistance to particular forms of power, Foucault encourages the possibility of changing power relations as such, since their own configuration is based on antagonism. In his opinion, domination (the total fusion of power relations, strategies of control, and disciplinary effects) essentially encounters resistance from within.

The key to Foucault's analysis of modern society is the interlocking of power and knowledge. The same applies to the work of Jean-François Lyotard. Our excerpts from *The Postmodern Condition: A Report on Knowledge* begin with criticism of the distinction between traditional and critical knowledge developed by Horkheimer. According to Lyotard, traditional theory portrays society as a unified adaptive system utilizing technological knowledge in order to maximize performative output (economic growth, political stability, etc.). Critical theory, by contrast, portrays society as inherently contradictory and susceptible to emancipatory reflection. Both views fail to recognize the true nature of the social bond, which incorporates traditional and critical aspects. The social bond consists of an interweaving of heterogeneous "language games" whose structure conforms neither to the technical transfer of information nor to the unconstrained achievement of mutual understanding between disinterested interlocutors. In Lyotard's opinion, consensus regarding the rules of a language game may serve to limit dissent temporarily, but the "agonistic" or "conflictual" aspect of the game requires speakers to displace the balance of power by surprising their interlocutors with "new moves," or innovative utterances. Even the most bureaucratically institutionalized language games (such as those in science and law) require occasional dissent from and transformation of the rules of the game in order to avoid entropy.

The implications of Lyotard's analysis of the social bond prove devastating for any global theory of legitimation. The modern demand for rational foundations, he argues, turns back upon itself. "Reason" delegitimates its own claim to universal validity. For Lyotard, a purely "positive" or factual science cannot legitimate the values and prescriptive norms that regulate its own discourse, since descriptive and prescriptive language games are radically heterogeneous. Efficiency alone cannot provide legitimation, since the criteria of efficiency—the goal toward which the system adapts itself—must be decided by the members of the system. Nevertheless, a critical theory guided by the criterion of unconstrained consensus will be just as useless in this regard. Habermas's theory of legitimation, Lyotard claims, rests on two false assumptions: "that it is possible for all speakers to come to agreement on which rules or metaprescriptions are universally valid for language games, when it is clear that language games are heteronomous, subject to heterogeneous sets of pragmatic rules" and that "the goal of dialogue is consensus" (333). The only concept of legitimacy and justice that takes into account the "postmodern" delegitimation of reason, Lyotard believes, is one that recognizes both the cybernetic (systemic) and social (agonistic) aspects as interlocking elements. So construed, the aim of postmodern politics would be resistance to entropic "terror," which threatens to close off innovation and disruption. This goal, Lyotard concludes, can only be achieved by permitting the public "free access to the memory and data banks" (334).

Contemporary critical theorists have only recently begun to respond to the challenge posed by Foucault and Lyotard. Habermas himself has been sympathetic to Foucault's "genealogical" analyses of power relations while criticizing their lack of normative foundations. In general, however, he believes that the poststructuralist dissolution of universal reason into a plurality of language games and power relations relativizes the distinction between strategic action and communication, domination and legitimate authority, power and knowledge to the point where political resistance becomes meaningless. Why be political if there is no ideal to be fought for, no subject to be emancipated?

These themes are developed in "Modernity: An Unfinished Project." Like Lyotard, Habermas underscores the subversive nature of a modern culture which continually undermines its own normative standards. Postmodernists seem to revel in the anarchy released by powers of aesthetic innovation and welcome the disruption of science, technology, and unifying reason. Neoconservatives, who desire a return to traditional moral authority and the capitalist work ethic, oppose this freedom for the very same reason. In Habermas's opinion, both are "conservative" in their hostility toward some aspect of modern culture. And both evince a postmodern disdain for modern reason, either in its scientific form or in its moral–aesthetic form. Yet Habermas does not think that the subversive nature of modern culture is so radical as to undermine the very standards of rationality that lend it cohesion. Contrary to the opinions of neoconservatives and "young" (poststructuralist) conservatives, modern culture is not inherently "paralogical" (to use Lyotard's expression) or self-contradictory. In Habermas's judgment, the transition to postmodernity is no more immanent within modernity than is the dialectic of enlightenment immanent within reason.

To begin with, for Habermas modern culture does not directly issue in the subversive effects—"hedonism, lack of social identification, incapacity for obedience, narcissism, and a withdrawal from competition for status and achievement" (346)—condemned by neoconservatives and celebrated by poststructural anarchists. Although Habermas (following Weber) argues that modern culture differentiates itself into autonomous aesthetic, ethical, and cognitive spheres of life (institutionalized respectively in art, law, and science), he also insists that a common thread of communicative rationality runs through all specialized disciplines. Communicative rationality, in turn, is responsible for ensuring transmission of tradition, integration of society, and socialization of free, responsible moral agents.

According to Habermas, the disintegrating effects bemoaned by neoconservatives are generated by the dynamics of economic growth and bureaucratic expansion, not by modern culture. Capitalism feeds off the rationalizing potential of cultural modernity only to turn against it. The functional imperatives of the system push for the expansion of instrumental modes of rationality and subvert the integrative achievements of an everyday life structured through communication. However, Habermas concedes that societal modernization under capitalism represents only one side of the problem of disintegration. The other side pertains to the splitting off of "elite" specialized disciplines that no longer speak to one another or to the average citizen.

Although, as Lyotard himself notes, one must guard against a "terroristic" overextension of any one sphere of discourse into other domains—the overextension of technological modes of thinking due to the overexpansion of economy and bureaucracy is a case in point—Habermas thinks it wrong to denounce (as Lyotard does) the unifying intentions of the Enlightenment as "terroristic reason." The point behind these intentions, Habermas claims, is not to do away with specialized disciplines but to make possible the revitalization of the average person's capacity to relate critically to existing traditions. Only by communicating specialized knowledge in a way that is accessible to popular experience can the average citizen learn to relate critically to his or her own cognitive, moral, and expressive sensibilities. The completion of the modern project—the enlightenment of average citizens who are capable of holding those possessing technical expertise rationally accountable for their power—demands nothing less than this.

The concluding essays in this anthology discuss the feminist response to critical theory. Although first-generation critical theorists touched on issues directly affecting the status of women in capitalist society, they seldom spoke about the peculiar oppression of women (Marcuse, who lived to see the women's liberation movement come to fruition, was a notable exception). Habermas, by contrast, has singled out the women's movement as one of the most important emancipatory movements to surface in the past two decades. Yet he, too, has had little to say about the form of oppression peculiar to women in modern society (he favorably notes, however, recent changes in the family and the work force toward greater gender equality). This neglect, however, has not prevented feminist philosophers sympathetic to his program from pointing out gender biases in it.

Nancy Fraser's "What's Critical About Critical Theory? The Case of Habermas and Gender" focuses on the distinction, mentioned above, between a communicatively structured "lifeworld" oriented toward "symbolic reproduction" (cultural transmission, social integration, and socialization) and an instrumentally structured, economic-bureaucratic "system" oriented toward "material reproduction." Habermas interprets this distinction in a way that assigns the family (childrearing) to the lifeworld and economy and state to the system. This interpretation, Fraser claims, ignores the extent to which the family contributes to the material reproduction of society and it undercuts the feminist critique of homemaking as unremunerated labor.

As noted above, Habermas's diagnosis of disintegrating tendencies in modern capitalism stresses the debilitating impact of the economic and administrative system on the family and public sphere, which rely on communicative action for their integration. Yet, according to Fraser, the principal form of alienation encountered by women arises from the debilitating impact of patriarchy, generated within the family, on the economic and administrative system. Since Habermas's diagnosis compels him to view any subsumption of the lifeworld under the system as inherently pathological, it follows that any attempt to restructure the family along the lines of an economic wage relationship would (following the Habermasian logic) disrupt the socialization process. In Fraser's opinion, however, the emancipation of homemakers might well require such a restructuration.

Habermas's diagnosis of social pathology, she claims, also neglects the gendered nature of worker, consumer, and client. For example, Habermas observes that the client-provider relationship between welfare recipients and the state undermines the freedom and dignity of the clients. However, as Fraser remarks, he nowhere provides an adequate explanation of this phenomenon in terms of institutionalized gender roles. Although women constitute the vast majority of welfare clients, it is men, not women, who experience welfare dependency most acutely. In Fraser's opinion, this is because the role of worker *as it has been institutionalized in our society* is primarily masculine. Men are raised to be independent and self-sufficient. Women are marginalized in "helping" professions in which they utilize their nurturing and caring skills or in part-time, low-paying, unskilled jobs. Whether they are homemakers or workers who supplement their husbands' incomes, women are not taught to think of themselves as fully independent, self-sufficient "breadwinners." Consequently, Fraser argues, welfare dependence is experienced differently by them. In short, women experience state paternalism as an extension of the patriarchal domination they have suffered under their entire lives.

Seyla Benhabib's essay "The Utopian Dimension in Communicative Ethics" provides an excellent clarification (and defense) of Habermas's ethics while pointing out its gender bias. By arguing that the legitimation of norms and institutions presupposes rational discussion aimed at critically evaluating and transforming existing needs and not merely agreeing on needs and interests already held in common, Habermas's ethics takes an important step in overcoming the "liberal" separation of personal questions concerning happiness and public questions concerning rights (freedom). Once the irrationality of needs is no longer taken for granted, the scope of rational agreement might extend beyond mutual acceptance of very broad private property rights, for example, to include restrictions on usage conformable to common interests and public goods (lower pollution, greater public control over distribution and production, etc.) as these have been publicly and rationally determined. The utopian break in Habermas's theory, Benhabib asserts, consists in redefining freedom in terms of a common life in which one's needs are rationally chosen in light of the needs of the concrete other rather than accepted as merely given—that is, as selfish entitlements one has a right to pursue, regardless of any impact on the freedom and happiness of others.

Despite the utopian dimension in Habermas's ethics, Benhabib argues that he still tends to distinguish moral-practical discourses aimed at discovering universalizable rights and duties from aesthetic-expressive discourses aimed at discovering common needs shared by particular communities. Habermas, she claims, thinks of the moral attitude in terms of a "generalized other" (Mead) or an impartial point of view that abstracts from the concrete differences and particular needs of individuals. On Habermas's interpretation, moral self-determination involves acting in accordance with universal principles. Aesthetic self-actualization, in contrast, involves a capacity to unfold a unique identity in concert with other unique personalities.

The separation of moral and aesthetic in Habermas's theory, Benhabib argues, displays a certain gender bias. Citing the empirical research of psychologist Carol Gilligan, she argues that in Western society female moral development has stressed competencies of caring, solidarity, love, sympathy, and bonding associated with the perspective of the "concrete other." This perspective has traditionally been relegated to the prerational and private sphere of familial, emotional bonding. Males develop along a path that emphasizes separation, independence, and competition. Consequently, males are more likely to develop aptitudes that favor abstract procedures of conflict resolution. The utopian dimension of Habermas's communicative ethic gives voice to both sets of competencies; his insistence on the transcendence of universal moral reason does not.

The preceding synopsis conveys the breadth and diversity of critical theory. It is a diversity informed by a single overarching theme: the fragility of moral reasoning that seeks comprehension of its own limits and possibilities. Whether moral reasoning can take on this philosophical burden and still enlighten political practice remains an open question. We can only hope that this anthology will further understanding of the complexity of the problem.

Left out of the preceding discussion is the all-important relationship between the selections we have surveyed and the particular historical events, both inside and outside the Frankfurt Institute, that bore directly upon their composition. We provide more historical documentation in the introductions prefacing each of the main sections.

NOTES

1. The Institute for Social Research was founded in Frankfurt, Germany, in 1923. In the 1930s and 1940s members of the institute emigrated to New York and California. The institute was reconstituted in Frankfurt in 1953. For further details on the history of the Institute for Social Research see Martin Jay, *The Dialectical Imagination: A History of the Frankfurt School and the Institute of Social Research, 1923–1950* (Boston: Little Brown, 1973).
2. First-generation critical theorists included Walter Benjamin, Leo Löwenthal, Erich Fromm, Franz Neumann, Friedrich Pollock, Otto Kirchheimer, Henryk Grossmann, and Arkadij

Gurland. Klaus Eder, Claus Offe, Albrecht Wellmer, and Axel Honneth comprise (along with Habermas) the most important second-generation critical theorists.

3. This sequence roughly corresponds to the chapter headings of the companion volume, *Critical Theory and Philosophy*.

4. A good example of Frankfurt School research combining statistical and theoretical (Freudian) approaches is the study *The Authoritarian Personality*, edited by T. W. Adorno, Else Frenkel-Brunswick, Daniel J. Levinson, and R. Nevitt Sanford (New York: Harper, 1950), which was undertaken in joint collaboration with the Berkeley Public Opinion Study Group.

5. This characterization of Marcuse and Horkheimer is admittedly one-sided. Marcuse never ceased to stress the historical nature of the instincts, while Horkheimer acknowledges certain universal tendencies operant within history as a whole.

6. One should not overlook the differences between Habermas's and Marcuse's appropriation of Freud. Marcuse, like Adorno, was generally skeptical of the therapeutic uses of Freudian psychoanalysis as a method of critical interpretation. Habermas, on the other hand, saw little value in the more speculative aspects of Freud's theory of instincts.

PART ONE

PHILOSOPHY AND CRITICAL THEORY

The selections that open this anthology deal with the relationship between philosophy and critical theory as seen by Theodor Adorno and Herbert Marcuse. Separated by twenty-five years, these essays also reflect the different philosophical temperaments of their authors.

Adorno (1903–1969) studied musicology, philosophy, sociology, and psychology at the University of Frankfurt, where he received a Ph.D. in 1924. He became affiliated with the Frankfurt School in 1931 (which he officially joined in 1938). Adorno was forced to emigrate following the Nazi takeover of Germany in 1933, eventually resettling in New York (1938) and later in Los Angeles (1941–1949). From 1956 to 1969 he was director of the reorganized Frankfurt Institute for Social Research.

The essay included here, "Why Philosophy?," originally appeared in an anthology of his work entitled *Eingriffe* (1963). It evinces the ironic defense of a philosophy that "once seemed obsolete, lives on because the moment to realize it was missed."[1] This pessimistic theme is developed in further detail in Adorno's late but difficult masterpiece *Negative Dialectics* (1966). The essay's critique of Heideggerian and Husserlian philosophy, however, is articulated more thoroughly in two other works by Adorno: *The Jargon of Authenticity* (1964) and *Against Epistemology* (1956).

Marcuse (1898–1978) studied with Edmund Husserl and Martin Heidegger before joining the Frankfurt Institute in 1933. He later emigrated to New York, and after the war taught at Columbia and Brandeis universities. He was among the leading spokesmen for the New Left during the 1960s and achieved wide popularity among students in France, Germany, and the United States. In 1964 he accepted an appointment as professor of philosophy at the University of California at San Diego.

Marcuse's contribution to the present discussion, "Philosophy and Critical Theory," first appeared in the *Zeitschrift für Sozialforschung* (1937). It reflects the generally positive assessment of the philosophical contributions of Hegel and the

---

[1] T. W. Adorno, *Negative Dialectics*, trans. E. B. Ashton (New York: Seabury, 1973), p. 3.

"early" Marx that was a trademark of his work from the late 1920s on (see, e.g., *Reason and Revolution: Hegel and the Rise of Social Theory* [1941] and *Studies in Critical Philosophy* [1972]). In contrast to Adorno's brooding reflections, this essay evinces a more optimistic (and certainly less problematic) faith in the power of philosophy to enlighten political practice.

Readers seeking more information regarding the philosophical roots of critical theory are urged to consult Chapter 1 of the companion volume, *Critical Theory and Philosophy*.

PHILOSOPHY AND CRITICAL THEORY

From the beginning the critical theory of society was constantly involved in philosophical as well as social issues and controversies. At the time of its origin, in the thirties and forties of the nineteenth century, philosophy was the most advanced form of consciousness, and by comparison real conditions in Germany were backward. Criticism of the established order there began as a critique of that consciousness, because otherwise it would have confronted its object at an earlier and less advanced historical stage than that which had already attained reality in countries outside Germany. Once critical theory had recognized the responsibility of economic conditions for the totality of the established world and comprehended the social framework in which reality was organized, philosophy became superfluous as an independent scientific discipline dealing with the structure of reality. Furthermore, problems bearing on the potentialities of man and of reason could now be approached from the standpoint of economics.

Philosophy thus appears within the economic concepts of materialist theory, each of which is more than an economic concept of the sort employed by the academic discipline of economics. It is more due to the theory's claim to explain the totality of man and his world in terms of his social being. Yet it would be false on that account to reduce these concepts to philosophical ones. To the contrary, the philosophical contents relevant to the theory are to be educed from the economic structure. They refer to conditions that, when forgotten, threaten the theory as a whole.

In the conviction of its founders the critical theory of society is essentially linked with materialism. This does not mean that it thereby sets itself up as a philosophical system in opposition to other philosophical systems. The theory of society is an economic, not a philosophical, system. There are two basic elements linking materialism to correct social theory: concern with human happiness, and the conviction that it can be attained only through a transformation of the material conditions of existence. The actual course of the transformation and the fundamental measures to be taken in order to arrive at a rational organization of society are prescribed by analysis of economic and political conditions in the given historical situation. The subsequent construction of the new society cannot be the object of theory, for it is to occur as the free creation of the liberated individuals. When reason has been realized as the rational organization of mankind, philosophy is left without an object. For philosophy, to the extent that it has been, up to the present, more than an occupation or a discipline within the given division of labor, has drawn its life from reason's not yet being reality.

Reason is the fundamental category of philosophical thought, the only one by means of which it has bound itself to human destiny. Philosophy wanted to discover the ultimate and most general grounds of Being. Under the name of reason it conceived the idea of an authentic Being in which all significant antitheses (of subject and object, essence and appearance, thought and being) were reconciled. Connected with this idea was the conviction that what exists is not immediately and already rational but must rather be brought to reason. Reason represents the highest potentiality of man and of existence; the two belong together. For when reason is accorded the status of substance, this means that at its highest level, as authentic reality, the world no longer stands opposed to the rational thought of men as mere material objectivity (*Gegenständlichkeit*). Rather, it is now comprehended by thought and defined as a concept (*Begriff*). That is, the external, antithetical character of material objectivity is overcome in a process through which the identity of subject and object is established as the rational, conceptual structure that is common to both. In its structure the world is considered accessible to reason, dependent on it, and dominated by it. In this form philosophy is idealism; it subsumes being under thought. But through this first thesis that made philosophy into rationalism and idealism it became critical philosophy as well. As the given world was bound up with rational thought and, indeed, ontologically dependent on it, all that contradicted reason or was not rational was posited as something that had to be overcome. Reason was established as a critical tribunal. In the philosophy of the bourgeois era reason took on the form of rational subjectivity. Man, the individual, was to examine and judge everything given by means of the power of his knowledge. Thus the concept of reason contains the concept of freedom as well. For such examination and judgment would be meaningless if man were not free to act in accordance with his insight and to bring what confronts him into accordance with reason.

Philosophy teaches us that all properties of mind subsist only through freedom, that all are only means for freedom, and that all seek and produce only freedom. To speculative philosophy belongs the knowledge that freedom is that alone which is true of mind.[1]

Hegel was only drawing a conclusion from the entire philosophical tradition when he identified reason and freedom. Freedom is the "formal element" of rationality, the only form in which reason can be.[2]

With the concept of reason as freedom, philosophy seems to reach its limit. What remains outstanding to the realization of reason is not a philosophical task. Hegel saw the history of philosophy as having reached its definitive conclusion at this point. However, this meant for mankind not a better future but the bad present that this condition perpetuates. Kant had, of course, written essays on universal history with cosmopolitan intent, and on perpetual peace. But his transcendental philosophy aroused the belief that the realization of reason through factual transformation was unnecessary, since individuals could become rational and free within the established order. In its basic concepts this philosophy fell prey to the order of the bourgeois epoch. In a world without reason, reason is only the semblance of rationality; in a state of general unfreedom, freedom is only a semblance of being free. This semblance is generated by the internalization of idealism. Reason and freedom become tasks that the individual is to fulfill within himself, and he can do so regardless of external conditions. Freedom does not contradict necessity, but, to the contrary, necessarily presupposes it. Only he is free who recognizes the necessary as necessary, thereby overcoming its mere necessity and elevating it to the sphere of reason. This is equivalent to asserting that a person born crippled, who cannot be cured at the given state of medical science, overcomes this necessity when he gives reason and freedom scope within his crippled existence, i.e. if from the start he always posits his needs, goals, and actions only as the needs, goals, and actions of a cripple. Idealist rationalism canceled the given antithesis of freedom and necessity so that freedom can never trespass upon necessity. Rather, it modestly sets up house within necessity. Hegel once said that this suspension of necessity "transfigures necessity into freedom."[3]

Freedom, however, can be the truth of necessity only when necessity is already true "in itself." Idealist rationalism's attachment to the status quo is distinguished by its particular conception of the relation of freedom and necessity. This attachment is the price it had to pay for the truth of its knowledge. It is already given in the orientation of the subject of idealist philosophy. This subject is rational only insofar as it is entirely self-sufficient. All that is "other" is alien and external to this subject and as such primarily suspect. For something to be true, it must be certain. For it to be certain, it must be posited by the subject as its own achievement. This holds equally for the *fundamentum inconcussum** of Descartes and the synthetic a priori judgments of Kant. Self-sufficiency and independence of all that is other and alien is the sole guarantee of the subject's freedom. What is not dependent on any other person or thing, what possesses itself, is free. Having excludes the other. Relating to the other in such a way that the subject really reaches and is united with it (or him) counts as loss and dependence. When Hegel ascribed to reason, as authentic reality, movement that "remains within itself," he could invoke Aristotle. From the beginning, philosophy was sure that the highest mode of being was being-within-itself (*Beisichselbstsein*).

This identity in the determination of authentic reality points to a deeper identity, property. Something is authentic when it is self-reliant, can preserve itself, and is not dependent on anything else. For idealism this sort of being is attained when the

---

* "a firm foundation" [Ed.].

subject has the world so that it cannot be deprived of it, that it disposes of it omnipresently, and that it appropriates it to the extent that in all otherness the subject is only with itself. However, the freedom attained by Descartes' *ego cogito*, Leibniz's monad, Kant's transcendental ego, Fichte's subject of original activity, and Hegel's world-spirit is not the freedom of pleasurable possession with which the Aristotelian God moved in his own happiness. It is rather the freedom of interminable, arduous labor. In the form that it assumed as authentic Being in modern philosophy, reason has to produce itself and its reality continuously in recalcitrant material. It exists only in this process. What reason is to accomplish is neither more nor less than the constitution of the world for the ego. Reason is supposed to create the universality and community in which the rational subject participates with other rational subjects. It is the basis of the possibility that, beyond the encounter of merely self-sufficient monads, a common life develops in a common world. But even this achievement does not lead beyond what already exists. It changes nothing. For the constitution of the world has always been effected prior to the actual action of the individual; thus he can never take his most authentic achievement into his own hands. The same characteristic agitation, which fears really taking what is and making something else out of it, prevails in all aspects of this rationalism. Development is proclaimed, but true development is "not a transformation, or becoming something else."[4] For at its conclusion it arrives at nothing that did not already exist "in itself" at the beginning. The absence of concrete development appeared to this philosophy as the greatest benefit. Precisely at its maturest stage, the inner statics of all its apparently so dynamic concepts become manifest.

Undoubtedly all these characteristics make idealist rationalism a bourgeois philosophy. And yet, merely on account of the single concept of reason, it is more than ideology, and in devoting oneself to it one does more than struggle against ideology. The concept of ideology has meaning only when oriented to the interest of theory in the transformation of the social structure. Neither a sociological nor a philosophical but rather a political concept, it considers a doctrine in relation not to the social conditions of its truth or to an absolute truth but rather to the interest of transformation.[5] Countless philosophical doctrines are mere ideology and, as illusions about socially relevant factors, readily integrate themselves into the general apparatus of domination. Idealist rationalism does not belong to this class, precisely to the extent that it is really idealistic. The conception of the domination of Being by reason is, after all, not only a postulate of idealism. With a sure instinct, the authoritarian state has fought classical idealism. Rationalism saw into important features of bourgeois society: the abstract ego, abstract reason, abstract freedom. To that extent it is correct consciousness. Pure reason was conceived as reason "independent" of all experience. The empirical world appears to make reason dependent; it manifests itself to reason with the character of "foreignness" (*Fremdartigkeit*).[6] Limiting reason to "pure" theoretical and practical achievement implies an avowal of bad facticity—but also concern with the right of the individual, with that in him which is more than "economic man," with what is left out of universal social exchange. Idealism tries to keep at least thought in a state of purity. It plays the peculiar double role of opposing both the true materialism of critical social theory and the false materialism of bourgeois practice. In idealism the individual protests the world by making both himself and the world free and rational in the realm of thought. This philosophy is in an essential sense individualistic. However, it comprehends the individual's uniqueness in terms of his self-sufficiency and "property"; all attempts to use the subject, construed in this sense, as the basis for constructing an intersubjective world have a dubious character. The alter ego always could be linked to the ego only in an abstract manner: it remained a problem of pure knowledge or pure ethics. Idealism's purity, too, is equivocal. To be sure, the highest truths of theoretical and of practical reason were to be pure and not based on facticity. But this purity could be saved only on the condition that facticity be left in impurity; the individual is surrendered to its untruth. Nevertheless, concern for the individual long kept idealism from giving its blessing to the sacrifice of the individual to the service of false collectives.

Rationalism's protest and critique remain idealistic and do not extend to the material conditions of existence. Hegel termed philosophy's abiding in the world of thought an "essential determination." Although philosophy reconciles antitheses in reason, it provides a "reconciliation not in reality, but in the world of ideas."[7] The materialist protest and materialist critique originated in the struggle of oppressed groups for better living conditions and remain permanently associated with the actual process of this struggle. Western philosophy had established reason as authentic reality. In the bourgeois epoch the reality of reason became the task that the free individual was to fulfill. The subject was the locus of reason and the source of the process by which objectivity was to become rational. The material conditions of life, however, allotted freedom to reason only in pure thought and pure will. But a social situation has come about in which the realization of reason no longer needs to be restricted to pure thought and will. If reason means shaping life according to men's free decision on the basis of their knowledge, then the demand for reason henceforth means the creation of a social organization in which individuals can collectively regulate their lives in accordance with their needs. With the realization of reason in such a society, philosophy would disappear. It was the task of social theory to demonstrate this possibility and lay the foundation for a transformation of the economic structure. By so doing, it could provide theoretical leadership for those strata which, by virtue of their historical situation, were to bring about the change. The interest of philosophy, concern with man, had found its new form in the interest of critical social theory. There is no philosophy alongside and outside this theory. For the philosophical construction of reason is replaced by the creation of a rational society. The philosophical ideals of a better world and of true Being are incorporated into the practical aim of struggling mankind, where they take on a human form.

What, however, if the development outlined by the theory does not occur? What if the forces that were to bring about the transformation are suppressed and appear to be defeated? Little as the theory's truth is thereby contradicted, it nevertheless appears then in a new light which illuminates new aspects and elements of its object. The new situation gives a new import to many demands and indices of the theory, whose changed function accords it in a more intensive sense the character of "critical theory."[8] Its critique is also directed at the avoidance of its full economic and political demands by many who invoke it. This situation compels theory anew to a sharper emphasis on its concern with the potentialities of man and with the individual's freedom, happiness, and rights contained in all of its analyses. For the theory, these are exclusively potentialities of the concrete social situation. They become relevant only as economic and political questions and as such bear on human relations in the productive process, the distribution of the product of social labor, and men's active participation in the economic and political administration of the whole. The more elements of the theory become reality—not only as the old order's evolution confirms the theory's predictions, but as the transition to the new order begins—the more urgent becomes the question of what the theory intended as its goal. For here, unlike in philosophical systems, human freedom is no phantom or arbitrary inwardness that leaves everything in the external world as it was. Rather, freedom here means a real potentiality, a social relationship on whose realization human destiny depends. At the given stage of development, the constructive character of critical theory emerges anew. From the beginning it did more than simply register and systematize facts. Its impulse came from the force with which it spoke against the facts and confronted bad facticity with its better potentialities. Like philosophy, it opposes making reality into a criterion in the manner of complacent positivism. But unlike philosophy, it always derives its goals only from present tendencies of the social process. Therefore it has no fear of the utopia that the new order is denounced as being. When truth cannot be realized within the established social order, it always appears to the latter as mere utopia. This transcendence speaks not against, but for, its truth. The utopian element was long the only progressive element in philosophy, as in the constructions of the best state and the highest pleasure, of perfect happiness and perpetual peace. The obstinacy that comes from adhering to truth against all appearances has given way in contemporary philosophy to whimsy and uninhibited opportunism. Critical theory preserves obstinacy as a genuine quality of philosophical thought.

The current situation emphasizes this quality. The reverse suffered by the progressive forces took place at a stage where the economic conditions for transformation were present. The new social situation expressed in the authoritarian state could be easily comprehended and predicted by means of the concepts worked out by the theory. It was not the failure of economic concepts that provided the impetus behind the new emphasis of the theory's claim that the transformation of economic conditions involves the transformation of the entirety of human existence. This claim is directed rather against a distorted interpretation and application of economics that is found in both practice and theoretical discussion. The discussion leads back to the question: In what way is the theory more than economics? From the beginning the critique of political economy established the difference by criticizing the entirety of social existence. In a society whose totality was determined by economic relations to the extent that the uncontrolled economy controlled all human relations, even the non-economic was contained in the economy. It appears that, if and when this control is removed, the rational organization of society toward which critical theory is oriented is more than a new form of economic regulation. The difference lies in the decisive factor, precisely the one that makes the society rational—the subordination of the economy to the individuals' needs. The transformation of society eliminates the original relation of substructure and superstructure. In a rational reality, the labor process should not determine the general existence of men; to the contrary, their needs should determine the labor process. Not that the labor process is regulated in accordance with a plan, but the interest determining the regulation becomes important: it is rational only if this interest is that of the freedom and happiness of the masses. Neglect of this element despoils the theory of one of its essential characteristics. It eradicates from the image of liberated mankind the idea of happiness that was to distinguish it from all previous mankind. Without freedom and happiness in the social relations of men, even the greatest increase of production and the abolition of private property in the means of production remain infected with the old injustice.

Critical theory has, of course, distinguished between various phases of realization and pointed out the unfreedoms and inequalities with which the new era inevitably will be burdened. Nevertheless, the transformed social existence must be determined by its ultimate goal even at its inception. In its concept of an ultimate goal, critical theory did not intend to replace the theological hereafter with a social one—with an ideal that appears in the new order as just another hereafter in virtue of its exclusive opposition to the beginning and its telescoping distance. By defending the endangered and victimized potentialities of man against cowardice and betrayal, critical theory is not to be supplemented by a philosophy. It only makes explicit what was always the foundation of its categories: the demand that through the abolition of previously existing material conditions of existence the totality of human relations be liberated. If critical theory, amidst today's desperation, indicates that the reality it intends must comprise the freedom and happiness of individuals, it is only following the direction given by its economic concepts. They are constructive concepts, which comprehend not only the given reality but, simultaneously, its abolition and the new reality that is to follow. In the theoretical reconstruction of the social process, the critique of current conditions and the analysis of their tendencies necessarily include future-oriented components. The transformation toward which this process tends and the existence that liberated mankind is to create for itself determine at the outset the establishment and unfolding of the first economic categories. Theory can invoke no facts in confirmation of the theoretical elements that point toward future freedom. From the viewpoint of theory all that is already attained is given only as something threatened and in the process of disappearing; the given is a positive fact, an element of the coming society, only when it is taken into the theoretical construction as something to be transformed. This construction is neither a supplement to nor an extension of economics. It is economics itself insofar as it deals with contents that transcend the realm of established economic conditions.

Unconditional adherence to its goal, which can be attained only in social struggle, lets theory continually confront the already attained with the not yet attained and newly threatened. The theory's interest in great philosophy is part of the same context of opposition to the established order. But critical theory is not concerned with the realization of ideals brought into social struggles from outside. In these struggles it identifies on one side the cause of freedom and on the other the cause of suppression and barbarism. If the latter seems to win in reality, it might easily appear as though critical theory were holding up a philosophical idea against factual development and its scientific analysis. Traditional science was in fact more subject to the powers that be than was great philosophy. It was not in science but in philosophy that traditional theory developed concepts oriented to the potentialities of man lying beyond his factual status. At the end of the *Critique of Pure Reason*, Kant cites the three questions in which "all the interest" of human reason "coalesces": What can I know?; What should I do?; What may I hope?[9] And in the introduction to his lectures on logic, he adds a fourth question encompassing the first three: What is man?[10] The answer to this question is conceived not as the description of human nature as it is actually found to be, but rather as the demonstration of what are found to be human potentialities. In the bourgeois period, philosophy distorted the meaning of both question and answers by equating human potentialities with those that are real within the established order. That is why they could be potentialities only of pure knowledge and pure will.

The transformation of a given status is not, of course, the business of philosophy. The philosopher can only participate in social struggles insofar as he is not a professional philosopher. This "division of labor," too, results from the modern separation of the mental from the material means of production, and philosophy cannot overcome it. The abstract character of philosophical work in the past and present is rooted in the social conditions of existence. Adhering to the abstractness of philosophy is more appropriate to circumstances and closer to truth than is the pseudophilosophical concreteness that condescends to social struggles. What is true in philosophical concepts was arrived at by abstracting from the concrete status of man and is true only in such abstraction. Reason, mind, morality, knowledge, and happiness are not only categories of bourgeois philosophy, but concerns of mankind. As such they must be preserved, if not derived anew. When critical theory examines the philosophical doctrines in which it was still possible to speak of man, it deals first with the camouflage and misinterpretation that characterized the discussion of man in the bourgeois period.

With this intention, several fundamental concepts of philosophy have been discussed in this journal [*Zeitschrift für Sozialforschung*]: truth and verification, rationalism and irrationalism, the role of logic, metaphysics and positivism, and the concept of essence. These were not merely analyzed sociologically, in order to correlate philosophical dogmas with social loci. Nor were specific philosophical contents "resolved" into social facts. To the extent that philosophy is more than ideology, every such attempt must come to nought. When critical theory comes to terms with philosophy, it is interested in the truth content of philosophical concepts and problems. It presupposes that they really contain truth. The enterprise of the sociology of knowledge, to the contrary, is occupied only with the untruths, not the truths of previous philosophy. To be sure, even the highest philosophical categories are connected with social facts, even if only with the most general fact that the struggle of man with nature has not been undertaken by mankind as a free subject but instead has taken place only in class society. This fact comes to expression in many "ontological differences" established by philosophy. Its traces can perhaps be found even in the very forms of conceptual thought: for example, in the determination of logic as essentially the logic of predication, or judgments about given objects of which predicates are variously asserted or denied. It was dialectical logic that first pointed out the shortcomings of this interpretation of judgment: the "contingency" of predication and the "externality" of the process of judgment, which let the subject of judgment appear "outside" as self-subsistent and the predicate "inside" as though in our heads.[11] Moreover, it is certainly true that many philosophical concepts are mere "foggy ideas" arising out of the domination of existence by an uncontrolled economy and, accordingly, are to be explained precisely by the material conditions of life.

But in its historical forms philosophy also contains insights into human and objective conditions whose truth points beyond previous society and thus cannot be completely reduced to it. Here belong not only the contents dealt with under such concepts as reason, mind, freedom, morality, universality, and essence, but also important achievements of epistemology, psychology, and logic. Their truth content, which surmounts their social conditioning, presupposes not an eternal consciousness that transcendentally constitutes the individual consciousness of historical subjects but only those particular historical subjects whose consciousness expresses itself in critical theory. It is only with and for this consciousness that the "surpassing" content becomes visible in its real truth. The truth that it recognizes in philosophy is not reducible to existing social conditions. This would be the case only in a form of existence where consciousness is no longer separated from being, enabling the rationality of thought to proceed from the rationality of social existence. Until then truth that is more than the truth of what is can be attained and intended only in opposition to established social relations. To this negative condition, at least, it is subject.

In the past, social relations concealed the meaning of truth. They formed a horizon of untruth that deprived the truth of its meaning. An example is the concept of universal consciousness, which preoccupied German Idealism. It contains the problem of the relation of the subject to the totality of society: How can universality as community (*Allgemeinheit*) become the subject without abolishing individuality?

The understanding that more than an epistemological or metaphysical problem is at issue here can be gained and evaluated only outside the limits of bourgeois thought. The philosophical solutions met with by the problem are to be found in the history of philosophy. No sociological analysis is necessary in order to understand Kant's theory of transcendental synthesis. It embodies an epistemological truth. The interpretation given to the Kantian position by critical theory[12] does not affect the internal philosophical difficulty. By connecting the problem of the universality of knowledge with that of society as a universal subject, it does not purport to provide a better philosophical solution. Critical theory means to show only the specific social conditions at the root of philosophy's inability to pose the problem in a more comprehensive way, and to indicate that any other solution lay beyond that philosophy's boundaries. The untruth inherent in all transcendental treatment of the problem thus comes into philosophy "from outside"; hence it can be overcome only outside philosophy. "Outside" does not mean that social factors affect consciousness from without as though the latter existed independently. It refers rather to a division within the social whole. Consciousness is "externally" conditioned by social existence to the very extent that in bourgeois society the social conditions of the individual are eternal to him and, as it were, overwhelm him from without. This externality made possible the abstract freedom of the thinking subject. Consequently, only its abolition would enable abstract freedom to disappear as part of the general transformation of the relationship between social being and consciousness.

If the theory's fundamental conception of the relation of social existence to consciousness is to be followed, this "outside" must be taken into consideration. In previous history there has been no pre-established harmony between correct thought and social being. In the bourgeois period, economic conditions determine philosophical thought insofar as it is the emancipated, self-reliant individual who thinks. In reality, he counts not in the concretion of his potentialities and needs but only in abstraction from his individuality, as the bearer of labor power, i.e. of useful functions in the process of the realization of capital. Correspondingly, he appears in philosophy only as an abstract subject, abstracted from his full humanity. If he pursues the idea of man, he must think in opposition to facticity. Wishing to conceive this idea in its philosophical purity and universality, he must abstract from the present state of affairs. This abstractness, this radical withdrawal from the given, at least clears a path along which the individual in bourgeois society can seek the truth and adhere to what is known. Beside concreteness and facticity, the thinking subject also leaves its misery "outside." But it cannot escape from itself, for it has incorporated the monadic isolation of the bourgeois individual into its premises. The subject thinks within a horizon of untruth that bars the door to real emancipation.

This horizon explains some of the characteristic features of bourgeois philosophy. One of them affects the idea of truth itself and would seem to relativize "sociologically" all its truths from the start: the coupling of truth and certainty. As such, this connection goes all the way back to ancient philosophy. But only in the modern period has it taken on the typical form that truth must prove itself as the guaranteed property of the individual, and that this proof is considered established only if the individual can continually reproduce the truth as his own achievement. The process of knowledge is never terminated, because in every act of cognition the individual must once again re-enact the "production of the world" and the categorical organization of experience. However, the process never gets any further because the restriction of "productive" cognition to the transcendental sphere makes any new form of the world impossible. The constitution of the world occurs behind the backs of the individuals; yet it is their work.

The corresponding social factors are clear. The progressive aspects of this construction of the world, namely the foundation of knowledge on the autonomy of the individual and the idea of cognition as an act and task to be continually re-enacted, are made ineffective by the life process of bourgeois society. But does this sociological limitation affect the true content of the construction, the essential connection of knowledge, freedom, and practice? Bourgeois society's domination reveals itself not only in the dependence of thought but also in the (abstract) independence of its contents. For this society determines consciousness such that the latter's activity and contents survive in the dimension of abstract reason; abstractness saves its truth. What is true is so only to the extent that it is not the truth about social reality. And just because it is not the latter, because it transcends this reality, it can become a matter for critical theory. Sociology that is interested only in the dependent and limited nature of consciousness has nothing to do with truth. Its research, useful in many ways, falsifies the interest and the goal of critical theory. In any case, what was linked, in past knowledge, to specific social structures disappears with them. In contrast, critical theory concerns itself with preventing the loss of the truths which past knowledge labored to attain.

This is not to assert the existence of eternal truths unfolding in changing historical forms of which they need only to be divested in order for their kernel of truth to be revealed. If reason, freedom, knowledge, and happiness really are transformed from abstract concepts into reality, then they will have as much and as little in common with their previous forms as the association of free men with competitive, commodity-producing society. Of course, to the identity of the basic social structure in previous history certainly corresponds an identity of certain universal truths, whose universal character is an essential component of their truth content. The struggle of authoritarian ideology against abstract universals has clearly exhibited this. That man is a rational being, that this being requires freedom, and that happiness is his highest good are all universal propositions whose progressive impetus derives precisely from their universality. Universality gives them an almost revolutionary character, for they claim that all, and not merely this or that particular person, should be rational, free, and happy. In a society whose reality gives the lie to all these universals, philosophy cannot make them concrete. Under such conditions, adherence to universality is more important than its philosophical destruction.

Critical theory's interest in the liberation of mankind binds it to certain ancient truths. It is at one with philosophy in maintaining that man can be more than a manipulable subject in the production process of class society. To the extent that philosophy has nevertheless made its peace with man's determination by economic conditions, it has allied itself with repression. That is the bad materialism that underlies the edifice of idealism: the consolation that in the material world everything is in order as it is. (Even when it has not been the personal conviction of the philosopher, this consolation has arisen almost automatically as part of the mode of thought of bourgeois idealism and constitutes its ultimate affinity with its time.) The other premise of this materialism is that the mind is not to make its demands in this world, but is to orient itself toward another realm that does not conflict with the material world. The materialism of bourgeois practice can quite easily come to terms with this attitude. The bad materialism of philosophy is overcome in the materialist theory of society. The latter opposes not only the production relations that gave rise to bad materialism, but every form of production that dominates man instead of being dominated by him: this idealism underlies its materialism. Its constructive concepts, too, have a residue of abstractness as long as the reality toward which they are directed is not yet given. Here, however, abstractness results not from avoiding the status quo, but from orientation toward the future status of man. It cannot be supplanted by another, correct theory of the established order (as idealist abstractness was replaced by the critique of political economy). It cannot be succeeded by a new theory, but only by rational reality itself. The abyss between rational and present reality cannot be bridged by conceptual thought. In order to retain what is not yet present as a goal in the present, phantasy is required. The essential connection of phantasy with philosophy is evident from the function attributed to it by philosophers, especially Aristotle and Kant, under the title of "imagination." Owing to its unique capacity to "intuit" an object though the latter be not present and to create something new out of given material of cognition, imagination denotes a considerable degree of independence from the given, of freedom amid a world of unfreedom. In surpassing what is present, it can anticipate the future. It is true that when Kant characterizes this "fundamental faculty of the human soul" as the a priori basis of all knowledge,[13] this restriction to the a priori diverts once again from the future to what is always past. Imagination succumbs to the general degradation of phantasy. To free it for the construction of a more beautiful and happier world remains the prerogative of children and fools. True, in phantasy one can imagine anything. But critical theory does not envision an endless horizon of possibilities.

The freedom of imagination disappears to the extent that real freedom becomes a real possibility. The limits of phantasy are thus no longer universal laws of essence (as the last bourgeois theory of knowledge that took seriously the meaning of phantasy so defined them),[14] but technical limits in the strictest sense. They are prescribed by the level of technological development. What critical theory is engaged in is not the depiction of a future world, although the response of phantasy to such a challenge would not perhaps be quite as absurd as we are led to believe. If phantasy were set free to answer, with precise reference to already existing technical material, the fundamental philosophical questions asked by Kant, all of sociology would be terrified at the utopian character of its answers. And yet the answers that phantasy could provide would be very close to the truth, certainly closer than those yielded by the rigorous conceptual analyses of philosophical anthropology. For it would determine what man is on the basis of what he really can be tomorrow. In replying to the question "What may I hope?," it would point less to eternal bliss and inner freedom than to the already possible unfolding and fulfillment of needs and wants. In a situation where such a future is a real possibility, phantasy is an important instrument in the task of continually holding the goal up to view. Phantasy does not relate to the other cognitive faculties as illusion to truth (which in fact, when it plumes itself on being the only truth, can perceive the truth of the future only as illusion). Without phantasy, all philosophical knowledge remains in the grip of the present or the past and severed from the future, which is the only link between philosophy and the real history of mankind.

Strong emphasis on the role of phantasy seems to contradict the rigorously scientific character that critical theory has always made a criterion of its concepts. This demand for scientific objectivity has brought materialist theory into unusual accord with idealist rationalism. While the latter could pursue its concern with man only in abstraction from given facts, it attempted to undo this abstractness by associating itself with science. Science never seriously called use-value into question. In their anxiety about scientific objectivity, the neo-Kantians are at one with Kant, as is Husserl with Descartes. How science was applied, whether its utility and productivity guaranteed its higher truth or were instead signs of general inhumanity—philosophy did not ask itself these questions. It was chiefly interested in the methodology of the sciences. The critical theory of society maintained primarily that the only task left for philosophy was elaborating the most general results of the sciences. It, too, took as its basis the viewpoint that science had sufficiently demonstrated its ability to serve the development of the productive forces and to open up new potentialities of a richer existence. But while the alliance between idealist philosophy and science was burdened from the beginning with sins engendered by the dependence of the sciences on established relations of domination, the critical theory of society presupposes the disengagement of science from this order. Thus the fateful fetishism of science is avoided here in principle. But this does not dispense the theory from a constant critique of scientific aims and methods which takes into account every new social situation. Scientific objectivity as such is never a sufficient guarantee of truth, especially in a situation where the truth speaks as strongly against the facts and is as well hidden behind them as today. Scientific predictability does not coincide with the futuristic mode in which the truth exists. Even the development of the productive forces and the evolution of technology know no uninterrupted progression from the old to the new society. For here, too, man himself is to determine progress: not "socialist" man, whose spiritual and moral regeneration is supposed to constitute the basis for planning the planners (a view that overlooks that "socialist" planning presupposes the disappearance of the abstract separation both of the subject from his activity and of the subject as universal from each individual subject), but the association of those men who bring about the transformation. Since what is to become of science and technology depends on them, science and technology cannot serve a priori as a conceptual model for critical theory.

Critical theory is, last but not least, critical of itself and of the social forces that make up its own basis. The philosophical element in the theory is a form of protest against the new "Economism," which would isolate the economic struggle and separate the economic from the political sphere. At an early stage, this view was countered with the criticism that the determining factors are the given situation of the entire society, the interrelationships of the various social strata, and relations of political power. The transformation of the economic structure must so reshape the organization of the entire society that, with the abolition of economic antagonisms between groups and individuals, the political sphere becomes to a great extent independent and determines the development of society. With the disappearance of the state, political relations would then become, in a hitherto unknown sense, general human relations: the organization of the administration of social wealth in the interest of liberated mankind.

The materialist theory of society is originally a nineteenth-century theory. Representing its relation to rationalism as one of "inheritance," it conceived this inheritance as it manifested itself in the nineteenth century. Much has changed since then. At that time the theory had comprehended, on the deepest level, the possibility of a coming barbarity, but the latter did not appear to be as imminent as the "conservative" abolition of what the nineteenth century represented: conservative of what the culture of bourgeois society, for all its poverty and injustice, had accomplished nonetheless for the development and happiness of the individual. What had already been achieved and what still remained to be done was clear enough. The entire impetus of the theory came from this interest in the individual, and it was not necessary to discuss it philosophically. The situation of inheritance has changed in the meantime. It is not a part of the nineteenth century, but authoritarian barbarity, that now separates the previous reality of reason from the form intended by the theory. More and more, the culture that was to have been abolished recedes into the past. Overlaid by an actuality in which the complete sacrifice of the individual has become a pervasive and almost unquestioned fact of life, that culture has vanished to the point where studying and comprehending it is no longer a matter of spiteful pride, but of sorrow. Critical theory must concern itself to a hitherto unknown extent with the past—precisely insofar as it is concerned with the future.

In a different form, the situation confronting the theory of society in the nineteenth century is being repeated today. Once again real conditions fall beneath the general level of history. Fettering the productive forces and keeping down the standard of life is characteristic of even the economically most developed countries. The reflection cast by the truth of the future in the philosophy of the past provides indications of factors that point beyond today's anachronistic conditions. Thus critical theory is still linked to these truths. They appear in it as part of a process: that of bringing to consciousness potentialities that have emerged within the maturing historical situation. They are preserved in the economic and political concepts of critical theory.

NOTES

1. Hegel, *Vorlesungen über die Philosophie der Geschichte* in *Werke*, 2d ed. (Berlin, 1840–47), IX, p. 22.
2. Hegel, *Vorlesungen über die Geschichte der Philosophie* in *Werke*, XIII, p. 34.
3. Hegel, *Enzyclopädie der philosophischen Wissenschaften*, par. 158, *op. cit.*, VI, p. 310.
4. Hegel, *Vorlesungen über die Geschichte der Philosophie, op. cit.*, p. 41.
5. See Max Horkheimer, "Ein neuer Ideologiebegriff?," *Grünbergs Archiv*, XV (1930), pp. 38–39.
6. Kant, *Nachlass Nr. 4728* in *Gesammelte Schriften*, Preussische Akademie der Wissenschaften, ed. (Berlin, 1900–1955), XVIII.
7. Hegel, *Vorlesungen über die Geschichte der Philosophie, op. cit.*, p. 67.
8. See Max Horkheimer, "Traditionelle und kritische Theorie," *Zeitschrift für Sozialforschung*, VI (1937), p. 245.
9. Kant, *Werke*, Ernst Cassirer, ed. (Berlin, 1911ff.), III, p. 540.
10. *Ibid.*, VIII, p. 344.
11. Hegel, *Enzyclopädie*, par. 166, *op. cit.*, p. 328.
12. See *Zeitschrift für Sozialforschung*, VI (1937), pp. 257ff.
13. Kant, *Kritik der reinen Vernunft, op. cit.*, p. 625.
14. Edmund Husserl, *Formale und transzendentale Logik* in *Jahrbuch für Philosophie*, X (Halle, 1929), p. 219.

THEODOR W. ADORNO

WHY PHILOSOPHY?

To a question like "Why Philosophy?," for the formulation of which I am myself responsible—although not unaware of its amateurish sound—most people would expect an answer along lines which assembled every imaginable difficulty and reservation, and eventually gave birth to an affirmative conclusion, hedged around with due limitations, confirming what had been rhetorically doubted. This all-too-familiar course discloses the conformist, apologetic approach, expressed in positive terms and counting on agreement in advance. That, indeed, is all one might expect from a professional lecturer in philosophy whose living depends on a continuance of such studies and whose own, tangible interests are damaged by any suggestion to the contrary. I have, nevertheless, some sort of right to pose the question, if only because I am not at all sure of the answer.

Anyone who is defending something that the spirit of an age rejects as out of date and obsolete is in an awkward position. The arguments put forward sound lame and overdone. He addresses his audience as though he is trying to talk them into buying something they don't want. This drawback has to be reckoned with by those who are not prepared to be dissuaded from philosophy. He knows that it is no longer suited to the modern techniques that control our lives—"technical" in the figurative, as well as in the literal, sense—and with which it was once so inextricably entwined. Nor is philosophy any longer a cultural medium transcending technical affairs, as it was in Hegel's time, for instance, when, for a few short decades, the tight little circle of German intellectuals exchanged ideas in the common language of philosophy. From about the time Kant died, philosophy came under a cloud because it had got out of step with the more exact sciences—and the physical sciences in particular—and forfeited its public position as the leading discipline. That trend is relevant to the crisis over the value of humanistic studies in education, and on this subject I need say little. The Kantian and Hegelian revivals, characterized by the appearance of the less imposing aspects of their namesakes' teachings, have left the situation substantially unchanged. Finally, caught up in the general urge to specialize, philosophy too settled into the grooves of a specialist study, that of the pure theory from which all incidental content has been purged. This involved denying the original philosophical concept—intellectual freedom, or refusal to acknowledge the supremacy of technical science. At the same time, by abstaining from a fixed content, be it a formal doctrine of logic or science, or the myth of pure being divorced from all that exists, "pure" philosophy declared itself bankrupt when confronted with the social objectives of the world around us. In this, of course, it was merely setting the seal to a process that broadly matched the course of its own historical development. Whole areas were continually being withdrawn from its sphere of influence and subjected to scientific method, so that it almost lost the power to choose between becoming a science itself or persisting in the form of a tiny, tolerated enclave, opposed thereby to what it set out to be—a universal system of truth. Even Newtonian physics had been known as "philosophy." The modern scientific intelligence would regard it as an archaic relic, a rudiment from that age of early Greek speculation in which bold explanations of natural phenomena and sublime metaphysical insight into the nature of things were still inextricably interwoven. For this reason, some resolute souls have announced that such archaic anachronisms constitute the only true philosophy and have sought to restore their one-time pre-eminence. But the schizophrenic mentality which casts about and seeks its own reunion in the harmonious unities of the past, falsifies the substance of its own quest. It is like working, by choice, in the medium of a primitive language. In philosophy, as much as elsewhere, restorations are doomed to failure. For philosophy needs to protect itself from cultural rantings, as well as from the magical incantations of ideologies. Neither should it be imagined that specialist work along the lines suggested by scientific method, or whatever else prides itself on being research, is philosophy. And, in the end, philosophical method that is free from all those things is diametrically opposed to current thinking. But nothing less frees it from the taint of apologetics. Philosophical speculation that satisfies the aims of genuine metaphysical enquiry, instead of sheepishly hiding behind the facts of its own history, draws its strength from its resistance to modern methodology and serves to counter the present-day nonchalant acceptance of the material world around us.

Even the greatest triumphs so far achieved in philosophical speculation, as exemplified in the work done by Hegel, no longer hold us. In accordance with the categories of public opinion—which apply to everyone—it is precisely those whose actions are public property, and who are thereby numbered among the dialecticians, that quote Hegelian differential dicta. No opinion rests upon personal conviction. Views are implicit from the direction taken by the subject-matter itself, its entire freedom to move, and freedom for our thought to follow it, being postulated by no less an authority than Hegel himself. The comprehensiveness claimed by traditional philosophical method, culminating in the thesis that reality is reasonable, is indistinguishable from apologetics, which has, however, been taken to absurd limits. By claiming to be an all-embracing system, philosophy runs the risk of ending in a series of crazy delusions. Immediately it abandons the claim to omniscience, however, and gives up the idea of crystallizing all truth within itself, it denies the whole weight of its own traditions. This is the price it must pay in exchanging its delusions for reality, in purging itself of crazy notions and linking reality with reason. It then loses its character of a self-sufficing and cogent body of justificatory proofs. Its place in society—which it would do well to promote and not to deny—corresponds to its own desperate need to define what, today, is defined by the hackneyed term of the absurd. Philosophy guided by a sense of responsibility for everything should no longer lay claim to a mastery of the absolute, should in fact renounce all such notions, in order not to betray them in the event, without, however, sacrificing the concept of truth itself. The province of philosophy lies in such contradictions as these. They confer on it a negative character. Kant's famous dictum that the path of criticism is the only one still open to us, belongs among those propositions by which the philosophy in which they originate, passes its test, inasmuch as the saying or axiom outlives the system which conceived it. The critical idea itself may indeed be included amongst the philosophical traditions that have been disrupted in the modern age. And while, in the meantime, the arena of every kind of knowledge has been invaded to so great an extent by scientific specializations—so that speculation along philosophic lines is attended by a kind of persecution complex and the ever-present fear that it must yield to rejection as a dilettante occupation, wherever it does light upon some substantial aspect of reality, the concept of original truth raises its reactionary head—and gobbles down undeserved credit for it. The more reified our world becomes, and the thicker the veil under which we hide the face of nature, the more the ideas around which that veil is spun are accepted as the only true experience of this world, and of natural phenomena. From the vaunted pre-Socratic era onwards, however, traditional philosophers have played a critical role. Xenophanes, to whose school of thought the concept of being is due which is, today, contrasted to any fixed philosophical notion, wanted to liberate natural forces from a mythological content. And then Aristotle saw through the Platonic trend towards elevating a proposition to the status of a being in itself. More recently, the scholastic dogmas were criticized by Descartes as being essentially opinions. Leibniz became the critic of the empirical method; then Kant refuted Leibniz and Hume at one and the same time; Hegel criticized Kant, and Marx came out against Hegel. In all these cases criticism was not merely a seasoning to what, thirty years ago would have been called, in the jargon of ontology, their "design." It did not seek to document attitudes that could be taken up according to taste or inclination. It had its being, rather, in the sphere of cogent argument. In criticism, these philosophers expressed their own truth. Criticism, rather than the passive acceptance of received theory, the unifying factor between the various problems, and an ingredient in each argument, has laid the foundations of what may be termed the constructive unity of the history of philosophy. In the progressive continuity of such lines of criticism, even those philosophies that base their teachings upon the supposedly eternal, a-temporal, verities, contain within themselves the crystallized metaphysical thought of their age.

Modern philosophical criticism should be conducted in the presence of two schools of thought which, in the spirit of our age, operate, willy-nilly, beyond the academic frontiers. They both diverge and, at the same time, run complementary to each other. In the Anglo-Saxon world especially, logical positivism, first inaugurated in the Viennese school, has gained ground to the point of virtual monopoly. In the sense that it is modern by reason of its remarkably consistent faculty of enlightenment, it strikes many as the doctrine most suited to the needs of a technological and scientifically-minded era. What it is unable to absorb—the indigestible residues—are the offshoots from metaphysics, the remains of a mythology it no longer heeds—or, in the terminology of those who know little of it, art. Against this—above all in the Germanic countries—there are the ontological approaches. The word ontology itself is somewhat out of favour, to judge at least from what Heidegger has published since "Sein und Zeit." His approach is an "archaic" one; while his French variant, existentialism, has remoulded the ontological framework in a spirit of enlightenment and with political commitment. The positivist and the ontological schools are anathema to each other. Heidegger's doctrine was—unjustly, by the way—attacked by Rudolf Carnap, one of the foremost exponents of the positivist school, as being devoid of sense. Positivist thinking, on the other hand, is looked on by ontologists of the Heidegger brand, as oblivious of being itself ("seinsvergessen"), and tending to vulgarize and cheapen the essential question. It is feared that too much preoccupation with the mere fact of existence—the tool of positivist views—will besmirch the hands of those who make use of it. All the more striking, then, is the coincident tendency of each of these standpoints. Metaphysics is their common enemy. The fact that it proceeds considerably beyond the limitations of known circumstance and is hence intolerable to the positivist, whose very name indicates an adherence to positive, existing and received evidence, requires no emphasis. But Heidegger too, schooled as he is in traditional metaphysics, has expressly tried to detach his work from its influence. He calls metaphysics, somewhat derogatorily, philosophy from the time of Aristotle at least—if not from that of Plato as well—inasmuch as it distinguishes between being and existing, idea and meaning—one might also say, using language of which Heidegger would, however, not approve—subject from object. Thinking that seeks to analyse and separate and break up the ideas suggested by the words that describe them, in short, all that Hegel called the operation and working efforts of "the concept," and equated with philosophy, is regarded as the betrayal of the latter, not even capable of being amended, but as being dictated by the nature of being itself. On these two counts, in both positivist theory and that of Heidegger—in his later work, at all events—the current is set against speculation. The idea which arises independently from, and indicatively of, the facts, and cannot be separated from them without leaving a residue behind—a remainder, as it were—is stigmatized as vain and profitless cerebration: according to Heidegger, however, ways of thinking that follow the typical pattern prescribed by the historical evolution of thought in the West at bottom fall short of the real truth. The latter comes to light of itself, and stands revealed: correct thinking is no more than the ability to perceive it. In the last resort, the final court of appeal for philosophy is philology. On this view of the common aversion to metaphysical method it appears less of a paradox than at first when we learn that Walter Bröcker, a disciple of Heidegger's working in Kiel, attempted to combine positivism and the philosophy of being by leaving the whole field of existence clear to positivist theory and superimposing over it, on a higher plane, the principles of the philosophy of being, in the form of a deliberately contrived mythology. Being, under which heading Heidegger's philosophy seems to range itself more and more closely is, for him, simply an impression made on the passive consciousness, in similarly direct independence from the mediation of the subject as the sensory data are for the positivists. The processes of thought are, for both, a necessary evil and held in less esteem, as involving tendentious risks. Thought loses the power of being something independent. The autonomy of reason is disappearing, inasmuch as it does not satisfy itself by measuring and comparing present and past data, and adjusting itself to them. By the same token, the concept of liberty of thought also disappears and, in effect, the idea of self-determination in human society. Most positivists, were they not deeply imbued with humanistic tendencies, would be obliged in practice to devise some form of adaption to the facts of existence which would render thought of no avail, and make it a mere anticipation or classification. With Heidegger, however, thought, in its character of a reverent, meaningless and passive listener to a continual reiteration of the formula of being, would lose its right to criticize and would be forced to capitulate indiscriminately to everything that might be referred to the equivocal superiority implied in the notion of being. Heidegger's absorption into Hitler's "Führerstaat" was not an opportunist manoeuvre: it followed from a philosophic attitude of mind in which the "Führer" and the dominant power of being were virtually identified.

Is philosophy still necessary, as it has been from time immemorial, as a critical method, as a check to the expanding influence of heteronomy? Is philosophical thought involved in a vain attempt to remain its own master and to convert a falsely imposed mythology and a resigned adaptation in accordance with its own standards of what is true and what is not true? Unless it were forbidden to do so, as it was in the Christian Athens of late antiquity, philosophy should provide a refuge for intellectual freedom and liberty, without having any hope, however, of being able to break the political trends that are stifling physical and mental freedoms throughout the world and continually sending powerful roots down into the substrata of philosophical discussion and argument. Changes in the substance of ideas always reflect something of external realities, however. But if those two heteronomous schools of thought exclude the truth, and can be shown to do so in a compelling manner, this not only adds a new link to the chain of hopeless philosophies but also gives some grounds for hoping that slavery and repression—evils in as little need of philosophical proof that they are evil as that they exist—may not, after all, have the last word. Criticism would have the task of establishing that the two dominant trends in philosophy were separate, insufficient, and yet irreconcilable aspects of truth, which had diverged in the course of historical evolution. Little as they lend themselves to fusion in what is known as a "synthesis," they would nevertheless call for critical reflection, each within itself. What is wrong with positivist theory is that it accepts the division of labour between the sciences, as it is socially enforced, as a standard of truth itself, admitting no theory in which the division of labour itself emerges clearly as being derived, an epiphenomenon the authority of which is falsely assumed. If philosophy wished to found a science in the present age of emancipation, and if she had seen her image as interpreted by Fichte and Hegel, as the only real science, the very general framework positivism borrowed from the sciences, and its refined and socially polished methods, would become a philosophy in an urge for self-justification—an example of thinking in a circle that appears to disturb the fanatical adherents of logical tidiness to a remarkably small extent. Philosophy resigned when she elevated to her own status the science which she alone was intended to illumine. The existence of science, telle quelle, as it appears in the weft and warp of social life, with all its inadequacies and irrationalities, has become the criterion of its own truth. Positivism, with its fanatical reverence for the reified veneer of facts, tends to become reified itself. With all its animosity towards mythology, it betrays the anti-mythological impulses of philosophy, throwing down what is merely man-made achievement and reducing its significance to the standards of its human origin.

Such a fundamental ontology, however, blinds itself to the mediatory role, not only of what is factual, but of concept. It suppresses recognition of the fact that the real entities, or whatever a progressive process of sublimation may call them, with which it confronts the facts of positivism, are still thought, subjective thinking, and mind. It is precisely the existence of subjectivity and subjective determination that takes us back to forms of existence that originate otherwise than entirely from the fact of being, in human social groupings, for example. In the sanctuary of the edifice in which the philosophy of repristination lies entrenched from the profanity of mere fact, as well as from the rationality of concepts, we come again upon the philosophical schism from which the heralds of unity, of indivisible wholes, imagined themselves immune. The words they use are necessarily concepts, inasmuch as they are intended to be meaningful at all; the philosophy of being wishes to be thought even after it has definitely turned towards archaism. Since, however, ideas, by their very nature, require some kind of complementarity; and since Hegel's unsurpassed speculative perception informs us that the mere thought of identity evokes, nay demands, the corresponding concept of non-identity against which alone we may demonstrate the idea of identity: the purest concepts still postulate their reverse aspect. Thought itself, of which all ideas are a function, cannot be represented in the absence of thinking activity, which the word thought implies. This retrospect already includes for its motive force what was, on an idealistic view, first formulated in the concept and what, from the viewpoint of mythological being, in addition to the concept, is an epiphenomenon, a third factor. Without the determination afforded by these two impulses, the third factor would be quite indeterminate; the mere mention of it goes beyond the fact of determination occasioned by such forces, the existence of which has been so assiduously denied. Even Kant's transcendental subject, from which transcendent, unsubjective being would gladly inherit the legacy, requires a complementary diversity to become a whole, just as, on the other hand, diversity requires the unifying complement of reason. Apart from the contents, which are those of the whole entity, the idea of the latter cannot be grasped, and the factual traces remaining in the contents are as little susceptible of exorcism as their differentiation from the concept of which they are a necessary ingredient. No unified concept, however formal or approximating to the abstractions of pure logic, can be detached—even in theory—from the subject-matter with which it is concerned: even the content of formal logic includes a material essence which pure logic prided itself on having eliminated. The basis of what Günther Anders has called the "pseudo-concretion" of Heidegger's philosophy of being, however—and of all the fallacious imposture to which it has given rise—resides in the fact that it claims to be pure of what it is ultimately in itself, and from the concreteness of which it profits. It celebrates victory in the course of a strategic withdrawal. Its mythical ambiguity merely camouflages the fixed interaction of impulse from which it is no more able to detach itself than the conditioned consciousness ever could. Because, in the mythology of being, the factual and the conceptual remain artificially confused, being is represented as on a higher plane than either existence or concept, and hence, in Kant's words, surreptitiously acquires absoluteness. It too is a product of reified consciousness, since it suppresses the human element in the most elevated concepts and idolizes them. Dialectics, however, insists upon the "mediation" of what is seemingly immediate, and upon the reciprocity at all levels of what is immediate and what requires intermediary processes. Dialectics is not a third approach but it represents an attempt, by means of an immanent criticism, to elevate philosophical viewpoints above themselves and above the despotism of such viewpoints. In contrast to the ingenuousness of a controlled, free consciousness which regards its own limitations and data as unlimited, philosophy would then have a binding obligation to be disingenuous. In a world which, permeated through and through with the structures of social order, is so heavily weighted against all individualistic tendencies that the individual has little other choice but to accept them for what they are, such naivety continually grows apace and takes on sinister connotations. What is forced upon the individual by an all-pervasive apparatus of his own construction, and in the toils of which he is held enmeshed, to the virtual exclusion of all spontaneous impulse, becomes natural to him. The reified consciousness is entirely naive, and yet it has also lost its naivety completely. The task before philosophy is to break up the seemingly obvious and the apparently incomprehensible.

The integration of philosophy and science, which showed itself in the earliest writings on metaphysics in the West, sought to liberate ideas from the tutelage of dogma, towards which they tended by reason of the despotic will, the negation of all freedom. At this, however, was aimed the postulate of the direct "association" of a lively intellectual activity in all branches of knowledge, the ineradicable criterion of "evidence" since the time of Spinoza. In purely logical terms, this was the anticipatory image of an actual situation in which man was free, at last, of any form of unseeing authority. The wheel has now come full circle, however. The appeal to science, the rules by which it functions, the absolute validity of the methods to which it owes its development, together constitute an authority which penalises free, untrammelled, "untrained" thinking and will not allow the minds of men to dwell on matters that do not bear the stamp of its approval. Science, the means to autonomy, has degenerated into an instrument of heteronomy. Its original raison d'être has become detached, a plaything of the slanderous comment, demeaned to an isolated existence in the limbo of speculative small-talk. The critical method of scientivism, which roundly refutes such ways of thinking is not, therefore, what its well-intentioned opponents reproach it for being, but is, rather, a destruction of what is already destructive. Criticism of the existing philosophies is not a plea for the disappearance of philosophy as such, or even for its replacement by a single discipline, social science, for instance. It may, in a formal and material way, even assist those forms of intellectual liberty that fail to find a foothold in the tide of present-day philosophic fashion. Speculation on a broad basis that proceeds consistently and works from the firm ground of progress towards an objective, is, on the other hand, also free in the sense that it refuses to be governed by the rules of organised knowledge. It directs the essence of its own accumulated experience towards the objects, strips away the social fabric that veils them, and gives them a new look. If philosophy could liberate itself from the aura of fearfulness spread about by the tyranny of current trends—from the ontological pressures to imagine only what is conceptually "pure"; and from the scientific compulsion to think solely along paths "in line with" the dictates of approved scientifically tested principle—it would be capable, in an atmosphere cleared of anxiety, of seeing what its inhibited perceptions had failed to descry. The dream of philosophic phenomenology, like the dream in which we imagine we are awake, of "getting at the facts," could only come true for a philosophy that hopes to acquire knowledge without waving the magic wand of intuition, but by reflecting upon subjective as well as objective intermediary phases, not, however, in accordance with the dogmatic primacy of a superimposed method which, instead of the objects desired, merely offers the phenomenological processes a series of fetishes, or "home-made" imaginings. Were not all positive phraseology so profoundly suspect, one might asseverate that, finally, what traditional philosophy has failed to achieve by confusing its own identity with what it wished to clarify, was revealed to a consciousness that was free and, at the same time, capable of "internal refraction." The attenuous weariness of a traditional philosophy that stems from the interplay of its own mutations is still potentially philosophy, since it possesses the latent dynamism of one which has broken the spell of its own evolution.

Problematic it may yet be, whether philosophy, as a form of occupation for the searching intellect, is still suited to the times; or whether it remains behind its present task, i.e. that of diagnosing the malady which is driving the world to disaster. The time for speculation seems to have gone. The obvious absurdity of the situation makes one boggle at the idea of understanding it. The abolition of philosophy was forecast more than a century ago. The fact that, in the East, Marxist philosophy has congealed to "diamat," as though such a philosophy were compatible with Marxist theory, is evidence of Marxism's divergence into a truncated, static dogma, refuting its own content; its retrogression, as they themselves call it, towards an ideology. Philosophers can continue their endeavours only if they deny the Marxist proposition of the obsolescence of reflection. Marx considered that opportunities to change society from top to bottom existed here and now. But it would be sheer obstinacy to stick to this expectation of Marx. The proletariat to which he addressed himself was not yet integrated into society; it was manifestly sunk in misery while the community still lacked the means of asserting its dominance, should the need arise. Philosophy, as a free and coherent body of thought, is in an entirely different position. Marx would have been the last to separate thought from the realities of historical evolution. Hegel was aware of the impermanence of art, and foretold its demise, associating its continued existence with a "consciousness of want." But what is right for art is applicable to philosophy, which contains an essence of truth in line with that expressed in art, although its methods are dissimilar. The undiminished continuance of suffering, anxiety and threats obliges thought which is unable to develop profitably to preserve itself. After missing its cue philosophy would then have to ask, without any illusions, why the world which could be a paradise on earth today, could become very hell tomorrow. Such knowledge would certainly be philosophical. To replace it in favour of practical politics which perpetuated necessarily the present situation, the condition it was the function of philosophy to criticize, would be anachronistic. Politics aimed at the formation of a reasonable and mature mankind remain under an evil spell, as long as they lack a theory that takes account of the totality that is false. That this does not mean that one should warm up idealism, but rather that one should accept the facts of social and political realities and their relative strengths goes without saying.

During the last forty or fifty years, philosophy has, generally quite spuriously, declared its opposition to idealism. What was genuine in this contention was its objection to decorative phraseology, intellectual conceit which ascribes absolute authority to the mind, and the glorification of this world, in the name of freedom. The anthropocentricity inherent in all idealistic theory is beyond aid; we need only call to mind the bare outlines of the changes taking place in cosmology during the last century and a half. Among the tasks awaiting the attention of philosophy, by no means the last is the adaptation, without amateurish analogies and syntheses, of the results of experience gained in the natural sciences, to the province of the mind. A deep and sterile gulf has grown up between such experience and what we call the world of the mind, to the point, in fact, that intellectual preoccupation with the mind itself and social phenomena appears, at times, like a vain conceit. If the sole purpose of philosophy consisted in bringing the human intellect to the stage where it could identify itself with what it has learned about natural phenomena, instead of leaving mankind to live out its life like a troglodyte sheltering behind its own knowledge of the cosmos in which the imprudent species, "homo," goes his graceless way, at least something would have been achieved. In view of this task, and of an unimpaired insight into the kinetic laws of society, it would hardly be tempted to claim to be able to set forth something like positive "meaning" to the world. To that extent it makes common cause with the positivist view, but still more with modern art, the manifestations of which remain beyond the ken of the greater part of what passes today for philosophic thinking. But the much overstated trend of neo-ontology against idealism ends, not in a dynamic restatement of its aims and purpose, but in resignation. Thought has allowed itself to become, as it were, intimidated, and no longer possesses the self-confidence to go beyond the mere reproduction of what is anyway. In contrast to such resigned attitudes, idealism at least retained an element of spontaneity. On the other hand, materialism, if carried to its logical conclusions, would mean the end of materialism, of man's blind, humiliating dependence on material circumstance. Far as the mind of man is from being absolute, it is not a mere duplication of brute fact either. It will only come to a proper awareness of things if it avoids its own limitations. The human mind's powers of resistance are the only criteria in philosophy today. It is as irreconcilable with reified consciousness as once Platonic enthusiasm was; its transcendence beyond the factual allows it to call the universally conditioned phenomena by their own names. It hopes for reconciliation with the non-identical that is being degraded continuously by affirmative philosophies. The latter regard everything in its functional aspect; even seeing in the adaptation to natural phenomena a pretext for subjugating the phenomenon of the mind. But what exists does not want to be manipulated. Anything that has function is bewitched in a functional world. Thought alone, unfettered by mental reservations, and freely admitting, without any illusions as to its inner sovereignty, its own absence of function and material impotence, may be vouchsafed a glimpse of a non-existent yet feasible order of things where men and things each occupy their appointed place. Philosophy is not outmoded simply because it is good-for-nothing; it should not even make that claim to attention if it wishes to avoid the heedless repetition of its cardinal sin, that of self-assertiveness.

That fault was a traditional one, inherited from the concept of a "philosophia perennis" in which the eternal verities were vested. Hegel sprang that trap with his remarkable adage that philosophy was the essence of a period, distilled by thought. He considered it such an evident requirement that he did not hesitate to define philosophy by it. He was the first to gain an insight into the temporal nucleus of time itself. He linked it to the belief that, by expressing its own stage of consciousness as a necessary, and dynamic, part of a whole, every significant philosophy also expressed itself as a whole. That this confidence, and the efficacy of the philosophy, was invalidated, diminishes not merely the emphatic claim of subsequent systems, but also their intrinsic quality. What was self-evident to Hegel, however, cannot by any means be said of the philosophies currently fashionable. They are no longer the essential substance of their times, expressed in ideas. In their "provincial" sphere, the ontologists are indeed doing themselves some good. This is duly parallelled by the impotent poverty of ideas evinced by the positivists. They have so modified the rules of the game that the reified consciousness of mindless "bright boys" may consider itself the cream of the "Zeitgeist." They are, however, but a symptom of the current mentality, and falsify what they want in the incorruptible virtue of those whom nobody will deceive. Both tendencies represent, at most, the spirit of regression, and Nietzsche's "Hinterweltler" (those remote from the main currents of life in the world) have literally reverted to being backwoodsmen. From such, philosophy, as the most advanced kind of awareness, should preserve itself, pervaded as it is with the possibility of becoming something different—and equal to the resistance of the forces of regression—should what it has absorbed and understood as so much ballast be raised to new, unforseen heights. If, in the face of such a claim—of which it is well aware—the philosophical archaism of today is evasive concerning the older kind of verity; if it treats casually the idea of progress, which it is engaged in obstructing, much as though it had got the better of it, we can put it down to humbug. No dialectic of progress could legitimatize an intellectual attitude that considers itself sound and "healthy" merely because it has not so far felt the pressures of that objectivity in which it is itself involved—and which ensures that the appeal to soundness directly strengthens the evil. That self-righteous meditation that treats the progressive type of consciousness with contempt is hackneyed. Reflections that go beyond the neo-ontological incantations, as well as beyond the "verities of fact" of the positivists, are not fashionable extremes, but are cogently motivated. As long as philosophy retains the slightest trace of the particular atmosphere diffused by the title of a book published more than thirty years ago by an early Kantian: "Aus der Philosophenecke" (Out of the Philosopher's Corner), it will continue to be the plaything of its detractors. Avuncular advice will not suffice to raise it above the hum and whirr of scientific activity. All wisdom has degenerated to the pontifical. Neither is philosophy turning to advantage the approach of that professor who, in the pre-Fascist era, experienced an urge to rectify the ills of the times, and examined Marlene Dietrich's film "The Blue Angel" in order to obtain, at first hand, an idea of how bad things really were. Excursions of that kind into tangible realities turn philosophy into the refuse of history, with the subject-matter of which it is confused, in the manner of a fetishistic belief in culture per se. A fair measure of the worth of a philosophy in these days would be its ability to counteract all such tendencies. It should not merely aim at the supercilious assembly of facts of various kinds and then take more or less arbitrary decisions, but it should seek, without mental reservations, to learn what those who cling to certain tenets wish to avoid, guided by the superstition that philosophy should, when all is said and done, have something constructive to offer. Rimbaud's phrase "Il faut être absolument moderne"* is not a programme of an aesthetic nature, nor one likely to appeal to lovers of neat and tidy schemes. It is a categorical imperative of philosophy. Those lines of enquiry that expressly seek to avoid it are the first to fall victims to historical bias. It does not hold the key to salvation, but allows some hope only to the movement of concept followed by the intellect wherever the path may lead.

---

* The statement has the force of an impersonal imperative: "One must be absolutely modern."

PART TWO

THE DIALECTIC OF ENLIGHTENMENT

The two selections in this part were written in Los Angeles between 1942 and 1944, among the darkest years for German emigrés fearful of a Nazi victory. Pessimism was further heightened in the case of Adorno and Horkheimer. They were convinced that an Allied victory would at most forestall what they perceived to be the inevitable spread of technological totalitarianism at work in all rationalized societies, including the capitalist democracies of the West. This conviction contrasts rather sharply with the views held by Adorno and Horkheimer in the 1930s. Although at that time they also warned about the ideological function of technology and science in capitalist society, they nonetheless continued to evince faith in the emancipatory power of reason. Indeed, Horkheimer himself insisted that the collaboration of philosophy and science was necessary for rational critique.

Max Horkheimer (1895–1971) studied with Edmund Husserl and Martin Heidegger before receiving his Ph.D. in 1922. He officially assumed the directorship of the Frankfurt Institute in 1931. After spending his wartime exile in America, he returned to Frankfurt to reestablish the institute, of which he was director from 1951 until 1956.

Horkheimer's essay "Means and Ends" is part of a larger collection of essays originally published in *Eclipse of Reason* (1947). The latter treats many of the themes developed in *Dialectic of Enlightenment* (1947), whose introductory essay, "The Concept of Enlightenment," we have also excerpted. Indeed, so similar is Horkheimer's thinking in *Eclipse of Reason* to that contained in *Dialectic of Enlightenment*, which he co-authored with Adorno, that, as he himself noted, "it would be difficult to say which of the ideas originated in his mind and which in my own; our philosophy is one."[1]

For more information concerning the sociological background and a more detailed discussion of the argument of *Dialectic of Enlightenment* and *Eclipse of Reason*, see *Critical Theory and Philosophy*, Chapters 3 and 4.

---

[1] M. Horkheimer, *Eclipse of Reason* (New York: Seabury, 1947), p. vii.

MAX HORKHEIMER

MEANS AND ENDS

When the ordinary man is asked to explain what is meant by the term reason, his reaction is almost always one of hesitation and embarrassment. It would be a mistake to interpret this as indicating wisdom too deep or thought too abstruse to be put into words. What it actually betrays is the feeling that there is nothing to inquire into, that the concept of reason is self-explanatory, that the question itself is superfluous. When pressed for an answer, the average man will say that reasonable things are things that are obviously useful, and that every reasonable man is supposed to be able to decide what is useful to him. Naturally the circumstances of each situation, as well as laws, customs, and traditions, should be taken into account. But the force that ultimately makes reasonable actions possible is the faculty of classification, inference, and deduction, no matter what the specific content—the abstract functioning of the thinking mechanism. This type of reason may be called subjective reason. It is essentially concerned with means and ends, with the adequacy of procedures for purposes more or less taken for granted and supposedly self-explanatory. It attaches little importance to the question whether the purposes as such are reasonable. If it concerns itself at all with ends, it takes for granted that they too are reasonable in the subjective sense, i.e. that they serve the subject's interest in relation to self-preservation—be it that of the single individual, or of the community on whose maintenance that of the individual depends. The idea that an aim can be reasonable for its own sake—on the basis of virtues that insight reveals it to have in itself—without reference to some kind of subjective gain or advantage, is utterly alien to subjective reason, even where it rises above the consideration of immediate utilitarian values and devotes itself to reflections about the social order as a whole.

However naive or superficial this definition of reason may seem, it is an important symptom of a profound change of outlook that has taken place in Western thinking in the course of the last centuries. For a long time, a diametrically opposite view of reason was prevalent. This view asserted the existence of reason as a force not only in the individual mind but also in the objective world—in relations among human beings and between social classes, in social institutions, and in nature and its manifestations. Great philosophical systems, such as those of Plato and Aristotle, scholasticism, and German idealism were founded on an objective theory of reason. It aimed at evolving a comprehensive system, or hierarchy, of all beings, including man and his aims. The degree of reasonableness of a man's life could be determined according to its harmony with this totality. Its objective structure, and not just man and his purposes, was to be the measuring rod for individual thoughts and actions. This concept of reason never precluded subjective reason, but regarded the latter as only a partial, limited expression of a universal rationality from which criteria for all things and beings were derived. The emphasis was on ends rather than on means. The supreme endeavor of this kind of thinking was to reconcile the objective order of the 'reasonable,' as philosophy conceived it, with human existence, including self-interest and self-preservation. Plato, for instance, undertakes in his *Republic* to prove that he who lives in the light of objective reason also lives a successful and happy life. The theory of objective reason did not focus on the co-ordination of behavior and aim, but on concepts—however mythological they sound to us today—on the idea of the greatest good, on the problem of human destiny, and on the way of realization of ultimate goals.

There is a fundamental difference between this theory, according to which reason is a principle inherent in reality, and the doctrine that reason is a subjective faculty of the mind. According to the latter, the subject alone can genuinely have reason: if we say that an institution or any other reality is reasonable, we usually mean that men have organized it reasonably, that they have applied to it, in a more or less technical way, their logical, calculative capacity. Ultimately subjective reason proves to be the ability to calculate probabilities and thereby to co-ordinate the right means with a given end. This definition seems to be in harmony with the ideas of many outstanding philosophers, particularly of English thinkers since the days of John Locke. Of course, Locke did not overlook other mental functions that might fall into the same category, for example discernment and reflection. But these functions certainly contribute to the co-ordination of means and ends, which is, after all, the social concern of science and, in a way, the *raison d'être* of theory in the social process of production.

In the subjectivist view, when 'reason' is used to connote a thing or an idea rather than an act, it refers exclusively to the relation of such an object or concept to a purpose, not to the object or concept itself. It means that the thing or the idea is good for something else. There is no reasonable aim as such, and to discuss the superiority of one aim over another in terms of reason becomes meaningless. From the subjective approach, such a discussion is possible only if both aims serve a third and higher one, that is, if they are means, not ends.[1]

The relation between these two concepts of reason is not merely one of opposition. Historically, both the subjective and the objective aspects of reason have been present from the outset, and the predominance of the former over the latter was achieved in the course of a long process. Reason in its proper sense of *logos*, or *ratio*, has always been essentially related to the subject, his faculty of thinking. All the terms denoting it were once subjective expressions; thus the Greek term stems from λέγειν, 'to say,' denoting the subjective faculty of speech. The subjective faculty of thinking was the critical agent that dissolved superstition. But in denouncing mythology as false objectivity, i.e. as a creation of the subject, it had to use concepts that it recognized as adequate. Thus it always developed an objectivity of its own. In Platonism, the Pythagorean theory of numbers, which originated in astral mythology, was transformed into the theory of ideas that attempts to define the supreme content of thinking as an absolute objectivity ultimately beyond, though related to, the faculty of thinking. The present crisis of reason consists fundamentally in the fact that at a certain point thinking either became incapable of conceiving such objectivity at all or began to negate it as a delusion. This process was gradually extended to include the objective content of every rational concept. In the end, no particular reality can seem reasonable *per se*; all the basic concepts, emptied of their content, have come to be only formal shells. As reason is subjectivized, it also becomes formalized.[2]

The formalization of reason has far-reaching theoretical and practical implications. If the subjectivist view holds true, thinking cannot be of any help in determining the desirability of any goal in itself. The acceptability of ideals, the criteria for our actions and beliefs, the leading principles of ethics and politics, all our ultimate decisions are made to depend upon factors other than reason. They are supposed to be matters of choice and predilection, and it has become meaningless to speak of truth in making practical, moral, or esthetic decisions. 'A judgment of fact,' says Russell,[3] one of the most objectivist thinkers among subjectivists, 'is capable of a property called "truth," which it has or does not have quite independently of what any one may think about it. . . . But . . . I see no property, analogous to "truth," that belongs or does not belong to an ethical judgment. This, it must be admitted, puts ethics in a different category from science.' However, Russell, more than others, is aware of the difficulties in which such a theory necessarily becomes involved. 'An inconsistent system may well contain less falsehood than a consistent one.'[4] Despite his philosophy, which holds 'ultimate ethical values to be subjective,'[5] he seems to differentiate between the objective moral qualities of human actions and our perception of them: 'What is horrible I will see as horrible.' He has the courage of inconsistency and thus, by disavowing certain aspects of his anti-dialectical logic, remains indeed a philosopher and a humanist at the same time. If he were to cling to his scientistic theory consistently, he would have to admit that there are no horrible actions or inhuman conditions, and that the evil he sees is just an illusion.

According to such theories, thought serves any particular endeavor, good or bad. It is a tool of all actions of society, but it must not try to set the patterns of social and individual life, which are assumed to be set by other forces. In lay discussion as well as in scientific, reason has come to be commonly regarded as an intellectual faculty of co-ordination, the efficiency of which can be increased by methodical use and by the removal of any non-intellectual factors, such as conscious or unconscious emotions.

Reason has never really directed social reality, but now reason has been so thoroughly purged of any specific trend or preference that it has finally renounced even the task of passing judgment on man's actions and way of life. Reason has turned them over for ultimate sanction to the conflicting interests to which our world actually seems abandoned.

This relegation of reason to a subordinate position is in sharp contrast to the ideas of the pioneers of bourgeois civilization, the spiritual and political representatives of the rising middle class, who were unanimous in declaring that reason plays a leading role in human behavior, perhaps even the predominant role. They defined a wise legislature as one whose laws conform to reason; national and international policies were judged according to whether they followed the lines of reason. Reason was supposed to regulate our preferences and our relations with other human beings and with nature. It was thought of as an entity, a spiritual power living in each man. This power was held to be the supreme arbiter—nay, more, the creative force behind the ideas and things to which we should devote our lives.

Today, when you are summoned into a traffic court, and the judge asks you whether your driving was reasonable, he means: Did you do everything in your power to protect your own and other people's lives and property, and to obey the law? He implicitly assumes that these values must be respected. What he questions is merely the adequacy of your behavior in terms of these generally recognized standards. In most cases, to be reasonable means not to be obstinate, which in turn points to conformity with reality as it is. The principle of adjustment is taken for granted. When the idea of reason was conceived, it was intended to achieve more than the mere regulation of the relation between means and ends: it was regarded as the instrument for understanding the ends, *for determining them.* Socrates died because he subjected the most sacred and most familiar ideas of his community and his country to the critique of the daimonion, or dialectical thought, as Plato called it. In doing so, he fought against both ideologic conservatism and relativism masked as progressiveness but actually subordinated to personal and professional interests. In other words, he fought against the subjective, formalistic reason advocated by the other Sophists. He undermined the sacred tradition of Greece, the Athenian way of life, thus preparing the soil for radically different forms of individual and social life. Socrates held that reason, conceived as universal insight, should determine beliefs, regulate relations between man and man, and between man and nature. . . .

The term objective reason thus on the one hand denotes as its essence a structure inherent in reality that by itself calls for a specific mode of behavior in each specific case, be it a practical or a theoretical attitude. This structure is accessible to him who takes upon himself the effort of dialectical thinking, or, identically, who is capable of *eros.* On the other hand, the term objective reason may also designate this very effort and ability to reflect such an objective order. Everybody is familiar with situations that by their very nature, and quite apart from the interests of the subject, call for a definite line of action—for example, a child or an animal on the verge of drowning, a starving population, or an individual illness. Each of these situations speaks, as it were, a language of itself. However, since they are only segments of reality, each of them may have to be neglected because there are more comprehensive structures demanding other lines of action equally independent of personal wishes and interests.

The philosophical systems of objective reason implied the conviction that an all-embracing or fundamental structure of being could be discovered and a conception of human destination derived from it. They understood science, when worthy of this name, as an implementation of such reflection or speculation. They were opposed to any epistemology that would reduce the objective basis of our insight to a chaos of unco-ordinated data, and identify our scientific work as the mere organization, classification, or computation of such data. The latter activities, in which subjective reason tends to see the main function of science, are in the light of the classical systems of objective reason subordinate to speculation. Objective reason aspires to replace traditional religion with methodical philosophical thought and insight and thus to become a source of tradition all by itself. Its attack on mythology is perhaps more serious than that of subjective reason, which, abstract and formalistic as it conceives itself to be, is inclined to abandon the fight with religion by setting up two different brackets, one for science and philosophy, and one for institutionalized mythology, thus recognizing both of them. For the philosophy of objective reason there is no such way out. Since it holds to the concept of objective truth, it must take a positive or a negative stand with regard to the content of established religion. Therefore the critique of social beliefs in the name of objective reason is much more portentous—although it is sometimes less direct and aggressive—than that put forward in the name of subjective reason. . . .

In the philosophical and political systems of rationalism, Christian ethics was secularized. The aims pursued in individual and social activity were derived from the assumption of the existence of certain innate ideas or self-evident intuitions, and thus linked to the concept of objective truth, although this truth was no longer regarded as being guaranteed by any dogma extraneous to the exigencies of thinking itself. Neither the church nor the rising philosophical systems separated wisdom, ethics, religion, and politics. But the fundamental unity of all human beliefs, rooted in a common Christian ontology, was gradually shattered, and the relativist tendencies that had been explicit in the pioneers of bourgeois ideology such as Montaigne, but had later been temporarily pushed into the background by rationalist metaphysics, asserted themselves victoriously in all cultural activities. . . .

Eventually the active controversy between religion and philosophy ended in a stalemate because the two were considered as separate branches of culture. People have gradually become reconciled to the idea that each lives its own life within the walls of its cultural compartment, tolerating the other. The neutralization of religion, now reduced to the status of one cultural good among others, contradicted its 'total' claim that it incorporates objective truth, and also emasculated it. Although religion remained respected on the surface, its neutralization paved the way for its elimination as the medium of spiritual objectivity and ultimately for the abolition of the concept of such an objectivity, itself patterned after the idea of the absoluteness of religious revelation.

In reality the contents of both philosophy and religion have been deeply affected by this seemingly peaceful settlement of their original conflict. The philosophers of the Enlightenment attacked religion in the name of reason; in the end what they killed was not the church but metaphysics and the objective concept of reason itself, the source of power of their own efforts. Reason as an organ for perceiving the true nature of reality and determining the guiding principles of our lives has come to be regarded as obsolete. Speculation is synonymous with metaphysics, and metaphysics with mythology and superstition. We might say that the history of reason or enlightenment from its beginnings in Greece down to the present has led to a state of affairs in which even the word reason is suspected of connoting some mythological entity. Reason has liquidated itself as an agency of ethical, moral, and religious insight. Bishop Berkeley, legitimate son of nominalism, Protestant zealot, and positivist enlightener all in one, directed an attack against such general concepts, including the concept of a general concept, two hundred years ago. In fact, the campaign has been victorious all along the line. Berkeley, in partial contradiction of his own theory, retained a few general concepts, such as mind, spirit, and cause. But they were efficiently eliminated by Hume, the father of modern positivism. . . .

All these consequences were contained in germ in the bourgeois idea of tolerance, which is ambivalent. On the one hand, tolerance means freedom from the rule of dogmatic authority; on the other, it furthers an attitude of neutrality toward all spiritual content, which is thus surrendered to relativism. Each cultural domain preserves its 'sovereignty' with regard to universal truth. The pattern of the social division of labor is automatically transferred to the life of the spirit, and this division of the realm of culture is a corollary to the replacement of universal objective truth by formalized, inherently relativist reason.

Self-interest, on which certain theories of natural law and hedonistic philosophies have tried to place primary emphasis, was held to be only one such insight, regarded as rooted in the objective structure of the universe and thus forming a part in the whole system of categories. In the industrial age, the idea of self-interest gradually gained the upper hand and finally suppressed the other motives considered fundamental to the functioning of society; this attitude dominated in the leading schools of thought and, during the liberalistic period, in the public mind. But the same process brought to the surface the contradictions between the theory of self-interest and the idea of the nation. Philosophy then was confronted with the alternative of accepting the anarchistic consequences of this theory or of falling prey to an irrational nationalism much more tainted with romanticism than were the theories of innate ideas that prevailed in the mercantilist period. . . .

This explains the tendency of liberalism to tilt over into fascism and of the intellectual and political representatives of liberalism to make their peace with its opposites. This tendency, so often demonstrated in recent European history, can be derived, apart from its economic causes, from the inner contradiction between the subjectivistic principle of self-interest and the idea of reason that it is alleged to express. Originally the political constitution was thought of as an expression of concrete principles founded in objective reason; the ideas of justice, equality, happiness, democracy, property, all were held to correspond to reason, to emanate from reason. Subsequently, the content of reason is reduced arbitrarily to the scope of merely a part of this content, to the frame of only one of its principles; the particular preempts the place of the universal. This *tour de force* in the realm of the intellectual lays the ground for the rule of force in the domain of the political.

Having given up autonomy, reason has become an instrument. In the formalistic aspect of subjective reason, stressed by positivism, its unrelatedness to objective content is emphasized; in its instrumental aspect, stressed by pragmatism, its surrender to heteronomous contents is emphasized. Reason has become completely harnessed to the social process. Its operational value, its role in the domination of men and nature, has been made the sole criterion. Concepts have been reduced to summaries of the characteristics that several specimens have in common. By denoting a similarity, concepts eliminate the bother of enumerating qualities and thus serve better to organize the material of knowledge. They are thought of as mere abbreviations of the items to which they refer. Any use transcending auxiliary, technical summarization of factual data has been eliminated as a last trace of superstition. Concepts have become 'streamlined,' rationalized, labor-saving devices. It is as if thinking itself has been reduced to the level of industrial processes, subjected to a close schedule—in short, made part and parcel of production. Toynbee[6] has described some of the consequences of this process for the writing of history. He speaks of the 'tendency for the potter to become the slave of his clay. . . . In the world of action, we know that it is disastrous to treat animals or human beings as though they were stocks and stones. Why should we suppose this treatment to be any less mistaken in the world of ideas?'

The more ideas have become automatic, instrumentalized, the less does anybody see in them thoughts with a meaning of their own. They are considered things, machines. Language has been reduced to just another tool in the gigantic apparatus of production in modern society. Every sentence that is not equivalent to an operation in that apparatus appears to the layman just as meaningless as it is held to be by contemporary semanticists who imply that the purely symbolic and operational, that is, the purely senseless sentence, makes sense. Meaning is supplanted by function or effect in the world of things and events. In so far as words are not used obviously to calculate technically relevant probabilities or for other practical purposes, among which even relaxation is included, they are in danger of being suspect as sales talk of some kind, for truth is no end in itself. . . .

What are the consequences of the formalization of reason? Justice, equality, happiness, tolerance, all the concepts that, as mentioned, were in preceding centuries supposed to be inherent in or sanctioned by reason, have lost their intellectual roots. They are still aims and ends, but there is no rational agency authorized to appraise and link them to an objective reality. Endorsed by venerable historical documents, they may still enjoy a certain prestige, and some are contained in the supreme law of the greatest countries. Nevertheless, they lack any confirmation by reason in its modern sense. Who can say that any one of these ideals is more closely related to truth than its opposite? According to the philosophy of the average modern intellectual, there is only one authority, namely, science, conceived as the classification of facts and the calculation of probabilities. The statement that justice and freedom are better in themselves than injustice and oppression is scientifically unverifiable and useless. It has come to sound as meaningless in itself as would the statement that red is more beautiful than blue, or that an egg is better than milk.

The more the concept of reason becomes emasculated, the more easily it lends itself to ideological manipulation and to propagation of even the most blatant lies. The advance of enlightenment dissolves the idea of objective reason, dogmatism, and superstition; but often reaction and obscurantism profit most from this development. Vested interests opposed to the traditional humanitarian values will appeal to neutralized, impotent reason in the name of 'common sense.' This devitalization of basic concepts can be followed through political history. In the American Constitutional Convention of 1787, John Dickinson of Pennsylvania contrasted experience with reason when he said: 'Experience must be our only guide. Reason may mislead us.'[7] He wished to caution against a too radical idealism. Later the concepts became so emptied of substance that they could be used synonymously to advocate oppression. Charles O'Conor, a celebrated lawyer of the period before the Civil War, once nominated for the presidency by a faction of the Democratic party, argued (after outlining the blessings of compulsory servitude): 'I insist that negro slavery is not unjust; it is just, wise, and beneficent . . . I insist that negro slavery . . . is ordained by nature . . . Yielding to the clear decree of nature, and the dictates of sound philosophy, we must pronounce that institution just, benign, lawful and proper.'[8] Though O'Conor still uses the words nature, philosophy, and justice, they are completely formalized and cannot stand up against what he considers to be facts and experience. Subjective reason conforms to anything. It lends itself as well to the uses of the adversaries as of the defenders of the traditional humanitarian values. It furnishes, as in O'Conor's instance, the ideology for profit and reaction as well as the ideology for progress and revolution. . . .

The basic ideals and concepts of rationalist metaphysics were rooted in the concept of the universally human, of mankind, and their formalization implies that they have been severed from their human content. How this dehumanization of thinking affects the very foundations of our civilization can be illustrated by analysis of the principle of the majority, which is inseparable from the principle of democracy. In the eyes of the average man, the principle of the majority is often not only a substitute for but an improvement upon objective reason: since men are after all the best judges of their own interests, the resolutions of a majority, it is thought, are certainly as valuable to a community as the intuitions of a so-called superior reason. However, the contradiction between intuition and the democratic principle, conceived in such crude terms, is only imaginary. For what does it mean to say that 'a man knows his own interests best'—how does he gain this knowledge, what evidences that his knowledge is correct? In the proposition, 'A man knows . . . best,' there is an implicit reference to an agency that is not totally arbitrary and that is incidental to some sort of reason underlying not only means but ends as well. If that agency should turn out to be again merely the majority, the whole argument would constitute a tautology.

The great philosophical tradition that contributed to the founding of modern democracy was not guilty of this tautology, for it based the principles of government upon more or less speculative assumptions—for instance, the assumption that the same spiritual substance or moral consciousness is present in each human being. In other words, respect for the majority was based on a conviction that did not itself depend on the resolutions of the majority. Locke still spoke of natural reason's agreeing with revelation in regard to human rights.[9] His theory of government refers to the affirmations of both reason and revelation. They are supposed to teach that men are 'by nature all free, equal, and independent.'[10]

Locke's theory of knowledge is an example of that treacherous lucidity of style which unites opposites by simply blurring the nuances. He did not care to differentiate too clearly between sensual and rational, atomistic and structural experience, nor did he indicate whether the state of nature from which he derived the natural law was inferred by logical processes or intuitively perceived. However, it seems to be sufficiently clear that freedom 'by nature' is not identical with freedom in fact. His political doctrine is based on rational insight and deductions rather than on empirical research.

The same may be said of Locke's disciple, Rousseau. When the latter declared that the renunciation of liberty is against the nature of man, because thereby 'man's actions would be deprived of all morality and his will deprived of all liberty,'[11] he knew very well that the renunciation of liberty was not against the empirical nature of man; he himself bitterly criticized individuals, groups, and nations for renouncing their freedom. He referred to man's spiritual substance rather than to a psychological attitude. His doctrine of the social contract is derived from a philosophical doctrine of man, according to which the principle of the majority rather than that of power corresponds to human nature as it is described in speculative thinking. In the history of social philosophy even the term 'common sense' is inseparably linked to the idea of self-evident truth. It was Thomas Reid who, twelve years before the time of Paine's famous pamphlet and the Declaration of Independence, identified the principles of common sense with self-evident truths and thus reconciled empiricism with rationalistic metaphysics.

Deprived of its rational foundation, the democratic principle becomes exclusively dependent upon the so-called interests of the people, and these are functions of blind or all too conscious economic forces. They do not offer any guarantee against tyranny.[12] In the period of the free market system, for instance, institutions based on the idea of human rights were accepted by many people as a good instrument for controlling the government and maintaining peace. But if the situation changes, if powerful economic groups find it useful to set up a dictatorship and abolish majority rule, no objection founded on reason can be opposed to their action. If they have a real chance of success, they would simply be foolish not to take it. The only consideration that could prevent them from doing so would be the possibility that their own interests would be endangered, and not concern over violation of a truth, of reason. Once the philosophical foundation of democracy has collapsed, the statement that dictatorship is bad is rationally valid only for those who are not its beneficiaries, and there is no theoretical obstacle to the transformation of this statement into its opposite.

The men who made the Constitution of the United States considered 'the fundamental law of every society, the *lex majoris partis*,'[13] but they were far from substituting the verdicts of the majority for those of reason. When they incorporated an ingenious system of checks and balances in the structure of government, they held, as Noah Webster put it, that 'the powers lodged in Congress are extensive, but it is presumed that they are not too extensive.'[14] He called the principle of the majority 'a doctrine as universally received as any intuitive truth'[15] and saw in it one among other natural ideas of similar dignity. For these men there was no principle that did not derive its authority from a metaphysical or religious source. Dickinson regarded the government and its trust as 'founded on the nature of man, that is, on the will of his Maker and . . . therefore sacred. It is then an offence against Heaven to violate that trust.'[16]

The majority principle in itself was certainly not considered to be a guarantee of justice. 'The majority,' says John Adams,[17] 'has eternally and without one exception, usurped over the rights of the minority.' These rights and all other fundamental principles were believed to be intuitive truths. They were taken over directly or indirectly from a philosophical tradition that at the time was still alive. They can be traced back through the history of Western thought to their religious and mythological roots, and it is from these origins that they had preserved the 'awfulness' that Dickinson mentions.

Subjective reason has no use for such inheritance. It reveals truth as habit and thereby strips it of its spiritual authority. Today the idea of the majority, deprived of its rational foundations, has assumed a completely irrational aspect. Every philosophical, ethical, and political idea—its lifeline connecting it with its historical origins having been severed—has a tendency to become the nucleus of a new mythology, and this is one of the reasons why the advance of enlightenment tends at certain points to revert to superstition and paranoia. The majority principle, in the form of popular verdicts on each and every matter, implemented by all kinds of polls and modern techniques of communication, has become the sovereign force to which thought must cater. It is a new god, not in the sense in which the heralds of the great revolutions conceived it, namely, as a power of resistance to existing injustice, but as a power of resistance to anything that does not conform. The more the judgment of the people is manipulated by all kinds of interests, the more is the majority presented as the arbiter in cultural life. It is supposed to justify the surrogates of culture in all its branches, down to the mass-deceiving products of popular art and literature. The greater the extent to which scientific propaganda makes of public opinion a mere tool for obscure forces, the more does public opinion appear a substitute for reason. This illusory triumph of democratic progress consumes the intellectual substance on which democracy has lived. . . .

It may be just as meaningless to call one particular way of living, one religion, one philosophy better or higher or truer than another. Since ends are no longer determined in the light of reason, it is also impossible to say that one economic or political system, no matter how cruel and despotic, is less reasonable than another. According to formalized reason, despotism, cruelty, oppression are not bad in themselves; no rational agency would endorse a verdict against dictatorship if its sponsors were likely to profit by it. Phrases like 'the dignity of man' either imply a dialectical advance in which the idea of divine right is preserved and transcended, or become hackneyed slogans that reveal their emptiness as soon as somebody inquires into their specific meaning. Their life depends, so to speak, on unconscious memories. If a group of enlightened people were about to fight even the greatest evil imaginable, subjective reason would make it almost impossible to point simply to the nature of the evil and to the nature of humanity, which make the fight imperative. Many would at once ask what the real motives are. It would have to be asserted that the reasons are realistic, that is to say, correspond to personal interests, even though, for the mass of the people, these latter may be more difficult to grasp than the silent appeal of the situation itself.

The fact that the average man still seems to be attached to the old ideals might be held to contradict this analysis. Formulated in general terms, the objection might be that there is a force that outweighs the destructive effects of formalized reason; namely, conformity to generally accepted values and behavior. After all, there are a large number of ideas that we have been taught to cherish and respect from our earliest childhood. Since these ideas and all the theoretical views connected with them are justified not by reason alone but also by almost universal consent, it would seem that they cannot be affected by the transformation of reason into a mere instrument. They draw their strength from our reverence for the community in which we live, from men who have given their lives for them, from the respect we owe to the founders of the few enlightened nations of our time. This objection actually expresses the weakness of the justification of allegedly objective content by past and present reputation. If tradition, so often denounced in modern scientific and political history, is now invoked as the measure of any ethical or religious truth, this truth has already been affected and must suffer from a lack of authenticity no less acutely than the principle that is supposed to justify it. In the centuries in which tradition still could play the role of evidence, the belief in it was itself derived from the belief in an objective truth. By now, the reference to tradition seems to have preserved but one function from those older times: it indicates that the consensus behind the principle that it seeks to reaffirm is economically or politically powerful. He who offends it is forewarned.

In the eighteenth century the conviction that man is endowed with certain rights was not a repetition of beliefs that were held by the community, nor even a repetition of beliefs handed down by forefathers. It was a reflection of the situation of the men who proclaimed these rights; it expressed a critique of conditions that imperatively called for change, and this demand was understood by and translated into philosophical thought and historical actions. The pathfinders of modern thought did not derive what is good from the law—they even broke the law—but they tried to reconcile the law with the good. Their role in history was not that of adapting their words and actions to the text of old documents or generally accepted doctrines: they themselves created the documents and brought about the acceptance of their doctrines. Today, those who cherish these doctrines and are deprived of an adequate philosophy may regard them either as expressions of mere subjective desires or as an established pattern deriving authority from the number of people who believe in it and the length of time of its existence. The very fact that tradition has to be invoked today shows that it has lost its hold on the people. No wonder that whole nations—and Germany is not alone in this—seem to have awakened one morning only to discover that their most cherished ideals were merely bubbles.

It is true that although the progress of subjective reason destroyed the theoretical basis of mythological, religious, and rationalistic ideas, civilized society has up until now been living on the residue of these ideas. But they tend to become more than ever a mere residue and are thus gradually losing their power of conviction. When the great religious and philosophical conceptions were alive, thinking people did not extol humility and brotherly love, justice and humanity because it was realistic to maintain such principles and odd and dangerous to deviate from them, or because these maxims were more in harmony with their supposedly free tastes than others. They held to such ideas because they saw in them elements of truth, because they connected them with the idea of *logos*, whether in the form of God or of a transcendental mind, or even of nature as an eternal principle. Not only were the highest aims thought of as having an objective meaning, an inherent significance, but even the humblest pursuits and fancies depended on a belief in the general desirability, the inherent value of their objects.

Mythological, objective origins, as they are being destroyed by subjective reason, do not merely pertain to great universal concepts, but are also at the bottom of apparently personal, entirely psychological behaviors and actions. They are all—down to the very emotions—evaporating, as they are being emptied of this objective content, this relation to supposedly objective truth. As children's games and adults' fancies originate in mythology, each joy was once related to a belief in an ultimate truth. . . .

These old forms of life smoldering under the surface of modern civilization still provide, in many cases, the warmth inherent in any delight, in any love of a thing for its own sake rather than for that of another thing. The pleasure of keeping a garden goes back to ancient times when gardens belonged to the gods and were cultivated for them. The sense of beauty in both nature and art is connected, by a thousand delicate threads, to these old superstitions.[18] If, by either flouting or flaunting the threads, modern man cuts them, the pleasure may continue for a while but its inner life is extinguished.

We cannot credit our enjoyment of a flower or of the atmosphere of a room to an autonomous esthetic instinct. Man's esthetic responsiveness relates in its prehistory to various forms of idolatry; his belief in the goodness or sacredness of a thing precedes his enjoyment of its beauty. This applies no less to such concepts as freedom and humanity. What has been said about the dignity of man is certainly applicable to the concepts of justice and equality. Such ideas must preserve the negative element, as the negation of the ancient stage of injustice or inequality, and at the same time conserve the original absolute significance rooted in their dreadful origins. Otherwise they become not only indifferent but untrue.

NOTES

1. The difference between this connotation of reason and the objectivistic conception resembles to a certain degree the difference between functional and substantial rationality as these words are used in the Max Weber school. Max Weber, however, adhered so definitely to the subjectivistic trend that he did not conceive of any rationality—not even a 'substantial' one by which man can discriminate one end from another. If our drives, intentions, and finally our ultimate decisions must *a priori* be irrational, substantial reason becomes an agency merely of correlation and is therefore itself essentially 'functional.' Although Weber's own and his followers' descriptions of the bureaucratization and monopolization of knowledge have illuminated much of the social aspect of the transition from objective to subjective reason (cf. particularly the analyses of Karl Mannheim in *Man and Society*, London, 1940), Max Weber's pessimism with regard to the possibility of rational insight and action, as expressed in his philosophy (cf., e.g., 'Wissenschaft als Beruf,' in *Gesammelte Aufsätze zur Wissenschaftslehre*, Tübingen, 1922), is itself a stepping-stone in the renunciation of philosophy and science as regards their aspiration of defining man's goal.
2. The terms subjectivization and formalization, though in many respects not identical in meaning, will be used as practically equivalent throughout this book.
3. 'Reply to Criticisms,' in *The Philosophy of Bertrand Russell*, Chicago, 1944, p. 723.
4. Ibid. p. 720.
5. Ibid.
6. *A Study of History*, 2d ed., London, 1935, vol. I, p. 7.
7. Cf. Morrison and Commager, *The Growth of the American Republic*, New York, 1942, vol. I, p. 281.
8. *A Speech at the Union Meeting—at the Academy of Music, New York City, December 19, 1859*, reprinted under title, 'Negro Slavery Not Unjust,' by the *New York Herald Tribune*.

9. *Locke on Civil Government*, Second Treatise, chap. V, Everyman's Library, p. 129.

10. Ibid. chap. VIII, p. 164.

11. *Contrat social*, vol. I, p. 4.

12. The anxiety of the editor of Tocqueville, in speaking of the negative aspects of the majority principle, was superfluous (cf. *Democracy in America*, New York, 1898, vol. I, pp. 334–5, note). The editor asserts that 'it is only a figure of speech to say that the majority of the people makes the laws,' and among other things reminds us that this is done in fact by their delegates. He could have added that if Tocqueville spoke of the tyranny of the majority, Jefferson, in a letter quoted by Tocqueville, spoke of 'the tyranny of the legislatures,' *The Writings of Thomas Jefferson*, Definitive Edition, Washington, D. C., 1905, vol. VII. p. 312. Jefferson was so suspicious of either department of government in a democracy, 'whether legislative or executive,' that he was opposed to maintenance of a standing army. Cf. ibid. p. 323.

13. Ibid. p. 324.

14. 'An Examination into the Leading Principles of the Federal Constitution . . . ,' in *Pamphlets on the Constitution of the United States*, ed. by Paul L. Ford, Brooklyn, N. Y., 1888, p. 45.

15. Ibid. p. 30.

16. Ibid. 'Letters of Fabius,' p. 181.

17. Charles Beard, *Economic Origin of Jeffersonian Democracy*, New York, 1915, p. 305.

18. Even the penchant for tidiness, a modern taste par excellence, seems to be rooted in the belief in magic. Sir James Frazer (*The Golden Bough*, vol. I, part I, p. 175) quotes a report on the natives of New Britain which concludes that 'the cleanliness which is usual in the houses, and consists in sweeping the floor carefully every day, is by no means based on a desire for cleanliness and neatness in themselves, but purely on the effort to put out of the way anything that might serve the ill-wisher as a charm.'

THEODOR W. ADORNO AND MAX HORKHEIMER

THE CONCEPT OF ENLIGHTENMENT

In the most general sense of progressive thought, the Enlightenment has always aimed at liberating men from fear and establishing their sovereignty. Yet the fully enlightened earth radiates disaster triumphant. The program of the Enlightenment was the disenchantment of the world; the dissolution of myths and the substitution of knowledge for fancy. Bacon, the "father of experimental philosophy,"[1] had defined its motives. . . .

Despite his lack of mathematics, Bacon's view was appropriate to the scientific attitude that prevailed after him. The concordance between the mind of man and the nature of things that he had in mind is patriarchal: the human mind, which overcomes superstition, is to hold sway over a disenchanted nature. Knowledge, which is power, knows no obstacles: neither in the enslavement of men nor in compliance with the world's rulers. As with all the ends of bourgeois economy in the factory and on the battlefield, origin is no bar to the dictates of the entrepreneurs: kings, no less directly than businessmen, control technology; it is as democratic as the economic system with which it is bound up. Technology is the essence of this knowledge. It does not work by concepts and images, by the fortunate insight, but refers to method, the exploitation of others' work, and capital. The "many things" which, according to Bacon, "are reserved," are themselves no more than instrumental: the radio as a sublimated printing press, the dive bomber as a more effective form of artillery, radio control as a more reliable compass. What men want to learn from nature is how to use it in order wholly to dominate it and other men. That is the only aim. Ruthlessly, in spite of itself, the Enlightenment has extinguished any trace of its own self-consciousness. . . . On the road to modern science, men renounce any claim to meaning. They substitute formula for concept, rule and probability for cause and motive. Cause was only the last philosophic concept which served as a yardstick for scientific criticism: so to speak because it alone among the old ideas still seemed to offer itself to scientific criticism, the latest secularization of the creative principle. Substance and quality, activity and suffering, being and existence: to define these concepts in a way appropriate to the times was a concern of philosophy after Bacon—but science managed without such categories. They were abandoned as *idola theatri** of the old metaphysics, and assessed as being even then memorials of the elements and powers of the prehistory for which life and death disclosed their nature in myths and became interwoven in them. The categories by which Western philosophy defined its everlasting natural order marked the spots once occupied by Oncus and Persephone, Ariadne and Nereus. The pre-Socratic cosmologies preserve the moment of transition. The moist, the indivisible, air, and fire, which they hold to be the primal matter of nature, are already rationalizations of the mythic mode of apprehension. Just as the images of generation from water and earth, which came from the Nile to the Greeks, became here hylozoistic principles, or elements, so all the equivocal multitude of mythical demons were intellectualized in the pure form of ontological essences. Finally, by means of the Platonic ideas, even the patriarchal gods of Olympus were absorbed in the philosophical *logos*. The Enlightenment, however, recognized the old powers in the Platonic and Aristotelian aspects of metaphysics, and opposed as superstition the claim that truth is predicable of universals. It asserted that in the authority of universal concepts, there was still discernible fear of the demonic spirits which men sought to portray in magic rituals, hoping thus to influence nature. From now on, matter would at last be mastered without any illusion of ruling or inherent powers, of hidden qualities. For the Enlightenment, whatever does not conform to the rule of computation and utility is suspect. So long as it can develop undisturbed by any outward repression, there is no holding it. In the process, it treats its own ideas of human rights exactly as it does the older universals. Every spiritual resistance it encounters serves merely to increase its strength.[2] Which means that enlightenment still recognizes itself even in myths. Whatever myths the resistance may appeal to, by virtue of the very fact that they become arguments in the process of opposition, they acknowledge the principle of dissolvent rationality for which they reproach the Enlightenment. Enlightenment is totalitarian.

. . . In advance, the Enlightenment recognizes as being and occurrence only what can be apprehended in unity: its ideal is the system from which all and everything follows. Its rationalist and empiricist versions do not part company on that point. Even though the individual schools may interpret the axioms differently, the structure of scientific unity has always been the same. Bacon's postulate of *una scientia universalis*,[3] whatever the number of fields of research, is as inimical to the unassignable as Leibniz's *mathesis universalis*** is to discontinuity. The multiplicity of forms is reduced to position and arrangement, history to fact, things to matter. According to Bacon, too, degrees of universality provide an unequivocal logical connection between first principles and observational judgments. De Maistre mocks him for haboring "*une idole d'échelle.*"[4]†† Formal logic was the major school of unified science. It

---

* "phantoms of the theatre" [Ed.]
† "a universal science" [Ed.]
** "a universal calculus" [Ed.]
†† "an idol to scale" [Ed.]

provided the Enlightenment thinkers with the schema of the calculability of the world. The mythologizing equation of Ideas with numbers in Plato's last writings expresses the longing of all demythologization: number became the canon of the Enlightenment. The same equations dominate bourgeois justice and commodity exchange. "Is not the rule, 'Si inaequalibus aequalia addas, omnia erunt inaequalia,'* an axiom of justice as well as of the mathematics? And is there not a true coincidence between commutative and distributive justice, and arithmetical and geometrical proportion?"5 Bourgeois society is ruled by equivalence. It makes the dissimilar comparable by reducing it to abstract quantities. To the Enlightenment, that which does not reduce to numbers, and ultimately to the one, becomes illusion; modern positivism writes it off as literature. Unity is the slogan from Parmenides to Russell. The destruction of gods and qualities alike is insisted upon.

Yet the myths which fell victim to the Enlightenment were its own products. In the scientific calculation of occurrence, the computation is annulled which thought had once transferred from occurrence into myths. Myth intended report, naming, the narration of the Beginning; but also presentation, confirmation, explanation: a tendency that grew stronger with the recording and collection of myths. Narrative became didactic at an early stage. Every ritual includes the idea of activity as a determined process which magic can nevertheless influence. This theoretical element in ritual won independence in the earliest national epics. The myths, as the tragedians came upon them, are already characterized by the discipline and power that Bacon celebrated as the "right mark." . . .

Myth turns into enlightenment, and nature into mere objectivity. Men pay for the increase of their power with alienation from that over which they exercise their power. Enlightenment behaves toward things as a dictator toward men. He knows them in so far as he can manipulate them. The man of science knows things in so far as he can make them. In this way their potentiality is turned to his own ends. In the metamorphosis the nature of things, as a substratum of domination, is revealed as always the same. This identity constitutes the unity of nature. It is a presupposition of the magical invocation as little as the unity of the subject. The shaman's rites were directed to the wind, the rain, the serpent without, or the demon in the sick man, but not to materials or specimens. . . . Like science, magic pursues aims, but seeks to achieve them by mimesis—not by progressively distancing itself from the object. It is not grounded in the "sovereignty of ideas," which the primitive, like the neurotic, is said to ascribe to himself;6 there can be no "over-evaluation of mental processes as against reality" where there is no radical distinction between thoughts and reality. The "unshakable confidence in the possibility of world domination,"7 which Freud anachronistically ascribes to magic, corresponds to realistic world domination only in terms of a more skilled science. The replacement of the milieu-bound practices of the medicine man by all-inclusive industrial technology required first of all the autonomy of ideas in regard to objects that was achieved in the reality-adjusted ego.

---

* "If you add equal to unequal things, everything will be unequal" [Ed.].

. . . Mythology itself set off the unending process of enlightenment in which ever and again, with the inevitability of necessity, every specific theoretic view succumbs to the destructive criticism that it is only a belief—until even the very notions of spirit, of truth and, indeed, enlightenment itself, have become animistic magic. The principle of fatal necessity, which brings low the heroes of myth and derives as a logical consequence from the pronouncement of the oracle, does not merely, when refined to the stringency of formal logic, rule in every rationalistic system of Western philosophy, but itself dominates the series of systems which begins with the hierarchy of the gods and, in a permanent twilight of the idols, hands down an identical content: anger against insufficient righteousness. Just as the myths already realize enlightenment, so enlightenment with every step becomes more deeply engulfed in mythology. It receives all its matter from the myths, in order to destroy them; and even as a judge it comes under the mythic curse. It wishes to extricate itself from the process of fate and retribution, while exercising retribution on that process. In the myths everything that happens must atone for having happened. And so it is in enlightenment: the fact becomes null and void, and might as well not have happened. The doctrine of the equivalence of action and reaction asserted the power of repetition over reality, long after men had renounced the illusion that by repetition they could identify themselves with the repeated reality and thus escape its power. But as the magical illusion fades away, the more relentlessly in the name of law repetition imprisons man in the cycle—that cycle whose objectification in the form of natural law he imagines will ensure his action as a free subject. The principle of immanence, the explanation of every event as repetition, that the Enlightenment upholds against mythic imagination, is the principle of myth itself. . . . Abstraction, the tool of enlightenment, treats its objects as did fate, the notion of which it rejects: it liquidates them. Under the leveling domination of abstraction (which makes everything in nature repeatable), and of industry (for which abstraction ordains repetition), the freedom themselves finally came to form that "herd" which Hegel[8] has declared to be the result of the Enlightenment.

The distance between subject and object, a presupposition of abstraction, is grounded in the distance from the thing itself which the master achieved through the mastered. . . . The universality of ideas as developed by discursive logic, domination in the conceptual sphere, is raised up on the basis of actual domination. The dissolution of the magical heritage, of the old diffuse ideas, by conceptual unity, expresses the hierarchical constitution of life determined by those who are free. The individuality that learned order and subordination in the subjection of the world, soon wholly equated truth with the regulative thought without whose fixed distinctions universal truth cannot exist. . . .

. . . The concept, which some would see as the sign-unit for whatever is comprised under it, has from the beginning been instead the product of dialectical thinking in which everything is always that which it is, only because it becomes that which it is not. That was the original form of objectifying definition, in which concept and thing are separated. . . . The symbols undertake a fetishistic function. In the process, the recurrence of nature which they signify is always the permanence of the social pressure which they represent. The dread objectified as a fixed image becomes the sign of the established domination of the privileged. Such is the fate of universal concepts, even when they have discarded everything pictorial. Even the deductive form of science reflects hierarchy and coercion. Just as the first categories represented the organized tribe and its power over the individual, so the whole logical order, dependency, connection, progression, and union of concepts is grounded in the corresponding conditions of social reality—that is, of the division of labor.[9] But of course this social character of categories of thought is not, as Durkheim asserts, an expression of social solidarity, but evidence of the inscrutable unity of society and domination. Domination lends increased consistency and force to the social whole in which it establishes itself. The division of labor to which domination tends serves the dominated whole for the end of self-preservation. But then the whole as whole, the manifestation of its immanent reason, necessarily leads to the execution of the particular. To the individual, domination appears to be the universal: reason in actuality. Through the division of labor imposed on them, the power of all the members of society—for whom as such there is no other course—amounts over and over again to the realization of the whole, whose rationality is reproduced in this way. What is done to all by the few always occurs as the subjection of individuals by the many: social repression always exhibits the masks of repression by a collective. It is this unity of the collectivity and domination, and not direct social universality, solidarity, which is expressed in thought forms. . . .

. . . Enlightenment is as totalitarian as any system. Its untruth does not consist in what its romantic enemies have always reproached it for: analytical method, return to elements, dissolution through reflective thought; but instead in the fact that for enlightenment the process is always decided from the start. When in mathematical procedure the unknown becomes the unknown quantity of an equation, this marks it as the well-known even before any value is inserted. Nature, before and after the quantum theory, is that which is to be comprehended mathematically; even what cannot be made to agree, indissolubility and irrationality, is converted by means of mathematical theorems. In the anticipatory identification of the wholly conceived and mathematized world with truth, enlightenment intends to secure itself against the return of the mythic. It confounds thought and mathematics. . . . Thinking objectifies itself to become an automatic, self-activating process; an impersonation of the machine that it produces itself so that ultimately the machine can replace it. . . . Mathematical procedure became, so to speak, the ritual of thinking. In spite of the axiomatic self-restriction, it establishes itself as necessary and objective: it turns thought into a thing, an instrument—which is its own term for it. . . . The more the machinery of thought subjects existence to itself, the more blind its resignation in reproducing existence. Hence enlightenment returns to mythology, which it never really knew how to elude. For in its figures mythology had the essence of the *status quo*: cycle, fate, and domination of the world reflected as the truth and deprived of hope. In both the pregnancy of the mythical image and the clarity of the scientific formula, the everlastingness of the factual is confirmed and mere existence pure and simple expressed as the meaning which it forbids. . . . The absorption of factuality, whether into legendary prehistory or into mathematical formalism, the symbolical relation of the contemporary to the mythic process in the rite or to the abstract category in science, makes the new appear as the predetermined, which is accordingly the old. . . .

In the enlightened world, mythology has entered into the profane. In its blank purity, the reality which has been cleansed of demons and their conceptual descendants assumes the numinous character which the ancient world attributed to demons. Under the title of brute facts, the social injustice from which they proceed is now as assuredly sacred a preserve as the medicine man was sacrosanct by reason of the protection of his gods. It is not merely that domination is paid for by the alienation of men from the objects dominated: with the objectification of spirit, the very relations of men—even those of the individual to himself—were bewitched. The individual is reduced to the nodal point of the conventional responses and modes of operation expected of him. Animism spiritualized the object, whereas industrialism objectifies the spirits of men. Automatically, the economic apparatus, even before total planning, equips commodities with the values which decide human behavior. Since, with the end of free exchange, commodities lost all their economic qualities except for fetishism, the latter has extended its arthritic influence over all aspects of social life. Through the countless agencies of mass production and its culture the conventionalized modes of behavior are impressed on the individual as the only natural, respectable, and rational ones. He defines himself only as a thing, as a static element, as success or failure. His yardstick is self-preservation, successful or unsuccessful approximation to the objectivity of his function and the models established for it. . . . In the end the transcendental subject of cognition is apparently abandoned as the last reminiscence of subjectivity and replaced by the much smoother work of automatic control mechanisms. Subjectivity has given way to the logic of the allegedly indifferent rules of the game, in order to dictate all the more unrestrainedly. Positivism, which finally did not spare thought itself, the chimera in a cerebral form, has removed the very last insulating instance between individual behavior and the social norm. The technical process, into which the subject has objectified itself after being removed from the consciousness, is free of the ambiguity of mythic thought as of all meaning altogether, because reason itself has become the mere instrument of the all-inclusive economic apparatus. It serves as a general tool, useful for the manufacture of all other tools, firmly directed toward its end, as fateful as the precisely calculated movement of material production, whose result for mankind is beyond all calculation. . . .

. . . The more complicated and precise the social, economic, and scientific apparatus with whose service the production system has long harmonized the body, the more impoverished the experiences which it can offer. The elimination of qualities, their conversion into functions, is translated from science by means of rationalized modes of labor to the experiential world of nations, and tends to approximate it once more to that of the amphibians. The regression of the masses today is their inability to hear the unheard-of with their own ears, to touch the unapprehended with their own hands—the new form of delusion which deposes every conquered mythic form. Through the mediation of the total society which embraces all relations and emotions, men are once again made to be that against which the evolutionary law of society, the principle of self, had turned: mere species beings, exactly like one another through isolation in the forcibly united collectivity. The oarsmen, who cannot speak to one another, are each of them yoked in the same rhythm as the modern worker in the factory, movie theater, and collective. The actual working conditions in society compel conformism—not the conscious influences which also made the suppressed men dumb and separated them from truth. The impotence of the worker is not merely a stratagem of the rulers, but the logical consequence of the industrial society into which the ancient Fate—in the very course of the effort to escape it—has finally changed.

But this logical necessity is not conclusive. It remains tied to domination, as both its reflection and its tool. Therefore its truth is no less questionable than its evidence is irrefutable. Of course thought has always sufficed concretely to characterize its own equivocation. It is the servant that the master cannot check as he wishes. Domination, ever since men settled down, and later in the commodity society, has become objectified as law and organization and must therefore restrict itself. The instrument achieves independence: the mediating instance of the spirit, independently of the will of the master, modifies the directness of economic injustice. The instruments of domination, which would encompass all—language, weapons, and finally machines— must allow themselves to be encompassed by all. Hence in domination the aspect of rationality prevails as one that is also different from it. The "objectivity" of the means, which makes it universally available, already implies the criticism of that domination as whose means thought arose. On the way from mythology to logistics, thought has lost the element of self-reflection, and today machinery disables men even as it nurtures them. But in the form of machines the alienated *ratio* moves toward a society which reconciles thought in its fixed form as a material and intellectual apparatus with free, live, thought, and refers to society itself as the real subject of thought. The specific origin of thought and its universal perspective have always been inseparable. Today, with the transformation of the world into industry, the perspective of universality, the social realization of thought, extends so far that in its behalf the rulers themselves disavow thought as mere ideology. . . . The masses are fed and quartered as the army of the unemployed. In their eyes, their reduction to mere objects of the administered life, which preforms every sector of modern existence including language and perception, represents objective necessity, against which they believe there is nothing they can do. Misery as the antithesis of power and powerlessness grows immeasurably, together with the capacity to remove all misery permanently. Each individual is unable to penetrate the forest of cliques and institutions which, from the highest levels of command to the last professional rackets, ensure the boundless persistence of status. For the union boss, let alone the director, the proletarian (should he ever come face to face with him) is nothing but a supernumerary example of the mass, while the boss in his turn has to tremble at the thought of his own liquidation.

The absurdity of a state of affairs in which the enforced power of the system over men grows with every step that takes it out of the power of nature, denounces the rationality of the rational society as obsolete. Its necessity is illusive, no less than the freedom of the entrepreneurs who ultimately reveal their compulsive nature in their inevitable wars and contracts. This illusion, in which a wholly enlightened mankind has lost itself, cannot be dissolved by a philosophy which, as the organ of domination, has to choose between command and obedience. Without being able to escape the confusion which still ensnares it in prehistory, it is nevertheless able to recognize the logic of either-or, of consequence and antimony, with which it radically emancipated itself from nature, as this very nature, unredeemed and self-alienated. Thinking, in whose mechanism of compulsion nature is reflected and persists, inescapably reflects its very own self as its own forgotten nature—as a mechanism of compulsion. Ideation is only an instrument. In thought, men distance themselves from nature in order thus imaginatively to present it to themselves—but only in order to determine how it is to be dominated. Like the thing, the material tool, which is held on to in different situations as the same thing, and hence divides the world as the chaotic, manysided, and disparate from the known, one, and identical, the concept is the ideal tool, fit to do service for everything, wherever it can be applied. And so thought becomes illusionary whenever it seeks to deny the divisive function, distancing and objectification. All mystic unification remains deception, the impotently inward trace of the absolved revolution. . . . Today, when Bacon's utopian vision that we should "command nature by action"—that is, in practice—has been realized on a tellurian scale, the nature of the thralldom that he ascribed to unsubjected nature is clear. It was domination itself. And knowledge, in which Bacon was certain the "sovereignty of man lieth hid," can now become the dissolution of domination. But in the face of such a possibility, and in the service of the present age, enlightenment becomes wholesale deception of the masses.

NOTES

1. Voltaire, *Lettres Philosophiques*, XII, *Œuvres Complètes* (Garnier: Paris, 1879), vol. XXII, p. 118.
2. Cf. Hegel, *Phänomenologie des Geistes* (*The Phenomenology of Spirit*), *Werke*, vol. II, pp. 410ff.
3. Bacon, *De Augmentis Scientiarum*, Works, vol. VIII, p. 152.
4. *Les Soirées de Saint-Pétersbourg* (5ième entretien), *Œuvres Complètes* (Lyon, 1891), vol. IV, p. 256.
5. Bacon, *Advancement of Learning*, Works, vol. II, p. 126.
6. Cf. Freud, *Totem und Tabu* (*Totem and Taboo*), *Gesammelte Werke*, vol. IX, pp. 106ff.
7. *Totem und Tabu*, p. 110.
8. *Phänomenologie des Geistes*, p. 424.
9. See E. Durkheim, *"De Quelques Formes Primitives de Classification,"* in: *L'Année Sociologique*, vol. IV, 1903, pp. 66ff.

PART THREE

CULTURE AND TECHNOLOGY AS IDEOLOGY

All the selections in this section were written in the fifties and sixties. "Freudian Theory and the Pattern of Fascist Propaganda" (1951) summarizes Adorno's Freudian critique of mass culture. Like the earlier study *The Authoritarian Personality* (1950), it argues that mass culture and authoritarianism go hand in hand. "How to Look at Television" (1954) applies the same psychoanalytical framework in examining the form and content of mass media. The sociological framework for both studies is laid out in "Society" (1966), where Adorno examines the role of market relations (commodification) in structuring a system that is at once functionally integrated and psychologically fragmented.

The remaining two selections specifically address the ideological and emancipatory aspects of modern technology. Originally published as Chapter 9 of *One-Dimensional Man: Studies in the Ideology of Advanced Industrial Society* (1964), "The Catastrophe of Liberation" develops the idea of a liberated form of technology that would no longer aim at domination. This idea partially reflects Marcuse's lifelong fascination with the philosophy of Martin Heidegger, who in later years held open the possibility of a poetic (or disclosive) technology that would replace the existing technology of total domination and ontological concealment.

Habermas's critique of Marcuse in "Technology and Science as 'Ideology' " (1968) articulates the distinction between communicative and instrumental reason that would mark his research for the next two decades. Habermas (b. 1929) worked as Adorno's assistant in Frankfurt from 1956 to 1959, where he heard Marcuse's lectures on Freud (one of which is reproduced in Part V). Shortly after assuming Horkheimer's chair of philosophy and sociology at Frankfurt, he, like Marcuse, became involved in radical student politics. During his tenure as director of the Max Planck Institute (1971–1983) and as professor of philosophy at the University of Frankfurt (since 1983), he became increasingly sympathetic to certain strands of Anglo-American philosophy—a tradition that had been held in low esteem by his predecessors. Habermas's essay is included in a volume of his work entitled *Toward a Rational Society* (1968).

Many of the selections contained in this part are discussed in greater detail in Chapters 2 and 4 of *Critical Theory and Philosophy*.

THEODOR W. ADORNO

SOCIETY

The idea of society confirms Nietzsche's insight that concepts "which are basically short-hand for process" elude verbal definition. For society is essentially process; its laws of movement tell more about it than whatever invariables might be deduced. Attempts to fix its limits end up with the same result. If one for instance defines society simply as mankind, including all the sub-groups into which it breaks down, out of which it is constructed, or if one, more simply still, calls it the totality of all human beings living in a given period, one misses thereby all the subtler implications of the concept. Such a formal definition presupposes that society is already a society of human beings, that society is itself already human, is immediately one with its subjects; as though the specifically social did not consist precisely in the imbalance of institutions over men, the latter coming little by little to be the incapacitated products of the former. In bygone ages, when things were perhaps different—in the stone age, for instance—the word society would scarcely have had the same meaning as it does under advanced capitalism. Over a century ago, the legal historian J. C. Bluntschli characterized "society" as a "concept of the third estate." It is that, and not only on account of the egalitarian tendencies which have worked their way down into it, distinguishing it from the feudal or absolutistic idea of "fine" or "high" society, but also because in its very structure this idea follows the model of middleclass society.

In particular it is not a classificatory concept, not for instance the highest abstraction of sociology under which all lesser social forms would be ranged. In this type of thinking one tends to confuse the current scientific ideal of a continuous and hierarchical ordering of categories with the very object of knowledge itself. The object meant by the concept society is not in itself rationally continuous. Nor is it to its elements as a universal to particulars; it is not merely a dynamic category, it is a functional one as well. And to this first, still quite abstract approximation, let us add a further qualification, namely the dependency of all individuals on the totality which they form. In such a totality, everyone is also dependent on everyone else. The whole survives only through the unity of the functions which its members fulfill. Each individual without exception must take some function on himself in order to prolong his existence; indeed, while his function lasts, he is taught to express his gratitude for it.

It is on account of this functional structure that the notion of society can not be grasped in any immediate fashion, nor is it susceptible of drastic verification, as are the laws of the natural sciences. Positivistic currents in sociology tend therefore to dismiss it as a mere philosophical survival. Yet such realism is itself unrealistic. For while the notion of society may not be deduced from any individual facts, nor on the other hand be apprehended as an individual fact itself, there is nonetheless no social fact which is not determined by society as a whole. Society appears as a whole behind each concrete social situation. Conflicts such as the characteristic ones between manager and employees are not some ultimate reality that is wholly comprehensible without reference to anything outside itself. They are rather the symptoms of deeper antagonisms. Yet one cannot subsume individual conflicts under those larger phenomena as the specific to the general. First and foremost, such antagonisms serve as the laws according to which such conflicts are located in time and space. Thus for example the so-called wage-satisfaction which is so popular in current management-sociology is only apparently related to the conditions in a given factory and in a given branch of production. In reality it depends on the whole price system as it is related to the specific branches; on the parallel forces which result in the price system in the first place and which far exceed the struggles between the various groups of entrepreneurs and workers, inasmuch as the latter have already been built into the system, and represent a voter potential that does not always correspond to their organizational affiliation. What is decisive, in the case of wage satisfaction as well as in all others, is the power structure, whether direct or indirect, the control by the entrepreneurs over the machinery of production. Without a concrete awareness of this fact, it is impossible adequately to understand any given individual situation without assigning to the part what really belongs to the whole. Just as social mediation cannot exist without that which is mediated, without its elements: individual human begins, institutions, situations; in the same way the latter cannot exist without the former's mediation. When details come to seem the strongest reality of all, on account of their tangible immediacy, they blind the eye to genuine perception.

Because society can neither be defined as a concept in the current logical sense, nor empirically demonstrated, while in the meantime social phenomena continue to call out for some kind of conceptualization, the proper organ of the latter is speculative *theory*. Only a thoroughgoing theory of society can tell us what society really is. Recently it has been objected that it is unscientific to insist on concepts such as that of society, inasmuch as truth and falsehood are characteristics of sentences alone, and not of ideas as a whole. Such an objection confuses a self-validation concept such as that of society with a traditional kind of definition. The former must develop as it is being understood, and cannot be fixed in arbitrary terminology to the benefit of some supposed mental tidiness.

The requirement that society must be defined through theory—a requirement, which is itself a theory of society—must further address itself to the suspicion that such theory lags far behind the model of the natural sciences, still tacitly assumed to binding on it. In the natural sciences theory represents a clear point of contact between well-defined concepts and repeatable experiments. A self-developing theory of society, however, need not concern itself with this intimidating model, given its enigmatic claim to mediation. For the objection measures the concept of society against the criterion of immediacy and presence, and if society is mediation, then these criteria have no validity for it. The next step is the ideal of knowledge of things from the inside: it is claimed that the theory of society entrenches itself behind such subjectivity. This would only serve to hinder progress in the sciences, so this argument runs, and in the most flourishing ones has been long since eliminated. Yet we must point out that society is both known and not known from the inside. Inasmuch as society remains a product of human activity, its living subjects are still able to recognize themselves in it, as from across a great distance, in a manner radically different than is the case for the objects of chemistry and physics. It is a fact that in middle-class society, rational action is objectively just as "comprehensible"* as it is motivated. This was the great lesson of the generation of Max Weber and Dilthey. Yet their ideal of comprehension remained onesided, insofar as it precluded everything in society that resisted identification by the observer. This was the sense of Durkheim's rule that one should treat social facts like objects, should first and foremost renounce any effort to "understand" them. He was firmly persuaded that society meets each individual primarily as that which is alien and threatening, as constraint. Insofar as that is true, genuine reflection on the nature of society would begin precisely where "comprehension" ceased. The scientific method which Durkheim stands for thus registers that Hegelian "second nature" which society comes to form, against its living members. This antithesis to Max Weber remains just as partial as the latter's thesis, in that it cannot transcend the idea of society's basic incomprehensibility any more than Weber can transcend that of society's basic comprehensibility. Yet this resistance of society to rational comprehension should be understood first and foremost as the sign of relationships between men which have grown increasingly independent of them, opaque, now standing off against human beings like some different substance. It ought to be the task of sociology today to comprehend the incomprehensible, the advance of human beings into the inhuman.

Besides which, the anti-theoretical concepts of that older sociology which had emerged from philosophy are themselves fragments of forgotten or repressed theory. The early twentieth-century German notion of comprehension is a mere secularization of the Hegelian absolute spirit, of the notion of a totality to be grasped; only it

---

* *Verstehen* and *Verstehbar* (here translated as "comprehension" and "comprehensibility") are technical terms used by Weber referring to the interpretative understanding of subjective meaning—in this instance the intentions, purposes, beliefs, and attitudes implicitly or explicitly motivating human action. Understanding is opposed to explanation, which seeks the causal antecedents underlying action in objective laws. [Ed.]

limits itself to particular acts, to characteristic images, without any consideration of that totality of society from which the phenomenon to be understood alone derives its meaning. Enthusiasm for the incomprehensible, on the other hand, transforms chronic social antagonisms into *quaestiones facti*. The situation itself, unreconciled, is contemplated without theory, in a kind of mental asceticism, and what is accepted thus ultimately comes to be glorified: society as a mechanism of collective constraint.

In the same way, with equally significant consequences, the dominant categories of contemporary sociology are also fragments of theoretical relationships which it refuses to recognize as such on account of its positivistic leanings. The notion of a "role" has for instance frequently been offered in recent years as one of the keys to sociology and to the understanding of human action in general. This notion is derived from the pure being-for-others of individual men, from that which binds them together with one another in social constraint, unreconciled, each unidentical with himself. Human beings find their "roles" in that structural mechanism of society which trains them to pure self-conservation at the same time that it denies them conservation of their Selves. The all-powerful principle of identity itself, the abstract interchangeability of social tasks, works towards the extinction of their personal identities. It is no accident that the notion of "role" (a notion which claims to be value-free) is derived from the theater, where actors are not in fact the identities they play at being. This divergence is merely an expression of underlying social antagonisms. A genuine theory of society ought to be able to move from such immediate observation of phenomena towards an understanding of their deeper social causes: why human beings today are still sworn to the playing of roles. The Marxist notion of character-masks, which not only anticipates the later category but deduces and founds it socially, was able to account for this implicitly. But if the science of society continues to operate with such concepts, at the same time drawing back in terror from that theory which puts them in perspective and gives them their ultimate meaning, then it merely ends up in the service of ideology. The concept of role, lifted without analysis from the social facade, helps perpetuate the monstrosity of role-playing itself.

A notion of society which was not satisfied to remain at that level would be a *critical* one. It would go far beyond the trivial idea that everything is interrelated. The emptiness and abstractness of this idea is not so much the sign of feeble thinking as it is that of a shabby permanency in the constitution of society itself: that of the market system in modern-day society. The first, objective abstraction takes place, not so much in scientific thought, as in the universal development of the exchange system itself; which happens independently of the qualitative attitudes of producer and consumer, of the mode of production, even of need, which the social mechanism tends to satisfy as a kind of secondary by-product. Profit comes first. A humanity fashioned into a vast network of consumers, the human beings who actually have the needs, have been socially pre-formed beyond anything which one might naively imagine, and this not only by the level of industrial development but also by the economic relationships themselves into which they enter, even though this is far more difficult to observe empirically. Above and beyond all specific forms of social differentiation, the abstraction implicit in the market system represents the domination of the general over the particular, of society over its captive membership. It is not at all a socially neutral phenomenon, as the logistics of reduction, of uniformity of work time might suggest. Behind the reduction of men to agents and bearers of exchange value lies the domination of men over men. This remains the basic fact, in spite of the difficulties with which from time to time many of the categories of political science are confronted. The form of the total system requires everyone to respect the law of exchange if he does not wish to be destroyed, irrespective of whether profit is his subjective motivation or not.

This universal law of the market system is not in the least invalidated by the survival of retrograde areas and archaic social forms in various parts of the world. The older theory of imperialism already pointed out the functional relationship between the economies of the advanced capitalistic countries and those of the non-capitalistic areas, as they were then called. The two were not merely juxtaposed, each maintained the other in existence. When old-fashioned colonialism was eliminated, all that was transformed into *political* interests and relationships. In this context, rational economic and developmental aid is scarcely a luxury. Within the exchange society, the pre-capitalistic remnants and enclaves are by no means something alien, mere relics of the past: they are vital necessities for the market system. Irrational institutions are useful to the stubborn irrationality of a society which is rational in its means but not in its ends. An institution such as the family, which finds its origins in nature and whose binary structure escapes regulation by the equivalency of exchange, owes its relative power of resistance to the fact that without its help, as an irrational component, certain specific modes of existence such as the small peasantry would hardly be able to survive, being themselves impossible to rationalize without the collapse of the entire middle-class edifice.

The process of increasing social rationalization, of universal extension of the market system, is not something that takes place beyond the specific social conflicts and antagonisms, or in spite of them. It works through those antagonisms themselves, the latter, at the same time tearing society apart in the process. For in the institution of exchange there is created and reproduced that antagonism which could at any time bring organized society to ultimate catastrophe and destroy it. The whole business keeps creaking and groaning on, at unspeakable human cost, only on account of the profit motive and the interiorization by individuals of the breach torn in society as a whole. Society remains class struggle, today just as in the period when that concept originated; the repression current in the eastern countries shows that things are no different there either. Although the prediction of increasing pauperization of the proletariat has not proved true over a long period of time, the disappearance of classes as such is mere illusion, epiphenomenon. It is quite possible that subjective class consciousness has weakened in the advanced countries; in America it was never very strong in the first place. But social theory is not supposed to be predicated on subjective awareness. And as society increasingly controls the very forms of consciousness itself, this is more and more the case. Even the oft-touted equilibrium between habits of consumption and possibilities for education is a subjective phenomenon, part of the consciousness of the individual member of society, rather than an objective social fact. And even from a subjective viewpoint the class relationship is not quite so easy to dismiss as the ruling ideology would have us believe. The most recent empirical sociological investigation has been able to distinguish essential differences in attitude between those assigned in a general statistical way to the upper and the lower classes. The lower classes have fewer illusions, are less "idealistic." The *happy few* hold such "materialism" against them. As in the past, workers today still see society as something split into an upper and a lower. It is well known that the formal possibility of equal education does not correspond in the least to the actual proportion of working class children in the schools and universities.

Screened from subjectivity, the difference between the classes grows objectively with the increasing concentration of capital. This plays a decisive part in the existence of individuals; if it were not so, the notion of class would merely be fetishization. Even though consumers' needs are growing more standardized—for the middle class, in contrast to the older feodality, has always been willing to moderate expenditures over intake, except in the first period of capitalist accumulation—the separation of social power from social helplessness has never been greater than it is now. Almost everyone knows from his own personal experience that his social existence can scarcely be said to have resulted from his own personal initiative; rather he has had to search for gaps, "openings," jobs from which to make a living, irrespective of what seem to him his own human possibilities or talents should he indeed still have any kind of vague inkling of the latter. The profoundly social-darwinistic notion of adaptation, borrowed from biology and applied to the so-called sciences of man in a normative manner, expresses this and is indeed its ideology. Not to speak of the degree to which the class situation has been transposed onto the relationship between nations, between the technically developed and underdeveloped countries.

That even so society goes on as successfully as it does is to be attributed to its control over the relationship of basic social forces, which has long since been extended to all the countries of the globe. This control necessarily reinforces the totalitarian tendencies of the social order, and is a political equivalent for and adaptation to the total penetration by the market economy. With this control, however, the very danger increases which such controls are designed to prevent, at least on this side of the Soviet and Chinese empires. It is not the fault of technical development or industrialization as such. The latter is only the image of human productivity itself, cybernetics and computers merely being an extension of the human senses: technical advancement is therefore only a moment in the dialectic between the forces of production and the relationships of production, and not some third thing, demonically self-sufficient. In the established order, industrialization functions in a centralistic way; on its own, it could function differently. Where people think they are closest to things, as with television, delivered into their very living room, nearness is itself mediated through social distance, through great concentration of power. Nothing offers a more striking symbol for the fact that people's lives, what they hold for the closest to them and the greatest reality, personal, maintained in being by them, actually receive their concrete content in large measure from above. Private life is, more than we can even imagine, mere re-privatization; the realities to which men hold have become unreal. "Life itself is a lifeless thing."

A rational and genuinely free society could do without administration as little as it could do without the division of labor itself. But all over the globe, administrations have tended under constraint towards a greater self-sufficiency and independence from their administered subjects, reducing the latter to objects of abstractly normed behavior. As Max Weber saw, such a tendency points back to the ultimate means-ends rationality of the economy itself. Because the latter is indifferent to its end, namely that of a rational society, and as long as it remains indifferent to such an end, for so long will it be irrational for its own subjects. The Expert is the rational form that such irrationality takes. His rationality is founded on specialization in technical and other processes, but has its ideological side as well. The ever smaller units into which the work process is divided begin to resemble each other again, once more losing their need for specialized qualifications.

Inasmuch as these massive social forces and institutions were once human ones, are essentially the reified work of living human beings, this appearance of self-sufficiency and independence in them would seem to be something ideological, a socially necessary mirage which one ought to be able to break through, to change. Yet such pure appearance is the *ens realissimum** in the immediate life of men. The force of gravity of social relationships serves only to strengthen that appearance more and more. In sharp contrast to the period around 1848, when the class struggle revealed itself as a conflict between a group immanent to society, the middle class, and one which was half outside it, the proletariat, Spencer's notion of integration, the very ground law of increasing social rationalization itself, has begun to seize on the very minds of those who are to be integrated into society. Both automatically and deliberately, subjects are hindered from coming to consciousness of themselves as subjects. The supply of goods that floods across them has that result, as does the industry of culture and countless other direct and indirect mechanisms of intellectual control. The culture industry sprang from the profit-making tendency of capital. It developed under the law of the market, the obligation to adapt your consumers to your goods, and then, by a dialectical reversal, ended up having the result of solidifying the existing forms of consciousness and the intellectual status quo. Society needs this tireless intellectual reduplication of everything that is, because without this praise of the monotonously alike and with waning efforts to justify that which exists on the

* "a most fundamental essence" [Ed.]

grounds of its mere existence, men would ultimately do away with this state of things in impatience.

Integration goes even further than this. That adaptation of men to social relationships and processes which constitutes history and without which it would have been difficult for the human race to survive has left its mark on them such that the very possibility of breaking free without terrible instinctual conflicts—even breaking free mentally—has come to seem a feeble and a distant one. Men have come to be— triumph of integration!—identified in their innermost behavior patterns with their fate in modern society. In a mockery of all the hopes of philosophy, subject and object have attained ultimate reconciliation. The process is fed by the fact that men owe their life to what is being done to them. The affective rearrangement of industry, the mass appeal of sports, the fetishization of consumers' goods, are all symptoms of this trend. The cement which once ideologies supplied is now furnished by these phenomena, which hold the massive social institutions together on the one hand, the psychological constitution of human beings on the other. If we were looking for an ideological justification of a situation in which men are little better than cogs to their own machines, we might claim without much exaggeration that present-day human beings serve as such an ideology in their own existence, for they seek of their own free will to perpetuate what is obviously a perversion of real life. So we come full circle. Men must act in order to change the present petrified conditions of existence, but the latter have left their mark so deeply on people, have deprived them of so much of their life and individuation, that they scarcely seem capable of the spontaneity necessary to do so. From this, apologists for the existing order draw new power for their argument that humanity is not yet ripe. Even to point the vicious circle out breaks a taboo of the integral society. Just as it hardly tolerates anything radically different, so also it keeps an eye out to make sure that anything which is thought or said serves some specific change or has, as they put it, something positive to offer. Thought is subjected to the subtlest censorship of the *terminus ad quem*: whenever it appears critically, it has to indicate the positive steps desired. If such positive goals turn out to be inaccessible to present thinking, why then thought itself ought to come across resigned and tired, as though such obstruction were its own fault and not the signature of the thing itself. That is the point at which society can be recognized as a universal block, both within men and outside them at the same time. Concrete and positive suggestions for change merely strengthen this hindrance, either as ways of administering the unadministrable, or by calling down repression from the monstrous totality itself. The concept and the theory of society are legitimate only when they do not allow themselves to be attracted by either of these solutions, when they merely hold in negative fashion to the basic possibility inherent in them: that of expressing the fact that such possibility is threatened with suffocation. Such awareness, without any preconceptions as to where it might lead, would be the first condition for an ultimate break in society's omnipotence.

Translated by F. R. Jameson

THEODOR W. ADORNO

HOW TO LOOK AT TELEVISION

The effect of television cannot be adequately expressed in terms of success or failure, likes or dislikes, approval or disapproval. Rather, an attempt should be made, with the aid of depth-psychological categories and previous knowledge of mass media, to crystallize a number of theoretical concepts by which the potential effect of television—its impact upon various layers of the spectator's personality—could be studied. It seems timely to investigate systematically socio-psychological stimuli typical of televised material both on a descriptive and psychodynamic level, to analyze their presuppositions as well as their total pattern, and to evaluate the effect they are likely to produce. This procedure may ultimately bring forth a number of recommendations on how to deal with these stimuli to produce the most desirable effect of television. By exposing the socio-psychological implications and mechanisms of television, often operating under the guise of fake realism, not only may the shows be improved, but, more important possibly, the public at large may be sensitized to the nefarious effect of some of these mechanisms.

We are not concerned with the effectiveness of any particular show or program; but, we are concerned with the nature of present-day television and its imagery. Yet, our approach is practical. The findings should be so close to the material, should rest on such a solid foundation of experience that they can be translated into precise recommendations and be made convincingly clear to large audiences.

Improvement of television is not conceived primarily on an artistic, purely aesthetic level, extraneous to present customs. This does not mean that we naïvely take for granted the dichotomy between autonomous art and mass media. We all know that their relationship is highly complex. Today's rigid division between what is called "long-haired" and "short-haired" art is the product of a long historical development. It would be romanticizing to assume that formerly art was entirely pure, that the creative artist thought only in terms of the inner consistency of the artifact and not also of its effect upon the spectators. Theatrical art, in particular, cannot be separated from audience reaction. Conversely, vestiges of the aesthetic claim to be something autonomous, a world unto itself, remain even within the most trivial product of mass culture. In fact, the present rigid division of art into autonomous and commercial aspects is itself largely a function of commercialization. It was hardly accidental that the slogan *l'art pour l'art* was coined polemically in the Paris of the first half of the nineteenth century, when literature really became large-scale business for the first time. Many of the cultural products bearing the anticommercial trademark "art for art's sake" show traces of commercialism in their appeal to the sensational or in the conspicuous display of material wealth and sensuous stimuli at the expense of the meaningfulness of the work. This trend was pronounced in the neo-Romantic theater of the first decades of our century.

OLDER AND RECENT POPULAR CULTURE

In order to do justice to all such complexities, much closer scrutiny of the background and development of modern mass media is required than communications research, generally limited to present conditions, is aware of. One would have to establish what the output of contemporary cultural industry has in common with older "low" or popular forms of art as well as with autonomous art and where the difference lies. Suffice it here to state that the archetypes of present popular culture were set comparatively early in the development of middle-class society—at about the turn of the seventeenth and the beginning of the eighteenth centuries in England. According to the studies of the English sociologist Ian Watt, the English novels of that period, particularly the works of Defoe and Richardson, marked the beginning of an approach to literary production that consciously created, served, and finally controlled a "market." Today the commercial production of cultural goods has become streamlined, and the impact of popular culture upon the individual has concomitantly increased. This process has not been confined to quantity, but has resulted in new qualities. While recent popular culture has absorbed all the elements and particularly all the "don't's" of its predecessor, it differs decisively in as much as it has developed into a *system*. Thus, popular culture is no longer confined to certain forms such as novels or dance music, but has seized all media of artistic expression. The structure and meaning of these forms show an amazing parallelism, even when they appear to have little in common on the surface (such as jazz and the detective novel). Their output has increased to such an extent that it is almost impossible for anyone to dodge them; and even those formerly aloof from popular culture—the rural population on one hand and the higher level of education on the other—are somehow affected. The more the system of "merchandising" culture is expanded, the more it tends also to assimilate the "serious" art of the past by adapting this art to the system's own requirements. The control is so extensive that any infraction of its rules is *a priori* stigmatized as "high-brow" and has but little chance to reach the population at large. The system's concerted effort results in what might be called the prevailing ideology of our time.

Certainly, there are many typical changes within today's pattern; e.g., men were formerly presented as erotically aggressive and women on the defensive, whereas this has been largely reversed in modern mass culture, as pointed out particularly by Wolfenstein and Leites. More important, however, is that the pattern itself, dimly perceptible in the early novels and basically preserved today, has by now become congealed and standardized. Above all, this rigid institutionalization transforms modern mass culture into a medium of undreamed of psychological control. The repetitiveness, the selfsameness, and the ubiquity of modern mass culture tend to make for automatized reactions and to weaken the forces of individual resistance.

When the journalist Defoe and the printer Richardson calculated the effect of their wares upon the audience, they had to speculate, to follow hunches; and therewith, a certain latitude to develop deviations remained. Such deviations have nowadays been reduced to a kind of multiple choice between very few alternatives. The following may serve as an illustration. The popular or semipopular novels of the first half of the nineteenth century, published in large quantities and serving mass consumption, were supposed to arouse tension in the reader. Although the victory of the good over the bad was generally provided for, the meandering and endless plots and subplots hardly allowed the readers of Sue and Dumas to be continuously aware of the moral. Readers could expect anything to happen. This no longer holds true. Every spectator of a television mystery knows with absolute certainty how it is going to end. Tension is but superficially maintained and is unlikely to have a serious effect any more. On the contrary, the spectator feels on safe ground all the time. This longing for "feeling on safe ground"—reflecting an infantile need for protection, rather than his desire for a thrill—is catered to. The element of excitement is preserved only with tongue in cheek. Such changes fall in line with the potential change from a freely competitive to a virtually "closed" society into which one wants to be admitted or from which one fears to be rejected. Everything somehow appears "predestined."

The increasing strength of modern mass culture is further enhanced by changes in the sociological structure of the audience. The old cultured elite does not exist any more; the modern intelligentsia only partially corresponds to it. At the same time, huge strata of the population formerly unacquainted with art have become cultural "consumers." Modern audiences, although probably less capable of the artistic sublimation bred by tradition, have become shrewder in their demands for perfection of technique and for reliability of information, as well as in their desire for "services"; and they have become more convinced of the consumers' potential power over the producer, no matter whether this power is actually wielded.

How changes within the audience have affected the meaning of popular culture may also be illustrated. The element of internalization played a decisive role in early Puritan popular novels of the Richardson type. This element no longer prevails, for it was based on the essential role of "inwardness" in both original Protestantism and earlier middle-class society. As the profound influence of the basic tenets of Protestantism has gradually receded, the cultural pattern has become more and more opposed to the "introvert." As Riesman puts it,

. . . the conformity of earlier generations of Americans of the type I term "inner-directed" was mainly assured by their internalization of adult authority. The middle-class urban American of today, the "other-directed," is, by contrast, in a characterological sense more the product of his peers—that is, in sociological terms, his "peer-groups," the other kids at school or in the block.[1]

This is reflected by popular culture. The accents on inwardness, inner conflicts, and psychological ambivalence (which play so large a role in earlier popular novels and on which their originality rests) have given way to complete externalization and consequently to an entirely unproblematic, cliché-like characterization. Yet the code of decency that governed the inner conflicts of the Pamelas, Clarissas, and Lovelaces remains almost literally intact.[2] The middle-class "ontology" is preserved in an almost fossilized way but is severed from the mentality of the middle classes. By being superimposed on people with whose living conditions and mental make-up it is no longer in accordance, this middle-class "ontology" assumes an increasingly authoritarian and at the same time hollow character.

The overt "naïveté" of older popular culture is avoided. Mass culture, if not sophisticated, must at least be up-to-date—that is to say, "realistic," or posing as realistic—in order to meet the expectations of a supposedly disillusioned, alert, and hard-boiled audience. Middle-class requirements bound up with internalization such as concentration, intellectual effort, and erudition have to be continuously lowered. This does not hold only for the United States, where historical memories are scarcer than in Europe; but it is universal, applying to England and Continental Europe as well.[3]

However, this apparent progress of enlightenment is more than counterbalanced by retrogressive traits. The earlier popular culture maintained a certain equilibrium between its social ideology and the actual social conditions under which its consumers lived. This probably helped to keep the border line between popular and serious art during the eighteenth century more fluid than it is today. Abbé Prévost was one of the founding fathers of French popular literature; but his *Manon Lescaut* is completely free from clichés, artistic vulgarisms, and calculated effects. Similarly, later in the eighteenth century, Mozart's *Zauberfloete* struck a balance between the "high" and the popular style which is almost unthinkable today.

The curse of modern mass culture seems to be its adherence to the almost unchanged ideology of early middle-class society, whereas the lives of its consumers are completely out of phase with this ideology. This is probably the reason for the gap between the overt and the hidden "message" of modern popular art. Although on an overt level the traditional values of English Puritan middle-class society are promulgated, the hidden message aims at a frame of mind which is no longer bound by these values. Rather, today's frame of mind transforms the traditional values into the norms of an increasingly hierarchical and authoritarian social structure. Even here it has to be admitted that authoritarian elements were also present in the older ideology which, of course, never fully expressed the truth. But the "message" of adjustment and unreflecting obedience seems to be dominant and all-pervasive today. Whether maintained values derived from religious ideas obtain a different meaning when severed from their root should be carefully examined. For example, the concept of the "purity" of women is one of the invariables of popular culture. In the earlier phase this concept is treated in terms of an inner conflict between concupiscence and the internalized Christian ideal of chastity, whereas in today's popular culture it is dogmatically posited as a value *per se*. Again, even the rudiments of this pattern are visible in productions such as *Pamela*. There, however, it seems a by-product; whereas in today's popular culture the idea that only the "nice girl" gets married and that she must get married at any price has come to be accepted before Richardson's conflicts even start.[4]

The more inarticulate and diffuse the audience of modern mass media seems to be, the more mass media tend to achieve their "*integration.*" The ideals of conformity and conventionalism were inherent in popular novels from the very beginning. Now, however, these ideals have been translated into rather clear-cut prescriptions of what to do and what not to do. The outcome of conflicts is pre-established, and all conflicts are mere sham. Society is always the winner, and the individual is only a puppet manipulated through social rules. True, conflicts of the nineteenth-century type— such as women running away from their husbands, the drabness of provincial life, and daily chores—occur frequently in today's magazine stories. However, with a regularity which challenges quantitative treatment, these conflicts are decided in favor of the very same conditions from which these women want to break away. The stories teach their readers that one has to be "realistic," that one has to give up romantic ideas, that one has to adjust oneself at any price, and that nothing more can be expected of any individual. The perennial middle-class conflict between individuality and society has been reduced to a dim memory, and the message is invariably that of identification with the *status quo*. This theme too is not new, but its unfailing universality invests it with an entirely different meaning. The constant plugging of conventional values seems to mean that these values have lost their substance, and it is feared that people would really follow their instinctual urges and conscious insights unless continuously reassured from outside that they must not do so. The less the message is really believed and the less it is in harmony with the actual existence of the spectators, the more categorically it is maintained in modern popular culture. One may speculate whether its inevitable hypocrisy is concomitant with punitiveness and sadistic sternness.

MULTILAYERED STRUCTURE

A depth-psychological approach to television has to be focused on its multilayered structure. Mass media are not simply the sum total of the actions they portray or of the messages that radiate from these actions. Mass media also consist of various layers of meaning superimposed on one another, all of which contribute to the effect. True, due to their calculative nature, these rationalized products seem to be more clear-cut in their meaning than authentic works of art which can never be boiled down to some unmistakable "message." But the heritage of polymorphic meaning has been taken over by cultural industry in as much as what it conveys becomes itself organized in order to enthrall the spectators on various psychological levels simultaneously. As a matter of fact, the hidden message may be more important than the overt since this hidden message will escape the controls of consciousness, will not be "looked through," will not be warded off by sales resistance, but is likely to sink into the spectator's mind.

Probably all the various levels in mass media involve *all* the mechanisms of consciousness and unconsciousness stressed by psychoanalysis. The difference between the surface content, the overt message of televised material, and its hidden meaning is generally marked and rather clear-cut. The rigid superimposition of various layers probably is one of the features by which mass media are distinguishable from the integrated products of autonomous art where the various layers are much more thoroughly fused. The full effect of the material on the spectator cannot be studied without consideration of the hidden meaning in conjunction with the overt one, and it is precisely this interplay of various layers which has hitherto been neglected and which will be our focus. This is in accordance with the assumption shared by numerous social scientists that certain political and social trends of our time, particularly those of a totalitarian nature, feed to a considerable extent on irrational and frequently unconscious motivations. Whether the conscious or the unconscious message of our material is more important is hard to predict and can be evaluated only after careful analysis. We do appreciate, however, that the overt message can be interpreted much more adequately in the light of psychodynamics— i.e., in its relation to instinctual urges as well as control—than by looking at the overt in a naïve way and by ignoring its implications and presuppositions.

The relation between overt and hidden message will prove highly complex in practice. Thus, the hidden message frequently aims at reinforcing conventionally rigid and "pseudorealistic" attitudes similar to the accepted ideas more rationalistically propagated by the surface message. Conversely, a number of repressed gratifications which play a large role on the hidden level are somehow allowed to manifest themselves on the surface in jests, off-color remarks, suggestive situations, and similar devices. All this interaction of various levels, however, points in some definite direction: the tendency to channelize audience reaction. This falls in line with the suspicion widely shared, though hard to corroborate by exact data, that the majority of television shows today aim at producing or at least reproducing the very smugness, intellectual passivity, and gullibility that seem to fit in with totalitarian creeds even if the explicit surface message of the shows may be antitotalitarian.

With the means of modern psychology, we will try to determine the primary prerequisites of shows eliciting mature, adult, and responsible reactions—implying not only in content but in the very way things are being looked at, the idea of autonomous individuals in a free democratic society. We perfectly realize that any definition of such an individual will be hazardous; but we know quite well what a human being deserving of the appellation "autonomous individual" should *not* be, and this "not" is actually the focal point of our consideration.

When we speak of the multilayered structure of television shows, we are thinking of various superimposed layers of different degrees of manifestness or hiddenness that are utilized by mass culture as a technological means of "handling" the audience. This was expressed felicitously by Leo Lowenthal when he coined the term "psychoanalysis in reverse." The implication is that somehow the psychoanalytic concept of a multilayered personality has been taken up by cultural industry, but that the concept is used in order to ensnare the consumer as completely as possible and in order to engage him psychodynamically in the service of premeditated effects. A clear-cut division into allowed gratifications, forbidden gratifications, and recurrence of the forbidden gratification in a somewhat modified and deflected form is carried through.

To illustrate the concept of the multilayered structure: the heroine of an extremely light comedy of pranks is a young schoolteacher who is not only underpaid but is incessantly fined by the caricature of a pompous and authoritarian school principal. Thus, she has no money for her meals and is actually starving. The supposedly funny situations consist mostly of her trying to hustle a meal from various acquaintances, but regularly without success. The mention of food and eating seems to induce laughter—an observation that can frequently be made and invites a study of its own.[5] Overtly, the play is just slight amusement mainly provided by the painful situations into which the heroine and her archopponent constantly run. The script does not try to "sell" any idea. The "hidden meaning" emerges simply by the way the story looks at human beings; thus the audience is invited to look at the characters in the same way without being made aware that indoctrination is present. The character of the underpaid, maltreated schoolteacher is an attempt to reach a compromise between prevailing scorn for the intellectual and the equally conventionalized respect for "culture." The heroine shows such an intellectual superiority and high-spiritedness that identification with her is invited, and compensation is offered for the inferiority of her position and that of her ilk in the social setup. Not only is the central character supposed to be very charming, but she wisecracks constantly. In terms of a set pattern of identification, the script implies: "If you are as humorous, good-natured, quickwitted, and charming as she is, do not worry about being paid a starvation wage. You can cope with your frustration in a humorous way; and your superior wit and cleverness put you not only above material privations, but also above the rest of mankind." In other words, the script is a shrewd method of promoting adjustment to humiliating conditions by presenting them as objectively comical and by giving a picture of a person who experiences even her own inadequate position as an object of fun apparently free of any resentment.

Of course, this latent message cannot be considered as unconscious in the strict psychological sense; but rather, as "inobtrusive," this message is hidden only by a style which does not pretend to touch anything serious and expects to be regarded as featherweight. Nevertheless, even such amusement tends to set patterns for the members of the audience without their being aware of it.

Another comedy of the same series is reminiscent of the funnies. A cranky old woman sets up the will of her cat (Mr. Casey) and makes as heirs some of the schoolteachers in the permanent cast. Later the actual inheritance is found to consist only of the cat's valueless toys. The plot is so constructed that each heir, at the reading of the will, is tempted to act as if he had known this person (Mr. Casey). The ultimate point is that the cat's owner had placed a hundred-dollar bill inside each of the toys; and the heirs run to the incinerator in order to recover their inheritance.

Some surface teachings are clearly observable. First, everybody is greedy and does not mind a little larceny, if he feels sure that he cannot be discovered—the attitude of the wise and realistic skeptic that is supposed to draw a smile from the audience. Second, the audience is told somewhat inconsistently: "Do not be greedy or you will be cheated." Beyond this, however, a more latent message may again be found. Fun is being poked at the universal daydream of the possibility of coming into an unexpected large inheritance. The audience is given to understand: "Don't expect the impossible, don't daydream, but be realistic." The denunciation of that archetypical daydream is enhanced by the association of the wish for unexpected and irrational blessings with dishonesty, hypocrisy, and a generally undignified attitude. The spectator is given to understand: "Those who dare daydream, who expect that money will fall to them from heaven, and who forget any caution about accepting an absurd will are at the same time those whom you might expect to be capable of cheating."

Here, an objection may be raised: Is such a sinister effect of the hidden message of television known to those who control, plan, write, and direct shows? Or it may even be asked: Are these traits possible projections of the unconscious of the decision-makers' own minds according to the widespread assumption that works of art can be properly understood in terms of psychological projections of their authors? As a matter of fact, it is this kind of reasoning that has led to the suggestion that a special socio-psychological study of decision makers in the field of television be made. We do not think that such a study would lead us very far. Even in the sphere of autonomous art, the idea of projection has been largely overrated. Although the authors' motivations certainly enter the artifact, they are by no means so all-determining as is often assumed. As soon as an artist has set himself his problem, it obtains some kind of impact of its own; and, in most cases, he has to follow the objective requirements of his product much more than his own urges of expression when he translates his primary conception into artistic reality. To be sure, these objective requirements do not play a decisive role in mass media which stress the effect on the spectator far beyond any artistic problem. However, the total setup here tends to limit the chances of the artists' projections utterly. Those who produce the material follow, often grumblingly, innumerable requirements, rules of thumb, set patterns, and mechanisms of controls which by necessity reduce to a minimum the range of any kind of artistic self-expression. The fact that most products of mass media are not produced by one individual but by collective collaboration, as happens to be true also with most of the illustrations so far discussed, is only one contributing factor to this generally prevailing condition. To study television shows in terms of the psychology of the authors would almost be tantamount to studying Ford cars in terms of the psycho-analysis of the late Mr. Ford.

PRESUMPTUOUSNESS

The typical psychological mechanisms utilized by television shows and the devices by which they are automatized function only within a small number of given frames of reference operative in television communication, and the socio-psychological effect largely depends on them. We are all familiar with the division of television content into various classes, such as light comedy, westerns, mysteries, so-called sophisti-cated plays, and others. These types have developed into formulas which, to a certain degree, pre-establish the attitudinal pattern of the spectator before he is confronted with any specific content and which largely determine the way in which any specific content is being perceived.

In order to understand television, it is, therefore, not enough to bring out the implications of various shows and types of shows; but an examination must be made of the presuppositions within which the implications function before a single word is spoken. Most important is that the typing of shows has gone so far that the spectator approaches each one with a set pattern of expectations before he faces the show itself—just as the radio listener who catches the beginning of Tschaikowsky's Piano Concerto as a theme song, knows automatically, "Aha, serious music!" or, when he hears organ music, responds equally automatically, "Aha, religion!" These halo effects of previous experiences may be psychologically as important as the implica-tions of the phenomena themselves for which they have set the stage; and these presuppositions should, therefore, be treated with equal care.

When a television show bears the title "Dante's Inferno," when the first shot is that of a night club by the same name, and when we find sitting at the bar a man with his hat on and at some distance from him a sad-looking, heavily made-up woman ordering another drink, we are almost certain that some murder will shortly be committed. The apparently individualized situation actually works only as a signal that moves our expectations into a definite direction. If we had never seen anything but "Dante's Inferno," we probably would not be sure about what was going to happen; but, as it is, we are actually given to understand by both subtle and not so subtle devices that this is a crime play, that we are entitled to expect some sinister and probably hideous and sadistic deeds of violence, that the hero will be saved from a situation from which he can hardly be expected to be saved, that the woman on the barstool is probably not the main criminal but is likely to lose her life as a gangster's moll, and so on. This conditioning to such universal patterns, however, scarcely stops at the television set.

The way the spectator is made to look at apparently everyday items, such as a night club, and to take as hints of possible crime common settings of his daily life, induces him to look at life itself as though it and its conflicts could generally be understood in such terms.[6] This, convincingly enough, may be the nucleus of truth in the old-fashioned arguments against all kinds of mass media for inciting criminality in the audience. The decisive thing is that this atmosphere of the normality of crime, its presentation in terms of an average expectation based on life situations, is never expressed in so many words but is established by the overwhelming wealth of material. It may affect certain spectator groups more deeply than the overt moral of crime and punishment regularly derived from such shows. What matters is not the importance of crime as a symbolic expression of otherwise controlled sexual or aggressive impulses, but the confusion of this symbolism with a pedantically maintained realism in all matters of direct sense perception. Thus, empirical life becomes infused with a kind of meaning that virtually excludes adequate experience no matter how obstinately the veneer of such "realism" is built up. This affects the social and psychological function of drama.

It is hard to establish whether the spectators of Greek tragedy really experienced the catharsis Aristotle described—in fact this theory, evolved after the age of tragedy was over, seems to have been a rationalization itself, an attempt to state the purpose of tragedy in pragmatic, quasi-scientific terms. Whatever the case, it seems pretty certain that those who saw the *Oresteia* of Aeschylus or Sophocles' *Oedipus* were not likely to translate these tragedies (the subject matter of which was known to everyone, and the interest in which was centered in artistic treatment) directly into everyday terms. This audience did not expect that on the next corner of Athens similar things would go on. Actually, pseudo realism allows for the direct and extremely primitive identifications achieved by popular culture; and it presents a façade of trivial buildings, rooms, dresses, and faces as though they were the promise of something thrilling and exciting taking place at any moment.

In order to establish this socio-psychological frame of reference, one would have to follow up systematically categories—such as the normality of crime or pseudo realism and many others—to determine their structural unity and to interpret the specific devices, symbols, and stereotypes in relation to this frame of reference. We hypothesize at this phase that the frames of reference and the individual devices will tend in the same direction.

Only against psychological backdrops such as pseudo realism and against implicit assumptions like the normality of crime can the specific stereotypes of television plays be interpreted. The very standardization indicated by the set frames of reference automatically produces a number of stereotypes. Also, the technology of television production makes stereotypy almost inevitable. The short time available for the preparation of scripts and the vast material continuously to be produced call for certain formulas. Moreover, in plays lasting only a quarter to half an hour each, it appears inevitable that the kind of person the audience faces each time should be indicated drastically through red and green lights. We are not dealing with the problem of the existence of stereotypes. Since stereotypes are an indispensable element of the organization and anticipation of experience, preventing us from falling into mental disorganization and chaos, no art can entirely dispense with them. Again, the functional change is what concerns us. The more stereotypes become reified and rigid in the present setup of cultural industry, the less people are likely to change their preconceived ideas with the progress of their experience. The more opaque and complicated modern life becomes, the more people are tempted to cling desperately to clichés which seem to bring some order into the otherwise ununderstandable. Thus, people may not only lose true insight into reality, but ultimately their very capacity for life experience may be dulled by the constant wearing of blue and pink spectacles.

STEREOTYPING

In coping with this danger, we may not do full justice to the meaning of some of the stereotypes which are to be dealt with. We should never forget that there are two sides to every psychodynamic phenomenon, the unconscious or id element and the rationalization. Although the latter is psychologically defined as a defense mechanism, it may very well contain some nonpsychological, objective truth which cannot simply be pushed aside on account of the psychological function of the rationalization. Thus some of the stereotypical messages, directed toward particularly weak spots in the mentality of large sectors of the population, may prove to be quite legitimate. However, it may be said with fairness that the questionable blessings of morals, such as "one should not chase after rainbows," are largely overshadowed by the threat of inducing people to mechanical simplifications by ways of distorting the world in such a way that it seems to fit into pre-established pigeonholes.

The example here selected, however, should indicate rather drastically the danger of stereotypy. A television play concerning a fascist dictator, a kind of hybrid between Mussolini and Peron, shows the dictator in a moment of crisis; and the content of the play is his inner and outer collapse. Whether the cause of his collapse is a popular upheaval or a military revolt is never made clear. But neither this issue nor any other of a social or political nature enters the plot itself. The course of events takes place exclusively on a private level. The dictator is just a heel who treats sadistically both his secretary and his "lovely and warm-hearted" wife. His antagonist, a general, was formerly in love with the wife; and they both still love each other, although the wife sticks loyally to her husband. Forced by her husband's brutality, she attempts flight, and is intercepted by the general who wants to save her. The turning point occurs when the guards surround the palace to defend the dictator's popular wife. As soon as they learn that she has departed, the guards quit; and the dictator, whose "inflated ego" explodes at the same time, gives up. The dictator is nothing but a bad, pompous, and cowardly man. He seems to act with extreme stupidity; nothing of the objective dynamics of dictatorship comes out. The impression is created that totalitarianism grows out of character disorders of ambitious politicians, and is overthrown by the honesty, courage, and warmth of those figures with whom the audience is supposed to identify. The standard device employed is that of the spurious personalization of objective issues. The representatives of ideas under attack, as in the case of the fascists here, are presented as villains in a ludicrous cloak-and-dagger fashion; whereas, those who fight for the "right cause" are personally idealized. This not only distracts from any real social issues but also enforces the psychologically extremely dangerous division of the world into black (the outgroup) and white (we, the ingroup). Certainly, no artistic production can deal with ideas or political creeds *in abstracto* but has to present them in terms of their concrete impact upon human beings; yet it would be utterly futile to present individuals as mere specimens of an abstraction, as puppets expressive of an idea. In order to deal with the concrete impact of totalitarian systems, it would be more commendable to show how the life of ordinary people is affected by terror and impotence than to cope with the phony psychology of the big shots, whose heroic role is silently endorsed by such a treatment even if they are pictured as villains. There seems to be hardly any question of the importance of an analysis of pseudo-personalization and its effect, by no means limited to television.

Although pseudo-personalization denotes the stereotyped way of "looking at things" in television, we should also point out certain stereotypes in the narrower sense. Many television plays could be characterized by the sobriquet "a pretty girl can do no wrong." The heroine of a light comedy is, to use George Legman's term, "a bitch heroine." She behaves toward her father in an incredibly inhuman and cruel manner only slightly rationalized as "merry pranks." But she is punished very slightly, if at all. True, in real life bad deeds are rarely punished at all, but this cannot be applied to television. Here, those who have developed the production code for the movies seem right: What matters in mass media is not what happens in real life, but rather the positive and negative "messages," prescriptions, and taboos that the spectator absorbs by means of identification with the material he is looking at. The punishment given to the pretty heroine only nominally fulfills the conventional requirements of the conscience for a second. But the spectator is given to understand that the heroine really gets away with everything just because she is pretty.

The attitude in question seems to be indicative of a universal penchant. In another sketch that belongs to a series dealing with the confidence racket, the attractive girl who is an active participant in the racket not only is paroled after having been sentenced to a long term, but also seems to have a good chance of marrying her victim. Her sex morality, of course, is unimpeachable. The spectator is supposed to like her at first sight as a modest and self-effacing character, and he must not be disappointed. Although it is discovered that she is a crook, the original identification must be restored, or rather maintained. The stereotype of the nice girl is so strong that not even the proof of her delinquency can destroy it; and, by hook or by crook, she must be what she appears to be. It goes without saying that such psychological models tend to confirm exploitative, demanding, and aggressive attitudes on the part of young girls—a character structure which has come to be known in psychoanalysis under the name of oral aggressiveness.

Sometimes such stereotypes are disguised as national American traits, a part of the American scene where the image of the haughty, egoistic, yet irresistible girl who plays havoc with poor dad has come to be a public institution. This way of reasoning is an insult to the American spirit. High-pressure publicity and continuous plugging to institutionalize some obnoxious type does not make the type a sacred symbol of folklore. Many considerations of an apparently anthropological nature today tend only to veil objectionable trends, as though they were of an ethnological, quasi-natural character. Incidentally, it is amazing to what degree television material even on superficial examination brings to mind psychoanalytic concepts with the qualification of being a psychoanalysis in reverse. Psychoanalysis has described the oral syndrome combining the antagonistic trends of aggressive and dependent traits. This character syndrome is closely indicated by the pretty girl that can do no wrong, who, while being aggressive against her father exploits him at the same time, depending on him as much as on the surface level she is set against him. The difference between the sketch and psychoanalysis is simply that the sketch exalts the very same syndrome which is treated by psychoanalysis as a reversion to infantile developmental phases and which the psychoanalyst tries to dissolve. It remains to be seen whether something similar applies as well to some types of male heroes, particularly the super-he-man. It may well be that he too can do no wrong.

Finally, we should deal with a rather widespread stereotype which, in as much as it is taken for granted by television, is further enhanced. At the same time, the example may serve to show that certain psychoanalytic interpretations of cultural stereotypes are not really too farfetched. The latent ideas that psychoanalysis attributes to certain stereotypes come to the surface. There is the extremely popular idea that the artist is not only maladjusted, introverted, and *a priori* somewhat funny; but that he is really an "aesthete," a weakling, and a "sissy." In other words, modern synthetic folklore tends to identify the artist with the homosexual and to respect only the "man of action" as a real, strong man. This idea is expressed in a surprisingly direct manner in one of the comedy scripts at our disposal. It portrays a young man who is not only the "dope" who appears so often on television but is also a shy, retiring, and accordingly untalented poet, whose moronic poems are ridiculed.[7] He is in love with a girl but is too weak and insecure to indulge in the necking practices she rather crudely suggests; the girl, on her part, is caricatured as a boy-chaser. As happens frequently in mass culture, the roles of the sexes are reversed—the girl is utterly aggressive, and the boy, utterly afraid of her, describes himself as "woman-handled" when she manages to kiss him. There are vulgar innuendos of homosexuality of which one may be quoted: The heroine tells her boy friend that another boy is in love with someone, and the boy friend asks, "What's he in love with?" She answers, "A girl, of course," and her boy friend replies, "Why, of course? Once before it was a neighbor's turtle, and what's more its name was Sam." This interpretation of the artist as innately incompetent and a social outcast (by the innuendo of sexual inversion) is worthy of examination.

We do not pretend that the individual illustrations and examples, or the theories by which they are interpreted, are basically new. But in view of the cultural and pedagogical problem presented by television, we do not think that the novelty of the specific findings should be a primary concern. We know from psychoanalysis that the reasoning "But we know all this!" is not infrequently a defense. This defense is made in order to dismiss insights as irrelevant because they are actually uncomfortable and make life more difficult for us than it already is by shaking our conscience when we are supposed to enjoy the "simple pleasures of life." The investigation of the television problems we have here indicated and illustrated by a few examples selected at random demands, most of all, taking seriously notions dimly familiar to most of us by putting them into their proper context and perspective and by checking them by pertinent material. We propose to concentrate on issues of which we are vaguely but uncomfortably aware, even at the expense of our discomfort's mounting, the further and the more systematically our studies proceed. The effort here required is of a moral nature itself: knowingly to face psychological mechanisms operating on various levels in order not to become blind and passive victims. We can change this medium of far-reaching potentialities only if we look at it in the same spirit which we hope will one day be expressed by its imagery.

NOTES

1. David Riesman, *The Lonely Crowd* (New Haven, 1950), p. v.
2. The evolution of the ideology of the extrovert has probably also its long history, particularly in the lower types of popular literature during the nineteenth century when the code of decency became divorced from its religious roots and therewith attained more and more the character of an opaque taboo. It seems likely, however, that in this respect the triumph of the films marked the decisive step. Reading as an act of perception and apperception probably carries with itself a certain kind of internalization; the act of reading a novel comes fairly close to a *monologue interieur*. Visualization in modern mass media makes for externalization. The idea of inwardness, still maintained in older portrait painting through the expressiveness of the face, gives way to unmistakable optical signals that can be grasped at a glance. Even if a character in a movie or television show is not what he appears to be, his appearance is treated in such a way as to leave no doubt about his true nature. Thus a villain who is not presented as a brute must at least be "suave," and his repulsive slickness and mild manner unambiguously indicate what we are to think of him.
3. It should be noted that the tendency against "erudition" was already present at the very beginning of popular culture, particularly in Defoe, who was consciously opposed to the learned literature of his day, and has become famous for having scorned every refinement of style and artistic construction in favor of an apparent faithfulness to "life."
4. One of the significant differences seems to be that in the eighteenth century the concept of

popular culture itself moving toward an emancipation from the absolutistic and semifeudal tradition had a progressive meaning stressing autonomy of the individual as being capable of making his own decisions. This means, among other things, that the early popular literature left space for authors who violently disagreed with the pattern set by Richardson and, nevertheless, obtained popularity of their own. The most prominent case in question is that of Fielding, whose first novel started as a parody of Richardson. It would be interesting to compare the popularity of Richardson and Fielding at that time. Fielding hardly achieved the same success as Richardson. Yet it would be absurd to assume that today's popular culture would allow the equivalent of a *Tom Jones*. This may illustrate the contention of the "rigidity" of today's popular culture. A crucial experiment would be to make an attempt to base a movie on a novel such as Evelyn Waugh's *The Loved One*. It is almost certain that the script would be rewritten and edited so often that nothing remotely similar to the idea of the original would be left.

5. The more rationality (the reality principle) is carried to extremes, the more its ultimate aim (actual gratification) tends, paradoxically, to appear as "immature" and ridiculous. Not only eating, but also uncontrolled manifestations of sexual impulses tend to provoke laughter in audiences—kisses in motion pictures have generally to be led up to, the stage has to be set for them, in order to avoid laughter. Yet mass culture never completely succeeds in wiping out potential laughter. Induced, of course, by the supposed infantilism of sensual pleasures, laughter can largely be accounted for by the mechanism of repression. Laughter is a defense against the forbidden fruit.

6. This relationship again should not be oversimplified. No matter to what extent modern mass media tend to blur the difference between reality and the aesthetic, our realistic spectators are still aware that all is "in fun." It cannot be assumed that the direct primary perception of reality takes place within the television frame of reference, although many movie-goers recall the alienation of familiar sights when leaving the theater: everything still has the appearance of being part of the movie plot. What is more important is the interpretation of reality in terms of psychological carry-overs, the preparedness to see ordinary objects as though some threatening mystery were hidden behind them. Such an attitude seems to be syntonic with mass delusions as suspicion of omnipresent graft, corruption, and conspiracy.

7. It could be argued that this very ridicule expresses that this boy is not meant to represent the artist but just the "dope." But this is probably too rationalistic. Again, as in the case of the schoolteacher, official respect for culture prevents caricaturing the artist as such. However, by characterizing the boy, among other things by his writing poetry, it is indirectly achieved that artistic activities and silliness are associated with each other. In many respects mass culture is organized much more by way of such associations than in strict logical terms. It may be added that quite frequently attacks on any social type seek protection by apparently presenting the object of the attack as an exception while it is understood by innuendo that he is considered as a specimen of the whole concept.

THEODOR W. ADORNO

FREUDIAN THEORY AND THE PATTERN OF FASCIST PROPAGANDA[1]

During the past decade the nature and content of the speeches and pamphlets of American fascist agitators have been subjected to intensive research by social scientists. Some of these studies, undertaken along the lines of content analysis, have finally led to a comprehensive presentation in the book, *Prophets of Deceit*, by L. Lowenthal and N. Guterman.[2] The over-all picture obtained is characterized by two main features. First, with the exception of some bizarre and completely negative recommendations: to put aliens into concentration camps or to expatriate Zionists, fascist propaganda material in this country is little concerned with concrete and tangible political issues. The overwhelming majority of all agitators' statements are directed *ad hominem*. They are obviously based on psychological calculations rather than on the intention to gain followers through the rational statement of rational aims. The term "rabble rouser," though objectionable because of its inherent contempt of the masses as such, is adequate insofar as it expresses the atmosphere of irrational emotional aggressiveness purposely promoted by our would-be Hitlers. If it is an impudence to call people "rabble," it is precisely the aim of the agitator to transform the very same people into "rabble," i.e., crowds bent to violent action without any sensible political aim, and to create the atmosphere of the pogrom. The universal purpose of these agitators is to instigate methodically what, since Gustave Le Bon's famous book, is commonly known as "the psychology of the masses."

Second, the agitators' approach is truly systematical and follows a rigidly set pattern of clear-cut "devices." This does not merely pertain to the ultimate unity of the political purpose: the abolition of democracy through mass support against the democratic principle, but even more so to the intrinsic nature of the content and presentation of propaganda itself. The similarity of the utterances of various agitators, from much-publicized figures such as Coughlin and Gerald Smith to provincial small-time hate mongers, is so great that it suffices in principle to analyze the statements of one of them in order to know them all.[3] Moreover, the speeches themselves are so monotonous that one meets with endless repetitions as soon as one is acquainted with the very limited number of stock devices. As a matter of fact, constant reiteration and scarcity of ideas are indispensable ingredients of the entire technique.

While the mechanical rigidity of the pattern is obvious and itself the expression of certain psychological aspects of fascist mentality, one cannot help feeling that propaganda material of the fascist brand forms a structural unit with a total common conception, be it conscious or unconscious, which determines every word that is said. This structural unit seems to refer to the implicit political conception as well as to the psychological essence. So far, only the detached and in a way isolated nature of each device has been given scientific attention; the psychoanalytic connotations of the devices have been stressed and elaborated. Now that the elements have been cleared up sufficiently, the time has come to focus attention on the psychological system as such—and it may not be entirely accidental that the term summons the association of paranoia—which comprises and begets these elements. This seems to be the more appropriate since otherwise the psychoanalytic interpretation of the individual devices will remain somewhat haphazard and arbitrary. A kind of theoretical frame of reference will have to be evolved. Inasmuch as the individual devices call almost irresistibly for psychoanalytic interpretation, it is but logical to postulate that this frame of reference should consist of the application of a more comprehensive, basic psychoanalytic theory to the agitator's over-all approach.

Such a frame of reference has been provided by Freud himself in his book *Group Psychology and the Analysis of the Ego*, published in English as early as 1922, and long before the danger of German fascism appeared to be acute.[4] It is not an overstatement if we say that Freud, though he was hardly interested in the political phase of the problem, clearly foresaw the rise and nature of fascist mass movements in purely psychological categories. If it is true that the analyst's unconscious perceives the unconscious of the patient, one may also presume that his theoretical intuitions are capable of anticipating tendencies still latent on a rational level but manifesting themselves on a deeper one. It may not have been perchance that after the first World War Freud turned his attention to narcissism and ego problems in the specific sense. The mechanisms and instinctual conflicts involved evidently play an increasingly important role in the present epoch, whereas, according to the testimony of practicing analysts, the "classical" neuroses such as conversion hysteria, which served as models for the method, now occur less frequently than at the time of Freud's own development when Charcot dealt with hysteria clinically and Ibsen made it the subject matter of some of his plays. According to Freud the problem of mass psychology is closely related to the new type of psychological affliction so characteristic of the era which for socio-economic reasons witnesses the decline of the individual and his subsequent weakness. While Freud did not concern himself with the social changes, it may be said that he developed within in the monadological confines of the individual the traces of its profound crisis and willingness to yield unquestioningly to powerful outside, collective agencies. Without ever devoting himself to the study of contemporary social developments, Freud has pointed to historical trends through the development of his own work, the choice of his subject matters, and the evolution of guiding concepts.

The method of Freud's book constitutes a dynamic interpretation of Le Bon's description of the mass mind and a critique of a few dogmatic concepts—magic words, as it were—which are employed by Le Bon and other pre-analytic psychologists as though they were keys for some startling phenomena. Foremost among these concepts is that of suggestion which, incidentally, still plays a large role as a stopgap in popular thinking about the spell exercised by Hitler and his like over the masses. Freud does not challenge the accuracy of Le Bon's well-known characterizations of masses as being largely de-individualized, irrational, easily influenced, prone to violent action and altogether of a regressive nature. What distinguishes him from Le Bon is rather the absence of the traditional contempt for the masses which is the *thema probandum** of most of the older psychologists. Instead of inferring from the usual descriptive findings that the masses are inferior per se and likely to remain so, he asks in the spirit of true enlightenment: what makes the masses into masses? He rejects the easy hypothesis of a social or herd instinct, which for him denotes the problem and not its solution. In addition to the purely psychological reasons he gives for this rejection, one might say that he is on safe ground also from the sociological point of view. The straightforward comparison of modern mass formations with biological phenomena can hardly be regarded as valid since the members of contemporary masses are, at least *prima facie* individuals, the children of a liberal, competitive and individualistic society, and conditioned to maintain themselves as independent, self-sustaining units; they are continuously admonished to be "rugged" and warned against surrender. Even if one were to assume that archaic, pre-individual instincts survive, one could not simply point to this inheritance but would have to explain why modern men revert to patterns of behavior which flagrantly contradict their own rational level and the present stage of enlightened technological civilization. This is precisely what Freud wants to do. He tries to find out which psychological forces result in the transformation of individuals into a mass. "If the individuals in the group are combined into a unity, there must surely be something to unite them, and this bond might be precisely the thing that is characteristic of a group."[5] This quest, however, is tantamount to an exposition of the fundamental issue of fascist manipulation. For the fascist demagogue, who has to win the support of millions of people for aims largely incompatible with their own rational self-interest, can do so only by artificially creating the *bond* Freud is looking for. If the demagogues' approach is at all realistic—and their popular success leaves no doubt that it is—it might be hypothesized that the bond in question is the very same the demagogue tries to produce synthetically; in fact, that it is the unifying principle behind his various devices.

In accordance with general psychoanalytic theory, Freud believes that the bond which integrates individuals into a mass, is of a *libidinal* nature. Earlier psychologists

* "proposition that must be approved" [Ed.]

have occasionally hit upon this aspect of mass psychology. "In McDougall's opinion men's emotions are stirred in a group to a pitch that they seldom or never attain under other conditions; and it is a pleasurable experience for those who are concerned to surrender themselves so unreservedly to their passions and thus to become merged in the group and to lose the sense of the limits of their individuality."[6] Freud goes beyond such observations by explaining the coherence of masses altogether in terms of the pleasure principle, that is to say, the actual or vicarious gratifications individuals obtain from surrendering to a mass. Hitler, by the way, was well aware of the libidinal source of mass formation through surrender when he attributed specifically female, passive features to the participants of his meetings, and thus also hinted at the role of unconscious homosexuality in mass psychology.[7] The most important consequence of Freud's introduction of libido into group psychology is that the traits generally ascribed to masses lose the deceptively primordial and irreducible character reflected by the arbitrary construct of specific mass or herd instincts. The latter are effects rather than causes. What is peculiar to the masses is, according to Freud, not so much a new quality as the manifestation of old ones usually hidden. "From our point of view we need not attribute so much importance to the appearance of new characteristics. For us it would be enough to say that in a group the individual is brought under conditions which allow him to throw off the repressions of his unconscious instincts."[8] This does not only dispense with auxiliary hypotheses *ad hoc* but also does justice to the simple fact that those who become submerged in masses are not primitive men but display primitive attitudes contradictory to their *normal* rational behavior. Yet, even the most trivial descriptions leave no doubt about the affinity of certain peculiarities of masses to archaic traits. Particular mention should be made here of the potential short cut from violent emotions to violent actions stressed by all authors on mass psychology, a phenomenon which in Freud's writings on primitive cultures leads to the assumption that the murder of the father of the primary horde is not imaginary but corresponds to prehistoric reality. In terms of dynamic theory the revival of such traits has to be understood as the result of a *conflict*. It may also help to explain some of the manifestations of fascist mentality which could hardly be grasped without the assumption of an antagonism between varied psychological forces. One has to think here above all of the psychological category of destructiveness with which Freud dealt in his *Civilization and its Discontent*. As a rebellion against civilization fascism is not simply the reoccurrence of the archaic but its reproduction in and by civilization itself. It is hardly adequate to define the forces of fascist rebellion simply as powerful id energies which throw off the pressure of the existing social order. Rather, this rebellion borrows its energies partly from other psychological agencies which are pressed into the service of the unconscious.

Since the libidinal bond between members of masses is obviously not of an uninhibited sexual nature, the problem arises as to which psychological mechanisms transform primary sexual energy into feelings which hold masses together. Freud copes with the problem by analyzing the phenomena covered by the terms suggestion and suggestibility. He recognizes suggestion as the "shelter" or "screen" concealing "love relationships." It is essential that the "love relationship" behind suggestion remains unconscious.[9] Freud dwells on the fact that in organized groups such as the Army or the Church there is either no mention of love whatsoever between the members, or it is expressed only in a sublimated and indirect way, through the mediation of some religious image in the love of whom the members unite and whose all-embracing love they are supposed to imitate in their attitude towards each other. It seems significant that in today's society with its artificially integrated fascist masses reference to love is almost completely excluded.[10] Hitler shunned the traditional role of the loving father and replaced it entirely by the negative one of threatening authority. The concept of love was relegated to the abstract notion of *Germany* and seldom mentioned without the epithet of "fanatical" through which even this love obtained a ring of hostility and aggressiveness against those not encompassed by it. It is one of the basic tenets of fascist leadership to keep primary libidinal energy on an unconscious level so as to divert its manifestations in a way suitable to political ends. The less an objective idea such as religious salvation plays a role in mass formation, and the more mass manipulation becomes the sole aim, the more thoroughly uninhibited love has to be repressed and moulded into obedience. There is too little in the content of fascist ideology that *could* be loved.

The libidinal pattern of fascism and the entire technique of fascist demagogues are authoritarian. This is where the techniques of the demagogue and the hypnotist coincide with the psychological mechanism by which individuals are made to undergo the regressions which reduce them to mere members of a group.

By the measures that he takes, the hypnotist awakens in the subject a portion of his archaic inheritance which had also made him compliant towards his parents and which had experienced an individual re-animation in his relation to his father: what is thus awakened is the idea of a paramount and dangerous personality, towards whom only a passive-masochistic attitude is possible, to whom one's will has to be surrendered—while to be alone with him, "to look him in the face," appears a hazardous enterprise. It is only in some such way as this that we can picture the relation of the individual member of the primal horde to the primal father . . . The uncanny and coercive characteristics of group formations, which are shown in their suggestion phenomena, may therefore with justice be traced back to the fact of their origin from the primal horde. The leader of the group is still the dreaded primal father; the group still wishes to be governed by unrestricted force; it has an extreme passion for authority; in Le Bon's phrase, it has a thirst for obedience. The primal father is the group ideal, which governs the ego in the place of the ego ideal. Hypnosis has a good claim to being described as a group of two; there remains as a definition for suggestion—a conviction which is not based upon perception and reasoning but upon an erotic tie.[11]

This actually defines the nature and content of fascist propaganda. It is psychological because of its irrational authoritarian aims which cannot be attained by means of rational convictions but only through the skillful awakening of "a portion of the subject's archaic inheritance." Fascist agitation is centered in the idea of the leader, no matter whether he actually leads or is only the mandatary of group interests, because only the psychological image of the leader is apt to reanimate the idea of the all-powerful and threatening primal father. This is the ultimate root of the otherwise enigmatic *personalization* of fascist propaganda, its incessant plugging of names and supposedly great men, instead of discussing objective causes. The formation of the imagery of an omnipotent and unbridled father figure, by far transcending the individual father and therewith apt to be enlarged into a "group ego," is the only way to promulgate the "passive-masochistic attitude . . . to whom one's will has to be surrendered," an attitude required of the fascist follower the more his political behavior becomes irreconcilable with his own rational interests as a private person as well as those of the group or class to which he actually belongs.[12] The follower's reawakened irrationality is, therefore, quite rational from the leader's viewpoint: it necessarily has to be "a conviction which is not based upon perception and reasoning but upon an erotic tie."

The mechanism which transforms libido into the bond between leader and followers, and between the followers themselves, is that of *identification*. A great part of Freud's book is devoted to its analysis.[13] It is impossible to discuss here the very subtle theoretical differentiation, particularly the one between identification and introjection. It should be noted, however, that the late Ernst Simmel, to whom we owe valuable contributions to the psychology of fascism, took up Freud's concept of the ambivalent nature of identification as a derivative of the oral phase of the organization of the libido,[14] and expanded it into an analytic theory of anti-Semitism.

We content ourselves with a few observations on the relevancy of the doctrine of identification to fascist propaganda and fascist mentality. It has been observed by several authors, and by Erik Homburger Erikson in particular, that the specifically fascist leader type does not seem to be a father figure such as for instance the king of former times. The inconsistency of this observation with Freud's theory of the leader as the primal father, however, is only superficial. His discussion of identification may well help us to understand, in terms of subjective dynamics, certain changes which are actually due to objective historical conditions. Identification is "the *earliest* expression of an emotional tie with another person," playing "a part in the early history of the Oedipus complex."[15] It may well be that this pre-oedipal component of identification helps to bring about the separation of the leader image as that of an all-powerful primal father from the actual father image. Since the child's identification with his father as an answer to the Oedipus complex is only a secondary phenomenon, infantile regression may go beyond this father image and through an "anaclitic" process reach a more archaic one. Moreover, the primitively narcissistic aspect of identification as an act of *devouring*, of making the beloved object part of oneself, may provide us with a clue to the fact that the modern leader image sometimes seems to be the enlargement of the subject's own personality, a collective projection of himself, rather than the image of the father whose role during the later phases of the subject's infancy may well have decreased in present-day society.[16] All these facets call for further clarification.

The essential role of narcissism in regard to the identifications which are at play in the formation of fascist groups is recognized in Freud's theory of *idealization*. "We see that the object is being treated in the same way as our own ego, so that when we are in love a considerable amount of narcissistic libido overflows on the object. It is even obvious, in many forms of love choice, that the object serves as a substitute for some unattained ego ideal of our own. We love it on account of the perfections which we have striven to reach for our own ego, and which we should now like to procure in this roundabout way as a means of satisfying our narcissism."[17] It is precisely this idealization of himself which the fascist leader tries to promote in his followers, and which is helped by the *Führer* ideology. The people he has to reckon with generally undergo the characteristic, modern conflict between a strongly developed rational, self-preserving ego agency[18] and the continuous failure to satisfy their own ego demands. This conflict results in strong narcissistic impulses which can be absorbed and satisfied only through idealization as the partial transfer of the narcissistic libido to the object. This, again, falls in line with the semblance of the leader image to an enlargement of the subject: by making the leader his ideal he loves himself, as it were, but gets rid of the stains of frustration and discontent which mar his picture of his own empirical self. This pattern of identification through idealization, the caricature of true, conscious solidarity, is, however, a collective one. It is effective in vast numbers of people with similar characterological dispositions and libidinal leanings. The fascist *community of the people* corresponds exactly to Freud's definition of a group as being "a number of individuals who have substituted one and the same object for their ego ideal and have consequently identified themselves with one another in their ego."[19] The leader image, in turn, borrows as it were its primal father-like omnipotence from collective strength.

Freud's psychological construction of the leader imagery is corroborated by its striking coincidence with the Fascist leader type, at least as far as its public build-up is concerned. His descriptions fit the picture of Hitler no less than idealizations into which the American demagogues try to style themselves. In order to allow narcissistic identification, the leader has to appear himself as absolutely narcissistic, and it is from this insight that Freud derives the portrait of the "primal father of the horde" which might as well be Hitler's.

He, at the very beginning of the history of mankind, was the *Superman*[20] whom Nietzsche only expected from the future. Even today the members of a group stand in need of the illusion that they are equally and justly loved by their leader; but the leader himself need love no one else, he may be of a masterly nature, absolutely narcissistic, but self-confident and independent. We know that love puts a check upon narcissism, and it would be possible to show how, by operating in this way, it became a factor of civilization.[21]

One of the most conspicuous features of the agitators' speeches, namely the absence of a positive program and of anything they might "give," as well as the paradoxical prevalence of threat and denial, is thus being accounted for: the leader can be loved only if he himself does not love. Yet, Freud is aware of another aspect of the leader image which apparently contradicts the first one. While appearing as a superman, the leader must at the same time work the miracle of appearing as an average person, just as Hitler posed as a composite of King-Kong and the suburban barber. This, too, Freud explains through his theory of narcissism. According to him,

the individual gives up his ego ideal and substitutes for it the group ideal as embodied in the leader. [However,] in many individuals the separation between the ego and the ego ideal is not very far advanced; the two still coincide readily; the ego has often preserved its earlier self-complacency. The selection of the leader is very much facilitated by this circumstance. He need only possess the typical qualities of the individuals concerned in a particularly clearly marked and pure form, and need only give an impression of greater force and of more freedom of libido; and in that case the need for a strong chief will often meet him half-way and invest him with a predominance to which he would otherwise perhaps have had no claim. The other members of the group, whose ego ideal would not, apart from this, have become embodied in his person without some correction, are then carried away with the rest by "suggestion," that is to say, by means of identification.[22]

Even the fascist leader's startling symptoms of inferiority, his resemblance to ham actors and asocial psychopaths, is thus anticipated in Freud's theory. For the sake of those parts of the follower's narcissistic libido which have not been thrown into the leader image but remain attached to the follower's own ego, the superman must still resemble the follower and appear as his "enlargement." Accordingly, one of the basic devices of personalized fascist propaganda is the concept of the "great little man," a person who suggests both omnipotence and the idea that he is just one of the folks, a plain, red-blooded American, untainted by material or spiritual wealth. Psychological ambivalence helps to work a social miracle. The leader image gratifies the follower's twofold wish to submit to authority and to be the authority himself. This fits into a world in which irrational control is exercised though it has lost its inner conviction through universal enlightenment. The people who obey the dictators also sense that the latter are superfluous. They reconcile this contradiction through the assumption that they are themselves the ruthless oppressor.

All the agitators' standard devices are designed along the line of Freud's exposé of what became later the basic structure of fascist demagoguery, the technique of personalization,[23] and the idea of the great little man. We limit ourselves to a few examples picked at random.

Freud gives an exhaustive account of the hierarchical element in irrational groups. "It is obvious that a soldier takes his superior, that is, really, the leader of the army, as his ideal, while he identifies himself with his equals, and derives from this community of their egos the obligations for giving mutual help and for sharing possessions which comradeship implies. But he becomes ridiculous if he tries to identify himself with the general,"[24] to wit, consciously and directly. The fascists, down to the last smalltime demagogue, continuously emphasize ritualistic ceremonies and hierarchical differentiations. The less hierarchy within the setup of a highly rationalized and quantified industrial society is warranted, the more artificial hierarchies with no objective *raison d'être* are built up and rigidly imposed by Fascists for purely psycho-technical reasons. It may be added, however, that this is not the only libidinous source involved. Thus hierarchical structures are in complete keeping with the wishes of the sadomasochistic character. Hitler's famous formula, *Verantwortung nach oben, Autorität nach unten* (responsibility towards above, authority toward below), nicely rationalizes this character's ambivalence.[25]

The tendency to tread on those below, which manifests itself so disastrously in the persecution of weak and helpless minorities, is as outspoken as the hatred against those outside. In practice, both tendencies quite frequently fall together. Freud's theory sheds light on the all-pervasive, rigid distinction between the beloved in-group and the rejected out-group. Throughout our culture this way of thinking and behaving has come to be regarded as self-evident to such a degree that the question of why people love what is like themselves and hate what is different is rarely asked seriously enough. Here as in many other instances, the productivity of Freud's approach lies in his questioning that which is generally accepted. Le Bon had noticed that the irrational crowd "goes directly to extremes."[26] Freud expands this observation and points out that the dichotomy between in- and out-group is of so deep-rooted a nature that it affects even those groups whose "ideas" apparently exclude such reactions. Already in 1921 he was therefore able to dispense with the liberalistic illusion that the progress of civilization would automatically bring about an increase of tolerance and a lessening of violence against out-groups.

Even during the kingdom of Christ those people who do not belong to the community of believers, who do not love him, and whom he does not love, stand outside this tie. Therefore a religion, even if it calls itself the religion of love, must be hard and unloving to those who do not belong to it. Fundamentally indeed every religion is in this same way a religion of love for all those whom it embraces; while cruelty and intolerance towards those who do not belong to it are natural to every religion. However difficult we may find it personally, we ought not to reproach believers too severely on this account: people who are unbelieving or indifferent are so much better off psychologically in this respect. If to-day that intolerance no longer shows itself so violent and cruel as in former centuries, we can scarcely conclude that there has been a softening in human manners. The cause is rather to be found in the undeniable weakening of religious feelings and the libidinal ties which depend upon them. If another group tie takes the place of the religious one—and the socialistic tie seems to be succeeding in doing so—, then there will be the same intolerance towards outsiders as in the age of the Wars of Religion.[27]

Freud's error in political prognosis, his blaming the "socialists" for what their German arch enemies did, is as striking as his prophecy of fascist destructiveness, the drive to eliminate the out-group.[28] As a matter of fact, neutralization of religion seems to have led to just the opposite of what the enlightener Freud anticipated: the division between believers and nonbelievers has been maintained and reified. However, it has become a structure in itself, independent of any ideational content, and is even more stubbornly defended since it lost its inner conviction. At the same time, the mitigating impact of the religious doctrine of love vanished. This is the essence of the "buck and sheep" device employed by all fascist demagogues. Since they do not recognize any spiritual criterion in regard to who is chosen and who is rejected, they substitute a pseudo-natural criterion such as the race,[29] which seems to be inescapable and can therefore be applied even more mercilessly than was the concept of heresy during the Middle Ages. Freud has succeeded in identifying the libidinal function of this device. It acts as a negatively integrating force. Since the positive libido is completely invested in the image of the primal father, the leader, and since few positive contents are available, a negative one has to be found. "The leader or the leading idea might also, so to speak, be negative; hatred against a particular person or institution might operate in just the same unifying way, and might call up the same kind of emotional ties as positive attachment."[30] It goes without saying that this negative integration feeds on the instinct of destructiveness to which Freud does not explicitly refer in his *Group Psychology*, the decisive role of which he has, however, recognized in his *Civilization and Its Discontents*. In the present context, Freud explains the hostility against the out-group with narcissism:

In the undisguised antipathies and aversions which people feel towards strangers with whom they have to do we may recognize the expression of self-love—of narcissism. This self-love works for the self-assertion of the individual, and behaves as though the occurrence of any divergence from his own particular lines of development involved a criticism of them and a demand for their alteration.[31]

The narcissistic *gain* provided by fascist propaganda is obvious. It suggests continuously, and sometimes in rather devious ways, that the follower, simply through belonging to the in-group, is better, higher and purer than those who are excluded. At the same time, any kind of critique or self-awareness is resented as a narcissistic loss, and elicits rage. It accounts for the violent reaction of all fascists against what they deem *zersetzend*,* that which debunks their own stubbornly maintained values, and it also explains the hostility of prejudiced persons against any kind of introspection. Concomitantly, the concentration of hostility upon the out-group does away with intolerance in one's own group to which one's relation would otherwise be highly ambivalent.

But the whole of this intolerance vanishes, temporarily or permanently, as the result of the formation of a group, and in a group. So long as a group formation persists or so far as it

* "subversive" [Ed.]

extends, individuals behave as though they were uniform, tolerate other people's peculiarities, put themselves on an equal level with them, and have no feeling of aversion towards them. Such a limitation of narcissism can, according to our theoretical views, only be produced by one factor, a libidinal tie with other people.[32]

This is the line pursued by the agitators' standard "unity trick." They emphasize their being different from the outsider but play down such differences within their own group and tend to level out distinctive qualities among themselves with the exception of the hierarchical one. "We are all in the same boat"; nobody should be better off; the snob, the intellectual, the pleasure seeker are always attacked. The undercurrent of malicious egalitarianism, of the brotherhood of all-comprising humiliation, is a component of fascist propaganda and Fascism itself. It found its symbol in Hitler's notorious command of the *Eintopfgericht.** The less they want the inherent social structure changed, the more they prate about social justice, meaning that no member of the "commmunity of the people" should indulge in individual pleasures. Repressive egalitarianism instead of realization of true equality through the abolition of repression, is part and parcel of the fascist mentality and reflected in the agitators' "If-you-only-knew" device which promises the vindictive revelation of all sorts of forbidden pleasures enjoyed by others. Freud interprets this phenomenon in terms of the transformation of individuals into members of a psychological "brother horde." Their coherence is a reaction formation against their primary jealousy of each other, pressed into the service of group coherence.

What appears later on in society in the shape of *Gemeingeist, esprit de corps*, ›group spirit‹, etc. does not belie its derivation from what was originally envy. No one must want to put himself forward, every one must be the same and have the same. Social justice means that we deny ourselves many things so that others may have to do without them as well, or, what is the same thing, may not be able to ask for them.[33]

It may be added that the ambivalence towards the brother has found a rather striking, ever-recurring expression in the agitators' technique. Freud and Rank have pointed out that in fairy tales small animals such as bees and ants "would be the brothers in the primal horde, just as in the same way in dream symbolism insects or vermin signify brothers and sisters (contemptuously, considered as babies)."[34] Since the members of the in-group have supposedly "succeeded in identifying themselves with one another by means of similar love for the same object,"[35] they cannot admit this contempt for each other. Thus, it is expressed by completely negative cathexis of these low animals, fused with hatred against the out-group, and projected upon the latter. Actually it is one of the favorite devices of Fascist agitators—examined in great detail by Leo Lowenthal[36]—to compare out-groups, all foreigners and particularly refugees and Jews, with low animals and vermin.

* "one-dish meal" [Ed.]

If we are entitled to assume a correspondence of Fascist propagandist stimuli to the mechanisms elaborated in Freud's *Group Psychology*, we have to ask ourselves the almost inevitable question: how did the fascist agitators, crude and semi-educated as they were, obtain knowledge of these mechanisms? Reference to the influence exercised by Hitler's *Mein Kampf* upon the American demagogues would not lead very far, since it seems impossible that Hitler's theoretical knowledge of group psychology went beyond the most trivial observations derived from a popularized Le Bon. Neither can it be maintained that Goebbels was a mastermind of propaganda and fully aware of the most advanced findings of modern depth psychology. Perusal of his speeches and selections from his recently published diaries give the impression of a person shrewd enough to play the game of power politics but utterly naive and superficial in regard to all societal or psychological issues below the surface of his own catchwords and newspaper editorials. The idea of the sophisticated and "radical" intellectual Goebbels is part of the devil's legend associated with his name and fostered by eager journalism; a legend, incidentally, which itself calls for psychoanalytic explanation. Goebbels himself thought in stereotypes and was completely under the spell of personalization. Thus we have to seek for sources other than erudition, for the much advertised fascist command of psychological techniques of mass manipulation. The foremost source seems to be the already mentioned basic identity of leader and follower which circumscribes one of the aspects of identification. The leader can guess the psychological wants and needs of those susceptible to his propaganda because he resembles them psychologically, and is distinguished from them by a capacity to express without inhibitions what is latent in them, rather than by any intrinsic superiority. The leaders are generally oral character types, with a compulsion to speak incessantly and to befool the others. The famous spell they exercise over their followers seems largely to depend on their orality: language itself, devoid of its rational significance, functions in a magical way and furthers those archaic regressions which reduce individuals to members of crowds. Since this very quality of uninhibited but largely associative speech presupposes at least a temporary lack of ego control, it may well indicate weakness rather than strength. The fascist agitators' boasting of strength is indeed frequently accompanied by hints at such weakness, particularly when begging for monetary contributions—hints which, to be sure, are skillfully merged with the idea of strength itself. In order successfully to meet the unconscious dispositions of his audience, the agitator so to speak simply turns his own unconscious outward. His particular character syndrome makes it possible for him to do exactly this, and experience has taught him consciously to exploit this faculty, to make rational use of his irrationality, similarly to the actor, or a certain type of journalist who knows how to sell their innervations and sensitivity. Without knowing it, he is thus able to speak and act in accord with psychological theory for the simple reason that the psychological theory is true. All he has to do in order to make the psychology of his audience click is shrewdly to exploit his own psychology.

The adequacy of the agitators' devices to the psychological basis of their aim is further enhanced by another factor. As we know, fascist agitations has by now come to be a profession, as it were, a livelihood. It had plenty of time to test the effectiveness of its various appeals and, through what might be called natural selection, only the most catchy ones have survived. Their effectiveness is itself a function of the psychology of the consumers. Through a process of "freezing," which can be observed throughout the techniques employed in modern mass culture, the surviving appeals have been standardized, similarly to the advertising slogans which proved to be most valuable in the promotion of business. This standardization, in turn, falls in line with stereotypical thinking, that is to say, with the "stereopathy" of those susceptible to this propaganda and their infantile wish for endless, unaltered repetition. It is hard to predict whether the latter psychological disposition will prevent the agitators' standard devices from becoming blunt through excessive application. In national-socialist Germany, everybody used to make fun of certain propagandistic phrases such as "blood and soil" (*Blut und Boden*), jokingly called *Blubo*, or the concept of the nordic race from which the parodistic verb *aufnorden* (to "northernize") was derived. Nevertheless, these appeals do not seem to have lost their attractiveness. Rather, their very "phonyness" may have been relished cynically and sadistically as an index for the fact that power alone decided one's fate in the Third Reich, that is, power unhampered by rational objectivity.

Furthermore, one may ask: why is the applied group psychology discussed here peculiar to Fascism rather than to most other movements that seek mass support? Even the most casual comparison of fascist propaganda with that of liberal, progressive parties will show this to be so. Yet, neither Freud nor Le Bon envisaged such a distinction. They spoke of crowds "as such," similar to the conceptualizations used by formal sociology, without differentiating between the political aims of the groups involved. As a matter of fact, both thought of traditional socialistic movements rather than of their opposite, though it should be noted that the Church and the Army—the examples chosen by Freud for the demonstration of his theory—are essentially conservative and hierarchical. Le Bon, on the other hand, is mainly concerned with nonorganized, spontaneous, ephemeral crowds. Only an explicit theory of society, by far transcending the range of psychology, can fully answer the question raised here. We content ourselves with a few suggestions. First, the objective aims of Fascism are largely irrational in so far as they contradict the material interests of great numbers of those whom they try to embrace, notwithstanding the prewar boom of the first years of the Hitler regime. The continuous danger of war inherent in Fascism spells destruction and the masses are at least preconsciously aware of it. Thus, Fascism does not altogether speak the untruth when it refers to its own irrational powers, however faked the mythology which ideologically rationalizes the irrational may be. Since it would be impossible for Fascism to win the masses through rational arguments, its propaganda must necessarily be deflected from discursive thinking; it must be oriented psychologically, and has to mobilize irrational, unconscious, regressive processes. This task is facilitated by the frame of mind of all those strata of the population who suffer from senseless frustrations and therefore develop a stunted, irrational mentality. It may well be the secret of fascist propaganda that it simply takes men for what they are: the true children of today's standardized mass culture, largely robbed of autonomy and spontaneity, instead of setting goals the realization of which would transcend the psychological *status quo* no less than the social one. Fascist propaganda has only to *reproduce* the existent mentality for its own purposes—it need not induce a change—and the compulsive repetition which is one of its foremost characteristics will be at one with the necessity for this continuous reproduction. It relies absolutely on the total structure as well as on each particular trait of the authoritarian character which is itself the product of an internalization of the irrational aspects of modern society. Under the prevailing conditions, the irrationality of fascist propaganda becomes rational in the sense of instinctual economy. For if the *status quo* is taken for granted and petrified, a much greater effort is needed to see through it than to adjust to it and to obtain at least some gratification through identification with the existent—the focal point of fascist propaganda. This may explain why ultrareactionary mass movements use the "psychology of the masses" to a much greater extent than do movements which show more faith in the masses. However, there is no doubt that even the most progressive political movement can deteriorate to the level of the "psychology of the crowd" and its manipulation, if its own rational content is shattered through the reversion to blind power.

The so-called psychology of Fascism is largely engendered by manipulation. Rationally calculated techniques bring about what is naively regarded as the "natural" irrationality of masses. This insight may help us to solve the problem of whether Fascism as a mass phenomenon can be explained at all in psychological terms. While there certainly exists potential susceptibility for Fascism among the masses, it is equally certain that the manipulation of the unconscious, the kind of suggestion explained by Freud in genetic terms, is indispensable for actualization of this potential. This, however, corroborates the assumption that Fascism as such is *not* a psychological issue and that any attempt to understand its roots and its historical role in psychological terms still remains on the level of ideologies such as the one of "irrational forces" promoted by Fascism itself. Although the Fascist agitator doubtlessly takes up certain tendencies within those he addresses, he does so as the mandatory of powerful economic and political interests. Psychological dispositions do not actually cause Fascism; rather, Fascism defines a psychological area which can be successfully exploited by the forces which promote it for entirely nonpsychological reasons of self-interest. What happens when masses are caught by Fascist propaganda is not a spontaneous primary expression of instincts and urges but a quasi-scientific revitalization of their psychology—the artificial regression described by Freud in his discussion of organized groups. The psychology of the masses has been taken over by their leaders and transformed into a means for their domination. It does not express itself directly through mass movements. This phenomenon is not entirely new but was foreshadowed throughout the counterrevolutionary movements of history. Far from being the source of Fascism, psychology has become one element among others in a superimposed system the very totality of which is necessitated by the potential of mass resistance—the masses' own rationality. The content of Freud's theory, the replacement of individual narcissism by identification with leader images, points into the direction of what might be called the appropriation of mass psychology by the oppressors. To be sure, this process has a psychological dimension, but it also indicates a growing tendency towards the abolition of psychological motivation in the old, liberalistic sense. Such motivation is systematically controlled and absorbed by social mechanisms which are directed from above. When the leaders become conscious of mass psychology and take it into their own hands, it ceases to exist in a certain sense. This potentiality is contained in the basic construct of psychoanalysis inasmuch as for Freud the concept of psychology is essentially a negative one. He defines the realm of psychology by the supremacy of the unconscious and postulates that what is it should become ego. The emancipation of man from the heteronomous rule of his unconscious would be tantamount to the abolition of his "psychology." Fascism furthers this abolition in the opposite sense through the perpetuation of dependence instead of the realization of potential freedom, through expropriation of the unconscious by social control instead of making the subjects conscious of their unconscious. For, while psychology always denotes some bondage of the individual, it also presupposes freedom in the sense of a certain self-sufficiency and autonomy of the individual. It is not accidental that the nineteenth century was the great era of psychological thought. In a thoroughly reified society, in which there are virtually no direct relationships between men, and in which each person has been reduced to a social atom, to a mere function of collectivity, the psychological processes, though they still persist in each individual, have ceased to appear as the determining forces of the social process. Thus the psychology of the individual has lost what Hegel would have called its substance. It is perhaps the greatest merit of Freud's book that though he restricted himself to the field of individual psychology and wisely abstained from introducing sociological factors from outside, he nevertheless reached the turning point where psychology abdicates. The psychological "impoverishment" of the subject that "surrendered itself to the object" which "it has substituted for its most important constituent"[37]; i.e., the superego, anticipates almost with *clairvoyance* the postpsychological de-individualized social atoms which form the fascist collectivities. In these social atoms the psychological dynamics of group formation have overreached themselves and are no longer a reality. The category of "phonyness" applies to the leaders as well as to the act of identification on the part of the masses and their supposed frenzy and hysteria. Just as little as people believe in the depth of their hearts that the Jews are the devil, do they completely believe in the leader. They do not really identify themselves with him but act this identification, perform their own enthusiasm, and thus participate in their leader's performance. It is through this performance that they strike a balance between their continuously mobilized instinctual urges and the historical stage of enlightenment they have reached, and which cannot be revoked arbitrarily. It is probably the suspicion of this fictitiousness of their own "group psychology" which makes fascist crowds so merciless and unapproachable. If they would stop to reason for a second, the whole performance would go to pieces, and they would be left to panic.

Freud came upon this element of "phonyness" within an unexpected context, namely, when he discussed hypnosis as a retrogression of individuals to the relation between primal horde and primal father.

As we know from other reactions, individuals have preserved a variable degree of personal aptitude for reviving old situations of this kind. Some knowledge that in spite of everything hypnosis is only a game, a deceptive renewal of these old impressions, may however remain behind and take care that there is a resistance against any too serious consequences of the suspension of the will in hypnosis.[38]

In the meantime, this game has been socialized, and the consequences have proved to be very serious. Freud made a distinction between hypnosis and group psychology by defining the former as taking place between two people only. However, the leaders' appropriation of mass psychology, the streamlining of their technique, has enabled them to collectivize the hypnotic spell. The Nazi battle cry of "Germany awake" hides its very opposite. The collectivization and institutionalization of the spell, on the other hand, have made the transference more and more indirect and precarious so that the aspect of performance, the "phonyness" of enthusiastic identification and of all the traditional dynamics of group psychology, have been tremendously increased. This increase may well terminate in sudden awareness of the untruth of the spell, and eventually in its collapse. Socialized hypnosis breeds within itself the forces which will do away with the spook of regression through remote control, and in the end awaken those who keep their eyes shut though they are no longer asleep.

NOTES

1. This article forms part of the author's continuing collaboration with Max Horkheimer.
2. Harper Brothers, New York, 1949. Cf. also: Leo Lowenthal and Norbert Guterman, "Portrait of the American Agitator," *Public Opinion Quart.*, (Fall) 1948, pp. 417ff.
3. This requires some qualification. There is a certain difference between those who, speculating rightly or wrongly on large-scale economic backing, try to maintain an air of respectability and deny that they are anti-Semites before coming down to the business of Jew baiting—and overt Nazis who want to act on their own, or at least make believe that they do, and indulge in the most violent and obscene language. Moreover, one might distinguish between agitators who play the old-fashioned, homely, Christian conservative and can easily be recognized by their hostility against the "dole," and those who, following a more streamlined modern version, appeal mostly to the youth and sometimes pretend to be revolutionary. However, such differences should not be overrated. The basic

structure of their speeches as well as their supply of devices is identical in spite of carefully fostered differences in overtones. What one has to face is a division of labor rather than genuine divergencies. It may be noted that the National Socialist Party shrewdly maintained differentiations of a similar kind, but that they never amounted to anything nor led to any serious clash of political ideas within the Party. The belief that the victims of June 30, 1934 were revolutionaries is mythological. The blood purge was a matter of rivalries between various rackets and had no bearing on social conflicts.

4. The German title, under which the book was published in 1921, is *Massenpsychologie und Ichanalyse*. The translator, James Strachey, rightly stresses that the term group here means the equivalent of Le Bon's *foule* and the German *Masse*. It may be added that in this book the term ego does not denote the specific psychological agency as described in Freud's later writings in contrast to the id and the superego; it simply means the individual. It is one of the most important implications of Freud's *Group Psychology* that he does not recognize an independent, hypostatized "mentality of the crowd," but reduces the phenomena observed and described by writers such as Le Bon and McDougall to regressions which take place in each one of the individuals who form a crowd and fall under its spell.

5. S. Freud, *Group Psychology and the Analysis of the Ego*, London, 1922, p. 7.

6. *Ibid.*, p. 27.

7. Freud's book does not follow up this phase of the problem but a passage in the addendum indicates that he was quite aware of it. "In the same way, love for women breaks through the group ties of race, of national separation, and of the social class system, and it thus produces important effects as a factor in civilization. It seems certain that homosexual love is far more compatible with group ties, even when it takes the shape of uninhibited sexual tendencies" (p. 123). This was certainly borne out under German Fascism where the borderline between overt and repressed homosexuality, just as that between overt and repressed sadism, was much more fluent than in liberal middle-class society.

8. *L.c.*, pp. 9 and 10.

9. " . . . love relationships . . . also constitute the essence of the group mind. Let us remember that the authorities make no mention of any such relations." (*Ibid.*, p. 40.)

10. Perhaps one of the reasons for this striking phenomenon is the fact that the masses whom the fascist agitator—prior to seizing power—has to face, are primarily not organized ones but the accidental crowds of the big city. The loosely knit character of such motley crowds makes it imperative that discipline and coherence be stressed at the expense of the centrifugal uncanalized urge to love. Part of the agitator's task consists in making the crowd believe that it is organized like the Army or the Church. Hence the tendency towards over-organization. A fetish is made of organization as such; it becomes an end instead of a means and this tendency prevails throughout the agitator's speeches.

11. *L.c.*, pp. 99–100. This key statement of Freud's theory of group psychology incidentally accounts for one of the most decisive observations about the Fascist personality: the externalization of the superego. The term "ego ideal" is Freud's earlier expression for what he later called superego. Its replacement through a "group ego" is exactly what happens to fascist personalities. They fail to develop an independent autonomous conscience and substitute for it an identification with collective authority which is as irrational as Freud described it, heteronomous, rigidly oppressive, largely alien to the individuals' own thinking and, therefore, easily exchangeable in spite of its structural rigidity. The

phenomenon is adequately expressed in the Nazi formula that what serves the German people is good. The pattern reoccurs in the speeches of American fascist demagogues who never appeal to their prospective followers' own conscience but incessantly invoke external, conventional, and stereotyped values which are taken for granted and treated as authoritatively valid without ever being subject to a process of living experience or discursive examination. As pointed out in detail in the book, *The Authoritarian Personality*, by T. W. Adorno, Else Frenkel-Brunswik, Daniel J. Levinson, and R. Nevitt Sanford (Harper Brothers, New York, 1950), prejudiced persons generally display belief in conventional values instead of making moral decisions of their own and regard as right "what is being done." Through identification they too tend to submit to a group ego at the expense of their own ego ideal which becomes virtually merged with external values.

12. The fact that the fascist follower's masochism is inevitably accompanied by sadistic impulses is in harmony with Freud's general theory of ambivalence, originally developed in connection with the oedipus complex. Since the fascist integration of individuals into masses satisfies them only vicariously, their resentment against the frustrations of civilization survives but is canalized to become compatible with the leader's aims; it is psychologically fused with authoritarian submissiveness. Though Freud does not pose the problem of what was later called "sado-masochism," he was nevertheless well aware of it, as evidenced by his acceptance of Le Bon's idea that "since a group is in no doubt as to what constitutes truth or error, and is conscious, moreover, of its own great strength, it is as intolerant as it is obedient to authority. It respects force and can only be slightly influenced by kindness, which it regards merely as a form of weakness. What it demands of its heroes is strength, or even violence. It wants to be ruled and oppressed and to fear its masters." (Freud, *op. cit.*, p. 17)

13. *Op. cit.*, pp. 58 ff.

14. *Ibid.*, p. 61.

15. *Ibid.*, p. 60.

16. Cf. Max Horkheimer, "Authoritarianism and the Family Today," *The Family: Its Function and Destiny*, ed., R. N. Anshen (Harper Brothers, New York, 1949).

17. Freud, *op. cit.*, p. 74.

18. The translation of Freud's book renders his term "*Instanz*" by "faculty," a word which, however, does not carry the hierarchical connotation of the German original. "Agency" seems to be more appropriate.

19. Freud, *l. c.*, p. 80.

20. It may not be superfluous to stress that Nietzsche's concept of the Superman has as little in common with this archaic imagery as his vision of the future with Fascism. Freud's allusion is obviously valid only for the "Superman" as he became popularized in cheap slogans.

21. *L. c.*, p. 93.

22. *Ibid.*, p. 102.

23. For further details on personalization cf. Freud, *l. c.*, p. 44, footnote, where he discusses the relation between ideas and leader personalities; and p. 53, where he defines as "secondary leaders" those essentially irrational ideas which hold groups together. In technological civilization, no *immediate* transference to the leader, unknown and distant as he actually is, is possible. What happens is rather a regressive re-personalization of

impersonal, detached social powers. This possibility was clearly envisaged by Freud. ". . . A common tendency, a wish in which a number of people can have a share, may . . . serve as a substitute. This abstraction, again, might be more or less completely embodied in the figure of what we might call a secondary leader."

24. *L. c.*, p. 110.
25. German folklore has a drastic symbol for this trait. It speaks of *Radfahrernaturen*, bicyclist's characters. Above they bow, they kick below.
26. Freud, *l. c.*, p. 16.
27. *L. c.*, pp. 50–51.
28. With regard to the role of "neutralized," diluted religion in the make-up of the Fascist mentality, cf. *The Authoritarian Personality*. Important psychoanalytic contributions to this whole area of problems are contained in Theodor Reik's *Der eigene und der fremde Gott*, and in Paul Federn's *Die vaterlose Gesellschaft*.
29. It may be noted that the ideology of race distinctly reflects the idea of primitive brotherhood revived, according to Freud, through the specific regression involved in mass formation. The notion of race shares two properties with brotherhood: it is supposedly "natural," a bond of "blood," and it is de-sexualized. In Fascism this similarity is kept unconscious. It mentions brotherhood comparatively rarely, and usually only in regard to Germans living *outside* the borders of the Reich ("Our Sudeten brothers"). This, of course, is partly due to recollections of the ideal of *fraternité* of the French Revolution, taboo to the Nazis.
30. *L. c.*, p. 53.
31. *L. c.*, pp. 55–56.
32. *L. c.*, p. 56.
33. *L. c.*, pp. 87–88.
34. *L. c.*, p. 114.
35. *L. c.*, p. 87.
36. Cf. *Prophets of Deceit*.
37. *L. c.*, p. 76.
38. *L. c.*, p. 99.

HERBERT MARCUSE

THE CATASTROPHE OF LIBERATION

Positive thinking and its neo-positivist philosophy counteract the historical content of rationality. This content is never an extraneous factor or meaning which can or cannot be included in the analysis; it enters into conceptual thought as constitutive factor and determines the validity of its concepts. To the degree to which the established society is irrational, the analysis in terms of historical rationality introduces into the concept the negative element—critique, contradiction, and transcendence.

This element cannot be assimilated with the positive. It changes the concept in its entirety, in its intent and validity. Thus, in the analysis of an economy, capitalist or not, which operates as an "independent" power over and above the individuals, the negative features (overproduction, unemployment, insecurity, waste, repression) are not comprehended as long as they appear merely as more or less inevitable by-products, as "the other side" of the story of growth and progress.

True, a totalitarian administration may promote the efficient exploitation of resources; the nuclear-military establishment may provide millions of jobs through enormous purchasing power; toil and ulcers may be the by-product of the acquisition of wealth and responsibility; deadly blunders and crimes on the part of the leaders may be merely the way of life. One is willing to admit economic and political madness—and one buys it. But this sort of knowledge of "the other side" is part and parcel of the solidification of the state of affairs, of the grand unification of opposites which counteracts qualitative change, because it pertains to a thoroughly hopeless or thoroughly preconditioned existence that has made its home in a world where even the irrational is Reason.

The tolerance of positive thinking is enforced tolerance—enforced not by any terroristic agency but by the overwhelming, anonymous power and efficiency of the technological society. As such it permeates the general consciousness—and the consciousness of the critic. The absorption of the negative by the positive is validated in the daily experience, which obfuscates the distinction between rational appearance and irrational reality. Here are some banal examples of this harmonization:

(1) I ride in a new automobile. I experience its beauty, shininess, power, convenience—but then I become aware of the fact that in a relatively short time it will deteriorate and need repair; that its beauty and surface are cheap, its power unnecessary, its size idiotic; and that I will not find a parking place. I come to think of *my* car as a product of one of the Big Three automobile corporations. The latter determine the appearance of my car and make its beauty as well as its cheapness, its power as well as its shakiness, its working as well as its obsolescence. In a way, I feel cheated. I believe that the car is not what it could be, that better cars could be made for less money. But the other guy has to live, too. Wages and taxes are too high; turnover is necessary; we have it much better than before. The tension between appearance and reality melts away and both merge in one rather pleasant feeling.

(2) I take a walk in the country. Everything is as it should be: Nature at its best. Birds, sun, soft grass, a view through the trees of the mountains, nobody around, no radio, no smell of gasoline. Then the path turns and ends on the highway. I am back among the billboards, service stations, motels, and roadhouses. I was in a National Park, and I now know that this was not reality. It was a "reservation," something that is being preserved like a species dying out. If it were not for the government, the billboards, hot dog stands, and motels would long since have invaded that piece of Nature. I am grateful to the government; we have it much better than before . . .

(3) The subway during evening rush hour. What I see of the people are tired faces and limbs, hatred and anger. I feel someone might at any moment draw a knife—just so. They read, or rather they are soaked in their newspaper or magazine or paperback. And yet, a couple of hours later, the same people, deodorized, washed, dressed-up or down, may be happy and tender, really smile, and forget (or remember). But most of them will probably have some awful togetherness or aloneness at home.

These examples may illustrate the happy marriage of the positive and the negative—the *objective* ambiguity which adheres to the data of experience. It is objective ambiguity because the shift in my sensations and reflections responds to the manner in which the experienced facts are actually interrelated. But this interrelation, if comprehended, shatters the harmonizing consciousness and its false realism. Critical thought strives to define the irrational character of the established rationality (which becomes increasingly obvious) and to define the tendencies which cause this rationality to generate its own transformation. "Its own" because, as historical totality, it has developed forces and capabilities which themselves become projects beyond the established totality. They are possibilities of the advancing technological rationality and, as such, they involve the whole of society. The technological transformation is at the same time political transformation, but the political change would turn into qualitative social change only to the degree to which it would alter the direction of technical progress—that is, develop a new technology. For the established technology has become an instrument of destructive politics.

Such qualitative change would be transition to a higher stage of civilization if technics were designed and utilized for the pacification of the struggle for existence. In order to indicate the disturbing implications of this statement, I submit that such a new direction of technical progress would be the catastrophe of the established direction, not merely the quantitative evolution of the prevailing (scientific and technological) rationality but rather its catastrophic transformation, the emergence of a new idea of Reason, theoretical and practical.

The new idea of Reason is expressed in Whitehead's proposition: "The function of Reason is to promote the art of life."[1] In view of this end, Reason is the "direction of the attack on the environment" which derives from the "threefold urge: (1) to live, (2) to live well, (3) to live better."[2]

Whitehead's propositions seem to describe the actual development of Reason as well as its failure. Or rather they seem to suggest that Reason is still to be discovered, recognized, and realized, for hitherto the historical function of Reason has also been to repress and even destroy the urge to live, to live well, and to live better—or to postpone and put an exorbitantly high price on the fulfillment of this urge.

In Whitehead's definition of the function of Reason, the term "art" connotes the element of determinate negation. Reason, in its application to society, has thus far been opposed to art, while art was granted the privilege of being rather irrational— not subject to scientific, technological, and operational Reason. The rationality of domination has separated the Reason of science and the Reason of art, or, it has falsified the Reason of art by integrating art into the universe of domination. It was a separation because, from the beginning, science contained the aesthetic Reason, the free play and even the folly of imagination, the fantasy of transformation; science indulged in the rationalization of possibilities. However, this free play retained the commitment to the prevailing unfreedom in which it was born and from which it abstracted; the possibilities with which science played were also those of liberation— of a higher truth.

Here is the original link (within the universe of domination and scarcity) between science, art, and philosophy. It is the consciousness of the discrepancy between the real and the possible, between the apparent and the authentic truth, and the effort to comprehend and to master this discrepancy. One of the primary forms in which this discrepancy found expression was the distinction between gods and men, finiteness and infinity, change and permanence. Something of this mythological interrelation between the real and the possible survived in scientific thought, and it continued to be directed toward a more rational and true reality. Mathematics was held to be real and "good" in the same sense as Plato's metaphysical Ideas. How then did the development of the former become *science*, while that of the latter remained metaphysics?

The most obvious answer is that, to a great extent, the *scientific* abstractions entered and proved their truth in the actual conquest and transformation of nature, while the *philosophic* abstractions did not—and could not. For the conquest and transformation of nature occurred within a law and order of life which philosophy transcended, subordinating it to the "good life" of a different law and order. And this other order, which presupposed a high degree of freedom from toil, ignorance, and poverty, was *unreal*, at the origins of philosophic thought and throughout its development, while scientific thought continued to be applicable to an increasingly powerful and universal *reality*. The final philosophic concepts remained indeed metaphysical; they were not and could not be verified in terms of the established universe of discourse and action.

But if this is the situation, then the case of metaphysics, and especially of the meaningfulness and truth of metaphysical propositions, is a historical case. That is, historical rather than purely epistemological conditions determine the truth, the cognitive value of such propositions. Like all propositions that claim truth, they must be verifiable; they must stay within the universe of possible experience. This universe is never co-extensive with the established one but extends to the limits of the world which can be created by transforming the established one, with the means which the latter has provided or withheld. The range of verifiability in this sense grows in the course of history. Thus, the speculations about the Good Life, the Good Society, Permanent Peace obtain an increasingly realistic content; on technological grounds, the metaphysical tends to become physical.

Moreover, if the truth of metaphysical propositions is determined by their historical content (i.e., by the degree to which they define historical possibilities), then the relation between metaphysics and science is strictly historical. In our own culture, at least, that part of Saint-Simon's Law of the Three Stages is still taken for granted which stipulates that the metaphysical *precedes* the scientific stage of civilization. But is this sequence a final one? Or does the scientific transformation of the world contain its own metaphysical transcendence?

At the advanced stage of industrial civilization, scientific rationality, translated into political power, appears to be the decisive factor in the development of historical alternatives. The question then arises: does this power tend toward its own negation—that is, toward the promotion of the "art of life"? Within the established societies, the continued application of scientific rationality would have reached a terminal point with the mechanization of all socially necessary but individually repressive labor ("socially necessary" here includes all performances which can be exercised more effectively by machines, even if these performances produce luxuries and waste rather than necessities). But this stage would also be the end and limit of the scientific rationality in its established structure and direction. Further progress would mean the *break*, the turn of quantity into quality. It would open the possibility of an essentially new human reality—namely, existence in free time on the basis of fulfilled vital needs. Under such conditions, the scientific project itself would be free for transutilitarian ends, and free for the "art of living" beyond the necessities and luxuries of domination. In other words, the completion of the technological reality would be not only the prerequisite, but also the rationale for *transcending* the technological reality.

This would mean reversal of the traditional relationship between science and metaphysics. The ideas defining reality in terms other than those of the exact or behavioral sciences would lose their metaphysical or emotive character as a result of the scientific transformation of the world; the scientific concepts could project and define the possible realities of a free and pacified existence. The elaboration of such concepts would mean more than the evolution of the prevailing sciences. It would involve the scientific rationality as a whole, which has thus far been committed to an unfree existence and would mean a new idea of science, of Reason.

If the completion of the technological project involves a break with the prevailing technological rationality, the break in turn depends on the continued existence of the technical base itself. For it is this base which has rendered possible the satisfaction of needs and the reduction of toil—it remains the very base of all forms of human freedom. The qualitative change rather lies in the reconstruction of this base—that is, in its development with a view of different ends.

I have stressed that this does not mean the revival of "values," spiritual or other, which are to supplement the scientific and technological transformation of man and nature. On the contrary, the historical achievement of science and technology has rendered possible the *translation of values into technical tasks*—the materialization of values. Consequently, what is at stake is the redefinition of values in *technical terms*, as elements in the technological process. The new ends, as technical ends, would then operate in the project and in the construction of the machinery, and not only in its utilization. Moreover, the new ends might assert themselves even in the construction of scientific hypotheses—in pure scientific theory. From the quantification of secondary qualities, science would proceed to the quantification of values.

For example, what is calculable is the minimum of labor with which, and the extent to which, the vital needs of all members of a society could be satisfied—provided the available resources were used for this end, without being restricted by other interests, and without impeding the accumulation of capital necessary for the development of the respective society. In other words; quantifiable is the available range of freedom from want. Or, calculable is the degree to which, under the same conditions, care could be provided for the ill, the infirm, and the aged—that is, quantifiable is the possible reduction of anxiety, the possible freedom from fear.

The obstacles that stand in the way of materialization are definable political obstacles. Industrial civilization has reached the point where, with respect to the aspirations of man for a human existence, the scientific abstraction from final causes becomes obsolete in science's own terms. Science itself has rendered it possible to make final causes the proper domain of science. Society,

"par une élévation et un élargissement du domaine technique, doit remettre à leur place, *comme techniques*, les problèmes de finalité, considérés à tort comme éthiques et parfois comme religieux. L'*inachèvement* des techniques sacralise les problèmes de finalité et asservit l'homme au respect de fins qu'il se représente comme des absolus."[3]

Under this aspect, "neutral" scientific method and technology become the science and technology of a historical phase which is being surpassed by its own achievements—which has reached its determinate negation. Instead of being separated from science and scientific method, and left to subjective preference and irrational, transcendental sanction, formerly metaphysical ideas of liberation may become the proper object of science. But this development confronts science with the unpleasant task of becoming *political*—of recognizing scientific consciousness as political consciousness, and the scientific enterprise as political enterprise. For the transformation of values into needs, of final causes into technical possibilities is a new stage in the conquest of oppressive, unmastered forces in society as well as in nature. It is an act of *liberation*:

"L'homme se libère de sa situation d'être asservi par la finalité du tout en apprenant à faire de la finalité, à organiser un tout finalisé qu'il juge et apprécie, pour n'avoir pas à subir passivement une intégration de fait." . . . "L'homme dépasse l'asservissement en organisant consciemment la finalité . . . "4

However, in constituting themselves *methodically* as political enterprise, science and technology would *pass beyond* the stage at which they were, because of their neutrality, *subjected* to politics and against their intent functioning as political instrumentalities. For the technological redefinition and the technical mastery of final causes *is* the construction, development, and utilization of resources (material and intellectual) *freed* from all *particular* interests which impede the satisfaction of human needs and the evolution of human faculties. In other words, it is the rational enterprise of man as man, of mankind. Technology thus may provide the historical correction of the premature identification of Reason and Freedom, according to which man can become and remain free in the progress of self-perpetuating productivity on the basis of oppression. To the extent to which technology has developed on this basis, the correction can never be the result of technical progress per se. It involves a political reversal.

Industrial society possesses the instrumentalities for transforming the metaphysical into the physical, the inner into the outer, the adventures of the mind into adventures of technology. The terrible phrases (and realities of) "engineers of the soul," "head shrinkers," "scientific management," "science of consumption," epitomize (in a miserable form) the progressing rationalization of the irrational, of the "spiritual"— the denial of the idealistic culture. But the consummation of technological rationality, while translating ideology into reality, would also transcend the materialistic antithesis to this culture. For the translation of values into needs is the twofold process of (1) material satisfaction (materialization of freedom) and (2) the free development of needs on the basis of satisfaction (non-repressive sublimation). In this process, the relation between the material and intellectual faculties and needs undergoes a fundamental change. The free play of thought and imagination assumes a rational and directing function in the realization of a pacified existence of man and nature. And the ideas of justice, freedom, and humanity then obtain their truth and good conscience on the sole ground on which they could ever have truth and good conscience—the satisfaction of man's material needs, the rational organization of the realm of necessity.

"Pacified existence." The phrase conveys poorly enough the intent to sum up, in one guiding idea, the tabooed and ridiculed *end* of technology, the repressed final cause behind the scientific enterprise. If this final cause were to materialize and become effective, the Logos of technics would open a universe of qualitatively different relations between man and man, and man and nature.

But at this point, a strong caveat must be stated—a warning against all technological fetishism. Such festishism has recently been exhibited mainly among Marxist critics of contemporary industrial society—ideas of the future omnipotence of technological man, of a "technological Eros," etc. The hard kernel of truth in these ideas demands an emphatic denunciation of the mystification which they express. Technics, as a universe of instrumentalities, may increase the weakness as well as the power of man. At the present stage, he is perhaps more powerless over his own apparatus than he ever was before.

The mystification is not removed by transferring technological omnipotence from particular groups to the new state and the central plan. Technology retains throughout its dependence on other than technological ends. The more technological rationality, freed from its exploitative features, determines social production, the more will it become dependent on political direction—on the collective effort to attain a pacified existence, with the goals which the free individuals may set for themselves.

"Pacification of existence" does not suggest an accumulation of power but rather the opposite. Peace and power, freedom and power, Eros and power may well be contraries! I shall presently try to show that the reconstruction of the material base of society with a view to pacification may involve a qualitative as well as quantitative *reduction* of power, in order to create the space and time for the development of productivity under self-determined incentives. The notion of such a reversal of power is a strong motive in dialectical theory.

To the degree to which the goal of pacification determines the Logos of technics, it alters the relation between technology and its primary object, Nature. Pacification presupposes mastery of Nature, which is and remains the object opposed to the developing subject. But there are two kinds of mastery: a repressive and a liberating one. The latter involves the reduction of misery, violence, and cruelty. In Nature as well as in History, the struggle for existence is the token of scarcity, suffering, and want. They are the qualities of blind matter, of the realm of immediacy in which life passively suffers its existence. This realm is gradually mediated in the course of the historical transformation of Nature; it becomes part of the human world, and to this extent, the qualities of Nature are historical qualities. In the process of civilization, Nature ceases to be mere Nature to the degree to which the struggle of blind forces is comprehended and mastered in the light of freedom.[5]

History is the negation of Nature. What is only natural is overcome and recreated by the power of Reason. The metaphysical notion that Nature comes to itself in history points to the unconquered limits of Reason. It claims them as historical limits—as a task yet to be accomplished, or rather yet to be undertaken. If Nature is in itself a rational, legitimate object of science, then it is the legitimate object not only of Reason as power but also of Reason as freedom; not only of domination but also of liberation. With the emergence of man as the *animal rationale*—capable of transforming Nature in accordance with the faculties of the mind and the capacities of matter—the merely natural, as the subrational, assumes negative status. It becomes a realm to be comprehended and organized by Reason.

And to the degree to which Reason succeeds in subjecting matter to rational standards and aims, all sub-rational existence appears to be want and privation, and their reduction becomes the historical task. Suffering, violence, and destruction are categories of the natural as well as human reality, of a helpless and heartless universe. The terrible notion that the sub-rational life of nature is destined to remain forever such a universe, is neither a philosophic nor a scientific one; it was pronounced by a different authority:

"When the Society for the Prevention of Cruelty to Animals asked the Pope for his support, he refused it, on the ground that human beings owe no duty to lower animals, and that ill-treating animals is not sinful. This is because animals have no souls."[6]

Materialism, which is not tainted by such ideological abuse of the soul, has a more universal and realistic concept of salvation. It admits the reality of Hell only at one definite place, here on earth, and asserts that this Hell was created by Man (and by Nature). Part of this Hell is the ill-treatment of animals—the work of a human society whose rationality is still the irrational.

All joy and all happiness derive from the ability to transcend Nature—a transcendence in which the mastery of Nature is itself subordinated to liberation and pacification of existence. All tranquillity, all delight is the result of conscious *mediation*, of autonomy and contradiction. Glorification of the natural is part of the ideology which protects an unnatural society in its struggle against liberation. The defamation of birth control is a striking example. In some backward areas of the world, it is also "natural" that black races are inferior to white, and that the dogs get the hindmost, and that business must be. It is also natural that big fish eat little fish—though it may not seem natural to the little fish. Civilization produces the means for freeing Nature from its own brutality, its own insufficiency, its own blindness, by virtue of the cognitive and transforming power of Reason. And Reason can fulfill this function only as post-technological rationality, in which technics is itself the instrumentality of pacification, organon of the "art of life." The function of Reason then converges with the function of *Art*.

The Greek notion of the affinity between art and technics may serve as a preliminary illustration. The artist possesses the ideas which, as final causes, guide the construction of certain things—just as the engineer possesses the ideas which guide, as final causes, the construction of a machine. For example, the idea of an abode for human beings determines the architect's construction of a house; the idea of wholesale nuclear explosion determines the construction of the apparatus which is to serve this purpose. Emphasis on the essential relation between art and technics points up the specific *rationality* of art.

Like technology, art creates another universe of thought and practice against and within the existing one. But in contrast to the technical universe, the artistic universe is one of illusion, semblance, *Schein*. However, this semblance is resemblance to a reality which exists as the threat and promise of the established one. In various forms of mask and silence, the artistic universe is organized by the images of a life without fear—in mask and silence because art is without power to bring about this life, and even without power to represent it adequately. Still, the powerless, illusory truth of art (which has never been more powerless and more illusory than today, when it has become an omnipresent ingredient of the administered society) testifies to the validity of its images. The more blatantly irrational the society becomes, the greater the rationality of the artistic universe.

Technological civilization establishes a specific relation between art and technics. I mentioned above the notion of a reversal of the Law of the Three Stages and of a "revalidation" of metaphysics *on the basis* of the scientific and technological transformation of the world. The same notion may now be extended to the relation between science-technology and art. The rationality of art, its ability to "project" existence, to define yet unrealized possibilities could then be envisaged as *validated by the functioning in the scientific-technological transformation of the world*. Rather than being the handmaiden of the established apparatus, beautifying its business and its misery, art would become a technique for destroying this business and this misery.

The technological rationality of art seems to be characterized by an aesthetic "reduction":

"Art is able to reduce the apparatus which the external appearance requires in order to preserve itself—reduction to the limits in which the external may become the manifestation of spirit and freedom."[7]

According to Hegel, art reduces the immediate contingency in which an object (or a totality of objects) exists, to a state in which the object takes on the form and quality of freedom. Such transformation is reduction because the contingent situation suffers requirements which are external, and which stand in the way of its free realization.

These requirements constitute an "apparatus" inasmuch as they are not merely natural but rather subject to free, rational change and development. Thus, the artistic transformation violates the natural object, but the violated is itself oppressive; thus the aesthetic transformation is liberation.

The aesthetic reduction appears in the technological transformation of Nature where and if it succeeds in linking mastery and liberation, directing mastery toward liberation. In this case, the conquest of Nature reduces the blindness, ferocity, and fertility of Nature—which implies reducing the ferocity of man against Nature. Cultivation of the soil is qualitatively different from destruction of the soil, extraction of natural resources from wasteful exploitation, clearing of forests from wholesale deforestation. Poverty, disease, and cancerous growth are natural as well as human ills—their reduction and removal is liberation of life. Civilization has achieved this "other," liberating transformation in its gardens and parks and reservations. But outside these small, protected areas, it has treated Nature as it has treated man—as an instrument of destructive productivity.

In the technology of pacification, aesthetic categories would enter to the degree to which the productive machinery is constructed with a view of the free play of faculties. But against all "technological Eros" and similar misconceptions, "labor cannot become play . . . " Marx's statement precludes rigidly all romantic interpretation of the "abolition of labor." The idea of such a millenium is as ideological in advanced industrial civilization as it was in the Middle Ages, and perhaps even more so. For man's struggle with Nature is increasingly a struggle with his society, whose powers over the individual become more "rational" and therefore more necessary than ever before. However, while the realm of necessity continues, its organization with a view of qualitatively different ends would change not only the mode, but also the extent of socially necessary production. And this change in turn would affect the human agents of production and their needs:

"Free time transforms its possessor into a different Subject, and as different Subject he enters the process of immediate production."[8]

I have recurrently emphasized the historical character of human needs. Above the animal level even the necessities of life in a free and rational society will be other than those produced in and for an irrational and unfree society. Again, it is the concept of "reduction" which may illustrate the difference.

In the contemporary era, the conquest of scarcity is still confined to small areas of advanced industrial society. Their prosperity covers up the Inferno inside and outside their borders; it also spreads a repressive productivity and "false needs." It is repressive precisely to the degree to which it promotes the satisfaction of needs which require continuing the rat race of catching up with one's peers and with planned obsolescence, enjoying freedom from using the brain, working with and for the means of destruction. The obvious comforts generated by this sort of productivity, and even more, the support which it gives to a system of profitable domination, facilitate its importation in less advanced areas of the world where the introduction of such a system still means tremendous progress in technical and human terms.

However, the close interrelation between technical and political-manipulative know-how, between profitable productivity and domination, lends to the conquest of scarcity the weapons for containing liberation. To a great extent, it is the sheer *quantity* of goods, services, work, and recreation in the overdeveloped countries which effectuates this containment. Consequently, qualitative change seems to presuppose a *quantitative* change in the advanced standard of living, namely, *reduction of overdevelopment.*

The standard of living attained in the most advanced industrial areas is not a suitable model of development if the aim is pacification. In view of what this standard has made of Man and Nature, the question must again be asked whether it is worth the sacrifices and the victims made in its defense. The question has ceased to be irresponsible since the "affluent society" has become a society of permanent mobilization against the risk of annihilation, and since the sale of its goods has been accompanied by moronization, the perpetuation of toil, and the promotion of frustration.

Under these circumstances, liberation from the affluent society does not mean return to healthy and robust poverty, moral cleanliness, and simplicity. On the contrary, the elimination of profitable waste would increase the social wealth available for distribution, and the end of permanent mobilization would reduce the social need for the denial of satisfactions that are the individual's own—denials which now find their compensation in the cult of fitness, strength, and regularity.

Today, in the prosperous warfare and welfare state, the human qualities of a pacified existence seem asocial and unpatriotic—qualities such as the refusal of all toughness, togetherness, and brutality; disobedience to the tyranny of the majority; profession of fear and weakness (the most rational reaction to this society!); a sensitive intelligence sickened by that which is being perpetrated; the commitment to the feeble and ridiculed actions of protest and refusal. These expressions of humanity, too, will be marred by necessary compromise—by the need to cover oneself, to be capable of cheating the cheaters, and to live and think in spite of them. In the totalitarian society, the human attitudes tend to become escapist attitudes, to follow Samuel Beckett's advice: "Don't wait to be hunted to hide. . . ."

Even such personal withdrawal of mental and physical energy from socially required activities and attitudes is today possible only for a few; it is only an inconsequential aspect of the redirection of energy which must precede pacification. Beyond the personal realm, self-determination presupposes free available energy which is not expended in superimposed material and intellectual labor. It must be free energy also in the sense that it is not channeled into the handling of goods and services which satisfy the individual, while rendering him incapable of achieving an existence of his own, unable to grasp the possibilities which are repelled by his satisfaction. Comfort, business, and job security in a society which prepares itself for and against nuclear destruction may serve as a universal example of enslaving contentment. Liberation of energy from the performances required to sustain destructive prosperity means decreasing the high standard of servitude in order to enable the individuals to develop that rationality which may render possible a pacified existence.

A new standard of living, adapted to the pacification of existence, also presupposes reduction in the future population. It is understandable, even reasonable, that industrial civilization considers legitimate the slaughter of millions of people in war, and the daily sacrifices of all those who have no adequate care and protection, but discovers its moral and religious scruples if it is the question of avoiding the production of more life in a society which is still geared to the planned annihilation of life in the National Interest, and to the unplanned deprivation of life on behalf of private interests. These moral scruples are understandable and reasonable because such a society needs an ever-increasing number of customers and supporters; the constantly regenerated excess capacity must be managed.

However, the requirements of profitable mass production are not necessarily identical with those of mankind. The problem is not only (and perhaps not even primarily) that of adequately feeding and caring for the growing population—it is first a problem of number, of mere quantity. There is more than poetic license in the indictment which Stefan George pronounced half a century ago: "Schon eure Zahl ist Frevel!"*

The crime is that of a society in which the growing population aggravates the struggle for existence in the face of its possible alleviation. The drive for more "living space" operates not only in international aggressiveness but also *within* the nation. Here, expansion has, in all forms of teamwork, community life, and fun, invaded the inner space of privacy and practically eliminated the possibility of that isolation in which the individual, thrown back on himself alone, can think and question and find. This sort of privacy—the sole condition that, on the basis of satisfied vital needs, can give meaning to freedom and independence of thought—has long since become the most expensive commodity, available only to the very rich (who don't use it). In this respect, too, "culture" reveals its feudal origins and limitations. It can become democratic only through the abolition of mass democracy, i.e., if society has succeeded in restoring the prerogatives of privacy by granting them to all and protecting them for each.

To the denial of freedom, even of the possibility of freedom, corresponds the granting of liberties where they strengthen the repression. The degree to which the population is allowed to break the peace wherever there still is peace and silence, to be ugly and to uglify things, to ooze familiarity, to offend against good form is frightening. It is

---

* "Your mere number is crime!" [Ed.]

frightening because it expresses the lawful and even organized effort to reject the Other in his own right, to prevent autonomy even in a small, reserved sphere of existence. In the overdeveloped countries, an ever-larger part of the population becomes one huge captive audience—captured not by a totalitarian regime but by the liberties of the citizens whose media of amusement and elevation compel the Other to partake of their sounds, sights, and smells.

Can a society which is incapable of protecting individual privacy even within one's four walls rightfully claim that it respects the individual and that it is a free society? To be sure, a free society is defined by more, and by more fundamental achievements, than private autonomy. And yet, the absence of the latter vitiates even the most conspicuous institutions of economic and political freedom—by denying freedom at its hidden roots. Massive socialization begins at home and arrests the development of consciousness and conscience. The attainment of autonomy demands conditions in which the repressed dimensions of experience can come to life again; their liberation demands repression of the heteronomous needs and satisfactions which organize life in this society. The more they have become the individual's own needs and satisfactions, the more would their repression appear to be an all but fatal deprivation. But precisely by virtue of this fatal character, it may create the primary subjective prerequisite for qualitative change—namely, the *redefinition of needs*.

To take an (unfortunately fantastic) example: the mere absence of all advertising and of all indoctrinating media of information and entertainment would plunge the individual into a traumatic void where he would have the chance to wonder and to think, to know himself (or rather the negative of himself) and his society. Deprived of his false fathers, leaders, friends, and representatives, he would have to learn his ABC's again. But the words and sentences which he would form might come out very differently, and so might his aspirations and fears.

To be sure, such a situation would be an unbearable nightmare. While the people can support the continuous creation of nuclear weapons, radioactive fallout, and questionable foodstuffs, they cannot (for this very reason!) tolerate being deprived of the entertainment and education which make them capable of reproducing the arrangements for their defense and/or destruction. The non-functioning of television and the allied media might thus begin to achieve what the inherent contradictions of capitalism did not achieve—the disintegration of the system. The creation of repressive needs has long since become part of socially necessary labor—necessary in the sense that without it, the established mode of production could not be sustained. Neither problems of psychology nor of aesthetics are at stake, but the material base of domination.

NOTES

1. A. N. Whitehead, *The Function of Reason* (Boston: Beacon Press, 1959), p. 5.
2. *Ibid.*, p. 8.
3. ". . . through a raising and enlarging of the technical sphere, must treat *as technical*

problems, questions of finality considered wrongly as ethical and sometimes religious. The *incompleteness* of technics makes a fetish of problems of finality and enslaves man to ends which he thinks of as absolutes." Gilbert Simondon, *loc. cit.* p. 151; my italics.

4. "Man liberates himself from his situation of being subjected to the finality of everything by learning to create finality, to organise a 'finalised' whole, which he judges and evaluates. Man overcomes enslavement by organising consciously finality." *Ibid.*, p. 103.

5. Hegel's concept of freedom presupposes consciousness throughout (in Hegel's terminology: self-consciousness). Consequently, the "realization" of Nature is not, and never can be, Nature's own work. But inasmuch as Nature is in itself negative (i.e., wanting in its own existence), the historical transformation of Nature by Man is, as the overcoming of this negativity, the liberation of Nature. Or, in Hegel's words, Nature is in its essence non-natural—"Geist."

6. Quoted in: Bertrand Russell, *Unpopular Essays* (New York: Simon and Schuster, 1950) p. 76.

7. Hegel, *Vorlesungen über die Aesthetik*, in: *Sämtliche Werke*, ed. H. Glockner (Stuttgart, Frommann, 1929), vol. XII, p. 217 f. See also Osmaston's translation, in: Hegel, *The Philosophy of Fine Art* (London, Bell and Sons, 1920), vol. I, p. 214.

8. Marx, *Grundrisse der Kritik der politischen Oekonomie* loc. cit., p. 559. (My translation.)

JÜRGEN HABERMAS

TECHNOLOGY AND SCIENCE AS "IDEOLOGY"

For Herbert Marcuse on his seventieth birthday, July 19, 1968

Max Weber introduced the concept of "rationality" in order to define the form of capitalist economic activity, bourgeois private law, and bureaucratic authority. Rationalization means, first of all, the extension of the areas of society subject to the criteria of rational decision. Second, social labor is industrialized, with the result that criteria of instrumental action also penetrate into other areas of life (urbanization of the mode of life, technification of transport and communication). Both trends exemplify the type of purposive-rational action, which refers to either the organization of means or choice between alternatives. Planning can be regarded as purposive-rational action of the second order. It aims at the establishment, improvement, or expansion of systems of purposive-rational action themselves.

The progressive "rationalization" of society is linked to the institutionalization of scientific and technical development. To the extent that technology and science permeate social institutions and thus transform them, old legitimations are destroyed. The secularization and "disenchantment" of action-orienting worldviews, of cultural tradition as a whole, is the obverse of the growing "rationality" of social action.

Herbert Marcuse has taken these analyses as a point of departure in order to demonstrate that the formal concept of rationality—which Weber derived from the purposive-rational action of the capitalist entrepreneur, the industrial wage laborer, the abstract legal person, and the modern administrative official and based on the criteria of science as well as technology—has specific substantive implications. Marcuse is convinced that what Weber called "rationalization" realizes not rationality as such but rather, in the name of rationality, a specific form of unacknowledged political domination. Because this sort of rationality extends to the correct choice among strategies, the appropriate application of technologies, and the efficient establishment of systems (with *presupposed* aims in *given* situations), it removes the total social framework of interests in which strategies are chosen, technologies applied, and systems established, from the scope of reflection and rational reconstruction. Moreover, this rationality extends only to relations of possible technical control and therefore requires a type of action that implies domination, whether of nature or of society. By virtue of its structure, purposive-rational action is the exercise of control. That is why, in accordance with this rationality, the "rationalization" of the conditions of life is synonymous with the institutionalization of a form of domination whose political character becomes unrecognizable: the technical reason of a social system of purposive-rational action does not lose its political content. Marcuse's critique of Weber comes to the conclusion that

the very concept of technical reason is perhaps ideological. Not only the application of technology but technology itself is domination (of nature and men)—methodical, scientific, calculated, calculating control. Specific purposes and interests of domination are not foisted upon technology "subsequently" and from the outside; they enter the very construction of the technical apparatus. Technology is always a historical-social *project*: in it is projected what a society and its ruling interests intend to do with men and things. Such a "purpose" of domination is "substantive" and to this extent belongs to the very form of technical reason.[1]

As early as 1956 Marcuse referred in a quite different context to the peculiar phenomenon that in industrially advanced capitalist societies domination tends to lose its exploitative and oppressive character and become "rational," without political domination thereby disappearing: "Domination is dependent only on the capacity and drive to maintain and extend the apparatus as a whole."[2] Domination is rational in that a system can be maintained which can allow itself to make the growth of the forces of production, coupled with scientific and technical progress, the basis of its legitimation although, at the same time, the level of the productive forces constitutes a potential in relation to which "the renunciations and burdens placed on individuals seem more and more unnecessary and irrational."[3] In Marcuse's judgment, the objectively superfluous repression can be recognized in the "intensified subjection of individuals to the enormous apparatus of production and distribution, in the deprivatization of free time, in the almost indistinguishable fusion of constructive and destructive social labor."[4] Paradoxically, however, this repression can disappear from the consciousness of the population because the legitimation of domination has assumed a new character: it refers to the "constantly increasing productivity and domination of nature which keeps individuals . . . living in increasing comfort."[5]

The institutionalized growth of the forces of production following from scientific and technical progress surpasses all historical proportions. From it the institutional framework draws its opportunity for legitimation. The thought that relations of production can be measured against the potential of developed productive forces is prevented because the existing relations of production present themselves as the technically necessary organizational form of a rationalized society. Here "rationality," in Weber's sense, shows its Janus face. It is no longer only a critical standard for the developmental level of the forces of production in relation to which the objectively superfluous, repressive character of historically obsolete relations of production can be exposed. It is also an apologetic standard through which these same relations of production can be justified as a functional institutional framework. Indeed, in relation to its apologetic serviceability, "rationality" is weakened as a critical standard and degraded to a corrective *within* the system: what can still be said is at best that society is "poorly programmed." At the stage of their scientific-technical development, then, the forces of production appear to enter a new constellation with the relations of production. Now they no longer function as the basis of a critique of prevailing legitimations in the interest of political enlightenment, but become instead the basis of legitimation. *This* is what Marcuse conceives of as world-historically new.

But if this is the case, must not the rationality embodied in systems of purposive-rational action be understood as specifically limited? Must not the rationality of science and technology, instead of being reducible to unvarying rules of logic and method have absorbed a substantive, historically derived, and therefore transitory *a priori* structure? Marcuse answers in the affirmative:

The principles of modern science were *a priori* structured in such a way that they could serve as conceptual instruments for a universe of self-propelling, productive control; theoretical operationalism came to correspond to practical operationalism. The scientific method which led to the ever-more-effective domination of nature thus came to provide the pure concepts as well as the instrumentalities for the ever-more-effective domination of man by man *through* the domination of nature . . . Today, domination perpetuates and extends itself not only through technology but *as* technology, and the latter provides the great legitimation of the expanding political power, which absorbs all spheres of culture.

In this universe, technology also provides the great rationalization of the unfreedom of man and demonstrates the "technical" impossibility of being autonomous, of determining one's own life. For this unfreedom appears neither as irrational nor as political, but rather as submission to the technical apparatus which enlarges the comforts of life and increases the productivity of labor. Technological rationality thus protects rather than cancels the legitimacy of domination and the instrumentalist horizon of reason opens on a rationally totalitarian society.[6]

Weber's "rationalization" is not only a long-term process of the transformation of social structures but simultaneously "rationalization" in Freud's sense: the true motive, the perpetuation of objectively obsolete domination, is concealed through the invocation of purposive-rational imperatives. This invocation is possible only because the rationality of science and technology is immanently one of control: the rationality of domination.

Marcuse owes this concept, according to which modern science is a historical formation, equally to Husserl's treatise on the crisis of European science and Heidegger's destruction of Western metaphysics. From the materialist position Ernst Bloch has developed the viewpoint that the rationality of modern science is, in its roots, distorted by capitalism in such a way as to rob modern technology of the innocence of a pure productive force. But Marcuse is the first to make the "political content of technical reason" the analytical point of departure for a theory of advanced capitalist society. Because he not only develops this viewpoint philosophically but also attempts to corroborate it through sociological analysis, the difficulties inherent in this conception become visible. I shall refer here to but one ambiguity contained in Marcuse's own conception.

If the phenomenon on which Marcuse bases his social analysis, i.e. the peculiar *fusion of technology and domination*, rationality and oppression, could not be interpreted otherwise than as a world "project," as Marcuse says in the language of Sartre's phenomenology, contained in the material *a priori* of the logic of science and technology and determined by class interest and historical situation, then social emancipation could not be conceived without a complementary revolutionary transformation of science and technology themselves. In several passages Marcuse is tempted to pursue this idea of a New Science in connection with the promise, familiar in Jewish and Protestant mysticism, of the "resurrection of fallen nature." This theme, well-known for having penetrated into Schelling's (and Baader's) philosophy via Swabian Pietism, returns in Marx's *Paris Manuscripts*, today constitutes the central thought of Bloch's philosophy, and, in reflected forms, also directs the more secret hopes of Walter Benjamin, Max Horkheimer, and Theodor W. Adorno. It is also present in Marcuse's thought:

The point which I am trying to make is that science, *by virtue of its own method* and concepts, has projected and promoted a universe in which the domination of nature has remained linked to the domination of man—a link which tends to be fatal to this universe as a whole. Nature, scientifically comprehended and mastered, reappears in the technical apparatus of production and destruction which sustains and improves the life of the individuals while subordinating them to the masters of the apparatus. Thus the rational hierarchy merges with the social one. If this is the case, then the change in the direction of progress, which might sever this fatal link, would also affect the very structure of science—the scientific project. Its hypotheses, without losing their rational character, would develop in an essentially different experimental context (that of a pacified world); consequently, science would arrive at essentially different concepts of nature and establish essentially different facts.[7]

In a logical fashion Marcuse envisages not only different modes of theory formation but a different scientific methodology in general. The transcendental framework within which nature would be made the object of a new experience would then no longer be the functional system of instrumental action. The viewpoint of possible technical control would be replaced by one of preserving, fostering, and releasing the potentialities of nature: "There are two kinds of mastery: a repressive and a liberating one."[8] To this view it must be objected that modern science can be interpreted as a historically unique project only if at least one alternative project is thinkable. And, in addition, an alternative New Science would have to include the definition of a New Technology. This is a sobering consideration because technology, if based at all on a project, can only be traced back to a "project" of the human species *as a whole*, and not to one that could be historically surpassed.

Arnold Gehlen has pointed out in what seems to me conclusive fashion that there is an immanent connection between the technology known to us and the structure of purposive-rational action. If we comprehend the behavioral system of action regulated by its own results as the conjunction of rational decision and instrumental action, then we can reconstruct the history of technology from the point of view of the step-by-step objectivation of the elements of that very system. In any case technological development lends itself to being interpreted as though the human species had taken the elementary components of the behavioral system of purposive-rational action, which is primarily rooted in the human organism, and projected them one after another onto the plane of technical instruments, thereby unburdening itself of the corresponding functions.[9] At first the functions of the motor apparatus (hands and legs) were augmented and replaced, followed by energy production (of the human body), the functions of the sensory apparatus (eyes, ears, and skin), and finally by the functions of the governing center (the brain). Technological development thus follows a logic that corresponds to the structure of purposive-rational action regulated by its own results, which is in fact the structure of *work*. Realizing this, it is impossible to envisage how, as long as the organization of human nature does not change and as long therefore as we have to achieve self-preservation through social labor and with the aid of means that substitute for work, we could renounce technology, more particularly *our* technology, in favor of a qualitatively different one.

Marcuse has in mind an alternative *attitude* to nature, but it does not admit of the idea of a New Technology. Instead of treating nature as the object of possible technical control, we can encounter her as an opposing partner in a possible interaction. We can seek out a fraternal rather than an exploited nature. At the level of an as yet incomplete intersubjectivity we can impute subjectivity to animals and plants, even to minerals, and try to communicate with nature instead of merely processing her under conditions of severed communication. And the idea that a still enchained subjectivity of nature cannot be unbound until men's communication among themselves is free from domination has retained, to say the least, a singular attraction. Only if men could communicate without compulsion and each could recognize himself in the other, could mankind possibly recognize nature as another subject: not, as idealism would have it, as its Other, but as a subject of which mankind itself is the Other.

Be that as it may, the achievements of technology, which are indispensable as such, could surely not be substituted for by an awakened nature. The alternative to existing technology, the project of nature as opposing partner instead of object, refers to an alternative structure of action: to symbolic interaction in distinction to purposive-rational action. This means, however, that the two projects are projections of work and of language, i.e. projects of the human species as a whole, and not of an individual epoch, a specific class, or a surpassable situation. The idea of a New Science will not stand up to logical scrutiny any more than that of a New Technology, if indeed science is to retain the meaning of modern science inherently oriented to possible technical control. For this function, as for scientific-technical progress in general, there is no more "humane" substitute.

Marcuse himself seems to doubt whether it is meaningful to relativize as a "project" the rationality of science and technology. In many passages of *One-Dimensional Man*, revolutionizing technological rationality means only a transformation of the institutional framework which would leave untouched the forces of production as such. The structure of scientific-technical progress would be conserved, and only the governing values would be changed. New values would be translated into technically solvable tasks. The *direction* of this progress would be new, but the standard of rationality itself would remain unchanged:

Technics, as a universe of instrumentalities, may increase the weakness as well as the power of man. At the present stage, he is perhaps more powerless over his own apparatus than he ever was before.[10]

This sentence reinstates the political innocence of the forces of production. Here Marcuse is only renewing the classical definition of the relationship between the productive forces and the production relations. But in so doing, he is as far from coming to grips with the new constellation at which he is aiming as he was with the assertion that the productive forces are thoroughly corrupted in their political implications. What is singular about the "rationality" of science and technology is that it characterizes the growing potential of self-surpassing productive forces which continually threaten the institutional framework *and at the same time*, set the standard of legitimation for the production relations that restrict this potential. The dichotomy of this rationality cannot be adequately represented either by historicizing the concept or by returning to the orthodox view: neither the model of the original sin of scientific-technical progress nor that of its innocence do it justice. The most sensible formulation of the matter in question seems to me to be the following:

The technological *a priori* is a political *a priori* inasmuch as the transformation of nature involves that of man, and inasmuch as the "man-made creations" issue from and reenter a societal ensemble. One may still insist that the machinery of the technological universe is "as such" indifferent towards political ends—it can revolutionize or retard a society. An electronic computer can serve equally in capitalist or socialist administrations; a cyclotron can be an equally efficient tool for a war party or a peace party. . . . However, when technics becomes the universal form of material production, it circumscribes an entire culture; it projects a historical totality—a "world."[11]

The difficulty, which Marcuse has only obscured with the notion of the political content of technical reason, is to determine in a categorially precise manner the meaning of the expansion of the rational form of science and technology, i.e. the rationality embodied in systems of purposive-rational action, to the proportions of a life form, of the "historical totality" of a life-world. This is the same process that Weber meant to designate and explain as the rationalization of society. I believe that neither Weber nor Marcuse has satisfactorily accounted for it. Therefore I should like to attempt to reformulate Weber's concept of rationalization in another frame of reference in order to discuss on this new basis Marcuse's critique of Weber, as well as his thesis of the double function of scientific-technical progress (as productive force and as ideology). I am proposing an interpretative scheme that, in the format of an essay, can be introduced but not seriously validated with regard to its utility. The historical generalizations thus serve only to clarify this scheme and are no substitute for its scientific substantiation.

By means of the concept of "rationalization" Weber attempted to grasp the repercussions of scientific-technical progress on the institutional framework of societies engaged in "modernization." He shared this interest with the classical sociological tradition in general, whose pairs of polar concepts all revolve about the same problem: how to construct a conceptual model of the institutional change brought about by the extension of subsystems of purposive-rational action. Status and contract, *Gemeinschaft* and *Gesellschaft*, mechanical and organic solidarity, informal and formal groups, primary and secondary groups, culture and civilization, traditional and bureaucratic authority, sacral and secular associations, military and industrial society, status group and class—all of these pairs of concepts represent as many attempts to grasp the structural change of the institutional framework of a traditional society on the way to becoming a modern one. Even Parsons' catalog of possible alternatives of value-orientations belongs in the list of these attempts, although he would not admit it. Parsons claims that his list systematically represents the decisions between alternative value-orientations that must be made by the subject of any action whatsoever, regardless of the particular or historical context. But if one examines the list, one can scarcely overlook the historical situation of the inquiry on which it is based. The four pairs of alternative value-orientations,

> *affectivity* versus *affective neutrality,*
> *particularism* versus *universalism,*
> *ascription* versus *achievement,*
> *diffuseness* versus *specificity,*

which are supposed to take into account *all* possible fundamental decisions, are tailored to an analysis of *one* historical process. In fact they define the relative dimensions of the modification of dominant attitudes in the transition from traditional to modern society. Subsystems of purposive-rational action do indeed demand orientation to the postponement of gratification, universal norms, individual achievement and active mastery, and specific and analytic relationships, rather than to the opposite orientations.

In order to reformulate what Weber called "rationalization," I should like to go beyond the subjective approach that Parsons shares with Weber and propose another categorical framework. I shall take as my starting point the fundamental distinction between *work* and *interaction.*[12]

By "work" or *purposive-rational action* I understand either instrumental action or rational choice or their conjunction. Instrumental action is governed by *technical rules* based on empirical knowledge. In every case they imply conditional predictions about observable events, physical or social. These predictions can prove correct or incorrect. The conduct of rational choice is governed by *strategies* based on analytic knowledge. They imply deductions from preference rules (value systems) and decision procedures; these propositions are either correctly or incorrectly deduced. Purposive-rational action realizes defined goals under given conditions. But while instrumental action organizes means that are appropriate or inappropriate according to criteria of an effective control of reality, strategic action depends only on the correct evaluation of possible alternative choices, which results from calculation supplemented by values and maxims.

By "interaction," on the other hand, I understand *communicative action*, symbolic interaction. It is governed by binding *consensual norms*, which define reciprocal expectations about behavior and which must be understood and recognized by at least two acting subjects. Social norms are enforced through sanctions. Their meaning is objectified in ordinary language communication. While the validity of technical rules and strategies depends on that of empirically true or analytically correct propositions, the validity of social norms is grounded only in the intersubjectivity of the mutual understanding of intentions and secured by the general recognition of obligations. Violation of a rule has a different consequence according to type. *Incompetent* behavior, which violates valid technical rules or strategies, is condemned per se to failure through lack of success; the "punishment" is built, so to speak, into its rebuff by reality. *Deviant* behavior, which violates consensual norms, provokes sanctions that are connected with the rules only externally, that is by convention. Learned rules of purposive-rational action supply us with *skills*, internalized norms with *personality structures*. Skills put us in a position to solve problems; motivations allow us to follow norms. The diagram below summarizes these definitions. They demand a more precise explanation, which I cannot give here. It is above all the bottom column which I am neglecting here, and it refers to the very problem for whose solution I am introducing the distinction between work and interaction.

In terms of the two types of action we can distinguish between social systems according to whether purposive-rational action or interaction predominates. The institutional framework of a society consists of norms that guide symbolic interaction. But there are subsystems such as (to keep to Weber's examples) the economic

	Institutional framework: symbolic interaction	Systems of purposive-rational (instrumental and strategic) action
action-orienting rules	social norms	technical rules
level of definition	intersubjectively shared ordinary language	context-free language
type of definition	reciprocal expectations about behavior	conditional predictions conditional imperatives
mechanisms of acquisition	role internalization	learning of skills and qualifications
function of action type	maintenance of institutions (conformity to norms on the basis of reciprocal enforcement)	problem-solving (goal attainment, defined in means-ends relations)
sanctions against violation of rules	punishment on the basis of conventional sanctions: failure against authority	inefficacy: failure in reality
"rationalization"	emancipation, individuation; extension of communication free of domination	growth of productive forces; extension of power of technical control

system or the state apparatus, in which primarily sets of purposive-rational action are institutionalized. These contrast with subsystems such as family and kinship structures, which, although linked to a number of tasks and skills, are primarily based on moral rules of interaction. So I shall distinguish generally at the analytic level between (1) the *institutional framework* of a society or the sociocultural life-world and (2) the *subsystems of purposive-rational action* that are "embedded" in it. Insofar as actions are determined by the institutional framework they are both guided and enforced by norms. Insofar as they are determined by subsystems of purposive-rational action, they conform to patterns of instrumental or strategic action. Of course, only institutionalization can guarantee that such action will in fact follow definite technical rules and expected strategies with adequate probability.

With the help of these distinctions we can reformulate Weber's concept of "rationalization."

The term "traditional society" has come to denote all social systems that generally meet the criteria of civilizations. The latter represent a specific stage in the evolution of the human species. They differ in several traits from more primitive social forms: (1) A centralized ruling power (state organization of political power in contrast to tribal organization); (2) The division of society into socioeconomic classes (distribution to individuals of social obligations and rewards according to class membership and not according to kinship status); (3) The prevalence of a central worldview (myth, complex religion) to the end of legitimating political power (thus converting power into authority). Civilizations are established on the basis of a relatively developed technology and of division of labor in the social process of production, which make possible a surplus product, i.e. a quantity of goods exceeding that needed for the satisfaction of immediate and elementary needs. They owe their existence to the solution of the problem that first arises with the production of a surplus product, namely, how to distribute wealth and labor both unequally and yet legitimately according to criteria other than those generated by a kinship system.[13]

In our context it is relevant that despite considerable differences in their level of development, civilizations, based on an economy dependent on agriculture and craft production, have tolerated technical innovation and organizational improvement only within definite limits. One indicator of the traditional limits to the development of the forces of production is that until about three hundred years ago no major social system had produced more than the equivalent of a maximum of two hundred dollars per capita per annum. The stable pattern of a precapitalist mode of production, preindustrial technology, and premodern science makes possible a typical relation of the institutional framework to subsystems of purposive-rational action. For despite considerable progress, these subsystems, developing out of the system of social labor and its stock of accumulated technically exploitable knowledge, never reached that measure of extension after which their "rationality" would have become an open threat to the authority of the cultural traditions that legitimate political power. The expression "traditional society" refers to the circumstance that the institutional framework is grounded in the unquestionable underpinning of legitimation constituted by mythical, religious or metaphysical interpretations of reality—cosmic as well as social—as a whole. "Traditional" societies exist as long as the development of subsystems of purposive-rational action keep within the limits of the legitimating efficacy of cultural traditions.[14] This is the basis for the "superiority" of the institutional framework, which does not preclude structural changes adapted to a potential surplus generated in the economic system but does preclude critically challenging the traditional form of legitimation. This immunity is a meaningful criterion for the delimitation of traditional societies from those which have crossed the threshold to modernization.

The "superiority criterion," consequently, is applicable to all forms of class society organized as a state in which principles of universally valid rationality (whether of technical or strategic means-ends relations) have not explicitly and successfully called into question the cultural validity of intersubjectively shared traditions, which function as legitimations of the political system. It is only since the capitalist mode of production has equipped the economic system with a self-propelling mechanism that ensures long-term continuous growth (despite crises) in the productivity of labor that the introduction of new technologies and strategies, i.e. innovation as such, has been institutionalized. As Marx and Schumpeter have proposed in their respective theories, the capitalist mode of production can be comprehended as a mechanism that guarantees the *permanent* expansion of subsystems of purposive-rational action and thereby overturns the traditionalist "superiority" of the institutional framework to the forces of production. Capitalism is the first mode of production in world history to institutionalize self-sustaining economic growth. It has generated an industrial system that could be freed from the institutional framework of capitalism and connected to mechanisms other than that of the utilization of capital in private form.

What characterizes the passage from traditional society to society commencing the process of modernization is *not* that structural modification of the institutional framework is necessitated under the pressure of relatively developed productive forces, for that is the mechanism of the evolution of the species from the very beginning. What is new is a level of development of the productive forces that makes permanent the extension of subsystems of purposive-rational action and thereby calls into question the traditional form of the legitimation of power. The older mythic, religious, and metaphysical worldviews obey the logic of interaction contexts. They answer the central questions of men's collective existence and of individual life history. Their themes are justice and freedom, violence and oppression, happiness and gratification, poverty, illness, and death. Their categories are victory and defeat, love and hate, salvation and damnation. Their logic accords with the grammar of systematically distorted communication and with the fateful causality of dissociated symbols and suppressed motives.[15] The rationality of language games, associated with communicative action, is confronted at the threshold of the modern period with the rationality of means-ends relations, associated with instrumental and strategic action. As soon as this confrontation can arise, the end of traditional society is in sight: the traditional form of legitimation breaks down.

Capitalism is defined by a mode of production that not only poses this problem but also solves it. It provides a legitimation of domination which is no longer called down from the lofty heights of cultural tradition but instead summoned up from the base of social labor. The institution of the market, in which private property owners exchange commodities—including the market on which propertyless private individuals exchange their labor power as their only commodity—promises that exchange relations will be and are just owing to equivalence. Even this bourgeois ideology of justice, by adopting the category of reciprocity, still employs a relation of communicative action as the basis of legitimation. But the principle of reciprocity is now the organizing principle of the sphere of production and reproduction itself. Thus on the base of a market economy, political domination can be legitimated henceforth "from below" rather than "from above" (through invocation of cultural tradition).

If we suppose that the division of society into socioeconomic classes derives from the differential distribution among social groups of the relevant means of production, and that this distribution itself is based on the institutionalization of relations of social force, then we may assume that in all civilizations this institutional framework has been identical with the system of political domination: traditional authority was political authority. Only with the emergence of the capitalist mode of production can the legitimation of the institutional framework be linked immediately with the system of social labor. Only then can the property order change from a *political relation* to a *production relation*, because it legitimates itself through the rationality of the market, the ideology of exchange society, and no longer through a legitimate power structure. It is now the political system which is justified in terms of the legitimate relations of production: this is the real meaning and function of rationalist natural law from Locke to Kant.[16] The institutional framework of society is only mediately political and immediately economic (the bourgeois constitutional state as "superstructure").

The superiority of the capitalist mode of production to its predecessors has these two roots: the establishment of an economic mechanism that renders permanent the expansion of subsystems of purposive-rational action, and the creation of an economic legitimation by means of which the political system can be adapted to the new requisites of rationality brought about by these developing subsystems. It is this process of adaptation that Weber comprehends as "rationalization." Within it we can distinguish between two tendencies: rationalization "from below" and rationalization "from above."

A permanent pressure for adaptation arises from below as soon as the new mode of production becomes fully operative through the institutionalization of a domestic market for goods and labor power and of the capitalist enterprise. In the system of social labor this institutionalization ensures cumulative progress in the forces of production and an ensuing horizontal extension of subsystems of purposive-rational action—at the cost of economic crises, to be sure. In this way traditional structures are increasingly subordinated to conditions of instrumental or strategic rationality: the organization of labor and of trade, the network of transportation, information, and communication, the institutions of private law, and, starting with financial administration, the state bureaucracy. Thus arises the substructure of a society under the compulsion of modernization. The latter eventually widens to take in all areas of life: the army, the school system, health services, and even the family. Whether in city or country, it induces an urbanization of the *form* of life. That is, it generates subcultures that train the individual to be able to "switch over" at any moment from an interaction context to purposive-rational action.

This pressure for rationalization coming from below is met by a compulsion to rationalize coming from above. For, measured against the new standards of purposive rationality, the power-legitimating and action-orienting traditions—especially mythological interpretations and religious worldviews—lose their cogency. On this level of generalization, what Weber termed "secularization" has two aspects. First, traditional worldviews and objectivations lose their power and validity *as* myth, *as* public religion, *as* customary ritual, *as* justifying metaphysics, *as* unquestionable tradition.

Instead, they are reshaped into subjective belief systems and ethics which ensure the private cogency of modern value-orientations (the "Protestant ethic"). Second, they are transformed into constructions that do both at once: criticize tradition and reorganize the released material of tradition according to the principles of formal law and the exchange of equivalents (rationalist natural law). Having become fragile, existing legitimations are replaced by new ones. The latter emerge from the critique of the dogmatism of traditional interpretations of the world and claim a scientific character. Yet they retain legitimating functions, thereby keeping actual power relations inaccessible to analysis and to public consciousness. It is in this way that ideologies in the restricted sense first came into being. They replace traditional legitimations of power by appearing in the mantle of modern science and by deriving their justification from the critique of ideology. Ideologies are coeval with the critique of ideology. In this sense there can be no prebourgeois "ideologies."

In this connection modern science assumes a singular function. In distinction from the philosophical sciences of the older sort, the empirical sciences have developed since Galileo's time within a methodological frame of reference that reflects the transcendental viewpoint of possible technical control. Hence the modern sciences produce knowledge which through its *form* (and not through the subjective intention of scientists) is technically exploitable knowledge, although the possible applications generally are realized afterwards. Science and technology were not interdependent until late into the nineteenth century. Until then modern science did not contribute to the acceleration of technical development nor, consequently, to the pressure toward rationalization from below. Rather, its contribution to the modernization process was indirect. Modern physics gave rise to a philosophical approach that interpreted nature and society according to a model borrowed from the natural sciences and induced, so to speak, the mechanistic worldview of the seventeenth century. The reconstruction of classical natural law was carried out in this framework. This modern natural law was the basis of the bourgeois revolutions of the seventeenth, eighteenth, and nineteenth centuries, through which the old legitimations of the power structure were finally destroyed.[17]

By the middle of the nineteenth century the capitalist mode of production had developed so fully in England and France that Marx was able to identify the locus of the institutional framework of society in the relations of production and at the same time criticize the legitimating basis constituted by the exchange of equivalents. He carried out the critique of bourgeois ideology in the form of *political economy*. His labor theory of value destroyed the semblance of freedom, by means of which the legal institution of the free labor contract had made unrecognizable the relationship of social force that underlay the wage-labor relationship. Marcuse's criticism of Weber is that the latter, disregarding this Marxian insight, upholds an abstract concept of rationalization, which not merely fails to express the specific class content of the adaptation of the institutional framework to the developing systems of purposive-rational action, but conceals it. Marcuse knows that the Marxian analysis can no longer be applied as it stands to advanced capitalist society, with which Weber was already confronted. But he wants to show through the example of Weber that the evolution of modern society in the framework of state-regulated capitalism cannot be conceptualized if liberal capitalism has not been analyzed adequately.

Since the last quarter of the nineteenth century two developmental tendencies have become noticeable in the most advanced capitalist countries: an increase in state intervention in order to secure the system's stability, and a growing interdependence of research and technology, which has turned the sciences into the leading productive force. Both tendencies have destroyed the particular constellation of institutional framework and subsystems of purposive-rational action which characterized liberal capitalism, thereby eliminating the conditions relevant for the application of political economy in the version correctly formulated by Marx for liberal capitalism. I believe that Marcuse's basic thesis, according to which technology and science today also take on the function of legitimating political power, is the key to analyzing the changed constellation.

The permanent regulation of the economic process by means of state intervention arose as a defense mechanism against the dysfunctional tendencies, which threaten the system, that capitalism generates when left to itself. Capitalism's actual development manifestly contradicted the capitalist idea of a bourgeois society, emancipated from domination, in which power is neutralized. The root ideology of just exchange, which Marx unmasked in theory, collapsed in practice. The form of capital utilization through private ownership could only be maintained by the governmental corrective of a social and economic policy that stabilized the business cycle. The institutional framework of society was repoliticized. It no longer coincides immediately with the relations of production, i.e. with an order of private law that secures capitalist economic activity and the corresponding general guarantees of order provided by the bourgeois state. But this means a change in the relation of the economy to the political system: politics is no longer *only* a phenomenon of the superstructure. If society no longer "autonomously" perpetuates itself through self-regulation as a sphere preceding and lying at the basis of the state—and its ability to do so was the really novel feature of the capitalist mode of production—then society and the state are no longer in the relationship that Marxian theory had defined as that of base and superstructure. Then, however, a critical theory of society can no longer be constructed in the exclusive form of a critique of political economy. A point of view that methodically isolates the economic laws of motion of society can claim to grasp the overall structure of social life in its essential categories only as long as politics depends on the economic base. It becomes inapplicable when the "base" has to be comprehended as in itself a function of governmental activity and political conflicts. According to Marx, the critique of political economy was the theory of bourgeois society only as *critique of ideology.* If, however, the ideology of just exchange disintegrates, then the power structure can no longer be criticized *immediately* at the level of the relations of production.

With the collapse of this ideology, political power requires a new legitimation. Now since the power indirectly exercised over the exchange process is itself operating under political control and state regulation, legitimation can no longer be derived from the unpolitical order constituted by the relations of production. To this extent the requirement for direct legitimation, which exists in precapitalist societies, reappears. On the other hand, the resuscitation of immediate political domination (in the traditional form of legitimation on the basis of cosmological worldviews) has become impossible. For traditions have already been disempowered. Moreover, in industrially developed societies the results of bourgeois emancipation from immediate political domination (civil and political rights and the mechanism of general elections) can be fully ignored only in periods of reaction. Formally democratic government in systems of state-regulated capitalism is subject to a need for legitimation which cannot be met by a return to a prebourgeois form. Hence the ideology of free exchange is replaced by a substitute program. The latter is oriented not to the social results of the institution of the market but to those of government action designed to compensate for the dysfunctions of free exchange. This policy combines the element of the bourgeois ideology of achievement (which, however, displaces assignment of status according to the standard of individual achievement from the market to the school system) with a guaranteed minimum level of welfare, which offers secure employment and a stable income. This substitute program obliges the political system to maintain stabilizing conditions for an economy that guards against risks to growth and guarantees social security and the chance for individual upward mobility. What is needed to this end is latitude for manipulation by state interventions that, at the cost of limiting the institutions of private law, secure the private form of capital utilization *and bind the masses' loyalty to this form.*

Insofar as government action is directed toward the economic system's stability and growth, politics now takes on a peculiarly negative character. For it is oriented toward the elimination of dysfunctions and the avoidance of risks that threaten the system: not, in other words, toward the *realization of practical goals* but toward the *solution of technical problems.* Claus Offe pointed this out in his paper at the 1968 Frankfurt Sociological Conference:

In this structure of the relation of economy and the state, "politics" degenerates into action that follows numerous and continually emerging "avoidance imperatives": the mass of differentiated social-scientific information that flows into the political system allows both the early identification of risk zones and the treatment of actual dangers. What is new about this structure is . . . that the risks to stability built into the mechanism of private capital utilization in highly organized markets, risks that can be manipulated, prescribe preventive actions and measures that *must* be accepted as long as they are to accord with the existing legitimation resources (i.e., substitute program).[18]

Offe perceives that through these preventive action-orientations, government activity is restricted to administratively soluble technical problems, so that practical questions evaporate, so to speak. *Practical substance is eliminated.*

Old-style politics was forced, merely through its traditional form of legitimation, to define itself in relation to practical goals: the "good life" was interpreted in a context defined by interaction relations. The same still held for the ideology of bourgeois society. The substitute program prevailing today, in contrast, is aimed exclusively at the functioning of a manipulated system. It eliminates practical questions and therewith precludes discussion about the adoption of standards; the latter could emerge only from a democratic decision-making process. The solution of technical problems is not dependent on public discussion. Rather, public discussions could render problematic the framework within which the tasks of government action present themselves as technical ones. Therefore the new politics of state interventionism requires a depoliticization of the mass of the population. To the extent that practical questions are eliminated, the public realm also loses its political function. At the same time, the institutional framework of society is still distinct from the systems of purposive-rational action themselves. Its organization continues to be a problem of *practice* linked to communication, not one of *technology*, no matter how scientifically guided. Hence, the bracketing out of practice associated with the new kind of politics is not automatic. The substitute program, which legitimates power today, leaves unfilled a vital need for legitimation: how will the depoliticization of the masses be made plausible to them? Marcuse would be able to answer: by having technology and science *also* take on the role of an ideology.

Since the end of the nineteenth century the other developmental tendency characteristic of advanced capitalism has become increasingly momentous: the scientization of technology. The institutional pressure to augment the productivity of labor through the introduction of new technology has always existed under capitalism. But innovations depended on sporadic inventions, which, while economically motivated, were still fortuitous in character. This changed as technical development entered into a feedback relation with the progress of the modern sciences. With the advent of large-scale industrial research, science, technology, and industrial utilization were fused into a system. Since then, industrial research has been linked up with research under government contract, which primarily promotes scientific and technical progress in the military sector. From there information flows back into the sectors of civilian production. Thus technology and science become a leading productive force, rendering inoperative the conditions for Marx's labor theory of value. It is no longer meaningful to calculate the amount of capital investment in research and development on the basis of the value of unskilled (simple) labor power, when scientific-technical progress has become an independent source of surplus value, in relation to which the only source of surplus value considered by Marx, namely the labor power of the immediate producers, plays an ever smaller role.[19]

As long as the productive forces were visibly linked to the rational decisions and instrumental action of men engaged in social production, they could be understood as the potential for a growing power of technical control and not be confused with the institutional framework in which they are embedded. However, with the institutionalization of scientific-technical progress, the potential of the productive forces has assumed a form owing to which men lose consciousness of the dualism of work and interaction.

It is true that social interests still determine the direction, functions, and pace of technical progress. But these interests define the social system so much as a whole that they coincide with the interest in maintaining the system. *As such* the private form of capital utilization and a distribution mechanism for social rewards that guarantees the loyalty of the masses are removed from discussion. The quasi-autonomous progress of science and technology then appears as an independent variable on which the most important single system variable, namely economic growth, depends. Thus arises a perspective in which the development of the social system *seems* to be determined by the logic of scientific-technical progress. The immanent law of this progress seems to produce objective exigencies, which must be obeyed by any politics oriented toward functional needs. But when this semblance has taken root effectively, then propaganda can refer to the role of technology and science in order to explain and legitimate why in modern societies the process of democratic decision-making about practical problems loses its function and "must" be replaced by plebiscitary decisions about alternative sets of leaders of administrative personnel. This technocracy thesis has been worked out in several versions on the intellectual level.[20] What seems to me more important is that it can also become a background ideology that penetrates into the consciousness of the depoliticized mass of the population, where it can take on legitimating power.[21] It is a singular achievement of this ideology to detach society's self-understanding from the frame of reference of communicative action and from the concepts of symbolic interaction and replace it with a scientific model. Accordingly the culturally defined self-understanding of a social life-world is replaced by the self-reification of men under categories of purposive-rational action and adaptive behavior.

The model according to which the planned reconstruction of society is to proceed is taken from systems analysis. It is possible in principle to comprehend and analyze individual enterprises and organizations, even political or economic subsystems and social systems as a whole, according to the pattern of self-regulated systems. It makes a difference, of course, whether we use a cybernetic frame of reference for analytic purpose or *organize* a given social system in accordance with this pattern as a man-machine system. But the transferral of the analytic model to the level of social organization is implied by the very approach taken by systems analysis. Carrying out this intention of an instinct-like self-stabilization of social systems yields the peculiar perspective that the structure of one of the two types of action, namely the behavioral system of purposive-rational action, not only predominates over the institutional framework but gradually absorbs communicative action as such. If, with Arnold Gehlen, one were to see the inner logic of technical development as the step-by-step disconnection of the behavioral system of purposive-rational action from the human organism and its transferral to machines, then the technocratic intention could be understood as the last stage of this development. For the first time man can not only, as *homo faber*, completely objectify himself and confront the achievements that have taken on independent life in his products; he can in addition, as *homo fabricatus*, be integrated into his technical apparatus if the structure of purposive-rational action can be successfully reproduced on the level of social systems. According to this idea the institutional framework of society—which previously was rooted in a different type of action—would now, in a fundamental reversal, be *absorbed* by the subsystems of purposive-rational action, which were embedded in it.

Of course this technocratic intention has not been realized anywhere even in its beginnings. But it serves as an ideology for the new politics, which is adapted to technical problems and brackets out practical questions. Furthermore it does correspond to certain developmental tendencies that could lead to a creeping erosion of what we have called the institutional framework. The manifest domination of the authoritarian state gives way to the manipulative compulsions of technical-operational administration. The moral realization of a normative order is a function of communicative action oriented to shared cultural meaning and presupposing the internalization of values. It is increasingly supplanted by conditioned behavior, while large organizations as such are increasingly patterned after the structure of purposive-rational action. The industrially most advanced societies seem to approximate the model of behavioral control steered by external stimuli rather than guided by norms. Indirect control through fabricated stimuli has increased, especially in areas of putative subjective freedom (such as electoral, consumer, and leisure behavior). Sociopsychologically, the era is typified less by the authoritarian personality than by the destructuring of the superego. The increase in *adaptive behavior* is, however, only the obverse of the dissolution of the sphere of linguistically mediated interaction by the structure of purposive-rational action. This is paralleled subjectively by the disappearance of the difference between purposive-rational action and interaction from the consciousness not only of the sciences of man, but of men themselves. The concealment of this difference proves the ideological power of the technocratic consciousness.

In consequence of the two tendencies that have been discussed, capitalist society has changed to the point where two key categories of Marxian theory, namely class struggle and ideology, can no longer be employed as they stand.

It was on the basis of the capitalist mode of production that the struggle of social classes as such was first constituted, thereby creating an objective situation from which the class structure of traditional society, with its immediately political constitution, could be *recognized* in retrospect. State-regulated capitalism, which emerged from a reaction against the dangers to the system produced by open class antagonism, suspends class conflict. The system of advanced capitalism is so defined by a policy of securing the loyalty of the wage-earning masses through rewards, that is, by avoiding conflict, that the conflict still built into the structure of society in virtue of the private mode of capital utilization is the very area of conflict which has the greatest probability of remaining latent. It recedes behind others, which, while conditioned by the mode of production, can no longer assume the form of class conflicts. In the paper cited, Claus Offe has analyzed this paradoxical state of affairs, showing that open conflicts about social interests break out with greater probability the less their frustration has dangerous consequences for the system. The needs with the greatest conflict potential are those on the periphery of the area of state intervention. They are far from the central conflict being kept in a state of latency and therefore they are not seen as having priority among dangers to be warded off. Conflicts are set off by these needs to the extent that disproportionately scattered state interventions produce backward areas of development and corresponding disparity tensions:

The disparity between areas of life grows above all in view of the differential state of development obtaining between the actually institutionalized and the possible level of technical and social progress. The disproportion between the most modern apparatuses for industrial and military purposes and the stagnating organization of the transport, health, and educational systems is just as well known an example of this disparity between areas of life as is the contradiction between rational planning and regulation in taxation and finance policy and the unplanned, haphazard development of cities and regions. Such contradictions can no longer be designated accurately as antagonisms between classes, yet they can still be interpreted as results of the still dominant process of the private utilization of capital and of a specifically capitalist power structure. In this process the prevailing interests are those which, without being clearly localizable, are in a position, on the basis of the established mechanism of the capitalist economy, to react to disturbances of the conditions of their stability by producing risks relevant to the system as a whole.[22]

The interests bearing on the maintenance of the mode of production can no longer be "clearly localized" in the social system as class interests. For the power structure, aimed as it is at avoiding dangers to the system, precisely excludes "domination" (as immediate political or economically mediated social force) exercised in such a manner that one class subject *confronts* another as an identifiable group.

This means not that class antagonisms have been abolished but that they have become *latent*. Class distinctions persist in the form of subcultural traditions and corresponding differences not only in the standard of living and life style but also in political attitude. The social structure also makes it probable that the class of wage earners will be hit harder than other groups by social disparities. And finally, the generalized interest in perpetuating the system is still anchored today, on the level of immediate life chances, in a structure of privilege. The concept of an interest that has become *completely* independent of living subjects would cancel itself out. But with the deflection of dangers to the system in state-regulated capitalism, the political system has incorporated an interest—which transcends latent class boundaries—in preserving the compensatory distribution façade.

Furthermore, the displacement of the conflict zone from the class boundary to the underprivileged regions of life does not mean at all that serious conflict potential has been disposed of. As the extreme example of racial conflict in the United States shows, so many consequences of disparity can accumulate in certain areas and groups that explosions resembling civil war can occur. But unless they are connected with protest potential from other sectors of society no conflicts arising from such underprivilege can really overturn the system—they can only provoke it to sharp reactions incompatible with formal democracy. For underprivileged groups are not social classes, nor do they ever even potentially represent the mass of the population. Their *disfranchisement* and pauperization no longer coincide with *exploitation*, because the system does not live off their labor. They can represent at most a past phase of exploitation. But they cannot through the withdrawal of cooperation attain the demands that they legitimately put forward. That is why these demands retain an appellative character. In the case of long-term nonconsideration of their legitimate demands underprivileged groups can in extreme situations react with desperate destruction and self-destruction. But as long as no coalitions are made with privileged groups, such a civil war lacks the chance of revolutionary success that class struggle possesses.

With a series of restrictions this model seems applicable even to the relations between the industrially advanced nations and the formerly colonial areas of the Third World. Here, too, growing disparity leads to a form of underprivilege that in the future surely will be increasingly less comprehensible through categories of exploitation. Economic interests are replaced on this level, however, with immediately military ones.

Be that as it may, in advanced capitalist society deprived and privileged groups no longer confront each other *as* socioeconomic classes—and to some extent the boundaries of underprivilege are no longer even specific to groups and instead run across population categories. Thus the fundamental relation that existed in all traditional societies and that came to the fore under liberal capitalism is mediatized, namely the class antagonism between partners who stand in an institutionalized relationship of force, economic exploitation, and political oppression to one another, and in which communication is so distorted and restricted that the legitimations serving as an ideological veil cannot be called into question. Hegel's concept of the ethical totality of a living relationship which is sundered because one subject does not reciprocally satisfy the needs of the other is no longer an appropriate model for the mediatized class structure of organized, advanced capitalism. The suspended dialectic of the ethical generates the peculiar semblance of *post-histoire*. The reason is that relative growth of the productive forces no longer represents *eo ipso* a potential that points beyond the existing framework with emancipatory consequences, in view of which legitimations of an existing power structure become enfeebled. For the leading productive force—controlled scientific-technical progress itself—has now become the basis of legitimation. Yet this new form of legitimation has cast off the old shape of *ideology*.

Technocratic consciousness is, on the one hand, "less ideological" than all previous ideologies. For it does not have the opaque force of a delusion that only transfigures the implementation of interests. On the other hand today's dominant, rather glassy background ideology, which makes a fetish of science, is more irresistible and farther-reaching than ideologies of the old type. For with the veiling of practical problems it not only justifies a *particular class's* interest in domination and represses *another class's* partial need for emancipation, but affects the human race's emancipatory interest as such.

Technocratic consciousness is not a rationalized, wishfulfilling fantasy, not an "illusion" in Freud's sense, in which a system of interaction is either represented or interpreted and grounded. Even bourgeois ideologies could be traced back to a basic pattern of just interactions, free of domination and mutually satisfactory. It was these ideologies which met the criteria of wish-fulfillment and substitute gratification; the communication on which they were based was so limited by repressions that the relation of force once institutionalized as the capital-labor relation could not even be called by name. But the technocratic consciousness is not based in the same way on the causality of dissociated symbols and unconscious motives, which generates both false consciousness and the power of reflection to which the critique of ideology is indebted. It is less vulnerable to reflection, because it is no longer *only* ideology. For it does not, in the manner of ideology, express a projection of the "good life" (which even if not identifiable with a bad reality, can at least be brought into virtually satisfactory accord with it). Of course the new ideology, like the old, serves to impede making the foundations of society the object of thought and reflection. Previously, social force lay at the basis of the relation between capitalist and wage-laborers. Today the basis is provided by structural conditions which predefine the tasks of system maintenance: the private form of capital utilization and a political form of distributing social rewards that guarantees mass loyalty. However, the old and new ideology differ in two ways.

First, the capital-labor relation today, because of its linkage to a loyalty-ensuring political distribution mechanism, no longer engenders uncorrected exploitation and oppression. The process through which the persisting class antagonism has been made virtual presupposes that the repression on which the latter is based first came to consciousness in history and *only then* was stabilized in a modified form as a property of the system. Technocratic consciousness, therefore, cannot rest in the same way on collective repression as did earlier ideologies. Second, mass loyalty today is created only with the aid of rewards for *privatized needs*. The achievements in virtue of which the system justifies itself may not in principle be interpreted politically. The acceptable interpretation is immediately in terms of allocations of money and leisure time (neutral with regard to their use), and mediately in terms of the technocratic justification of the occlusion of practical questions. Hence the new ideology is distinguished from its predecessor in that it severs the criteria for justifying the organization of social life from any normative regulation of interaction, thus depoliticizing them. It anchors them instead in functions of a putative system of purposive-rational action.

Technocratic consciousness reflects not the sundering of an ethical situation but the repression of "ethics" as such as a category of life. The common, positivist way of thinking renders inert the frame of reference of interaction in ordinary language, in which domination and ideology both arise under conditions of distorted communication and can be reflectively detected and broken down. The depoliticization of the mass of the population, which is legitimated through technocratic consciousness, is at the same time men's self-objectification in categories equally of both purposive-rational action and adaptive behavior. The reified models of the sciences migrate into the sociocultural life-world and gain objective power over the latter's self-understanding. The ideological nucleus of this consciousness is *the elimination of the distinction between the practical and the technical.* It reflects, but does not objectively account for, the new constellation of a disempowered institutional framework and systems of purposive-rational action that have taken on a life of their own.

The new ideology consequently violates an interest grounded in one of the two fundamental conditions of our cultural existence: in language, or more precisely, in the form of socialization and individuation determined by communication in ordinary language. This interest extends to the maintenance of intersubjectivity of mutual understanding as well as to the creation of communication without domination. Technocratic consciousness makes this practical interest disappear behind the interest in the expansion of our power of technical control. Thus the reflection that the new ideology calls for must penetrate beyond the level of particular historical class interests to disclose the fundamental interests of mankind as such, engaged in the process of self-constitution.[23]

If the relativization of the field of application of the concept of ideology and the theory of class be confirmed, then the category framework developed by Marx in the basic assumptions of historical materialism requires a new formulation. The model of forces of production and relations of production would have to be replaced by the more abstract one of work and interaction. The relations of production designate a level on which the institutional framework was anchored only during the phase of the development of liberal capitalism, and not either before or after. To be sure, the productive forces, in which the learning processes organized in the subsystems of purposive-rational action accumulate, have been from the very beginning the motive force of social evolution. But, they do not appear, as Marx supposed, *under all circumstances* to be a potential for liberation and to set off emancipatory movements—at least not once the continual growth of the productive forces has become dependent on scientific-technical progress that has *also* taken on functions of *legitimating political power.* I suspect that the frame of reference developed in terms of the analogous, but more general relation of institutional framework (interaction) and subsystems of purposive-rational action ("work" in the broad sense of instrumental and strategic action) is more suited to reconstructing the sociocultural phases of the history of mankind.

There are several indications that during the long initial phase until the end of the Mesolithic period, purposive-rational actions could only be motivated at all through ritual attachment to interactions. A profane realm of subsystems of purposive-rational action seems to have separated out from the institutional framework of symbolic interaction in the first settled cultures, based on the domestication of animals and cultivation of plants. But it was probably only in civilizations, that is under the conditions of a class society organized as a state that the differentiation of work and interaction went far enough for the subsystems to yield technically exploitable knowledge that could be stored and expanded relatively independently of mythical and religious interpretations of the world. At the same time social norms became separated from power-legitimating traditions, so that "culture" attained a certain independence from "institutions." The threshold of the modern period would then be characterized by that process of rationalization which commenced with loss of the "superiority" of the institutional framework to the subsystems of purposive-rational action. Traditional legitimations could now be criticized against the standards of rationality of means-ends relations. Concurrently, information from the area of technically exploitable knowledge infiltrated tradition and compelled a reconstruction of traditional world interpretations along the lines of scientific standards.

We have followed this process of "rationalization from above" up to the point where technology and science themselves in the form of a common positivistic way of thinking, articulated as technocratic consciousness, began to take the role of a substitute ideology for the demolished bourgeois ideologies. This point was reached with the critique of bourgeois ideologies. It introduced ambiguity into the concept of rationalization. This ambiguity was deciphered by Horkheimer and Adorno as the dialectic of enlightenment, which has been refined by Marcuse as the thesis that technology and science themselves become ideological.

From the very beginning the pattern of human sociocultural development has been determined by a growing power of technical control over the external conditions of existence on the one hand, and a more or less passive adaptation of the institutional framework to the expanded subsystems of purposive-rational action on the other. Purposive-rational action represents the form of *active* adaptation, which distinguishes the collective *self*-preservation of societal subjects from the preservation of the species characteristic of other animals. We know how to bring the relevant conditions of life under control, that is, we know how to adapt the environment to our needs culturally rather than adapting ourselves to external nature. In contrast, changes of the institutional framework, to the extent that they are derived immediately or mediately from new technologies or improved strategies (in the areas of production, transportation, weaponry, etc.) have not taken the same form of active adaptation. In general such modifications follow the pattern of *passive* adaptation. They are not the result of planned purposive-rational action geared to its own consequences, but the product of fortuitous, undirected development. Yet it was impossible to become conscious of this disproportion between active and passive adaptation as long as the dynamics of capitalist development remained concealed by bourgeois ideologies. Only with the critique of bourgeois ideologies did this disproportion enter public consciousness.

The most impressive witness to this experience is still the *Communist Manifesto*. In rapturous words Marx eulogizes the revolutionary role of the bourgeoisie:

The bourgeoisie cannot exist without constantly revolutionizing the instruments of production, and thereby the relations of production, and with them the whole relations of society.

In another passage he writes:

The bourgeoisie, during its rule of scarce one hundred years, has created more massive and more colossal productive forces than have all preceding generations together. Subjection of nature's forces to man, machinery, application of chemistry to industry and agriculture, steam navigation, railways, electric telegraphs, clearing of whole continents for cultivation, canalization of rivers, whole populations conjured out of the ground . . .

Marx also perceives the reaction of this development back upon the institutional framework:

All fixed, fast-frozen relations, with their train of ancient and venerable prejudices and opinions, are swept away, all new-formed ones become antiquated before they can ossify. All that is solid melts into air, all that is holy is profaned, and man is at last compelled to face with sober senses his real conditions of life and his relations with his kind.

It is with regard to the disproportion between the passive adaptation of the institutional framework and the "active subjection of nature" that the assertion that men make their history, but not with will or consciousness, was formulated. It was the aim of Marx's critique to transform the secondary adaptation of the institutional framework as well into an active one, and to bring under control the structural change of society itself. This would overcome a fundamental condition of all previous history and complete the self-constitution of mankind: the end of prehistory. But this idea was ambiguous.

Marx, to be sure, viewed the problem of making history with will and consciousness as one of the *practical* mastery of previously ungoverned processes of social development. Others, however, have understood it as a *technical* problem. They want to bring society under control in the same way as nature by reconstructing it according to the pattern of self-regulated systems of purposive-rational action and adaptive behavior. This intention is to be found not only among technocrats of capitalist planning but also among those of bureaucratic socialism. Only the technocratic consciousness obscures the fact that this reconstruction could be achieved at no less a cost than closing off the only dimension that is essential, because it is susceptible to humanization, *as* a structure of interactions mediated by ordinary language. In the future the repertoire of control techniques will be considerably expanded. On Herman Kahn's list of the most probable technical innovations of the next thirty years I observe among the first fifty items a large number of techniques of behavioral and personality change:

30. new and possibly pervasive techniques for surveillance, monitoring and control of individuals and organizations;
33. new and more reliable "educational" and propaganda techniques affecting human behavior—public and private;
34. practical use of direct electronic communication with and stimulation of the brain;
37. new and relatively effective counterinsurgency techniques;
39. new and more varied drugs for control of fatigue, relaxation, alertness, mood, personality, perceptions, and fantasies;
41. improved capability to "change" sex;
42. other genetic control or influence over the basic constitution of an individual.[24]

A prediction of this sort is extremely controversial. Nevertheless, it points to an area of future possibilities of detaching human behavior from a normative system linked to the grammar of language-games and integrating it instead into self-regulated subsystems of the man-machine type by means of immediate physical or psychological control. Today the psychotechnic manipulation of behavior can already liquidate the old fashioned detour through norms that are internalized but capable of reflection. Behavioral control could be instituted at an even deeper level tomorrow through biotechnic intervention in the endocrine regulating system, not to mention the even greater consequences of intervening in the genetic transmission of inherited information. If this occurred, old regions of consciousness developed in ordinary-language communication would of necessity completely dry up. At this stage of human engineering, if the end of psychological manipulation could be spoken of in the same sense as the end of ideology is today, the spontaneous alienation derived from the uncontrolled lag of the institutional framework would be overcome. But the self-objectivation of man would have fulfilled itself in planned alienation—men would make their history with will, but without consciousness.

I am not asserting that this cybernetic dream of the instinct-like self-stabilization of societies is being fulfilled or that it is even realizable. I do think, however, that it follows through certain vague but basic assumptions of technocratic consciousness to their conclusion as a negative utopia and thus denotes an evolutionary trend that is taking shape under the slick domination of technology and science as ideology. Above all, it becomes clear against this background that *two concepts of rationalization* must be distinguished. At the level of subsystems of purposive-rational action, scientific-technical progress has already compelled the reorganization of social institutions and sectors, and necessitates it on an even larger scale than heretofore. But this process of the development of the productive forces can be a potential for liberation if and only if it does not replace rationalization on another level. *Rationalization at the level of the institutional framework* can occur only in the medium of symbolic interaction itself, that is, through *removing restrictions on communication*. Public, unrestricted discussion, free from domination, of the suitability and desirability of action-orienting principles and norms in the light of the sociocultural repercussions of developing subsystems of purposive-rational action—such communication at all levels of political and repoliticized decision-making processes is the only medium in which anything like "rationalization" is possible.

In such a process of generalized reflection institutions would alter their specific composition, going beyond the limit of a mere change in legitimation. A rationalization of social norms would, in fact, be characterized by a decreasing degree of repressiveness (which at the level of personality structure should increase average tolerance of ambivalence in the face of role conflicts), a decreasing degree of rigidity (which should multiply the chances of an individually stable self-presentation in everyday interactions), and approximation to a type of behavioral control that would allow role distance and the flexible application of norms that, while well-internalized, would be accessible to reflection. Rationalization measured by changes in these three dimensions does not lead, as does the rationalization of purposive-rational subsystems, to an increase in technical control over objectified processes of nature and society. It does not lead per se to the better functioning of social systems, but would furnish the members of society with the opportunity for further emancipation and progressive individuation. The growth of productive forces is not the same as the intention of the "good life." It can at best serve it.

I do not even think that the model of a technologically possible surplus that cannot be used in full measure within a repressively maintained institutional framework (Marx speaks of "fettered" forces of production) is appropriate to state-regulated capitalism. Today, better utilization of an unrealized potential leads to improvement of the economic-industrial apparatus, but no longer *eo ipso* to a transformation of the institutional framework with emancipatory consequences. The question is not whether we completely *utilize* an available or creatable potential, but whether we *choose* what we want for the purpose of the pacification and gratification of existence. But it must be immediately noted that we are only posing this question and cannot answer it in advance. For the solution demands precisely that unrestricted communication about the goals of life activity and conduct against which advanced capitalism, structurally dependent on a depoliticized public realm, puts up a strong resistance.

A new conflict zone, in place of the virtualized class antagonism and apart from the disparity conflicts at the margins of the system, can only emerge where advanced capitalist society has to immunize itself, by depoliticizing the masses of the population, against the questioning of its technocratic background ideology: in the public sphere administered through the mass media. For only here is it possible to buttress the concealment of the difference between progress in systems of purposive-rational action and emancipatory transformations of the institutional framework, between technical and practical problems. And it is necessary for the system to conceal this difference. Publicly administered definitions extend to *what* we want for our lives, but not to *how* we would like to live if we could find out, with regard to attainable potentials, how we *could* live.

Who will activate this conflict zone is hard to predict. Neither the old class antagonism nor the new type of underprivilege contains a protest potential whose origins make it tend toward the repoliticization of the desiccated public sphere. For the present, the only protest potential that gravitates toward the new conflict zone owing to identifiable interests is arising among certain groups of university, college, and high school students. Here we can make three observations:

1. Protesting students are a privileged group, which advances no interests that proceed immediately from its social situation or that could be satisfied in conformity with the system through an augmentation of social rewards. The first American studies of student activists conclude that they are predominantly not from upwardly mobile sections of the student body, but rather from sections with privileged status recruited from economically advantaged social strata.[25]

2. For plausible reasons the legitimations offered by the political system do not seem convincing to this group. The welfare-state substitute program for decrepit bourgeois ideologies presupposes a certain status and achievement orientation. According to the studies cited, student activists are less privatistically oriented to professional careers and future families than other students. Their academic achievements, which tend to be above average, and their social origins do not promote a horizon of expectations determined by anticipated exigencies of the labor market. Active students, who relatively frequently are in the social sciences and humanities, tend to be immune to technocratic consciousness because, although for varying motives, their primary experiences in their own intellectual work in neither case accord with the basic technocratic assumptions.

3. Among this group, conflict cannot break out because of the extent of the discipline and burdens imposed, but only because of their quality. Students are not fighting for a larger share of social rewards in the prevalent categories: income and leisure time. Instead, their protest is directed against the very category of reward itself. The few available data confirm the supposition that the protest of youth from bourgeois homes no longer coincides with the pattern of authority conflict typical of previous generations. Student activists tend to have parents who share their critical attitude. They have been brought up relatively frequently with more psychological understanding and according to more liberal educational principles than comparable inactive groups.[26] Their socialization seems to have been achieved in subcultures freed from immediate economic compulsion, in which the traditions of bourgeois morality and their petit-bourgeois derivatives have lost their function. This means that training for switching over to value-orientations of purposive-rational action no longer includes fetishizing this form of action. These educational techniques make possible experiences and favor orientations that clash with the conserved life form of

an economy of poverty. What can take shape on this basis is a lack of understanding in principle for the reproduction of virtues and sacrifices that have become superfluous—a lack of understanding why despite the advanced stage of technological development the life of the individual is still determined by the dictates of professional careers, the ethics of status competition, and by values of possessive individualism and available substitute gratifications: why the institutionalized struggle for existence, the discipline of alienated labor, and the eradication of sensuality and aesthetic gratification are perpetuated. To this sensibility the structural elimination of practical problems from a depoliticized public realm must become unbearable. However, it will give rise to a political force only if this sensibility comes into contact with a problem that the system cannot solve. For the future I see *one* such problem. The amount of social wealth produced by industrially advanced capitalism and the technical and organizational conditions under which this wealth is produced make it ever more difficult to link status assignment in an even subjectively convincing manner to the mechanism for the evaluation of individual achievement.[27] In the long run therefore, student protest could permanently destroy this crumbling achievement-ideology, and thus bring down the already fragile legitimating basis of advanced capitalism, which rests only on depoliticization.

NOTES

1. Herbert Marcuse, "Industrialization and Capitalism in the Work of Max Weber," in *Negations: Essays in Critical Theory*, with translations from the German by Jeremy J. Shapiro (Boston, 1968), pp. 223 f.
2. Herbert Marcuse, "Freedom and Freud's Theory of the Instincts," in *Five Lectures*, translations by Jeremy J. Shapiro and Shierry M. Weber (Boston, 1970), p. 16.
3. *Ibid.*, p. 3.
4. *Ibid.*
5. *Ibid.*
6. Herbert Marcuse, *One-Dimensional Man* (Boston, 1964).
7. *Ibid.*, pp. 166 f.
8. *Ibid.*, p. 236.
9. "This law expresses an intratechnical occurrence, a process that man has not willed as a whole. Rather, it takes place, as it were, behind his back, instinctively extending through the entire history of human culture. Furthermore, in accordance with this law, technology cannot evolve beyond the stage of the greatest possible automation, for there are no further specifiable regions of human achievement that could be objectified." Arnold Gehlen, "Anthropologische Ansicht der Technik," in *Technik im technischen Zeitalter*, Hans Freyer *et al.*, eds. (Düsseldorf, 1965).
10. Marcuse, *One-Dimensional Man*, p. 235.
11. *Ibid.*, p. 154.
12. On the context of these concepts in the history of philosophy, see my contribution to the *Festschrift* for Karl Löwith: "Arbeit und Interaktion: Bemerkungen zu Hegels Jenenser Realphilosophie," in *Natur und Geschichte. Karl Löwith zum 70. Geburtstag*, Hermann

Braun and Manfred Riedel, eds. (Stuttgart, 1967). This essay is reprinted in *Technik und Wissenschaft als 'Ideologie'* (Frankfurt am Main, 1968) and will appear in English in *Theory and Practice*, to be published by Beacon Press.

13. Gerhard E. Lenski, *Power and Privilege: A Theory of Social Stratification* (New York, 1966).

14. See Peter L. Berger, *The Sacred Canopy* (New York, 1967).

15. See my study *Erkenntnis und Interesse* (Frankfurt am Main, 1968), to be published by Beacon Press as *Cognition and Human Interests*.

16. See Leo Strauss, *Natural Right and History* (Chicago, 1963); C. B. MacPherson, *The Political Theory of Possessive Individualism* (London, 1962); and Jürgen Habermas, "Die klassische Lehre von der Politik in ihrem Verhältnis zur Sozialphilosophie," in *Theorie und Praxis*, 2d ed. (Neuwied, 1967), to appear in *Theory and Practice*.

17. See Jürgen Habermas, "Naturrecht und Revolution," in *Theorie und Praxis*.

18. Claus Offe, "Politische Herrschaft und Klassenstrukturen," in Gisela Kress and Dieter Senghass, eds., *Politikwissenschaft* (Frankfurt am Main, 1969). The quotation in the text is from the original manuscript, which differs in formulation from the published text.

19. The most recent explication of this is Eugen Löbl, *Geistige Arbeit—die wahre Quelle des Reichtums*, translated from the Czech by Leopold Grünwald (Vienna, 1968).

20. See Helmut Schelsky, *Der Mensch in der wissenschaftlichen Zivilisation* (Cologne-Opladen, 1961); Jacques Ellul, *The Technological Society* (New York, 1967); and Arnold Gehlen, "Über kulturelle Kristallisationen," in *Studien zur Anthropologie und Soziologie (Berlin, 1963)*, and "Über kulturelle Evolution," in *Die Philosophie und die Frage nach dem Fortschritt*, M. Hahn and F. Wiedmann, eds. (Munich, 1964).

21. To my knowledge there are no empirical studies concerned specifically with the propagation of this background ideology. We are dependent on extrapolations from the findings of other investigations.

22. Offe, op. cit.

23. See my essay "Erkenntnis und Interesse" in *Technik und Wissenschaft als 'Ideologie.'* It will appear in English as an appendix to *Cognition and Human Interests*.

24. Herman Kahn and Anthony J. Wiener, "The Next Thirty-Three Years: A Framework for Speculation," in *Toward the Year 2000: Work in Progress*, Daniel Bell, ed. (Boston, 1969), pp. 80 f.

25. Seymour Martin Lipset and Philip G. Altbach, "Student Politics and Higher Education in the U.S.A.," in *Student Politics*, Seymour Martin Lipset, ed. (New York, 1967); Richard W. Flacks, "The Liberated Generation: An Exploration of the Roots of Student Protest," in *Journal of Social Issues*, 23:3, pp. 52-75; and Kenneth Keniston, "The Sources of Student Dissent," *ibid.*, pp. 108 ff.

26. In Flacks' words, "Activists are more radical than their parents; but activists' parents are decidedly more liberal than others of their status. . . . Activism is related to a complex of values, not ostensibly political, shared by both the students and their parents. . . . Activists' parents are more 'permissive' than parents of non-activists."

27. See Robert L. Heilbroner, *The Limits of American Capitalism* (New York, 1966).

PART FOUR

ETHICS AND CRITICAL THEORY

The essays in this part address the general problem of the quest for happiness within the bounds of universal reason. The first selection, "On Hedonism," originally appeared in *Zeitschrift für Sozialforschung* in 1938 and is also contained in the volume of Marcuse's essays entitled *Negations*. In this essay, Marcuse attempts a reevaluation of hedonism as a philosophical position that would reconcile individual happiness and the general good of the community. Against the traditional conception of pleasure as the satisfaction of needs and wants, Marcuse invokes the Epicurean conception of a "true" pleasure in order to reconcile the antithesis between reason and sensuality. Thus philosophical hedonism, like critical theory, calls for a new social organization that would allow for "true pleasure" or enjoyment by free individuals.

The second selection, "Materialism and Morality," also originally appeared in *Zeitschrift für Sozialforschung*, in 1933. In this reassessment of Kantian morality, Horkheimer raises many of the questions addressed by Marcuse in "On Hedonism." He, too, emphasizes the gap between individual happiness and the general good in bourgeois society. Horkheimer, however, calls for the continual reassessment of cultural values and goals because of changing historical circumstances. Arguing for historical materialism, Horkheimer sees both the possibility for a renewed commitment to the goals of justice, freedom, and equality and the necessity of redefining these goals in accordance with changing historical conditions.

Habermas's contribution is excerpted from his book *Legitimation Crisis* (1973). In the first section, "The Relation of Practical Questions to Truth," he analyzes what it means to rationally follow a norm of action. Habermas maintains that only in a communicative situation, in which the only force is "that of the better argument" and the only motive that of "the cooperative search for the truth," can the question of whether or not to adopt a particular norm be answered. Thus he asserts that moral questions concerning actions to be taken do admit of truth. In the second section, "The Model of the Suppression of Generalizable Interests," he attempts to distinguish between norms that regulate generalizable interests and norms that are based on force. He maintains that establishing generalizable interests remains one of the central goals of a critical theory of society.

For a detailed discussion of the question of the moral foundations of critical theory, see Chapters 7 and 8 of *Philosophy and Critical Theory*.

HERBERT MARCUSE

ON HEDONISM

The idealist philosophy of the bourgeois era attempted to comprehend the universal, which was supposed to realize itself in and through isolated individuals, under the notion of reason. The individual appears as an ego isolated from and against others in its drives, thoughts, and interests. This isolating individuation is overcome and a common world constructed through the reduction of concrete individuality to the subject of mere thought, the rational ego. Operating among men who at first follow only their particular interests, the laws of reason eventually succeed in bringing about community. The universal validity of at least some forms of intuition and of thought can be securely established, and certain general maxims of conduct can be derived from the rationality of the person. Insofar as the individual partakes of universality only as a rational being and not with the empirical manifold of his needs, wants, and capacities, this idea of reason implicitly contains the sacrifice of the individual. His full development could not be admitted into the realm of reason. The gratification of his wants and capacities, his happiness, appears as an arbitrary and subjective element that cannot be brought into consonance with the universal validity of the highest principle of human action.

For it is every man's own special feeling of pleasure and pain that decides in what he is to place his happiness, and even in the same subject this will vary with the difference of his wants according as this feeling changes, and thus a law which is *subjectively necessary* (as a law of nature) is *objectively* a very *contingent* practical principle, which can and must be very different in different subjects, and therefore can never furnish a law . . .[1]

Happiness is of no matter, for happiness does not lead beyond the individual in all his contingency and imperfection. Hegel saw the history of humanity as burdened with this irredeemable misfortune. Individuals must be sacrificed for the sake of the universal, for there is no pre-established harmony between the general and the particular interest, or between reason and happiness. The progress of reason realizes itself against the happiness of individuals.

Happy is he who has adapted his existence to his particular character, will, and choice and thus enjoys himself in his existence. History is not the stage of happiness. In it, the periods of happiness are empty pages . . .[2]

The universal follows its course in disregard of individuals, and history, when comprehended, appears as the monstrous Calvary of the spirit.

Hegel fought against eudaemonism in the interest of historical progress. As such, the eudaemonistic principle of "making happiness and pleasure the highest good" is not false, according to Hegel. Rather, the baseness of eudaemonism is that it transposes the fulfillment of desire and the happiness of individuals into a "vulgar world and reality." In accordance with this eudaemonism, the individual is supposed to be reconciled to this common and base world. The individual should "trust in this world and yield himself to it and be able to devote himself to it without sin."[3] Eudaemonism sins against historical reason, according to Hegel, in that it lets the culmination of human existence be prescribed and tainted by bad empirical reality.

Hegel's critique of eudaemonism expresses insight into the required objectivity of happiness. If happiness is no more than the immediate gratification of particular interests, then eudaemonism contains an irrational principle that keeps men within whatever forms of life are given. Human happiness should be something other than personal contentment. Its own title points beyond mere subjectivity.

Both ancient and bourgeois eudaemonism viewed happiness essentially as such a subjective condition. Insofar as men can and should attain happiness within the status prescribed them by the established social order, this doctrine contains a moment of resignation and approbation. Eudaemonism comes into contradiction with the principle of the critical autonomy of reason.

The contraposition of happiness and reason goes all the way back to ancient philosophy. The relegation of happiness to chance, to that which cannot be controlled and is not dominated, to the irrational power of conditions that are essentially external to the individual, so that happiness at most "supervenes" on its aims and goals—this resigned relationship to happiness is contained in the Greek concept of *tycheie*.[4]* One is happy in the realm of "external goods," which do not fall within the freedom of the individual, but rather are subject to the opaque contingency of the social order of life. True felicity, the fulfillment of individuals' highest potentialities, thus cannot consist in what is commonly called happiness, but must be sought in the world of the soul and the mind.

It is against this internalization of happiness, which accepts as inevitable the anarchy and unfreedom of the external conditions of existence, that the hedonistic trends of philosophy have protested. By identifying happiness with pleasure, they were demanding that man's sensual and sensuous potentialities and needs, too, should find satisfaction—that in them, too, man should enjoy his existence without sinning

* "Fortune," good or bad [Ed.]

against his essence, without guilt and shame. In the principle of hedonism, in an abstract and undeveloped form, the demand for the freedom of the individual is extended into the realm of the material conditions of life. Insofar as the materialistic protest of hedonism preserves an otherwise proscribed element of human liberation, it is linked with the interest of critical theory.

Two types of hedonism are commonly distinguished: the Cyrenaic and the Epicurean trends. The Cyrenaics' point of departure is the thesis that the fulfillment of specific instincts and wants of the individual is associated with the feeling of pleasure. Happiness consists in having these individual pleasures as often as possible.

> Our end is particular pleasure, whereas happiness is the sum total of all individual pleasures, in which are included both past and future pleasures. Particular pleasure is desirable for its own sake, whereas happiness is desirable not for its own sake, but for the sake of particular pleasures.[5]

What the individual instincts and wants may be makes no difference; their moral evaluation is not based upon their "nature." They are a matter of custom, of social convention.[6] Pleasure is all that matters. It is the only happiness that the individual is allotted. ". . . pleasure does not differ from pleasure nor is one pleasure more pleasant than another."[7]

And now the materialist protest against internalization:

> . . . bodily pleasures are far better than mental pleasures, and bodily pains far worse than mental pains . . .[8]

Even rebellion against sacrificing the individual to the hypostatized community is preserved: "It was reasonable . . . for the good man not to risk his life in the defence of his country, for he would never throw wisdom away to benefit the unwise."[9]

This hedonism fails to differentiate not only between individual pleasures but also between the individuals who enjoy them. They are to gratify themselves just as they are, and the world is to become an object of possible enjoyment just as it is. In its relegation of happiness to immediate abandon and immediate enjoyment, hedonism accords with circumstances located in the structure of antagonistic society itself; they become clear only in their developed form.

In this form of society, the world as it is can become an object of enjoyment only when everything in it, men and things, is accepted as it appears. Its essence, that is, those potentialities which emerge as the highest on the basis of the attained level of the productive forces and of knowledge, is not present to the subject of enjoyment. For since the life process is not determined by the true interests of individuals creating, in solidarity, their existence through contending with nature, these potentialities are not realized in the decisive social relations. They can only appear to consciousness as lost, atrophied, and repressed. Any relationship to men and things going beyond their immediacy, any deeper understanding, would immediately come upon their essence, upon that which they could be and are not, and would then suffer from their appearance. Appearance becomes visible in the light of unrealized potentialities. Then it is no longer one beautiful moment among others so much as something evanescent which is lost and cannot be restored. Faults and blemishes of the objects of enjoyment are then burdened with the general ugliness and general unhappiness, whereas in immediacy they can even become a source of pleasure. Contingency in relations to men and things and the accompanying obstacles, losses, and renunciations become an expression of the anarchy and injustice of the whole, of a society in which even the most personal relations are determined by the economic law of value.

In this society, all human relationships transcending immediate encounter are not relations of happiness: especially not relationships in the labor process, which is regulated with regard not to the needs and capacities of individuals but rather to profit on capital and the production of commodities. Human relations are class relations, and their typical form is the free labor contract. This contractual character of human relationships has spread from the sphere of production to all of social life. Relationships function only in their reified form, mediated through the class distribution of the material output of the contractual partners. If this functional depersonalization were ever breached, not merely by that backslapping familiarity which only underscores the reciprocal functional distance separating men but rather by mutual concern and solidarity, it would be impossible for men to return to their normal social functions and positions. The contractual structure upon which this society is based would be broken.

Contract, however, does not encompass all interpersonal relations. Society has released a whole dimension of relationships whose value is supposed to consist precisely in their not being determined by contractual achievements and contractual services. These are relationships in which individuals are in the relation of "persons" to one another and in which they are supposed to realize their personality. Love, friendship, and companionship are such personal relations, to which Western culture has relegated man's highest earthly happiness. But they cannot sustain happiness, precisely when they are what they are intended to be. If they are really to guarantee an essential and permanent community among individuals, they must be based on comprehending understanding of the other. They must contain uncompromising knowledge. To this knowledge the other reveals himself not merely in the uninterrupted immediacy of sensual appearance that can be desired and enjoyed as beautiful, through satisfaction with appearance, but rather in his essence, as he really is. His image will thus include ugliness, injustice, inconstancy, decay, and ephemerality not as subjective properties that could be overcome by understanding concern but rather as the effects of the intervention of social necessities into the personal sphere. These necessities actually constitute the instincts, wants, and interests of the person in this society. Accordingly the very essence of the person expresses itself in modes of behavior to which the other (or the person himself) reacts with disappointment, concern, sympathy, anxiety, infidelity, jealousy, and sorrow. Culture has transfigured these feelings and given them tragic consecration. In fact, they subvert reification. In the behavior to which they are a response, the individual wants to release himself from a situation whose social law he has hitherto obeyed, whether marriage, occupation, or any other obligation in which he has accepted morality. He wants to follow his passions. In an order of unfreedom, however, passion is deeply disorderly and hence immoral. When not diverted toward generally desired goals, it leads to unhappiness.

This is not the only way in which personal relations are linked to pain and unhappiness. The development of personality also means the development of knowledge: insight into the structures of the reality in which one lives. These structures being what they are, every step of cognition removes the individual from immediate abandonment to appearance and from ready acceptance of the ideology that conceals its essence. Thus knowledge destroys proffered happiness. If the individual really acts on his knowledge, he is led either to struggle against the status quo or to renunciation. Knowledge does not help him attain happiness, yet without it he reverts to reified relationships. This is an inescapable dilemma. Enjoyment and truth, happiness and the essential relations of individuals are disjunctions.

By not concealing this dichotomy, consistent hedonism fulfilled a progressive function. It did not pretend that, in an anarchic society, happiness could be found in a developed, harmonic "personality" based on the highest achievements of culture. Hedonism is useless as ideology and in no way admits of being employed to justify an order associated with the suppression of freedom and the sacrifice of the individual. For such a purpose it must first be morally internalized or revised in a utilitarian sense. Hedonism advocates happiness equally for all individuals. It does not hypostatize a community in which happiness is negated without regard to the individuals. It is meaningful to speak of the progress of universal reason realizing itself in the face of the unhappiness of individuals, but general happiness apart from the happiness of individuals is a meaningless phrase.

Hedonism is the opposite pole to the philosophy of reason. In abstract fashion, both movements of thought have preserved potentialities of existing society that point to a real human society. The philosophy of reason has emphasized the development of the productive forces, the free rational shaping of the conditions of life, the domination of nature, and the critical autonomy of the associated individuals. Hedonism has stressed the comprehensive unfolding and fulfillment of individual wants and needs, emancipation from an inhuman labor process, and liberation of the world for the purposes of enjoyment. In society up to the present, the two doctrines have been incompatible, as are the principles that they represent. The idea of reason aims at universality, at a society in which the antagonistic interests of "empirical" individuals are canceled. To this community, however, the real fulfillment of individuals and their happiness remains alien and external; they must be sacrificed. There is no harmony between the general and the particular interest, between reason and happiness. If the individual believes that both interests are in accord, he becomes the victim of a necessary and salutary illusion; reason outwits the individuals. The true interest (of universality) reifies itself in opposition to the individuals and becomes a power that overwhelms them.

Hedonism wants to preserve the development and gratification of the individual as a goal within an anarchic and impoverished reality. But the protest against the reified community and against the meaningless sacrifices which are made to it leads only deeper into isolation and opposition between individuals as long as the historical forces that could transform the established society into a true community have not matured and are not comprehended. For hedonism, happiness remains something exclusively subjective. The particular interest of the individual, just as it is, is affirmed as the true interest and is justified against every and all community. This is the limit of hedonism: its attachment to the individualism of competition. Its concept of happiness can be derived only by abstracting from all universality and community. Abstract happiness corresponds to the abstract freedom of the monadic individual. The concrete objectivity of happiness is a concept for which hedonism finds no evidence.

This inevitable entanglement of even the most radical eudaemonism is a proper target of Hegel's critique. For it reconciles particular happiness with general unhappiness. Hedonism is not untrue because the individual is supposed to seek and find his happiness in a world of injustice and of misery. To the contrary, the hedonistic principle as such rebels often enough against this order. If it were ever to take hold of the masses, they would scarcely tolerate unfreedom and would be made completely unsuited for heroic domestication. The apologetic aspect of hedonism is located at a deeper level. It is to be found in hedonism's abstract conception of the subjective side of happiness, in its inability to distinguish between true and false wants and interests and between true and false enjoyment. It accepts the wants and interests of individuals as simply given and as valuable in themselves. Yet these wants and interests themselves, and not merely their gratification, already contain the stunted growth, the repression, and the untruth with which men grow up in class society. The affirmation of the one already contains the affirmation of the other.

The inability of hedonism to apply the category of truth to happiness, its fundamental relativism, is not a logical or epistemological fault of a philosophical system. It can be neither corrected within the system nor eliminated by a more comprehensive and better philosophical system. It originates in the form of social relations to which hedonism is linked, and all attempts to avoid it through immanent differentiation lead to new contradictions.

The second type of hedonism, the Epicurean, represents such an attempt at immanent differentiation. The identification of the highest good with pleasure is retained, but a specific kind of pleasure is, as "true" pleasure, opposed to all others. The undifferentiated gratification of whatever wants are given is all too often obviously followed by pain, whose magnitude is the basis for a differentiation of individual pleasures. There are wants and desires whose satisfaction is succeeded by pain that only serves to stimulate new desires, detroying man's peace of mind and health. Therefore

. . . we do not choose every pleasure whatsoever, but ofttimes pass over many pleasures when a greater annoyance ensues from them. And ofttimes we consider pains superior to pleasures when submission to the pains for a long time brings us as a consequence a greater pleasure.[10]

Reason, whose foresight makes possible a comparison of the values of momentary pleasure and later pain, becomes the adjudicator of pleasure. It may itself even become the highest pleasure.

It is not an unbroken succession of drinking-bouts and of revelry, not sexual love, not the enjoyment of the fish and other delicacies . . . which produce a pleasant life; it is sober reasoning, searching out the grounds of every choice and avoidance, and banishing those beliefs through which the greatest tumults take possession of the soul.[11]

Reason grants man that moderate enjoyment which reduces risk and offers the prospect of permanently balanced health. The differentiating evaluation of pleasure ensues therefore with regard to the greatest possible security and permanence of pleasure. This method expresses fear of the insecurity and badness of the conditions of life, the invincible limitation of enjoyment. It is a negative hedonism. Its principle is less the pleasure to be striven for than the pain to be avoided. The truth against which pleasure is to be measured is only evasion of conflict with the established order: the socially permitted if not desired form of pleasure. The "sage's" tranquility is the goal: an idea in which the concept of pleasure as well as the concept of the sage are deprived of their meaning. Pleasure perishes, inasmuch as the cautious, measured, and withdrawn relationship of the individual to men and things resists their dominion over him precisely where this dominion brings real happiness: as enjoyable abandon. In the antagonistic ordering of existence, happiness is encountered as something withdrawn from the autonomy of the individual, something that can be neither achieved nor controlled by reason. The element of extraneousness, contingency, and gratuitousness is here an essential component of happiness. It is just in this externality, in this innocent, unburdened, harmonious conjunction of the individual with something in the world, that pleasure consists. In the historical situation of individuals up to the present, it is not what reason has achieved nor what the soul experiences that can be called happiness (for these are necessarily tainted with unhappiness). To the contrary, only "externalized" pleasure, i.e. sensuality, can be called happiness. In reified social relationships, sensuality, and not reason, is the "organ" of happiness.

In the antithesis of reason and sensuality (or sensuousness), as it has been worked out in the development of philosophy, sensuality has increasingly acquired the character of a lower, baser human faculty, a realm lying on this side of true and false and of correct and incorrect, a region of dull, undiscriminating instincts. Only in epistemology has the connection between sensuousness and truth been preserved. Here the decisive aspect of sensuality has been retained: receptivity that is open and that opens itself (to experience). This quality contradicts sensuality's allegedly dull instinctual character. Precisely through this receptivity, this open abandon to objects (men and things), sensuality can become a source of happiness. For in it, in complete immediacy, the individual's isolation is overcome. Objects can occur to him here without their essential mediation through the social life process and, consequently, without their unhappy side becoming constitutive of pleasure. In the process of knowledge, in reason, quite the reverse holds. Here the individual's spontaneity necessarily comes up against the object as against something foreign. Reason must overcome the latter quality and comprehend the object in its essence, not only as it is presented and appears but as it has become. The method of reason has always been held to be the way of attaining clarity about the origin and principle of beings. This method implicitly referred to history. To be sure, history was understood not as real history but only transcendentally. Nevertheless, that process of comprehension worthy of the title of reason absorbed enough of the mutability, the insecurity, the conflicts, and suffering of reality to make the application of the term "pleasure" appear false in this realm. When Plato and Aristotle connected reason with pleasure, they did not establish reason as one of (or the best of) the individual pleasures in the sense of the hedonists. Rather, reason appears as the highest human potentiality and therefore, necessarily, as the highest human pleasure. Here, in the fight against hedonism, the concept of pleasure is taken out of the sphere to which the hedonists had relegated it and held up in opposition to this entire sphere.

The situation is different when, as in the case of Epicurus, reason is made a pleasure or pleasure is made reasonable within hedonism itself. This gives rise to that ideal of the satisfied sage in which both pleasure as well as reason have lost their meaning. The sage, then, would be the person whose reason and whose pleasure never go too far. They never are followed through to the end because, if they were, they would come upon knowledge that negates enjoyment. The sage's reason would be so limited from the start that it would only be occupied with the calculation of risks and with the psychic technique of extracting the best from everything. Such reason has abdicated its claim to truth. It appears only as subjective cunning and private expertise, calmly acquiescing in the persistence of general unreason and enjoying not so much what is allotted or occurs to it as itself.

Hedonism embodies a correct judgment about society. That the receptivity of sensuality and not the spontaneity of reason is the source of happiness results from antagonistic work relations. They are the real form of the attained level of human reason. It is in them that the extent of possible freedom and possible happiness is decided. If this form is one in which the productive forces are disposed of in the interest of the smallest social groups, in which the majority of men are separated from the means of production, and in which labor is performed not in accordance with the capacities and needs of individuals but according to the requirements of the process of profitable production, then happiness cannot be general within it. Happiness is restricted to the sphere of consumption. Radical hedonism was formulated in the ancient world and draws a moral conclusion from the slave economy. Labor and happiness are essentially separated. They belong to different modes of existence.

Some men are slaves in their essence, others are free men. In the modern epoch the principle of labor has become general. Everyone is supposed to work and everyone is supposed to be rewarded in accordance with his work. But since the distribution of social labor proceeds according to the opaque necessity of the capitalist law of value, no rational relation is established between production and consumption, between labor and enjoyment. Gratification occurs as a contingency that is to be accepted. Reason rules only behind the backs of individuals in the reproduction of the whole that takes place despite anarchy. For the individual in pursuit of his own interests, reason's role is at most a personal calculation in choosing among given possibilities. And it is in this atrophied form that reason depreciated to the idea of the sage. If reason cannot be effective in the process of production as free communal decision about the state of human existence (within specific historical and natural conditions), then it can certainly not be effective in the process of consumption.

The restriction of happiness to the sphere of consumption, which appears separated from the process of production, stabilizes the particularity and the subjectivity of happiness in a society in which rational unity of the process of production and consumption, of labor and enjoyment, has not been brought about. The rejection by idealistic ethics of hedonism just because of the latter's essential particularity and subjectivity is founded upon a justified criticism: Does not happiness, with its immanent demand for increase and permanence, require that, within happiness itself, the isolation of individuals, the reification of human relations, and the contingency of gratification be done away with? Must not happiness become compatible with truth? On the other hand, none other than isolation, reification, and contingency have been the dimensions of happiness in previous society. Hedonism, therefore, has been right precisely in its falsehood insofar as it has preserved the demand for happiness against every idealization of unhappiness. The truth of hedonism would be its abolition by and preservation in a new principle of social organization, not in a different philosophical principle.

Philosophy has attempted in various ways to save the objectivity of happiness and to comprehend it under the category of truth and universality. Such attempts are to be found in ancient eudaemonism, in the Catholic philosophy of the Middle Ages, in humanism, and in the French Enlightenment. If inquiry into the possible objectivity of happiness is not extended to the structure of the social organization of humanity, its result is bound to run aground on social contradictions. Inasmuch, however, as the philosophical critique at least refers decisively to the historical problem at hand as a task of historical practice, we shall discuss in what follows the first and most important controversy with hedonism.

Plato's critique of hedonism (on two different levels in the *Gorgias* and *Philebus*) worked out for the first time the concept of true and false wants and true and false pleasure. Here truth and falsehood are categories that are supposed to be applicable to every individual pleasure. The critique takes its departure from the essential conjunction of pleasure and pain. Every pleasure is connected with pain, since pleasure is the removal and fulfillment of a want (lack, privation) that as such is felt as painful. Pleasure, therefore, cannot be "the good" or happiness, because it contains its own opposite: unless it were possible to find an "unmixed" pleasure, one essentially separated from pain. In the *Philebus* (51 b ff.) what remains as unmixed, true pleasure is in the last analysis only pleasure in lines, sounds, and colors that are "beautiful in themselves," in other words, enjoyment released from all painful desire and restricted to inorganic objects. This enjoyment is obviously too empty to be happiness. Designating inorganic entities as the object of pure pleasure shows decisively that in the given form of existential relations true pleasure is not only separated from the soul, which, as the seat of desire and longing, is necessarily also the source of pain, but is also separated from all essential personal relationships. Unmixed pleasure is to be had only in those things which are most removed from the social life process. The receptivity of open abandonment to the object of enjoyment, which Plato recognizes as the precondition of pleasure, remains only in complete externality, in which all essential relations between man and man are silenced. Happiness is thus situated at the antipode of internalization and inwardness.

Plato's earlier solution of the problem of true pleasure takes another direction. In the *Gorgias* he proceeds directly to the question of the social order within which the individual is to fulfill himself. This order itself as the highest norm against which individual pleasures are to be measured is not a subject of discussion; it is accepted in its given form. Bad wants and bad pleasures are those which destroy the just order of the soul and which prevent the individual from attaining his true potentialities. It is the community, however, within which individuals live and through which alone "the heavens and the earth, gods and men are bound together" (508 a) that decides these potentialities and thus the truth and falsehood of wants and pleasures. The concept of the order of the soul turns into that of the order of the community and the concept of the individually "just" into that of justice (504). Whether the individuals enjoy the right pleasure depends on the right ordering of the polis. The generality of happiness is posed as a problem. Only those wants may be satisfied which make the individual a good citizen. They are true wants, and the pleasure associated with their gratification is true pleasure. The others are not to be fulfilled. It is the task of the statesman to look after the general interest and to bring the satisfaction of particular interests into accord with it. The possibility of such harmony, the authentic social question, is not pursued further in the *Gorgias* (although the critique of major Greek statesmen at least suggests social criticism).

Inasmuch as true and false pleasure are contraposed, happiness is subjected to the criterion of truth. If human existence is to come in pleasure to its highest fulfillment, to felicity, then not every sensation of pleasure can in itself be happiness. Plato's critique of hedonism traces the givens of wants and of pleasures back to the individuals who "have" them. This conceptual regress is made necessary by the fact that both the sick and the healthy, the good and the bad, the crazy and the normal feel pleasure in like manner (at least with respect to the fact of pleasure).[12] What is common to all of these cannot be the highest. There must be a truth of happiness on the basis of which the happiness of the individual can be judged. Pleasure must be susceptible to distinction according to truth and falsehood and to justice and injustice if (in case pleasure is happiness) the happiness of men is not to be inseparably associated with unhappiness. The basis of such a distinction, however, cannot lie in the individual sensation of pleasure as such, for both the sick and the healthy and the bad and the good feel real pleasure. Nevertheless, just as an idea can be false even though it be a real idea, so too a pleasure can be false without the reality of the sensation of pleasure being denied (*Philebus* 36). This is more than a mere analogy. Here a cognitive function in the strictest sense is attributed to pleasure, for it reveals beings as objects of enjoyment. On the basis of its "intentional" character, pleasure is thus made accessible to the question of truth. A pleasure is untrue when the object that it intends is not "in itself" pleasurable (according to the exposition of the *Philebus*, when it can only be encountered mixed with pain). But the question of truth does not regard only the object but also the subject of pleasure. This is made possible through Plato's interpretation of pleasure as belonging not merely to sensuousness (*aesthesis*) alone but also to the psyche (*Philebus* 33 f.). Psychic forces (such as desire, expectation, memory) are necessary for every sensation of pleasure, so that in pleasure the whole man is involved. With respect to the latter the question of truth arrives at the same point that had been reached in the *Gorgias*: that "good" men have true pleasure and "bad" men have false pleasure (*Philebus* 40 b, c).

The essential connection of the good of man with the truth of pleasure at which Plato's discussion of hedonism arrives makes of pleasure a moral problem. For it is the concrete form of the "community" that ultimately decides on this connection. Pleasure is subject to the claim of society and enters the realm of duty—duty to oneself and to others. The truth of the particular interest and its gratification is determined by the truth of the general interest. The agreement of the two is not immediate. Rather, it is mediated through the subjection of the particular to the requirements of generality. Within a society that requires morality (as an objective, general code of ethics opposed to the subjective wants and interests of individuals) for its existence, an amoral attitude is intolerable, for the latter destroys the bases of communal order. The amoral man violates the law of a society that, even if in a bad form, guarantees the preservation of social life. He does so, furthermore, without linking himself to a better, true society. For he remains in the given, "corrupted" structure of instincts and wants. Morality is the expression of the antagonism between the particular and the general interest. It is the code of those demands which are a matter of life and death for the society's self-preservation.[13] Insofar as particular interests are not really incorporated into and fulfilled in the society, such demands appear to the individual as commands coming from outside himself. If left to itself, pleasure as the immediate gratification of the merely particular interest must come into conflict with the interest of the hypostatized social community. In contrast to the isolated individual, society represents what is historically right. It demands the repression of all pleasure that violates the decisive social taboo. It forbids the satisfaction of those wants which would shatter the foundations of the established order.

The moralization of pleasure is called for by the existence of antagonistic society. It is the historical form in which this society unites the satisfaction of particular wants and instincts with the general interest, and it has had a progressive function in the development of the social labor process.[14] The hedonistic protest of the individual who is isolated in his particular interest is amoral. The amoral, beyond-good-and-evil attitude can be progressive only within a historical practice that leads beyond the already attained form of this process and fights for a new, true community against the established one. Only then does this attitude represent more than a merely particular interest. Isolated from the historical struggle for a better organization of the conditions of life, in which the individual has to engage himself in concrete social groups and tasks and thus gives up his amorality, amoral thought and action can, of course, escape from morality (if its subject is economically independent enough). But the ruling social law maintains its power over the amoral individual both in his wants and in the objects of their satisfaction. They originated under this law, and only the latter's transformation could overcome morality. Amoral rebellion, however, stops short of this decisive sphere. It wants to avoid morality as well as its social basis within the given order. Dodging the latter's contradictions, this amoral rebellion really remains beyond good and evil. It puts itself beyond the bounds of even that morality which links the established order with a more rational and happy society.

The attempt to save the objectivity of happiness, expressed for the first time in Plato's critique of hedonism, takes two directions in the advance toward an objective formulation of the concept of happiness. On the one hand, the gratification of the individual, his best possible existence, is measured against the "essence of man" in such a way that the highest potentialities open to man in his historical situation take precedence in development and gratification over all others in which man is not free but rather dependent on what is "external." On the other hand, the essence of man can develop only within society, whose actual organization participates in determining the realization of those potentialities and therefore also determines happiness. In Platonic and Aristotelian ethics both aspects, the personal and the social, are still joined. In the ethics of the modern period, in the form in which they have become prevalent since the Reformation, society is to a great extent relieved of responsibility for human potentialities. The latter are supposed to subsist exclusively in the individual himself, in his autonomy. The unconditioned freedom of the person becomes the measure of the "highest good." Since, however, this freedom is only abstract in the real world and coexists with social unfreedom and unhappiness, it becomes, in idealist ethics, programmatically separated from happiness. The latter increasingly takes on the character of irrational, bodily gratification, of mere enjoyment and therefore of inferiority:

. . . reason can never be persuaded that the existence of a man who merely lives for *enjoyment*
. . . has a worth in itself. . . . Only through what he does without reference to enjoyment, in full

freedom and independently of what nature can procure for him passively, does he give an absolute worth to his being, as the existence of a person; and happiness, with the whole abundance of its pleasures, is far from being an unconditioned good.[15]

The duress of the disciplining process of modern society comes to expression: the happiness of the individual is at best a worthless accident of his life. In the determination of the highest good, happiness is completely subordinated to virtue. Happiness may be only the "morally conditioned although necessary consequence" of morality. A "necessary connection" between the ethics of conviction and happiness becomes possible only through the assumption of a "purely intellectual determining principle" of human action and of an "intelligible author of nature."[16] The harmony of virtue and happiness belongs to those beautiful relations for whose realization the world beyond is necessary.

The unconditional manner, however, in which German idealism adhered to the principle of freedom as the condition of the highest good serves to emphasize more than ever the inner connection between happiness and freedom. The concrete form of human freedom determines the form of human happiness. Comprehension of the connection between happiness and freedom was already expressed in the ancient critique of hedonism. Happiness, as the fulfillment of all potentialities of the individual, presupposes freedom: at root, it is freedom. Conceptual analysis reveals them to be ultimately identical. Because freedom does not reign in the material conditions of the external world, because there happiness and contingency are almost identical, and because on the other hand the individual's freedom was maintained as a condition of the "highest good," felicity could not be made to reside in the external world. This motive is at work in Platonic and Aristotelian ethics. In the moral critique of the bourgeois period, too, hedonism is rejected from the standpoint of the concept of freedom. Kant rejected the principle of pleasure as something merely contingent which contradicted the autonomy of the person. And Fichte called pleasure essentially "involuntary" since it presupposes an agreement of the "external world" with the instincts and wants of the subject, whose realization does not fall within the range of the subject's freedom. In the happiness of pleasure, the individual is thus "alienated from himself."[17] This position presupposes that the subject's unfreedom in relation to the good things of the external world cannot be abolished and that the free person is therefore necessarily debased if his happiness is located in this relation. For the ancient critique the highest good was still supposed really to be the highest happiness. But now factual unfreedom is ontologized, and both freedom and happiness are so internalized that in the process happiness is excluded. The attempt to include happiness in the autonomous development of the person is abandoned, and a virtue is made out of the abstract freedom that accompanies social unfreedom.

The gratification of instincts and wants falls into ill repute; in any case, it lies beneath the human sphere with which philosophy is to concern itself. Moral commands can be followed without one's wants having been fulfilled to more than the physiological minimum; with this proposition, to be sure, a decisive achievement of modern society receives philosophical recognition. Man educated to internalization will not be easily induced, even under extreme wretchedness and injustice, to struggle against the established order.

In the moral concept of the highest good an untruth of hedonism is supposed to be eliminated: the mere subjectivity of happiness. Happiness remains an "element" of the highest good, but it stays subject to the universality of the moral law. This law is a law of reason: happiness is linked to knowledge and taken out of the dimension of mere feeling. Real happiness presupposes knowledge of the truth: that men know what they can attain as the highest potential of their existence, that they know their true interest. Individuals can feel happy and yet not be happy, because they do not even know real happiness. How, though, is one to judge of the reality of happiness? What is the criterion of its truth? In the ancient critique of hedonism this question became the political question of the right organization of the polis. The Christian ethics of the Middle Ages saw the answer to it in divine justice. The rigoristic morality of the bourgeois period made freedom the criterion of truth. But this was defined as the abstract freedom of the rational being and, in contrast to it, happiness remained external and contingent. The moral interpretation of happiness, its subjection to a universal law of reason, tolerated both the essential isolation of the autonomous person and his actual limitation.

Critical theory[18] comes to the question of the truth and universality of happiness in the elucidation of the concepts with which it seeks to determine the rational form of society. One of these determinations circumscribing the association of free men contains the explicit demand that each individual share in the social product according to his needs. With the comprehensive development of individuals and of the productive forces, society can inscribe on its banner, "From each according to his abilities, to each according to his needs." Here reappears the old hedonistic definition which seeks happiness in the comprehensive gratification of needs and wants. The needs and wants to be gratified should become the regulating principle of the labor process. But the wants of liberated men and the enjoyment of their satisfaction will have a different form from wants and satisfaction in a state of unfreedom, even if they are physiologically the same. In a social organization that opposes atomized individuals to one another in classes and leaves their particular freedom to the mechanism of an uncontrolled economic system, unfreedom is already operative in the needs and wants themselves: how much more so in enjoyment. The way want and enjoyment appear here, they do not even require general freedom. The development of the productive forces, the growing domination of nature, the extension and refinement of the production of commodities, money, and universal reification have created, along with new needs, new possibilities for enjoyment. But these given possibilities for enjoyment confront men who objectively, due to their economic status, as well as subjectively, due to their education and disciplining, are largely incapable of enjoyment. From the discrepancy between what exist as objects of possible enjoyment and the way in which these objects are understood, taken, and used arises the question of the truth of the condition of happiness in this society. Acts intending enjoyment do not achieve the fulfillment of their own intention; even when they fulfill themselves, they remain untrue.

Enjoyment is an attitude or mode of conduct toward things and human beings. The former, unless they have been made generally available by nature or by social regulation, are commodities accessible to corresponding purchasing power. For the great majority of humanity, only the very cheapest portion of these commodities is available. They become objects of enjoyment as commodities, and their origin is preserved within them—even enjoyment has a class character. The cheap is not as good as the dear. Precisely insofar as they lie outside the labor process, relations between men are essentially relations between members of the same class. For the majority, one's partner in pleasure will also be one's partner in the poverty of the same class. These conditions of life are a paltry showplace for happiness. The continual pressure under which the great masses must be kept for the reproduction of this society has only been augmented by the monopolistic accumulation of wealth. Any growth of enjoyment would endanger necessary discipline and make difficult the punctual and reliable coordination of the masses who keep the apparatus of the whole in operation. The economic regulation of enjoyment is supplemented by the police and the administration of justice. Pleasure wants essentially its own augmentation and refinement. The unfolding of the personality must not be merely spiritual. Industrial society has differentiated and intensified the objective world in such a manner that only an extremely differentiated and intensified sensuality can respond adequately to it. Modern technology contains all the means necessary to extract from things and bodies their mobility, beauty, and softness in order to bring them closer and make them available. Both the wants corresponding to these potentialities and the sensual organs through which they can be assimilated have been developed. What man can perceive, feel, and do in the midst of advanced civilization corresponds to the newly opened-up wealth of the world. But only those groups with the greatest purchasing power can take advantage of the expanded capacities and their gratification. The development of sensuality is only one part of the development of the productive forces; the need to fetter them is rooted in the antagonistic social system within which this development has taken place. There are many ways in which the ruled strata can be educated to diversion and substitute gratification. Here sports and a wide variety of permitted popular entertainment fulfill their historical function. In authoritarian states sadistic terror against enemies of the regime has found unforeseen modes of organized discharge. At the movies the common man can regularly participate in the glamour of the world of the stars and yet be aware at the same time that it is only a film and that there, too, there is splendor, bitterness, trouble, guilt, atonement, and the triumph of the good. The labor process, in which the laborer's organs atrophy and are coarsened, guarantees that the sensuousness of the lower strata does not develop beyond the technically necessary minimum. What is allowed beyond this as immediate enjoyment is circumscribed by the penal code.

It is not only the masses, however, in whom enjoyment cannot achieve the fulfillment of all subjective and objective potentialities, as it intends. Where the prevailing social relationship is the relation of men to one another as owners of commodities and where the value of every commodity is determined by the abstract labor time applied to it, enjoyment has no value in itself. For all that it is in this society, it is in separation from labor. In enjoyment the individual expends no labor power, nor does he reproduce labor power. He behaves as and acknowledges himself to be a private person. When value, the standard of the equity of exchange, is created only by abstract labor, then pleasure may not be a value. For if it were, social justice would be called into question. Indeed, it would reveal itself as striking injustice. The legitimation of pleasure as a value would, in fact, invert what is "all the news that's fit to print."

For every modern man the value of a thing is the value of the labor that was necessary to produce it. Value is thus coated with the laborer's sweat, which pastes up the flaming sword that separates culture from paradise. It is dangerous to associate conceptually pleasure and pain with value. For the question then arises whether those who produce values have more pleasure or more pain. And one could come upon the thought that value may be in inverse proportion to pleasure.[19]

The danger of this conceptual association was recognized as early as at the origins of bourgeois society. The worthlessness of mere pleasure was inculcated by all means into the consciousness of individuals.

Nowhere does the connection between the devaluation of enjoyment and its social justification manifest itself as clearly as in the interpretation of sexual pleasure. The latter—pragmatically or morally—is rationalized and appears as a mere means to an end lying outside of itself, in the service of a smooth subordination of the individual to the established form of the labor process. As a hygienic value sexual pleasure is supposed to contribute to physical and mental health, which promotes the normal functioning of man within the given order. According to Spinoza, "sensual pleasure" may only "be sought as means," and above all as hygienic means. We may "indulge ourselves with pleasures only insofar as they are necessary for preserving health."[20] Leibniz declares that "voluptuousness of the senses must be used, according to the rules of reason, as a nourishment, medication, or tonic."[21] Fichte brings sexuality into immediate conjunction with the renovation of the social labor process:

The real station, the honor and worth of the human being, and quite particularly of man in his morally natural existence, consists without doubt in his capacity as original progenitor to produce out of himself new men, new commanders of nature: beyond his earthly existence and for all eternity to establish new masters of nature. . . . It would consequently be absolute dishonor, the abnegation of authentic human and manly honor, if the capacity bestowed for the exercise of that privilege were made into a means of sensual pleasure. What is above all of nature and intended to reproduce dominion over her would become secondary and subject to one of nature's urges: pleasure. . . . [This absolute worthlessness is] lewdness—the use of the faculty of generation for mere pleasure, without intending its purpose or consciously willing it.[22]

Only when sexual relations are placed under the express purpose of the production of new labor power for the process of the social domination of nature is their enjoyment worthy of a human being and sanctioned. Later representatives of idealist ethics turned away from such frankness. Hermann Cohen considers the mere procreation of men an "animalistic" process and demands the purification of sexual pleasure by means of a truly ethical purpose. Only in love based on fidelity is sexual intercourse raised to the sphere of morality, making "sexual love" into a "characteristic of the pure will to the formation of ethical self-consciousness."[23] In the authoritarian phase of the bourgeois order, the attachment of love to the form of marriage comes into open contradiction to the state's need of a strong military and economic reserve army. The "experience of love" is "not unconditionally bound to marriage." But love should be "the presupposition and condition of marriage and of childbearing in marriage." Not the begetting of children as such, but the procreation of industrious and useful children is decisive. "Racial hygiene, social anthropology, and other medical-anthropological disciplines [give consideration] in a very meritorious way to valuable aspects even of human procreation."[24]

The unpurified, unrationalized release of sexual relationships would be the strongest release of enjoyment as such and the total devaluation of labor for its own sake. No human being could tolerate the tension between labor as valuable in itself and the freedom of enjoyment. The dreariness and injustice of work conditions would penetrate explosively the consciousness of individuals and make impossible their peaceful subordination to the social system of the bourgeois world.

The function of labor within this society determines its attitude with respect to enjoyment. The latter may not be meaningful in itself or remain unrationalized. Instead it must receive its value from elsewhere. "Pleasure . . . and pain are withdrawn from any justification or motivation by the will to labor; rather, they provide this will with the stimulus to labor," which would then be subsumed under the principle of the satisfaction of wants. "Hedonism is the limit of a self-justification of the will to labor"[25] and contradicts the basic interest of the established order. The internalization and spiritualization by means of which enjoyment is refined to the level of culture, which helps reproduce the whole and thus proves its social value, is subject to this conviction. For the immediate producer the restriction of enjoyment operates immediately, without any moral mediation, through the working day, which leaves only a brief period of "leisure time" for enjoyment and puts it in the service of relaxation and the recreation of energy or labor power. The usufructuaries of the labor process are affected by the same valuation. That their enjoyment consists of doing and having what actually produces no value, creates a kind of social guilt feeling that leads to a rationalization of enjoyment. As representation, relaxation, and display of the splendor of those who are on top and bear the greatest responsibility, this enjoyment is discharged almost as a burden or duty.

The creation of social guilt feeling is a decisive achievement of education. The prevailing law of value is mirrored in the continually renewed conviction that everyone, left completely to himself, must earn a living in the general competitive struggle, if only in order to be enabled to continue to earn it in the future, and that everyone is rewarded in proportion to the labor power he has expended. Happiness, however, cannot be earned in this fashion. The goal of labor is not supposed to be happiness, and its remuneration is not enjoyment but profit or wages, i.e. the possibility of working more in the future. For the perpetuation of this labor process, those instincts and wants which could undermine the normal relation of labor and enjoyment (as the extent of the absence of labor) and the institutions that secure it (such as the family or marriage) must be diverted or repressed. This diversion and repression is not always linked to cultural progress. Many instincts and wants first become false and destructive due to the false forms into which their satisfaction is channeled, while the attained level of objective development would permit their true gratification—true because they could fulfill themselves in their original intention of "unmixed" pleasure. Such are the repressed cruelty that leads to sadistic terror and the repressed self-abandon that leads to masochistic subjection. In their authentic intention as forms of the sexual instinct they can result in augmented pleasure not only for the subject but for the object as well. They are then no longer connected with destruction.[26] But precisely the increased differentiation of pleasure is intolerable in a society that requires such wants to be gratified in a repressed form. Augmented pleasure would represent immediately increased liberation of the individual, for it would demand freedom in the choice of object, in the knowledge and in the realization of his potentialities, and freedom of time and of place. All these demands violate the law of life of the established society. The taboo on pleasure has been most stubbornly maintained due to the innermost connection of happiness and freedom. This taboo has extended far into the ranks of the historical opposition to the given order, distorting the problem and its solutions.[27]

The designation of happiness as the condition of the comprehensive gratification of the individual's needs and wants is abstract and incorrect as long as it accepts needs and wants as ultimate data in their present form. For as such they are beyond neither good and evil nor true and false. As historical facts they are subject to questioning as to their "right": Are they of such a sort that their gratification can fulfill the subjective and objective potentialities of individuals? For many forms of want characteristic of the prevailing human condition, this question would have to be answered in the negative in view of the already attained stage of social development. For the latter makes possible a truer happiness than that which men attain for themselves today. Pleasure in the abasement of another as well as self-abasement under a stronger will, pleasure in the manifold surrogates for sexuality, in meaningless sacrifices, in the heroism of war are false pleasures because the drives and needs that fulfill themselves in them make men less free, blinder, and more wretched than they have to be. They are the drives and needs of individuals who were raised in an antagonistic society. To the extent to which they do not completely disappear in a new form of social organization, modes of their gratification are conceivable in which the most extreme potentialities of men can really unfold happiness. This liberation of potentialities is a matter of social practice. What men, with their developed sensuous and psychic organs and the wealth created by their work, can undertake to attain the highest measure of happiness rests with this practice. Understood in this way, happiness can no longer or in any way be merely subjective: it enters the realm of men's communal thought and action.

Where society utilizes the developed productive forces only in fettered form, it is not just the gratifications but the very wants themselves that are falsified. Insofar as they extend beyond the subsistence minimum, they come to expression only in proportion to their effective demand. Class situation, especially the situation of the individual in the labor process, is active in them, for this situation has formed the (bodily and spiritual) organs and capacities of men and the horizon of their demands. Since these appear as wants only in their stunted form, with all their repressions, renunciations, adaptations, and rationalizations, they can normally be satisfied within the given social framework. Because they are themselves already unfree, the false happiness of their fulfillment is possible in unfreedom.

In critical theory, the concept of happiness has been freed from any ties with bourgeois conformism and relativism. Instead, it has become a part of general, objective truth, valid for all individuals insofar as all their interests are preserved in it. Only in view of the historical possibility of general freedom is it meaningful to designate as untrue even actual, really perceived happiness in the previous and present conditions of existence. It is the individual's interest that expresses itself in his wants, and their gratification corresponds to this interest. That there is any happiness at all in a society governed by blind laws is a blessing. Through this happiness, the individual in this society can feel secure and protected from ultimate desperation. Rigoristic morality sins against the cheerless form in which humanity has survived. All hedonism is right in opposing it. Only today, at the highest stage of development of the established order, when the objective forces making for a higher order of humanity have become mature, and only in connection with the theory and practice linked to such a transformation, may the critique of the totality of the established order also take as its object the happiness that this order provides. It appears that individuals raised to be integrated into the antagonistic labor process cannot be judges of their own happiness. They have been prevented from knowing their true interest. Thus it is possible for them to designate their condition as happy and, without external compulsion, embrace the system that oppresses them. The results of modern plebiscites prove that men separated from possible truth can be brought to vote against themselves. As long as individuals see their interest only as getting along within the given order, such plebiscites pose no problems for the authoritarian apparatus. Terror merely supplements the delusions of the governed. Appeal to interest is untrue.

In view of the possibility of a happier real state of humanity the interest of the individual is no longer an ultimate datum. There are true and false interests even with regard to the individual. His factual, immediate interest is not in itself his true interest. It is not as though the true interest were that which demanded, on the grounds of lesser risk and greater chance of enjoyment, the sacrifice of an immediate interest. Such calculation of happiness stays within the general framework of false interest and can at best facilitate the choice of the better false happiness. It cannot be in the true interest of the individual to want his own and others' vitiation—not even in the true interest of those whose power can only be maintained at the cost of such vitiation. At the attained level of development power can no longer enjoy the world which it dominates. For if it were to cease working and continually renewing the bloody and destructive process of its mere reproduction, it would be instantly lost. Even the powers that be have something to gain.

That the true interest of individuals is the interest of freedom, that true individual freedom can coexist with real general freedom and, indeed, is possible only in conjunction with it, that happiness ultimately consists in freedom—these are not propositions of philosophical anthropology about the nature of man but descriptions of a historical situation which humanity has achieved for itself in the struggle with nature. The individuals whose happiness is at stake in making good use of this situation have grown up in the school of capitalism. To the high intensification and differentiation of their abilities and of their world corresponds the social shackling of this development. Insofar as unfreedom is already present in wants and not just in their gratification, they must be the first to be liberated—not through an act of education or of the moral renewal of man but through an economic and political process encompassing the disposal over the means of production by the community, the reorientation of the productive process toward the needs and wants of the whole society, the shortening of the working day, and the active participation of the individuals in the administration of the whole. When all present subjective and objective potentialities of development have been unbound, the needs and wants themselves will change. Those based on the social compulsion of repression, on injustice, and on filth and poverty would necessarily disappear. There may still be the sick, the insane, and the criminal. The realm of necessity persists; struggle with nature and even among men continues. Thus the reproduction of the whole will continue to be associated with privations for the individual. Particular interest will not coincide immediately with true interest. The difference between particular and true interest, nevertheless, is something other than the difference between particular interest and a hypostatized general interest that suppresses the individuals. In his relation to an authentic general interest, the individual would relate to truth; the demands and decisions of the whole would then preserve the individual interest and eventually promote his happiness. If the true interest, furthermore, must be represented by a general law forbidding specific wants and gratifications, such a law will no longer be a front for the particular interest of groups that maintain their power against the general interest through usurpation. Rather, it will express the rational decision of free individuals. Having come of age, men themselves will have to confront and deal with their wants. Their responsibility will be infinitely greater, because they will no longer have the false pleasure of masochistic security in the strong protection of a heteronomous power. The internal, real union of duty and happiness (and not a union effected in the world beyond), which idealist ethics had doubted, is possible only in freedom. This was Kant's intention when he founded the concept of duty on the autonomy of the person. Through its limitation to the freedom of the pure will, autonomy limits itself in favor of a social order that it could only admit in an abstract form.

If individuals, having attained majority, reject particular wants or a particular pleasure as bad, this would occur on the basis of the autonomous recognition of their true interest: the preservation of general freedom. Consequently it would occur in the interest of happiness itself, which can only exist in general freedom as the fulfillment of all developed potentialities. It was the ancient desideratum of hedonism to join in thought both happiness and truth. The problem was insoluble. For as long as an anarchic, unfree society determined the truth, the latter could only manifest itself either in the particular interest of the isolated individual or in the necessities of the hypostatized general interest, the society. In the first case its form (generality) was lost; in the second, its content (particularity). The truth to which the liberated individual relates in happiness is both general and particular. The subject is no longer isolated in its interest against others. His life can be happy beyond the contingency of the moment, because his conditions of existence are no longer determined by a labor process which creates wealth only through the perpetuation of poverty and privation. Instead they are regulated through the rational self-administration of the whole in which the subject participates actively. The individual can relate to others as equals and to the world as his world, no longer alienated from him. Mutual understanding will no longer be permeated by unhappiness, since insight and passion will no longer come into conflict with a reified form of human relationship.

General happiness presupposes knowledge of the true interest: that the social life-process be administered in a manner which brings into harmony the freedom of individuals and the preservation of the whole on the basis of given objective historical and natural conditions. With the development of social antagonisms the connection of happiness with knowledge was obscured. The abstract reason of isolated individuals is certainly powerless over a happiness abandoned to contingency. But this very social development has also brought forth the forces which can once again bring about that connection. For the immediate producers, isolating individuation has already been abolished extensively within unfreedom: the individual has no property to preserve that can only be enjoyed at the expense of others. His interest drives him not to competition or into interest groups based in turn upon competition but rather to militant solidarity. The first goal of struggle is only a particular social group's interest in better, more humane conditions of life. But this particular interest cannot be pursued without bettering and making more humane the conditions of life of the whole and liberating the entire society. In the monopolistic phase of bourgeois society, when the preservation of the general interest on the part of the groups fighting for transformation is obvious enough, the efforts of the beneficiaries of the Establishment are directed toward splitting that solidarity. Bureaucratization, increase of wage differentials, and immediate corruption of the workers are intended to root contradictions even among these strata. Their true interest requires not piecemeal change but the reconstruction of the productive process. When this has been achieved, general reason can no longer outwit the particular interest behind the backs of the individuals. To the contrary, the particular interest becomes the active and cognitive force of the process through which generality, embodied in the community, is advanced. Only at this point in society is "the truth of *particular* satisfactions . . . the *general* satisfaction that, as happiness, the thinking will sets itself as goal."[28]

Hegel pointed out that general progress comes about in history only through particular interests, for only particular interest can stir the individual to the passion of historical struggle. "The particular interest of passion is therefore inseparable from the activity of the universal; for it is from the particular and determinate and from its negation, that the universal results."[29] When this inseparability rests on the cunning of reason, it entails the unhappiness of individuals. In the passion with which they pursue their particular interests, they wear themselves out and are destroyed. Hegel called it a "horrible comfort" that "historical men have not been what is called happy."[30] If no higher form of historical reason is possible than the antagonistic organization of humanity, then this horror cannot be thought away. It is true, of course, that men intend not happiness but, in each case, specific ends whose fulfillment then brings happiness. In the specific goals which are aimed at in solidary struggle for a rational society, happiness is no longer merely an attendant contingency. It is built into the very structure of the new order of the conditions of existence that have been demanded. Happiness ceases to be a mere subjective state of feeling when general concern for the potentialities of individuals is effective at the level of the liberated needs and wants of the subjects.

For Hegel, then, the struggle for the higher generality, or form of society, of the future becomes in the present the cause of particular individuals and groups, and this constitutes the tragic situation of world-historical persons. They attack social conditions in which—even if badly—the life of the whole reproduces itself. They fight against a concrete form of reason without empirical proof of the practicability of the future form which they represent. They offend against that which, within limits at least, has proven true. Their rationality necessarily operates in a particular, irrational, explosive form, and their critique of decadence and anarchy appears anarchic and destructive. Individuals who hold so fast to the Idea[31] that it permeates their existence are unyielding and stubborn. Common sense cannot distinguish between them and criminals, and in fact in the given order they are criminals like Socrates in Athens.[32] Universality and reason have become their own passion. The formalistic conformist, for whom one want is just as valid as another, knows of them as selfish characters who are dangerous. He sees how the critique of the appearance of freedom in the present and the knowledge of the future reality of freedom already constitute their happiness, because in them the blunt separation of here and there, today and tomorrow, the exclusive, defensive ego-feeling of bourgeois existence is overcome—but he cannot understand it. Whatever he may say, they are to him exalted, at best religious. For of themselves, thinks the conformist, people have only their own advantage in mind. Their paradoxical situation is apparent only to few.

Just as the attainable form of happiness can only be realized through the particular interest of only those social strata whose liberation leads not to the domination of particular interests over the community but to the general liberation of humanity, the same holds for the correct knowledge required by this form. This interest requires its ideology as a veil over the structure of truth in order to justify itself as a general interest. This interest, by its very nature, implies thinking to the end all realizable potentialities (which in the bourgeois period found their social limit in the danger of a material transformation of the whole) and keeping to the goal of their realization. The loss of correct knowledge would entail the loss of happiness as well, for the compulsion and necessity of an uncontrollable situation would once again win its contingent power over men. Freedom of knowledge is a part of real freedom, which can only exist together with common decision and action on the basis of what is known to be true. The essential role of truth for the happiness of individuals makes the characterization of happiness as pleasure and enjoyment appear insufficient. When knowledge of truth is no longer linked to knowledge of guilt, poverty, and injustice, it is no longer forced to remain external to a happiness ceded to immediate, sensual relationships. Even the most personal human relations can be opened to happiness in a really guiltless knowledge. Perhaps they would thereby become, in fact, that free community in life of which idealist morality had expected the highest unfolding of individuality. Knowledge will no longer disturb pleasure. Perhaps it can even become pleasure, which the ancient idea of *nous* had dared to see as the highest determination of knowledge. The bogey of the unchained voluptuary who would abandon himself only to his sensual wants is rooted in the separation of intellectual from material productive forces and the separation of the labor process from the process of consumption. Overcoming this separation belongs to the preconditions of freedom. The development of material wants must go together with the development of psychic and mental wants. The organization of technology, science, and art changes with their changed utilization and changed content. When they are no longer under the compulsion of a system of production based on the unhappiness of the majority, and of the pressures of rationalization, internalization, and sublimation, then mind and spirit can only mean an augmentation of happiness. Hedonism is both abolished and preserved in critical theory and practice. If freedom prevails in the spiritual and mental side of life, i.e. in culture, and if culture is no longer subject to the compulsion of internalization, then it becomes meaningless to restrict happiness to sensual pleasure.

The reality of happiness is the reality of freedom as the self-determination of liberated humanity in its common struggle with nature. "The truth of particular satisfactions is the *general* [*allgemeine*] satisfaction that, as happiness, the thinking will sets itself as goal." But this happiness is at first "generality of content only as representation, as abstraction, only as something that *should* be." Its truth is "the *universal* [*allgemeine*] determinacy of the will in itself, i.e. its own self-determination: *freedom.*"[33] For idealism, freedom was also reason: "the substance of" and "that alone which is true of spirit."[34] In their completed form both, happiness and reason, coincide. Hegel did not believe that the realization of this form by bringing about a new form of the social organization of humanity could become the task of historical practice. Under the title of the "ideal," however, he represented happiness as a "stage of world development" that is simultaneously one of reason and freedom: as the abolition of the antithesis, characteristic of the bourgeois stage of development, between individuals isolated in their particular interests, on the one hand, and the hypostatized general interest as the state that perpetuates itself through the sacrifice of individuals, on the other.

In the ideal . . . particular individuality is supposed to remain precisely in undissolved harmony with the substantial; and insofar as the ideal partakes of the freedom and independence of subjectivity, to that extent the surrounding world of conditions and developmental structures may not possess any essential objectivity belonging to itself quite apart from the subjective and the individual. For the ideal individual should be self-contained. The objective world should still be part of what is incontestably his and not move or develop by itself, detached from the individuality of subjects. Otherwise the subject becomes merely subordinate to a world that is complete in itself.[35]

NOTES

1. Kant, *Critique of Practical Reason*, 6th ed., trans. by T. H. Abbott (London: Longmans, 1909), pp. 112–113.
2. Hegel, *Vorlesungen über die Philosophie der Geschichte* in *Werke*, 2d ed., E. Gans, K. Hegel, *et al.*, eds. (Berlin, 1840–47), IX, p. 34.
3. Hegel, *Glauben und Wissen* in *Werke*, I, pp. 8ff.
4. Aristotle *Politics*, 1323 b 27ff., *Magna Moralia*, 1206 b 30ff., *Politics*, 1332 a 30.
5. Diogenes Laertius, *Lives of Eminent Philosophers*, trans. by R. D. Hicks (2 vols.; New York: Putnam, 1925), I, p. 217.
6. *Ibid.*, p. 221.
7. *Ibid.*, p. 217.
8. *Ibid.*, p. 219.
9. *Ibid.*, p. 227.
10. *Ibid.*, II, p. 655.
11. *Ibid.*, p. 657.
12. *Gorgias* 497–498.
13. Cf. *Zeitschrift für Sozialforschung*, II (1933), pp. 169ff.
14. Cf. *Zeitschrift für Sozialforschung*, V (1936), pp. 190–191, 201–202.
15. Kant, *Kritik of Judgement*, trans. by J. H. Bernard (New York: Macmillan, 1892), p. 52 (with changes in translation).

16. Kant, *Kritik der praktischen Vernunft* in *Werke*, Ernst Cassirer, ed. (Berlin, 1912ff.), V, pp. 125 and 129.
17. Fichte, *System der Sittenlehre* in *Werke*, Fritz Medicus, ed. (Leipzig, n.d.), II, p. 540.
18. By critical theory we mean here social theory as presented in the fundamental essays of the *Zeitschrift für Sozialforschung* on the basis of dialectical philosophy and the critique of political economy. See the essay "Philosophy and Critical Theory" in this volume.
19. Hermann Cohen, *Ethik des reinen Willens*, 3d ed. (Berlin, 1931), p. 163.
20. Spinoza, *On the Improvement of the Understanding*, trans. by R. H. M. Elwes, in *Selections*, J. Wild, ed. (New York: Scribner's, 1930), pp. 4 and 6.
21. Leibniz, *Von der Glückseligkeit* in *Opera Philosophica*, J. E. Erdmann, ed. (Berlin, 1840), p. 672.
22. Fichte, *Die Staatslehre* (1813) in *Werke*, VI, pp. 523–524.
23. Hermann Cohen, *op. cit.*, p. 584.
24. Bruno Bauch, *Grundzüge der Ethik* (Stuttgart, 1933), pp. 240–241.
25. A. Görland, *Ethik als Kritik der Weltgeschichte* (Leipzig, 1914), pp. 119–120.
26. Cf. *Zeitschrift für Sozialforschung*, V (1936), pp. 229ff.
27. Even in the case of the firmest advocates of bourgeois sexual reform, the taboo of pleasure still appears, concealed in ethical or psychological rationalizations.
28. Hegel, *Enzyclopädie* in *Werke*, VII, p. 372 (§478).
29. Hegel, *Vorlesungen über die Philosophie der Geschichte, op. cit.*, p. 41.
30. *Ibid.*, p. 39.
31. *Translator's note*: That is, they pursue in practice what they have rationally come to know as the tendencies immanent in the status quo—tendencies that can be realized only by transforming the status quo. For this Hegelian use of "Idea" as substance developing both subjectively and objectively through a dialectical process, see Herbert Marcuse, *Reason and Revolution* (Boston: Beacon Press, 1960). pp. 164ff., and "The Concept of Essence," *Negations*, pp. 67ff. and 82ff.
32. Cf. Hegel, *Vorlesungen über die Geschichte der Philosophie* in *Werke*, XIV, p. 101.
33. Hegel, *Enzyclopädie, op. cit.* (§478, 480).
34. Hegel, *Vorlesungen über die Philosophie der Geschichte, op. cit.*, p. 22.
35. Hegel, *Vorlesungen über die Ästhetik* in *Werke*, X, Part 1, pp. 227–228.

MAX HORKHEIMER

MATERIALISM AND MORALITY

That human beings autonomously attempt to decide whether their actions are good or evil appears to be a late historical phenomenon.[1] A highly-developed European individual can bring into the light of clear consciousness and morally evaluate not just important decisions, but also those primarily instinctual and habitual reactions of which his life for the most part consists. However, human actions appear more compulsive as their subjects belong to earlier historical formations. The capacity to subject instinctual reactions to moral criticism and to change them on the basis of individual considerations could only develop with the growing differentiation of society. Even the authority principle of the Middle Ages, the undermining of which marks the starting-point of modern moral inquiry, is an expression of a later phase of this process. The unbroken religious faith which preceded the dominance of this principle was an already tremendously complicated mediation between naive experience and instinctual reaction; therefore, the medieval criterion of tradition sanctioned by the church (whose exclusive validity surely still carried a strongly compulsive character) already indicates a moral conflict. When Augustine[2] declares: "*Ego vero evangelio non crederem nisi me catholicae ecclesiae commoveret auctoritas,*"* this affirmation already presupposes—as Dilthey[3] recognized—a doubting of faith. The social life-process of the modern period has presently so advanced human powers that at least the members of certain strata in the most developed countries are capable, in a relatively wide range of their existence, of not merely following instinct or habit, but of choosing autonomously among several possible aims. The exercise of this capacity admittedly takes place on a much smaller scale than is commonly believed. Even if the deliberations concerning the technique and the means which should be applied to a given purpose have become extremely refined in many areas of social and individual life, the aims of human beings nonetheless continue to be rigidly fixed. Precisely in those actions which in their totality are socially and historically significant, human

---

* "I would not believe in the true gospel if the authority of the Catholic church were not moving me to do so" [Ed.].

beings in general behave in a quite typical manner, that is, in conformity with a definite scheme of motives which are characteristic of their social group. Only in non-essential, private affairs do people occasionally examine their motives conscientiously and apply their intellectual powers to the determination of goals. Within contemporary society and especially among younger people, nonetheless, proper goals have been energetically questioned. As the principle of authority was undermined and a significant number of individuals acquired substantial decision-making power over the conduct of their lives, the need emerged for a spiritual guideline which could substitute for this principle's eroding bases in orienting the individual in this world. The acquisition of moral principles was important for members of the higher social strata, since their position constantly demanded that they make intervening decisions of which they had earlier been absolved by authority. At the same time, a rationally grounded morality for the purpose of dominating the masses in the state became all the more necessary when a mode of action that diverged from the their life-interests was demanded of them.

The idealist philosophers of the modern period met this need through axiomatic construction. In accordance with the conditions which, since the Renaissance, force the individual back upon himself, they sought to authenticate these maxims with reason—that is, with reasons that are in principle generally accessible. As distinctive as the systems of Leibniz, Spinoza, and of the Enlightenment may be, they all bear the marks of an effort to justify a particular kind of behavior as that which is proper for all times on the basis of the eternal constitution of the world and of the individual. They therefore make a claim to unconditional validity. Those standards characterized as correct are admittedly quite general for the most part and offer—with the exception of several materialist and militant theories of the French Enlightenment—few definite directives. In the last centuries, life has demanded too much capacity for conformity to both religion and morality for substantively elaborated precepts to preserve even the appearance of permanence. Even modern moral philosophers who decisively attack the formalism of earlier moral teachings hardly diverge from them in this respect. "Ethics does not teach directly what ought here and now to happen in any given case," writes Nicolai Hartmann,[4] "but in general how that is constituted which ought to happen universally. . . . Ethics furnishes the bird's-eye view from which the actual can be seen objectively." Idealist moral philosophy purchases the belief in its own unconditionality by taking no position with respect to an historical moment. It does not take sides. Though its perceptions may accord perfectly well with or even benefit a group of individuals in collective historical struggle, it nonetheless prescribes no position. Hartmann declares: "What a man ought to do, when he is confronted with a serious conflict that is fraught with responsibility, is this: to decide according to his best conscience; that is, according to his own living sense of the relative height of the respective values . . ."[5] Ethics "does not mix itself up with the conflicts of life, gives no precepts coined *ad hoc*; it is no code, as law is, of commandments and prohibitions. It turns its attention directly to the creative in man, challenges it afresh in every new case to observe, to divine, as it were, what ought here and now to happen."[6] Morality is understood in this connection as an eternal category. The judgment of character and actions as good or evil should always be possible, just as judging statements true or false, or objective forms beautiful or ugly is part of the human essence. Despite the most vigorous discussions concerning the possibility or impossibility of an eternal morality, more recent philosophers understand one another's concepts. The mutability of the content, the innate quality of certain statements is asserted and contested, but the capacity for moral value judgments as a rule is held to be an essential characteristic of human nature of at least equal rank with that of theoretical knowledge [Erkenntnis]. A new category of virtue has entered philosophy since the Renaissance: moral virtue. It has little in common with either the ethical conceptions of the Greeks, which concerned the best path to happiness, or the religious ethics of the Middle Ages. Although connections exist between it and these phenomena, the fundamental feature of the modern problem of morality has its roots in the bourgeois order. Insofar as certain economic elements of that order are found in earlier societies, aspects of this problem appear in them as well; morality can itself, however, only be understood from the standpoint of the general life situation of the epoch now about to end.

The moral conception of the bourgeoisie came to its purest expression in Kant's formulation of the categorical imperative. "Act only according to that maxim by which you can at the same time will that it should become a universal law."[7] According to Kant, actions which conform to this principle and which occur immediately for its sake distinguish themselves from all others through the quality of morality. He himself explained wherein "the specific mark"[8] distinguishing this imperative from all other rules of action could be sought: in the "renunciation of all interest." Even if reason itself takes a pure and immediate interest in moral actions,[9] they do not occur out of an interest in the object, nor out of necessity. Acting out of duty is contrasted with acting out of interest. Virtue does not consist in acting contrary to one's individual purposes, but rather independently of them. The individual should liberate himself from his interest.

As is well known, Kant's view was contested from various directions, including Schiller and Schleiermacher. Interest-free action was even declared impossible. "[W]hat is an interest other than the working of a motive upon the Will? Therefore where a motive moves the Will, there the latter has an interest; but where the Will is affected by no motive, there in truth it can be as little active, as a stone is able to leave its place without being pushed or pulled," says Schopenhauer.[10] Certainly Kant did not want moral action understood as action without motive, even if he viewed acting out of interest as the natural law of human beings. On the contrary, the moral impulsion[11] lies in respect for the moral law [Sittengesetz]. But Schopenhauer's critique, which he transformed positively [ins Positive] through the construction of his own ethics, hits one thing on the mark: to the moral agent in the Kantian sense, the actual reasons for action remain obscure. The reason that the general should stand above the particular is unknown to him, nor is it clear how in the individual harmony is to be achieved between them. The imperative, which "of itself finds entrance into the mind and yet gains reluctant reverence (though not always obedience)"[12] leaves the individual in a certain uneasiness and unclarity. In his soul, a struggle plays itself out between personal interest and the vague conception of a general interest, between individual and general objectives. Yet it remains obscure how a rational decision according to criteria is possible between the two. There arises an endless reflection and constant turmoil which in principle is not to be overcome. Because this problematic, which plays itself out in the inner lives of human beings, necessarily derives from their role in the social life-process, the Kantian philosophy, as its faithful reflection, is a consummate expression of its age.

The foundation of this spiritual [seelische] situation is easily recognized upon consideration of the structure of the bourgeois order. The social whole lives through unleashing the possessive instincts of all individuals. The whole is maintained insofar as they concern themselves with profit, with the conservation and multiplication of their own property. Each is left to care for himself as best he can. But because thereby he must produce things that others need, the general needs are fulfilled through activities which are apparently independent of one another and which only seem to serve the individual's own welfare. The fact that in this order the production of total social needs coincides with the subjects' striving after possessions has stamped the psychic apparatus of its members. In all epochs, human beings have accommodated themselves in their entire being to the life-conditions of society: a consequence of this accommodation in the modern period is that human powers orient themselves to the promotion of individual advantage. Neither the feelings of the individual nor his consciousness, neither the form of his happiness nor his conception of God escape this life-dominating principle. Even in the most refined and seemingly remote impulses of the individual, the function bringing these to bear in society still makes itself felt. In this era, economic advantage is the natural law under which individual life proceeds. To this natural law of individuals, the categorical imperative holds up the "general natural law," the law [Lebensgesetz] of human society as a standard of comparison. This would be meaningless unless particular interests and the needs of the generality intersected, not highly imperfectly, but necessarily. That this does not occur, however, is the inadequacy of the bourgeois economic form: there exists no rational connection between the free competition of individuals as the mediating and the existence of the entire society as the mediated. The process takes place not under the control of a conscious will, but as a natural occurrence. The life of the generality arises blindly, accidentally, and badly out of the chaotic activity of individuals, industries, and states. This irrationality expresses itself in the suffering of the majority of all human beings. The individual, completely absorbed in the concern for himself and "his own," thus promotes the life of the whole not merely without clear consciousness; rather, through his labor he effects both the welfare and the misery of others. It never becomes apparent to what extent and for which individuals his labor means the one or the other. No unambiguous connection can be drawn between one's own labor and larger social considerations. This problem, which only society itself could rationally solve through the systematic incorporation of each member into a consciously directed labor process, manifests itself in the bourgeois epoch as a conflict in the inner life of its subjects.

To be sure, with the liberation of the individual from the overarching unities of the Middle Ages, the individual acquired the consciousness of itself as an independent being. This self-consciousness is, however, abstract: the manner in which each individual contributes to the workings of the entire society through his labor, and is at the same time influenced by it, remains completely obscure. All of them cooperate in the good or bad development of the entire society, and yet it appears as a natural occurrence. One's role in this whole, without which the essence of the individual cannot be determined, cannot be perceived. Hence each necessarily has a false consciousness about his existence, which he is able to comprehend only in psychological categories as the sum of supposedly free decisions. Given the lack of a rational organization of the social whole that his labor benefits, he cannot recognize himself in his true connection to it and knows himself only as an individual whom the whole affects somewhat, without it ever becoming clear how and how much his egoistic activity actually affects it. The whole thus appears as an admonition, as a demand, and troubles precisely the progressive individuals at their labor, in the call of conscience and in moral deliberation.[13]

Materialism reveals—and not so generally as was just suggested, but paying particular heed to the various periods and social classes—the actual relationships from which the moral problems are derived and reflected, if only in a distorted fashion, in the doctrines of moral philosophy. The idea of morality, as it was formulated by Kant, contains the truth that the mode of action informed by the natural law of economic advantage is not necessarily the rational mode. It does not, as might be supposed, oppose the interest of the individual to feelings or even to the return to blind obedience; neither interest nor reason is maligned, but instead reason recognizes that it need not exclusively serve the natural law, i.e., individual advantage, when it has absorbed the natural law of the whole into its will. The individual, of course, cannot fulfill the demand to rationally shape the whole. Mastery of the overall process of society by human beings can only be achieved when it has overcome its anarchic form and constituted itself as a real subject—that is, through historical deed. Such a deed issues not from the individual, but rather from a constellation of social groups, in the dynamics of which conscience certainly plays an important role. Moral anxiety by no means burdens the labor of individuals in the production process alone; their entire being is affected by it. Whenever human beings follow the law which is natural to them in this society, they attend immediately only to the affairs of the subject of interests which bears their name. The reason of the bourgeois individual extends beyond his particular purposes, insofar as he is not just this determinate X with his private worries and wishes, but, at the same time, one who can ask himself what concern these worries of X actually are to him even as they immediately affect his personal existence—insofar, that is, as he is not this mere X but rather a member of human society—the "autonomous" will of Kant's commandment stirs within him. As Kant consistently argued,[14] the interest of another is in this connection equally contingent as one's own, for the relation of the strivings of Y to life of the generality is for X, as a rule, no more transparent than his own. Whoever, in the economic situation of the bourgeois, is incapable of experiencing the whole conflict is retarded in his development; he lacks a type of reaction which belongs to individuals of this period.

Therefore, morality is not simply dismissed by materialism as mere ideology or false consciousness. Rather it is understood as a human phenomenon which is not to be overcome for the duration of the bourgeois epoch. Its philosophical expression, however, is in many respects distorted. Above all, the solution of the problem does not lie in the observance of rigidly formulated commandments. In attempting to apply the Kantian imperative it quickly becomes clear that the generality with which the moral will is concerned would not be helped in the least. Even if all were to observe it, even if all were to lead a virtuous life in its sense, the same confusion would reign. Nothing essential would be changed.

Kant's four examples of moral action place this helplessness and powerlessness of the good will in bold relief: in the first, a desperate man turns away from suicide in consideration of the moral law. His decision to reject suicide is so dubious, however, that the reader is astonished that Kant does not seriously pursue it. Why should a person "who, through a series of misfortunes which has grown into hopelessness, tires of this life,"[15] not at the same time be able to will that the maxim of this action become a universal law? Is not this world in such a condition that a rational actor would perceive the possibility of that escape route as a consolation? Hume's essay on suicide, in which he proves himself a true Enlightenment figure, while written and published long before the *Foundations of the Metaphysics of Morals*, nonetheless serves as a response to Kant's peculiar opinion. "A man, who retires from life," he says, "does no harm to society: He only ceases to do good; which, if it is an injury, is of the lowest kind. . . . But suppose that it is no longer in my power to promote the interest of society; suppose that I am a burthen to it; suppose that my life hinders some person from being much more useful to society. In such cases my resignation of life must not only be innocent but laudable. And most people who lie under any temptation to abandon existence, are in some such situation; those, who have health, or power, or authority, have commonly better reason to be in humour with the world."[16] Kant's deliberations, which take no notice of the contradictions in society, seem quite lame in comparison with this voice!

In the second example, someone avoids obtaining money by the false promise of later repayment. Kant has him morally reflect that if everyone were to do this, in the end no promise would be taken seriously. In order to evaluate this example, it would be necessary to know the purpose for the money and the relationship between the two contracting parties. Sometimes Kant defends his moral solution with as much artificiality as when he discusses reasons for lying.[17] In the third example, the disregard for reality proves more ominous than in the first. A rich man finds in himself a certain talent, but is too indolent to develop it. Kant says that he could not possibly want all others to remain idle in his situation, and that he therefore must undergo the effort. But, contrary to Kant's view, the will of the gifted man would dissuade him from summoning all of the competitors (if any are present) in one arena. In the context of a competitive society, if he should decide to subject himself to the school of hard knocks, he must wish precisely that his will does not become a universal rule. The fourth example deals with charity. Kant recommends it not on the basis of respecting the moral law but with the not very persuasive argument that even a rich person may require charity someday. If this example is supposed to concern not a few measly pennies but rather a really tempting amount, the rich person would do right to prefer the secure present to the questionable future. But if this problem is considered not egoistically, but rather morally in the Kantian sense—that is, with a view to universality—then the rich person's theory regarding what is good for society at large will be quite different from that of the beggar: the former will declare with the utmost sincerity that large contributions are detrimental. If it concerns higher matters, such as taxes [*soziale Lasten*] or wages, then there will be as many beliefs about what befits universal law as social groups.

That each acts according to his conscience is not enough to put an end either to the chaos or to the resulting misery. The formal directive that one should remain pure and have a will without contradiction does not constitute a standard that could remove the basis of moral uneasiness. Is there no misdeed that has been committed at some time or other in all good conscience? It is not whether individuals consider their action reconcilable with the universal law of nature [*Naturgesetz der Allgemeinheit*], but the extent to which it is actually reconcilable with it that is decisive for the happiness of humanity. The belief that a good will—as important a motive as this may be—is the highest Good, i.e., the evaluation of an action only according to its intent and not also according to what it means in the given historical moment, is an idealist illusion. From this ideological side of the Kantian conception of morality a direct path leads to the modern mysticism of sacrifice and obedience, which otherwise only unjustly lays claim to Kant's authority. If the development and happy employment of social powers is the highest aim, it is not enough to see to a virtuous soul [*Innere*] or to the mere intellect—for instance, to suppress the instinct for acquisition through discipline— but to see the achievement of the external arrangements which can bring about happiness. What is important is not just how men do things, but what they do: precisely when the chips are down, the motives of those who pursue a goal matter less than that they achieve it. Of course, the object and situation of action involve the soul of the acting individual, for the internal and the external are as much moments of the historical dialectic as they are of the life of individuals. But the prevalent tendency in bourgeois morality to lay exclusive value upon conviction proves to be a position that inhibits progress, especially in the present. Not conscious of duty, enthusiasm, and sacrifice *as such*, but conscious of duty, enthusiasm and sacrifice *for what* decides the fate of humanity in the face of the prevailing peril. A will that is prepared to sacrifice may clearly become a good tool in the service of any power, even the most reactionary; the relation of its content to the entire society, however, is not given by conscience but by the correct theory.

This idealist trait, according to which the world would be in order as long as everything were in order in Spirit, lacks a distinction between fantasy and reality. Idealist philosophy proves itself to be a refined form of the primitive belief in the omnipotence of thought—that is, magic—but it comprises only one side of Kant's teaching. Kantianism has a very active relation to reality. As we have shown above, the categorical imperative cannot be meaningfully realized in a society of isolated individuals. Its necessary implication is thus the transformation of this society. The individual to whom the imperative appeals and whose shaping is its sole aim, would also have to disappear. Bourgeois morality points beyond the order upon which it first becomes possible and necessary. If people want to act in such a way that their maxim is fit to become universal law, they must bring about an order in which this consideration does not remain as dubious as in the cases enumerated by Kant, but rather in which it can really be carried out according to criteria. Society must then be constructed so that it establishes its own interests and those of all its members in a rational fashion: only under this condition is it meaningful for the individual, who finds himself involved in such a project subjectively and objectively, to organize his life on this basis. If in modern ethics the negative characteristics of Kant's view— namely the transformation-hindering subjectivism—is developed instead of this dynamic trait which points beyond the given relations, then the reason for this lies less with Kant than in subsequent history.

The Kantian doctrine does contain the impossible concept of an eternal commandment addressed to free subjects, but it also anticipates the end of morality. Therein is expressed the contradiction with which the bourgeoisie had been saddled throughout its entire epoch: it created and clung to an order which is in tension with its own concept of reason. Kant asserts the absoluteness of morality and must necessarily proclaim its transcendence, must view it as transitory. Morality rests upon the distinction between interest and duty. The task of reconciling both was put to bourgeois society by its protagonists, but the philosophical exponents of "enlightened self-interest" (Bentham) hardly dared to declare it fulfilled. This fulfillment is impossible in the prevailing form of society, for in it humanity has neither voice nor consciousness, except perhaps in theory which, in contradiction to public opinion, criticizes particular interests that pretend to be universal. The doctrine that the precondition of morality in the bourgeois sense, the distinction between particular and general interests, could be dissolved by historical action had been a part of early bourgeois materialist anthropology. Helvetius held that[18] one can "only make men happy if one reconciles their personal interest with the general. Under the condition of this principle it is apparent that morality is only a vain science if it is not fused with politics and legislation, from which I conclude that the philosophers must consider matters from the same standpoint as the legislator if they want to prove useful.

Without, of course, being animated by the same spirit. The concern of the moralist is to fashion the laws; the legislator secures their execution by impressing upon them the seal of his power." Kant also considered the reconciliation of happiness and duty to be possible in a better society. There is for him "no conflict of practice with theory,"[19] "the pure principles of right have objective reality, i.e., they may be applied."[20] It is his conviction that the true task of politics is to "accord with the public's universal end, happiness,"[21] even though political maxims may not "be derived from the welfare or happiness which a single state expects from obedience to them, and thus not from the end which one of them proposes for itself."[22] Accordingly, neither a single state nor any power group may make itself the universal. In the last analysis, according to Kant, genuine politics is concerned not with the reconciliation of individual interests with those of such particularities, but rather with the achievement of the end whose principle is given through pure reason. If he preferred to define this end not as the condition of the greatest possible happiness, but as the constitution of the greatest human freedom according to laws,[23] he did not allow any contradiction between freedom and happiness but declared that one follows from the other. Kant always emphasized the fundamental distinction between interest and duty not with respect to the perfected order itself, but rather with respect to the human beings which aspire to it. In society, viewed as an end, the purposes of any given individual could exist together with those of all the others; in it, the private purposes of the individuals might be different with respect to their content, but there need be no necessary mutual obstruction. Moral action would coincide with the natural law, or in any case would not lead to conflict with it. Despite clear phrases about the possibility of this future society, Kant wavered regarding the extent of its realization [*Verwirklichung*]; in the formulation of the *Critique of Pure Reason* it was his conviction that the realization [*Durchführung*] of the ideal can "pass beyond any and every specified limit."[24] He had harsh words for so-called "politic" men, who pride themselves on their praxis but who in reality only fawn on the powers that be, because they claimed that human nature precludes the possibility of improvement in the Idea. To them, "the legal constitution in force at any time is . . . the best, but when it is amended from above, this amendment always seems best, too."[25] The philosopher does not skeptically refer to how he "knows men," but rather knows "Man" and knows "what can be made of him."[26] There is no valid objection of anthropology against the overcoming of bad social relations. Kant's arguments against the psychological defense of absolutism are valid for every epoch in which the human sciences (among other sciences) are exploited for the struggle against progress. What Schopenhauer called the "setting up [of] a moral utopia"[27]—the fulfillment of morality and simultaneously its overcoming—is for Kant no illusion, but the goal of politics.

Kant's philosophy reveals utopian elements: they lie not in the idea of a perfect constitution, but rather in his undialectical conception of a continuous approach to it. According to his conviction, all determinations of bourgeois society return to themselves as identical in that final state; only they are better reconciled with each other than in the present. Even Kant regards the categories[28] of the prevailing system as eternal. The order he postulates as a goal would be composed of autonomously acting individuals whose individual decisions smoothly yield the welfare of the whole. This ideal is indeed a utopia; as in every utopia, the yearning thought forms a beautiful vision from the unchanged elements of the present. The harmony of the interests of all in Kant's utopia can only be understood as a preestablished harmony, as a charitable miracle. In contrast, science takes account of the fact that historical transformation also changes the elements of the earlier condition at the same time.

The materialist theory of society overcomes the utopian character of Kant's conception of a perfect constitution. After all, the disparate interests of individuals are not ultimate facts; they have their basis not in an independent psychological constitution, but in the material relations and total social situation of the individual. The absolutely incommensurable disparity of interests derives from the disparity of ownership; human beings today stand against one another as functions of various economic powers, of which each reveals to the other contradictory developmental tendencies. Only when this antagonistic economic form, the introduction of which once meant tremendous progress (including among others things the developmental possibility of self-conscious human beings), has been replaced by a society in which productive property is administered in the general interest, not just from "good intentions" but with rational necessity, will the concordance of individual ends stop appearing miraculous. Individuals will then cease to be merely the exponents of private ends. Each is no longer simply a monad, but rather, in Kant's language, a "joint" or "limb" of society at large [ein "Glied" der Allgemeinheit].

This expression, which characterizes a dynamic element in the moral phenomenon pointing beyond itself to a more rational society, has an unhappy function in modern sociology. It is supposed to prompt human beings, who despair of this mechanism run amok that is contemporary society, to give themselves over blindly to the particular "whole" into whose realm they have fallen by birth or by fate, regardless of the role it happens to play in human history. The organological expression in this connection is understood in a way that runs precisely counter to Kant. Instead of referring to an era in which human relations will really be governed by reason, it points toward outmoded levels of society in which all processes were mediated simply by instinct, tradition, and obedience. Kant employs the image of the organism in order to indicate the frictionless functioning of the future society, but does not thereby deny the role of rational thought. Today, by contrast, the image of the organism characterizes a system of dependency and economic inequality that can no longer justify itself before the mature critical understanding of human beings and which thus requires metaphysical phrases in order to reconcile them to it. The organism is drawn into the matter in order to rationalize—as an eternal relationship based on blind nature—the fact that certain people decide and others execute their decision, a state of affairs made questionable by the growth of all forces. Suffering human beings are supposed to be satisfied today, as in the time of Menenius Agrippa, with the thought that their role in the whole is as innate to them as are the joints in the animal body. Obdurate natural dependency is held up as an example to the members [*Gliedern*] of society. In contradistinction to idealist sociology, which believes that it puts an end to injustice insofar as it strives to remove from people's heads the mounting consciousness of that injustice, Kantian moral theory tends toward a society in which the material arrangements are indeed linked together [*gegliedert*], but in which the development and happiness of individuals is neither subordinated to a sequence of stages nor surrendered up to fate. "That there should be no schism in the body; but that the members should have the same care one for another," as it says in the New Testament.29 With Kant, the organism is defined precisely by the concept of ends. Organic operation, according to him, always refers to the "causality of a concept,"30 that is, to purpose and planning.

In the future society toward which the moral consciousness aspires, the life of the whole and of the individuals is produced not merely as a natural effect, but as the consequence of rational designs that take account of the happiness of the individuals in equal measure. In place of the blind mechanism of economic struggles which presently condition happiness and—for the greater part of humanity—unhappiness emerges the purposive application of the wealth of human and material powers of production. According to Kant, each individual "gives universal laws while also [being] subject to these laws."31 The individual is "legislating" not merely in the juridical sense of formal democracy, but so that it itself, with its possibilities in the total social reality, might find just as much respect as all others. In Kant's sense, no specific totality [*Ganzheit*] has the status of an absolute end, only individuals: only they have reason. Kant demonstrated the idea of this dignified [*menschenwürdigen*] society, in which morality loses its basis, through his analysis of moral consciousness; this dignified society appears as its demand and consequence. Hegel made this society the foundation of his philosophy. According to him, rationality consists concretely in the unity of objective and subjective freedom; that is, in the unity of the general will and the individuals who carry out its ends.32 Naturally Hegel considered this condition—like his liberalistic teachers of political economy [*Nationalökonomie*]—as already realized in his time. Morality as a human power distinct from interest played no major role in his system. With Hegel's definitive metaphysics of history as the driving force, it was no longer necessary. Hegel's concept of Spirit, however, contains the same ideal expressed in the bourgeois world and Kant's philosophy. The theory of its realization leads from philosophy to the critique of political economy.

With the recognition that the will and the appeal to it have their roots in the contemporary mode of production and, like other forms of life, will change with it, morality is simultaneously comprehended and made mortal. In an epoch in which the domination of the possessive instincts is the natural law of humanity, and in which by Kant's definition each individual sees the other above all as a means to his own ends, morality represents the concern for the development and happiness of life as a whole. Even the opponents of traditional morality presuppose such an indeterminate moral sentiment. In the Foreword to *The Genealogy of Morals*, Nietzsche reveals that the materialist question, "Under what conditions did man deem those value judgments good and evil?" is followed immediately by the moral one: "And what value have they themselves? Have they so far inhibited or advanced human development? Are they a sign of need, impoverishment, of deformation of life? Or, on the other hand, do they betray the fullness, the power, the will of life, its courage, its optimism, its future?" As a standard, the universal conception of humanity is as operative here as it is in Kant. Nietzsche, however, commended very perverse means for human liberation in a period when conditions for a more prosperous form of organization were already visible; his challenge to humanity in his time, that it must "set its goal above itself— not in a false world, however, but in one which would be a continuation of human- ity"[33] applies to himself, for his practical suggestions all rest upon a false extrapola- tion. From his psychological investigation of the individuals that act under the natural law of their personal interest he concluded that the universal fulfillment of that for which they strove—namely security and happiness—would have to produce a soci- ety of philistines [Spiessbürger], the world of the "last" men. He failed to recognize that the characteristics of the present which he so detested derive precisely from the dearth of propitious conditions for society at large. With the spread of reason that he feared, with its application to all of the relations of society, those negative characteristics—which in truth rest upon the concentration of all the instincts on private advantage—must be transformed, as must ideas and indeed the drives themselves. Through his ignorance of dialectics Nietzsche foresaw the same "dearth of justice" that Kant had seen. "If it were as we would like, all morality would transform itself into self-interest."[34] But in reality, self-interest would transform itself into morality, or rather the two would merge in a new form of human interest that would accord with the more rational condition. Nietzsche's theory of history misses the mark; he places the end [*Ziel*] in a perverse world, if not quite in another one, because he misunderstands the movement of the contemporary world due to his ignorance of economic laws. His own moral philosophy, however, contains the same elements as that which he struggles against. He fumes against himself.

Bergson claims as well that moral philosophy contains the notion of the progress of humanity. ". . . *de la société réelle dont nous sommes nous nous transportons par la pensée à la société idéale, vers elle montre notre hommage quand nous nous inclinons devant la dignité humaine en nous, quand nous déclarons agir par respect de nous- mêmes.*"[35]* He claims that morality has two aspects: a "natural" one which arises from society's accommodation to its life-conditions—consisting in socially func- tional [*zweckmässigen*] reactions consolidated in customs, characteristic of primi- tive tribes, civilized nations, and brutish associations—and a truly human aspect, the "*élan d'amour.*" This second aspect contains within itself "*le sentiment d'un*

* ". . . from the real society, of which we are a part, we transport ourselves in thought to the ideal society, we pay homage to it when we bow before the human dignity in us, when we declare that we act out of respect for ourselves" [Ed.]

progrès"[36]* and is no longer oriented to the preservation and security of the particular association to which the individual happens to belong, but is oriented rather to humanity. The difference between the two aspects, one of which appears as the *"pression sociale"*† and the other as the *"marche en avant,"*‡ is none other than Kant's distinction between natural law and respect for humanity. Even today Bergson's vision extends deep enough to hit upon the distinction between publicly esteemed sentiment and forward-pointing morality. The *"tendances innées et fondamentales de l'homme actuel"*[37]§ are aimed at family, interest formations, and nation, and necessarily include possible enmity between groups. Hate, but not in the least the solidarity of forward-pointing moral sentiment, belongs to this purposeful [*zweckvoller*] love. *"C'est qu'entre la nation, si grande soit-elle, et l'humanité, il y a toute la distance du fini à l'indéfini, du clos à l'ouvert."*[38]‖ As with Nietzsche, Bergson indeed loses his sharpness of vision in the face of the question of how the ideal society prescribed by genuine morality is to be realized, which of the present forces work against it, who promulgates it, and who sides with it. Here he repeats the theory of the heroes, *"dont chacun représente, comme eût fait l'apparition d'une nouvelle espéce, un effort d'évolution créatrice."*[39]# According to old superstition they are to arise only in isolation and at the beginning of long periods of time. Indeed, Bergson is so certain of their rarity that he forgets to ask whether today these heroes of the *"société idéale"*** might not ultimately exist in abundance and in struggles, unless philosophers were to regard them in a manner other than that which is peculiar to the "closed soul." In this forgetting, in the indifference to the mortal struggles for that society which is anticipated in morality, in the deficient connection with the forces which are driving forward, is that bit of immorality which can presently be discovered even in genuine philosophy.

Materialism sees morality as the life expression of determinate individuals and seeks to understand it in terms of the conditions for its emergence and passing away, not for the sake of truth in itself, but in connection with determinate historical forces. Materialism understands itself as the effort to abolish existing misery. The features it discerns in the historical phenomenon of morality figure into its consideration only on the condition of a determinate practical interest. Materialism presumes no transhistorical authority behind morality. The fear which moral precepts—be they ever so spiritualized—still carry from their origin in religious authority is foreign to mate-

---

* "the feeling of progress" [Ed.]

† "social pressure" [Ed.]

‡ "march forward" [Ed.]

§ "innate and fundamental tendencies in man today" [Ed.]

‖ "Between the nation, as big as it may be, and humanity, there is the entire distance from the finite to the indefinite, from the closed to the open" [Ed.]

". . . of which each one represents, as would have done the appearance of a new species, an effort of creative evolution" [Ed.]

** "ideal society" [Ed.]

rialism. The consequences of all human actions work themselves out exclusively in the spatio-temporal world. As long as they have no effect on their author [*Urheber*] in this world, he has nothing to fear from them. Even the splendor in which philosophers—as well as public opinion in general—cloak "ethical" conduct, all arguments by which they recommend it, cannot withstand the test of reason. With the notion that one could investigate the "field of distinctive values"[40] in a manner similar to other inquiries, the "value research" of Scheler and Hartmann has only hit upon another method of the solution of an impossible task; the grounding of practices in mere philosophy. The very idea of a science of "the structure and order of the realm of values" necessarily entails such a promulgation of commandments. For even if this knowledge is characterized as "in a rudimentary stage,"[41] an "Ought[42]," which in certain cases is transformed "into the Ought-to-Do of the subject,"[43] still clings to all values the ethicist strives to discover. Despite the explanation that decision is constantly in the conscience of the subject, and despite the universality that indeed belongs to the essence of the philosophical doctrine of morality, it is claimed that there exist differences of degree in behavior conformity: "Thus, for example, brotherly love is evidently higher in value than justice, love for the remotest higher than brotherly love, and personal love (as it appears) higher than either. Likewise bravery stands higher than self-control, faith and fidelity higher than bravery, radiant virtue and personality again higher than these."[44] But such assertions, whose content moreover is only diffusely connected with moral sentiment due to the reactionary character of philosophy since Kant, have the same commandmentlike character of the categorical imperative. They are the mystified expression of spiritual [*seelische*] states of affairs in which "*pression social*" and "*élan d'amour*" indeed enter into a connection which is difficult to analyze. There is no eternal realm of values. The needs and wishes, the interests and passions of human beings change in relation to the historical process. Psychology and other auxiliary sciences of history must join together to explain the accepted values and their change at any given time.

Binding moral laws do not exist. Materialism finds no transcendent authority over human beings which would distinguish between goodwill and the lust for profit, kindness and cruelty, avarice and self-sacrifice. Logic likewise remains silent and grants no pre-eminence to moral conviction. All attempts to ground morality in terms of temporal prudence rather than the hereafter—as the cited examples show, even Kant didn't resist this inclination—are based on an illusion of harmony. First of all, in most cases morality and prudence diverge. Morality does not admit of any grounding—neither by means of intuition nor of argument. But it does involve a psychic constitution. To describe the latter, to make its personal conditions and its mechanisms of transmission intelligible, is the business of psychology. Characteristic of moral sentiment is an interest which diverges from "natural law" and which has nothing to do with private acquisition and possession. At present all human impulses are determined, whether through such law or mere convention. It follows from the definitions of the bourgeois thinkers that in this period even love falls under the category of property. *"Videmus . . . quod ille, qui amat necessario conatur rem, quam amat, praesentum habere et conservare,"** says Spinoza.[45] Kant describes marriage as the "joining together of two people of the opposite sex for the lifelong mutual ownership of their sexual attributes"[46] and speaks of the "equality of possessions" of the married couple not merely in terms of material goods, but also in terms of "two people who mutually own each other."[47] Modern accounts, if not completely ideological, still contain similar definitions. According to Freud, the sexual aim of the infantile instinct [*Trieb*], in which according to his teachings the essential features of the instinctual life of the adult are also to be discovered, consists in "obtaining satisfaction by means of an appropriate stimulation of the [selected] erotogenic zone . . ."[48] Accordingly, the loved person appears mainly as the means to fulfill said stimulation. On this point, one is struck by the way in which Freud's theory is an elaboration of Kant's definition of marriage.

Moral sentiment is to be distinguished from this kind of love, and Kant is right to distinguish the former not only from egoism, but from any such "inclination." He indicates the psychic state of affairs by his doctrine that in morality (as opposed to that which is the rule in the bourgeois world), a person is to be not simply a means, but always at the same time an end. Moral sentiment has something to do with love, for "love, reverence, yearning for perfection, longing, all these things are inherent in an end."[49] However, this love has nothing to do with the person as economic subject or as an item in the property of the one who loves, but rather as a potential member of a happy humanity. It is not directed at the role and standing of a particular individual in civil life, but at its needs and powers, which point towards the future. Unless the aim of a future happy life for all men, which admittedly arises not on the basis of a revelation but out of the privation of the present, is included in the description of this love, it proves impossible to define. Love wishes the free development of the creative powers of all human beings as such. To love it appears as if all living beings have a claim to happiness, for which it would not in the least ask any justification or grounds. It stands in primordial contradiction to stringency, even though there may be psychic processes which sustain both moments in themselves. In bourgeois society, training in strict morality more often stood in service to natural law rather than under the badge of liberation from it. Not the rod of punishment, but the climax of the Ninth Symphony is the expression of moral sentiment.

This sentiment is active today in a twofold manner. First, as compassion. In Kant's period social production mediated by private acquisition was progressive; today it signifies the senseless crippling of powers and their misuse for purposes of destruction. The struggle of great economic power groups, played out on a world scale, is conducted amid the atrophy of kind human inclinations, the proclamation of overt and covert lies, and the development of an immeasurable hatred. Humanity has

---

* "We see that the man who loves necessarily attempts to keep at hand and to retain that which he loves" [Ed.].

become so rich in the bourgeois period, and has at its disposal such great natural and human auxiliary powers, that it could exist united by worthy objectives. The need to veil this state of affairs, which is transparent in every respect, gives rise to a sphere of hypocrisy which extends not only to international relations, but which penetrates into even the most private relations; it results in a diminution of cultural endeavors (including science) and a brutalization of personal and public life, such that spiritual and material misery are compounded. At no time has the poverty of humanity stood in such crying contradiction to its potential wealth, at no time have all powers been so horribly fettered as in this generation, where children go hungry and the hands of the fathers are busy turning out bombs. It appears as if the world is being driven into a catastrophe—rather, as if it already finds itself in one—which can only be compared, within known history, to the fall of antiquity. The futility of the fate of the individual, already caused by the irrationality and barren naturalness of the production process, has risen to the most striking characteristic of contemporary existence. Whoever is fortunate could, as regards their inner worth, just as easily take the place of the most unfortunate, and vice-versa. Everyone is given up to blind chance. The course of one's existence has no relation to one's inner possibilities; one's role in the present society has for the most part no relation to that which could be achieved in a rational society. Accordingly, the behavior of the moral agent is not capable of being oriented to one's dignity; the extent to which dispositions and deeds are really meritorious does not come to light in the chaotic present, "the real morality of actions, their merit or guilt, even that of our own conduct, . . . remains entirely hidden from us."[50] We view human beings not as subjects of their fate, but rather as objects of a blind occurrence of nature, to which the response of a moral sentiment is compassion.

That Kant did not see compassion as based on a moral sentiment can be explained in terms of the historical situation. He could expect from the uninterrupted progress of free competition an increase in general happiness, for he beheld the coming of a world dominated by this principle. All the same, even in his time compassion could not be separated from morality. As long as the individual and the whole have not really become one, as long as it is not the case that the easy death of the individual freed from fear is looked upon by the individual itself as something external, because he rightly knows his essential purposes to be looked after by society at large—as long, therefore, as morality still has a reason for existence—compassion will have its place in it. Indeed, compassion may outlast it; for morality belongs to that determinate form of human relations based on the bourgeois mode of production. With the transformation of these relations through their rational arrangement, morality will, at the very least, step into the background. Human beings may then struggle in concert against their own pains and maladies—what medicine will achieve, once it is freed from its present social fetters, is not to be foreseen—although suffering and death will continue to hold sway in nature. The solidarity of human beings, however, is a part of the solidarity of life in general. The progress in the realization of the one will also strengthen the inclination toward the other. Animals need human beings [*Die*

Tiere bedürfen des Menschen]. It is the accomplishment of Schopenhauer's philosophy to have wholly illuminated the unity between us and them. The greater gifts of human beings, above all reason, do not annul [*aufheben*] the communion which they feel with animals. While the traits of human beings have a certain impact, the relationship of their happiness and misery with the life of animals is manifest.

The other form in which morality today finds appropriate expression is politics. The happiness of the general public is consistently characterized as its proper aim by the great moral philosophers. To be sure, Kant had to deceive himself about the structure of future society, since he considered the form of the contemporary one to be eternal. The materialist critique of political economy was the first to show that the realization of the ideal, in terms of which the present society was established—namely the union of general and particular interest—can take place only by transforming its conditions. Today it is claimed that the bourgeois ideals of Freedom, Equality, and Justice have proven themselves to be poor ones; however, it is not the ideals of the bourgeoisie but conditions which do not correspond to them that are untenable. The battle-cries of the Enlightenment and of the French Revolution are valid now more than ever. The dialectical critique of the world, which is borne along by them, consists precisely in the demonstration that they have retained their actuality rather than lost it on the basis of reality. These ideas and values are nothing but the isolated traits of the rational society, as they are anticipated in morality as a necessary goal. Politics in accord with this goal therefore must not abandon these demands, but realize them—not, however, by clinging in a utopian manner to definitions which are historically conditioned [*zeitbedingt*]—but in conformity with their meaning. The content of the ideas is not eternal, but is subject to historical change—not, as one might suppose, because "Spirit" of itself capriciously infringed upon the principle of identity—but because the human impulses which demand something better take different forms according to the historical material with which they have to work. The unity of such concepts results less from the invariability of their elements than from the historical development of the circumstances under which their realization is necessary.

In materialist theory, the main point is not to maintain concepts unchanged, but to improve the lot of humanity [*Allgemeinheit*]. In the struggle to achieve this, ideas have altered their content. Today, the freedom of the individual demands submitting their economic independence to a plan. The presupposition of the ideas of Equality and Justice hitherto was the prevailing inequality of economic and human subjects; these presuppositions disappear in a unified society, for therein these ideas lose their meaning. "Equality exists only in contrast to inequality, justice to injustice; they are therefore still burdened with the contrast to the old, previous history, hence with the old society itself."[51] Hitherto, these concepts took their determinate content from the relations of the free market, which with time were supposed to function to the benefit of all. Today they have transformed themselves into the concrete image of a better society, which will be born out of the present one, if humanity does not first sink into barbarism.

The concept of Justice, which played a decisive role as a battle-cry in the struggle for a rational organization of society, is older than morality. It is as old as class society, i.e., as old as known European history itself. As a universal principle to be realized in this world, Justice, in connection with Freedom and Equality, first found recognition in bourgeois philosophy; though only today have the resources of humanity become great enough for their adequate realization as an immediate historical task. The intense struggle for their fulfillment marks our epoch of transition.

In previous history, every task of culture was possible only on the basis of a division between ruler and ruled. The suffering that is connected with the continual reproduction of the masses at a particular level and especially with every advance, which, so to speak, represents the social costs, has never been distributed equitably. The reason for this is not to be found, as the high-minded philosophers of the eighteenth century thought, in the avarice and depravity of the rulers, but in the disproportion between the powers and needs of human beings. Right up till the present, the general level of development of the whole of society (including the upper class) conditioned, in view of the available tools, the subordination of the masses at work and thus in life generally. Their coarseness corresponded to the inability of the rulers to raise them to a higher stage of development, and both moments were constantly reproduced along with the harshness of social life, which changes only slowly. Historical humanity, in danger of sinking into chaos, had no choice but to abandon the relation of domination. The emergence and dissemination of cultural values cannot be separated from this division. Leaving aside the material goods which result from a production process based on the division of labor, the products of art and science, the refined forms of intercourse among men, their sense of an intellectual life, all point to their origin in a society which distributes burdens and pleasures unequally.

It has often been asserted that class division, which has left its imprint on all previous history, is a continuation of the inequality in nature. The genera of animals may be divided up into predators and prey, such that some genera are both at the same time, whereas others are principally only one of the two. Even within genera there are spatially separated groups, which appear to be in part blessed by fortune, in part pursued by a series of inconceivable blows of fate. In turn, the pain and death of the individuals within the groups and genera are unequally distributed, and depend on circumstances which lack any meaningful connection to the life of the those so affected. The inequality which is constantly determined by the lifeprocess of society is related to that inequality which pertains to the whole of nature. Both of these permeate the life of humanity, in that the natural diversity of external form and abilities, not to mention diseases and further circumstances of death, further complicate social inequality. Of course, the degree to which these natural differences are operative in society depends on historical development; they have different consequences at the various levels of different social structures: the appearance of the same disease can mean quite different things for members of different social circles. Attention, pedagogical artifice, and a range of gratifications afford the poorly gifted wealthy child the opportunity to develop the aptitudes which still remain, whereas the slow child of poor people struggling for existence will go to ruin mentally as well as physically: this child's shortcomings will be intensified throughout its life, its hopeful first steps will come to nothing.

In this history of humanity, in which inequality constitutes such a fundamental trait, a certain human reaction repeatedly became apparent, whether as its other side or as its effect. The abolition of inequality has been demanded at different times and in different places by not only the dominated classes, but renegades from the ruling classes who pronounced inequality evil. The equality which was to be brought about (and which, in the materialist view, developed with the exchange relationship) has been understood in various ways. From the basic demand that everyone should receive an equal share of the consumer goods produced by society (e.g., in early Christendom) to the proposition that to each should be allotted that share which corresponds to their labor (e.g., Proudhon), to the thought that the most sensitive should be the least burdened (Nietzsche), there is an exceedingly wide range of ideas about the correct state of affairs. All of them make reference to the point that happiness, insofar as it is possible for each person in comparison with others on the basis of their lot in society, is not to be determined by fortuitous, capricious factors which are external to the individual—in other words: that the degree of inequality of the life-conditions of individuals at least be no greater than that dictated by the maintenance of the total social supply of goods at the given level. That is the universal content of the concept of Justice; according to this concept, the social inequality prevailing at any given time requires a rational foundation. It ceases to be considered as Good, and becomes something that should be overcome.

It is an achievement of recent times to have made this principle universal. Yet in this same period there has certainly been no lack of defenders of inequality and eulogists for the blindness in nature and society. But if philosophers representative of past epochs, such as Aristotle and Thomas Aquinas, had extolled the differences in people's fate as an eternal value, then the Enlightenment (in connection with old humanistic doctrines, to be sure) described inequality as an evil to be abolished. In the French Revolution, Equality was raised to a principle of the constitution. Recognition of this principle was not mere inspiration or, in Bergson's terms, an incursion of open morality into the sphere of closed morality. Rather its recognition belonged in that epoch to the process whereby the entire society conformed to the changing life-conditions. The latter puts this recognition into effect on the strength of the dynamic residing in it, as with every living being, both continuously as well as by leaps and bounds. The idea of Equality "*résulte logiquement des transformations réelle de nos sociétés.*"52* The idea of Equality necessarily brings that of Freedom to the fore. If indeed no individual is initially less worthy than another of developing and finding satisfaction in reality, it follows that the utilization of coercion by one group against the other must be acknowledged as evil. The concept of Justice is as inseparable from that of Freedom as it is from that of Equality.

* ". . . results logically from the real transformations of our societies" [Ed.]

From the beginning, the proclamation of Equality as a constitutional principle was not only an advance for thought, but a danger as well. As the sublation of determinate inequalities (which were no longer necessary, which were indeed hindrances in the context of the expanded powers of human beings) in fact came to pass in the new constellation of legal relations, this step was proclaimed withal as the realization of Equality in general. It became unclear whether the social equality of human beings was still a demand to be met or a description of reality. The French Revolution had not only helped the universal concept of Justice to gain theoretical recognition, but had to a great extent realized it at that time as well. This concept came to dominate the ideas of the nineteenth century and turned into the decisive feature of all thought, indeed even into the feeling of the European and American world. But the institutions which at the time aptly embodied the principle have grown old, as has the overall constitution of bourgeois society. At the time, equality before the law had signified a step forward in the direction of Justice, inequality of property notwithstanding; today it has become inadequate because of this economic inequality. Freedom of public expression was a weapon in the struggle for better conditions; today it acts primarily to the advantage of conditions which have become obsolete. Sanctity of property was a protection of bourgeois labor against the clutches of the authorities; today it brings in its wake monopolization, the expropriation of additional bourgeois strata and the tying up of social resources.

The alliance struck between the ruling power and the ideas of the bourgeoisie since the victory of the French Revolution confounds thought for this reason: these propelling ideas are alienated from and set against their logical proponents, the progressive forces of society. But it is precisely in the present, as humanity confronts the danger of ruin, that humanity is charged with their realization. The abolition of economic inequality, which would soon have to lead to a far-reaching abolition of the distinction between the rulers and ruled, signifies for the first time today not an abandonment of cultural values, but on the contrary their redemption. While the unequal distribution of power was among the prerequisites of culture in earlier epochs, today it has become a threat to the same. Forces which benefit from wretched social relations presently make use of those ideas to avert the possible change needed by humanity. They snatch these ideas from those who have a genuine interest in their realization. The present confusion in the ideological [weltanschaulichem] domain is a consequence of this. The provisions of justice, which today find expression in the institutions of a merely formal democracy and in the ideas of those raised in its spirit, have lost any clear connection to their origin. Otherwise, they would now be levelled at the ruling powers which fetter the development of humanity, just as they were during the time when the latter understood the bourgeoisie itself in a productive sense—except that today the change would signify a much more decisive step. However, although the powerful themselves have for centuries proclaimed the principles of a good order to be holy, they are willing to twist them around or betray them the instant that their meaningful application no longer serves their interest, but runs against it. Indeed, they are ready to throw overboard and pull from the curriculum all the ideals which the fathers of the bourgeois revolution championed, worked for, and fought for, as soon as people are developed and desperate enough to no longer apply them mechanically to the preservation of institutions, but to apply them dialectically to the realization of a better order. In many places, the requirements of internal and external control entail that all progressive elements of bourgeois morality be stifled or deliberately eliminated. There is a steady increase in the number of countries where those values that aim at the happiness of individuals have fallen into disrepute; it appears that the period in which the bourgeois world produced morality was too short to be maintained at the level of generality in flesh and blood. It is not only secular morality which rests on such shaky ground; the same can be said of whatever elements of kindness and charity made their way into the soul as a result of Christianity (the civilizing influence which preceded secular morality), such that in a few decades even these forces could atrophy. The moral sentiment in governments, peoples, and spokesmen of the civilized [*gebildeten*] world is so weak that, although it is indeed expressed at gatherings on the occasions of earthquakes and mine disasters, it is nevertheless easily silenced and forgotten in the face of the monstrous injustice which takes place for the sake of pure property interests, i.e., in the enforcement of the "natural law" and amidst the mockery of all bourgeois values.

The appeal to morality is more powerless than ever, but it is not even needed. In contrast to the idealistic belief in the cry of conscience as a decisive force in history, this hope is foreign to materialist thinking. Yet because materialism itself belongs to the efforts to attain a better society, it well knows where the elements of morality that are pushing forward are active today. They are produced time and again, under the immense pressure which weighs heavily upon a large segment of society, in the will to create rational relations which correspond to the present state of development. The part of humanity which necessarily counts on this change, due to its situation, already contains (and attracts ever more) forces for whom realizing a better society is a matter of great importance. It is also psychologically prepared for it, since its role in the production process forces it to rely less on the unlikely increase of property than on the employment of its labor power. These conditions facilitate the generation of personalities in which the acquisitive instincts are not of prime importance. If the inheritance of morality thus passes on to new classes, there are nevertheless many proletarians who exhibit those bourgeois traits under the domination of the natural law.[53] The works of later bourgeois writers such as Zola, Maupassant, Ibsen, and Tolstoy constitute testimonials to moral goodness. But in any case, the common efforts of that part of humanity guided by knowledge contain so much genuine solidarity with respect to their liberation, and that of all of humanity, so little concern about their private existence, so few thoughts of possessions and property, that they already seem to manifest the sensibility [*Lebensgefühl*] of a future humanity. In existing society, the putative consciousness of equality generally overlooks the actual inequality in human beings, and thus embraces untruth, whereas the forces pressing for change place actual inequality in the forefront. The authentic concept of Equality contains knowledge of its negative: contemporary human beings differ not only in terms of economic fortunes, but also in terms of their intellectual and moral qualities. A Bavarian farmer differs radically from a factory worker in Berlin. But the certainty that the differences are based on transient conditions—and above all that inequalities of power and happiness, as they have become entrenched today through the structure of society, no longer correspond to the developed forces of production—engenders a respect for the inner possibilities of the individual and for that "which can be made out of him" (Kant), a feeling of independence and goodwill, which politics must positively connect with if it is concerned to build a free society.

There is no obligation to this politics, any more than there is an obligation to compassion. Obligations refer back to commands and contracts, which do not exist in this case. Nonetheless, materialism recognizes in compassion, as well as in progressive politics, productive forces historically related to bourgeois morality. According to materialism, however, not just the explicit forms of command, but the ideas of duty and metaphysical obligation [*Schuld*], and above all the maligning of desire and pleasure constrain the present social dynamic. Materialist theory certainly does not afford to the political actor the solace that he will necessarily achieve his objective; it is not a metaphysics of history, but rather a changing image of the world, evolving in relation to the practical efforts towards its improvement. The knowledge of tendencies contained in this image offers no clear prognosis of historical development. Even if those who maintain that the theory could be misleading "only" in regard to the pace of development and not its direction, were correct (a frightful "only," since it concerns the agonies of generations), merely formal time could, after all, turn around and affect the quality of the content, i.e., humanity could be thrown back to earlier stages of development simply because the struggle lasted too long. But even the sheer certainty that such a new order would come to pass would not alone provide even the slightest of grounds on which to affirm or precipitate this new order. That something in the world gains power is no reason to revere it. The ancient myth of the rulers, that that which has power must also be good, passed into occidental philosophy by way of Aristotle's doctrine of the unity of reality and perfection. Protestantism reaffirmed this myth in its belief in God as the lord of history and the regulator of the world. It dominates the whole of life in present-day Europe and America. The blind worship of success determines men even in the most private expressions of life. For the materialist, the mere presence of a historical force, or its prospects, does not constitute its recommendation. The materialist asks how this historical force, at a given moment, relates to materialist values and acts according to the concrete situation. In the prevailing social conditions, such action is burdened by the unhappy situation that compassion and politics, the two forms in which moral sentiment finds expression today can only rarely be brought into rational relationship. Regard for those close at hand and those far away, support for the individual and for humanity are contradictory in most cases. Even the best harden some place in their hearts.

The insight that morality cannot be proven, that not a single value admits of a purely theoretical grounding, separates materialism from the idealist currents of philosophy. But both the derivation and the concrete application of the principle within the sphere of knowledge [*Wissenschaft*] are completely different. In idealist philosophy this principle is necessarily connected with the doctrine of the absolutely free subject. Just as the subject (at least according to later exponents) supposedly produces knowledge of itself, so too is the positing of value thought to be subjective. Without any foundation at all, it issues from autonomous Spirit, from "the intellectus." Nikolaus Cusanus already teaches: "But for the power of judgement and of comparison there ceases to be any evaluation, and with it value must fall as well. Herefrom springs the wonder of the mind since without it everything created would have been without value."[54] Even though, according to Cusanus, the autonomous subject does not of itself produce the *essence* of value, it nonetheless freely decides how much of that essence is accorded to each object. In this creative activity, it is supposed to be similar to God, even, as it were, another God itself. Since Cusanus, this doctrine has been definitive in science and philosophy. Thus, the differences in the value of things are by no means material; the object in itself is indifferent to value. Science can indeed describe the human acts which posit value, but cannot itself decide among them. In modern methodology this principle is formulated as the demand for value-neutrality [*Wertfreiheit*]. Max Weber's view is characteristic of the main tendencies of idealistic philosophy (with the exception of theories of objective value), which display mostly romantic, or in any case anti-democratic tendencies. It is his view "that we are *cultural* beings, endowed with the capacity and the will to take a deliberate attitude towards the world and to lend it significance . . . Undoubtedly, all evaluative ideas are 'subjective.' "[55] As a result of this doctrine, idealist philosophy and science rule out any value judgement. Indeed, in recent decades it has increasingly been made a duty of the human or cultural sciences not to develop a connection with larger social objectives, but establish and classify "theory-free" facts. The application of earlier bourgeois objectives—above all the greatest happiness of all— to those areas of inquiry [*Wissenschaften*] would necessarily lead to increasing conflicts. In the original works of the bourgeoisie these motives are absolutely decisive. Even the originators of positivism defended themselves against the neutral degeneration of knowledge [*Wissenschaft*], in contrast to many of their later disciples. "The 'dispersive speciality' of the present race of scientific men," writes John Stuart Mill in his work on Auguste Comte, "who, unlike their predecessors, have a positive aversion to enlarged views, and seldom either know or care for any of the interests of mankind beyond the narrow limits of their pursuit, is dwelt on by M. Comte as one of the great and growing evils of the time, and the one which most retards moral and intellectual regeneration. To contend against it is one of the main purposes towards which he thinks the forces of society should be directed."[56] Such voices are rare among today's progressive scholars. They must be satisfied with defending their work against the increasing predominance of those who, without respect for rigor or integrity, would like knowledge to return to its subjugation under questionable goals, and would reduce it to the hand-maiden of whatever power happens to hold sway. In seeking to protect knowledge and the interest in truth from the present invading barbarism, those scholars render a service to civilization similar to where, through education, genuine bourgeois values still have respect in the public mind.[57]

Materialism recognizes the unconditional respect for truth as a necessary if not sufficient condition of science. It knows that interests stemming from social and personal circumstances also condition research, whether the researcher [der Urheber der Wissenschaft] at any given time knows it or not. On both a small and a large scale, historical factors are operative not only in the choice of objects, but in the direction of attention and abstraction as well. In each case, the result has its origin in a determinate interrelation between investigators and objects. But in contrast to idealist philosophy, materialism does not trace the interests and objectives that are operative on the part of the subject back to the independent creative activity of this subject, to free will. On the contrary, they are themselves seen as a result of a development in which both subjective and objective moments have a part. Even exchange value in the economy is not based on free valuation, but rather ensues from the life-process of society, in which use-values are determining factors. The undialectical concept of the free subject is foreign to materialism. Materialism is also well aware of itself as conditioned. Apart from personal nuances, this latter is to be sought in connection with those forces devoted to the realization of the aims stated above. Because materialist science never takes its eyes from these aims, it does not assume the character of false impartiality, but is consciously biased [akzentuiert]. It is concerned not so much with originality as with the extension of the theoretical knowledge already attained on this course.

Materialism breaks from present-day positivism in its acknowledgment of the decisive significance of theory, as contrasted with the mere compiling of facts. Certainly no such division pertains between materialism and concrete research, which often arrive at the same findings [Erkenntnisse]. Some positivists have grasped the relation of morality and praxis to theory through an intimate acquaintance with social problems. "Loin que la pratique se déduise de la théorie, c'est la théorie qui, jusqu'à présent, est une sorte de projection abstraite de la morale pratiquée dans une société donnée, à une époque donnée."[58*] Theory is a cohesive body of insights [Zusammenhang von Erkenntnissen] stemming from a determinate praxis and out of determinate objectives. The world reveals a consistent image to whomever looks at it from a consistent point of view—an image which changes, to be sure, with the historicity of acting and knowing individuals. Praxis already organizes the material of individual knowing. The demand to establish theory-free facts is false, it this is to mean that subjective factors are not already operative in the given objective facts. Understood productively, it can only mean that the description is veracious [wahrhaftig]. The whole cognitive structure from which every description gets its meaning, and which description should serve in return, even theory itself ranks among the strivings

---

* "Far from the practice being deduced from the theory, it is the theory which, up until now, is a sort of abstract projection of the morality practiced in a given society, at a given time" [Ed.].

of the human beings that create it. These may arise from private whims, from reactionary interests, or from the needs of a developing humanity.

NOTES

1. Translators' comment on some terms in the article: *Allgemeinheit*: As used by Horkheimer, this term usually has a triple meaning that encompasses the Kantian "universality," the Hegelian "generality," and the more common meaning "society at large." Where the term contains all three of these aspects (which in "Materialism and Morality" is most of the time), it has been rendered as "generality." The term is thus quasi-technical in the translation, since it connotes "society at large" much more weakly than does "*Allgemeinheit*." It is nevertheless the least distorting among the possible choices; where the term more strongly has one of the other connotations, it has been rendered either as "universality" or "society at large."

Aufheben: The choice for the translator in regard to this bugaboo is to either render it according to whether it is used "positively" (supercede, transcend) or "negatively" (annul, abolish), or to pick one term and render it consistently. Although the former alternative is often chosen by translators of material from the Hegelian and Marxist traditions, we have opted for the latter alternative and have chosen the homely "sublate" or "sublation" wherever it has the Hegelian/Marxist shading, which it most often does. Although this technical term was once derided as "baroque" in this journal, none of the other available renderings in English carry both the positive and negative senses of the term (supersession comes the closest, but still connotes neither the *preservation* of contradiction at a higher level of unity, nor any sense of annulment) or sustains this unity in opposition across contexts. Cf. *The Logic of Hegel* [the *Lesser Logic*, tr. Wm. Wallace, 2nd ed., London, 1904, p. 180, and *The Science of Logic*, tr. A.V. Miller, London, 1969, pp. 106f.]

Gebot: In light of Kant's use of the term, we find the usual "precept" (Beck's choice) too weak and "command" (Paton's choice) too imprecise. *Ein Gebot* has the character of a *law*, with all the connotations of universality that this term has in Kant. Neither "precept" nor "command" catches this. At one point in the *Grundlegung*, Kant in fact equates "*Gesetze*" and "*Gebote*" (Akadamie-Ausgabe, p. 416). We therefore have adopted the term "commandment," which is also the rendering in the English abstract of "*Materialisimus und Moral*" that is appended to the original in the *Zeitschrift für Sozialforschung*. Although the German "*Gebot*" does not inherently have the strong biblical connotation of "commandment," neither do we feel this connotation to be completely off the mark, either. The term "precept" we have reserved for "[*moralische*] *Vorschrift*."

Moral: In the above mentioned English abstract of "*Materialismus und Moral*," the title is rendered "Materialism and Ethics." However, Horkheimer consistently distinguishes *Ethik* from *Moral* in the article; while both could be rendered as "moral philosophy," only the latter retains the connotation of a moment in the totality, and since this is the primary focus of the article, we have retained this distinction and always rendered derivatives of *Ethik* as "ethics" or "ethical," and *Moral* as "morality" or "moral philosophy."

moralisches Gefühl: In their translations of Kant's *Grundlegung zur Metaphysik der Sitten*, both H.J. Paton and L.W. Beck render this as "moral feeling." Yet the term in German is Kant's own rendering of "moral sentiment," the term used by the Scottish moralists, whose "heteronomous" ethical theories Kant is (often only implicitly) criticizing in the *Grundlegung*; we have thus always rendered it as "moral sentiment" (which is also the rendering that appears in the *ZfS*'s abstract mentioned above).

Wissenschaft: "Science" is always a translation of *Wissenschaft*, but this latter term can also mean "scholarship," "knowledge," etc., depending on the context. Its connotations are as philosophical and humanities-oriented as they are "scientistic," which should be borne in mind as the word "science" is encountered in the article.

2. Cf. esp. Manich. 6.
3. Cf. *Gesammelte Schriften* [*Collected Writings*] vol. II, Leipzig and Berlin, 1921, p. 110 ff.
4. Nicolai Hartmann, *Ethics*, vol. 1, tr. Stanton Coit, London, 1932, p. 29.
5. Nicolai Hartmann, *Ethics*, vol. 2, tr. Stanton Coit, London, 1932, p. 285.
6. *Ethics*, vol. 1, p. 30.
7. Kant, *Foundations of the Metaphysics of Morals*, tr. Louis White Beck, New York, 1959, p. 39.
8. *Ibid.*, p. 50.
9. *Ibid.*, pp. 67ff.
10. Schopenhauer, *The Basis of Morality*, tr. Author B. Bullock, London, 1915, p. 99.
11. [Translators' note: "moralisch Triebfeder"—in Kant's own technical language, this is actually a contradiction in terms; cf. *Grundlegung zur Metaphysik der Sitten*. Ak. Aus. p. 63. "Impulsion" follows Paton's rendering in his translation of the *Grundlegung*: Beck renders this as "incentive," but also recommends "urge."]
12. Kant, *Critique of Practical Reason*. tr. L.W. Beck, Indianapolis, 1956, p. 89.
13. The psychological theory of conscience, as developed for example by Freud in his work *The Ego and the Id*, (tr. James Strachey, New York, 1960, pp. 18ff., esp. p. 27), is thoroughly reconcilable with this explanation. Psychology provides knowledge about the mechanism by which the predisposition for morality reproduces itself and strikes firm roots in the individual. The ground of existence of this mechanism, however, lies deeper than in the individual soul.
14. Cf. e.g., *Foundations*, p. 51.
15. *Ibid.*, p. 39.
16. Hume, "On Suicide," in Hume's *Ethical Writings*, ed. Alasdair MacIntyre, London, 1965, pp. 304–305.
17. Cf. Kant, Akademie-Ausgabe, vol. 8, pp. 425ff. ["Über ein vermeintliches Recht, aus Menschenliebe zu lügen"].
18. "De L'Esprit," *Oeuvres complètes*, Part I (London, 1780) p. 206.
19. Kant, "Perpetual Peace," in *On History*, ed. Louis White Beck, New York, 1963, p. 117.
20. *Ibid.*, p. 129.
21. *Ibid.*, p. 134.
22. *Ibid.*, p. 127.
23. Cf. Kant, *Critique of Pure Reason*, tr. Norman Kemp Smith, New York, St. Martin's Press, 1965, p. 312.
24. *Ibid.*
25. "Perpetual Peace," p. 121. [Translators' note: in the original, Horkheimer cites p. 370 of the Ak. Aus.; in fact, the passage is to be found on p. 373 of the same.]
26. *Ibid.*

27. Schopenhauer, *op. cit.*, p. 100.
28. [Translators' note: reading the *"Kategorie"* of the original as *"Kategorien."*]
29. 1 Corinthians, Ch. 12, Verse 25.
30. Cf. Kant, *The Critique of Judgement*, tr. James C. Meredith, London, 1952, section 10, p. 61 (First Part) and section 64, pp. 16ff. (Second Part).
31. Kant, *Foundations, op. cit.*, p. 52.
32. Cf. e.g., *Hegel's Philosophy of Right*, tr. T. M. Knox, London, Oxford, and New York, 1952, Sec. 258, pp. 155ff.
33. "Explanatory Notes to *Thus Spake Zarathustra*," tr. Anthony M. Ludovici, in *The Complete Works of Friedrich Nietzsche*, vol. 16, ed. Oscar Levy, New York, 1964 (reissue), p. 269.
34. Kant, *"Reflexionen zur Metaphysik,"* in *Handschriftlicher Nachlass*, Akademie Edition, vol. 18, p. 454.
35. *Les deux sources de la morale et de la religion.* Paris, 1932, p. 66.
36. *Ibid.*, p. 41.
37. *Ibid.*, p. 54.
38. *Loc. cit.*
39. *Ibid.*, p. 98.
40. Hartmann, *Ethics*, vol. 1, p. 86.
41. *Ethics*, vol. 2, p. 23.
42. *Ethics*, vol. 1, p. 247.
43. *Ibid.*, p. 259.
44. *Ethics*, vol. 2, p. 387.
45. Spinoza, *Ethica*, Pars III, Propos. XIII, Schol.
46. *Metaphysische Anfangsgründe der Rechtslehre*, Sec. 24, Akademie-Ausgabe, vol. 6, p. 277.
47. *Ibid.*, sec. 26, p. 278.
48. Freud, *Three Essays on the Theory of Sexuality*, tr. James Strachey, New York, 1962, p. 50.
49. Nietzsche, *loc. cit.*, modified translation.
50. Kant, *Critique of Pure Reason*, p. 475 (note).
51. Engels, Vorarbeiten zum "Anti-Dühring," Marx-Engels-Archiv, vol. 2, Frankfurt a.M., 1927, p. 408.
52. Bouglé, *Les idées égalitaires*, Paris, 1925, p. 248.
53. *"Die psychoanalytische Charakterologie und ihre Bedeutung für die Sozialpsychologie"* [The Psychoanalytic Theory of the Personality and its Significance for Social Psychology], *Zeitschrift für Sozialforschung*, 1932, p. 268ff., esp. p. 274.
54. De ludo globi II, 236f., cited in Cassirer, *Individuum und Kosmos in der Philosophie der Renaissance*, Berlin, 1927, p. 46.
55. Max Weber, " 'Objectivity' in Social Science and Social Policy," ed. Edward A. Shils and Henry A. Finch, New York, 1949, pp. 81, 83.
56. John Stuart Mill, *The Positive Philosophy of Auguste Comte*, Boston, 1866, p. 88.
57. Cf., e.g., the discussion led by Ed. Claparède at the meeting of the Société francaise de Philosophie on March 12, 1932 (vid. the Bulletin of this society, July/September 1932, published by Armand Colin in Paris).
58. Lévy-Bruhl, *La morale et la science des moeurs*, ninth impression, Paris, 1927, p. 98.

JÜRGEN HABERMAS

SELECTIONS FROM LEGITIMATION CRISIS

THE RELATION OF PRACTICAL QUESTIONS TO TRUTH

Since Hume the dualism between "is" and "ought," between facts and values, has been thoroughly clarified. It signifies the impossibility of logically deriving prescriptive sentences or value judgments from descriptive sentences or statements.[1] In analytic philosophy this has been the point of departure for a noncognitivist treatment of practical questions in which we distinguish between empiricist and decisionist lines of argument. They converge in the conviction that moral controversies cannot, in the final analysis, be decided with reason because the value premises from which we infer moral sentences are irrational. The empiricist assumptions are that we employ practical sentences either to express the attitudes and needs of the speaker or to bring about or to manipulate behavioral dispositions in the hearer. In analytic philosophy, primarily semantic and pragmatic investigations of the emotive meaning of moral expressions have been carried out along this line (Stevenson, Monro).[2] The decisionistic assumptions are that practical sentences belong to an autonomous domain that is subject to a logic different from that governing theoretical-empirical sentences and that connected with belief acts or decisions, rather than experiences. In analytic philosophy, primarily logical investigations—into questions of a deontic logic (von Wright) or, generally, into the formal structure of prescriptive languages (Hare)—have arisen from this line of thought.[3]

I shall choose as an example an instructive essay of K. H. Ilting, which connects arguments of both types in order to reject the cognitivist claim to justification of practical sentences. By means of language analysis, Ilting attempts to rehabilitate Carl Schmitt's version of the Hobbesian position.[4] He makes the prior decision—not further grounded—to derive norms from demand sentences [*Forderungssätzen*] or imperatives. The elementary demand sentence signifies: (*a*) that the speaker wants something to be the case, and (*b*) that he wants the hearer to adopt and to actualize the state of affairs desired by him. (*a*) is a definite volition; (*b*) is a demand [*Aufforderung*]. Ilting draws a further distinction between the thought that the demand contains, the appeal to the will of the hearer to adopt this thought and to act according to it, and, finally, the volitional act of the hearer by which he accepts or refuses the appeal. The decision to follow the imperative of another is neither logically nor causally "effected" by the demand; "Only that can be expected to which the hearer is himself inclined or to which he can be moved by the threat of a greater evil." What use the hearer makes of his choice [*Willkür*] in the face of an imperative depends on empirical motives alone.

If two imperatives are connected on the basis of reciprocity in such a way that both parties agree to accede to each other's demands, we speak of a *contract* [*Vertrag*]. A contract is grounded in a norm that both parties to the contract "recognize."

The recognition of the common norm creates certain behavioral expectations which can make it appear advisable to one of the participants to accomplish something which is in the other's interest. With that, however, the demand that the other for his part now accomplish what has been agreed to ceases to be a mere expectation which he may accept or refuse according to choice (as in the case of an imperative). It becomes a *claim* which he has already previously recognized as a condition of his action.

The imperativist construction proposed by Ilting for the reconstruction of systems of norms is favorable to the aims of non-cognitivism. Since the cognitive component of demand sentences (wishes, commands) is limited to the propositional content ("the desired state of affairs," the "thought" which the demand contains), and since volitional acts (decisions, beliefs, attitudes) are motivated only empirically (that is, bring needs and interests into play), as soon as a norm comes into force through the choice [*Willkür*] of the contracting parties, it too can contain nothing that would admit of cognitive support or disputation, that is, of justification or objection. It would be meaningless to try to "justify" practical sentences otherwise than by reference to the fact of an empirically motivated contractual agreement.

It is no longer meaningful to look for a justification of the mutually recognized contractual norm. Both parties had a sufficient motive to recognize the contractual norm . . . Just as little can one . . . meaningfully demand a justification of the norm that contractual agreements are to be kept.

The proposed construction (whose explicit content, incidentally, might be difficult to reconcile with its own status) is to be evaluated in the light of its aim: to explain as completely as possible the meaning and the achievement of norms. But it cannot at all adequately explain *one* central element of the meaning of norms, namely the "ought" or normative validity. A norm has a binding character—therein consists its validity claim. But if only empirical motives (such as inclinations, interests, and fear of sanctions) sustain the agreement, it is impossible to see why a party to the contract should continue to feel bound to the norms when his original motives change. Ilting's construction is unsuitable because it does not permit us to give an account of the decisive *difference between obeying concrete commands and following intersubjectively recognized norms.* Thus, Ilting finds it necessary to introduce the auxiliary hypothesis "that the recognition of a 'fundamental norm' is always presupposed in the recognition of any other norm; the recognition of a norm is to be regarded as an act of the will which might in the future also be brought to bear against the will itself." But what motive could there be for recognizing such a paradoxical fundamental norm? The validity of norms cannot be grounded on an obligation to oneself not to change them, for the original constellation of interests can change at any time, and norms that are made independent of their interest-basis lack, according to Ilting's own construction, any sense of normative regulation at all. If, on the other hand, one wishes to avoid the difficulty of normatively fixing fleeting constellations of interest for an undetermined time and to allow for revisions, then it must be possible to distinguish valid motives for revision. If any given change in motives is sufficient cause for changing norms, then we cannot plausibly distinguish the validity claim of a norm from the imperative meaning of a demand. If, on the other hand, there can be only empirical motives, one is as good as the other—each is justified by its mere existence. The only motives that can be distinguished from others are those for which we can adduce reasons.

From this reflection, it follows that we cannot explain the validity claim of norms without recourse to rationally motivated agreement or at least to the conviction that consensus on a recommended norm could be brought about *with reasons.* In that case the model of contracting parties who need know only what an imperative means is inadequate. The appropriate model is rather the communication community [*Kommunikationsgemeinschaft*] of those affected, who as participants in a practical discourse test the validity claims of norms and, to the extent that they accept them with reasons, arrive at the conviction that in the given circumstances the proposed norms are "right." The validity claim of norms is grounded not in the irrational volitional acts of the contracting parties, but in the rationally motivated recognition of norms, which may be questioned at any time. The cognitive component of norms is, thus, not limited to the propositional content of the normed behavioral expectations. The normative-validity claim is itself cognitive in the sense of the supposition (however counterfactual) that it could be discursively redeemed—that is, grounded in consensus of the participants through argumentation.

An ethics developed along imperativist lines lacks the proper dimension of possible justification of practical sentences: moral argumentation. As the examples of Max Weber and Karl Popper show, there are certainly positions which leave room for the possibility of moral argument and retain, nevertheless, a decisionistic treatment of the value problematic. The reason for this lies in a narrow concept of rationality that permits only deductive arguments. Since a valid deductive argument can neither produce new information nor contribute anything to the truth-values of its components, moral argumentation is limited to two tasks: analytically testing the consistency of the value premises (or the preference system taken as a basis); and empirically testing the realizability of goals selected from value perspectives. This kind of "rational critique of values" in no way changes the irrationality of the choice of the preference system itself.

Hans Albert goes a step further in the metaethical application of the principles of *critical rationalism.*[5] If—as in critical rationalism—one gives up the idea of justification [*Begründung*] in science, while retaining the fallibilistically interpreted possibility of critical testing, then the renunciation of claims to justification in ethics need not automatically have decisionistic consequences. Because cognitive claims, like practical claims, are subject to rationally motivated evaluation from selected points of view, Albert affirms the possibility of critically testing practical sentences in a somewhat analogous way to that in which theoretical-empirical sentences are tested. Since he involves the "active search for contradictions" in the discussion of value problems, moral argumentation can assume—beyond the tasks of testing the consistency of values and the realizability of goals—the productive task of critically developing values and norms.

Of course, no value judgment can, as we know, be directly deduced from statements of fact. But certain value judgments can, in the light of revised convictions about the facts, prove to be incompatible with certain value convictions which we previously held . . . From the fact that we discover new moral ideas which make previous solutions to moral problems appear questionable, there can indeed result another kind of critique. In the light of such ideas, certain problematic features of these solutions, which have previously gone unnoticed or been taken as self-evident, often first become perceptible. There results in this way a new problem situation, as happens in science with the appearance of new ideas.[6]

In this way, Albert introduces into Popperian criticism the idea already developed in the pragmatist tradition (especially by Dewey) of a rational clarification and critical development of inherited value systems.[7] To be sure, even this program remains noncognitivist at its core, because it retains the alternative between decisions, which cannot be rationally motivated, and proofs or justifications, which are possible only through deductive arguments. Even the "bridge principles" introduced *ad hoc* cannot bridge this gap. The idea developed in critical rationalism of renouncing proof or confirmation in favor of the elimination of untruths cannot vindicate the power of discursively attained, rational consensus against the Weberian pluralism of value systems, gods, and demons. The empiricist and/or decisionist barriers, which immunize the so-called pluralism of values against the efforts of practical reason, cannot be overcome so long as the power of argumentation is sought only in the power of refuting deductive arguments.

In contrast, Peirce and Toulmin have both seen the rationally motivating force of argumentation in the fact that the progress of knowledge takes place through substantial arguments.[8] The latter are based on logical inferences, but they are not exhausted in deductive systems of statements. Substantial arguments serve to redeem or to criticize validity claims, whether the claims to truth implicit in assertions or the claims to correctness connected with norms (of action and evaluation) or implied in recommendations and warnings. They have the force to convince the participants in a discourse of a validity claim, that is, *to provide rational grounds for* the recognition of validity claims. Substantial arguments are explanations and justifications, that is, pragmatic unities, in which not sentences but speech acts (sentences employed in utterances) are connected. The systematic aspect of their connection has to be clarified within the framework of a logic of discourse.[9] In theoretical discourses— which serve to ground assertions—consensus is produced according to rules of argumentation different from those obtaining in practical discourses—which serve to justify recommended norms. However, in both cases the goal is the same: a rationally motivated decision about the recognition (or rejection) of validity claims.

What *rationally motivated recognition* of the validity claim of a norm of action means follows from the discursive procedures of motivation. Discourse can be understood as that form of communication that is removed from contexts of experience and action and whose structure assures us: that the bracketed validity claims of assertions, recommendations, or warnings are the exclusive object of discussion; that participants, themes and contributions are not restricted except with reference to the goal of testing the validity claims in questions; that no force except that of the better argument is exercised; and that, as a result, all motives except that of the cooperative search for truth are excluded. If under these conditions a consensus about the recommendation to accept a norm arises argumentatively, that is, on the basis of hypothetically proposed, alternative justifications, then this consensus expresses a "rational will." Since all those affected have, in principle, at least the chance to participate in the practical deliberation, the "rationality" of the discursively formed will consists in the fact that the reciprocal behavioral expectations raised to normative status afford validity to a *common* interest ascertained *without deception*. The interest is common because the constraint-free consensus permits only what *all* can want; it is free of deception because even the interpretations of needs in which *each individual* must be able to recognize what he wants become the object of discursive will-formation. The discursively formed will may be called "rational" because the formal properties of discourse and of the deliberative situation sufficiently guarantee that a consensus can arise only through appropriately interpreted, *generalizable* interests, by which I mean needs *that can be communicatively shared*. The limits of a decisionistic treatment of practical questions are overcome as soon as argumentation is expected to test the generaliz*ability* of interests, instead of being resigned to an impenetrable pluralism of apparently ultimate value orientations (or belief-acts or attitudes). It is not the fact of this pluralism that is here disputed, but the assertion that it is impossible to separate by argumentation generalizable interests from those that are and remain particular. Albert mentions, to be sure, various types of more or less contingent "bridge principles." But he does not mention the only principle in which practical reason expresses itself, namely, the principle of universalization.

Only on this principle do cognitivist and non-cognitivist approaches in ethics part ways. In analytic philosophy, the "good-reasons approach" (which begins with the question of the extent to which "better" reasons can be given for action X than for action Y) has led to the renewal of a strategic-utilitarian, contractual morality that distinguishes fundamental duties by the possibility of their universal validity (Grice).[10] Another line of argument goes back to Kant in order to disconnect the categorical imperative from the context of transcendental philosophy and to reconstruct it, in terms of language analysis, as the "principle of universality" or the "generalization argument" (Baier, Singer).[11] The methodical philosophy of the Erlangen School also understands its theory of moral argument as a renewal of the critique of practical reason (Lorenzen, Schwemmer).[12] In the present context, we are interested less in the proposed norming of the language of discussion permitted in the deliberation of practical questions than in the introduction of the "moral principle" that obliges each participant in a practical discourse to transfer his subjective desires into generalizable desires. Thus Lorenzen also speaks of the principle of *transsubjectivity.*

The introduction of maxims of universalization (of whatever type) raises the consequent problem of the circular justification of a principle that, supposedly, first makes possible the justification of norms. Paul Lorenzen admits to a residual decisionistic problematic when he calls the recognition of the moral principle an "act of faith . . . if one defines faith in a negative sense as the acceptance of something which is not justified."[13] But he removes the arbitrary character of this act of faith insofar as he claims that methodical exercise of the practice of deliberation trains one to a rational attitude. Reason cannot be demonstrated but can, to a certain degree, be inculcated by socialization. Schwemmer gives this interpretation a different turn, if I understand him correctly, in that he has recourse to the prior understanding [*Vorverständnis*] of the intersubjective practice of speaking and acting exercised in unreflected [*naturwüchsigen*] contexts of action, on the one hand, and to the motive arising therein to settle conflicts *without force*, on the other. But methodical philosophy's claim to ultimate foundations makes it necessary for Schwemmer too to stylize a "first" decision:

The moral principle is established on the basis of a common practice which I have here attempted step by step to motivate and to make understandable. In this common action, we have so transformed our desires that we recognized the common transformation of desires as the fulfillment of our original desires (motives) which brought us to take up a common practice in the first place. What is required for the common establishment of the moral principles is participation in common practice, to this extent a "decision" which is not justified through further speech. And this participation first makes possible rational action which takes account of and understands the desires of others.[14]

The difficulties in Schwemmer's construction are analyzed in a work by Looser, Uscher, Maciejewski, and Menne:

A necessary condition for beginning the construction of normed speech is that the individuals who make this beginning already stand in a *common* context of speech and action, and agree therein, through a pre-form [*Vorform*] of "practical deliberation" (*Schwemmer*), to undertake *in common* the construction of a well-founded mode of speech. That this anticipation is achieved under unclarified conditions is shown by the fact that the Erlangen attempt does not conceive itself as a historically identified endeavor which could be understood as the consequence of acquiring and pushing through the principle of resolving practical questions in communication free of force, that is, discursively. Instead, the decision between talk and force is itself still placed in the construction of practical philosophy.[15]

The problematic that arises with the introduction of a moral principle is disposed of as soon as one sees that the expectation of discursive redemption of normative-validity claims is already contained in the structure of intersubjectivity and makes specially introduced maxims of universalization superfluous. In taking up a practical discourse, we unavoidably suppose an ideal speech situation that, on the strength of its formal properties, allows consensus only through *generalizable* interests. A cognitivist linguistic ethics [*Sprachethik*] has no need of principles. It is based only on fundamental norms of rational speech that we must always presuppose if we discourse at all. This, if you will, transcendental character of ordinary language, which is also implicitly claimed by the Erlangen School as the basis for the construction of normed speech, can (as I hope to show) be reconstructed in the framework of a universal pragmatic.[16]

THE MODEL OF THE SUPPRESSION OF GENERALIZABLE INTERESTS

Our excursion into the contemporary discussion of ethics was intended to support the assertion that practical questions admit of truth. If this is so, justifiable norms can be distinguished from norms that merely stabilize relations of force. Insofar as norms express generalizable interests, they are based on a *rational consensus* (or they would find such a consensus if practical discourse could take place). Insofar as norms do not regulate generalizable interests, they are based on force [*Gewalt*]; in the latter context we use the term normative power [*Macht*].

There is, however, one case of normative power that is distinguished by being indirectly justifiable: *compromise*. A normed adjustment between particular interests is called a compromise if it takes place under conditions of a balance of power between the parties involved. The separation of powers is an ordering principle intended to guarantee such a balance of power in the domain of particular interests in order to make compromises possible. Another ordering principle is realized in bourgeois civil law, which delimits autonomous domains of action for the strategic pursuit of individual interests. It presupposes a balance of power between private persons and makes compromises on non-generalizable interests unnecessary. In both cases, universalistic principles that admit of justification are employed—with the proviso, to be sure, that the generalizability of the regulated interests can be denied. This proviso can, in turn, be tested only through discourse. For this reason, separation of powers and democracy are not of equal rank as political-ordering principles.

That democratic will-formation turns into repression if it is not kept within limits by the freedom-guaranteeing principle of the separation of powers, is a theme of the counter-enlightenment that was renewed by Helmut Schelsky in connection with the German federal elections of November, 1972:

> According to its oft declared, fundamental political constitution, the Federal Republic represents a harmony of both principles in a liberal-democratic [*freiheitlich-demokratischen*] order. It is perhaps no accident that the principle of freedom precedes that of democracy in this formula. But if those in power then programmatically announce the priority of "more democracy" in this fundamental order based on principles, then the acceptance of "less freedom" is tacitly, and without admitting it, bound up with that program.[17]

The gravity of this dilemma disappears as soon as we see that: (*a*) separation of powers may legitimately be introduced only where the domains of interests to be regulated cannot be justified discursively and thus require compromises; and that (*b*) demarcating particular from generalizable interests in a manner that admits of consensus is possible only by means of discursive will-formation. Counter to the Schelsky's diagnosis furthermore, it is the Social Democrats who—with the postulate of "equal rights for labor and capital"—are reclaiming, for example, separation of powers in a domain of interests that was, to be sure, previously removed from discursive will-formation, but in which there is certainly no lack of generalizable interests. Even if a "class-compromise" came about in advanced capitalism under conditions of a balance of power, the justifiability of the compromise would remain questionable as long as it excluded the possibility of discursively testing whether it was in fact a matter, on both sides, of particular interests that did not permit of a rational will and were thus accessible only to compromise.

A compromise can be justified as a compromise only if both conditions are met; a balance of power among the parties involved and the non-generalizability of the negotiated interests exist. If even one of these *general* conditions of *compromise formation* is not fulfilled, we are dealing with a pseudo-compromise [*Scheinkompromiss*]. In complex societies *pseudo-compromises* are an important form of legitimation. But historically they are not the rule. In traditional and liberal-capitalist societies, it is rather the *ideological form* of justification, which either asserts or counterfactually supposes a generalizability of interests, that is dominant. In this case, legitimations consist of interpretations, of narrative presentations or (for example in natural law) of systematized explanations and chains of argument, that have the double function of proving that the validity claims of norm systems are legitimate and of avoiding thematization and testing of discursive-validity claims. The specific achievement of such ideologies consists in the inconspicuous manner in which communication is systematically limited.[18] A social theory critical of ideology can, therefore, identify the normative power built into the institutional system of a society only if it starts from the *model of the suppression of generalizable interests* and compares normative structures existing at a given time with the hypothetical state of a system of norms formed, *ceteris paribus*, discursively. Such a counterfactually projected reconstruction—for which P. Lorenzen proposes the procedure of "normative genesis"[19]—can be guided by the question (justified, in my opinion, by considerations from universal pragmatics): how would the members of a social system, at a given stage in the development of productive forces, have collectively and bindingly interpreted their needs (and which norms would they have accepted as justified) if they could and would have decided on organization of social intercourse through discursive will-formation, with adequate knowledge of the limiting conditions and functional imperatives of their society?[20] Of course, the model of the suppression of generalizable interests—which explains at one and the same time the *functional necessity* of the apparent legitimation of domination and the *logical possibility* of undermining normative-validity claims by a critique of ideology—can be made fruitful for social theory only by making empirical assumptions.

We can start from the position that the orientation of action toward institutionalized values is unproblematic only as long as the normatively prescribed distribution of opportunities for the legitimate satisfaction of needs rests on an actual consensus. But as soon as a difference of opinion arises, the "injustice" of the repression of generalizable interests can be recognized in the categories of the interpretive system obtaining at the time. This consciousness of conflicts of interest is, as a rule, sufficient motive for replacing value-oriented action with interest-guided action. The pattern of communicative action gives way then, in politically relevant domains of behavior, to that type of behavior for which the competition for scarce goods supplies the model, that is, strategic action. Thus, I use the term "interests" for needs that are—to the extent of the withdrawal of legitimation and the rising of the consciousness of conflict—rendered subjective and detached, as it were, from the crystallizations of commonly shared values supported by tradition (and made binding in norms of action).

These assumptions of conflict theory can be connected with the discourse model at two levels. I make the empirical assumption that the interest constellations of the parties involved, which are revealed in cases of conflict, coincide sufficiently with interests that would have to find expression among those involved if they *were* to enter into practical discourse. Furthermore, I make the methodological assumption that it is meaningful and possible to reconstruct (even for the normal case of norms recognized without conflict) the hidden interest positions of involved individuals or groups by counterfactually imagining [*fingieren*] the limit case of a conflict between the involved parties in which they would be forced to consciously perceive their interests and strategically assert them, instead of satisfying basic interests simply by actualizing institutional values as is normally the case. Marx too had to make these or equivalent assumptions in the analysis of class struggles. He had: (*a*) to draw a general distinction between particular and general interests; (*b*) to understand the consciousness of justified and, at the same time, suppressed interests as a sufficient motive for conflict; and (c) to attribute, with reason, interest positions to social groups. The social scientist can only hypothetically project this ascription of interests; indeed a direct confirmation of this hypothesis would be possible only in the form of a practical discourse among the very individuals or groups involved. An indirect confirmation on the basis of observable conflicts is possible to the extent that the ascribed interest positions can be connected with predictions about conflict motivations.

Claus Offe provides an instructive survey of alternative attempts to "establish a critical standard for determining the selectivity of a political system and thereby to avoid the complementary difficulties of systems-theoretic and of behavioristic procedures (which are unable to conceptualize the non-events of suppressed, that is, latent, claims and needs.)"[21] Three of the alternatives mentioned are, for essential and easily seen reasons, inapplicable.

- "A need potential can be defined *anthropologically*. The totality of unfulfilled needs appears then as a non-fact, as an indicator of the selectivity of a political system, of its greater or lesser character of domination" (p. 85). None of the drive theories put forward until now, however, has succeeded even in making it plausible that the assumption of an invariant need structure in human beings is both meaningful and empirically testable. Through the example of the most prominent and well-thought-out drive theory, namely, the psychoanalytic, it can be convincingly shown, in my opinion, that theoretical predictions about the range of variation of aggressive and libidinal drive potentials are not possible.[22]
- In the framework of an *objectivistic philosophy of history*, the attribution of interests can be projected on the basis of observable structural features. However, teleological historical constructions acquiesce in a circular structure of proof and, for this reason, cannot make their empirical reference plausible.

  Such a method, which only supposedly stands in the succession of Marxist "orthodoxy," runs the danger of raising to a theoretical premise what is to be demonstrated by analysis (the class character of the organizations of political domination) and, at the same time, of reducing to insignificance the historical particularities of the selectivity of a concrete institutional system—whether or not it can be brought into agreement with the dogmatically advanced class concept (p. 86ff.).

- Finally, there is the *normative-analytic* approach, which is dependent upon declared options for more or less conventionally introduced goal states. Social-scientific systems analysis proceeds normatively in this sense, since there is as yet no theory that enables us to make up for the backwards state of social-scientific functionalism in comparison to biocybernetics and to grasp goal states of social systems in a non-arbitrary way.[23] Normativistically employed systems analysis has a weak empirical content because it can only chance upon causally effective mechanisms from arbitrarily chosen functional points of reference.

Its analytical limitedness is grounded in the circumstance that it cannot distinguish between *systematic* selectivity of an institutional system on the one hand, and merely accidental non-fulfillment of given norms (which could be fulfilled while retaining the selective structures) on the other (p. 86).

The remaining strategies mentioned by Offe are on another level. They can be understood as the search for empirical indicators of suppressed interests.

- One can proceed *immanently* in playing off "claim" and "reality" against one another. This method is commonly employed in the critical literature on constitutional law (constitutional claim versus constitutional reality). It carries with it, however, the burden of proof for the thesis that there is not merely a tendency for the unactualized claim to which the critique refers to be violated, but that this violation is systematic (p. 88).
- One can identify *rules of exclusion* codified in a political system—perhaps in the form of procedural rules of administrative law, civil laws, and penal laws. Such a procedure for analyzing structural selectivity is inadequate in so far as it can hardly be supposed that a social system itself designates in codified form the totality of restrictions effective within it (p. 88).
- A further possibility would be confronting political-administrative processes not with their own or with constitutional pretensions . . . but with the *unintended*, yet *systematically arising* "misunderstandings" and *over-interpretations* which they evoke (p. 89).

(One should not, of course, rely on the political system's making rejected claims sufficiently evident at all times.)

- Finally, one can adopt comparative procedures, identifying the rules of exclusion which distinguish one political system from another with the help of a *ceteris paribus* clause. . . . [But], for one thing, those selectivities which are common to the systems compared do not come into view; for another, conditions which would justify a rigorous application of the *ceteris paribus* clause are scarcely ever met with (p. 87).

These shortcomings in the search for indicators are trivial as long as the theoretical concept for which indicators are sought is lacking. Observed discrepancy between legal norms and legal reality, codified rules of exclusion, discrepancy between actual level of claims and politically permitted level of satisfaction, repressions that become visible in international comparison—all of these phenomena have the same status as other conflict phenomena: they can be called upon in crisis analysis only if they can be ordered in a theoretical system for description and evaluation. A version of the advocacy model based on principles presents itself for this purpose. I do not mean by this the empirical feedback of critique on the goals of conflict groups—goals that are chosen on the basis of pre-theoretical experiences, that is, with partisanship. For the latter formulation would render partisanship immune to demands for foundations.

Instead, the advocacy role of the critical theory of society would consist in ascertaining generalizable, though nevertheless suppressed, interests in a representatively simulated discourse between groups that are differentiated (or could be nonarbitrarily differentiated) from one another by articulated, or at least virtual, opposition of interests. A discourse carried through as advocacy can lead only to a hypothetical result.[24] But pointed indicators for testing such hypotheses can be sought in the abovementioned dimensions with some hope of success.

NOTES

1. K. R. Popper, *The Open Society and Its Enemies*, 2 vols. (Princeton, 1950), vol. 1, chap. 5, "Nature and Convention."
2. L. Stevenson, *Ethics and Language* (New Haven, 1950); D. H. Monro, *Empiricism and Ethics* (Cambridge, 1967).
3. R. M. Hare, *The Language of Morals* (Oxford, 1952).
4. K. H. Ilting, "Anerkennung," in *Probleme der Ethik* (Freiburg, 1972).
5. H. Albert, *Traktat über kritische Vernunft* (Tübingen, 1968), chap. 3, p. 55ff. J. Mittelstrass (*Das praktische Fundament der Wissenschaft*, p. 18) is certainly correct in remarking that the trilemma of Popper and Albert results from the ungrounded equation of deductive justification [*Begründung*] with justification in general. K. O. Apel, *Das Apriori der Kommunikationsgemeinschaft*, vol. II of *Transformation der Philsophie* (Frankfurt, 1973), p. 405ff., distinguishes deductive from transcendental justification and traces the unreflectiveness of critical rationalism to a characteristic neglect of the pragmatic dimension of argumentation.

   Under the presupposition of abstracting from the pragmatic dimension of signs there is no human *subject* of argumentation and therefore also no possibility of a reflection on the conditions of possibility of argumentation which are *always presupposed by us*. Instead, there is the infinite hierarchy of *meta*-languages, *meta*-theories, etc., in which the *reflective competence* of man as the *subject of argumentation* is simultaneously made perceptible and concealed . . . And yet we know very well that our *reflective competence*—more precisely, the self-reflection of the human subject of thought operations, which is bracketed out *a priori* at the level of syntactic-semantic systems—is hidden behind the aporia of infinite regress and makes possible, for example, something like an undecidability *proof* in the sense of Gödel. In other words, precisely in the confirmation that the subjective conditions of possibility of argumentation *cannot be objectivated* in a syntactic-semantic *model* of argumentation is expressed the self-reflective knowledge of the transcendental-pragmatic subject of argumentation. (p. 406ff).

6. Albert, *Trakatat über kritische Vernunft*, p. 78.
7. J. Dewey, *The Quest for Certainty* (New York, 1929).
8. S. Toulmin, *The Uses of Argument*; on Peirce see K. O. Apel, "Von Kant zu Peirce. Die semiotische Transformation der Transzendentalen Logik," in *Transformation der Philosophie*, 2:157ff.
9. J. Habermas, "Wahrheitstheorien."
10. R. Grice, *The Grounds of Moral Judgement* (Cambridge, 1967).
11. K. Baier, *The Moral Point of View* (Ithaca, 1958); M. G. Singer, *Generalization in Ethics* (London, 1963).

12. P. Lorenzen, *Normative Logic and Ethics* (Mannheim, 1969); "Szientismus versus Dialektik," in *Festschrift für Gadamer* (Tübingen, 1970), 1:57ff.; O. Schwemmer, *Philosophie der Praxis* (Frankfurt, 1971); S. Blasche and O. Schwemmer, "Methode und Dialektik," in M. Riedel, ed., *Rehabilitierung der praktischen Philosophie I* (Freiburg, 1972), p. 457ff.
13. P. Lorenzen, *Normative Logic and Ethics*, p. 74.
14. O. Schwemmer, *Philosophie der Praxis*, p. 194.
15. Cited from manuscript; soon to appear in a volume on practical philosophy edited by F. Kambartel for the *Theorie-Diskussion* series, Suhrkamp Verlag.
16. Cf. also K. O. Apel, "Das Apriori der Kommunikationsgemeinschaft und die Ethik," in *Transformation der Philosophie*, 2:358ff. In this fascinating essay, in which Apel summarizes his large-scale attempt at reconstruction, the fundamental assumption of communicative ethics is developed: "with the presupposition of intersubjective consensus the search for truth must also anticipate the morality of an ideal communication community." (p. 405) Even with Apel there arises, to be sure, a residual decisionistic problematic.

Whoever poses the—in my opinion, quite meaningful—question of the justification of the moral principle already *takes part* in the discussion. And one can "make him aware"—quite in the manner proposed by Lorenzen and Schwemmer of a reconstruction of reason—of what he has "already" accepted, and that he should accept this principle through intentional affirmation as the *condition of the possibility and of the validity of argumentation*. Whoever does not comprehend or accept this withdraws from the discussion. But anyone who does not participate in the discussion cannot pose the question of the justification of fundamental ethical principles. Thus, it is *meaningless* to talk of the meaninglessness of his question and to recommend to him a valiant decision to believe. (pp. 420-21)

That "intentional affirmation" can, however, only be stylized to an intentional act as long as one disregards the fact that discourses are not only contingently, but systematically admitted into a life-context whose peculiarly fragile *facticity consists* in the recognition of discursive-validity claims. Anyone who does not participate, or is not ready to participate in argumentation stands nevertheless "already" in contexts of *communicative action*. In doing so, he has already naively recognized the validity claims—however counterfactually raised—that are contained in speech acts and that can be redeemed only discursively. Otherwise he would have had to detach himself from the communicatively established language game of everyday practice. The *fundamental* error of methodological solipsism extends to the assumption of the possibility not only of monological *thought*, but also of monological *action*. It is absurd to imagine that a subject capable of speech and action could permanently realize the limit case of communicative action, that is, the monological role of acting instrumentally and strategically, without losing his identity. The socio-cultural form of life of communicatively socialized individuals produces the "transcendental illusion" of pure communicative action in *every* interaction context and, at the same time, it structurally refers *every* interaction context to the possibility of an ideal speech situation in which the validity claims accepted in action can be tested discursively. (Habermas and Luhmann, *Sozialtechnologie?*, p. 136f.) If one understands the communication community *in the first place* as a community of interaction and not of argumentation, as action and not as discourse, then the relation—important from the perspective of emancipation—of the "real" to the "ideal" communication community (Apel, "Das Apriori der Kommunikationsgemeinschaft," p. 429ff.) can also be examined from the point of view of idealizations of pure communicative action (cf. my introduction to the English edition of *Theory and Practice*, Boston, 1973, p. 1ff., and my "Postscript to *Knowledge and Human Interests*," *Philosophy of the Social Sciences*, 3 (1973): p. 157-89).

17. H. Schelsky, "Mehr Demokratie oder mehr Freiheit?," *Frankfurter Allgemeine Zeitung*, Jan. 20, 1973, p. 7.
18. J. Habermas, "Der Universalitätsanspruch der Hermeneutik," in *Hermeneutik und Ideologiekritik* (Frankfurt, 1971), p. 120ff.
19. P. Lorenzen, "Szientismus versus Dialektik."
20. J. Habermas, "Einige Bemerkungen zum Problem der Begründung von Werturteilen," in *Verhandlungen des 9. Deutschen Kongress für Philosophie* (Meisenheim, 1972), p. 89ff.
21. C. Offe, "Klassenherrschaft und politisches System," p. 85.
22. Habermas, *Knowledge and Human Interests*, p. 284ff.
23. Compare the abovementioned dissertation of R. Döbert; also G. Schmid, "N. Luhmanns funktional-strukturelle Systemtheorie," in *Politische Vierteljahreschrift* (1970), p. 186ff.
24. J. Habermas, *Toward a Rational Society*, p. 74ff.

PART FIVE

THE FOUNDATIONS AND METHODS OF CRITICAL THEORY

he three essays in this section raise questions concerning critical theory's foundations and methodology. The first, "Freedom and Freud's Theory of the Instincts," was originally given as a lecture in the late 1950s, then revised and published as part of Marcuse's *Five Lectures* (trans. 1970). Marcuse examines several tensions in Freud's work, in particular concerning the problematic conception of the instincts and domination in Freud's *Civilization and Its Discontents* (1930). Marcuse argues that according to Freud's conception of the instincts freedom becomes an impossible concept: everything is prescribed for the individual in one way or another. Marcuse also discusses the tension between the life and death instincts in Freud (*eros* and *thanatos*). Marcuse's critique of Freud holds out the possibility of a civilization that strives for happiness and freedom without resorting to domination.

Horkheimer's contribution, "Traditional and Critical Theory," is excerpted from the longer essay contained in *Critical Theory. Selected Essays: Max Horkheimer.* This programmatic essay originally appeared in *Zeitschrift für Sozialforschung* in 1937. In this essay, Horkheimer sets out to define what is meant by a critical theory. He carefully develops an argument for an interdisciplinary approach to the study of society combining the methods of science, philosophy, history, and sociology.

The final selection in this part is reprinted from the English translation of Habermas's book *Knowledge and Human Interests* (1968). It was originally an inaugural address he gave in 1965. In this address he reexamines the notion of a critical theory calling for the reintegration of the methods of the empirical-analytical sciences with the methods of the historical-hermeneutical sciences. Habermas argues that no form of knowledge is interest-free. He privileges self-reflection as a form of knowledge that renders explicit the connection between knowledge and interest: In self-reflection the subject recognizes the confluence of knowledge for the sake of knowledge and the subject's interest in autonomy and responsibility. Ultimately, Habermas asserts, we must recognize that knowledge and interest are one.

For a more detailed discussion of methodological questions and their relation to Freud see Chapter 6 of *Philosophy and Critical Theory*.

HERBERT MARCUSE

FREEDOM AND FREUD'S THEORY OF INSTINCTS

A discussion of Freudian theory from the standpoint of political science and philosophy requires some justification—in part because Freud repeatedly emphasized the scientific and empirical character of his work. The justification must be two-fold: first, it must show that the structure of Freudian theory is open to and in fact *encourages* consideration in political terms, that this theory, which appears to be purely biological, is fundamentally social and historical. Second, it must show on the one hand to what extent psychology today is an essential part of political science, and on the other hand to what extent the Freudian theory of instincts (which is the only thing we will be concerned with here) makes it possible to understand the hidden nature of certain decisive tendencies in current politics.

We will begin with the second aspect of the justification. Our concern is not with introducing psychological concepts into political science or with explaining political processes in psychological terms. That would mean attempting to explain what is basic in terms of what is based on it. Rather, psychology in its inner structure must reveal itself to be political. The psyche appears more and more immediately to be a piece of the social totality, so that individuation is almost synonymous with apathy and even with guilt, but also with the principle of negation, of possible revolution. Moreover, the totality of which the psyche is a part becomes to an increasing extent less "society" than "politics." That is, society has fallen prey to and become identified with domination.

We must identify at the outset what we mean by "domination," because the content of this notion is central to Freudian instinct theory. Domination is in effect whenever the individual's goals and purposes and the means of striving for and attaining them are prescribed to him and performed by him as something prescribed. Domination can be exercised by men, by nature, by things—it can also be internal, exercised by the individual on himself, and appear in the form of autonomy. This second form plays a decisive role in Freudian instinct theory: the superego absorbs the authoritarian models, the father and his representatives, and makes their commands and prohibitions its own laws, the individual's conscience. Mastery of drives becomes the individual's own accomplishment—autonomy.

Under these circumstances, however, freedom becomes an impossible concept, for there is nothing that is not prescribed for the individual in some way or other. And in fact freedom can be defined only within the framework of domination, if previous history is to provide a guide to the definition of freedom. Freedom is *a form of domination*: the one in which the means provided satisfy the needs of the individual with a minimum of displeasure and renunciation. In this sense freedom is completely historical, and the degree of freedom can be determined only historically; capacities and needs as well as the minimum of renunciation differ depending on the level of cultural development and are subject to objective conditions. But it is precisely the fact of being objectively, historically conditioned that makes the distinction between freedom and domination transcend any merely subjective valuation: like human needs and capacities themselves, the means of satisfying the needs produced at a particular level of culture are socially given facts, present in material and mental productive forces and in the possibilities for their application. Civilization can use these possibilities in the interest of individual gratification of needs and so will be organized under the aspect of freedom. Under optimal conditions domination is reduced to a rational division of labor and experience; freedom and happiness converge. On the other hand, individual satisfaction itself may be subordinated to a social need that limits and diverts these possibilities; in that case the social and the individual needs become separate, and civilization is operating through domination.

Hitherto existing culture has been organized in the form of domination insofar as social needs have been determined by the interests of the ruling groups at any given time, and this interest has defined the needs of other groups and the means and limitations of their satisfactions. Contemporary civilization has developed social wealth to a point where the renunciations and burdens placed on individuals seem more and more unnecessary and irrational. The irrationality of unfreedom is most crassly expressed in the intensified subjection of individuals to the enormous apparatus of production and distribution, in the de-privatization of free time, in the almost indistinguishable fusion of constructive and destructive social labor. And it is precisely this fusion that is the condition of the constantly increasing productivity and domination of nature which keeps individuals—or at least the majority of them in the advanced countries—living in increasing comfort. Thus irrationality becomes the form of social *reason*, becomes the rational universal. Psychologically—and that is all that concerns us here—the difference between domination and freedom is becoming smaller. The individual reproduces on the deepest level, in his instinctual structure, the values and behavior patterns that serve to maintain domination, while domination becomes increasingly less autonomous, less "personal," more objective and universal. What actually dominates is the economic, political, and cultural apparatus, which has become an indivisible unity constructed by social labor.

To be sure, the individual has always reproduced domination from within himself, and to the extent that domination represented and developed the whole, this reproduction has been of service to rational self-preservation and self-development. From the outset the whole has asserted itself in the sacrifice of the happiness and the freedom of a great part of mankind; it has always contained a self-contradiction, which has been embodied in the political and spiritual forces striving toward a different form of life. What is peculiar to the present stage is the neutralization of this contradiction—the mastering of the tension between the given form of life and its negation, a refusal in the name of the greater freedom which is historically possible. Where the neutralization of this contradiction is now most advanced, the possible is scarcely still known and desired, especially by those on whose knowing and willing its realization depends, those who alone could make it something really possible. In the most technically advanced centers of the contemporary world, society has been hammered into a unity as never before; what is possible is defined and realized by the forces that have brought about this unity; the future is to remain theirs, and individuals are to desire and bring about this future "in freedom."

"In freedom"—for compulsion presupposes a contradiction that can express itself in resistance. The totalitarian state is only one of the forms—a form perhaps already obsolete—in which the battle against the historical possibility of liberation takes place. The other, the democratic form, rejects terror because it is strong and rich enough to preserve and reproduce itself without terror: most individuals are in fact better off in this form. But what determines its historical direction is not this fact, but the way it organizes and utilizes the productive forces at its disposal. It, too, maintains society at the attained level, despite all technical progress. It, too, works against the new forms of freedom that are historically possible. In this sense its rationality, too, is regressive, although it works with more painless and more comfortable means and methods. But that it does so should not repress the consciousness that in the democratic form freedom is played off against its complete realization, reality against possibility.

To compare potential freedom with existing freedom, to see the latter in the light of the former, presupposes that at the present stage of civilization much of the toil, renunciation, and regulation imposed upon men is no longer justified by scarcity, the struggle for existence, poverty, and weakness. Society could afford a high degree of instinctual liberation without losing what it has accomplished or putting a stop to its progress. The basic trend of such liberation, as indicated by Freudian theory, would be the recovery of a large part of the instinctual energy diverted to alienated labor, and its release for the fulfillment of the autonomously developing needs of individuals. That would in fact also be *desublimation*—but a desublimation that would not destroy the "spiritualized" manifestations of human energy but rather take them as projects for and possibilities of happy satisfaction. The result would be not a reversion to the prehistory of civilization but rather a fundamental change in the content and goal of civilization, in the principle cf progress. I shall try to explain this elsewhere;[1] here I should simply like to point out that the realization of this possibility presupposes fundamentally changed social and cultural institutions. In the existing culture that progression appears as a catastrophe, and the battle against it as a necessity, with the result that the forces tending toward it are paralyzed.

Freudian instinct theory reveals this neutralization of the dynamic of freedom in terms of psychology, and Freud made visible its necessity, its consequences for the individual, and its limits. We will formulate these dimensions in the form of theses, using but also going beyond the concepts of Freudian instinct theory.

Within the framework of civilization which has become historical reality, freedom is possibly only on the basis of unfreedom, that is, on the basis of instinctual suppression. For in terms of its instinctual structure, the organism is directed toward procuring pleasure; it is dominated by the *pleasure principle*: the instincts strive for pleasurable release of tension, for painless satisfaction of needs. They resist delay of gratification, limitation and sublimation of pleasure, nonlibidinal work. But culture *is* sublimation: postponed, methodically controlled satisfaction which presupposes unhappiness. The "struggle for existence," "scarcity," and cooperation all compel renunciation and repression in the interest of security, order, and living together. Cultural progress consists in the ever greater and more conscious production of the technical, material, and intellectual conditions of progress—in work, itself unsatisfying, on the means of satisfaction. Freedom in civilization has its internal limit in the necessity of gaining and maintaining labor power in the organism—of transforming him from a subject-object of pleasure into a subject-object of work. This is the social content of the overcoming of the pleasure principle through the *reality principle*, which becomes from earliest childhood the dominant principle in the psychic processes. Only this transformation, which leaves an unhealable wound in men, makes them fit for society and thus for life, for without secure cooperation it is impossible to survive in a hostile and niggardly environment. It is only this traumatic transformation, which is an "alienation" of man from nature in the authentic sense, an alienation from his own nature, that makes man capable of enjoyment; only the instinct that has been restrained and mastered raises the merely natural satisfaction of need to pleasure that is experienced and comprehended—to happiness.

But from then on all happiness is only of a sort that is consonant with social restrictions, and man's growing freedom is based on unfreedom. According to Freud's theory this intertwining is inevitable and indissoluble. In order to understand this we must pursue his theory of instincts a little further. In doing so we will proceed from the late version of the theory, developed after 1920. It is the metapsychological, even metaphysical version, but perhaps precisely for that reason it is also the one that contains the deepest and most revolutionary nucleus of Freudian theory.

The organism develops through the activity of two original basic instincts: the *life* instinct (sexuality, which Freud for the most part now calls *Eros*) and the *death* instinct, the destructive instinct. While the former strives for the binding of living substance into ever larger and more permanent units, the death instinct desires regression to the condition before birth, without needs and thus without pain. It strives for the annihilation of life, for reversion to inorganic matter. The organism equipped with such an antagonistic instinctual structure finds itself in an environment which is too poor and too hostile for the immediate gratification of the life instincts. Eros desires life under the pleasure principle, but the environment stands in the way of this goal. Thus as soon as the life instinct has subjected the death instinct to itself (a subjection which is simultaneous with the beginning and the continuation of life), the environment compels a decisive modification of the instincts: in part they are diverted from their original goal or inhibited on the way to it, in part the area of their activity is limited and their direction is changed.* The result of this modification is gratification which is inhibited, delayed, and vicarious but also secure, useful, and relatively lasting.

Thus the psychic dynamic takes the form of a constant struggle of three basic forces: Eros, the death instinct, and the outside world. Corresponding to these three forces are the three basic principles which according to Freud determine the functions of the psychic apparatus: the *pleasure principle*, the *Nirvana principle*, and the *reality principle*. If the pleasure principle stands for the unlimited unfolding of the life instinct, and the Nirvana principle for regression into the painless condition before birth, then the reality principle signifies the totality of the modifications of those instincts compelled by the outside world; it signifies "reason" as reality itself.

It seems that there is a dichotomy hidden behind the tripartite division: if the death instinct presses for the annihilation of life because life is the predominance of displeasure, tension, and need, then the Nirvana principle too would be a form of the pleasure principle, and the death instinct would be dangerously close to Eros. On the other hand, Eros itself seems to partake of the nature of the death instinct: the striving for pacification, for making pleasure eternal, indicates an instinctual resistance in Eros as well to the continual appearance of new tensions, to giving up a pleasurable equilibrium once reached. This resistance, if not hostile to life, is nevertheless static and thus "antagonistic to progress." Freud saw the original unity of the two opposing instincts: he spoke of the "*conservative nature*" common to them, of the "inner weight" and "inertia" of all life. He rejected this thought—in fear, one might almost say—and maintained the duality of Eros and the death instinct, the pleasure principle and the Nirvana principle, despite the difficulty, which he emphasized several times, of demonstrating any drives in the organism other than originally libidinous ones. It is the effective "mixture" of the two fundamental instincts that defines life: although forced into the service of Eros, the death instinct retains the energy proper to it, except that this destructive energy is diverted from the organism itself and directed toward the outside world in the form of socially useful aggression—toward nature and sanctioned enemies—or, in the form of conscience, of morality, it is used by the superego for the socially useful mastery of one's own drives.

The instincts of destruction become of service to the life instincts in this form, but only in that the latter are decisively transformed. Freud devoted the major portion of his work to analyzing the transformations of Eros; here we shall emphasize only what

* The "plasticity" of the instincts which this theory presupposes should suffice to refute the notion that the instincts are essentially unalterable biological substrata: only the "energy" of the instincts and—to some extent—their "localization" remain fundamentally unchanged.

is decisive for the fate of freedom. Eros as the life-instinct is sexuality, and sexuality in its original function is "deriving pleasure from the zones of the body," no more and no less. Freud expressly adds: a pleasure which only "afterwards is placed in the service of reproduction."[2] This indicates the polymorphous-perverse character of sexuality: in terms of their object, the instincts are indifferent with respect to one's own and other bodies; above all they are not localized in specific parts of the body or limited to special functions. The primacy of genital sexuality and of reproduction, which then becomes reproduction in monogamous marriage, is to a certain extent a subsequent development—a late achievement of the reality principle, that is, a historical achievement of human society in its necessary struggle against the pleasure principle, which is not compatible with society. Originally* the organism in its totality and in all its activities and relationships is a potential field for sexuality, dominated by the pleasure principle. And precisely for this reason it must be *desexualized* in order to carry out unpleasurable work, in order, in fact, to live in a context of unpleasurable work.

Here we can bring out only the two most important aspects of the process of desexualization which Freud describes: first the blocking off of the so-called "partial instincts," that is, of pre- and non-genital sexuality, which proceed from the body as a total erogenous zone. The partial instincts either lose their independence, become subservient to genitality and thereby to reproduction by being made into preliminary stages, or they become sublimated and, if there is resistance, suppressed and tabooed as perversions. Second, sexuality and the sexual object are desensualized in "love"—the ethical taming and inhibiting of Eros. This is one of the greatest achievements of civilization—and one of the latest. It alone makes the patriarchal monogamous family the healthy "nucleus" of society.

The overcoming of the Oedipus complex is the precondition for this. In this process Eros, which originally includes everything, is reduced to the special function of genital sexuality and its accompaniments. Eroticism is limited to the socially acceptable minimum. Now Eros is no longer the life instinct governing the whole organism and striving to become the formative principle for the human and natural environment; it has become a private matter for which there is neither time nor place in the necessary social relations of men, labor relations, and Eros becomes "general" only as the reproductive function. The suppression of instincts—for sublimation is also suppression—becomes the basic condition of life in civilized society.

This biological-psychological transformation determines the fundamental experience of human existence and the goal of human life. Life is experienced as a struggle

---

* The notion of "origin" as Freud uses it has simultaneously structural—functional—and temporal, ontogenetic, and phylogenetic significance. The "original" structure of the instincts was the one which dominated in the prehistory of the species. It is transformed during the course of history but continues to be effective as a substratum, preconscious and unconscious, in the history of the individual and the species— most obviously so in early childhood. The idea that mankind, in general and in its individuals, is still dominated by "archaic" powers is one of Freud's most profound insights.

with one's self and the environment; it is suffered and won by conquests. Its substance is unpleasure, not pleasure. Happiness is a reward, relaxation, coincidence, a moment—in any case, not the goal of existence. That goal is rather *labor*. And labor is essentially alienated labor. Only in privileged situations does man work "for himself" in his occupation, does he satisfy his own needs, sublimated and unsublimated, in his occupation; normally he is busy all day long carrying out a prescribed social function, while his self-fulfillment, if there is any, is limited to a scanty free time. The social structuring of time is patterned on the structuring of the instincts completed in childhood; only the limitation of Eros makes possible the limitation of free, that is, pleasurable time to a minimum deducted from full-time labor. And time, like existence itself, is divided into the primary content "alienated labor" and the secondary content "non-labor."

But the structuring of the instincts that dethrones the pleasure principle also makes possible ethics, which has become increasingly more decisive in the development of Western civilization. The individual reproduces *instinctively* the cultural negation of the pleasure principle, renunciation, the pathos of labor: in the repressively modified instincts social legislation becomes the individual's own legislation; the necessary unfreedom appears as an act of his autonomy and thus as freedom. If the Freudian theory of the instincts had stopped here, it would be little more than the psychological grounding of the idealist concept of freedom, which in turn had given a philosophical foundation to the facts of cultural domination. This philosophical concept defines freedom in opposition to pleasure, so that the control, even the suppression of instinctual sensuous aims appears to be a condition of the possibility of freedom. For Kant, freedom is essentially moral—inner, intelligible—freedom and as such it is *compulsion*: "The less man can be physically compelled but the more he can rather be morally compelled (through the mere mental representation of duty), the more free he is."[3] The step from the realm of necessity to the realm of freedom here is progress from physical to moral compulsion, but the object of the compulsion remains the same: man as a member of the "sensuous world." And the moral compulsion is not only moral; it has its own very physical institutions. From the family to the factory to the army, they surround the individual as the effective embodiments of the reality principle. Political freedom is developed on this double basis of moral compulsion: wrung from absolutism in bloody street conflicts and battles, it is set up, secured, and neutralized in the self-discipline and self-renunciation of individuals. They have learned that their inalienable freedom is subject to duties not the least of which is the suppression of instinctual drives. Moral and physical compulsion have a common denominator—*domination*.

Domination is the internal logic of the development of civilization. In acknowledging it, Freud is at one with idealistic ethics and with liberal-bourgeois politics. Freedom must contain compulsion: scarcity, the struggle for existence, and the amoral nature of the instincts make the suppression of instinctual drives indispensable; the alternative is progress or barbarism. It must be emphasized again that for

Freud the most fundamental reason for the necessity to suppress the instincts is the integral claim of the pleasure principle, that is, the fact that the organism is constitutionally directed toward calm through fulfillment, gratification, peace. The "conservative nature" of the instincts makes them unproductive in the deepest sense: unproductive for the alienated productivity that is the motor of cultural progress, so unproductive that even the self-preservation of the organism is not an original goal as long as self-preservation means predominance of displeasure. In Freud's late instinct theory there is no longer an independent drive for self-preservation: it is a manifestation either of Eros or of aggression. For this reason unproductiveness and conservatism must be overcome if the species is to develop a civilized communal life. Calm and peace and the pleasure principle are worth nothing in the struggle for existence: "The program for becoming happy which the pleasure principle presses upon us cannot be fulfilled."[4]

The repressive transformation of the instincts becomes the biological constitution of the organism: history rules even in the instinctual structure; culture becomes nature as soon as the individual learns to affirm and to reproduce the reality principle from within himself, through his instincts. In limiting Eros to the partial function of sexuality and making the destructive instinct useful, the individual becomes, *in his very nature*, the subject-object of socially useful labor, of the domination of men and nature. Technology too is born of suppression; even the highest achievements for making human existence less burdensome bear witness to their origin in the rape of nature and in the deadening of human nature. "Individual freedom is not a product of civilization."[5]

As soon as civilized society establishes itself the repressive transformation of the instincts becomes the psychological basis of a *threefold domination*: first, domination over one's self, over one's own nature, over the sensual drives that want only pleasure and gratification; second, domination of the labor achieved by such disciplined and controlled individuals; and third, domination of outward nature, science, and technology. And to domination subdivided in this way belongs the *threefold freedom* proper to it: first, freedom from the mere necessity of satisfying one's drives, that is, freedom for renunciation and thus for socially acceptable pleasure—moral freedom; second, freedom from arbitrary violence and from the anarchy of the struggle for existence, social freedom characterized by the division of labor, with legal rights and duties—political freedom; and third, freedom from the power of nature, that is, the mastery of nature, freedom to change the world through human reason—intellectual freedom.

The psychic substance common to these three aspects of freedom is *unfreedom*: domination of one's instincts, domination that society makes into second nature and that perpetuates the institutions of domination. But civilized unfreedom is oppression of a particular kind: it is rational unfreedom, rational domination. It is rational to the extent that it makes possible the ascent from a human animal to a human being, from nature to civilization. But does it remain rational when civilization has developed completely?

This is the point at which the Freudian theory of the instincts questions the development of civilization. The question arose in the course of psychoanalytic practice, of clinical experience, which for Freud opened the way to theory. Thus it is in the individual and from the point of view of the individual—and in fact from the point of view of the sick, neurotic individual—that civilization is put into question. The sickness is one's individual fate, private history; but in psychoanalysis the private reveals itself to be a particular instance of the general destiny, of the traumatic wound that the repressive transformation of the instincts has inflicted on man. When Freud then asks what civilization has made of man, he is contrasting civilization not with the idea of some "natural" condition but rather with the historically developing needs of individuals and with the possibilities for their fulfillment.

Freud's answer has already been indicated in what has been said. The more civilization progresses, the more powerful its apparatus for the development and gratification of social needs becomes, the more oppressive are the sacrifices that it has to impose on individuals in order to maintain the necessary instinctual structure.

The thesis contained in the Freudian theory asserts that repression increases with cultural progress because the aggression to be suppressed increases. The assertion seems more than questionable when we compare present freedoms with previous ones. Sexual morality is certainly much more relaxed than it was in the nineteenth century. Certainly the patriarchal authority structure and with it the family as the agency of education, of "socialization" of the individual, has been considerably weakened. Certainly political liberties in the Western world are much more wide-spread than they were previously, even though the substance of the fascist period is alive in them again and there is no need to prove the growth of aggression. Nevertheless, when we consider the greater liberality of public and private morality, the essential connection that, according to Freud, existed between these facts and the instinctual dynamic is by no means immediately evident. But the present situation appears in another light when we apply the Freudian categories to it more concretely.

There are two orientations for this examination of Freudian instinct theory. The first is in terms of the *reification and automatization of the ego*. According to Freudian instinct theory, the reality principle works primarily through the processes that occur between the id, the ego, and the superego, between the unconscious, the conscious, and the outside world. The ego, or rather the conscious part of the ego, fights a battle on two fronts, against the id and against the outside world, with frequently shifting alliances. Essentially, the struggle centers on the degree of instinctual freedom to be allowed and the modifications, sublimations, and repressions to be carried out. The conscious ego plays a leading role in this struggle. The decision is really *its* decision; it is, at least in the normal case of the mature individual, the responsible master of the psychic processes. But this mastery has undergone a crucial change. Franz Alexander pointed out that the ego becomes "corporeal," so to speak, and that its reactions to the outside world and to the instinctual desires emerging from the id become increasingly "automatic." The conscious processes of confrontation are replaced to an increasing degree by immediate, almost physical reactions in which comprehending consciousness, thought, and even one's own feelings play a very small role. It is as though the free space which the individual has at his disposal for his psychic processes has been greatly narrowed down; it is no longer possible for something like an individual psyche with its own demands and decisions to develop; the space is occupied by public, social forces. This reduction of the relatively autonomous ego is empirically observable in people's frozen gestures, and in the growing passivity of leisuretime activities, which become more and more inescapably de-privatized, centralized, universalized in the bad sense, and as such controlled. This process is the psychic correlate of the social overpowering of the opposition, the impotence of criticism, technical coordination, and the permanent mobilization of the collective.

The second change is the *strengthening* of *extra-familial* authority. The social development that has dethroned the individual as an economic subject has also reduced, to an extreme degree, the individualistic function of the family in favor of more effective powers. The younger generation is taught the reality principle less through the family than outside the family; it learns socially useful reactions and ways of behaving outside of the protected private sphere of the family. The modern father is not a very effective representative of the reality principle, and the loosening of sexual morality makes it easier to overcome the Oedipus complex: the struggle against the father loses much of its decisive psychological significance. But the effect of this is to strengthen rather than to weaken the omnipotence of domination. Precisely insofar as the family was something private it stood against public power or at least was different from it; the more the family is now controlled by public power, that is, the more the models and examples are taken from outside it, the more unified and uninterrupted becomes the "socialization" of the young generation in the interest of public power, as a part of public power. Here too the psychic space in which independence and difference could emerge is limited and occupied.

In order to make the historical function of these psychic changes evident, we must try to see them in connection with contemporary political structures. The defining characteristic of these structures has been called *mass democracy*. Without discussing whether we are justified in using this concept, we will outline its main components briefly: in mass democracy the real elements of politics are no longer identifiable individual groups but rather unified—or politically integrated— *totalities*. There are two dominant units; first, the giant production-and-distribution apparatus of modern industry, and second, the masses which serve this apparatus. Having control of the apparatus, or even of its key positions, means having control of the masses in such a way, in fact, that this control seems to result automatically from the division of labor, to be its technical result, the rationale of the functioning apparatus that spans and maintains the whole society. Thus domination appears as a technical-administrative quality, and this quality fuses the different groups that hold the key positions in the apparatus—economic, political, military—into a technical-administrative collective that represents the whole.

On the other hand, the groups that serve the apparatus are united into the masses, the people, through a technical necessity; the people become the object of administration even where they, the "sovereign," delegate power freely and control it democratically.

This technical-administrative collectivization appears as the expression of objective reason, that is, as the form in which the whole reproduces and extends itself. All freedoms are predetermined and preformed by it and subordinated not so much to political force as to the rational demands of the apparatus. The latter encompasses the public and private existence of individuals, of those who administer it as well as those who are administered, it encompasses work time and free time, service and relaxation, nature and culture. But in doing so the apparatus invades the inner sphere of the person himself, his instincts and his intelligence, and this occurs differently than in the earlier stages of the development: it no longer occurs primarily as the intervention of a brutal external, personal, or natural force, no longer even as the free working of competition, of the economy, but rather as completely objectified technological reason, which appears doubly rational, methodically controlled—and legitimized.

Thus the masses are no longer simply those who are dominated, but rather the governed who are *no longer in opposition*, or whose opposition itself is integrated into the positive whole, as a calculable and manipulable corrective that demands improvements in the apparatus. What was previously a political subject has become an object, and the antagonistic interests that were previously irreconcilable seem to have passed over into a true collective interest.

With this, however, the political picture as a whole has been transformed. There is no longer an autonomous subject across from the object, a subject that governs and in doing so pursues its own definable interests and goals. *Domination tends to become neutral, interchangeable*, without the totality itself being changed by this change; domination is dependent only on the capacity and the drive to maintain and extend the apparatus as a whole. One visible political expression of this neutralization is the increasing resemblance in the most advanced countries of political parties previously opposed to one another, of their strategy and their goals, the growing unification of political language and political symbols, and the supranational and even supracontinental unification that is taking place despite all resistance and that does not stop even at countries with very different political systems. Might the neutralization of contradictions and the tendency to increasing international resemblance finally determine the relationship of the two opposing total systems, those of the Western and Eastern worlds? There are signs of this.

This political digression may help to illuminate the historical function of the psychic dynamic uncovered by Freud. The political collectivization has its counterpart in the neutralization of the psychic structure, which was briefly described above: the unification of the ego and the superego through which the ego's free confrontation with paternal authority is absorbed by social reason. To the technical-administrative quality of domination correspond the automatization and reification of the ego, in which free actions become rigidified to reactions.

But the ego that has been robbed of its independent power to structure its instincts, and delivered over to the superego is all the more a subject of destruction and all the less a subject of Eros. For the superego is the social agent of repression and the locus of the socially useful destruction stored up in the psyche. *Thus it seems that the psychic atoms of contemporary society are themselves as explosive as is social productivity.* Behind the technical-administrative rational quality of the unification appears the danger of the irrationality that has still not been mastered—in Freud's language, the harshness of the sacrifice that existing civilization must demand of individuals.

As productivity increases, the taboos and instinctual prohibitions on which social productivity rests have to be guarded with ever greater anxiety. Might we say, going beyond Freud, that this is so because the temptation to enjoy this increasing productivity in freedom and happiness becomes increasingly strong and increasingly rational? In any case Freud speaks of an "intensification of the feeling of guilt" in the progress of civilization, of its increase "perhaps to extremes that the individual finds hard to tolerate."[6] And he sees in this feeling of guilt the "expression of the conflict of ambivalence, of the perpetual struggle between Eros and the destructive or death instinct."[7] This is Freud's revolutionary insight: the conflict that is decisive for the fate of civilization is that between the reality of repression and the almost equally real possibility of doing away with repression, between the increase of Eros necessary for civilization and the equally necessary suppression of its claims for pleasure. To the extent that the emancipation of Eros can be more and more clearly envisaged as social wealth increases, its repression becomes harsher and harsher. And thus just as this repression weakens Eros' power to bind the death instinct, it also releases destructive energy from its bonds and frees aggression to a hitherto unknown extent, which in turn makes more intensive control and manipulation a political necessity.

This is the fatal dialectic of civilization, which, according to Freud, has no solution—just as the struggle between Eros and the death instinct, productivity and destruction has no solution. But if we are justified in seeing in this conflict the contradiction between socially necessary oppression and the historical possibility of going beyond it, then the increasing "feeling of guilt" would be characterized by the same contradiction: the guilt then lies not only in the continued existence of prohibited instinctual impulses—hostility toward the father and desire for the mother—but also in the acceptance and even complicity with suppression, that is, in reinstating, internalizing, and defying paternal authority and thus domination as such. What on more primitive cultural levels was—perhaps—not only a social but also a biological necessity for the further development of the species has become, at the height of civilization, a merely social, political "necessity" for maintaining the status quo. The incest taboo was the historical and structural *prima causa* for the whole chain of taboos and repressions that characterize patriarchal-monogamous society. These perpetuate the subordination of gratification to a productivity that transcends itself and destroys itself, and perpetuates the mutilation of Eros, of the life instincts. Hence the feeling of guilt about a freedom that one has both missed and betrayed.

Freud's definition of the conflict in civilization as the expression of the eternal struggle between Eros and the death instinct points to an internal contradiction in Freudian theory, which contradiction, in turn, as a genuine one, contains the possibility of its own solution, a possibility that psychoanalysis has almost repressed. Freud emphasizes that "civilization obeys an inner erotic impulse that tells it to unite men in an increasingly intimately bound mass."[8] If this is true, how can what Freud repeatedly emphasized as the amoral and asocial, even anti-moral and anti-social nature of Eros be at the same time one that "creates civilization"? How can the integral claim of the pleasure principle, which outweighs even the drive for self-preservation, how can the polymorphous-perverse character of sexuality be an erotic impulse to civilization? It does not help to assign the two sides of the contradiction to two successive stages of development; Freud ascribes both sides to the original nature of Eros. Instead we must sustain the contradiction itself and find in it the way to its solution.

When Freud ascribes the goal of "uniting the organic in ever greater units,"[9] of "producing and preserving ever greater units,"[10] to the sexual drives, this striving is at work in every process that preserves life, from the first union of the germ cells to the formation of cultural communities: society and nation. This drive stands under the aegis of the pleasure principle: it is precisely the polymorphous character of sexuality that drives beyond the special function to which it is limited, toward gaining more intensive and extensive pleasure, toward the generation of libidinous ties with one's fellow men, the production of a libidinous, that is, happy environment. Civilization arises from pleasure: we must hold fast to this thesis in all its provocativeness. Freud writes: "The same process occurs in the social relations of men that psychoanalytic research has become familiar with in regard to the course of development of individual libido. Libido involves itself in gratifying the major needs of life and chooses for its first objects the persons who participate in this activity. And as with the individual, so in the development of mankind as a whole, love alone, in the sense of turning from egoism to altruism, has acted as the force of civilization."[11] It is Eros, not Agape, it is the drive that has not yet been split into sublimated and unsublimated energy, from which this effect proceeds. The *work* that has contributed so essentially to the development of man from animal is *originally libidinous.* Freud states expressly that sexual as well as sublimated love is "connected to communal labor."[12] Man begins working because he finds pleasure in work, not only after work, pleasure in the play of his faculties and the fulfillment of his life needs, not as a means of life but as life itself. Man begins the cultivation of nature and of himself, cooperation, in order to secure and perpetuate the gaining of pleasure. It is perhaps Géza Róheim who has most penetratingly presented and tried to prove this thesis.

If this is so, however, the Freudian conception of the relationship between civilization and the dynamic of the instincts is in need of a decisive correction. The conflict between the pleasure principle and the reality principle would then be neither biologically necessary nor insoluble nor soluble only through a repressive transformation of the instincts. And the repressive solution would then be not a natural process extended into history and compelled by an ineluctable struggle for existence, weakness, and hostility, but rather a sociohistorical process which has become part of nature. The traumatic transformation of the organism into an instrument of alienated labor is *not* the psychic condition of civilization as such but only of civilization as domination, that is, of a specific form of civilization. Constitutional unfreedom would not be the condition of freedom in civilization but rather only of freedom in a civilization organized on the basis of domination, which in fact is what existing civilization is.

Freud actually did derive the fate of the instincts from that of domination: it is the despotism of the primal father that forces the development of the instincts into the path which then becomes the psychological foundation for rational, domination-based civilization, which, however, never abandoned its roots in the original domination. Since the rebellion of the sons and brothers against the primal father[13] and the reestablishment and internalization of paternal authority, domination, religion, and morality have been intimately connected, and in such a way that the latter provide the psychological foundation for the permanence and the legitimized organization—the "reason"—of domination but at the same time make domination universal. Just as all share in the guilt, the rebellion, so all must make sacrifices, including those who now rule. The masters, like the servants, submit to limitations on their instinctual gratification, on pleasure. But just as repression of the instincts makes every servant "master in his own house," so it also reproduces masters over all houses: with instinctual repression social domination fortifies its position as universal reason. This takes place in the *organization of labor.*

The development of domination through the organization of labor is a process the study of which belongs to political economy rather than psychology. But the somatic-psychic preconditions for this development which Freud uncovered make it possible to pinpoint the hypothetical point at which civilization based on instinctual repression stops being historically "rational" and reproducing historical reason. To demonstrate that this is possible let me summarize again the main factors in the dynamic of the instincts insofar as they are decisive for the labor process: first, repressive modifications of sexuality make the organism free to be used as an instrument of unpleasurable but socially useful labor. Second, if this labor is a lifelong chief occupation, that is, has become the universal means of life, then the original direction of the instincts is so distorted that the content of life is no longer gratification but rather working toward it. Third, in this way civilization reproduces itself on an increasingly extended scale. The energy won from sexuality and sublimated constantly increases the psychic "investment fund" for the increasing productivity of labor (technical progress). Fourth, increasing productivity of labor increases the possibility of enjoyment and thus the potential reversal of the socially compelled relationship between labor and enjoyment, labor time and free time. But the domination reproduced in the existing relationships also reproduces sublimation on an increasing scale: the goods produced for enjoyment remain commodities, the enjoyment of which presupposes further labor within existing relationships. Gratification remains a by-product of ungratifying labor. Increasing productivity itself becomes the necessity which it was to eliminate. Thus, fifth, the sacrifices that socialized individuals have imposed on themselves since the fall of the primal father become increasingly more irrational the more obviously reason has fulfilled its purpose and eliminated the original state of need. And the guilt which the sacrifices were to expiate through the deification and internalization of the father (religion and morality) remains unexpiated, because with the reestablishment of patriarchal authority, although in the form of rational universality, the—suppressed—wish for its annihilation remains alive. Indeed, the guilt becomes increasingly oppressive as this domination reveals its archaic character in the light of historical possibilities for liberation.

At this stage of development unfreedom appears no longer as the fundamental condition of rational freedom but rather as a limitation on freedom. The achievements of domination-based civilization have undermined the necessity for unfreedom; the degree of domination of nature and of social wealth attained makes it possible to reduce ungratifying labor to a minimum; quantity is transformed into quality, free time can become the content of life and work can become the free play of human capacities. In this way the repressive structure of the instincts would be explosively transformed: the instinctual energies that would no longer be caught up in ungratifying work would become free and, as Eros, would strive to universalize libidinous relationships and develop a libidinous civilization. But although in the light of this possibility the necessity of instinctual repression appears irrational, it remains not only a social but also a biological necessity for men in existing society. For the repression of the instincts reproduced renunciation in the individuals themselves, and the apparatus of need-gratification that they have constructed reproduces the individuals themselves in the form of labor power.

We have already said that the Freudian theory of the instincts in its fundamental conception seems to represent the psychological counterpart of the ethical-idealist notion of freedom. Despite Freud's mechanistic-materialist notion of the soul, freedom contains its own repression, its own unfreedom, because without this unfreedom man would fall back to the animal level: "Individual freedom is not a product of civilization." And just as idealist ethics interprets the freedom that suppresses sensuousness as an ontological structure and sees in it the "essence" of human freedom, so Freud sees in the repression of the instincts both a cultural and a natural necessity: scarcity, the struggle for existence, and the anarchical character of the instincts place limits on freedom which cannot be trespassed. We can now follow these parallels further. A second essential moment of the idealist notion of freedom, most clearly expressed in existential philosophy, is transcendence: human freedom is the possibility, even the necessity, of going beyond, negating every given situation in existence, because in relation to men's possibilities every situation itself is negativity, a barrier, "something other." Human existence thus seems, to use Sartre's notion, an eternal "project," which never reaches fulfillment, plenitude, rest: the contradiction between in-itself and for-itself can never be solved in a real being-in-and-for-itself. This negativity of the notion of freedom also finds its psychological formulation in Freud's instinct theory.

This becomes evident when we remember the "conservative nature" of the instincts, which produces the lifelong conflict between the pleasure principle and the reality principle. The basic instincts are striving essentially for gratification, perpetuation of pleasure, but the fulfillment of this striving would be the *death* of man, both his natural and his sociohistorical death: natural death in being the condition before birth, historical death in being the state before civilization. Sublimation is the psychological transcendence in which civilized freedom consists, the negation of a negativity which itself still remains negative—not only because it is repression of sensuality but also because it perpetuates itself as transcendence: the productivity of renunciation, which spurs itself on endlessly. But what in idealist ethics remains wrapped up and concealed in an ontological structure and in this form is transfigured as the crown of humanity appears in Freud as a traumatic wound, a disease that culture has inflicted on man and that cries out for healing. Increasing destruction and constriction, growing anxiety, "discontent with civilization" that grows out of the suppression of the wish for happiness, out of the sacrifice of the possibility of happiness—all this is not the other side of civilized freedom but its inner logic, and must be controlled and supervised all the more strictly the nearer civilization, in progressing, brings the possibility of happiness and the more it transforms a utopian fantasy into to an undertaking that can be directed by science and knowledge.

Thus Freud reveals the actual negativity of freedom, and in refusing to transfigure it idealistically he preserves the idea of another possible freedom in which the repression of the instincts would be abolished along with political oppression, while the achievements of repression would be preserved. In Freud there is nothing like a return to nature or to natural man: the process of civilization is irreversible. If instinctual repression can be done away with to the point where the existing relationship of labor and enjoyment can be reversed, the archaic sublimation of erotic energy can be revoked. If, therefore, sensuousness and reason, happiness and freedom can be brought into harmony or even unity, this is possible only at the height of the development of civilization, where the state of absolute need and lack could be done away with, technically at least, and where the struggle for existence no longer need be a struggle for the means of existence.

Freud was more than skeptical with regard to this possibility. He was all the more so in that he had seen the profound connection between growing productivity and growing destruction, between increasing control of nature and increasing control of men, long before the atom and hydrogen bombs and before that total mobilization that began with the period of fascism and evidently has not yet reached its peak. He saw that men must be kept in line with ever better and more effective means the greater social wealth becomes, the wealth that would be able to satisfy their freely—not manipulated—developing needs. This is perhaps the final reason for Freud's assertion that the progress of civilization has intensified guilt feeling to almost unbearable heights—the feeling of guilt about the prohibited instinctual wishes that are still active despite almost lifelong repression. He maintained that these forbidden and living instinctual impulses are directed in the final instance toward the father and mother; but in his late work they are distinguished increasingly clearly from their first biological-psychological form. The feeling of guilt is now defined as "the expression of the conflict of ambivalence, of the eternal struggle between Eros and the destruction or death instinct."[14] And a puzzling statement reads: "What began with the father is completed in the masses."[15] Civilization obeys "an inner erotic impulse" when it unites men in "intimately connected" communities; it obeys the pleasure principle. But Eros is connected to the death instinct, the pleasure principle to the Nirvana principle. The conflict has to be fought out—and "as long as this community knows only the form of the family," it expresses itself in the Oedipus complex. To understand the full import of the Freudian conception one must be aware of the way the forces are distributed in this conflict. The father, in forbidding the son the mother he desires, represents Eros, which restricts the regression of the death instinct—and thereby, repressive Eros, which limits the pleasure principle to pleasure compatible with life but also with society, and thus releases destructive energy. There is a corresponding ambivalence of love and hate in the relationship to the father. The mother is the goal of Eros and of the death instinct: behind the sexual wish stands the wish for regression to the condition before birth, the undifferentiated union of the pleasure principle and the Nirvana principle *on this side* of the reality principle and thus without ambivalence, pure libido. The erotic impulse to civilization then extends beyond the family and joins greater and greater social groups, the conflict becomes intensified "in forms that depend on the past": paternal domination extends itself triumphantly and thus the ambivalence conflict does too. At the height of civilization it plays itself out in and against the masses, who have incorporated the father into themselves. And the more universal domination becomes, the more universal becomes the destruction that it releases. The conflict between Eros and the death instinct belongs to the innermost essence of the development of civilization, *as long as it occurs in forms that "depend on the past."*

Thus the thought Freud expresses so often is emphasized again—that the history of mankind is still dominated by "archaic" powers, that prehistory and early history are still at work in us. The "return of the repressed" takes place at the fearful turning points of history: in the hatred of and rebellion against the father, in the deification and restoration of paternal authority. The erotic impulses to civilization that strive for the union of happiness and freedom fall prey to domination over and over again, and protest suffocates in destruction. Only seldom and cautiously did Freud express the hope that civilization would finally realize at some date the freedom that it could have realized for so long and thus conquer the archaic powers. *Civilization and Its Discontents* closes with the words: "Men have brought their powers of subduing the forces of nature to such a pitch that by using them they could now very easily exterminate one another to the last man. They know this—hence arises a great part of their current unrest, their dejection, their mood of apprehension. And now it may be expected that the other of the two 'heavenly forces,' eternal Eros, will put forth his strength so as to maintain himself alongside of his equally immortal adversary."[16]

That was written in 1930. In the time that has passed since then there has been truly no trace of the opponent's growing retaliation, of the approach of that happy freedom, of Eros as creator of civilization. Or does perhaps the increasing activity of destruction, which presents an ever more rational face, indicate that civilization is proceeding toward a catastrophe that will pull the archaic forces down with it in its collapse and thus clear the way to a higher stage?

NOTES

1. See this text, pp. 28–43. "This text" refers to the collection of essays from which this selection is excerpted. The collection is Marcuse's *Five Lectures* (Boston: Beacon Press, 1970).
2. Sigmund Freud, "Abriss der Psychoanalyse" (Outline of Psychoanalysis), *Gesammelte Werke*, 18 vols. (London and Frankfurt: S. Fischer Verlag, 1940-1968), 17:75. All subsequent references to the collected works of Freud are taken from this edition.
3. Immanuel Kant, "Metaphysische Anfangsgründe der Tugendlehre," *Die Metaphysik der Sitten*, in two parts (Königsberg: Nicolovius, 1797), 2:6.
4. Sigmund Freud, "Das Unbehagen in der Kultur" (Civilization and Its Discontents), *Gesammelte Werke*, 14:442.
5. *Ibid.*, 14:455.
6. *Ibid.*, 14:493.
7. *Ibid.*, 14:492.
8. *Ibid.*
9. Sigmund Freud, "Jenseits des Lustprinzips" (Beyond the Pleasure Principle), *Gesammelte Werke*, 13:45.
10. Sigmund Freud, "Abriss der Psychoanalyse" (Outline of Psychoanalysis), *Gesammelte Werke*, 17:71.
11. Sigmund Freud, "Massenpsychologie und Ich-Analyse" (Group Psychology and the Analysis of the Ego), *Gesammelte Werke*, 13:112.
12. *Ibid.*, 13:113.
13. See *Five Lectures*, pp. 28–43.
14. Sigmund Freud, "Das Unbehagen in der Kultur" (Civilization and Its Discontents), *Gesammelte Werke*, 14:492.
15. *Ibid.*, 14:492 f.
16. Sigmund Freud, *Civilization and Its Discontents* (New York: Doubleday, Anchor edition, 1958), p. 105.

MAX HORKHEIMER

TRADITIONAL AND CRITICAL THEORY

What is "theory"? The question seems a rather easy one for contemporary science. Theory for most researchers is the sum-total of propositions about a subject, the propositions being so linked with each other that a few are basic and the rest derive from these. The smaller the number of primary principles in comparison with the derivations, the more perfect the theory. The real validity of the theory depends on the derived propositions being consonant with the actual facts. If experience and theory contradict each other, one of the two must be reexamined. Either the scientist has failed to observe correctly or something is wrong with the principles of the theory. . . .

The derivation as usually practiced in mathematics is to be applied to all science. The order in the world is captured by a deductive chain of thought.

Those long chains of deductive reasoning, simple and easy as they are, of which geometricians make use in order to arrive at the most difficult demonstrations, had caused me to imagine that all those things which fall under the cognizance of men might very likely be mutually related in the same fashion; and that, provided only that we abstain from receiving anything as true which is not so, and always retain the order which is necessary in order to deduce the one conclusion from the other, there can be nothing so remote that we cannot reach to it, nor so recondite that we cannot discover it. [1]

Depending on the logician's own general philosophical outlook, the most universal propositions from which the deduction begins are themselves regarded as experiential judgments, as inductions (as with John Stuart Mill), as evident insights (as in rationalist and phenomenological schools), or as arbitrary postulates (as in the modern axiomatic approach). In the most advanced logic of the present time, as represented by Husserl's *Logische Untersuchungen*, theory is defined "as an enclosed system of propositions for a science as a whole."[2] Theory in the fullest sense is "a systematically linked set of propositions, taking the form of a systematically unified deduction."[3] Science is "a certain totality of propositions . . . , emerging in one or other manner from theoretical work, in the systematic order of which propositions a certain totality of objects acquires definition."[4] The basic requirement which any theoretical system must satisfy is that all the parts should intermesh thoroughly and without friction. Harmony, which includes lack of contradictions, and the absence of superfluous, purely dogmatic elements which have no influence on the observable phenomena, are necessary conditions, according to Weyl.[5]

In so far as this traditional conception of theory shows a tendency, it is towards a purely mathematical system of symbols. As elements of the theory, as components of the propositions and conclusions, there are ever fewer names of experiential objects and ever more numerous mathematical symbols. Even the logical operations themselves have already been so rationalized that, in large areas of natural science at least, theory formation has become a matter of mathematical construction.

The sciences of man and society have attempted to follow the lead of the natural sciences with their great successes. The difference between those schools of social science which are more oriented to the investigation of facts and those which concentrate more on principles has nothing directly to do with the concept of theory as such. The assiduous collecting of facts in all the disciplines dealing with social life, the gathering of great masses of detail in connection with problems, the empirical inquiries, through careful questionnaires and other means, which are a major part of scholarly activity, especially in the Anglo-Saxon universities since Spencer's time— all this adds up to a pattern which is, outwardly, much like the rest of life in a society dominated by industrial production techniques. . . .

There can be no doubt, in fact, that the various schools of sociology have an identical conception of theory and that it is the same as theory in the natural sciences. Empirically oriented sociologists have the same idea of what a fully elaborated theory should be as their theoretically oriented brethren. The former, indeed, are persuaded that in view of the complexity of social problems and the present state of science any concern with general principles must be regarded as indolent and idle. If theoretical work is to be done, it must be done with an eye unwaveringly on the facts; there can be no thought in the foreseeable future of comprehensive theoretical statements. These scholars are much enamored of the methods of exact formulation and, in particular, of mathematical procedures, which are especially congenial to the conception of theory described above. . . . There is always, on the one hand, the conceptually formulated knowledge and, on the other, the facts to be subsumed under it. Such a subsumption or establishing of a relation between the simple perception or verification of a fact and the conceptual structure of our knowing is called its theoretical explanation.

. . . For Weber, the historian's explanations, like those of the expert in criminal law, rest not on the fullest possible enumeration of all pertinent circumstances but on the establishment of a connection between those elements of an event which are significant for historical continuity, and particular, determinative happenings. This connection, for example the judgment that a war resulted from the policies of a statesman who knew what he was about, logically supposes that, had such a policy not existed, some other effect would have followed. If one maintains a particular causal nexus between historical events, one is necessarily implying that had the nexus not existed, then in accordance with the rules that govern our experience another effect would have followed in the given circumstances. The rules of experience here are nothing but the formulations of our knowledge concerning economic, social, and psychological interconnections. With the help of these we reconstruct the probable course of events, going beyond the event itself to what will serve as explanation.[6] We are thus working with conditional propositions as applied to a given situation. If circumstances a, b, c, and d are given, then event q must be expected; if d is lacking, event r; if g is added, event s, and so on. This kind of calculation is a logical tool of history as it is of science. It is in this fashion that theory in the traditional sense is actually elaborated.

What scientists in various fields regard as the essence of theory thus corresponds, in fact, to the immediate tasks they set for themselves. The manipulation of physical nature and of specific economic and social mechanisms demand alike the amassing of a body of knowledge such as is supplied in an ordered set of hypotheses. The technological advances of the bourgeois period are inseparably linked to this function of the pursuit of science. On the one hand, it made the facts fruitful for the kind of scientific knowledge that would have practical application in the circumstances, and, on the other, it made possible the application of knowledge already possessed. Beyond doubt, such work is a moment in the continuous transformation and development of the material foundations of that society. But the conception of theory was absolutized, as though it were grounded in the inner nature of knowledge as such or justified in some other ahistorical way, and thus it became a reified, ideological category.

As a matter of fact, the fruitfulness of newly discovered factual connections for the renewal of existent knowledge, and the application of such knowledge to the facts, do not derive from purely logical or methodological sources but can rather be understood only in the context of real social processes. When a discovery occasions the restructuring of current ideas, this is not due exclusively to logical considerations or, more particularly, to the contradiction between the discovery and particular elements in current views. If this were the only real issue, one could always think up further hypotheses by which one could avoid changing the theory as a whole. That new views in fact win out is due to concrete historical circumstances, even if the scientist himself may be determined to change his views only by immanent motives. Modern theoreticians of knowledge do not deny the importance of historical circumstance, even if among the most influential nonscientific factors they assign more importance to genius and accident than to social conditions. . . .

The traditional idea of theory is based on scientific activity as carried on within the division of labor at a particular stage in the latter's development. It corresponds to the activity of the scholar which takes place alongside all the other activities of a society but in no immediately clear connection with them. In this view of theory, therefore, the real social function of science is not made manifest; it speaks not of what theory means in human life, but only of what it means in the isolated sphere in which for historical reasons it comes into existence. Yet as a matter of fact the life of society is the result of all the work done in the various sectors of production. Even if therefore the division of labor in the capitalist system functions but poorly, its branches, including science, do not become for that reason self-sufficient and independent. They are particular instances of the way in which society comes to grips with nature and maintains its own inherited form. They are moments in the social process of production, even if they be almost or entirely unproductive in the narrower sense. Neither the structures of industrial and agrarian production nor the separation of the so-called guiding and executory functions, services, and works, or of intellectual and manual operations are eternal or natural states of affairs. They emerge rather from the mode of production practiced in particular forms of society. The seeming self-sufficiency enjoyed by work processes whose course is supposedly determined by the very nature of the object corresponds to the seeming freedom of the economic subject in bourgeois society. The latter believe they are acting according to personal determinations, whereas in fact even in their most complicated calculations they but exemplify the working of an incalculable social mechanism. . . .

The whole perceptible world as present to a member of bourgeois society and as interpreted within a traditional worldview which is in continuous interaction with that given world, is seen by the perceiver as a sum-total of facts; it is there and must be accepted. The classificatory thinking of each individual is one of those social reactions by which men try to adapt to reality in a way that best meets their needs. But there is at this point an essential difference between the individual and society. The world which is given to the individual and which he must accept and take into account is, in its present and continuing form, a product of the activity of society as a whole. The objects we perceive in our surroundings—cities, villages, fields, and woods—bear the mark of having been worked on by man. It is not only in clothing and appearance, in outward form and emotional make-up that men are the product of history. Even the way they see and hear is inseparable from the social life-process as it has evolved over the millennia. The facts which our senses present to us are socially preformed in two ways: through the historical character of the object perceived and through the historical character of the perceiving organ. Both are not simply natural; they are shaped by human activity, and yet the individual perceives himself as receptive and passive in the act of perception. The opposition of passivity and activity, which appears in knowledge theory as a dualism of sense-perception and understanding, does not hold for society, however, in the same measure as for the individual. The individual sees himself as passive and dependent, but society, though made up of individuals, is an active subject, even if a nonconscious one and, to that extent, a subject only in an improper sense. This difference in the existence of man and society is an expression of the cleavage which has up to now affected the historical forms of social life. The existence of society has either been founded directly on oppression or been the blind outcome of conflicting forces, but in any event not the result of conscious spontaneity on the part of free individuals. Therefore the meaning of "activity" and "passivity" changes according as these concepts are applied to society or to individual. In the bourgeois economic mode the activity of society is blind and concrete, that of individuals abstract and conscious.

Human production also always has an element of planning to it. To the extent then that the facts which the individual and his theory encounter are socially produced, there must be rationality in them, even if in a restricted sense. But social action always involves, in addition, available knowledge and its application. The perceived fact is therefore co-determined by human ideas and concepts, even before its conscious theoretical elaboration by the knowing individual. Nor are we to think here only of experiments in natural science. The so-called purity of objective event to be achieved by the experimental procedure is, of course, obviously connected with technological conditions, and the connection of these in turn with the material process of production is evident. But it is easy here to confuse two questions: the question of the mediation of the factual through the activity of society as a whole, and the question of the influence of the measuring instrument, that is, of a particular action, upon the object being observed. The latter problem, which continually plagues physics, is no more closely connected with the problem that concerns us here than is the problem of perception generally, including perception in everyday life. Man's physiological apparatus for sensation itself largely anticipates the order followed in physical experiment. As man reflectively records reality, he separates and rejoins pieces of it, and concentrates on some particulars while failing to notice others. This process is just as much a result of the modern mode of production, as the perception of a man in a tribe of primitive hunters and fishers is the result of the conditions of his existence (as well, of course, as of the object of perception). . . .

At least Kant understood that behind the discrepancy between fact and theory which the scholar experiences in his professional work, there lies a deeper unity, namely, the general subjectivity upon which individual knowledge depends. The activity of society thus appears to be a transcendental power, that is, the sum-total of spiritual factors. However, Kant's claim that its reality is sunk in obscurity, that is, that it is irrational despite all its rationality, is not without its kernel of truth. The bourgeois type of economy, despite all the ingenuity of the competing individuals within it, is not governed by any plan; it is not consciously directed to a general goal; the life of society as a whole proceeds from this economy only at the cost of excessive friction, in a stunted form, and almost, as it were, accidentally. The internal difficulties in the supreme concepts of Kantian philosophy, especially the ego of transcendental subjectivity, pure or original apperception, and consciousness-in-itself, show the depth and honesty of his thinking. The two-sidedness of these Kantian concepts, that is, their supreme unity and purposefulness, on the one hand, and their obscurity, unknownness, and impenetrability, on the other, reflects exactly the contradiction-filled form of human activity in the modern period. The collaboration of men in society is the mode of existence which reason urges upon them, and so they do apply their powers and thus confirm their own rationality. But at the same time their work and its results are alienated from them, and the whole process with all its waste of work-power and human life, and with its wars and all its senseless wretchedness, seems to be an unchangeable force of nature, a fate beyond man's control. . . .

We must go on now to add that there is a human activity which has society itself for its object.[7] The aim of this activity is not simply to eliminate one or other abuse, for it regards such abuses as necessarily connected with the way in which the social structure is organized. Although it itself emerges from the social structure, its purpose is not, either in its conscious intention or in its objective significance, the better functioning of any element in the structure. On the contrary, it is suspicious of the very categories of better, useful, appropriate, productive, and valuable, as these are understood in the present order, and refuses to take them as nonscientific presuppositions about which one can do nothing. The individual as a rule must simply accept the basic conditions of his existence as given and strive to fulfill them; he finds his satisfaction and praise in accomplishing as well as he can the tasks connected with his place in society and in courageously doing his duty despite all the sharp criticism he may choose to exercise in particular matters. But the critical attitude of which we are speaking is wholly distrustful of the rules of conduct with which society as presently constituted provides each of its members. The separation between individual and society in virtue of which the individual accepts as natural the limits prescribed for his activity is relativized in critical theory. The latter considers the overall framework which is conditioned by the blind interaction of individual activities (that is, the existent division of labor and the class distinctions) to be a function which originates in human action and therefore is a possible object of planful decision and rational determination of goals.

The two-sided character of the social totality in its present form becomes, for men who adopt the critical attitude, a conscious opposition. In recognizing the present form of economy and the whole culture which it generates to be the product of human work as well as the organization which mankind was capable of and has provided for itself in the present era, these men identify themselves with this totality and conceive it as will and reason. It is their own world. At the same time, however, they experience the fact that society is comparable to nonhuman natural processes, to pure mechanisms, because cultural forms which are supported by war and oppression are not the creations of a unified, self-conscious will. That world is not their own but the world of capital.

Previous history thus cannot really be understood; only the individuals and specific groups in it are intelligible, and even these not totally, since their internal dependence on an inhuman society means that even in their conscious action such individuals and groups are still in good measure mechanical functions. The identification, then, of men of critical mind with their society is marked by tension, and the tension characterizes all the concepts of the critical way of thinking. Thus, such thinkers interpret the economic categories of work, value, and productivity exactly as they are interpreted in the existing order, and they regard any other interpretation as pure idealism. But at the same time they consider it rank dishonesty simply to accept the interpretation; the critical acceptance of the categories which rule social life contains simultaneously their condemnation. This dialectical character of the self-interpretation of contemporary man is what, in the last analysis, also causes the obscurity of the Kantian critique of reason. Reason cannot become transparent to itself as long as men act as members of an organism which lacks reason. Organism as a naturally developing and declining unity cannot be a sort of model for society, but only a form of deadened existence from which society must emancipate itself. An attitude which aims at such an emancipation and at an alteration of society as a whole might well be of service in theoretical work carried on within reality as presently ordered. But it lacks the pragmatic character which attaches to traditional thought as a socially useful professional activity.

In traditional theoretical thinking, the genesis of particular objective facts, the practical application of the conceptual systems by which it grasps the facts, and the role of such systems in action, are all taken to be external to the theoretical thinking itself. This alienation, which finds expression in philosophical terminology as the separation of value and research, knowledge and action, and other polarities, protects the savant from the tensions we have indicated and provides an assured framework for his activity. Yet a kind of thinking which does not accept this framework seems to have the ground taken out from under it. . . .

. . . Its opposition to the traditional concept of theory springs in general from a difference not so much of objects as of subjects. For men of the critical mind, the facts, as they emerge from the work of society, are not extrinsic in the same degree as they are for the savant or for members of other professions who all think like little savants. The latter look towards a new kind of organization of work. But in so far as the objective realities given in perception are conceived as products which in principle should be under human control and, in the future at least, will in fact come under it, these realities lose the character of pure factuality.

The scholarly specialist "as" scientist regards social reality and its products as extrinsic to him, and "as" citizen exercises his interest in them through political articles, membership in political parties or social service organizations, and participation in elections. But he does not unify these two activities, and his other activities as well, except, at best, by psychological interpretation. Critical thinking, on the contrary, is motivated today by the effort really to transcend the tension and to abolish the opposition between the individual's purposefulness, spontaneity, and rationality, and those work-process relationships on which society is built. Critical thought has a concept of man as in conflict with himself until this opposition is removed. If activity governed by reason is proper to man, then existent social practice, which forms the individual's life down to its least details, is inhuman, and this inhumanity affects everything that goes on in the society. There will always be something that is extrinsic to man's intellectual and material activity, namely nature as the totality of as yet unmastered elements with which society must deal. But when situations which really depend on man alone, the relationships of men in their work, and the course of man's own history are also accounted part of "nature," the resultant extrinsicality is not only not a suprahistorical eternal category (even pure nature in the sense described is not that), but it is a sign of contemptible weakness. To surrender to such weakness is nonhuman and irrational. . . .

Critical thought and its theory are opposed to both the types of thinking just described. Critical thinking is the function neither of the isolated individual nor of a sum-total of individuals. Its subject is rather a definite individual in his real relation to other individuals and groups, in his conflict with a particular class, and, finally, in the resultant web of relationships with the social totality and with nature. . . .

How is critical thought related to experience? One might maintain that if such thought were not simply to classify but also to determine for itself the goals which classification serves, in other words its own fundamental direction, it would remain locked up within itself, as happened to idealist philosophy. If it did not take refuge in utopian fantasy, it would be reduced to the formalistic fighting of sham battles. The attempt legitimately to determine practical goals by thinking must always fail. If thought were not content with the role given to it in existent society, if it were not to engage in theory in the traditional sense of the word, it would necessarily have to return to illusions long since laid bare.

The fault in such reflections as these on the role of thought is that thinking is understood in a detachedly departmentalized and therefore spiritualist way, as it is today under existing conditions of the division of labor. . . . Now, inasmuch as every individual in modern times has been required to make his own the purposes of society as a whole and to recognize these in society, there is the possibility that men would become aware of and concentrate their attention upon the path which the social work process has taken without any definite theory behind it, as a result of disparate forces interacting, and with the despair of the masses acting as a decisive factor at major turning points. Thought does not spin such a possibility out of itself but rather becomes aware of its own proper function. In the course of history men have come to know their own activity and thus to recognize the contradiction that marks their existence. . . .

Yet, as far as the role of experience is concerned, there is a difference between traditional and critical theory. The viewpoints which the latter derives from historical analysis as the goals of human activity, especially the idea of a reasonable organization of society that will meet the needs of the whole community, are immanent in human work but are not correctly grasped by individuals or by the common mind. A certain concern is also required if these tendencies are to be perceived and expressed. According to Marx and Engels such a concern is necessarily generated in the proletariat. . . .

But it must be added that even the situation of the proletariat is, in this society, no guarantee of correct knowledge. The proletariat may indeed have experience of meaninglessness in the form of continuing and increasing wretchedness and injustice in its own life. Yet this awareness is prevented from becoming a social force by the differentiation of social structure which is still imposed on the proletariat from above and by the opposition between personal class interests which is transcended only at very special moments. Even to the proletariat the world superficially seems quite different than it really is. Even an outlook which could grasp that no opposition really exists between the proletariat's own true interests and those of society as a whole, and would therefore derive its principles of action from the thoughts and feelings of the masses, would fall into slavish dependence on the status quo. The intellectual is satisfied to proclaim with reverent admiration the creative strength of the proletariat and finds satisfaction in adapting himself to it and in canonizing it. He fails to see that such an evasion of theoretical effort (which the passivity of his own thinking spares him) and of temporary opposition to the masses (which active theoretical effort on his part might force upon him) only makes the masses blinder and weaker than they need be. His own thinking should in fact be a critical, promotive factor in the development of the masses. . . .

If critical theory consisted essentially in formulations of the feelings and ideas of one class at any given moment, it would not be structurally different from the special branches of science. It would be engaged in describing the psychological contents typical of certain social groups; it would be social psychology. The relation of being to consciousness is different in different classes of society. If we take seriously the ideas by which the bourgeoisie explains its own order—free exchange, free competition, harmony of interests, and so on—and if we follow them to their logical conclusion, they manifest their inner contradiction and therewith their real opposition to the bourgeois order. The simple description of bourgeois self-awareness thus does not give us the truth about this class of men. Similarly, a systematic presentation of the contents of proletarian consciousness cannot provide a true picture of proletarian existence and interests. . . .

If, however, the theoretician and his specific object are seen as forming a dynamic unity with the oppressed class, so that his presentation of societal contradictions is not merely an expression of the concrete historical situation but also a force within it to stimulate change, then his real function emerges. The course of the conflict between the advanced sectors of the class and the individuals who speak out the truth concerning it, as well as of the conflict between the most advanced sectors with their theoreticians and the rest of the class, is to be understood as a process of interactions in which awareness comes to flower along with its liberating but also its aggressive forces which incite while also requiring discipline. The sharpness of the conflict shows in the ever present possibility of tension between the theoretician and the class which his thinking is to serve. The unity of the social forces which promise liberation is at the same time their distinction (in Hegel's sense); it exists only as a conflict which continually threatens the subjects caught up in it. This truth becomes clearly evident in the person of the theoretician; he exercises an aggressive critique not only against the conscious defenders of the status quo but also against distracting, conformist, or utopian tendencies within his own household. . . .

One thing which this way of thinking has in common with fantasy is that an image of the future which springs indeed from a deep understanding of the present determines men's thoughts and actions even in periods when the course of events seems to be leading far away from such a future and seems to justify every reaction except belief in fulfillment. It is not the arbitrariness and supposed independence of fantasy that is the common bond here, but its obstinacy. Within the most advanced group it is the theoretician who must have this obstinacy. The theoretician of the ruling class, perhaps after difficult beginnings, may reach a relatively assured position, but, on the other hand, the theoretician is also at times an enemy and criminal, at times a solitary utopian; even after his death the question of what he really was is not decided. The historical significance of his work is not self-evident; it rather depends on men speaking and acting in such a way as to justify it. It is not a finished and fixed historical creation. . . .

Our consideration of the various functions of traditional and critical theory brings to light the difference in their logical structure. The primary propositions of traditional theory define universal concepts under which all facts in the field in question are to be subsumed; for example, the concept of a physical process in physics or an organic process in biology. . . .

The critical theory of society also begins with abstract determinations; in dealing with the present era it begins with the characterization of an economy based on exchange.[8] The concepts Marx uses, such as commodity, value, and money, can function as genera when, for example, concrete social relations are judged to be relations of exchange and when there is question of the commodity character of goods. But the theory is not satisfied to relate concepts of reality by way of hypotheses. The theory begins with an outline of the mechanism by which bourgeois society, after dismantling feudal regulations, the guild system, and vassalage, did not immediately fall apart under the pressure of its own anarchic principle but managed to survive. The regulatory effects of exchange are brought out on which bourgeois economy is founded. The conception of the interaction of society and nature, which is already exercising its influence here, as well as the idea of a unified period of society, of its self-preservation, and so on, spring from a radical analysis, guided by concern for the future, of the historical process. The relation of the primary conceptual interconnections to the world of facts is not essentially a relation of classes to instances. It is because of its inner dynamism that the exchange relationship, which the theory outlines, dominates social reality, as, for example, the assimilation of food largely dominates the organic life of plant and brute beast. . . .

Thus the critical theory of society begins with the idea of the simple exchange of commodities and defines the idea with the help of relatively universal concepts. It then moves further, using all knowledge available and taking suitable material from the research of others as well as from specialized research. Without denying its own principles as established by the special discipline of political economy, the theory shows how an exchange economy, given the condition of men (which, of course, changes under the very influence of such an economy), must necessarily lead to a heightening of those social tensions which in the present historical era lead in turn to wars and revolutions.

The necessity just mentioned, as well as the abstractness of the concepts, are both like and unlike the same phenomena in traditional theory. In both types of theory there is a strict deduction if the claim of validity for general definitions is shown to include a claim that certain factual relations will occur. For example, if you are dealing with electricity, such and such an event must occur because such and such characteristics belong to the very concept of electricity. To the extent that the critical theory of society deduces present conditions from the concept of simple exchange, it includes this kind of necessity, although it is relatively unimportant that the hypothetical form of statement be used. That is, the stress is not on the idea that wherever a society based on simple exchange prevails, capitalism must develop—although this is true. The stress is rather on the fact that the existent capitalist society, which has spread all over the world from Europe and for which the theory is declared valid, derives from the basic relation of exchange. Even the classificatory judgments of specialized science have a fundamentally hypothetical character, and existential judgments are allowed, if at all, only in certain areas, namely the descriptive and practical parts of the discipline.[9] But the critical theory of society is, in its totality, the unfolding of a single existential judgment. To put it in broad terms, the theory says that the basic form of the historically given commodity economy on which modern history rests contains in itself the internal and external tensions of the modern era; it generates these tensions over and over again in an increasingly heightened form; and after a period of progress, development of human powers, and emancipation for the individual, after an enormous extension of human control over nature, it finally hinders further development and drives humanity into a new barbarism. . . .

Even the critical theory, which stands in opposition to other theories, derives its statements about real relationships from basic universal concepts, as we have indicated, and therefore presents the relationships as necessary. Thus both kinds of theoretical structure are alike when it comes to logical necessity. But there is a difference as soon as we turn from logical to real necessity, the necessity involved in factual sequences. The biologist's statement that internal processes cause a plant to wither or that certain processes in the human organism lead to its destruction leaves untouched the question whether any influences can alter the character of these processes or change them totally. Even when an illness is said to be curable, the fact that the necessary curative measures are actually taken is regarded as purely extrinsic to the curability, a matter of technology and therefore nonessential as far as the theory as such is concerned. The necessity which rules society can be regarded as biological in the sense described, and the unique character of critical theory can therefore be called in question on the grounds that in biology as in other natural sciences particular sequences of events can be theoretically constructed just as they are in the critical theory of society. The development of society, in this view, would simply be a particular series of events, for the presentation of which conclusions from various other areas of research are used, just as a doctor in the course of an illness or a geologist dealing with the earth's prehistory has to apply various other disciplines. Society here would be the individual reality which is evaluated on the basis of theories in the special sciences.

However many valid analogies there may be between these different intellectual endeavors, there is nonetheless a decisive difference when it comes to the relation of subject and object and therefore to the necessity of the event being judged. The object with which the scientific specialist deals is not affected at all by his own theory. Subject and object are kept strictly apart. Even if it turns out that at a later point in time the objective event is influenced by human intervention, to science this is just another fact. The objective occurrence is independent of the theory, and this independence is part of its necessity: the observer as such can effect no change in the object. A consciously critical attitude, however, is part of the development of society: the construing of the course of history as the necessary product of an economic mechanism simultaneously contains both a protest against this order of things, a protest generated by the order itself, and the idea of self-determination for the human race, that is the idea of a state of affairs in which man's actions no longer flow from a mechanism but from his own decision. The judgment passed on the necessity inherent in the previous course of events implies here a struggle to change it from a blind to a meaningful necessity. If we think of the object of the theory in separation from the theory, we falsify it and fall into quietism or conformism. Every part of the theory presupposes the critique of the existing order and the struggle against it along lines determined by the theory itself.

The theoreticians of knowledge who started with physics had reason, even if they were not wholly right, to condemn the confusion of cause and operation of forces and to substitute the idea of condition or function for the idea of cause. For the kind of thinking which simply registers facts there are always only series of phenomena, never forces and counterforces; but this, of course, says something about this kind of thinking, not about nature. If such a method is applied to society, the result is statistics and descriptive sociology, and these can be important for many purposes, even for critical theory.

For traditional science either everything is necessary or nothing is necessary, according as necessity means the independence of event from observer or the possibility of absolutely certain prediction. But to the extent that the subject does not totally isolate himself, even as thinker, from the social struggles of which he is a part and to the extent that he does not think of knowledge and action as distinct concepts, necessity acquires another meaning for him. If he encounters necessity which is not mastered by man, it takes shape either as that realm of nature which despite the far-reaching conquests still to come will never wholly vanish, or as the weakness of the society of previous ages in carrying on the struggle with nature in a consciously and purposefully organized way. Here we do have forces and counterforces. Both elements in this concept of necessity—the power of nature and the weakness of society—are interconnected and are based on the experienced effort of man to emancipate himself from coercion by nature and from those forms of social life and of the juridical, political, and cultural orders which have become a straitjacket for him. The struggle on two fronts, against nature and against society's weakness, is part of the effective striving for a future condition of things in which whatever man wills is also necessary and in which the necessity of the object becomes the necessity of a rationally mastered event. . . .

Critical theory does not have one doctrinal substance today, another tomorrow. The changes in it do not mean a shift to a wholly new outlook, as long as the age itself does not radically change. The stability of the theory is due to the fact that amid all change in society the basic economic structure, the class relationship in its simplest form, and therefore the idea of the supersression of these two remain identical. The decisive substantive elements in the theory are conditioned by these unchanging factors and they themselves therefore cannot change until there has been a historical transformation of society. On the other hand, however, history does not stand still until such a point of transformation has been reached. The historical development of the conflicts in which the critical theory is involved leads to a reassignment of degrees of relative importance to individual elements of the theory, forces further concretizations, and determines which results of specialized science are to be significant for critical theory and practice at any given time.

In order to explain more fully what is meant, we shall use the concept of the social class which disposes of the means of production. In the liberalist period economic predominance was in great measure connected with legal ownership of the means of production. The large class of private property owners exercised leadership in the society, and the whole culture of the age bears the impress of this fact. Industry was still broken up into a large number of independent enterprises which were small by modern standards. The directors of factories, as was suitable for this stage of technological development, were either one or more of the owners or their direct appointees. Once, however, the development of technology in the last century had led to a rapidly increasing concentration and centralization of capital, the legal owners were largely excluded from the management of the huge combines which absorbed their small factories, and management became something quite distinct from ownership before the law. Industrial magnates, the leaders of the economy, came into being.

. . . Once the legal owners are cut off from the real productive process and lose their influence, their horizon narrows; they become increasingly unfitted for important social positions, and finally the share which they still have in industry due to ownership and which they have done nothing to augment comes to seem socially useless and morally dubious. These and other changes are accompanied by the rise of ideologies centering on the great personality and the distinction between productive and parasitic capitalists. The idea of a right with a fixed content and independent of society at large loses its importance. The very same sector of society which brutally maintains its private power to dispose of the means of production (and this power is at the heart of the prevailing social order) sponsors political doctrines which claim that unproductive property and parasitic incomes must disappear. The circle of really powerful men grows narrower, but the possibility increases of deliberately constructing ideologies, of establishing a double standard of truth (knowledge for insiders, a cooked-up story for the people), and of cynicism about truth and thought generally. The end result of the process is a society dominated no longer by independent owners but by cliques of industrial and political leaders.

Such changes do not leave the structure of the critical theory untouched. It does not indeed fall victim to the illusion that property and profit no longer play a key role, an illusion carefully fostered in the social sciences. On the one hand, even earlier it had regarded juridical relations not as the substance but as the surface of what was really going on in society. It knows that the disposition of men and things remains in the hands of a particular social group which is in competition with other economic power groups, less so at home but all the more fiercely at the international level. Profit continues to come from the same social sources and must in the last analysis be increased by the same means as before. On the other hand, in the judgment of the critical theorist the loss of all rights with a determined content, a loss conditioned by the concentration of economic power and given its fullest form in the authoritarian state, has brought with it the disappearance not only of an ideology but also of a cultural factor which has a positive value and not simply a negative one.

When the theory takes into account these changes in the inner structure of the entrepreneurial class, it is led to differentiate others of its concepts as well. The dependence of culture on social relationships must change as the latter change, even in details, if society indeed be a single whole. Even in the liberalist period political and moral interpretations of individuals could be derived from their economic situation. Admiration for nobility of character, fidelity to one's word, independence of judgment, and so forth, are traits of a society of relatively independent economic subjects who enter into contractual relationships with each other. But this cultural dependence was in good measure psychologically mediated, and morality itself acquired a kind of stability because of its function in the individual. (The truth that dependence on the economy thoroughly pervaded even this morality was brought home when in the recent threat to the economic position of the liberalist bourgeoisie the attitude of freedom and independence began to disintegrate.) Under the conditions of monopolistic capitalism, however, even such a relative individual independence is a thing of the past. The individual no longer has any ideas of his own. The content of mass belief, in which no one really believes, is an immediate product of the ruling economic and political bureaucracies, and its disciples secretly follow their own atomistic and therefore untrue interests; they act as mere functions of the economic machine.

The concept of the dependence of the cultural on the economic has thus changed. . . . This influence of social development on the structure of the theory is part of the theory's doctrinal content. Thus new contents are not just mechanically added to already existent parts. Since the theory is a unified whole which has its proper meaning only in relation to the contemporary situation, the theory as a whole is caught up in an evolution. The evolution does not change the theory's foundations, of course, any more than recent changes essentially alter the object which the theory reflects, namely contemporary society. Yet even the apparently more remote concepts of the theory are drawn into the evolution. The logical difficulties which understanding meets in every thought that attempts to reflect a living totality are due chiefly to this fact. . . .

There are no general criteria for judging the critical theory as a whole, for it is always based on the recurrence of events and thus on a self-reproducing totality. Nor is there a social class by whose acceptance of the theory one could be guided. It is possible for the consciousness of every social stratum today to be limited and corrupted by ideology, however much, for its circumstances, it may be bent on truth. For all its insight into the individual steps in social change and for all the agreement of its elements with the most advanced traditional theories, the critical theory has no specific influence on its side, except concern for the abolition of social injustice. This negative formulation, if we wish to express it abstractly, is the materialist content of the idealist concept of reason.

In a historical period like the present true theory is more critical than affirmative, just as the society that corresponds to it cannot be called "productive." The future of humanity depends on the existence today of the critical attitude, which of course contains within it elements from traditional theories and from our declining culture generally. Mankind has already been abandoned by a science which in its imaginary self-sufficiency thinks of the shaping of practice, which it serves and to which it belongs, simply as something lying outside its borders and is content with this separation of thought and action. Yet the characteristic mark of the thinker's activity is to determine for itself what it is to accomplish and serve, and this not in fragmentary fashion but totally. Its own nature, therefore, turns it towards a changing of history and the establishment of justice among men. Behind the loud calls for "social spirit" and "national community," the opposition between individual and society grows ever greater. The self-definition of science grows ever more abstract. But conformism in thought and the insistence that thinking is a fixed vocation, a self-enclosed realm within society as a whole, betrays the very essence of thought.

Translated by Matthew J. O'Connell

NOTES

1. Descartes, *Discourse on Method*, in *The Philosophical Works of Descartes*, tr. by Elizabeth S. Haldane and G. R. T. Ross (Cambridge: Cambridge University Press, 1931²), volume 1, p. 92.
2. Edmund Husserl, *Formale und transzendentale Logik* (Halle, 1929), p. 89.
3. Husserl, *op. cit.,* p. 79.
4. Husserl, *op. cit.,* p. 91.
5. Hermann Weyl, *Philosophie der Naturwissenschaft*, in *Handbuch der Philosophie*, Part 2 (Munich-Berlin, 1927), pp. 118ff.
6. Max Weber, "Critical Studies in the Logic of the Cultural Sciences I: A Critique of Eduard Meyer's Methodological Views," in *Max Weber on the Methodology of the Social Sciences*, ed. and tr. by Edward A. Shils and Henry A. Finch (Glencoe: Free Press, 1949), pp. 113-63.
7. In the following pages this activity is called "critical" activity. The term is used here less in the sense it has in the idealist critique of pure reason than in the sense it has in the dialectical critique of political economy. It points to an essential espect of the dialectical theory of society.
8. On the logical structure of the critique of political economy, cf. the essay "Zum Problem der Wahrheit," in Horkheimer, *Kritische Theorie*, vol. I (Frankfurt, 1968), p. 265ff.
9. There are connections between the forms of judgment and the historical periods. A brief indication will show what is meant. The classificatory judgment is typical of prebourgeois society: this is the way it is, and man can do nothing about it. The hypothetical and disjunctive forms belong especially to the bourgeois world: under certain circumstances this effect can take place; it is either thus or so. Critical theory maintains: it need not be so; man can change reality, and the necessary conditions for such change already exist.

JÜRGEN HABERMAS

KNOWLEDGE AND HUMAN INTERESTS: A GENERAL PERSPECTIVE

I

n 1802, during the summer semester at Jena, Schelling gave his Lectures on the Method of Academic Study. In the language of German Idealism he emphatically renewed the concept of theory that has defined the tradition of great philosophy since its beginnings.

The fear of speculation, the ostensible rush from the theoretical to the practical, brings about the same shallowness in action that it does in knowledge. It is by studying a strictly theoretical philosophy that we become most immediately acquainted with Ideas, and only Ideas provide action with energy and ethical significance. [1]

The *only* knowledge that can truly orient action is knowledge that frees itself from mere human interests and is based on Ideas—in other words, knowledge that has taken a theoretical attitude.

The word "theory" has religious origins. The *theoros* was the representative sent by Greek cities to public celebrations. [2] Through *theoria*, that is through looking on, he abandoned himself to the sacred events. In philosophical language, *theoria* was transferred to contemplation of the cosmos. In this form, theory already presupposed the demarcation between Being and time that is the foundation of ontology. This separation is first found in the poem of Parmenides and returns in Plato's *Timaeus*. It reserves to *logos* a realm of Being purged of inconstancy and uncertainty and leaves to *doxa* the realm of the mutable and perishable. When the philosopher views the immortal order, he cannot help bringing himself into accord with the proportions of the cosmos and reproducing them internally. He manifests these proportions, which he sees in the motions of nature and the harmonic series of music, within himself; he forms himself through mimesis. Through the soul's likening itself to the ordered motion of the cosmos, theory enters the conduct of life. In *ethos* theory molds life to its form and is reflected in the conduct of those who subject themselves to its discipline.

This concept of theory and of life in theory has defined philosophy since its beginnings. The distinction between theory in this traditional sense and theory in the sense of critique was the object of one of Max Horkheimer's most important studies.[3] Today, a generation later, I should like to reexamine this theme,[4] starting with Husserl's *The Crisis of the European Sciences*, which appeared at about the same time as Horkheimer's.[5] Husserl used as his frame of reference the very concept of theory that Horkheimer was countering with that of critical theory. Husserl was concerned with crisis: not with crises in the sciences, but with their crisis as science. For "in our vital state of need this science has nothing to say to us." Like almost all philosophers before him, Husserl, without second thought, took as the norm of his critique an idea of knowledge that preserves the Platonic connection of pure theory with the conduct of life. What ultimately produces a scientific culture is not the information content of theories but the formation among theorists themselves of a thoughtful and enlightened mode of life. The evolution of the European mind seemed to be aiming at the creation of a scientific culture of this sort. After 1933, however, Husserl saw this historical tendency endangered. He was convinced that the danger was threatening not from without but from within. He attributed the crisis to the circumstance that the most advanced disciplines, especially physics, had degenerated from the status of true theory.

II

Let us consider this thesis. There is a real connection between the positivistic self-understanding of the sciences and traditional ontology. The *empirical-analytic* sciences develop their theories in a self-understanding that automatically generates continuity with the beginnings of philosophical thought. For both are committed to a theoretical attitude that frees those who take it from dogmatic association with the natural interests of life and their irritating influence; and both share the cosmological intention of describing the universe theoretically in its lawlike order, just as it is. In contrast, the *historical-hermeneutic* sciences, which are concerned with the sphere of transitory things and mere opinion, cannot be linked up so smoothly with this tradition—they have nothing to do with cosmology. But they, too, comprise a *scientistic consciousness*, based on the model of science. For even the symbolic meanings of tradition seem capable of being brought together in a cosmos of facts in ideal simultaneity. Much as the cultural sciences may comprehend their facts through understanding and little though they may be concerned with discovering general laws, they nevertheless share with the empirical-analytic sciences the methodological consciousness of describing a structured reality within the horizon of the theoretical attitude. Historicism has become the positivism of the cultural and social sciences.

Positivism has also permeated the self-understanding of the *social sciences*, whether they obey the methodological demands of an empirical-analytic behavioral science or orient themselves to the pattern of normative-analytic sciences, based on presuppositions about maxims of action.[6] In this field of inquiry, which is so close to practice, the concept of value-freedom (or ethical neutrality) has simply reaffirmed the ethos that modern science owes to the beginnings of theoretical thought in Greek philosophy: psychologically an unconditional commitment to theory and epistemologically the severance of knowledge from interest. This is represented in logic by the distinction between descriptive and prescriptive statements, which makes grammatically obligatory the filtering out of merely emotive from cognitive contents.

Yet the very term "value freedom" reminds us that the postulates associated with it no longer correspond to the classical meaning of theory. To dissociate values from facts means counterposing an abstract Ought to pure Being. Values are the nominalistic by-products of a centuries-long critique of the emphatic concept of Being to which theory was once exclusively oriented. The very term "values," which neo-Kantianism brought into philosophical currency, and in relation to which science is supposed to preserve neutrality, renounces the connection between the two that theory originally intended.

Thus, although the sciences share the concept of theory with the major tradition of philosophy, they destroy its classical claim. They borrow two elements from the philosophical heritage: the methodological meaning of the theoretical attitude and the basic ontological assumption of a structure of the world independent of the knower. On the other hand, however, they have abandoned the connection of *theoria* and *kosmos*, of *mimesis* and *bios theoretikos* that was assumed from Plato through Husserl. What was once supposed to comprise the practical efficacy of theory has now fallen prey to methodological prohibitions. The conception of theory as a process of cultivation of the person has become apocryphal. Today it appears to us that the mimetic conformity of the soul to the proportions of the universe, which seemed accessible to contemplation, had only taken theoretical knowledge into the service of the internalization of norms and thus estranged it from its legitimate task.

III

In fact the sciences had to lose the specific significance for life that Husserl would like to regenerate through the renovation of pure theory. I shall reconstruct his critique in three steps. It is directed in the first place against the objectivism of the sciences, for which the world appears objectively as a universe of facts whose lawlike connection can be grasped descriptively. In truth, however, knowledge of the apparently objective world of facts has its transcendental basis in the prescientific world. The possible objects of scientific analysis are constituted a priori in the self-evidence of our primary life-world. In this layer phenomenology discloses the products of a meaning-generative subjectivity. Second, Husserl would like to show that this productive subjectivity disappears under the cover of an objectivistic self-understanding, because the sciences have not radically freed themselves from interests rooted in the primary life-world. Only phenomenology breaks with the naive attitude in favor of a rigorously contemplative one and definitively frees knowledge from interest. Third, Husserl identifies transcendental self-reflection, to which he accords the name of phenomenological description, with theory in the traditional sense. The philosopher owes the theoretical attitude to a transposition that liberates him from the fabric of empirical interests. In this regard theory is "unpractical." But this does not cut it off from practical life. For, according to the traditional concept, it is precisely the consistent abstinence of theory that produces action-orienting culture. Once the theoretical attitude has been adopted, it is capable in turn of being mediated with the practical attitude:

This occurs in the form of a novel practice . . . , whose aim is to elevate mankind to all forms of veridical norms through universal scientific reason, to transform it into a fundamentally new humanity, capable of absolute self-responsibility on the basis of absolute theoretical insight.

If we recall the situation of thirty years ago, the prospect of rising barbarism, we can respect this invocation of the therapeutic power of phenomenological description; but it is unfounded. At best, phenomenology grasps transcendental norms in accordance with which consciousness necessarily operates. It describes (in Kantian terms) laws of pure reason, but not norms of a universal legislation derived from practical reason, which a free will could obey. Why, then, does Husserl believe that he can claim practical efficacy for phenomenology as pure theory? He errs because he does not discern the connection of positivism, which he justifiably criticizes, with the ontology from which he unconsciously borrows the traditional concept of theory.

Husserl rightly criticizes the objectivist illusion that deludes the sciences with the image of a reality-in-itself consisting of facts structured in a lawlike manner; it conceals the constitution of these facts, and thereby prevents consciousness of the interlocking of knowledge with interests from the life-world. Because phenomenology brings this to consciousness, it is itself, in Husserl's view, free of such interests. It thus earns the title of pure theory unjustly claimed by the sciences. It is to this freeing of knowledge from interest that Husserl attaches the expectation of practical efficacy. But the error is clear. Theory in the sense of the classical tradition only had an impact on life because it was thought to have discovered in the cosmic order an ideal world structure, including the prototype for the order of the human world. Only as cosmology was *theoria* also capable of orienting human action. Thus Husserl cannot expect self-formative processes to originate in a phenomenology that, as transcendental philosophy, purifies the classical theory of its cosmological contents, conserving something like the theoretical attitude only in an abstract manner. Theory had educational and cultural implications not because it had freed knowledge from interest. To the contrary, it did so because it derived *pseudonormative power* from *the concealment of its actual interest.* While criticizing the objectivist self-understanding of the sciences, Husserl succumbs to another objectivism, which was always attached to the traditional concept of theory.

IV

In the Greek tradition, the same forces that philosophy reduces to powers of the soul still appeared as gods and superhuman powers. Philosophy domesticated them and banished them to the realm of the soul as internalized demons. If from this point of view we regard the drives and affects that enmesh man in the empirical interests of his inconstant and contingent activity, then the attitude of pure theory, which promises *purification* from these very affects, takes on a new meaning: disinterested contemplation then obviously signifies emancipation. The release of knowledge from interest was not supposed to purify theory from the obfuscations of subjectivity but inversely to provide the subject with an ecstatic purification from the passions. What indicates the new stage of emancipation is that catharsis is now no longer attained through mystery cults but established in the will of individuals themselves by means of theory. In the communication structure of the polis, individuation has progressed to the point where the identity of the individual ego as a stable entity can only be developed through identification with abstract laws of cosmic order. Consciousness, emancipated from archaic powers, now anchors itself in the unity of a stable cosmos and the identity of immutable Being.

Thus it was only by means of ontological distinctions that theory originally could take cognizance of a self-subsistent world purged of demons. At the same time, the illusion of pure theory served as a protection against regression to an earlier stage that had been surpassed. Had it been possible to detect that the identity of pure Being was an objectivistic illusion, ego identity would not have been able to take shape on its basis. The repression of interest appertained to this interest itself.

If this interpretation is valid, then the two most influential aspects of the Greek tradition, the theoretical attitude and the basic ontological assumption of a structured, self-subsistent world, appear in a connection that they explicitly prohibit: the connection of knowledge with human interests. Hence we return to Husserl's critique of the objectivism of the sciences. But this connection turns *against* Husserl. Our reason for suspecting the presence of an unacknowledged connection between knowledge and interest is not that the sciences have abandoned the classical concept of theory, but that they have not completely abandoned it. The suspicion of objectivism exists because of the *ontological illusion of pure theory* that the sciences still deceptively share with the philosophical tradition *after casting off its practical content.*

With Husserl we shall designate as objectivistic an attitude that naively correlates theoretical propositions with matters of fact. This attitude presumes that the relations between empirical variables represented in theoretical propositions are self-existent. At the same time, it suppresses the transcendental framework that is the precondition of the meaning of the validity of such propositions. As soon as these statements are understood in relation to the prior frame of reference to which they are affixed, the objectivist illusion dissolves and makes visible a knowledge-constitutive interest.

There are three categories of processes of inquiry for which a specific connection between logical-methodological rules and knowledge-constitutive interests can be demonstrated. This demonstration is the task of a critical philosophy of science that escapes the snares of positivism.[7] The approach of the empirical-analytic sciences incorporates a *technical* cognitive interest; that of the historical-hermeneutic sciences incorporates a *practical* one; and the approach of critically oriented sciences incorporates the *emancipatory* cognitive interest that, as we saw, was at the root of traditional theories. I should like to clarify this thesis by means of a few examples.

V

In the *empirical-analytic sciences* the frame of reference that prejudges the meaning of possible statements establishes rules both for the construction of theories and for their critical testing.[8] Theories comprise hypothetico-deductive connections of propositions, which permit the deduction of lawlike hypotheses with empirical content. The latter can be interpreted as statements about the covariance of observable events; given a set of initial conditions, they make predictions possible. Empirical-analytic knowledge is thus possible predictive knowledge. However, the *meaning* of such predictions, that is their technical exploitability, is established only by the rules according to which we apply theories to reality.

In controlled observation, which often takes the form of an experiment, we generate initial conditions and measure the results of operations carried out under these conditions. Empiricism attempts to ground the objectivist illusion in observations expressed in basic statements. These observations are supposed to be reliable in providing immediate evidence without the admixture of subjectivity. In reality basic statements are not simple representations of facts in themselves, but express the success or failure of our operations. We can say that facts and the relations between them are apprehended descriptively. But this way of talking must not conceal that as such the facts relevant to the empirical sciences are first constituted through an a priori organization of our experience in the behavioral system of instrumental action.

Taken together, these two factors, that is the logical structure of admissible systems of propositions and the type of conditions for corroboration suggest that theories of the empirical sciences disclose reality subject to the constitutive interest in the possible securing and expansion, through information, of feed-back-monitored action. This is the cognitive interest in technical control over objectified processes.

The *historical-hermeneutic sciences* gain knowledge in a different methodological framework. Here the meaning of the validity of propositions is not constituted in the frame of reference of technical control. The levels of formalized language and objectified experience have not yet been divorced. For theories are not constructed deductively and experience is not organized with regard to the success of operations.

Access to the facts is provided by the understanding of meaning, not observation. The verification of lawlike hypotheses in the empirical-analytic sciences has its counterpart here in the interpretation of texts. Thus the rules of hermeneutics determine the possible meaning of the validity of statements of the cultural sciences.[9]

Historicism has taken the understanding of meaning, in which mental facts are supposed to be given in direct evidence, and grafted onto it the objectivist illusion of pure theory. It appears as though the interpreter transposes himself into the horizon of the world or language from which a text derives its meaning. But here, too, the facts are first constituted in relation to the standards that establish them. Just as positivist self-understanding does not take into account explicitly the connection between measurement operations and feedback control, so it eliminates from consideration the interpreter's pre-understanding. Hermeneutic knowledge is always mediated through this pre-understanding, which is derived from the interpreter's initial situation. The world of traditional meaning discloses itself to the interpreter only to the extent that his own world becomes clarified at the same time. The subject of understanding establishes communication between both worlds. He comprehends the substantive content of tradition by *applying* tradition to himself and his situation.

If, however, methodological rules unite interpretation and application in this way, then this suggests that hermeneutic inquiry discloses reality subject to a constitutive interest in the preservation and expansion of the intersubjectivity of possible action-orienting mutual understanding. The understanding of meaning is directed in its very structure toward the attainment of possible consensus among actors in the framework of a self-understanding derived from tradition. This we shall call the *practical* cognitive interest, in contrast to the technical.

The systematic *sciences of social action*, that is economics, sociology, and political science, have the goal, as do the empirical-analytic sciences, of producing nomological knowledge.[10] A critical social science, however, will not remain satisfied with this. It is concerned with going beyond this goal to determine when theoretical statements grasp invariant regularities of social action as such and when they express ideologically frozen relations of dependence that can in principle be transformed. To the extent that this is the case, the *critique of ideology*, as well, moreover, as *psychoanalysis*, take into account that information about lawlike connections sets off a process of reflection in the consciousness of those whom the laws are about. Thus the level of unreflected consciousness, which is one of the initial conditions of such laws, can be transformed. Of course, to this end a critically mediated knowledge of laws cannot through reflection alone render a law itself inoperative, but it can render it inapplicable.

The methodological framework that determines the meaning of the validity of critical propositions of this category is established by the concept of *self-reflection*. The latter releases the subject from dependence on hypostatized powers. Self-reflection is determined by an emancipatory cognitive interest. Critically oriented sciences share this interest with philosophy.

However, as long as philosophy remains caught in ontology, it is itself subject to an objectivism that disguises the connection of its knowledge with the human interest in autonomy and responsibility (*Mündigkeit*). There is only one way in which it can acquire the power that it vainly claims for itself in virtue of its seeming freedom from presuppositions: by acknowledging its dependence on this interest and turning against its own illusion of pure theory the critique it directs at the objectivism of the sciences.[11]

VI

The concept of knowledge-constitutive human interests already conjoins the two elements whose relation still has to be explained: knowledge and interest. From everyday experience we know that ideas serve often enough to furnish our actions with justifying motives in place of the real ones. What is called rationalization at this level is called ideology at the level of collective action. In both cases the manifest content of statements is falsified by consciousness' unreflected tie to interests, despite its illusion of autonomy. The discipline of trained thought thus correctly aims at excluding such interests. In all the sciences routines have been developed that guard against the subjectivity of opinion, and a new discipline, the sociology of knowledge, has emerged to counter the uncontrolled influence of interests on a deeper level, which derive less from the individual than from the objective situation of social groups. But this accounts for only one side of the problem. Because science must secure the objectivity of its statements against the pressure and seduction of particular interests, it deludes itself about the fundamental interests to which it owes not only its impetus but *the conditions of possible objectivity* themselves.

Orientation toward technical control, toward mutual understanding in the conduct of life, and toward emancipation from seemingly "natural" constraint establish the specific viewpoints from which we can apprehend reality as such in any way whatsoever. By becoming aware of the impossibility of getting beyond these transcendental limits, a part of nature acquires, through us, autonomy in nature. If knowledge could ever outwit its innate human interest, it would be by comprehending that the mediation of subject and object that philosophical consciousness attributes exclusively to *its own* synthesis is produced originally by interests. The mind can become aware of this natural basis reflexively. Nevertheless, its power extends into the very logic of inquiry.

Representations and descriptions are never independent of standards. And the choice of these standards is based on attitudes that require critical consideration by means of arguments, because they cannot be either logically deduced or empirically demonstrated. Fundamental methodological decisions, for example such basic distinctions as those between categorial and noncategorial being, between analytic and synthetic statements, or between descriptive and emotive meaning, have the singular character of being neither arbitrary nor compelling.[12] They prove appropriate or inappropriate. For their criterion is the metalogical necessity of interests that we can neither prescribe nor represent, but with which we must instead come to terms. Therefore my first thesis is this: *The achievements of the transcendental subject have their basis in the natural history of the human species.*

Taken by itself this thesis could lead to the misunderstanding that reason is an organ of adaptation for men just as claws and teeth are for animals. True, it does serve this function. But the human interests that have emerged in man's natural history, to which we have traced back the three knowledge-constitutive interests, derive both from nature and *from the cultural break* with nature. Along with the tendency to realize natural drives they have incorporated the tendency toward release from the constraint of nature. Even the interest in self-preservation, natural as it seems, is represented by a social system that compensates for the lacks in man's organic equipment and secures his historical existence *against* the force of nature threatening from without. But society is not only a system of self-preservation. An enticing natural force, present in the individual as libido, has detached itself from the behavioral system of self-preservation and urges toward utopian fulfillment. These individual demands, which do not initially accord with the requirement of collective self-preservation, are also absorbed by the social system. That is why the cognitive processes to which social life is indissolubly linked function not only as means to the reproduction of life; for in equal measure they themselves determine the definitions of this life. What may appear as naked survival is always in its roots a historical phenomenon. For it is subject to the criterion of what a society intends for itself as *the good life.* My *second thesis* is thus that *knowledge equally serves as an instrument and transcends mere self-preservation.*

The specific viewpoints from which, with transcendental necessity, we apprehend reality ground three categories of possible knowledge: information that expands our power of technical control; interpretations that make possible the orientation of action within common traditions; and analyses that free consciousness from its dependence on hypostatized powers. These viewpoints originate in the interest structure of a species that is linked in its roots to definite means of social organization: work, language, and power. The human species secures its existence in systems of social labor and self-assertion through violence, through tradition-bound social life in ordinary-language communication, and with the aid of ego identities that at every level of individuation reconsolidate the consciousness of the individual in relation to the norms of the group. Accordingly the interests constitutive of knowledge are linked to the functions of an ego that adapts itself to its external conditions through learning processes, is initiated into the communication system of a social life-world by means of self-formative processes, and constructs an identity in the conflict between instinctual aims and social constraints. In turn these achievements become part of the productive forces accumulated by a society, the cultural tradition through which a society interprets itself, and the legitimations that a society accepts or criticizes. My *third thesis* is thus that *knowledge-constitutive interests take form in the medium of work, language, and power.*

However, the configuration of knowledge and interest is not the same in all categories. It is true that at this level it is always illusory to suppose an autonomy, free of presuppositions, in which knowing first grasps reality theoretically, only to be taken subsequently into the service of interests alien to it. But the mind can always reflect back upon the interest structure that joins subject and object a priori: this is reserved to self-reflection. If the latter cannot cancel out interest, it can to a certain extent make up for it.

It is no accident that the standards of self-reflection are exempted from the singular state of suspension in which those of all other cognitive processes require critical evaluation. They possess theoretical certainty. The human interest in autonomy and responsibility is not mere fancy, for it can be apprehended a priori. What raises us out of nature is the only thing whose nature we can know: *language*. Through its structure, autonomy and responsibility are posited for us. Our first sentence expresses unequivocally the intention of universal and unconstrained consensus. Taken together, autonomy and responsibility constitute the only Idea the we possess a priori in the sense of the philosophical tradition. Perhaps that is why the language of German Idealism, according to which "reason" contains both will and consciousness as its elements, is not quite obsolete. Reason also means the will to reason. In self-reflection knowledge for the sake of knowledge attains congruence with the interest in autonomy and responsibility. The emancipatory cognitive interest aims at the pursuit of reflection as such. My *fourth thesis* is thus that *in the power of self-reflection, knowledge and interest are one.*

However, only in an emancipated society, whose members' autonomy and responsibility had been realized, would communication have developed into the non-authoritarian and universally practiced dialogue from which both our model of reciprocally constituted ego identity and our idea of true consensus are always implicitly derived. To this extent the truth of statements is based on anticipating the realization of the good life. The ontological illusion of pure theory behind which knowledge-constitutive interests become invisible promotes the fiction that Socratic dialogue is possible everywhere and at any time. From the beginning philosophy has presumed that the autonomy and responsibility posited with the structure of language are not only anticipated but real. It is pure theory, wanting to derive everything from itself, that succumbs to unacknowledged external conditions and becomes ideological. Only when philosophy discovers in the dialectical course of history the traces of violence that deform repeated attempts at dialogue and recurrently close off the path to unconstrained communication does it further the process whose suspension it otherwise legitimates: mankind's evolution toward autonomy and responsibility. My *fifth thesis* is thus that *the unity of knowledge and interest proves itself in a dialectic that takes the historical traces of suppressed dialogue and reconstructs what has been suppressed.*

VII

The sciences have retained one characteristic of philosophy: the illusion of pure theory. This illusion does not determine the practice of scientific research but only its self-understanding. And to the extent that this self-understanding reacts back upon scientific practice, it even has its point.

The glory of the sciences is their unswerving application of their methods without reflecting on knowledge-constitutive interests. From knowing not what they do methodologically, they are that much surer of their discipline, that is of methodical progress within an unproblematic framework. False consciousness has a protective function. For the sciences lack the means of dealing with the risks that appear once the connection of knowledge and human interest has been comprehended on the level of self-reflection. It was possible for fascism to give birth to the freak of a national physics and Stalinism to that of a Soviet Marxist genetics (which deserves to be taken more seriously than the former) only because the illusion of objectivism was lacking. It would have been able to provide immunity against the more dangerous bewitchments of misguided reflection.

But the praise of objectivism has its limits. Husserl's critique was right to attack it, if not with the right means. As soon as the objectivist illusion is turned into an affirmative *Weltanschauung*, methodologically unconscious necessity is perverted to the dubious virtue of a scientistic profession of faith. Objectivism in no way prevents the sciences from intervening in the conduct of life, as Husserl thought it did. They are integrated into it in any case. But they do not of themselves develop their practical efficacy in the direction of a growing rationality of action.

Instead, the positivist self-understanding of the *nomological sciences* lends countenance to the substitution of technology for enlightened action. It directs the utilization of scientific information from an illusory viewpoint, namely that *the practical mastery of history can be reduced to technical control of objectified processes*. The objectivist self-understanding of the *hermeneutic sciences* is of no lesser consequence. It defends sterilized knowledge against the reflected appropriation of active traditions and locks up history in a museum. Guided by the objectivist attitude of theory as the image of facts, the nomological and hermeneutical sciences reinforce each other with regard to their practical consequences. The latter displace our connection with tradition into the realm of the arbitrary, while the former, on the levelled-off basis of the repression of history, squeeze the conduct of life into the behavioral system of instrumental action. The dimension in which acting subjects could arrive rationally at agreement about goals and purposes is surrendered to the obscure area of mere decision among reified value systems and irrational beliefs.[13] When this dimension, abandoned by all men of good will, is subjected to reflection that relates to history objectivistically, as did the philosophical tradition, then positivism triumphs at the highest level of thought, as with Comte. This happens when critique uncritically abdicates its own connection with the emancipatory knowledge-constitutive interest in favor of pure theory. This sort of high-flown critique projects the undecided process of the evolution of the human species onto the level of a philosophy of history that dogmatically issues instructions for action. *A delusive philosophy of history, however, is only the obverse of deluded decisionism.* Bureaucratically prescribed partisanship goes only too well with contemplatively misunderstood value freedom.

These practical consequences of a restricted, scientistic consciousness of the sciences[14] can be countered by a critique that destroys the illusion of objectivism. Contrary to Husserl's expectations, objectivism is eliminated not through the power of renewed *theoria* but through demonstrating what it conceals: the connection of knowledge and interest. Philosophy remains true to its classic tradition by renouncing it. The insight that the truth of statements is linked in the last analysis to the intention of the good and true life can be preserved today only on the ruins of ontology. However even this philosophy remains a specialty alongside of the sciences and outside public consciousness as long as the heritage that it has critically abandoned lives on in the positivistic self-understanding of the sciences.

NOTES

1. Friedrich W. J. von Schelling, *Werke*, edited by Manfred Schröter (Munich: Beck, 1958–59), 3:299.
2. Bruno Snell, "Theorie und Praxis," in *Die Entdeckung des Geistes*, 3d ed. (Hamburg: Claassen, 1955), p. 401 ff.; Georg Picht, "Der Sinn der Unterscheidung von Theorie und Praxis in der griechischen Philosophie," in *Evangelische Ethik* (1964), 8:321 ff.
3. "Traditionelle und kritische Theorie," in *Zeitschrift für Sozialforschung*, 6:245 ff. Reprinted in Max Horkheimer, *Kritische Theorie*, edited by Alfred Schmidt (Frankfurt am Main: Fischer, 1968), pp. 137–191.
4. The appendix was the basis of my inaugural lecture at the University of Frankfurt am Main on June 28, 1965. Bibliographical notes are restricted to a few references.
5. *Die Krisis der europäischen Wissenschaften und die transzendentale Phänomenologie in Gesammelte Werke* (The Hague: Martinus Nijhoff, 1950), vol. 6.
6. See Gérard Gäfgen, *Theorie der wirtschaftlichen Entscheidung* (Tübingen: Mohr, 1963).
7. This path has been marked out by Karl-Otto Apel. See *Transformation der Philosophie* (Frankfurt: Suhrkump, 1973), 2 vols. Chapter 10, n. 1, above.
8. See Popper's *The Logic of Scientific Discovery*, and my paper "Analytische Wissenschaftstheorie," in *Zeugnisse* (Frankfurt am Main: Europäische Verlagsanstalt, 1963), p. 473 ff.
9. I concur with the analyses in Part II of Hans-Georg Gadamer, *Wahrheit und Methode*.
10. Ernst Topitsch, editor, *Logik der Sozialwissenschaften* (Cologne: 1965).
11. Theodor W. Adorno, *Zur Metakritik der Erkenntnistheorie*.
12. Morton White, *Toward Reunion in Philosophy* (Cambridge: Harvard University Press, 1956).
13. See my essay "Dogmatismus, Vernunft und Entscheidung" (Dogmatism, Reason, and Decision) in *Theorie und Praxis*.

14. In *One-Dimensional Man* (Boston: Beacon, 1964) Herbert Marcuse has analyzed the dangers of the reduction of reason to technical rationality and the reduction of society to the dimension of technical control. In another context, Helmut Schelsky has made the same diagnosis:

> With a scientific civilization that man himself creates according to plan, a new peril has entered the world: the danger that man will develop himself only in external actions of altering the environment, and keep and deal with everything, himself and other human beings, at this object level of constructive action. This new self-alienation of man, which can rob him of his own and others' identity . . . is the danger of the creator losing himself in his work, the constructor in his construction. Man may recoil from completely transcending himself toward self-produced objectivity, toward constructed being; yet he works incessantly at extending this process of scientific self-objectification.

See Schelsky's *Einsamkeit und Freiheit* (Hamburg: 1963), p. 299.

PART SIX

COMMUNICATION AND SOCIAL CRISIS

he first selection reprinted in this part is excerpted from the eleventh lecture of Habermas's *The Philosophical Discourse of Modernity* (1985). In this essay, Habermas outlines the advantages of a communicative over a subject-centered model of reason. He critiques the traditional subject–object paradigm for its tendency to issue in the dialectic of enlightenment and recommends a communicative paradigm that emphasizes intersubjective understanding and reciprocal recognition.

"What Does a Legitimation Crisis Mean Today? Legitimation Problems in Late Capitalism," also by Habermas, originally appeared in the journal *Social Research* in 1973. Here, Habermas describes the structural features of late-capitalist societies and diagnoses crisis tendencies concerning legitimation and motivation. Habermas's discussion touches on many of the crises facing the world today, including threats to the ecological, anthropological and international balances. His essay concludes with a theoretical explanation of these crisis tendencies that offers his vision of the direction any possible solution must take.

For a fuller discussion of Habermas's work, see Chapter 7 of *Philosophy and Critical Theory*.

JÜRGEN HABERMAS

AN ALTERNATIVE WAY OUT OF THE PHILOSOPHY OF THE SUBJECT: COMMUNICATIVE VERSUS SUBJECT-CENTERED REASON

f we can presuppose for a moment the model of action oriented to reaching understanding that I have developed elsewhere,[1] the objectifying attitude in which the knowing subject regards itself as it would entities in the external world is no longer *privileged*. Fundamental to the paradigm of mutual understanding is, rather, the performative attitude of participants in interaction, who coordinate their plans for action by coming to an understanding about something in the world. When ego carries out a speech act and alter takes up a position with regard to it, the two parties enter into an interpersonal relationship. The latter is structured by the system of reciprocally interlocked perspectives among speakers, hearers, and non-participants who happen to be present at the time. On the level of grammar, this corresponds to the system of personal pronouns. Whoever has been trained in this system has learned how, in the performative attitude, to take up and to transform into one another the perspectives of the first, second, and third persons.

Now this attitude of participants in linguistically mediated interaction makes possible a *different* relationship of the subject to itself from the sort of objectifying attitude that an observer assumes toward entities in the external world. The transcendental-empirical doubling of the relation to self is only unavoidable so long as there is no alternative to this observer-perspective; only then does the subject have to view itself as the dominating counterpart to the world as a whole or as an entity appearing within it. No mediation is possible between the extramundane stance of the transcendental I and the intramundane stance of the empirical I. As soon as linguistically generated intersubjectivity gains primacy, this alternative no longer applies. Then ego stands within an interpersonal relationship that allows him to relate to himself as a participant in an interaction from the perspective of alter. And indeed this reflection undertaken from the perspective of the participant escapes the kind of objectification inevitable from the reflexively applied perspective of the observer. Everything gets frozen into an object under the gaze of the third person, whether directed inwardly or outwardly. The first person, who turns back upon himself in a performative attitude from the angle of vision of the second person, can *recapitulate* [*nachvollziehen*] the acts it just carried out. In place of reflectively objectified knowledge—the knowledge proper to self-consciousness—we have a recapitulating reconstruction of knowledge already employed. . . .

[E]vidence from more recent ethology, especially experiments with the artificially induced acquisition of language by chimpanzees, teaches us that it is not the use of propositions per se, but only the *communicative use* of propositionally differentiated language that is proper to our sociocultural form of life and is constitutive for the level of a genuinely social reproduction of life. In terms of language philosophy, the equiprimordiality and equal value of the three fundamental linguistic functions come into view as soon as we abandon the analytic level of the judgment or the sentence and expand our analysis to speech acts, precisely to the communicative use of sentences. Elementary speech acts display a structure in which three components are mutually combined: the propositional component for representing (or mentioning) states of affairs; the illocutionary component for taking up interpersonal relationships; and finally, the linguistic components that bring the intention of the speaker to expression. The clarification, in terms of speech-act theory, of the complex linguistic functions of representation, the establishment of interpersonal relationships, and the expression of one's own subjective experiences has far-reaching consequences for (a) the theory of meaning, (b) the ontological presuppositions of the theory of communication, and (c) the concept of rationality itself. Here I will only point out these consequences to the extent that they are directly relevant to (d) a *new orientation* for the critique of instrumental reason.

(a) Truth-condition semantics, as it has been developed from Frege to Dummett and Davidson, proceeds—as does the Husserlian theory of meaning—from the logocentric assumption that the truth reference of the assertoric sentence (and the indirect truth reference of intentional sentences related to the implementation of plans) offers a suitable point of departure for the explication of the linguistic accomplishment of mutual understanding generally. Thus, this theory arrives at the principle that we understand a sentence when we know the conditions under which it is true. (For understanding intentional and imperative sentences it requires a corresponding knowledge of "conditions for success."[2]) The pragmatically expanded theory of meaning overcomes this fixation on the fact-mirroring function of language. Like truth-condition semantics, it affirms an internal connection between meaning and validity, but it does not reduce this to the validity proper to truth. Correlative to the three fundamental functions of language, each elementary speech act as a whole can be contested under three different aspects of validity. The hearer can reject the utterance of a speaker *in toto* by either disputing the *truth* of the proposition asserted in it (or of the existential presuppositions of its propositional content), or the *rightness* of the speech act in view of the normative context of the utterance (or the legitimacy of the presupposed context itself), or the *truthfulness* of the intention expressed by the speaker (that is, the agreement of what is meant with what is stated). Hence, the internal connection of meaning and validity holds for the *entire spectrum* of linguistic meanings—and not just for the meaning of expressions that can be expanded into assertoric sentences. It holds true not only for constative speech acts, but for any given speech act, that we understand its meaning when we know the conditions under which it can be accepted as valid.

(b) If, however, not just constative but also regulative and expressive speech acts can be connected with validity claims and accepted as valid or rejected as invalid, the basic, ontological framework of the philosophy of consciousness (which has remained normative for linguistic philosophy as well, with exceptions such as Austin) proves to be too narrow. The "world" to which subjects can relate with their representations or propositions was hitherto conceived of as the totality of objects or existing states of affairs. The objective world is considered the correlative of all true assertoric sentences. But if normative rightness and subjective truthfulness are introduced as validity claims analogous to truth, "worlds" analogous to the world of facts have to be postulated for legitimately regulated interpersonal relationships and for attributable subjective experiences—a "world" not only for what is "objective," which appears to us in the attitude of the third person, but also one for what it normative, to which we feel obliged in the attitude of addresses, as well as one for what is subjective, which we either disclose or conceal to a public in the attitude of the first person. With any speech act, the speaker takes up a relation to something in the objective world, something in a common social world, and something in his own subjective world. The legacy of logocentrism is still noticeable in the terminological difficulty of expanding the ontological concept of "world" in this way.

The phenomenological concept (elaborated by Heidegger in particular) of a referential context, a lifeworld, that forms the unquestioned context for processes of mutual understanding—behind the backs of participants in interaction, so to speak— needs a corresponding expansion. Participants draw from this *lifeworld* not just consensual patterns of interpretation (the background knowledge from which propositional contents are fed), but also normatively reliable patterns of social relations (the tacitly presupposed solidarities on which illocutionary acts are based) and the competences acquired in socialization processes (the background of the speaker's intentions).

(c) "Rationality" refers in the first instance to the disposition of speaking and acting subjects to acquire and use fallible knowledge. As long as the basic concepts of the philosophy of consciousness lead us to understand knowledge exclusively as knowledge of something in the objective world, rationality is assessed by how the isolated subject orients himself to representational and propositional contents. Subject-centered reason finds its criteria in standards of truth and success that govern the relationships of knowing and purposively acting subjects to the world of possible objects or states of affairs. By contrast, as soon as we conceive of knowledge as communicatively mediated, rationality is assessed in terms of the capacity of responsible participants in interaction to orient themselves in relation to validity claims geared to intersubjective recognition. Communicative reason finds its criteria in the argumentative procedures for directly or indirectly redeeming claims to propositional truth, normative rightness, subjective truthfulness, and aesthetic harmony.[3]

Thus, a procedural concept of rationality can be worked out in terms of the interdependence of various forms of argumentation, that is to say, with the help of a pragmatic logic of argumentation. This concept is richer than that of purposive rationality, which is tailored to the cognitive-instrumental dimension, because it integrates the moral-practical as well as the aesthetic-expressive domains; it is an explicitation of the rational potential built into the validity basis of speech. This communicative rationality recalls older ideas of logos, inasmuch as it brings along with it the connotations of a noncoercively unifying, consensus-building force of a discourse in which the participants overcome their at first subjectively biased views in favor of a rationally motivated agreement. Communicative reason is expressed in a decentered understanding of the world.

(d) From this perspective, both cognitive-instrumental mastery of an objectivated nature (and society) and narcissistically overinflated autonomy (in the sense of purposively rational self-assertion) are derivative moments that have been rendered independent from the communicative structures of the life-world, that is, from the intersubjectivity of relationships of mutual understanding and relationships of reciprocal recognition. Subject-centered reason is the *product of division and usurpation*, indeed of a social process in the course of which a subordinated moment assumes the place of the whole, without having the power to assimilate the structure of the whole. Horkheimer and Adorno have, like Foucault, described this process of a self-overburdening and self-reifying subjectivity as a world-historical process. But both sides missed its deeper irony, which consists in the fact that the communicative potential of reason first had to be released in the patterns of modern lifeworlds before the unfettered imperatives of the economic and administrative subsystems could react back on the vulnerable practice of everyday life and could thereby promote the cognitive-instrumental dimension to domination over the suppressed moments of practical reason. The communicative potential of reason has been simultaneously developed and distorted in the course of capitalist modernization.

The paradoxical contemporaneity and interdependence of the two processes can only be grasped if the false alternative set up by Max Weber, with his opposition between substantive and formal rationality, is overcome. Its underlying assumption is that the disenchantment of religious-metaphysical world views robs rationality, along with the contents of tradition, of all substantive connotations and thereby strips it of its power to have a structure-forming influence on the lifeworld beyond the purposive-rational organization of means. As opposed to this, I would like to insist that, despite its purely procedural character as disburdened of all religious and metaphysical mortgages, communicative reason is directly implicated in social life-processes insofar as acts of mutual understanding take on the role of a mechanism for coordinating action. The network of communicative actions is nourished by resources of the lifeworld and is at the same time the *medium* by which concrete forms of life are reproduced. . . .

There is a more serious question: whether the concepts of communicative action and of the transcending force of universalistic validity claims do not reestablish an idealism that is incompatible with the naturalistic insights of historical materialism. Does not a lifeworld that is supposed to be reproduced only via the medium of action oriented to mutual understanding get cut off from its material life processes? Naturally, the lifeworld is materially reproduced by way of the results and consequences of the goal-directed actions with which its members intervene in the world. But these instrumental actions are interlaced with communicative ones insofar as they represent the execution of plans that are linked to the plans of other interaction participants by way of common definitions of situations and processes of mutual understanding. Along these paths, the solutions to problems in the sphere of social labor are also plugged into the medium of action oriented by mutual understanding. The theory of communicative action takes into account the fact that the symbolic reproduction of the lifeworld and its material reproduction are internally interdependent.

It is not so simple to counter the suspicion that with the concept of action oriented to validity claims the idealism of a pure, nonsituated reason slips in again, and the dichotomies between the realms of the transcendental and the empirical are given new life in another form.

There is no pure reason that might don linguistic clothing only in the second place. Reason is by its very nature incarnated in contexts of communicative action and in structures of the lifeworld.[4] To the extent that the plans and actions of different actors are interconnected in historical time and across social space through the use of speech oriented toward mutual agreement, taking yes/no positions on criticizable validity claims, however implicitly, gains a key function in *everyday* practice. Agreement arrived at through communication, which is measured by the intersubjective recognition of validity claims, makes possible a networking of social interactions and lifeworld contexts. Of course, these validity claims have a Janus face: As claims, they transcend any local context; at the same time, they have to be raised here and now and be de facto recognized if they are going to bear the agreement of interaction participants that is needed for effective cooperation. The transcendent moment of *universal* validity bursts every provinciality asunder; the obligatory moment of accepted validity claims renders them carriers of a *context-bound* everyday practice. Inasmuch as communicative agents reciprocally raise validity claims with their speech acts, they are relying on the potential of assailable grounds. Hence, a moment of *unconditionality* is built into *factual* processes of mutual understanding—the validity laid claim to is distinguished from the social currency of a de facto established practice and yet serves it as the foundation of an existing consensus. The validity claimed for propositions and norms transcends spaces and times, *"blots out" space and time*; but the claim is always raised *here and now*, in specific contexts, and is either accepted or rejected with factual consequences for action. Karl-Otto Apel speaks in a suggestive way about the entwinement of the real communication community with an ideal one.[5]

The communicative practice of everyday life is, as it were, reflected in itself. This "reflection" is no longer a matter of the cognitive subject relating to itself in an objectivating manner. The stratification of discourse and action built into communicative action takes the place of this prelinguistic and isolated reflection. For factually raised validity claims point directly or indirectly to arguments by which they can be worked out and in some cases resolved. This argumentative debate about hypothetical validity claims can be described as the reflective form of communicative action: a relation-to-self that does without the compulsion to objectification found in the basic concepts of the philosophy of the subject. That is to say, the "vis-à-vis" of proponents and opponents reproduces at a reflective level that basic form of intersubjective relationship which always mediates the self-relation of the speaker through the performative relation to an addressee. The tense interconnection of the ideal and the real is also, and especially clearly, manifest in discourse itself. Once participants enter into argumentation, they cannot avoid supposing, in a reciprocal way, that the conditions for an ideal speech situation have been sufficiently met. And yet they realize that their discourse is never definitively "purified" of the motives and compulsions that have been filtered out. As little as we can do without the supposition of a purified discourse, we have equally to make do with "unpurified" discourse.

At the end of the fifth lecture, I indicated that the internal connection between contexts of justification and contexts of discovery, between validity and genesis, is never utterly severed. The task of justification, or, in other words, the critique of validity claims carried out from the perspective of a participant, cannot ultimately be separated from a genetic consideration that issues in an ideology critique—carried out from a third-person perspective—of the mixing of power claims and validity claims. Ever since Plato and Democritus, the history of philosophy has been dominated by two opposed impulses: One relentlessly elaborates the transcendent power of abstractive reason and the emancipatory unconditionality of the intelligible, whereas the other strives to unmask the imaginary purity of reason in a materialist fashion.

In contrast, dialectical thought has enlisted the subversive power of materialism to undercut these false alternatives. It does not respond to the banishment of everything empirical from the realm of ideas merely by scornfully reducing relationships of validity to the powers that triumph behind their back. Rather, the theory of communicative action regards the dialectic of knowing and not knowing as embedded within the dialectic of successful and unsuccessful mutual understanding.

Communicative reason makes itself felt in the binding force of intersubjective understanding and reciprocal recognition. At the same time, it circumscribes the universe of a common form of life. Within this universe, the irrational cannot be separated from the rational in the same way as, according to Parmenides, ignorance could be separated from the kind of knowledge that, as the absolutely affirmative, rules over the "nothing." Following Jacob Böhme and Isaac Luria, Schelling correctly insisted that mistakes, crimes, and deceptions are not simply without reason; they are forms of manifestation of the inversion of reason. The violation of claims to truth, correctness, and sincerity affects the whole permeated by the bond of reason. There is no escape and no refuge for the few who are in the truth and are supposed to take their leave of the many who stay behind in the darkness of their blindness, as the day takes leave of the night. Any violation of the structures of rational life together, to which all lay claim, affects everyone equally. This is what the young Hegel meant by the ethical totality that is disrupted by the deed of the criminal and that can only be restored by insight into the indivisibility of suffering due to alienation. The same idea motivates Klaus Heinrich in his confrontation of Parmenides with Jonah.

In the idea of the convenant made by Yahweh with the people of Israel, there is the germ of the dialectic of betrayal and avenging force: "Keeping the covenant with God is the symbol of fidelity; breaking this covenant is the model of betrayal. To keep faith with God is to keep faith with life-giving Being itself—in oneself and others. To deny it in any domain of being means breaking the covenant with God and betraying one's own foundation. . . . Thus, betrayal of another is simultaneously betrayal of oneself; and every protest against betrayal is not just protest in one's own name, but in the name of the other at the same time. . . . The idea that each being is potentially a 'covenant partner' in the fight against betrayal, including anyone who betrays himself and me, is the only counterbalance against the stoic resignation already formulated by Parmenides when he made a cut between those who know and the mass of the ignorant. The concept of 'enlightenment' familiar to us is unthinkable without the concept of a potentially universal confederation against betrayal."[6] Peirce and Mead were the first to raise this religious motif of a confederation to philosophical status in the form of a consensus theory of truth and a communication theory of society. The theory of communicative action joins itself with this pragmatist tradition; like Hegel in his early fragment on crime and punishment, it, too, lets itself be guided by an intuition that can be expressed in the concepts of the Old Testament as follows: In the restlessness of the real conditions of life, there broods an ambivalence that is due to the dialectic of betrayal and avenging force.[7]

In fact, we can by no means always, or even only often, fulfill those improbable pragmatic presuppositions from which we nevertheless set forth in day-to-day communicative practice—and, in the sense of transcendental necessity, from which we *have to* set forth. For this reason, sociocultural forms of life stand under the structural restrictions of a communicative reason *at once claimed and denied*.

The reason operating in communicative action not only stands under, so to speak, external, situational constraints; its own conditions of possibility necessitate its branching out into the dimensions of historical time, social space, and body-centered experiences. That is to say, the rational potential of speech is interwoven with the *resources* of any particular given lifeworld. To the extent that the lifeworld fulfills the resource function, it has the character of an intuitive, unshakeably certain, and holistic knowledge, which cannot be made problematic at will—and in this respect it does not represent "knowledge" in any strict sense of the word. This amalgam of background assumptions, solidarities, and skills bred through socialization constitutes a conservative counterweight against the risk of dissent inherent in processes of reaching understanding that work through validity claims.

As a resource from which interaction participants support utterances capable of reaching consensus, the lifeworld constitutes an equivalent for what the philosophy of the subject had ascribed to consciousness in general as synthetic accomplishments. Now, of course, the generative accomplishments are related not to the form but to the content of possible mutual understanding. To this extent, *concrete* forms of life replace transcendental consciousness in its function of creating unity. In culturally embodied self-understandings, intuitively present group solidarities, and the competences of socialized individuals that are brought into play as know-how, the reason expressed in communicative action is mediated with the traditions, social practices, and body-centered complexes of experience that coalesce into *particular* totalities. These particular forms of life, which only emerge in the plural, are certainly not connected with each other only through a web of family resemblances; they exhibit structures common to lifeworlds in general. But these universal structures are only stamped on particular life forms through the medium of action oriented to mutual understanding by which they have to be reproduced. This explains why the importance of these universal structures can increase in the course of historical processes of differentiation. This is also the key to the rationalization of the lifeworld and to the successive release of the rational potential contained in communicative action. This historical tendency can account for the normative content of a modernity threatened by self-destruction without drawing upon the constructions of the philosophy of history.

NOTES

1. Jürgen Habermas, "Remarks on the Concept of Communicative Action," in G. Seebass and R. Tuomela, eds., *Social Action* (Dordrecht, 1985), pp. 151–178.
2. Ernst Tugendhat, *Einführung in die sprachanalytische Philosophie* (Frankfurt, 1976).
3. Albrecht Wellmer has shown that the harmony of a work of art—aesthetic truth, as it is called—can by no means be reduced, without further ado, to authenticity or sincerity; see his "Truth, Semblance and Reconciliation," *Telos* 62 (1984/85):89–115.
4. J. H. Hamann, "Metakritik über den Purismus der Vernunft," in J. Simon, ed., *Schriften zur Sprache* (Frankfurt, 1967), pp. 213ff.

5. Karl-Otto Apel, *Towards a Transformation of Philosophy* (London, 1980), pp. 225ff. See also my response to Mary Hesse in John Thompson and David Held, eds., *Habermas: Critical Debates* (Cambridge, MA, and London, 1982), pp. 276ff.

6. K. Heinrich, *Versuch über die Schwierigkeit nein zu sagen* (Frankfurt, 1964), p. 20; see also his *Parmenides und Jona* (Frankfurt, 1966).

7. H. Brunkhorst, "Kommunikative Vernunft und rächende Gewalt," *Sozialwissenschaftliche Literatur-Rundschau* 8/9 (1983):7–34.

JÜRGEN HABERMAS

WHAT DOES A LEGITIMATION CRISIS MEAN TODAY? LEGITIMATION PROBLEMS IN LATE CAPITALISM

The expression 'late capitalism' implicitly asserts that, even in state-regulated capitalism, social developments are still passing through 'contradictions' or crises. I would therefore like to begin by elucidating the concept of *crisis.*

Prior to its use in economics, we are familiar with the concept of crisis in medicine. It refers to that phase of a disease in which it is decided whether the self-healing powers of the organism are sufficient for recovery. The critical process, the disease, seems to be something objective. A contagious disease, for instance, affects the organism from outside. The deviations of the organism from what it should be—i.e. the patient's normal condition—can be observed and, if necessary, measured with the help of indicators. The patient's consciousness plays no part in this. How the patient feels and how he experiences his illness is at most a symptom of events that he himself can barely influence. Nevertheless, we would not speak of a crisis in a medical situation of life or death if the patient were not trapped in this process with all his subjectivity. A crisis cannot be separated from the victim's inner view. He experiences his impotence toward the objectivity of his illness only because he is a subject doomed to passivity and temporarily unable to be a subject in full possession of his strength.

Crisis suggests the notion of an objective power depriving a subject of part of his normal sovereignty. If we interpret a process as a crisis, we are tacitly giving it a normative meaning. When the crisis is resolved, the trapped subject is liberated.

This becomes clearer when we pass from the medical to the dramaturgical notion of crisis. In classical aesthetics from Aristotle to Hegel, crisis signifies the turning point of a fateful process which, although fully objective, does not simply break in from the outside. There is a contradiction expressed in the catastrophic culmination of a conflict of action, and that contradiction is inherent in the very structure of the system of action and in the personality systems of the characters. Fate is revealed in conflicting norms that destroy the identities of the characters unless they in turn manage to regain their freedom by smashing the mythical power of fate.

The notion of crisis developed by classical tragedy has its counterpart in the notion of crisis to be found in the doctrine of salvation. Recurring throughout the philosophy of history in the eighteenth century, this figure of thought enters the evolutionary social theories of the nineteenth century. Marx is the first to develop a sociological concept of system crisis. It is against that background that we now speak of social or economic crises. In any discussion of, say, the great economic crisis in the early thirties, the Marxist overtones are unmistakable.

Since capitalist societies have the capacity of steadily developing technological productive forces, Marx conceives an economic crisis as a crisis-ridden process of economic growth. Accumulation of capital is tied to the acquisition of surplus. This means for Marx that economic growth is regulated by a mechanism that both establishes and conceals a power relationship. Thus the model of rising complexity is contradictory in the sense that the economic system keeps creating new and more problems as it solves others. The total accumulation of capital passes through periodic devaluations of capital components: this forms the cycle of crises, which Marx in his time was able to observe. He tried to explain the classical type of crisis by applying the theory of value with the help of the law of the tendential fall of the rate of profit. But that is outside my purpose at the moment. My question is really, 'Is late capitalism following the same or similar self-destructive pattern of development as classical—i.e. competitive—capitalism? Or has the organizing principle of late capitalism changed so greatly that the accumulation process no longer generates any problems jeopardizing its existence?

My starting point will be a rough descriptive model of the most important structural features of late-capitalist societies. I will then mention three crisis tendencies which today, though not specific to the system, are major topics of discussion. And finally, I will deal with various explanations of the crisis tendencies in late capitalism.

STRUCTURAL FEATURES OF LATE-CAPITALIST SOCIETIES

The expression 'organized or state-regulated capitalism' refers to two classes of phenomena both of which can be traced back to the advanced stage of the accumulation process. One such class is the process of economic concentration (the creation of national and by now even multinational corporations) and the organization of markets for goods, capital, and labour. On the other hand, the interventionist state keeps filling the increasing functional gaps in the market. The spread of oligopolistic market structures certainly spells the end of competitive capitalism. But no matter how far companies may see into the future or extend their control over the environment, the steering mechanism of the market will continue to function as long as investments are determined by company profits. At the same time, by complementing and partially replacing the market mechanism, government intervention means the end of liberal capitalism. But no matter how much the state may restrict the owner of goods in his private autonomous activity, there will be no political planning to allocate scarce resources as long as the overall societal priorities develop naturally— i.e. as indirect results of the strategies of private enterprise. In advanced capitalist societies, the economic, the administrative, and the legitimation systems can be characterized as follows.

The Economic System

During the 1960s, various authors, using the example of the United States, developed a three-sector model based on the distinction between the private and public areas. Private production is market-oriented, one sector still regulated by competition, another by the market strategies of the oligopolies that tolerate a competitive fringe. However, the public area, especially in the wake of armament and space-travel production, has witnessed the rise of great industries which, in their investment decisions, can operate independently of the market. These are either enterprises directly controlled by the government or private firms living on government contracts. The monopolistic and the public sectors are dominated by capital-intensive industries; the competitive sector is dominated by labour-intensive industries. In the monopolistic and the public sectors, the industries are faced with powerful unions. But in the competitive sector, labour is not as well organized, and the salary levels are correspondingly different. In the monopolistic sector, we can observe relatively rapid progress in production. However, in the public sector, the companies do not need to be, and in the competitive sector they cannot be, that efficient.

The Administrative System

The state apparatus regulates the overall economic cycle by means of global planning. On the other hand, it also improves the conditions for utilizing capital.

Global planning is limited by private autonomous use of the means of production (the investment freedom of private enterprises cannot be restricted). It is limited on the other hand by the general purpose of crisis management. There are fiscal and financial measures to regulate cycles, as well as individual measures to regulate investments and overall demand (credits, price guarantees, subsidies, loans, secondary redistribution of income, government contracts based on business-cycle policies, indirect labour-market policies, etc.). All these measures have the reactive character of avoidance strategies within the context of a well-known preference system. This system is determined by a didactically demanded compromise between competing imperatives: steady growth, stability of money value, full employment, and balance of trade.

Global planning manipulates the marginal conditions of decisions made by private enterprise. It does so in order to correct the market mechanism by neutralizing dysfunctional side effects. The state, however, supplants the market mechanism wherever the government creates and improves conditions for utilizing excess accumulated capital. It does so:

(1) by 'strengthening the competitive capacity of the nation', by organizing supranational economic blocks, by an imperialistic safeguarding of international stratification, etc.;

(2) by unproductive government consumption (armament and space-travel industry);

(3) by politically structured guidance of capital in sectors neglected by an autonomous market;

(4) by improving the material infrastructure (transportation, education and health, vocation centres, urban and regional planning, housing, etc.);

(5) by improving the immaterial infrastructure (promotion of scientific research, capital expenditure in research and development, intermediary of patents, etc.);

(6) by increasing the productivity of human labour (universal education, vocational schooling, programmes of training and re-education, etc.);

(7) by paying for the social costs and real consequences of private production (unemployment, welfare, ecological damage).

The Legitimation System

With the functional weaknesses of the market and the dysfunctional side effects of the market mechanism, the basic bourgeois ideology of fair exchange also collapsed. Yet there is a need for even greater legitimation. The government apparatus no longer merely safeguards the prerequisites for the production process. It also, on its own initiative, intervenes in that process. It must therefore be legitimated in the growing realms of state intervention, even though there is now no possibility of reverting to the traditions that have been undermined and worn out in competitive capitalism. The universalistic value systems of bourgeois ideology have made civil rights, including suffrage, universal. Independent of general elections, legitimation can thus be gotten only in extraordinary circumstances and temporarily. The resulting problem is resolved through formal democracy.

A wide participation by the citizens in the process of shaping political will—i.e. genuine democracy—would have to expose the contradiction between administratively socialized production and a still private form of acquiring the produced values. In order to keep the contradiction from being thematized, one thing is necessary. The administrative system has to be sufficiently independent of the shaping of legitimating will. This occurs in a legitimation process that elicits mass loyalty but avoids participation. In the midst of an objectively politicized society, the members enjoy the status of passive citizens with the right to withhold their acclaim. The private autonomous decision about investments is complemented by the civil privatism of the population.

Class Structure

The structures of late capitalism can be regarded as a kind of reaction formation. To stave off the system crisis, late-capitalist societies focus all socially integrative strength on the conflict that is structurally most probable. They do so in order all the more effectively to keep that conflict latent.

In this connection, an important part is played by the quasi-political wage structure, which depends on negotiations between companies and unions. Price fixing, which has replaced price competition in the oligopolistic markets, has its counterpart in the labour market. The great industries almost administratively control the prices in their marketing territories. Likewise, through wage negotiations, they achieve quasi-political compromises with their union adversaries. In those industrial branches of the monopolistic and public sectors that are crucial to economic development, the commodity known as labour has a 'political' price. The 'wage-scale partners' find a broad zone of compromise, since increased labour costs can be passed on into the prices, and the middle-range demands made by both sides against the government tend to converge. The main consequences of immunizing the original conflict zone are as follows: (1) disparate wage developments; (2) a permanent inflation with the corresponding short-lived redistribution of incomes to the disadvantages of unorganized wage earners and other marginal groups; (3) a permanent crisis in government finances, coupled with public poverty—i.e. pauperization of public transportation, education, housing, and health; (4) an insufficient balance of disproportionate economic developments, both sectoral (e.g. agricultural) and regional (marginal areas).

Since World War II, the most advanced capitalist countries have kept the class conflict latent in its essential areas. They have extended the business cycle, transforming the periodic pressures of capital devaluation into a permanent inflationary crisis with milder cyclical fluctuations. And they have filtered down the dysfunctional side effects of the intercepted economic crisis and scattered them over quasi-groups (such as consumers, school children and their parents, transportation users, the sick, the elderly) or divided groups difficult to organize. This process breaks down the social identity of the classes and fragments class consciousness. In the class compromise now part of the structure of late capitalism, nearly everyone both participates and is affected as an individual—although, with the clear and sometimes growing unequal distribution of monetary values and power, one can well distinguish between those belonging more to the one or to the other category.

THREE DEVELOPING CRISES

The rapid growth processes of late-capitalist societies have confronted the system of world society with new problems. These problems cannot be regarded as crisis phenomena specific to the system, even though the possibilities of coping with the crises are specific to the system and therefore limited. I am thinking of the disturbance of the ecological balance, the violation of the personality system (alienation), and the explosive strain on international relations.

The Ecological Balance

If physically economic growth can be traced back to the technologically sophisticated use of more energy to increase the productivity of human labour, then the societal formation of capitalism is remarkable for impressively solving the problem of economic growth. To be sure, capital accumulation originally pushes economic growth ahead, so there is no option for the conscious steering of this process. The growth imperatives originally followed by capitalism have meanwhile achieved a global validity by way of system competition and worldwide diffusion (despite the stagnation or even retrogressive trends in some Third World countries).

The mechanisms of growth are forcing an increase of both population and production on a worldwide scale. The economic needs of a growing population and the productive exploitation of nature are faced with material restrictions: on the one hand, finite resources (cultivable and inhabitable land, fresh water, metals, minerals, etc.); on the other hand, irreplaceable ecological systems that absorb pollutants such as fallout, carbon dioxide, and waste heat. Forrester and others have estimated the limits of the exponential growth of population, industrial production, exploitation of natural resources, and environmental pollution. To be sure, their estimates have rather weak empirical foundations. The mechanisms of population growth are as little known as the maximum limits of the earth's potential for absorbing even the major pollutants. Moreover, we cannot forecast technological development accurately enough to know which raw materials will be replaced or renovated by future technology.

However, despite any optimistic assurances, we are able to indicate (if not precisely determine) *one* absolute limitation on growth: the thermal strain on the environment due to consumption of energy. If economic growth is necessarily coupled with increasing consumption of energy, and if all natural energy that is transformed into economically useful energy is ultimately released as heat, it will eventually raise the temperature of the atmosphere. Again, determining the deadline is not easy. Nevertheless, these reflections show that an exponential growth of population and production—i.e. an expanded control over external nature—will some day run up against the limits of the biological capacity of the environment.

This is not limited to complex societal systems. Specific to these systems are the possibilities of warding off dangers to the ecology. Late-capitalist societies would have a very hard time limiting their growth without abandoning their principle of organization, because an overall shift from spontaneous capitalist growth to qualitative growth would require production planning in terms of use-values.

The Anthropological Balance

While the disturbance of the ecological balance points out the negative aspect of the exploitation of natural resources, there are no sure signals for the capacity limits of personality systems. I doubt whether it is possible to identify such things as psychological constants of human nature that inwardly limit the socialization process. I do, however, see a limitation in the kind of socializing that societal systems have been using to create motives for action. Our behaviour is oriented by norms requiring justification and by interpretative systems guaranteeing identity. Such a communicative organization of behaviour can become an obstacle in complex societies for a simple reason. The adaptive capacity in organizations increases proportionately as the administrative authorities become independent of the particular motivations of the members. The choice and achievement of organization goals in systems of high intrinsic complexity have to be independent of the influx of narrowly delimited motives. This requires a generalized willingness to comply (in political systems, such willingness has the form of legitimation). As long as socialization brings inner nature into a communicative behavioural organization, no legitimation for norms of action could conceivably secure an unmotivated acceptance of decisions. In regard to decisions whose contents are still undetermined, people will comply if convinced that those decisions are based on a legitimate norm of action. If the motives for acting were no longer to pass through norms requiring justification, and if the personality structures no longer had to find their unity under interpretative systems guaranteeing identity, then (and only then) the unmotivated acceptance of decisions would become an irreproachable routine, and the readiness to comply could thus be produced to any desirable degree.

The International Balance

The dangers of destroying the world system with thermonuclear weapons are on a different level. The accumulated potential for annihilation is a result of the advanced stage of productive forces. Its basis is technologically neutral, and so the productive forces can also take the form of destructive forces (which has happened because international communication is still undeveloped). Today, mortal damage to the natural substratum of global society is quite possible. International communication is therefore governed by a historically new imperative of self-limitation. Once again, this is not limited to all highly militarized societal systems, but the possibilities of tackling this problem have limits specific to the systems. An actual disarmament may be unlikely because of the forces behind capitalist and post-capitalist class societies. Yet regulating the arms race is not basically incompatible with the structure of late-capitalist societies if it is possible to increase technologically the use-value of capital to the degree that the capacity effect of the government's demand for unproductive consumer goods can be balanced.

DISTURBANCES SPECIFIC TO THE SYSTEM

I would now like to leave these three global consequences of late-capitalist growth and investigate disturbances specific to the system. I will start with a thesis, widespread among Marxists, that the basic capitalist structures continue unaltered and create economic crises in altered manifestations. In late capitalism, the state pursues the politics of capital with other means. This thesis occurs in two versions.

Orthodox state-theory maintains that the activities of the interventionist state, no less than the exchange processes in liberal capitalism, obey economic laws. The altered manifestations (the crisis of state finances and permanent inflation, growing disparities between public poverty and private wealth, etc.) are due to the fact that the self-regulation of the realization process is governed by power rather than by exchange. However, the crisis tendency is determined, as much as ever, by the law of value, the structurally forced asymmetry in the exchange of wage labour for capital. As a result, state activity cannot permanently compensate for the tendency of falling rates of profit. It can at best mediate that trend—i.e. consummate it with political means. The replacement of market functions by state functions does not alter the unconscious nature of the overall economic process. This is shown by the narrow limits of the state's possibilities for manipulation. The state cannot substantially intervene in the property structure without causing an investment strike. Neither can it manage permanently to avoid cyclical stagnation tendencies of the accumulation process—i.e. stagnation tendencies that are created endogenously.

A revisionist version of the Marxist theory of the state is current among leading economists in the German Democratic Republic. According to this version, the state apparatus, instead of naturally obeying the logic of the law of value, is consciously supporting the interests of united monopoly capitalists. This agency theory, adapted to late capitalism, regards the state not as a blind organ of the realization process but as a potent supreme capitalist who makes the accumulation of capital the substance of his political planning. The high degree of the socialization of production brings together the individual interests of the large corporations and the interest in maintaining the system. And all the more so because its existence is threatened internally by forces transcending the system. This leads to an overall capitalist interest, which the united monopolies sustain with the aid of the state apparatus.

I consider both versions of the theory of economic crises inadequate. One version underestimates the state, the other overestimates it.

In regard to the orthodox thesis, I wonder if the state-controlled organization of scientific and technological progress and the system of collective bargaining (a system producing a class compromise, especially in the capital- and growth-intensive economic sectors) have not altered the mode of production. The state, having been drawn into the process of production, has modified the determinants of the process of utilizing capital. On the basis of a partial class compromise, the administrative system has gained a limited planning capacity. This can be used within the framework of the democratic acquisition of legitimation for purposes of reactive avoidance of crises. The cycle of crises is deactivated and rendered less harmful in its social consequences. It is replaced by inflation and a permanent crisis of public finances. The question as to whether these surrogates indicate a successful halting of the economic crisis or merely its temporary shift into the political system is an empirical one. Ultimately, this depends on whether the indirectly productive capital invested in research, development, and education can continue the process of accumulation. It can manage to do so by making labour more productive, raising the rate of surplus value, and cheapening the fixed components of capital.

The revisionist theory has elicited the following reservations. For one thing, we cannot empirically support the assumption that the state apparatus, no matter in whose interest, can actively plan, as well as draft and carry through, a central economic strategy. The theory of state-monopoly capitalism (akin to Western theories of technocracy) fails to recognize the limits of administrative planning in late capitalism. Bureaucracies for planning always reactively avoid crises. The various bureaucracies are not fully coordinated, and because of their limited capacity for perceiving and steering, they tend to depend largely on the influence of their clients. It is because of this very inefficiency that organized partial interests have a chance to penetrate the administrative apparatus. Nor can we empirically support the other assumption that the state is active as the agent of the united monopolists. The theory of state-monopoly capitalism (akin to Western elite theories) overrates the significance of personal contacts and direct influence. Studies on the recruiting, make-up, and interaction of the various power elites fail to explain cogently the functional connections between the economic and administrative systems.

In my opinion, the late-capitalist state can be properly understood neither as the unconscious executive organ of economic laws nor as a systematic agent of the united monopoly capitalists. Instead, I would join Claus Offe in advocating the theory that late-capitalist societies are faced with two difficulties caused by the state's having to intervene in the growing functional gaps of the market. We can regard the state as a system that uses legitimate power. Its output consists in sovereignly executing administrative decisions. To this end, it needs an input of mass loyalty that is as unspecific as possible. Both directions can lead to crisis-like disturbances. Output crises have the form of the efficiency crisis. The administrative system fails to fulfil the steering imperative that it has taken over from the economic system. This results in the disorganization of different areas of life. Input crises have the form of the legitimation crisis. The legitimation system fails to maintain the necessary level of mass loyalty. We can clarify this with the example of the acute difficulties in public finances, with which all late-capitalist societies are now struggling.

The government budget, as I have said, is burdened with the public expenses of an increasingly socialized production. It bears the costs of international competition and of the demand for unproductive consumer goods (armament and space-travel). It bears the costs for the infrastructural output (transportation and communication, scientific and technological progress, vocational training). It bears the costs of the social consumption indirectly concerned with production (housing, transportation, health, leisure, general education, social security). It bears the costs of providing for the unemployed. And finally, it bears the externalized costs of environmental damage caused by private production. Ultimately, these expenses have to be met by taxes. The state apparatus thus has two simultaneous tasks. It has to levy the necessary taxes from profits and income and employ them so efficiently as to prevent any crises from disturbing growth. In addition the selective raising of taxes, the recognizable priority model of their utilization, and the administrative performance have to function in such a way as to satisfy the resulting need for legitimation. If the state fails in the former task, the result is a deficit in administrative efficiency. If it fails in the latter task, the result is a deficit in legitimation.

THEOREMS OF THE LEGITIMATION CRISIS

I would like to restrict myself to the legitimation problem. There is nothing mysterious about its genesis. Legitimate power has to be available for administrative planning. The functions accruing to the state apparatus in late capitalism and the expansion of social areas treated by administration increase the need for legitimation. Liberal capitalism constituted itself in the forms of bourgeois democracy, which is easy to explain in terms of the bourgeois revolution. As a result, the growing need for legitimation now has to work with the means of political democracy (on the basis of universal suffrage). The formal democratic means, however, are expensive. After all, the state apparatus does not just see itself in the role of the supreme capitalist facing the conflicting interests of the various capital factions. It also has to consider the generalizable interests of the population as far as necessary to retain mass loyalty and prevent a conflict-ridden withdrawal of legitimation. The state has to gauge these three interest areas (individual capitalism, state capitalism, and generalizable interests), in order to find a compromise for competing demands. A theorem of crisis has to explain not only why the state apparatus encounters difficulties but also why certain problems remain unsolved in the long run.

First, an obvious objection. The state can avoid legitimation problems to the extent that it can manage to make the administrative system independent of the formation of legitimating will. To that end, it can, say, separate expressive symbols (which create a universal willingness to follow) from the instrumental functions of administration. Well-known strategies of this sort are: the personalizing of objective issues, the symbolic use of inquiries, expert opinions, legal incantations, etc. Advertising techniques, borrowed from oligopolistic competition, both confirm and exploit current structures of prejudice. By resorting to emotional appeals, they arouse unconscious motives, occupy certain contents positively, and devalue others. The public, which is engineered for purposes of legitimation, primarily has the function of structuring attention by means of areas of themes and thereby of pushing uncomfortable themes, problems, and arguments below the threshold of attention. As Niklas Luhmann put it, the political system takes over tasks of ideology planning.

The scope for manipulation, however, is narrowly delimited, for the cultural system remains peculiarly resistant to administrative control. There is no administrative creation of meaning, there is at best an ideological erosion of cultural values. The acquisition of legitimation is self-destructive as soon as the mode of acquisition is exposed. Thus there is a systematic limit for attempts at making up for legitimation deficits by means of well-aimed manipulation. This limit is the structural dissimilarity between areas of administrative action and cultural tradition.

A crisis argument, to be sure, can be constructed out of these considerations only with the viewpoint that the expansion of state activity has the side-effect of disproportionately increasing the need for legitimation. I regard such an overproportionate increase as likely because things that are taken for granted culturally, and have so far been external conditions of the political systems, are now being drawn into the planning area of administration. This process thematizes traditions which previously were not part of public programming, much less of practical discourse. An example of such direct administrative processing of cultural tradition is educational planning, especially the planning of the curriculum. Hitherto, the school administration merely had to codify a given naturally evolved canon. But now the planning of the curriculum is based on the premise that the tradition models can also be different. Administrative planning creates a universal compulsion for justification toward a sphere that was actually distinguished by the power of self-legitimation.

In regard to the direct disturbance of things that were culturally taken for granted, there are further examples in regional and urban planning (private ownership of land), health planning ('classless hospital'), and family planning and marriage-law planning (which are shaking sexual taboos and facilitating emancipation).

An awareness of contingency is created not just for contents of tradition but also for the techniques of tradition—i.e. socialization. Among pre-school children, formal schooling is already competing with family upbringing. The new problems afflicting the educational routine, and the widespread awareness of these problems, are reflected by, among other indications, a new type of pedagogical and psychological writing addressed to the general public.

On all these levels, administrative planning has unintentional effects of disquieting and publicizing. These effects weaken the justification potential of traditions that have been forced out of their natural condition. Once they are no longer indisputable, their demands for validity can be stabilized only by way of discourse. Thus, the forcible shift of things that have been culturally taken for granted further politicizes areas of life that previously could be assigned to the private domain. However, this spells danger for bourgeois privatism, which is informally assured by the structures of the public. I see signs of this danger in strivings for participation and in models for alternatives, such as have developed particularly in secondary and primary schools, in the press, the church, theatres, publishing, etc.

These arguments support the contention that late-capitalist societies are afflicted with serious problems of legitimation. But do these arguments suffice to explain why these problems cannot be solved? Do they explain the prediction of a crisis in legitimation? Let us assume the state apparatus could succeed in making labour more productive and in distributing the gains in productivity in such a way as to assure an economic growth free of crises (if not disturbances). Such growth would nevertheless proceed in terms of priorities independent of the generalizable interests of the population. The priority models that Galbraith has analysed from the viewpoint of 'private wealth versus public poverty' result from a class structure which, as always, is still being kept latent. This structure is ultimately the cause of the legitimation deficit.

We have seen that the state cannot simply take over the cultural system and that, in fact, the expansion of areas for state planning creates problems for things that are culturally taken for granted. 'Meaning' is an increasingly scarce resource, which is why those expectations that are governed by concrete and identifiable needs—i.e. that can be checked by their success—keep mounting in the civil population. The rising level of aspirations is proportionate to the growing need for legitimation. The resource of 'value', siphoned off by the tax office, has to make up for the scanty resource of 'meaning'. Missing legitimations have to be replaced by social rewards such as money, time, and security. A crisis of legitimation arises as soon as the demands for these rewards mount more rapidly than the available mass of values, or if expectations come about that are different and cannot be satisfied by those categories of rewards conforming with the present system.

Why then should not the level of demands keep within operable limits? As long as the welfare state's programming in connection with a widespread technocratic consciousness (which makes uninfluenceable system-restraints responsible for bottlenecks) maintains a sufficient amount of civil privatism, then the legitimation emergencies do not have to turn into crises. To be sure, the democratic form of legitimation could cause expenses that cannot be covered if that form drives the competing parties to outdo one another in their platforms and thereby raise the expectations of the population higher and higher. Granted, this argument could be amply demonstrated empirically. But we would still have to explain why late-capitalist societies even bother to retain formal democracy. Merely in terms of the administrative system, formal democracy could just as easily be replaced by a variant—a conservative, authoritarian welfare state that reduces the political participation of the citizens to a harmless level; or a Fascist authoritarian state that keeps the population toeing the mark on a relatively high level of permanent mobilization. Evidently, both variants are in the long run less compatible with developed capitalism than a party state based on mass democracy. The socio-cultural system creates demands that cannot be satisfied in authoritarian systems.

This reflection leads me to the following thesis: only a rigid socio-cultural system, incapable of being randomly functionalized for the needs of the administrative system, could explain how legitimation difficulties result in a legitimation crisis. This development must therefore be based on a motivation crisis—i.e. a discrepancy between the need for motives that the state and the occupational system announce and the supply of motivation offered by the socio-cultural system.

THEOREMS OF THE MOTIVATION CRISIS

The most important motivation contributed by the socio-cultural system in late-capitalist societies consists in syndromes of civil and family/vocational privatism. Civil privatism means strong interests in the administrative system's output and minor participation in the process of will-formation (high-output orientation versus low-input orientation). Civil privatism thus corresponds to the structures of a depoliticized public. Family and vocational privatism complements civil privatism. It consists of a family orientation with consumer and leisure interests, and of a career orientation consistent with status competition. This privatism thus corresponds to the structures of educational and occupational systems regulated by competitive performance.

The motivational syndromes mentioned are vital to the political and economic system. However, bourgeois ideologies have components directly relevant to privatistic orientations, and social changes deprive those components of their basis. A brief outline may clarify this.

Performance Ideology

According to bourgeois notions which have remained constant from the beginnings of modern natural law to contemporary election speeches, social rewards should be distributed on the basis of individual achievement. The distribution of gratifications should correlate to every individual's performance. A basic condition is equal opportunity to participate in a competition which is regulated in such a way that external influences can be neutralized. One such allocation mechanism was the market. But ever since the general public realized that social violence is practised in the forms of exchange, the market has been losing its credibility as a mechanism for distributing rewards based on performance. Thus, in the more recent versions of performance ideology, market success is being replaced by the professional success mediated by formal schooling. However, this version can claim credibility only when the following conditions have been fulfilled:

(1) equal opportunity of access to higher schools;

(2) non-discriminatory evaluation standards for school performance;

(3) synchronic developments of the educational and occupational systems;

(4) work processes whose objective structure permits evaluation according to performances that can be ascribed to individuals.

'School justice' in terms of opportunity of access and standards of evaluation has increased in all advanced capitalist societies at least to some degree. But a counter-trend can be observed in the two other dimensions. The expansion of the educational system is becoming more and more independent of changes in the occupational system, so that ultimately the connection between formal schooling and professional success will most likely loosen. At the same time, there are more and more areas in which production structures and work dynamics make it increasingly difficult to evaluate individual performance. Instead, the extrafunctional elements of occupational roles are becoming more and more important for conferring occupational status.

Moreover, fragmented and monotonous work processes are increasingly entering sectors in which previously a personal identity could be developed through the vocational role. An intrinsic motivation for performance is getting less and less support from the structure of the work process in market-dependent work areas. An instrumentalist attitude toward work is spreading even in the traditionally bourgeois professions (white-collar workers, professionals). A performance motivation coming from outside can, however, be sufficiently stimulated by wage income only if:

(1) the reserve army on the labour market exercises an effective competitive pressure;

(2) a sufficient income differential exists between the lower wage groups and the inactive work population.

Both conditions are not necessarily met today. Even in capitalist countries with chronic unemployment (such as the United States), the division of the labour market (into organized and competitive sectors) interferes with the natural mechanism of competition. With a mounting poverty line (recognized by the welfare state), the living standards of the lower income groups and the groups temporarily released from the labour process are mutually assimilating on the other side in the sub-proletarian strata.

Possessive Individualism
Bourgeois society sees itself as an instrumental group that accumulates social wealth only by way of private wealth—i.e. guarantees economic growth and general welfare through competition between strategically acting private persons. Collective goals, under such circumstances, can be achieved only by way of individual utility orientations. This preference system, of course, presupposes:

(1) that the private economic subjects can with subjective unambiguity recognize and calculate needs that remain constant over given time periods;

(2) that this need can be satisfied by individually demandable goods (normally, by way of monetary decisions that conform to the system).

Both presuppositions are no longer fulfilled as a matter of course in the developed capitalist societies. These societies have reached a level of societal wealth far beyond warding off a few fundamental hazards to life and the satisfying of basic needs. This is why the individualistic system of preference is becoming vague. The steady interpreting and reinterpreting of needs is becoming a matter of the collective formation of the will, a fact which opens the alternatives of either free and quasi-political communication among consumers as citizens or massive manipulation—i.e. strong indirect steering. The greater the degree of freedom for the preference system of the de-manders, the more urgent the problem of sales policies for the suppliers—at least if they are to maintain the illusion that the consumers can make private and autonomous decisions. Opportunistic adjustment of the consumers to market strategies is the ironical form of every consumer autonomy, which is to be maintained as the facade of possessive individualism. In addition, with increasing socialization of production, the quota of collective commodities among the consumer goods keeps growing. The urban living conditions in complex societies are more and more dependent on an infrastructure (transportation, leisure, health, education, etc.) that is withdrawing further and further from the forms of differential demand and private appropriation.

Exchange-value Orientation

Here I have to mention the tendencies that weaken the socialization effects of the market, especially the increase of those parts of the population that do not reproduce their lives through income from work (students, welfare recipients, social security recipients, invalids, criminals, soldiers, etc.) as well as the expansion of areas of activity in which, as in civil service or in teaching, abstract work is replaced by concrete work. In addition, the relevance that leisure acquires with fewer working hours (and higher real income), compared with the relevance of issues within the occupational sphere of life, does not in the long run privilege those needs that can be satisfied monetarily.

The erosion of bourgeois tradition brings out normative structures that are no longer appropriate to reproducing civil and family and professional privatism. The now dominant components of cultural heritage crystallize around a faith in science, a 'postauratic' art, and universalistic values. Irreversible developments have occurred in each of these areas. As a result, functional inequalities of the economic and the political systems are blocked by cultural barriers, and they can be broken down only at the psychological cost of regressions—i.e. with extraordinary motivational dam-age. German fascism was an example of the wasteful attempt at a collectively organized regression of consciousness below the thresholds of fundamental scientistic convictions, modern art, and universalistic law and morals.

Scientism

The political consequences of the authority enjoyed by the scientific system in developed societies are ambivalent. The rise of modern science established a demand for discursive justification, and traditionalistic attitudes cannot hold out against that demand. On the other hand, short-lived popular syntheses of scientific data (which have replaced global interpretations) guarantee the authority of science in the ab-stract. The authority known as 'science' can thus cover both things: the broadly effective criticism of any prejudice, as well as the new esoterics of specialized knowledge and expertise. A self-affirmation of the sciences can further a positivistic common sense on the part of the depoliticized public. Yet scientism establishes standards by which it can also be criticized itself and found guilty of residual dogmatism. Theories of technocracy and of democratic elitism, asserting the necessity of an institutionalized civic privatism, come forth with the presumption of theories. But this does not make them immune to criticism.

Postauratic Art

The consequences of modern art are somewhat less ambivalent. The modern age has radicalized the autonomy of bourgeois art in regard to the external purposes for which art could be used. For the first time, bourgeois society itself produced a counterculture against the bourgeois life style of possessive individualism, performance, and practicality. The *Bohème*, first established in Paris, the capital of the nineteenth century, embodies a critical demand that had arisen, unpolemically still, in the aura of the bourgeois artwork. The alter ego of the businessman, the 'human being', whom the bourgeois used to encounter in the lonesome contemplation of the artwork, soon split away from him. In the shape of the artistic avant garde, it confronted him as a hostile, at best seductive, force. In artistic beauty, the bourgeoisie had been able to experience its own ideals and the (as always) fictitious redemption of the promise of happiness which was merely suspended in everyday life. In radicalized art, however, the bourgeois soon had to recognize the negation of social practice as its complement.

Modern art is the outer covering in which the transformation of bourgeois art into a counter-culture was prepared. Surrealism marks the historical moment when modern art programmatically destroyed the outer covering of no-longer beautiful illusion in order to enter life desublimated. The levelling of the different reality degrees of art and life was accelerated (although not, as Walter Benjamin assumed, introduced) by the new techniques of mass reproduction and mass reception. Modern art had already sloughed off the aura of classical bourgeois art in that the art work made the production process visible and presented itself as a made product. But art enters the ensemble of utility values only when abandoning its autonomous status. The process is certainly ambivalent. It can signify the degeneration of art into a propagandistic mass art or commercialized mass culture, or else its transformation into a subversive counter-culture.

Universalist Morality

The blockage which bourgeois ideologies, stripped of their functional components, create for developing the political and economic system, is even clearer in the moral system than in the authority of science and the self-disintegration of modern art. The moment traditional societies enter a process of modernization, the growing complexity results in steering problems that necessitate an accelerated change of social norms. The tempo inherent in natural cultural tradition has to be heightened. This leads to bourgeois formal law which permits releasing the norm contents from the dogmatic structure of mere tradition and defining them in terms of intention. The legal norms are uncoupled from the corps of privatized moral norms. In addition, they need to be created (and justified) according to principles. Abstract law counts only for that area pacified by state power. But the morality of bourgeois private persons, a morality likewise raised to the level of universal principles, encounters no barrier in the continuing natural condition between the states. Since principled morality is sanctioned only by the purely inward authority of the conscience, its claim to universality conflicts with public morality, which is still bound to a concrete state-subject. This is the conflict between the cosmopolitanism of the human being and the loyalties of the citizen.

If we follow the developmental logic of overall societal systems of norms (leaving the area of historical examples), we can settle that conflict. But its resolution is conceivable only under certain conditions. The dichotomy between inner and outer morality has to disappear. The contrast between morally and legally regulated areas has to be relativized. And the validity of *all* norms has to be tied to the discursive formation of the will of the people potentially affected.

Competitive capitalism for the first time gave a binding force to strictly universalistic value systems. This occurred because the system of exchange had to be regulated universalistically and because the exchange of equivalents offered a basic ideology effective in the bourgeois class. In organized capitalism, the bottom drops out of this legitimation model. At the same time, new and increased demands for legitimation arise. However, the system of science cannot intentionally fall behind an attained stage of cumulative knowledge. Similarly, the moral system, once practical discourse has been admitted, cannot simply make us forget a collectively attained stage of moral consciousness.

I would like to conclude with a final reflection. If no sufficient concordance exists between the normative structures that still have some power today and the politico-economic system, then we can still avoid motivation crises by uncoupling the cultural system. Culture would then become a non-obligatory leisure occupation or the object of professional knowledge. This solution would be blocked if the basic convictions of a communicative ethics and the experience complexes of counter-cultures (in which postauratic art is embodied) acquired a motive-forming power determining typical socialization processes. Such a conjecture is supported by several behaviour syndromes spreading more and more among young people—either retreat as a reaction to an exorbitant claim on the personality resources; or protest as a result of an autonomous ego organization that cannot be stabilized without conflicts under given conditions. On the activist side we find the student movements, revolts by high-school students and apprentices, pacifists, women's lib. The retreatist side is represented by hippies, Jesus people, the drug subculture, phenomena of undermotivation in schools, etc. These are the primary areas for checking our hypothesis that late-capitalist societies are endangered by a collapse of legitimation.

PART SEVEN

CRITICAL THEORY AND ITS CRITICS

The final selections in this anthology represent critical evaluations of critical theory from postmodern, poststructuralist, and feminist perspectives. We have also included an essay by Habermas that addresses some of the issues raised by his critics.

The first selection, Michel Foucault's essay "The Subject and Power," originally appeared as an appendix to a work devoted to his thought by Hubert Dreyfus and Paul Rabinow entitled *Michel Foucault: Beyond Hermeneutics and Structuralism* (1982). In this essay he presents an overview of the central themes that occupied his historical studies such as *Discipline and Punish* (1975) and *The History of Sexuality: Volume I* (1976). Here Foucault focuses on the general question of how a human being becomes a subject. His discussion of the ways in which power is exercised relates to many of the problems and concerns raised by members of the Frankfurt School. One of the crucial points of contention between Foucault and Habermas regards the relationship of the subject to power. Foucault argues that the constitution of subjectivity entails that subjects at once exercise and are subjected to power. For Foucault there is no rational, moral foundation for critique of the sort Habermas defends. Habermas's indirect reply to Foucault is contained in *The Philosophical Discourse of Modernity* (1985).

Written from the perspective of postmodernism, Jean-François Lyotard's study entitled *The Postmodern Condition: A Report on Knowledge* (1979), takes issue with the Frankfurt School's conception of the social bond. Lyotard prefers to describe the social relation in terms of what he calls language games. Thus, for Lyotard, the question of legitimation raised by Habermas needs to be understood in the context of fragmented relations between disciplines and discourses. In place of the common linguistic bond that enables universal consensus in Habermas's work, Lyotard sees heterogeneous language games that work toward multiplicity and difference.

Habermas's contribution to this debate, "Modernity: An Unfinished Project," is translated in its entirety here for the first time. An abridged version previously appeared with the title "Modernity versus Postmodernity" in *New German Critique*

No. 22 (Winter 1981). Habermas originally gave this lecture in 1980 when he received the Adorno Prize from the city of Frankfurt. In this essay he addresses many of the issues raised by Lyotard and indirectly answers some of Foucault's criticisms. Habermas here reiterates his commitment to the modern project of rational enlightenment.

The fourth selection, "What's Critical About Critical Theory? The Case of Habermas and Gender," introduces the key question of gender into the critical evaluation of society. The essay appears in a volume of Nancy Fraser's work entitled *Unruly Practices: Power, Discourse and Gender in Contemporary Social Theory* (1989). In this essay, Fraser locates certain gender biases in Habermas's analysis of social institutions. These biases produce a theory that allows for the perpetuation of male dominance and female subordination. Fraser suggests a reevaluation of certain aspects of Habermas's theory in view of producing a critical theory sensitive to gender specificity.

The final selection, "The Utopian Dimension in Communicative Ethics" by Seyla Benhabib, offers another feminist critique of Habermas's work. Relying on the research of Carol Gilligan into gender differences in moral development, Benhabib argues that Habermas's adherence to a conception of the generalized other reveals a gender bias in his theory. Benhabib maintains that this conception of the generalized other restricts the utopian dimension of Habermas's work. By substituting a notion of the concrete other, Benhabib offers a vision of the full utopian potential of Habermas's theory. For a complete discussion of the tension between norm and utopia in Habermas's work, see Benhabib's book *Critique, Norm and Utopia: A Study of the Foundations of Critical Theory* (1986).

For a detailed discussion of postmodern, poststructuralist, and feminist critiques of critical theory (including Habermas's response to these criticisms), see Chapter 8 and the Postscript of *Philosophy and Critical Theory*.

MICHEL FOUCAULT

THE SUBJECT AND POWER

WHY STUDY POWER?
THE QUESTION OF THE SUBJECT

The ideas which I would like to discuss here represent neither a theory nor a methodology.

I would like to say, first of all, what has been the goal of my work during the last twenty years. It has not been to analyze the phenomena of power, nor to elaborate the foundations of such an analysis.

My objective, instead, has been to create a history of the different modes by which, in our culture, human beings are made subjects. My work has dealt with three modes of objectification which transform human beings into subjects.

The first are the modes of inquiry which try to give themselves the status of sciences; for example, the objectivizing of the speaking subject in *grammaire générale*, philology, and linguistics. Or again, in this first mode, the objectivizing of the productive subject, the subject who labors, in the analysis of wealth and of economics. Or, a third example, the objectivizing of the sheer fact of being alive in natural history or biology.

In the second part of my work, I have studied the objectivizing of the subject in what I shall call "dividing practices." The subject is either divided inside himself or divided from others. This process objectivizes him. Examples are the mad and the sane, the sick and the healthy, the criminals and the "good boys."

Finally, I have sought to study—it is my current work—the way a human being turns him- or herself into a subject. For example, I have chosen the domain of sexuality—how men have learned to recognize themselves as subjects of "sexuality."

Thus it is not power, but the subject, which is the general theme of my research.

It is true that I became quite involved with the question of power. It soon appeared to me that, while the human subject is placed in relations of production and of signification, he is equally placed in power relations which are very complex. Now, it seemed to me that economic history and theory provided a good instrument for relations of production; that linguistics and semiotics offered instruments for studying relations of signification; but for power relations we had no tools of study. We had recourse only to ways of thinking about power based on legal models, that is: What legitimates power? Or we had recourse to ways of thinking about power based on institutional models, that is: What is the state?

It was therefore necessary to expand the dimensions of a definition of power if one wanted to use this definition in studying the objectivizing of the subject.

Do we need a theory of power? Since a theory assumes a prior objectification, it cannot be asserted as a basis for analytical work. But this analytical work cannot proceed without an ongoing conceptualization. And this conceptualization implies critical thought—a constant checking.

The first thing to check is what I should call the "conceptual needs." I mean that the conceptualization should not be founded on a theory of the object—the conceptualized object is not the single criterion of a good conceptualization. We have to know the historical conditions which motivate our conceptualization. We need a historical awareness of our present circumstance.

The second thing to check is the type of reality with which we are dealing.

A writer in a well-known French newspaper once expressed his surprise: "Why is the notion of power raised by so many people today? Is it such an important subject? Is it so independent that it can be discussed without taking into account other problems?"

This writer's surprise amazes me. I feel skeptical about the assumption that this question has been raised for the first time in the twentieth century. Anyway, for us it is not only a theoretical question, but a part of our experience. I'd like to mention only two "pathological forms"—those two "diseases of power"—fascism and Stalinism. One of the numerous reasons why they are, for us, so puzzling, is that in spite of their historical uniqueness they are not quite original. They used and extended mechanisms already present in most other societies. More than that: in spite of their own internal madness, they used to a large extent the ideas and the devices of our political rationality.

What we need is a new economy of power relations—the word *economy* being used in its theoretical and practical sense. To put it in other words: since Kant, the role of philosophy is to prevent reason from going beyond the limits of what is given in experience; but from the same moment—that is, since the development of the modern state and the political management of society—the role of philosophy is also to keep watch over the excessive powers of political rationality. Which is a rather high expectation.

Everybody is aware of such banal facts. But the fact that they're banal does not mean they don't exist. What we have to do with banal facts is to discover—or try to discover—which specific and perhaps original problem is connected with them.

The relationship between rationalization and excesses of political power is evident. And we should not need to wait for bureaucracy or concentration camps to recognize the existence of such relations. But the problem is: What to do with such an evident fact?

Shall we try reason? To my mind, nothing would be more sterile. First, because the field has nothing to do with guilt or innocence. Second, because it is senseless to refer to reason as the contrary entity to nonreason. Lastly, because such a trial would trap us into playing the arbitrary and boring part of either the rationalist or the irrationalist.

Shall we investigate this kind of rationalism which seems to be specific to our modern culture and which originates in *Aufklärung*? I think that was the approach of some of the members of the Frankfurt School. My purpose, however, is not to start a discussion of their works, although they are most important and valuable. Rather, I would suggest another way of investigating the links between rationalization and power.

It may be wise not to take as a whole the rationalization of society or of culture, but to analyze such a process in several fields, each with reference to a fundamental experience: madness, illness, death, crime, sexuality, and so forth.

I think that the word *rationalization* is dangerous. What we have to do is analyze specific rationalities rather than always invoking the progress of rationalization in general.

Even if the *Aufklärung* has been a very important phase in our history and in the development of political technology, I think we have to refer to much more remote processes if we want to understand how we have been trapped in our own history.

I would like to suggest another way to go further towards a new economy of power relations, a way which is more empirical, more directly related to our present situation, and which implies more relations between theory and practice. It consists of taking the forms of resistance against different forms of power as a starting point. To use another metaphor, it consists of using this resistance as a chemical catalyst so as to bring to light power relations, locate their position, find out their point of application and the methods used. Rather than analyzing power from the point of view of its internal rationality, it consists of analyzing power relations through the antagonism of strategies.

For example, to find out what our society means by sanity, perhaps we should investigate what is happening in the field of insanity.

And what we mean by legality in the field of illegality.

And, in order to understand what power relations are about, perhaps we should investigate the forms of resistance and attempts made to dissociate these relations.

As a starting point, let us take a series of oppositions which have developed over the last few years: opposition to the power of men over women, of parents over children, of psychiatry over the mentally ill, of medicine over the population, of administration over the ways people live.

It is not enough to say that these are antiauthority struggles; we must try to define more precisely what they have in common.

1) They are "transversal" struggles; that is, they are not limited to one country. Of course, they develop more easily and to a greater extent in certain countries, but they are not confined to a particular political or economic form of government.

2) The aim of these struggles is the power effects as such. For example, the medical profession is not criticized primarily because it is a profit-making concern, but because it exercises an uncontrolled power over people's bodies, their health and their life and death.

3) These are "immediate" struggles for two reasons. In such struggles people criticize instances of power which are the closest to them, those which exercise their action on individuals. They do not look for the "chief enemy," but for the immediate enemy. Nor do they expect to find a solution to their problem at a future date (that is, liberations, revolutions, end of class struggle). In comparison with a theoretical scale of explanations or a revolutionary order which polarizes the historian, they are anarchistic struggles.

But these are not their most original points. The following seem to me to be more specific.

4) They are struggles which question the status of the individual: on the one hand, they assert the right to be different and they underline everything which makes individuals truly individual. On the other hand, they attack everything which separates the individual, breaks his links with others, splits up community life, forces the individual back on himself and ties him to his own identity in a constraining way.

These struggles are not exactly for or against the "individual," but rather they are struggles against the "government of individualization."

5) They are an opposition to the effects of power which are linked with knowledge, competence, and qualification: struggles against the privileges of knowledge. But they are also an opposition against secrecy, deformation, and mystifying representations imposed on people.

There is nothing "scientistic" in this (that is, a dogmatic belief in the value of scientific knowledge), but neither is it a skeptical or relativistic refusal of all verified truth. What is questioned is the way in which knowledge circulates and functions, its relations to power. In short, the *régime du savoir*.

6) Finally, all these present struggles revolve around the question: Who are we? They are a refusal of these abstractions, of economic and ideological state violence which ignore who we are individually, and also a refusal of a scientific or administrative inquisition which determines who one is.

To sum up, the main objective of these struggles is to attack not so much "such or such" an institution of power, or group, or elite, or class, but rather a technique, a form of power.

This form of power applies itself to immediate everyday life which categorizes the individual, marks him by his own individuality, attaches him to his own identity, imposes a law of truth on him which he must recognize and which others have to recognize in him. It is a form of power which makes individuals subjects. There are two meanings of the word *subject*: subject to someone else by control and dependence, and tied to his own identity by a conscience or self-knowledge. Both meanings suggest a form of power which subjugates and makes subject to.

Generally, it can be said that there are three types of struggles: either against forms of domination (ethnic, social, and religious); against forms of exploitation which separate individuals from what they produce; or against that which ties the individual to himself and submits him to others in this way (struggles against subjection, against forms of subjectivity and submission).

I think that in history, you can find a lot of examples of these three kinds of social struggles, either isolated from each other, or mixed together. But even when they are mixed, one of them, most of the time, prevails. For instance, in the feudal societies, the struggles against the forms of ethnic or social domination were prevalent, even though economic exploitation could have been very important among the revolt's causes.

In the nineteenth century, the struggle against exploitation came into the foreground.

And nowadays, the struggle against the forms of subjection—against the submission of subjectivity—is becoming more and more important, even though the struggles against forms of domination and exploitation have not disappeared. Quite the contrary.

I suspect that it is not the first time that our society has been confronted with this kind of struggle. All those movements which took place in the fifteenth and sixteenth centuries and which had the Reformation as their main expression and result should be analyzed as a great crisis of the Western experience of subjectivity and a revolt against the kind of religious and moral power which gave form, during the Middle Ages, to this subjectivity. The need to take a direct part in spiritual life, in the work of salvation, in the truth which lies in the Book—all that was a struggle for a new subjectivity.

I know what objections can be made. We can say that all types of subjection are derived phenomena, that they are merely the consequences of other economic and social processes: forces of production, class struggle, and ideological structures which determine the form of subjectivity.

It is certain that the mechanisms of subjection cannot be studied outside their relation to the mechanisms of exploitation and domination. But they do not merely constitute the "terminal" of more fundamental mechanisms. They entertain complex and circular relations with other forms.

The reason this kind of struggle tends to prevail in our society is due to the fact that since the sixteenth ·century, a new political form of power has been continuously developing. This new political structure, as everybody knows, is the state. But most of the time, the state is envisioned as a kind of political power which ignores individuals, looking only at the interests of the totality or, I should say, of a class or a group among the citizens.

That's quite true. But I'd like to underline the fact that the state's power (and that's one of the reasons for its strength) is both an individualizing and a totalizing form of power. Never, I think, in the history of human societies—even in the old Chinese society—has there been such a tricky combination in the same political structures of individualization techniques, and of totalization procedures.

This is due to the fact that the modern Western state has integrated in a new political shape, an old power technique which originated in Christian institutions. We can call this power technique the pastoral power.

First of all, a few words about this pastoral power.

It has often been said that Christianity brought into being a code of ethics fundamentally different from that of the ancient world. Less emphasis is usually placed on the fact that it proposed and spread new power relations throughout the ancient world.

Christianity is the only religion which has organized itself as a Church. And as such, it postulates in principle that certain individuals can, by their religious quality, serve others not as princes, magistrates, prophets, fortune-tellers, benefactors, educationalists, and so on, but as pastors. However, this word designates a very special form of power.

1) It is a form of power whose ultimate aim is to assure individual salvation in the next world.

2) Pastoral power is not merely a form of power which commands; it must also be prepared to sacrifice itself for the life and salvation of the flock. Therefore, it is different from royal power, which demands a sacrifice from its subjects to save the throne.

3) It is a form of power which does not look after just the whole community, but each individual in particular, during his entire life.

4) Finally, this form of power cannot be exercised without knowing the inside of people's minds, without exploring their souls, without making them reveal their innermost secrets. It implies a knowledge of the conscience and an ability to direct it.

This form of power is salvation oriented (as opposed to political power). It is oblative (as opposed to the principle of sovereignty); it is individualizing (as opposed to legal power); it is coextensive and continuous with life; it is linked with a production of truth—the truth of the individual himself.

But all this is part of history, you will say; the pastorate has, if not disappeared, at least lost the main part of its efficiency.

This is true, but I think we should distinguish between two aspects of pastoral power—between the ecclesiastical institutionalization which has ceased or at least lost its vitality since the eighteenth century, and its function, which has spread and multiplied outside the ecclesiastical institution.

An important phenomenon took place around the eighteenth century—it was a new distribution, a new organization of this kind of individualizing power.

I don't think that we should consider the "modern state" as an entity which was developed above individuals, ignoring what they are and even their very existence, but on the contrary as a very sophisticated structure, in which individuals can be integrated, under one condition: that this individuality would be shaped in a new form, and submitted to a set of very specific patterns.

In a way, we can see the state as a modern matrix of individualization, or a new form of pastoral power.

A few more words about this new pastoral power.

1) We may observe a change in its objective. It was no longer a question of leading people to their salvation in the next world, but rather ensuring it in this world. And in this context, the word *salvation* takes on different meanings: health, well-being (that is, sufficient wealth, standard of living), security, protection against accidents. A series of "worldly" aims took the place of the religious aims of the traditional pastorate, all the more easily because the latter, for various reasons, had followed in an accessory way a certain number of these aims; we only have to think of the role of medicine and its welfare function assured for a long time by the Catholic and Protestant churches.

2) Concurrently the officials of pastoral power increased. Sometimes this form of power was exerted by state apparatus or, in any case, by a public institution such as the police. (We should not forget that in the eighteenth century the police force was not invented only for maintaining law and order, nor for assisting governments in their struggle against their enemies, but for assuring urban supplies, hygiene, health and standards considered necessary for handicrafts and commerce.) Sometimes the power was exercised by private ventures, welfare societies, benefactors and generally by philanthropists. But ancient institutions, for example the family, were also mobilized at this time to take on pastoral functions. It was also exercised by complex structures such as medicine, which included private initiatives with the sale of services on market economy principles, but which also included public institutions such as hospitals.

3) Finally, the multiplication of the aims and agents of pastoral power focused the development of knowledge of man around two roles: one, globalizing and quantitative, concerning the population; the other, analytical, concerning the individual.

And this implies that power of a pastoral type, which over centuries—for more than a millennium—had been linked to a defined religious institution, suddenly spread out into the whole social body; it found support in a multitude of institutions. And, instead of a pastoral power and a political power, more or less linked to each other, more or less rival, there was an individualizing "tactic" which characterized a series of powers: those of the family, medicine, psychiatry, education, and employers.

At the end of the eighteenth century Kant wrote, in a German newspaper—the *Berliner Monatschrift*—a short text. The title was *Was heisst Aufklärung?* It was for a long time, and it is still, considered a work of relatively small importance.

But I can't help finding it very interesting and puzzling because it was the first time a philosopher proposed as a philosophical task to investigate not only the metaphysical system or the foundations of scientific knowledge, but a historical event—a recent, even a contemporary event.

When in 1784 Kant asked, Was heisst Aufklärung?, he meant, What's going on just now? What's happening to us? What is this world, this period, this precise moment in which we are living?

Or in other words: What are we? as *Aufklärer*, as part of the Enlightenment? Compare this with the Cartesian question: Who am I? I, as a unique but universal and unhistorical subject? I, for Descartes is everyone, anywhere at any moment?

But Kant asks something else: What are we? in a very precise moment of history. Kant's question appears as an analysis of both us and our present.

I think that this aspect of philosophy took on more and more importance. Hegel, Nietzsche. . . .

The other aspect of "universal philosophy" didn't disappear. But the task of philosophy as a critical analysis of our world is something which is more and more important. Maybe the most certain of all philosophical problems is the problem of the present time, and of what we are, in this very moment.

Maybe the target nowadays is not to discover what we are, but to refuse what we are. We have to imagine and to build up what we could be to get rid of this kind of political "double bind," which is the simultaneous individualization and totalization of modern power structures.

The conclusion would be that the political, ethical, social, philosophical problem of our days is not to try to liberate the individual from the state, and from the state's institutions, but to liberate us both from the state and from the type of individualization which is linked to the state. We have to promote new forms of subjectivity through the refusal of this kind of individuality which has been imposed on us for several centuries.

HOW IS POWER EXERCISED?

For some people, asking questions about the "how" of power would limit them to describing its effects without ever relating those effects either to causes or to a basic nature. It would make this power a mysterious substance which they might hesitate to interrogate in itself, no doubt because they would prefer *not* to call it into question. By proceeding this way, which is never explicitly justified, they seem to suspect the presence of a kind of fatalism. But does not their very distrust indicate a presupposition that power is something which exists with three distinct qualities: its origin, its basic nature, and its manifestations?

If, for the time being, I grant a certain privileged position to the question of "how" it is not because I would wish to eliminate the questions of "what" and "why." Rather it is that I wish to present these questions in a different way; better still, to know if it is legitimate to imagine a power which unites in itself a what, a why, and a how. To put it bluntly, I would say that to begin the analysis with a "how" is to suggest that power as such does not exist. At the very least it is to ask oneself what contents one has in mind when using this all-embracing and reifying term; it is to suspect that an extremely complex configuration of realities is allowed to escape when one treads endlessly in the double question: What is power? and Where does power come from? The little question, What happens? although flat and empirical, once it is scrutinized is seen to avoid accusing a metaphysics or an ontology of power of being fraudulent; rather it attempts a critical investigation into the thematics of power.

"How," not in the sense of "How does it manifest itself?" but "By what means is it exercised?" and "What happens when individuals exert (as they say) power over others?"
As far as this power is concerned, it is first necessary to distinguish that which is exerted over things and gives the ability to modify, use, consume, or destroy them—a power which stems from aptitudes directly inherent in the body or relayed by external instruments. Let us say that here it is a question of "capacity." On the other hand, what characterizes the power we are analyzing is that it brings into play relations between individuals (or between groups). For let us not deceive ourselves; if we speak of the structures or the mechanisms of power, it is only insofar as we suppose that certain persons exercise power over others. The term "power" designates relationships between partners (and by that I am not thinking of a zero-sum game, but simply, and for the moment staying in the most general terms, of an ensemble of actions which induce others and follow from one another).

It is necessary also to distinguish power relations from relationships of communication which transmit information by means of a language, a system of signs, or any other symbolic medium. No doubt communicating is always a certain way of acting upon another person or persons. But the production and circulation of elements of meaning can have as their objective or as their consequence certain results in the realm of power; the latter are not simply an aspect of the former. Whether or not they pass through systems of communication, power relations have a specific nature. Power relations, relationships of communication, objective capacities should not therefore be confused. This is not to say that there is a question of three separate domains. Nor that there is on one hand the field of things, of perfected technique, work, and the transformation of the real; on the other that of signs, communication, reciprocity, and the production of meaning; finally that of the domination of the means of constraint, of inequality and the action of men upon other men.[1] It is a question of three types of relationships which in fact always overlap one another, support one another reciprocally, and use each other mutually as means to an end. The application of objective capacities in their most elementary forms implies relationships of communication (whether in the form of previously acquired information or of shared work); it is tied also to power relations (whether they consist of obligatory tasks, of gestures imposed by tradition or apprenticeship, of subdivisions and the more or less obligatory distribution of labor). Relationships of communication imply finalized activities (even if only the correct putting into operation of elements of meaning) and, by virtue of the modifying the field of information between partners, produce effects of power. They can scarcely be dissociated from activities brought to their final term, be they those which permit the exercise of this power (such as training techniques, processes of domination, the means by which obedience is obtained) or those which in order to develop their potential call upon relations of power (the division of labor and the hierarchy of tasks).

Of course the coordination between these three types of relationships is neither uniform nor constant. In a given society there is no general type of equilibrium between finalized activities, systems of communication, and power relations. Rather there are diverse forms, diverse places, diverse circumstances or occasions in which these interrelationships establish themselves according to a specific model. But there are also "blocks" in which the adjustment of abilities, the resources of communication, and power relations constitute regulated and concerted systems. Take for example an educational institution: the disposal of its space, the meticulous regulations which govern its internal life, the different activities which are organized there, the diverse persons who live there or meet one another, each with his own function, his well-defined character—all these things constitute a block of capacity-communication-power. The activity which ensures apprenticeship and the acquisition of aptitudes or types of behavior is developed there by means of a whole ensemble of regulated communications (lessons, questions and answers, orders, exhortations, coded signs of obedience, differentiation marks of the "value" of each person and of the levels of knowledge) and by the means of a whole series of power processes (enclosure, surveillance, reward and punishment, the pyramidal hierarchy).

These blocks, in which the putting into operation of technical capacities, the game of communications, and the relationships of power are adjusted to one another according to considered formulae, constitute what one might call, enlarging a little the sense of the word, disciplines. The empirical analysis of certain disciplines as they have been historically constituted presents for this very reason a certain interest. This is so because the disciplines show, first, according to artificially clear and decanted systems, the manner in which systems of objective finality and systems of communication and power can be welded together. They also display different models of articulation, sometimes giving preeminence to power relations and obedience (as in those disciplines of a monastic or penitential type), sometimes to finalize activities (as in the disciplines of workshops or hospitals), sometimes to relationships of communication (as in the disciplines of apprenticeship), sometimes also to a saturation of the three types of relationship (as perhaps in military discipline, where a plethora of signs indicates, to the point of redundancy, tightly knit power relations calculated with care to produce a certain number of technical effects).

What is to be understood by the disciplining of societies in Europe since the eighteenth century is not, of course, that the individuals who are part of them become more and more obedient, nor that they set about assembling in barracks, schools, or prisons; rather that an increasingly better invigilated process of adjustment has been sought after—more and more rational and economic—between productive activities, resources of communication, and the play of power relations.

To approach the theme of power by an analysis of "how" is therefore to introduce several critical shifts in relation to the supposition of a fundamental power. It is to give oneself as the object of analysis power relations and not power itself—power relations which are distinct from objective abilities as well as from relations of communication. This is as much as saying that power relations can be grasped in the diversity of their logical sequence, their abilities, and their interrelationships.

What constitutes the specific nature of power?

The exercise of power is not simply a relationship between partners, individual or collective; it is a way in which certain actions modify others. Which is to say, of course, that something called Power, with or without a capital letter, which is assumed to exist universally in a concentrated or diffused form, does not exist. Power exists only when it is put into action, even if, of course, it is integrated into a disparate field of possibilities brought to bear upon permanent structures. This also means that power is not a function of consent. In itself it is not a renunciation of freedom, a transference of rights, the power of each and all delegated to a few (which does not prevent the possibility that consent may be a condition for the existence or the maintenance of power); the relationship of power can be the result of a prior or permanent consent, but it is not by nature the manifestation of a consensus.

Is this to say that one must seek the character proper to power relations in the violence which must have been its primitive form, its permanent secret and its last resource, that which in the final analysis appears as its real nature when it is forced to throw aside its mask and to show itself as it really is? In effect, what defines a relationship of power is that it is a mode of action which does not act directly and immediately on others. Instead it acts upon their actions: an action upon an action, on existing actions or on those which may arise in the present or the future. A relationship of violence acts upon a body or upon things; it forces, it bends, it breaks on the wheel, it destroys, or it closes the door on all possibilities. Its opposite pole can only be passivity, and if it comes up against any resistance it has no other option but to try to minimize it. On the other hand a power relationship can only be articulated on the basis of two elements which are each indispensable if it is really to be a power relationship: that "the other" (the one over whom power is exercised) be thoroughly recognized and maintained to the very end as a person who acts; and that, faced with a relationship of power, a whole field of responses, reactions, results, and possible inventions may open up.

Obviously the bringing into play of power relations does not exclude the use of violence any more than it does the obtaining of consent; no doubt the exercise of power can never do without one or the other, often both at the same time. But even though consensus and violence are the instruments or the results, they do not constitute the principle or the basic nature of power. The exercise of power can produce as much acceptance as may be wished for: it can pile up the dead and shelter itself behind whatever threats it can imagine. In itself the exercise of power is not violence; nor is it a consent which, implicitly, is renewable. It is a total structure of actions brought to bear upon possible actions; it incites, it induces, it seduces, it makes easier or more difficult; in the extreme it constrains or forbids absolutely; it is nevertheless always a way of acting upon an acting subject or acting subjects by virtue of their acting or being capable of action. A set of actions upon other actions.

Perhaps the equivocal nature of the term *conduct* is one of the best aids for coming to terms with the specificity of power relations. For to "conduct" is at the same time to "lead" others (according to mechanisms of coercion which are, to varying degrees, strict) and a way of behaving within a more or less open field of possibilities.[2] The exercise of power consists in guiding the possibility of conduct and putting in order the possible outcome. Basically power is less a confrontation between two adversaries or the linking of one to the other than a question of government. This word must be allowed the very broad meaning which it had in the sixteenth century. "Government" did not refer only to political structures or to the management of states; rather it designated the way in which the conduct of individuals or of groups might be directed: the government of children, of souls, of communities, of families, of the sick. It did not only cover the legitimately constituted forms of political or economic subjection, but also modes of action, more or less considered and calculated, which were destined to act upon the possibilities of action of other people. To govern, in this sense, is to structure the possible field of action of others. The relationship proper to power would not therefore be sought on the side of violence or of struggle, nor on that of voluntary linking (all of which can, at best, only be the instruments of power), but rather in the area of the singular mode of action, neither warlike nor juridical, which is government.

When one defines the exercise of power as a mode of action upon the actions of others, when one characterizes these actions by the government of men by other men—in the broadest sense of the term—one includes an important element: freedom. Power is exercised only over free subjects, and only insofar as they are free. By this we mean individual or collective subjects who are faced with a field of possibilities in which several ways of behaving, several reactions and diverse comportments may be realized. Where the determining factors saturate the whole there is no relationship of power; slavery is not a power relationship when man is in chains. (In this case it is a question of a physical relationship of constraint.) Consequently there is no face to face confrontation of power and freedom which is mutually exclusive (freedom disappears everywhere power is exercised), but a much more complicated interplay. In this game freedom may well appear as the condition for the exercise of power (at the same time its precondition, since freedom must exist for power to be exerted, and also its permanent support, since without the possibility of recalcitrance, power would be equivalent to a physical determination).

The relationship between power and freedom's refusal to submit cannot therefore be separated. The crucial problem of power is not that of voluntary servitude (how could we seek to be slaves?). At the very heart of the power relationship, and constantly provoking it, are the recalcitrance of the will and the intransigence of freedom. Rather than speaking of an essential freedom, it would be better to speak of an "agonism"[3]—of a relationship which is at the same time reciprocal incitation and struggle; less of a face-to-face confrontation which paralyzes both sides than a permanent provocation.

How is one to analyze the power relationship?

One can analyze such relationships, or rather I should say that it is perfectly legitimate to do so, by focusing on carefully defined institutions. The latter constitute a privileged point of observation, diversified, concentrated, put in order, and carried through to the highest point of their efficacity. It is here that, as a first approximation, one might expect to see the appearance of the form and logic of their elementary mechanisms. However, the analysis of power relations as one finds them in certain circumscribed institutions presents a certain number of problems. First, the fact that an important part of the mechanisms put into operation by an institution are designed to ensure its own preservation brings with it the risk of deciphering functions which are essentially reproductive, especially in power relations between institutions. Second, in analyzing power relations from the standpoint of institutions one lays oneself open to seeking the explanation and the origin of the former in the latter, that is to say finally, to explain power to power. Finally, insofar as institutions act essentially by bringing into play two elements, explicit or tacit regulations and an apparatus, one risks giving to one or the other an exaggerated privilege in the relations of power and hence to see in the latter only modulations of the law and of coercion.

This does not deny the importance of institutions on the establishment of power relations. Instead I wish to suggest that one must analyze institutions from the standpoint of power relations, rather than vice versa, and that the fundamental point of anchorage of the relationships, even if they are embodied and crystallized in an institution, is to be found outside the institution.

Let us come back to the definition of the exercise of power as a way in which certain actions may structure the field of other possible actions. What therefore would be proper to a relationship of power is that it be a mode of action upon actions. That is to say, power relations are rooted deep in the social nexus, not reconstituted "above" society as a supplementary structure whose radical effacement one could perhaps dream of. In any case, to live in society is to live in such a way that action upon other actions is possible—and in fact ongoing. A society without power relations can only be an abstraction. Which, be it said in passing, makes all the more politically necessary the analysis of power relations in a given society, their historical formation, the source of their strength or fragility, the conditions which are necessary to transform some or to abolish others. For to say that there cannot be a society without power relations is not to say either that those which are established are necessary, or, in any case, that power constitutes a fatality at the heart of societies, such that it cannot be undermined. Instead I would say that the analysis, elaboration, and bringing into question of power relations and the "agonism" between power relations and the intransitivity of freedom is a permanent political task inherent in all social existence.

Concretely the analysis of power relations demands that a certain number of points be established:

1) *The system of differentiations* which permits one to act upon the actions of others: differentiations determined by the law or by traditions of status and privilege; economic differences in the appropriation of riches and goods, shifts in the processes of production, linguistic or cultural differences, differences in know-how and competence, and so forth. Every relationship of power puts into operation differentiations which are at the same time its conditions and its results.

2) *The types of objectives* pursued by those who act upon the actions of others: the maintenance of privileges, the accumulation of profits, the bringing into operation of statutory authority, the exercise of a function or of a trade.

3) *The means of bringing power relations into being:* according to whether power is exercised by the threat of arms, by the effects of the word, by means of economic disparities, by more or less complex means of control, by systems of surveillance, with or without archives, according to rules which are or are not explicit, fixed or modifiable, with or without the technological means to put all these things into action.

4) *Forms of institutionalization:* these may mix traditional predispositions, legal structures, phenomena relating to custom or to fashion (such as one sees in the institution of the family); they can also take the form of an apparatus closed in upon itself, with its specific *loci*, its own regulations, its hierarchical structures which are carefully defined, a relative autonomy in its functioning (such as scholastic or military institutions); they can also form very complex systems endowed with multiple apparatuses, as in the case of the state, whose function is the taking of everything under its wing, the bringing into being of general surveillance, the principle of regulation and, to a certain extent also, the distribution of all power relations in a given social ensemble.

5) *The degrees of rationalization:* the bringing into play of power relations as action in a field of possibilities may be more or less elaborate in relation to the effectiveness of the instruments and the certainty of the results (greater or lesser technological refinements employed in the exercise of power) or again in proportion to the possible cost (be it the economic cost of the means brought into operation, or the cost in terms of reaction constituted by the resistance which is encountered). The exercise of power is not a naked fact, an institutional right, nor is it a structure which holds out or is smashed: it is elaborated, transformed, organized; it endows itself with processes which are more or less adjusted to the situation.

One sees why the analysis of power relations within a society cannot be reduced to the study of a series of institutions, not even to the study of all those institutions which would merit the name "political." Power relations are rooted in the system of social networks. This is not to say, however, that there is a primary and fundamental principle of power which dominates society down to the smallest detail; but, taking as point of departure the possibility of action upon the action of others (which is coextensive with every social relationship), multiple forms of individual disparity, of objectives, of the given application of power over ourselves or others, of, in varying degrees, partial or universal institutionalization, of more or less deliberate organization, one can define different forms of power. The forms and the specific situations of the government of men by one another in a given society are multiple; they are superimposed, they cross, impose their own limits, sometimes cancel one another out, sometimes reinforce one another. It is certain that in contemporary societies the state is not simply one of the forms or specific situations of the exercise of power— even if it is the most important—but that in a certain way all other forms of power relation must refer to it. But this is not because they are derived from it; it is rather because power relations have come more and more under state control (although this state control has not taken the same form in pedagogical, judicial, economic, or family systems). In referring here to the restricted sense of the word *government*, one could say that power relations have been progressively governmentalized, that is to say, elaborated, rationalized, and centralized in the form of, or under the auspices of, state institutions.

Relations of power and relations of strategy
The word *strategy* is currently employed in three ways. First, to designate the means employed to attain a certain end; it is a question of rationality functioning to arrive at an objective. Second, to designate the manner in which a partner in a certain game acts with regard to what he thinks should be the action of the others and what he considers the others think to be his own; it is the way in which one seeks to have the advantage over others. Third, to designate the procedures used in a situation of confrontation to deprive the opponent of his means of combat and to reduce him to giving up the struggle; it is a question therefore of the means destined to obtain victory. These three meanings come together in situations of confrontation—war or games—where the objective is to act upon an adversary in such a manner as to render the struggle impossible for him. So strategy is defined by the choice of winning solutions. But it must be borne in mind that this is a very special type of situation and that there are others in which the distinctions between the different senses of the word *strategy* must be maintained.

Referring to the first sense I have indicated, one may call power strategy the totality of the means put into operation to implement power effectively or to maintain it. One may also speak of a strategy proper to power relations insofar as they constitute modes of action upon possible action, the action of others. One can therefore interpret the mechanisms brought into play in power relations in terms of strategies. But most important is obviously the relationship between power relations and confrontation strategies. For, if it is true that at the heart of power relations and as a permanent condition of their existence there is an insubordination and a certain essential obstinacy on the part of the principles of freedom, then there is no relationship of power without the means of escape or possible flight. Every power relationship implies, at least *in potentia*, a strategy of struggle, in which the two forces are not superimposed, do not lose their specific nature, or do not finally become confused. Each constitutes for the other a kind of permanent limit, a point of possible reversal. A relationship of confrontation reaches its term, its final moment (and the victory of one of the two adversaries) when stable mechanisms replace the free play of antagonistic reactions. Through such mechanisms one can direct, in a fairly constant manner and with reasonable certainty, the conduct of others. For a relationship of confrontation, from the moment it is not a struggle to the death, the fixing of a power relationship becomes a target—at one and the same time its fulfillment and its suspension. And in return the strategy of struggle also constitutes a frontier for the relationship of power, the line at which, instead of manipulating and inducing actions in a calculated manner, one must be content with reacting to them after the event. It would not be possible for power relations to exist without points of insubordination which, by definition, are means of escape. Accordingly, every intensification, every extension of power relations to make the insubordinate submit can only result in the limits of power. The latter reaches its final term either in a type of action which reduces the other to total impotence (in which case victory over the adversary replaces the exercise of power) or by a confrontation with those whom one governs and their transformation into adversaries. Which is to say that every strategy of confrontation dreams of becoming a relationship of power and every relationship of power leans toward the idea that, if it follows its own line of development and comes up against direct confrontation, it may become the winning strategy.

In effect, between a relationship of power and a strategy of struggle there is a reciprocal appeal, a perpetual linking and a perpetual reversal. At every moment the relationship of power may become a confrontation between two adversaries. Equally, the relationship between adversaries in society may, at every moment, give place to the putting into operation of mechanisms of power. The consequence of this instability is the ability to decipher the same events and the same transformations either from inside the history of struggle or from the standpoint of the power relationships. The interpretations which result will not consist of the same elements of meaning or the same links or the same types of intelligibility, although they refer to the same historical fabric and each of the two analyses must have reference to the other. In fact it is precisely the disparities between the two readings which make visible those fundamental phenomena of "domination" which are present in a large number of human societies.

Domination is in fact a general structure of power whose ramifications and consequences can sometimes be found descending to the most incalcitrant fibers of society. But at the same time it is a strategic situation more or less taken for granted and consolidated by means of a long-term confrontation between adversaries. It can certainly happen that the fact of domination may only be the transcription of a mechanism of power resulting from confrontation and its consequences (a political structure stemming from invasion); it may also be that a relationship of struggle between two adversaries is the result of power relations with the conflicts and cleavages which ensue. But what makes the domination of a group, a caste, or a class, together with the resistance and revolts which that domination comes up against, a central phenomenon in the history of societies is that they manifest in a massive and universalizing form, at the level of the whole social body, the locking together of power relations with relations of strategy and the results proceeding from their interaction.

NOTES

1. When Habermas distinguishes between domination, communication, and finalized activity, I do not think that he sees in them three separate domains, but rather three "transcendentals."

2. Foucault is playing on the double meaning in French of the verb *conduire*—to lead or to drive, and *se conduire*—to behave or conduct oneself, whence *la conduite*, conduct or behavior. (Translator's note)

3. Foucault's neologism is based on the Greek ἀγώνισμα, meaning "a combat." The term would hence imply a physical contest in which the opponents develop a strategy of reaction and of mutual taunting, as in a wrestling match. (Translator's note)

JEAN-FRANÇOIS LYOTARD

FROM THE POSTMODERN CONDITION: A REPORT ON KNOWLEDGE

THE NATURE OF THE SOCIAL BOND: THE MODERN ALTERNATIVE

If we wish to discuss knowledge in the most highly developed contemporary society, we must answer the preliminary question of what methodological representation to apply to that society. Simplifying to the extreme, it is fair to say that in principle there have been, at least over the last half-century, two basic representational models for society: either society forms a functional whole, or it is divided in two. An illustration of the first model is suggested by Talcott Parsons (at least the postwar Parsons) and his school, and of the second, by the Marxist current (all of its component schools, whatever differences they may have, accept both the principle of class struggle and dialectics as a duality operating within society).[1]

This methodological split, which defines two major kinds of discourse on society, has been handed down from the nineteenth century. The idea that society forms an organic whole, in the absence of which it ceases to be a society (and sociology ceases to have an object of study), dominated the minds of the founders of the French school. Added detail was supplied by functionalism; it took yet another turn in the 1950s with Parsons's conception of society as a self-regulating system. The theoretical and even material model is no longer the living organism; it is provided by cybernetics, which, during and after the Second World War, expanded the model's applications.

In Parsons's work, the principle behind the system is still, if I may say so, optimistic: it corresponds to the stabilization of the growth economies and societies of abundance under the aegis of a moderate welfare state.[2] In the work of contemporary German theorists, *systemtheorie* is technocratic, even cynical, not to mention despairing: the harmony between the needs and hopes of individuals or groups and the functions guaranteed by the system is now only a secondary component of its functioning. The true goal of the system, the reason it programs itself like a computer, is the optimization of the global relationship between input and output—in other words, performativity. Even when its rules are in the process of changing and innovations are occurring, even when its dysfunctions (such as strikes, crises, unemployment, or political revolutions) inspire hope and lead to belief in an alternative, even then what is actually taking place is only an internal readjustment, and its result can be no more than an increase in the system's "viability." The only alternative to this kind of performance improvement is entropy, or decline.[3]

Here again, while avoiding the simplifications inherent in a sociology of social theory, it is difficult to deny at least a parallel between this "hard" technocratic version of society and the ascetic effort that was demanded (the fact that it was done in name of "advanced liberalism" is beside the point) of the most highly developed industrial societies in order to make them competitive—and thus optimize their "rationality"—within the framework of the resumption of economic world war in the 1960s.

Even taking into account the massive displacement intervening between the thought of a man like Comte and the thought of Luhmann, we can discern a common conception of the social: society is a unified totality, a "unicity." Parsons formulates this clearly: "The most essential condition of successful dynamic analysis is a continual and systematic reference of every problem to the state of the system as a whole. . . . A process or set of conditions either 'contributes' to the maintenance (or development) of the system or it is 'dysfunctional' in that it detracts from the integration, effectiveness, etc., of the system."[4] The "technocrats"[5] also subscribe to this idea. Whence its credibility: it has the means to become a reality, and that is all the proof it needs. This is what Horkheimer called the "paranoia" of reason.[6]

But this realism of systemic self-regulation, and this perfectly sealed circle of facts and interpretations, can be judged paranoid only if one has, or claims to have, at one's disposal a viewpoint that is in principle immune from their allure. This is the function of the principle of class struggle in theories of society based on the work of Marx.

"Traditional" theory is always in danger of being incorporated into the programming of the social whole as a simple tool for the optimization of its performance; this is because its desire for a unitary and totalizing truth lends itself to the unitary and totalizing practice of the system's managers. "Critical" theory,[7] based on a principle of dualism and wary of syntheses and reconciliations, should be in a position to avoid this fate. What guides Marxism, then, is a different model of society, and a different conception of the function of the knowledge that can be produced by society and acquired from it. This model was born of the struggles accompanying the process of capitalism's encroachment upon traditional civil societies. There is insufficient space here to chart the vicissitudes of these struggles, which fill more than a century of social, political, and ideological history. We will have to content ourselves with a glance at the balance sheet, which is possible for us to tally today now that their fate is known: in countries with liberal or advanced liberal management, the struggles and their instruments have been transformed into regulators of the system; in communist countries, the totalizing model and its totalitarian effect have made a comeback in the name of Marxism itself, and the struggles in question have simply been deprived of the right to exist.[8] Everywhere, the Critique of political economy (the subtitle of Marx's *Capital*) and its correlate, the critique of alienated society, are used in one way or another as aids in programming the system.[9]

Of course, certain minorities, such as the Frankfurt School or the group *Socialisme ou barbarie*,[10] preserved and refined the critical model in opposition to this process. But the social foundation of the principle of division, or class struggle, was blurred to the point of losing all of its radicality; we cannot conceal the fact that the critical model in the end lost its theoretical standing and was reduced to the status of a "utopia" or "hope,"[11] a token protest raised in the name of man or reason or creativity, or again of some social category—such as the Third World or the students[12]—on which is conferred in extremis the henceforth improbable function of critical subject.

The sole purpose of this schematic (or skeletal) reminder has been to specify the problematic in which I intend to frame the question of knowledge in advanced industrial societies. For it is impossible to know what the state of knowledge is—in other words, the problems its development and distribution are facing today—without knowing something of the society within which it is situated. And today more than ever, knowing about that society involves first of all choosing what approach the inquiry will take, and that necessarily means choosing how society can answer. One can decide that the principal role of knowledge is as an indispensable element in the functioning of society, and act in accordance with that decision, only if one has already decided that society is a giant machine.[13]

Conversely, one can count on its critical function, and orient its development and distribution in that direction, only after it has been decided that society does not form an integrated whole, but remains haunted by a principle of opposition.[14] The alternative seems clear: it is a choice between the homogeneity and the intrinsic duality of the social, between functional and critical knowledge. But the decision seems difficult, or arbitrary.

It is tempting to avoid the decision altogether by distinguishing two kinds of knowledge. One, the positivist kind, would be directly applicable to technologies bearing on men and materials, and would lend itself to operating as an indispensable productive force within the system. The other—the critical, reflexive, or hermeneutic kind—by reflecting directly or indirectly on values or aims, would resist any such "recuperation."[15]

THE NATURE OF THE SOCIAL BOND: THE POSTMODERN PERSPECTIVE

I find this partition solution unacceptable. I suggest that the alternative it attempts to resolve, but only reproduces, is no longer relevant for the societies with which we are concerned and that the solution itself is still caught within a type of oppositional thinking that is out of step with the most vital modes of postmodern knowledge. As I have already said, economic "redeployment" in the current phase of capitalism, aided by a shift in techniques and technology, goes hand in hand with a change in the function of the State: the image of society this syndrome suggests necessitates a serious revision of the alternate approaches considered. For brevity's sake, suffice it to say that functions of regulation, and therefore of reproduction, are being and will be further withdrawn from administrators and entrusted to machines. Increasingly, the central question is becoming who will have access to the information these machines must have in storage to guarantee that the right decisions are made. Access to data is, and will continue to be, the prerogative of experts of all stripes. The ruling class is and will continue to be the class of decision makers. Even now it is no longer composed of the traditional political class, but of a composite layer of corporate leaders, high-level administrators, and the heads of the major professional, labor, political, and religious organizations.[16]

What is new in all of this is that the old poles of attraction represented by nation-states, parties, professions, institutions, and historical traditions are losing their attraction. And it does not look as though they will be replaced, at least not on their former scale. The Trilateral Commission is not a popular pole of attraction. "Identifying" with the great names, the heroes of contemporary history, is becoming more and more difficult.[17] Dedicating oneself to "catching up with Germany," the life goal the French president [Giscard d'Estaing at the time this book was published in France] seems to be offering his countrymen, is not exactly exciting. But then again, it is not exactly a life goal. It depends on each individual's industriousness. Each individual is referred to himself. And each of us knows that our *self* does not amount to much.[18]

This breaking up of the grand Narratives (discussed below, sections 9 and 10) leads to what some authors analyze in terms of the dissolution of the social bond and the disintegration of social aggregates into a mass of individual atoms thrown into the absurdity of Brownian motion.[19] Nothing of the kind is happening: this point of view, it seems to me, is haunted by the paradisaic representation of a lost "organic" society.

A *self* does not amount to much, but no self is an island; each exists in a fabric of relations that is now more complex and mobile than ever before. Young or old, man or woman, rich or poor, a person is always located at "nodal points" of specific communication circuits, however tiny these may be.[20] Or better: one is always located at a post through which various kinds of messages pass. No one, not even the least privileged among us, is ever entirely powerless over the messages that traverse and position him at the post of sender, addressee, or referent. One's mobility in relation to these language game effects (language games, of course, are what this is all about) is tolerable, at least within certain limits (and the limits are vague); it is even solicited by regulatory mechanisms, and in particular by the self-adjustments the system undertakes in order to improve its performance. It may even be said that the system can and must encourage such movement to the extent that it combats its own entropy; the novelty of an unexpected "move," with its correlative displacement of a partner or group of partners, can supply the system with that increased performativity it forever demands and consumes.[21]

It should now be clear from which perspective I chose language games as my general methodological approach. I am not claiming that the *entirety* of social relations is of this nature—that will remain an open question. But there is no need to resort to some fiction of social origins to establish that language games are the minimum relation required for society to exist: even before he is born, if only by virtue of the name he is given, the human child is already positioned as the referent in the story recounted by those around him, in relation to which he will inevitably chart his course.[22] Or more simply still, the question of the social bond, insofar as it is a question, is itself a language game, the game of inquiry. It immediately positions the person who asks, as well as the addressee and the referent asked about: it is already the social bond.

On the other hand, in a society whose communication component is becoming more prominent day by day, both as a reality and as an issue,[23] it is clear that language assumes a new importance. It would be superficial to reduce its significance to the traditional alternative between manipulatory speech and the unilateral transmission of messages on the one hand, and free expression and dialogue on the other.

A word on this last point. If the problem is described simply in terms of communication theory, two things are overlooked: first, messages have quite different forms and effects depending on whether they are, for example, denotatives, prescriptives, evaluatives, performatives, etc. It is clear that what is important is not simply the fact that they communicate information. Reducing them to this function is to adopt an outlook which unduly privileges the system's own interests and point of view. A cybernetic machine does indeed run on information, but the goals programmed into it, for example, originate in prescriptive and evaluative statements it has no way to correct in the course of its functioning—for example, maximizing its own performance. How can one guarantee that performance maximization is the best goal for the social system in every case? In any case the "atoms" forming its matter are competent to handle statements such as these—and this question in particular.

Second, the trivial cybernetic version of information theory misses something of decisive importance, to which I have already called attention: the agonistic aspect of society. The atoms are placed at the crossroads of pragmatic relationships, but they are also displaced by the messages that traverse them, in perpetual motion. Each language partner, when a "move" pertaining to him is made, undergoes a "displacement," an alteration of some kind that not only affects him in his capacity as addressee and referent, but also as sender. These "moves" necessarily provoke "countermoves"—and everyone knows that a countermove that is merely reactional is not a "good" move. Reactional countermoves are no more than programmed effects in the opponent's strategy; they play into his hands and thus have no effect on the balance of power. That is why it is important to increase displacement in the games, and even to disorient it, in such a way as to make an unexpected "move" (a new statement).

What is needed if we are to understand social relations in this manner, on whatever scale we choose, is not only a theory of communication, but a theory of games which accepts agonistics as a founding principle. In this context, it is easy to see that the essential element of newness is not simply "innovation." Support for this approach can be found in the work of a number of contemporary sociologists,[24] in addition to linguists and philosophers of language.

This "atomization" of the social into flexible networks of language games may seem far removed from the modern reality, which is depicted, on the contrary, as afflicted with bureaucratic paralysis.[25] The objection will be made, at least, that the weight of certain institutions imposes limits on the games, and thus restricts the inventiveness of the players in making their moves. But I think this can be taken into account without causing any particular difficulty.

In the ordinary use of discourse—for example, in a discussion between two friends—the interlocutors use any available ammunition, changing games from one utterance to the next: questions, requests, assertions, and narratives are launched pell-mell into battle. The war is not without rules,[26] but the rules allow and encourage the greatest possible flexibility of utterance.

From this point of view, an institution differs from a conversation in that it always requires supplementary constraints for statements to be declared admissible within its bounds. The constraints function to filter discursive potentials, interrupting possible connections in the communication networks: there are things that should not be said. They also privilege certain classes of statements (sometimes only one) whose predominance characterizes the discourse of the particular institution: there are things that should be said, and there are ways of saying them. Thus: orders in the army, prayer in church, denotation in the schools, narration in families, questions in philosophy, performativity in businesses. Bureaucratization is the outer limit of this tendency.

However, this hypothesis about the institution is still too "unwieldy": its point of departure is an overly "reifying" view of what is institutionalized. We know today that the limits the institution imposes on potential language "moves" are never established once and for all (even if they have been formally defined).[27] Rather, the limits are themselves the stakes and provisional results of language strategies, within the institution and without. Examples: Does the university have a place for language experiments (poetics)? Can you tell stories in a cabinet meeting? Advocate a cause in the barracks? The answers are clear: yes, if the university opens creative workshops; yes, if the cabinet works with prospective scenarios; yes, if the limits of the old institution are displaced.[28] Reciprocally, it can be said that the boundaries only stabilize when they cease to be stakes in the game.

This, I think, is the appropriate approach to contemporary institutions of knowledge.

DELEGITIMATION

In contemporary society and culture—postindustrial society, post-modern culture[29]—the question of the legitimation of knowledge is formulated in different terms. The grand narrative has lost its credibility, regardless of what mode of unification it uses, regardless of whether it is a speculative narrative or a narrative of emancipation.

The decline of narrative can be seen as an effect of the blossoming of techniques and technologies since the Second World War, which has shifted emphasis from the ends of action to its means; it can also be seen as an effect of the redeployment of advanced liberal capitalism after its retreat under the protection of Keynesianism during the period 1930-60, a renewal that has eliminated the communist alternative and valorized the individual enjoyment of goods and services.

Anytime we go searching for causes in this way we are bound to be disappointed. Even if we adopted one or the other of these hypotheses, we would still have to detail the correlation between the tendencies mentioned and the decline of the unifying and legitimating power of the grand narratives of speculation and emancipation.

It is, of course, understandable that both capitalist renewal and prosperity and the disorienting upsurge of technology would have an impact on the status of knowledge. But in order to understand how contemporary science could have been susceptible to those effects long before they took place, we must first locate the seeds of "delegitimation"[30] and nihilism that were inherent in the grand narratives of the nineteenth century.

First of all, the speculative apparatus maintains an ambigious relation to knowledge. It shows that knowledge is only worthy of that name to the extent that it reduplicates itself ("lifts itself up," *hebt sich auf*; is sublated) by citing its own statements in a second-level discourse (autonymy) that functions to legitimate them. This is as much as to say that, in its immediacy, denotative discourse bearing on a certain referent (a living organism, a chemical property, a physical phenomenon, etc.) does not really know what it thinks it knows. Positive science is not a form of knowledge. And speculation feeds on its suppression. The Hegelian speculative narrative thus harbors a certain skepticism toward positive learning, as Hegel himself admits.[31]

A science that has not legitimated itself is not a true science; if the discourse that was meant to legitimate it seems to belong to a prescientific form of knowledge, like a "vulgar" narrative, it is demoted to the lowest rank, that of an ideology or instrument of power. And this always happens if the rules of the science game that discourse denounces as empirical are applied to science itself.

Take for example the speculative statement: "A scientific statement is knowledge if and only if it can take its place in a universal process of engendering." The question is: Is this statement knowledge as it itself defines it? Only if it can take its place in a universal process of engendering. Which it can. All it has to do is to presuppose that such a process exists (the Life of spirit) and that it is itself an expression of that process. This presupposition, in fact, is indispensable to the speculative language game. Without it, the language of legitimation would not be legitimate; it would accompany science in a nosedive into nonsense, at least if we take idealism's word for it.

But this presupposition can also be understood in a totally different sense, one which takes us in the direction of postmodern culture: we could say, in keeping with the perspective we adopted earlier, that this presupposition defines the set of rules one must accept in order to play the speculative game.[32] Such an appraisal assumes first that we accept that the "positive" sciences represent the general mode of knowledge and second, that we understand this language to imply certain formal and axiomatic presuppositions that it must always make explicit. This is exactly what Nietzsche is doing, though with a different terminology, when he shows that "European nihilism" resulted from the truth requirement of science being turned back against itself.[33]

There thus arises an idea of perspective that is not far removed, at least in this respect, from the idea of language games. What we have here is a process of delegitimation fueled by the demand for legitimation itself. The "crisis" of scientific knowledge, signs of which have been accumulating since the end of the nineteenth century, is not born of a chance proliferation of sciences, itself an effect of progress in technology and the expansion of capitalism. It represents, rather, an internal erosion of the legitimacy principle of knowledge. There is erosion at work inside the speculative game, and by loosening the weave of the encyclopedic net in which each science was to find its place, it eventually sets them free.

The classical dividing lines between the various fields of science are thus called into question—disciplines disappear, overlappings occur at the borders between sciences, and from these new territories are born. The speculative hierarchy of learning gives way to an immanent and, as it were, "flat" network of areas of inquiry, the respective frontiers of which are in constant flux. The old "faculties" splinter into institutes and foundations of all kinds, and the universities lose their function of speculative legitimation. Stripped of the responsibility for research (which was stifled by the speculative narrative), they limit themselves to the transmission of what is judged to be established knowledge, and through didactics they guarantee the replication of teachers rather than the production of researchers. This is the state in which Nietzsche finds and condemns them.[34]

The potential for erosion intrinsic to the other legitimation procedure, the emancipation apparatus flowing from the *Aufklärung*, is no less extensive than the one at work within speculative discourse. But it touches a different aspect. Its distinguishing characteristic is that it grounds the legitimation of science and truth in the autonomy of interlocutors involved in ethical, social, and political praxis. As we have seen, there are immediate problems with this form of legitimation: the difference between a denotative statement with cognitive value and a prescriptive statement with practical value is one of relevance, therefore of competence. There is nothing to prove that if a statement describing a real situation is true, it follows that a prescriptive statement based upon it (the effect of which will necessarily be a modification of that reality) will be just.

Take, for example, a closed door. Between "The door is closed" and "Open the door" there is no relation of consequence as defined in propositional logic. The two statements belong to two autonomous sets of rules defining different kinds of relevance, and therefore of competence. Here, the effect of dividing reason into cognitive or theoretical reason on the one hand, and practical reason on the other, is to attack the legitimacy of the discourse of science. Not directly, but indirectly, by revealing that it is a language game with its own rules (of which the a priori conditions of knowledge in Kant provide a first glimpse) and that it has no special calling to supervise the game of praxis (nor the game of aesthetics, for that matter). The game of science is thus put on a par with the others.

If this "delegitimation" is pursued in the slightest and if its scope is widened (as Wittgenstein does in his own way, and thinkers such as Martin Buber and Emmanuel Lévinas in theirs)[35] the road is then open for an important current of postmodernity: science plays its own game; it is incapable of legitimating the other language games. The game of prescription, for example, escapes it. But above all, it is incapable of legitimating itself, as speculation assumed it could.

The social subject itself seems to dissolve in this dissemination of language games. The social bond is linguistic, but is not woven with a single thread. It is a fabric formed by the intersection of at least two (and in reality an indeterminate number) of language games, obeying different rules. Wittgenstein writes: "Our language can be seen as an ancient city: a maze of little streets and squares, of old and new houses, and of houses with additions from various periods; and this surrounded by a multitude of new boroughs with straight regular streets and uniform houses."[36] And to drive home that the principle of unitotality—or synthesis under the authority of a metadiscourse of knowledge—is inapplicable, he subjects the "town" of language to the old sorites paradox by asking: "how many houses or streets does it take before a town begins to be a town?"[37]

New languages are added to the old ones, forming suburbs of the old town: "the symbolism of chemistry and the notation of the infinitesimal calculus."[38] Thirty-five years later we can add to the list: machine languages, the matrices of game theory, new systems of musical notation, systems of notation for nondenotative forms of logic (temporal logics, deontic logics, modal logics), the language of the genetic code, graphs of phonological structures, and so on.

We may form a pessimistic impression of this splintering: nobody speaks all of those languages, they have no universal metalanguage, the project of the system-subject is a failure, the goal of emancipation has nothing to do with science, we are all stuck in the positivism of this or that discipline of learning, the learned scholars have turned into scientists, the diminished tasks of research have become compartmentalized and no one can master them all.[39] Speculative or humanistic philosophy is forced to relinquish its legitimation duties,[40] which explains why philosophy is facing a crisis wherever it persists in arrogating such functions and is reduced to the study of systems of logic or the history of ideas where it has been realistic enough to surrender them.[41]

Turn-of-the-century Vienna was weaned on this pessimism: not just artists such as Musil, Kraus, Hofmannsthal, Loos, Schönberg, and Broch, but also the philosophers Mach and Wittgenstein.[42] They carried awareness of and theoretical and artistic responsibility for delegitimation as far as it could be taken. We can say today that the mourning process has been completed. There is no need to start all over again. Wittgenstein's strength is that he did not opt for the positivism that was being developed by the Vienna Circle,[43] but outlined in his investigation of language games a kind of legitimation not based on performativity. That is what the postmodern world is all about. Most people have lost the nostalgia for the lost narrative. It in no way follows that they are reduced to barbarity. What saves them from it is their knowledge that legitimation can only spring from their own linguistic practice and communicational interaction. Science "smiling into its beard" at every other belief has taught them the harsh austerity of realism.[44]

LEGITIMATION BY PARALOGY

Let us say at this point that the facts we have presented concerning the problem of the legitimation of knowledge today are sufficient for our purposes. We no longer have recourse to the grand narratives—we can resort neither to the dialectic of Spirit nor even to the emancipation of humanity as a validation for postmodern scientific discourse. But as we have just seen, the little narrative [*petit récit*] remains the quintessential form of imaginative invention, most particularly in science.[45] In addition, the principle of consensus as a criterion of validation seems to be inadequate. It has two formulations. In the first, consensus is an agreement between men, defined as knowing intellects and free wills, and is obtained through dialogue. This is the form elaborated by Habermas, but his conception is based on the validity of the narrative of emancipation. In the second, consensus is a component of the system, which manipulates it in order to maintain and improve its performance.[46] It is the object of administrative procedures, in Luhmann's sense. In this case, its only validity is as an instrument to be used toward achieving the real goal, which is what legitimates the system—power.

The problem is therefore to determine whether it is possible to have a form of legitimation based solely on paralogy. Paralogy must be distinguished from innovation: the latter is under the command of the system, or at least used by it to improve its efficiency; the former is a move (the importance of which is often not recognized until later) played in the pragmatics of knowledge. The fact that it is in reality frequently, but not necessarily, the case that one is transformed into the other presents no difficulties for the hypothesis.

Returning to the description of scientific pragmatics (section 7), it is now dissension that must be emphasized. Consensus is a horizon that is never reached. Research that takes place under the aegis of a paradigm[47] tends to stabilize; it is like the exploitation of a technological, economic, or artistic "idea." It cannot be discounted. But what is striking is that someone always comes along to disturb the order of "reason." It is necessary to posit the existence of a power that destabilizes the capacity for explanation, manifested in the promulgation of new norms for understanding or, if one prefers, in a proposal to establish new rules circumscribing a new field of research for the language of science. This, in the context of scientific discussion, is the same process Thom calls morphogenesis. It is not without rules (there are classes of catastrophes), but it is always locally determined. Applied to scientific discussion and placed in a temporal framework, this property implies that "discoveries" are unpredictable. In terms of the idea of transparency, it is a factor that generates blind spots and defers consensus.[48]

This summary makes it easy to see that systems theory and the kind of legitimation it proposes have no scientific basis whatsoever; science itself does not function according to this theory's paradigm of the system, and contemporary science excludes the possibility of using such a paradigm to describe society.

In this context, let us examine two important points in Luhmann's argument. On the one hand, the system can only function by reducing complexity, and on the other, it must induce the adaptation of individual aspirations to its own ends.[49] The reduction in complexity is required to maintain the system's power capability. If all messages could circulate freely among all individuals, the quantity of the information that would have to be taken into account before making the correct choice would delay decisions considerably, thereby lowering performativity. Speed, in effect, is a power component of the system.

The objection will be made that these molecular opinions must indeed be taken into account if the risk of serious disturbances is to be avoided. Luhmann replies—and this is the second point—that it is possible to guide individual aspirations through a process of "quasi-apprenticeship," "free of all disturbance," in order to make them compatible with the system's decisions. The decisions do not have to respect individuals' aspirations: the aspirations have to aspire to the decisions, or at least to their effects. Administrative procedures should make individuals "want" what the system needs in order to perform well.[50] It is easy to see what role telematics technology could play in this.

It cannot be denied that there is persuasive force in the idea that context control and domination are inherently better than their absence. The performativity criterion has its "advantages." It excludes in principle adherence to a metaphysical discourse; it requires the renunciation of fables; it demands clear minds and cold wills; it replaces the definition of essences with the calculation of interactions; it makes the "players" assume responsibility not only for the statements they propose, but also for the rules to which they submit those statements in order to render them acceptable. It brings the pragmatic functions of knowledge clearly to light, to the extent that they seem to relate to the criterion of efficiency: the pragmatics of argumentation, of the production of proof, of the transmission of learning, and of the apprenticeship of the imagination.

It also contributes to elevating all language games to self-knowledge, even those not within the realm of canonical knowledge. It tends to jolt everyday discourse into a kind of metadiscourse: ordinary statements are now displaying a propensity for self-citation, and the various pragmatic posts are tending to make an indirect connection even to current messages concerning them.[51] Finally, it suggests that the problems of internal communication experienced by the scientific community in the course of its work of dismantling and remounting its languages are comparable in nature to the problems experienced by the social collectivity when, deprived of its narrative culture, it must reexamine its own internal communication and in the process question the nature of the legitimacy of the decisions made in its name.

At risk of scandalizing the reader, I would also say that the system can count severity among its advantages. Within the framework of the power criterion, a request (that is, a form of prescription) gains nothing in legitimacy by virtue of being based on the hardship of an unmet need. Rights do not flow from hardship, but from the fact that the alleviation of hardship improves the system's performance. The needs of the most underprivileged should not be used as a system regulator as a matter of principle: since the means of satisfying them is already known, their actual satisfaction will not improve the system's performance, but only increase its expenditures. The only counterindication is that not satisfying them can destabilize the whole. It is against the nature of force to be ruled by weakness. But it is in its nature to induce new requests meant to lead to a redefinition of the norms of "life."[52] In this sense, the system seems to be a vanguard machine dragging humanity after it, dehumanizing it in order to rehumanize it at a different level of normative capacity. The technocrats declare that they cannot trust what society designates as its needs; they "know" that society cannot know its own needs since they are not variables independent of the new technologies.[53] Such is the arrogance of the decision makers—and their blindness.

What their "arrogance" means is that they identify themselves with the social system conceived as a totality in quest of its most performative unity possible. If we look at the pragmatics of science, we learn that such an identification is impossible: in principle, no scientist embodies knowledge or neglects the "needs" of a research project, or the aspirations of a researcher, on the pretext that they do not add to the performance of "science" as a whole. The response a researcher usually makes to a request is: "We'll have to see, tell me your story."[54] In principle, he does not prejudge that a case has already been closed or that the power of "science" will suffer if it is reopened. In fact, the opposite is true.

Of course, it does not always happen like this in reality. Countless scientists have seen their "move" ignored or repressed, sometimes for decades, because it too abruptly destabilized the accepted positions, not only in the university and scientific hierarchy, but also in the problematic.[55] The stronger the "move," the more likely it is to be denied the minimum consensus, precisely because it changes the rules of the game upon which consensus had been based. But when the institution of knowledge functions in this manner, it is acting like an ordinary power center whose behavior is governed by a principle of homeostasis.

Such behavior is terrorist, as is the behavior of the system described by Luhmann. By terror I mean the efficiency gained by eliminating, or threatening to eliminate, a player from the language game one shares with him. He is silenced or consents, not because he has been refuted, but because his ability to participate has been threatened (there are many ways to prevent someone from playing). The decision makers' arrogance, which in principle has no equivalent in the sciences, consists in the exercise of terror. It says: "Adapt your aspirations to our ends—or else."[56]

Even permissiveness toward the various games is made conditional on performativity. The redefinition of the norms of life consists in enhancing the system's competence for power. That this is the case is particularly evident in the introduction of telematics technology: the technocrats see in telematics a promise of liberalization and enrichment in the interactions between interlocutors; but what makes this process attractive for them is that it will result in new tensions in the system, and these will lead to an improvement in its performativity.[57]

To the extent that science is differential, its pragmatics provides the antimodel of a stable system. A statement is deemed worth retaining the moment it marks a difference from what is already known, and after an argument and proof in support of it has been found. Science is a model of an "open system,"[58] in which a statement becomes relevant if it "generates ideas," that is, if it generates other statements and other game rules. Science possesses no general metalanguage in which all other languages can be transcribed and evaluated. This is what prevents its identification with the system and, all things considered, with terror. If the division between decision makers and executors exists in the scientific community (and it does), it is a fact of the socioeconomic system and not of the pragmatics of science itself. It is in fact one of the major obstacles to the imaginative development of knowledge.

The general question of legitimation becomes: What is the relationship between the antimodel of the pragmatics of science and society? Is it applicable to the vast clouds of language material constituting a society? Or is it limited to the game of learning? And if so, what role does it play with respect to the social bond? Is it an impossible ideal of an open community? Is it an essential component for the subset of decision makers, who force on society the performance criterion they reject for themselves. Or, conversely, is it a refusal to cooperate with the authorities, a move in the direction of counterculture, with the attendant risk that all possibility for research will be foreclosed due to lack of funding?[59]

From the beginning of this study, I have emphasized the differences (not only formal, but also pragmatic) between the various language games, especially between denotative, or knowledge, games and prescriptive, or action, games. The pragmatics of science is centered on denotative utterances, which are the foundation upon which it builds institutions of learning (institutes, centers, universities, etc.). But its postmodern development brings a decisive "fact" to the fore: even discussions of denotative statements need to have rules. Rules are not denotative but prescriptive utterances, which we are better off calling metaprescriptive utterances to avoid confusion (they prescribe what the moves of language games must be in order to be admissible). The function of the differential or imaginative or paralogical activity of the current pragmatics of science is to point out these metaprescriptives (science's "presuppositions")[60] and to petition the players to accept different ones. The only legitimation that can make this kind of request admissible is that it will generate ideas, in other words, new statements.

Social pragmatics does not have the "simplicity" of scientific pragmatics. It is a monster formed by the interweaving of various networks of heteromorphous classes of utterances (denotative, prescriptive, performative, technical, evaluative, etc.). There is no reason to think that it would be possible to determine metaprescriptives common to all of these language games or that a revisable consensus like the one in force at a given moment in the scientific community could embrace the totality of metaprescriptions regulating the totality of statements circulating in the social collectivity. As a matter of fact, the contemporary decline of narratives of legitimation—be they traditional or "modern" (the emancipation of humanity, the realization of the Idea)—is tied to the abandonment of this belief. It is its absence for which the ideology of the "system," with its pretensions to totality, tries to compensate and which it expresses in the cynicism of its criterion of performance.

For this reason, it seems neither possible, nor even prudent, to follow Habermas in orienting our treatment of the problem of legitimation in the direction of a search for universal consensus[61] through what he calls *Diskurs*, in other words, a dialogue of argumentation.[62]

This would be to make two assumptions. The first is that it is possible for all speakers to come to agreement on which rules or metaprescriptions are universally valid for language games, when it is clear that language games are heteromorphous, subject to heterogeneous sets of pragmatic rules.

The second assumption is that the goal of dialogue is consensus. But as I have shown in the analysis of the pragmatics of science, consensus is only a particular state of discussion, not its end. Its end, on the contrary, is paralogy. This double observation (the heterogeneity of the rules and the search for dissent) destroys a belief that still underlies Habermas's research, namely, that humanity as a collective (universal) subject seeks its common emancipation through the regularization of the "moves" permitted in all language games and that the legitimacy of any statement resides in its contributing to that emancipation.[63]

It is easy to see what function this recourse plays in Habermas's argument against Luhmann. *Diskurs* is his ultimate weapon against the theory of the stable system. The cause is good, but the argument is not.[64] Consensus has become an outmoded and suspect value. But justice as a value is neither outmoded nor suspect. We must thus arrive at an idea and practice of justice that is not linked to that of consensus.

A recognition of the heteromorphous nature of language games is a first step in that direction. This obviously implies a renunciation of terror, which assumes that they are isomorphic and tries to make them so. The second step is the principle that any consensus on the rules defining a game and the "moves" playable within it *must* be local, in other words, agreed on by its present players and subject to eventual cancellation. The orientation then favors a multiplicity of finite meta-arguments, by which I mean argumentation that concerns metaprescriptives and is limited in space and time.

This orientation corresponds to the course that the evolution of social interaction is currently taking; the temporary contract is in practice supplanting permanent institutions in the professional, emotional, sexual, cultural, family, and international domains, as well as in political affairs. This evolution is of course ambiguous: the temporary contract is favored by the system due to its greater flexibility, lower cost, and the creative turmoil of its accompanying motivations—all of these factors contribute to increased operativity. In any case, there is no question here of proposing a "pure" alternative to the system: we all now know, as the 1970s come to a close, that an attempt at an alternative of that kind would end up resembling the system it was meant to replace. We should be happy that the tendency toward the temporary contract is ambiguous: it is not totally subordinated to the goal of the system, yet the system tolerates it. This bears witness to the existence of another goal within the system: knowledge of language games as such and the decision to assume responsibility for their rules and effects. Their most significant effect is precisely what validates the adoption of rules—the quest for paralogy.

We are finally in a position to understand how the computerization of society affects this problematic. It could become the "dream" instrument for controlling and regulating the market system, extended to include knowledge itself and governed exclusively by the performativity principle. In that case, it would inevitably involve the use of terror. But it could also aid groups discussing metaprescriptives by supplying them with the information they usually lack for making knowledgeable decisions. The line to follow for computerization to take the second of these two paths is, in principle, quite simple: give the public free access to the memory and data banks.[65] Language games would then be games of perfect information at any given moment. But they would also be non-zero-sum games, and by virtue of that fact discussion would never risk fixating in a position of minimax equilibrium because it had exhausted its stakes. For the stakes would be knowledge (or information, if you will), and the reserve of knowledge—language's reserve of possible utterances—is inexhaustible. This sketches the outline of a politics that would respect both the desire for justice and the desire for the unknown.

NOTES

1. See in particular Talcott Parsons, *The Social System* (Glencoe, Ill.: Free Press, 1967), and *Sociological Theory and Modern Society* (New York: Free Press, 1967). A bibliography of Marxist theory of contemporary society would fill more than fifty pages. The reader can

consult the useful summary (dossiers and critical bibliography) provided by Pierre Souyri, *Le Marxisme après Marx* (Paris: Flammarion, 1970). An interesting view of the conflict between these two great currents of social theory and of their intermixing is given by A. W. Gouldner, *The Coming Crisis of Western Sociology* (New York: Basic Books, 1970). This conflict occupies an important place in the thought of Habermas, who is simultaneously the heir of the Frankfurt School and in a polemical relationship with the German theory of the social system, especially that of Luhmann.

2. This optimism appears clearly in the conclusions of Robert Lynd, *Knowledge for What?* (Princeton, N.J.: Princeton University Press, 1939), p. 239; quoted by Max Horkheimer, *Eclipse of Reason* (Oxford: Oxford University Press, 1947): in modern society, science must replace religion ("worn threadbare") in defining the aims of life.

3. Helmut Schelsky, *Der Mensch in der Wissenschaftlichen Zivilisation* (Köln und Opladen: Arbeitsgemeinschaft für Forschung des Landes Nordrhein-Westfalen, Geisteswissenschaften Heft 96), pp. 24ff: "The sovereignty of the State is no longer manifested by simple fact that it monopolizes the use of violence (Max Weber) or possesses emergency powers (Carl Schmitt), but primarily by the fact that the State determines the degree of effectiveness of all of the technical means existing within it, reserving their greatest effectiveness for itself, while at the same time exempting its own use of these instruments from the limitations it applies to their use by others." It will be said that this is a theory of the State, not of the system. But Schelsky adds: "In the process, the State's choice of goals is subordinated to the law that I have already mentioned as being the universal law of scientific civilization: namely that the means determine the ends, or rather, that the technical possibilities dictate what use is made of them." Habermas invokes against this law the fact that sets of technical means and systems of finalized rational action never develop autonomously: cf. "Dogmatism, Reason, and Decision: On Theory and Practice in Our Scientific Civilization" [trans. John Viertel, in *Theory and Practice* (Boston: Beacon, 1973)]. See too Jacques Ellul, *La Technique ou l'enjeu du siècle* (Paris: Armand Colin, 1954), and *Le Système technicien* (Paris: Calmann-Lévy, 1977). That strikes, and in general the strong pressure brought to bear by powerful workers' organizations, produce a tension that is in the long run beneficial to the performance of the system is stated clearly by C. Levinson, a union leader; he attributes the technical and managerial advance of American industry to this tension (quoted by H.-F. de Virieu, *Le Matin*, special number, "Que veut Giscard?" December 1978).

4. Talcott Parsons, *Essays in Sociological Theory Pure and Applied*, rev. ed. (Glencoe, Ill.: Free Press, 1954), pp. 216-18.

5. I am using this word in the sense of John Kenneth Galbraith's term *technostructure* as presented in *The New Industrial State* (Boston: Houghton Mifflin, 1967), or Raymond Aron's term *technico-bureaucratic structure* in *Dix-huit leçons sur la société industrielle* (Paris: Gallimard, 1962) [Eng. trans. M. K. Bottomore, *Eighteen Lectures on Industrial Society* (London: Weidenfeld and Nicholson, 1967)], not in a sense associated with the term *bureaucracy*. The term *bureaucracy* is much "harder" because it is sociopolitical as much as it is economical, and because it descends from the critique of Bolshevik power by the worker's Opposition (Kollontaï) and the critique of Stalinism by the Trotskyist opposition. See on this subject Claude Lefort, *Eléments d'une critique de la bureaucratie* (Genève: Droz, 1971), in which the critique is extended to bureaucratic society as a whole.

6. *Eclipse of Reason*, p. 183.

7. Max Horkheimer, "Traditionnelle und kritische Theorie" (1937), [Eng. trans. in J. O'Connell et al., trans., *Critical Theory: Selected Essays* (New York: Herder & Herder, 1972)].

8. See Claude Lefort, *Eléments d'une critique* and *Un homme en trop* (Paris: Seuil, 1976); Cornelius Castoriadis, *La Société bureaucratique* (Paris: Union Générale d'Édition, 1973).

9. See for example J. P. Garnier, *Le Marxisme lénifiant* (Paris: Le Sycomore, 1979).

10. This was the title of the "organ of critique and revolutionary orientation" published between 1949 and 1965 by a group whose principal editors, under various pseudonyms, were C. de Beaumont, D. Blanchard, C. Castoriadis, S. de Diesbach, C. Lefort, J.-F. Lyotard, A. Maso, D. Mothé, P. Simon, P. Souyri.

11. Ernest Bloch, *Das Prinzip Hoffnung* (Frankfurt: Suhrkamp Verlag, 1959). See G. Raulet, ed., *Utopie-Marxisme selon E. Bloch* (Paris: Payot, 1976).

12. This is an allusion to the theoretical bunglings occasioned by the Algerian and Vietnam wars, and the student movement of the 1960s. A historical survey of these is given by Alain Schapp and Pierre Vidal-Naquet in their introduction to the *Journal de la Commune étudiante* (Paris: Seuil, 1969) [Eng. trans. Maria Jolas, *The French Student Uprising, November 1967–June 1968* (Boston: Beacon, 1971)].

13. Lewis Mumford, *The Myth of the Machine: Technics and Human Development*, 2 vols. (New York: Harcourt, Brace, 1967).

14. An appeal that was intended to secure intellectuals' participation in the system is nonetheless imbued with hesitation between these two hypotheses: P. Nemo, "La Nouvelle Responsabilité des clercs," *Le Monde*, 8 September 1978.

15. The origin of the theoretical opposition between *Naturwissenschaft* and *Geisteswissenschaft* is to be found in the work of Wilhelm Dilthey (1863–1911).

16. M. Albert, a commission member of the French Plan, writes: "The Plan is a governmental research department. . . . It is also a great meeting place where ideas ferment, where points of view clash and where change is prepared. . . . We must not be alone. Others must enlighten us. . . ." (*L'Expansion*, November 1978). On the problem of decision, see G. Gafgen, *Theorie der wissenschaftlichen Entscheidung* (Tübingen, 1963); L. Sfez, *Critique de la décision* (1973; Presses de la Fondation nationale des sciences politiques, 1976).

17. Think of the waning of names such as Stalin, Mao, and Castro as the eponyms of revolution over the last twenty years; consider the erosion of the image of the President in the United States since the Watergate affair.

18. This is a central theme in Robert Musil, *Der Mann ohne Eigenschaften* (1930–33; Hamburg: Rowolt, 1952) [Eng. trans. Eithne Wilkins and Ernest Kaiser, *The Man without Qualities* (London: Secker and Warburg, 1953–60)]. In a free commentary, J. Bouveresse underlines the affinity of this theme of the "dereliction" of the self with the "crisis" of science at the beginning of the twentieth century and with Mach's epistemology; he cites the following evidence: "Given the state of science in particular, a man is made only of what people say he is or of what is done with what he is. . . . The world is one in which lived events have become independent of man. . . . It is a world of happening, of what happens without its happening to anyone, and without anyone's being responsible" ("La problématique du sujet dans *L'Homme sans qualités*," *Noroît* (Arras) 234 and 235 (December 1978 and January 1979); the published text was not revised by the author.

19. Jean Baudrillard, *A l'ombre des majorités silencieuses, ou la fin du social* (Fontenay-sous-bois: Cahiers Utopie 4, 1978) [Eng. trans. *In the Shadow of the Silent Majority* (New York: Semiotexte, 1983)].

20. This is the vocabulary of systems theory. See for example P. Nemo, "La Nouvelle Responsabilité": "Think of society as a system, in the cybernetic sense. This system is a communication grid with intersections where messages converge and are redistributed. . . ."

21. An example of this is given by J.-P. Garnier, *Le Marxisme lénifiant*, "The role of the Center for Information on Social Innovation, directed by H. Dougier and F. Bloch-Lainé, is to inventory, analyze, and distribute information on new experiences of daily life (education, health, justice, cultural activities, town planning and architecture, etc.). This data bank on 'alternative practices' lends its services to those state organs whose job it is to see to it that 'civil society' remains a civilized society: the Commissariat au Plan, the Secrétariat à l'action sociale, DATAR, etc."

22. Freud in particular stressed this form of "predestination." See Marthe Robert, *Roman des origines, origine du roman* (Paris: Grasset, 1972).

23. See the work of Michel Serres, especially *Hermés I-IV* (Paris: Editions de Minuit, 1969–77).

24. For example, Erving Goffman, *The Presentation of Self in Everyday Life* (Garden City, N.Y.: Doubleday, 1959); Gouldner, *The Coming Crisis* (note 37), chap. 10; Alain Touraine et al., *Lutte étudiante* (Paris: Seuil, 1978); M. Callon, "Sociologie des techniques?" *Pandore* 2 (February 1979): 28–32; Watzlawick et al., *Pragmatics of Human Communication*.

25. See note 5. The theme of general bureaucratization as the future of modern societies was first developed by B. Rizzi, *La Bureaucratisation du monde* (Paris: B. Rizzi, 1939).

26. See H. P. Grice, "Logic and Conversation" in Peter Cole and Jeremy Morgan, eds., *Speech Acts III, Syntax and Semantics* (New York: Academic Press, 1975), pp. 59–82.

27. For a phenomenological approach to the problem, see Maurice Merleau-Ponty, *Résumés de cours*, ed. Claude Lefort (Paris: Gallimard, 1968), the course for 1954–55. For a psycho-sociological approach, see R. Loureau, *L'Analyse institutionnelle* (Paris: Editions de Minuit, 1970).

28. M. Callon, "Sociologie des techniques?" p. 30: "Sociologics is the movement by which actors constitute and institute differences, or frontiers, between what is social and what is not, what is imaginary and what is real: the outline of these frontiers is open to dispute, and no consensus can be achieved except in cases of total domination." Compare this with what Alain Touraine calls permanent sociology in *La voix et le regard*.

29. Certain scientific aspects of postmodernism are inventoried by Ihab Hassan in "Culture, Indeterminacy, and Immanence: Margins of the (Postmodern) Age," *Humanities in Society* 1 (1978): 51–85.

30. Claus Mueller uses the expression "a process of delegitimation" in *The Politics of Communication* (New York: Oxford University Press, 1973), p. 164.

31. "Road of doubt . . . road of despair . . . skepticism," writes Hegel in the preface to the *Phenomenology of Spirit* to describe the effect of the speculative drive on natural knowledge.

32. For fear of encumbering this account, I have postponed until a later study the exposition of

this group of rules. [See "Analyzing Speculative Discourse as Language-Game," *The Oxford Literary Review* 4, no. 3 (1981): 59–67.]

33. Nietzsche, "Der europäische Nihilismus" (MS. N VII 3); "der Nihilism, ein normaler Zustand" (MS. W II 1); "Kritik der Nihilism" (MS. W VII 3); "Zum Plane" (MS. W II 1), in *Nietzshes Werke kritische Gesamtausgabe*, vol. 7, pts. 1 and 2 (1887–89) (Berlin: De Gruyter, 1970). These texts have been the object of a commentary by K. Ryjik, *Nietzsche, le manuscrit de Lenzer Heide* (typescript, Département de philosophie, Université de Paris VIII [Vincennes]).

34. "On the future of our educational institutions," in *Complete Works* (note 35), vol. 3.

35. Martin Buber, *Ich und Du* (Berlin: Schocken Verlag, 1922) [Eng. trans. Ronald G. Smith, *I and Thou* (New York: Charles Scribner's Sons, 1937)], and *Dialogisches Leben* (Zürich: Müller, 1947); Emmanuel Lévinas, *Totalité et Infinité* (La Haye: Nijhoff, 1961) [Eng. trans. Alphonso Lingis, *Totality and Infinity: An Essay on Exteriority* (Pittsburgh: Duquesne University Press, 1969)], and "Martin Buber und die Erkenntnis theorie" (1958), in *Philosophen des 20. Jahrhunderts* (Stuttgart: Kohlhammer, 1963) [Fr. trans. "Martin Buber et la théorie de la connaissance," in *Noms Propres* (Montpellier: Fata Morgana, 1976)].

36. *Philosophical Investigations*, sec. 18, p. 8.

37. Ibid.

38. Ibid.

39. See for example, "La taylorisation de la recherche," in *(Auto) critique de la science*, pp. 291–93. And especially D. J. de Solla Price, *Little Science, Big Science* (New York: Columbia University Press, 1963), who emphasizes the split between a small number of highly productive researchers (evaluated in terms of publication) and a large mass of researchers with low productivity. The number of the latter grows as the square of the former, so that the number of high productivity researchers only really increases every twenty years. Price concludes that science considered as a social entity is "undemocratic" (p. 59) and that "the eminent scientist" is a hundred years ahead of "the minimal one" (p. 56).

40. See J. T. Desanti, "Sur le rapport traditionnel des sciences et de la philosophie," in *La Philosophie silencieuse, ou critique des philosophies de la science* (Paris: Seuil, 1975).

41. The reclassification of academic philosophy as one of the human sciences in this respect has a significance far beyond simply professional concerns. I do not think that philosophy as legitimation is condemned to disappear, but it is possible that it will not be able to carry out this work, or at least advance it, without revising its ties to the university institution. See on this matter the preamble to the *Projet d'un institut polytechnique de philosophie* (typescript, Département de philosophie, Université de Paris VIII [Vincennes], 1979).

42. See Allan Janik and Stephan Toulmin, *Wittgenstein's Vienna* (New York: Simon & Schuster, 1973), and J. Piel, ed., "Vienne début d'un siècle," *Critique*, 339–40 (1975).

43. See Jürgen Habermas, "Dogmatismus, Vernunft unt Entscheidung—Zu Theorie und Praxis in der verwissenschaftlichen Zivilisation" (1963), in *Theorie und Praxis* [*Theory and Practice*, abr. ed. of 4th German ed., trans. John Viertel (Boston: Beacon Press, 1971)].

44. "Science Smiling into its Beard" is the title of chap. 72, vol. 1 of Musil's *The Man Without Qualities*. Cited and discussed by J. Bouveresse, "La Problématique du sujet" (note 18).

45. It has not been possible within the limits of this study to analyze the form assumed by the return of narrative in discourses of legitimation. Examples are: the study of open systems, local determinism, antimethod—in general, everything that I group under the name *paralogy*.

46. Nora and Minc, for example, attribute Japan's success in the field of computers to an "intensity of social consensus" that they judge to be specific to Japanese society (*L'Informatisation de la Société* [note 9], p. 4). They write in their conclusion: "The dynamics of extended social computerization leads to a fragile society: such a society is constructed with a view to facilitating consensus, but already presupposes its existence, and comes to a standstill if that consensus cannot be realized" (p. 125). Y. Stourdzé, "Les États-Unis" (note 20), emphasizes the fact that the current tendency to deregulate, destabilize, and weaken administration is encouraged by society's loss of confidence in the State's performance capability.

47. In Kuhn's sense.

48. Pomian ("Catastrophes") shows that this type of functioning bears no relation to Hegelian dialectics.

49. "What the legitimation of decisions accordingly entails is fundamentally an effective learning process, with a minimum of friction, within the social system. This is an aspect of the more general question 'How do aspirations change, how can the political-administrative subsystem, itself only part of society, nevertheless structure expectations in society through its decisions?' The effectiveness of the activity of what is only a part, for the whole, will in large measure depend on how well it succeeds in integrating new expectations into already existing systems—whether these are persons or social systems—without thereby provoking considerable functional disturbances." (Niklas Luhmann, *Legitimation durch Verfahren* [note 160], p. 35).

50. This hypothesis is developed in David Riesman's earlier studies. See Riesman, *The Lonely Crowd* (New Haven: Yale University Press, 1950); W. H. Whyte, *The Organization Man* (New York: Simon & Schuster, 1956); Herbert Marcuse, *One Dimensional Man* (Boston: Beacon, 1966).

51. Josette Rey-Debove (*Le Métalangage* [note 117], pp. 228ff.) notes the proliferation of marks of indirect discourse or autonymic connotation in contemporary daily language. As she reminds us, "indirect discourse cannot be trusted."

52. As Georges Canguilhem says, "man is only truly healthy when he is capable of a number of norms, when he is more than normal" ("Le Normal et la pathologique" [1951], in *La Connaissance de la vie* [Paris: Hachette, 1952], p. 210) [Eng. trans. Carolyn Fawcett, *On the Normal and the Pathological* (Boston: D. Reidel, 1978)].

53. E. E. David, Jr. (*La Recherche* 21 (1972):211) comments that society can only be aware of the needs it feels in the present state of its technological milieu. It is of the nature of the basic sciences to discover unknown properties which remodel the technical milieu and create unpredictable needs. He cites as examples the use of solid materials as amplifiers and the rapid development of the physics of solids. This "negative regulation" of social interactions and needs by the object of contemporary techniques is critiqued by R. Jaulin, "Le Mythe technologique," *Revue de l'entreprise* 26, special "Ethnotechnology" issue (March 1979): 49–55. This is a review of A. G. Haudricourt, "La Technologie culturelle, essai de méthodologie," in Gille, *Historie des techniques* (note 154).

54. Medawar (*Art of the Soluble*, pp. 151–52) compares scientists' written and spoken styles. The former must be "inductive" or they will not be considered; as for the second, Medawar makes a list of expressions often heard in laboratories, including, "My results don't make a story yet." He concludes, "Scientists are building explanatory structures, *telling stories.* . . ."

55. For a famous example, see Lewis S. Feuer, *Einstein and the Generations of Science* (New York: Basic Books, 1974). As Moscovici emphasizes in his introduction to the French translation [trans. Alexandre, *Einstein et le conflit des générations* (Bruxelles' Complexe, 1979)], "Relativity was born in a makeshift 'academy' formed by friends, not one of whom was a physicist; all were engineers or amateur philosophers."

56. Orwell's paradox. The bureaucrat speaks: "We are not content with negative obedience, nor even with the most abject submission. When finally you do surrender to us, it must be of your own free will" (1984 [New York: Harcourt, Brace, 1949], p. 258). In language game terminology the paradox would be expressed as a "Be free," or a "Want what you want," and is analyzed by Watzlawick et al., *Pragmatics of Human Communication* (note 11), pp. 203–7. On these paradoxes, see J. M. Salanskis, "Genèses 'actuelles' et genèses 'sérielles' de l'inconsistant et de l'hétérogeme," *Critique 379* (1978): 1155–73.

57. See Nora and Minc's description of the tensions that mass computerization will inevitably produce in French society (*L'Informatisation de la société* [note 9], introduction).

58. Cf. the discussion of open systems in Watzlawick et al., *Pragmatics of Human Communication: A Study of Interactional Patterns, Pathologies, and Paradoxes* (New York: Norton, 1967), pp. 117–48. The concept of open systems theory is the subject of a study by J. M. Salanskis, *Le Systématique ouvert* (forthcoming).

59. After the separation of Church and State, Paul Feyerabend (*Against Method*), demands in the same "lay" spirit the separation of Science and State. But what about Science and Money?

60. This is at least one way of understanding this term, which comes from Ducrot's problematic, *Dire et ne pas dire* (Paris: Hermann, 1972).

61. *Legitimationsprobleme im Spätkapitalismus* (Frankfurt: Suhrkamp, 1973), passim, especially pp. 21–22: "Language functions in the manner of a transformer . . . changing cognitions into propositions, needs and feelings into normative expectations (commands, values). This transformation produces the far-reaching distinction between the subjectivity of intention, willing, of pleasure and unpleasure on the one hand, and expressions and norms with a *pretension to universality* on the other. Universality signifies the objectivity of knowledge and the legitimacy of prevailing norms; both assure the community [*Gemeinsamkeit*] constitutive of lived social experience." We see that by formulating the problematic in this way, the question of legitimacy is fixated on one type of reply, universality. This on the one hand presupposes that the legitimation of the subject of knowledge is identical to that of the subject of action (in opposition to Kant's critique, which dissociates conceptual universality, appropriate to the former, and ideal universality, or "suprasensible nature," which forms the horizon of the latter, and on the other hand it maintains that consensus (*Gemeinschaft*) is the only possible horizon for the life of humanity.

62. Ibid., p. 20. The subordination of the metaprescriptives of prescription (i.e., the normalization of laws) to *Diskurs* is explicit, for example, on p. 144: "The normative pretension to

validity is itself cognitive in the sense that it always assumes it could be accepted in a rational discussion."

63. Garbis Kortian, *Métacritique* (Paris: Editions de Minuit, 1979) [Eng. trans. John Raffan, *Metacritique: The Philosophical Argument of Jürgen Habermas* (Cambridge: Cambridge University Press, 1980)], pt. 5, examines this enlightenment aspect of Habermas's thought. See by the same author, "Le Discours philosphique et son objet," *Critique 384* (1979): 407–19.

64. See J. Poulain, ("Vers une pragmatique nucléaire" [note 28]), and for a more general discussion of the pragmatics of Searle and Gehlen, see J. Poulain, "Pragmatique de la parole et pragmatique de la vie," *Phi zéro* 7, no. 1 (Université de Montréal, September 1978): 5–50.

65. See Tricot et al., *Informatique et libertés*, government report (La Documentation française, 1975); L. Joinet, "Les 'pièges liberaticides' de l'informatique," *Le Monde diplomatique* 300 (March 1979): these traps (*pièges*) are "the application of the technique of 'social profiles' to the management of the mass of the population; the logic of security produced by the automatization of society." See too the documents and analysis in *Interférences* 1 and 2 (Winter 1974–Spring 1975), the theme of which is the establishment of popular networks of multimedia communication. Topics treated include: amateur radios (especially their role in Quebec during the FLQ affair of October 1970 and that of the "Front commun" in May 1972); community radios in the United States and Canada; the impact of computers on editorial work in the press; pirate radios (before their development in Italy); administrative files, the IBM monopoly, computer sabotage. The municipality of Yverdon (Canton of Vaud), having voted to buy a computer (operational in 1981), enacted a certain number of rules: exclusive authority of the municipal council to decide which data are collected, to whom and under what conditions they are communicated; access for all citizens to all data (on payment); the right of every citizen to see the entries on his file (about 50), to correct them and address a complaint about them to the municipal council and if need be to the Council of State; the right of all citizens to know (on request) which data concerning them is communicated and to whom (*La Semaine media* 18, 1 March 1979, 9).

JÜRGEN HABERMAS

MODERNITY: AN UNFINISHED PROJECT*

Now, after the painters and the filmmakers, the architects have also been admitted to the Biennale in Venice. The response to this first architecture Biennale has been disappointment. Those who exhibited in Venice formed an avant-garde with the fronts reversed. Under the slogan "the presence of the past," they sacrificed the tradition of modernity to a new historicism: "The fact that the whole Modern Movement drew its sustenance from its confrontation with the past, that Frank Lloyd Wright would not have been thinkable without Japan, Le Corbusier without classical antiquity and Mediterranean architecture, and Mies van der Rohe without Schinkel and Behrens, is passed over in silence." With this comment the *Frankfurter Allgemeine Zeitung*'s critic W. Pehnt[1] introduces his thesis, a thesis that goes beyond this event to provide a diagnosis of our times: "Postmodernity presents itself decisively as Antimodernity."

This statement refers to an affective current that has penetrated all spheres of intellectual activity and called into being theories of a post-Enlightenment, post-modernity, and posthistory, in short, a new conservatism. Adorno and his work stand in contrast to this current.

Adorno subscribed so wholeheartedly to the spirit of modernity that he sensed the presence of an affective response to the affront of modernity even in the attempt to distinguish an authentic modernity from mere modernism. Hence it may not be inappropriate to express my gratitude for an Adorno Prize by pursuing the question of the current status of the modernist point of view. Is modernity as passé as the postmodernists claim it is? Or is the much-proclaimed postmodernity itself "phony"? Is *postmodern* a cliché under which all the antagonisms cultural moder-nity has evoked since the middle of the nineteenth century have been unobtrusively passed on?

* This text formed the basis of a talk I gave at the Paulskirche in Frankfurt on 11 September 1980, when was awarded the city's Adorno Prize.

THE OLD AND THE NEW

Those who, like Adorno, conceive of "modernity" as beginning around 1850 look at it through the eyes of Baudelaire and avant-garde art. Let me elucidate this concept of cultural modernity through a brief look at its long prehistory, which has been illuminated by Hans Robert Jauss.[2] The word *modern* was first used in the late fifth century to delimit the present, which had become officially Christian, from the heathen and Roman past. With varying contents, the term *modernity* repeatedly expresses the consciousness of an era that relates itself to the past of classical antiquity in order to conceive itself as the result of a transition from the old to the new. This is not true merely of the Renaissance, with which the modern age [*Neuzeit*] begins *for us*; people also thought of themselves as "modern" at the time of Charlemagne, in the twelfth century, and during the Enlightenment—that is, whenever the consciousness of a new era in Europe developed through a renewed relationship to classical antiquity. In this process, *antiquitas*, antiquity, was considered a normative model to be imitated, up to the famous *querelle des anciens et des modernes*; that is, the dispute with the adherents of classicistic taste in late-seventeenth-century France. Only with the French Enlightenment's ideals of perfection and the notion, inspired by modern science, of the infinite progress of knowledge and an infinite advance toward social and moral betterment was the spell that the classical works of antiquity exerted on the spirit of those *early* moderns at each point gradually broken. Ultimately modernity, opposing the romantic to the classical, sought its past in an idealized Middle Ages. During the course of the nineteenth century this romanticism produced a radicalized consciousness of modernity that detached itself from all historical connections and retained only an abstract opposition to tradition and history as a whole.

At that point, what was considered modern was what helped the spontaneously self-renewing historical contemporaneity of the *Zeitgeist* to achieve objective expression. The signature of such works is the New, which will be surpassed and devalued by the innovation that constitutes the next style. But while the merely modish becomes outmoded when displaced into the past, the modern retains a secret link with the classical. Classical has always meant what survives through the ages. The emphatically modern no longer derives this force from the authority of a past age; it derives it solely from the authenticity of a contemporary relevance that is now in the past. This transformation of present-day relevance into relevance that is now in the past is both destructive and productive; as Jauss observed, it is modernity itself that creates its classicity—these days we speak of "classical modernity" as though the term were unproblematic. Adorno opposes the distinction between modernity and modernism because "without the subjective mind-set [*Gesinnung*] inspired by the New no objective modernity can crystallize."[3]

THE AESTHETIC MODERN MENTALITY

The aesthetic modern mentality took on clearer contours with Baudelaire and his theory of art, which was influenced by Edgar Allen Poe. It developed in the avant-garde movements and ultimately reached its high point in Surrealism and the Dadaists' Café Voltaire. It is characterized by attitudes crystallized around an altered consciousness of time. This consciousness is expressed in the spatial metaphor of a vanguard—that is, an avant-garde that scouts unknown territory, exposing itself to the risks of sudden and shocking encounters, conquering an as-yet uninhabited future, and orienting itself in an as-yet unsurveyed terrain. But the forward orientation, the anticipation of an undefined, contingent future, and the cult of the New actually mean the glorification of a present that repeatedly gives birth to new, subjectively defined pasts. It is not simply that the new time consciousness, which penetrates into philosophy as well with Bergson, expresses the experience of a society that has been mobilized, a history that has been speeded up, and an everyday life without continuity. What is expressed in the new value accorded the transitory and the ephemeral and in the celebration of dynamism is the longing for an immaculate and unchanging present. Modernism, a self-negating movement, is "nostalgia for true presence." This, says Octavio Paz, "is the secret theme of the best modernist writers."[4]

This also explains modernism's abstract opposition to history, which is no longer structured as an organized process of transmission that guarantees continuity. Individual epochs lose their distinctive characteristics; instead, the present has a heroic affinity with what is most distant on the one hand and what is closest on the other: Decadence recognizes itself immediately in the barbaric, the wild, and the primitive. An anarchistic intention of exploding the continuum of history accounts for the subversive force of an aesthetic consciousness that rebels against the normalizing achievements of tradition, that is sustained by the experience of rebelling against everything normative, and that neutralizes both the morally good and the practical, a consciousness that continually stages a dialectic of secrecy and scandal, addicted to the fascination of the fright evoked by the act of profanation and at the same time in flight from the trivial results of that profanation. Thus for Adorno "the stigma of disruption are modernity's seals of authenticity, that through which modernity negates in desperation the closed character of the eternally invariant; explosion is one of modernity's invariants. Antitraditionalist energy becomes a devouring maelstrom. In this sense modernity is myth turned against itself; myth's timelessness becomes the catastrophe of the moment that disrupts temporal continuity."[5]

The time consciousness articulated in avant-garde art is not simply antihistorical, of course; it is directed only against the false normativity of an understanding of history derived from the imitation of models, an understanding whose traces persist even in Gadamer's philosophical hermeneutics. This time consciousness avails itself of the objectified pasts made available by historicist scholarship but at the same time rebels against the neutralization of criteria that historicism practices when it locks history up in the museum. In the same spirit, Walter Benjamin construes the relation of modernity to history *posthistoricistically*. He recalls the French Revolution's conception of itself: "It evoked ancient Rome the way fashion evokes costumes of the past. Fashion has a flair for the topical, no matter where it stirs in the thickets of long ago."[6] And just as for Robespierre ancient Rome was a past charged with Nowness [*Jetztzeit*], so the historian has to grasp the constellation "which his own era has formed with a definite earlier one." This is how Benjamin grounds his concept of "the present as the 'time of the now' [*Jetztzeit*] which is shot through with chips of Messianic time."[7] Since then this spirit of aesthetic modernity has aged. In the 1960s it was, of course, recited again. But with the 1970s behind us, we must admit that modernism finds almost no resonance today. Even during the 1960s Octavio Paz, a partisan of modernity, noted with melancholy that "the avant-garde of 1967 repeats the deeds and gestures of the avant-garde of 1917. We are experiencing the end of the idea of modern art."[8] Following Peter Bürger's work, we now speak of post-avant-garde art, a term that acknowledges the failure of the Surrealist revolt. But what is the significance of this failure? Does it signal the demise of modernity? Does a post-avant-garde mean a transition to postmodernity?

This is in fact how Daniel Bell, a well-known social theorist and the most brilliant of the American neoconservatives, understands the matter. In an interesting book, the *Cultural Contradictions of Capitalism*,[9] Bell develops the thesis that the crisis phenomenon of the developed societies of the West can be traced to a split between culture and society, between cultural modernity and the demands of the economic and administrative systems. Avant-garde art has penetrated the values of daily life and infected the lifeworld with the modernist mentality. Modernism is the great seducer, bringing about the dominance of the principle of unrestricted self-realization, the demand for authentic experience of the self, and the subjectivism of an overstimulated sensibility, and unleashing hedonistic motives that are incompatible with the discipline of professional life and in general with the moral bases of a purposive-rational mode of life. Hence Bell, like Arnold Gehlen in Germany, puts the blame for the dissolution of the Protestant ethic, something that had disturbed Max Weber earlier, on an "adversary culture"; that is, a culture whose modernism arouses hostility to the conventions and virtues of a daily life rationalized under economic and administrative imperatives.

On the other hand, on this reading the impulse of modernity is supposed to be definitively exhausted and the avant-garde finished; while still being propagated, it is no longer creative. This poses the question for neoconservatism of how norms can be established that will set limits on libertinage, restore discipline and the work ethic, and oppose the virtues of individual competitiveness to the leveling effects of the welfare state. Bell considers a religious revival the only solution; it would link up with quasi-natural traditions that are immune to criticism, permit clearly defined identities, and provide the individual with existential security.

CULTURAL MODERNITY AND SOCIAL MODERNIZATION

One cannot, of course, simply conjure up authoritative beliefs. Thus the only practical result of analyses like Bell's is an imperative we have seen in Germany as well: intellectual and political confrontation with the intellectual bearers of cultural modernity. To cite Peter Steinfels, a thoughtful observer of the new style the neoconservatives imposed on the intellectual scene in the 1970s:

The struggle takes the form of exposing every manifestation of what could be considered an oppositionist mentality and tracing its "logic" so as to link it to various expressions of extremism: drawing the connection between modernism and nihilism . . . between government regulation and totalitarianism, between criticism of arms expenditures and subservience to Communism, between Women's Liberation or homosexual rights and the destruction of the family . . . between the Left generally and terrorism, anti-Semitism, and fascism. [10]

Steinfels is referring only to the United States here, but the parallels are obvious. The personalizing and bitterness that characterize the abuse of intellectuals fomented by anti-Enlightenment intellectuals in Germany as well as in the United States cannot be explained in psychological terms; rather, it has its roots in the analytic weaknesses of neoconservative doctrine itself.

For neoconservatism displaces the burdensome consequences of a more or less successful capitalist modernization of economy and society onto cultural modernity. Because it conceals the connections between the processes of social modernization it welcomes on the one hand and the crisis of motivation it laments on the other and does not reveal the social-structural causes of altered attitudes toward work, consumer habits, levels of demand, and leisure-time orientation, it can attribute something that looks like hedonism, lack of social identification, incapacity for obedience, narcissism, and a withdrawal from competition for status and achievement directly to a culture that in fact plays only a very mediated role in the process. What is put in place of these unanalyzed causes is the intellectuals who continue to consider themselves committed to the project of modernity. To be sure, Daniel Bell sees a further connection between the erosion of bourgeois values and the consumerism of a society that has shifted to mass production. Even Bell, however, unimpressed by his own argument, traces the new permissiveness first and foremost to the spread of a life-style that initially developed in the elite countercultures of bohemian artists. This of course is only a variation on a misunderstanding to which the avant-garde itself has already fallen prey—the idea that the mission of art is to fulfill its indirect promise of happiness through the spread to society as a whole of the artistic life-style that has been defined as its opposite.

Bell remarks of the period in which aesthetic modernity originated that "radical in economics, the bourgeoisie became conservative in morals and cultural taste." [11] If that were correct, one could see neoconservatism as a return to a tried-and-true pattern of the bourgeois mentality. But that is too simple. For the mood that feeds neoconservatism today is by no means derived from discontent with the antinomian consequences of a culture that has transgressed its boundaries and broken out of the museums and into life. This discontent is not evoked by modernist intellectuals; it is rooted in more fundamental reactions to a social modernization that, under pressure from the imperatives of economic growth and state administration, intervenes further and further into the ecology of developed forms of life, into the communicative infrastructure of historical lifeworlds. Thus neopopulist protests are only giving pointed expression to widespread fears of a destruction of urban and natural milieus, the destruction of forms of communal human life. Multiple occasions for discontent and protest arise wherever a one-sided modernization guided by criteria of economic and administrative rationality penetrates into spheres of life centered around tasks of cultural transmission, social integration, and socialization, spheres of life that are guided by other criteria, namely those of communicative rationality. But it is precisely from these social processes that neoconservative doctrines divert attention; they project the causes they conceal onto an autonomous subversive culture and its advocates.

To be sure, cultural modernity generates its own aporias as well. And positions that proclaim a postmodernity, recommend a return to premodernity, or radically reject modernity, invoke these aporias. Aside from the problematic consequences of *social* modernization, motives for doubt and despair with the project of modernity arise from the *internal viewpoint* of cultural development.

THE PROJECT OF ENLIGHTENMENT

The idea of modernity is intimately tied up with the development of European art, but what I have called the project of modernity comes into focus only when we abandon the usual concentration on art. For Max Weber, what characterized cultural modernity was the separation of the substantive reason expressed in religious and metaphysical worldviews into three moments, the connections between which (through the form of argumentative justification) were now merely formal ones. Since the worldviews in question have disintegrated and their traditional problems have been distributed among the specific perspectives of truth, normative rightness, and authenticity or beauty—that is, can be treated *as* questions of knowledge, justice, or taste—what we have in the modern world is a differentiation of the value spheres of science and scholarship, morality, and art. Scientific discourse, moral and legal inquiry, and art production and criticism are institutionalized in the corresponding cultural systems as matters for experts. The professionalized treatment of cultural transmission in terms of abstract considerations of validity puts the emphasis on the logical structures intrinsic to each of these knowledge-complexes—the cognitive-instrumental, the moral-practical (*Eigengesetzlichkeiten*), and the aesthetic-expressive. From now on there will also be *internal* histories of science and scholarship, moral and legal theory, and art. These are not linear developments, to be sure, but they are learning processes nevertheless. That is one side.

On the other side, the distance between these expert cultures and the general public has increased. The increases in culture produced by specialized treatment and reflection do not *automatically* become the property of everyday practice. Instead, with cultural rationalization there is a danger that the lifeworld, its traditional substance having been devalued, will become *impoverished*. The project of modernity, formulated in the eighteenth century by the Enlightenment *philosophes*, consists of a relentless development of the objectivating sciences, the universalistic bases of morality and law, and autonomous art in accordance with their internal logic but at the same time a release of the cognitive potentials thus accumulated from their esoteric high forms and their utilization in praxis; that is, in the rational organization of living conditions and social relations. Proponents of the Enlightenment like Condorcet still held the extravagant expectation that the arts and sciences would further not only the control of the forces of nature but also the understanding of self and world, moral progress, justice in social institutions, and even human happiness.

The twentieth century has not left us much of this optimism. But the problem has remained, and as before there is a difference of opinion: should we hold to the intentions of the Enlightenment, battered as they may be, or should we abandon the project of modernity? Where cognitive potentials do not result in technical progress, economic growth, and rational administration, should we want to see them checked so that they do not effect a life-praxis dependent on blind traditions?

Even among the philosophers who currently form something like a rearguard of the Enlightenment the project of modernity is strangely splintered. Each places his trust in only one of the moments into which reason has become differentiated. Popper, and I am referring to the theorist of the open society, who has not yet let himself be appropriated by the neoconservatives, holds to the enlightening force of scientific criticism, whose effects extend into the political domain; for this he pays the price of moral skepticism and a general indifference to the aesthetic. Paul Lorenzen is concerned with how a methodically constructed artificial language in which practical reason will be brought to bear can be effective in reforming everyday life. His conception, however, channels science and scholarship into the narrow paths of justifications analogous to moral-practical justifications, and he too neglects the aesthetic. In Adorno, conversely, the emphatic claim to reason has withdrawn into the accusatory gestures of the esoteric work of art, while morality is no longer susceptible of justification, and philosophy is left with the sole task of indicating, through indirect discourse, the critical content concealed in art.

The differentiation of science and scholarship, morality, and art with which Max Weber characterized the rationalism of Western culture, means *both* the specialized treatment of special sectors *and* their detachment from the stream of tradition, which continues in quasi-natural form in the hermeneutics of everyday life. This detachment is the problem to which the autonomous development of the differentiated value spheres gives rise; it has also evoked abortive attempts to "sublate" the expert cultures. We can see that best in art.

KANT AND THE AUTONOMY OF THE AESTHETIC

Simplifying, one can discern a line of progressive autonomization in the development of modern art. A subject domain categorized exclusively in terms of the beautiful was first constituted in the Renaissance. Then in the course of the eighteenth century, literature, the fine arts, and music were institutionalized as domains of activity separate from ecclesiastical and court life. Finally, around the middle of the nineteenth century an aestheticist conception of art emerged that obliged the artist to produce his works in accordance with the consciousness of *l'art pour l'art*. With this the autonomy of the aesthetic was constituted as a project.

In the first phase of this process, then, the cognitive structures of a new domain, distinct from the complex of science and scholarship and morality, emerged. Later it became the job of philosophical aesthetics to clarify these structures. Kant labored energetically to specify the distinctive nature of the aesthetic domain. His point of departure was the analysis of the judgment of taste, whose object is something subjective, the free play of the imagination, but which does not indicate mere preference but instead is oriented to intersubjective agreement.

Although aesthetic objects belong neither to the sphere of phenomena known with the help of the categories of the understanding nor to the sphere of free actions subject to the laws of practical reason, works of art (and of natural beauty) are accessible to objective judgment. The beautiful constitutes a further domain of validity alongside those of truth and morality, a domain that forms the basis for the link between art and art criticism. One "speaks of beauty as if it were a property of things."[12] Beauty pertains, of course, only to the *representation* of a thing, just as the judgment of taste refers only to the relationship between the mental representation of an object and the feeling of pleasure or displeasure. Only in the medium of semblance (*Medium des Scheins*) can an object to perceived *as* an aesthetic object; only as a fictive object can it affect the sensibility in such a way that it can represent what evades the conceptual character of objectivating thought and moral judgment. Kant characterizes the state of mind evoked by the play of the representational capacities, a state set in motion aesthetically, as *disinterested* pleasure. The quality of a work, then, is defined independently of its connections with practical life.

Whereas the fundamental concepts of classical aesthetics I have mentioned—that is, taste and criticism, beautiful semblance, disinterestedness, and the transcendance of the work—serve first and foremost to delimit the aesthetic from the other spheres of value and from everyday life, the concept of the *genius* required for the production of a work of art has a positive definition. Kant calls genius "the exemplary originality of the natural gifts of a subject in the free employment of his cognitive faculties."[13] When we separate the concept of genius from its romantic origins, we can say, paraphrasing freely: The talented artist can give authentic expression to what he experiences in his concentrated dealings with a decentered subjectivity that is released from the constraints of knowledge and action.

The autonomy of the aesthetic—that is, the objectification of a self-experiencing, decentered subjectivity, the exclusion of the spatio-temporal structures of everyday life, the break with the conventions of perception and purposeful activity, and the dialectic of revelation and shock—could emerge as consciousness of modernity only with the gesture of modernism, and only after two further conditions had been fulfilled. Those conditions were, first, the institutionalization of art production independent of the market and of a nonpurposeful enjoyment of art mediated by criticism; and second, an aestheticist self-understanding on the part of artists and also critics, who conceive themselves less as advocates of the public than as interpreters who form part of the process of art production itself. At that point, a movement could get under way in painting and literature that some consider to have been anticipated in Baudelaire's art criticism: colors, lines, sounds, and movements stop serving primarily representation; the media of representation and the techniques of production advance to become aesthetic objects in their own right. And Adorno can begin his *Aesthetic Theory* with the statement "We now take it for granted that nothing concerned with art is taken for granted any more, either in art or in its relation to the whole, not even its right to exist."[14]

THE FALSE SUBLATION OF CULTURE

Art's right to exist, of course, would not have been called into question by Surrealism if modern art had not contained a promise of happiness that concerned its "relationship to the whole." In Schiller the promise that aesthetic contemplation makes but does not fulfill still had the explicit form of a utopia extending beyond art. The line of this aesthetic utopia extends to Marcuse's lament over the affirmative character of culture, a lament he formulated as a critique of ideology. But even in Baudelaire, who repeats the *promesse de bonheur*, the utopia of reconciliation had been turned around to become a critical reflection of the unreconciled character of the social world. The more distant from life art becomes, the more it withdraws into the untouchability of perfect autonomy, the more painfully this lack of reconciliation comes to consciousness. This pain was reflected in the boundless *ennui* of Baudelaire, the outsider who identified with the ragpickers of Paris.

Along such pathways of feeling gather the explosive energies that are finally discharged in rebellion, in the violent attempt to explode the sphere of art, which has only a semblance of autarchy, and to force reconciliation through this sacrifice. Adorno sees very clearly why the Surrealist program "renounces art without, however, being able to shake it off."[15] Attempts to eliminate the discrepancy between art and life, fiction and practice, and illusion and reality; attempts to eliminate the distinction between artifact and object of utility, between something produced and something found, between deliberate shaping and spontaneous impulse; attempts to declare everything art and everyone an artist, to abolish all criteria, to assimilate aesthetic judgments to the expression of subjective experiences—these undertakings, which have been well studied, can now be seen to be nonsense experiments that involuntarily illuminate all the more brightly the very structures of art they were intended to dissolve: the medium of semblance, the transcendence of the work, the concentrated and planful character of artistic production, and the cognitive status of the judgment of taste.[16] Ironically, the radical attempt to sublate art legitimates the categories with which classical aesthetics circumscribed its object domain. In the process, of course, the categories themselves have undergone a change.

The failure of the Surrealist revolt confirms the double error of a false sublation. On the one hand, when the containers of an autonomously developed cultural sphere are shattered, its contents disintegrate. When meaning is desublimated and form destructured, nothing is left; no emancipatory effect is produced. The other error, however, is of more consequence. In the communicative practice of everyday life, cognitive interpretations, moral expectations, expressions, and evaluations must interpenetrate one another. The processes of reaching understanding in the lifeworld require the *whole breadth* of cultural transmission. Hence a rationalized everyday life could not be redeemed from the rigidity of cultural impoverishment through the forcible opening of *one* cultural domain, in this case art, and the establishment of a link with *one* of the specialized complexes of knowledge. At best, such an attempt merely replaces one form of one-sidedness and one abstraction with another.

There are parallels in the domains of theoretical knowledge and morality to this program and its unsuccessful practice of false sublation. They are less clearly defined. Like art, science and scholarship on the one hand and moral and legal theory on the other have become autonomous. But the two spheres remain linked to specialized forms of praxis. The one is linked to scientized technology, the other to a legally organized administrative practice dependent on moral justification. And yet, institutionalized science and scholarship and the moral-practical discussions that have been separated off into the legal system have become so distant from everyday life that the program of the Enlightenment could be transformed into a false sublation in these spheres as well.

There has been talk of the "sublation of philosophy" since the days of the Young Hegelians, and the question of the relationship of theory and practice has been raised since Marx. Here, the intellectuals, however, have allied themselves with the workers' movement. It is only on the edges of this social movement that sectarian groups have found room to play out their program of a sublation of philosophy the way the Surrealists played out their sublation of art. The consequences of dogmatism and moral rigorism reveal the same error as in the Surrealist project: when the practice of everyday life that is designed for an unconstrained interplay between the cognitive, the moral-practical, and the aesthetic-expressive, becomes reified, it cannot be cured by being linked with a *single* cultural domain that has been opened by force. Nor should imitation of the life-styles of extraordinary representatives of the value spheres—in other words, generalization of the subversive forces that Nietzsche, Bakunin, and Baudelaire expressed in their individual lives—be confused with the institutionalization and the practical utilization of the knowledge accumulated in science and scholarship, morality, and art.

In specific situations, terrorist activities may be connected with the overextension of one of the cultural moments and thus with the tendency to aestheticize politics, to replace politics by moral rigorism, or to force politics under the dogmatism of a doctrine.

Such relatively impalpable connections, however, should not mislead us into denouncing the intentions of an intransigent Enlightenment as the offspring of a "terroristic reason." Those who lump the project of modernity together with the state of mind of individual terrorists and their sensationalistic public actions are just as short-sighted as those who claim that the incomparably more continual and extensive bureaucratic terrorism practiced in darkness, in the cellars of the military and the secret police, in camps and psychiatric institutions, is the raison d'être of the modern state (and its positivistically eroded legal domination), simply because this kind of terrorism makes use of the coercive means of the state apparatus.

ALTERNATIVES TO THE FALSE SUBLATION OF CULTURE

I believe we would do better to learn from the aberrations that have accompanied the project of modernity and the mistakes of these extravagant programs of sublation than to abandon modernity and its project. Perhaps a way out of the aporias of cultural modernity can be at least suggested, using the example of the reception of art. Since art criticism developed during the Romantic period it has contained countercurrents, which have become more starkly polarized since the emergence of the avant-garde movements. Art criticism claims both the role of a productive supplement to the work of art and the role of an advocate on behalf of the general public's need for interpretation. Bourgeois art addresses *both* of these expectations to its public: on the one hand, the layperson who enjoyed art should educate himself to the level of the expert, and on the other hand, the layperson could act as a connoisseur who relates aesthetic experience to his own life-problems. Perhaps this second, seemingly more harmless mode of reception lost its radical character through its confused relationship to the first mode.

Artistic production, to be sure, of necessity atrophies semantically if it is not carried on as a specialized treatment of autonomous problems, a matter for experts, without regard to exoteric needs. All those involved (including the critic as a technically trained recipient) commit themselves to examining the problems they deal with in terms of an abstract criterion of validity. This concentration on one and only one dimension, however, breaks down as soon as aesthetic experience is brought into the context of an individual life history or a collective form of life. The reception of art by the layperson, or rather the person who is an expert in daily life, takes a different course than the reception of art by a professional critic who is concerned with development in purely artistic terms. Albrecht Wellmer has pointed out to me that an aesthetic experience that is not translated primarily into judgments of taste alters its status. When it is related to life-problems or used on an exploratory basis to illuminate a life-historical situation, it enters into a language game that is no longer that of art criticism. In that case aesthetic experience not only revitalizes the need-interpretations in the light of which we perceive the world; it also influences cognitive interpretations and normative expectations and alters the way in which these moments refer to one another.

An example of the exploratory, life-orienting force that can emanate from an encounter with a great painting at a crisis point in the individual's life is depicted by Peter Weiss, who has his hero wander through Paris after a desperate return from the Spanish Civil War and anticipate in his imagination the encounter with Géricault's painting of the shipwrecked men that will shortly take place in the Louvre. A specific variant of the mode of reception I am talking about is captured still better by the heroic process of appropriation the same author depicts in the first volume of his *Aesthetik des Widerstandes*. A group of young people in Berlin in 1937, workers who are politically motivated and eager to learn, are acquiring the means to grasp the history, including the social history, of European painting through evening high-school classes. Out of the hard stone of the objective spirit they are hewing the pieces they assimilate, taking them into the experiential horizon of their milieu, which is as far removed from traditional education as it is from the existing regime, and turning them around until they begin to glow:

Our conception of a culture only seldom harmonized with what presented itself as a giant reservoir of commodities, stored-up discoveries, and illuminations. As people without property, we approached what had been accumulated at first fearfully, full of awe, until it became clear to us that we had to provide our own evaluation of all this, that the overall concept could be usable only if it said something about our life circumstances as well as the difficulties and peculiarities of our thought processes.[17]

In examples like these, where the expert culture is appropriated from the perspective of the lifeworld, something of the intention of the doomed Surrealist revolt, and even more of Brecht's and even Benjamin's experimental reflections on the reception of nonauratic works of art, has been preserved. One might pursue similar reflections on the spheres of science and scholarship and morality if one considered that the human, social, and behavioral sciences are by no means *fully* divorced from the structures of action-orienting knowledge, and that the focusing of universalist ethics on questions of justice is an abstraction that needs to be linked to the problems of the good life it initially excludes.

Modern culture can be successfully linked back up to a practice of everyday life that is dependent on vital traditions but impoverished by mere traditionalism only if social modernization *too* can be guided into *other*, noncapitalist directions, and if the lifeworld can develop, on its own, institutions that will lie outside the borders of the inherent dynamics of the economic and administrative systems.

THREE CONSERVATISMS

If I am not mistaken, the prospects for this are not good. A climate that promotes tendencies critical of modernism has arisen in virtually the whole of the Western world. In the process, the disillusionment resulting from the failure of programs for the false sublation of art and philosophy and the aporias of cultural modernity that have become apparent serve as pretexts for the conservative positions. Let me distinguish briefly between the antimodernism of the Young Conservatives, the premodernism of the Old Conservatives, and the postmodernism of the New Conservatives.

The *Young Conservatives* appropriate the fundamental experience of aesthetic modernity, namely the revelation of a decentered subjectivity emancipated from the constraints of cognition and purposefulness and from the imperatives of labor and utility—and use it to escape from the modern world. They base an implacable antimodernism on a modernist attitude. They transpose the spontaneous forces of the imagination, the experience of the self, and affectivity onto the sphere of the distant and archaic, and they set up a dualistic opposition between instrumental reason and a principle accessible only through evocation, be it sovereignty or the will to power, Being or a Dionysian force of the poetic. In France this line extends from George Bataille through Foucault to Derrida. Over all of them, of course, hovers the spirit of Nietzsche, resurrected in the 1970s.

The *Old Conservatives* do not allow themselves to be contaminated by cultural modernity. They observe the disintegration of substantive reason, the differentiation of science, morality, and art, and the modern understanding of the world and its merely procedural rationality with suspicion and advocate (and here Max Weber discerned a regression to material rationality) a return to positions prior to modernity. Neo-Aristotelianism in particular has enjoyed a certain success. These days the ecological problematic allows it to call for a renewal of cosmological ethics. Along this line, which emanates from Leo Strauss, one finds interesting works by Hans Jonas and Robert Spaemann, for example.

The *New Conservatives* take the most affirmative position on the accomplishments of modernity. They welcome the development of modern science as long as it oversteps its own sphere only to further technical progress, capitalistic growth, and rational administration. For the rest, they advocate a politics of defusing the explosive contents of cultural modernity. One of their theses asserts that science and scholarship, correctly understood, have in any case become meaningless as far as orientation within the lifeworld is concerned. A further thesis is that politics is to be exempted, as far as possible, from the requirements of moral-practical justification. And a third thesis asserts the pure immanence of art, disputes its utopian contents, and appeals to its illusionary character, with the aim of confining aesthetic experience within the private sphere. Here one could adduce the early Wittgenstein, Carl Schmitt in his middle period, and Gottfried Benn in his late period. With science and scholarship, morality, and art definitively confined within autonomous spheres split off from the lifeworld and administered by specialists, all that remains of cultural modernity is what one has left after renouncing the project of modernity. The resulting space is to be filled by traditions which are to be spared demands for justification; it is, of course, difficult to see how these traditions are to survive in the modern world except through governmental backing.

This typology, like any typology, is a simplification, but it may be of some use in analyzing current intellectual and political controversies. I fear that antimodernist ideas, with a touch of premodernism added to them, are gaining ground in the circles around the Greens and the alternative groups. In the shift in consciousness within the political parties, on the other hand, we see the result of the ideological shift, namely an alliance of postmodernity with premodernity. None of the parties seems to me to have a monopoly on neoconservatism or abuse of intellectuals. Hence—and especially after the clarifications you provided in your introductory remarks, Mayor Wallmann—I have good reason to be grateful for the liberal spirit in which the city of Frankfurt has bestowed on me a prize bearing the name of Adorno, a son of the city who, as a philosopher and a writer, has shaped the image of the intellectual as scarcely anyone else in West Germany has, and who has become a model for intellectuals.

Translated by Shierry Nicholsen

NOTES

1. W. Pehnt, "Die Postmoderne als Lunapark," *Frankfurter Allgemeine Zeitung*, August 18, 1980, p. 17.
2. Hans Robert Jauss, "Literarische Tradition und gegenwärtiges Bewusstsein der Moderne," in Jauss, *Literaturgeschichte als Provokation* (Frankfurt am Main: Suhrkamp, 1970), pp. 11ff.
3. Theodor W. Adorno, *Aesthetische Theorie*, Volume 7 of his *Gesammelte Schriften* (Frankfurt am Main: Suhrkamp, 1970), p. 45. (This and the following translations from *Aesthetische Theorie* are by Shierry Nicholsen; the corresponding page in the English translation by Christian Lenhardt, *Aesthetic Theory* [London and Boston: Routledge & Kegan Paul, 1984], is p. 38.)
4. Octavio Paz, *Essays* (Frankfurt am Main: Suhrkamp, 1979) vol. 2, p. 159.
5. Adorno, *Aesthetische Theorie*, p. 41; *Aesthetic Theory*, p. 34.
6. Walter Benjamin, "Theses on the Philosophy of History," in *Illuminations*, trans. Harry Zohn (New York: Schocken, 1969), p. 261.
7. Benjamin, p. 263.
8. Paz, p. 329.
9. Daniel Bell, *The Cultural Contradictions of Capitalism* (New York: Basic Books, 1976).

10. Peter Steinfels, *The Neoconservatives* (New York: Simon & Schuster, 1979), p. 65.
11. Bell, p. 17.
12. Immanuel Kant, *Kritik der Urteilskraft*, par. 7. (Translated by J. H. Bernard, *Kant's Critique of Judgment* [London and New York: Macmillan, 1982], p. 58.)
13. Kant, *Kritik der Urteilskraft*, par. 49; Bernard, p. 203.
14. Adorno, *Aesthetische Theorie*, p. 9; *Aesthetic Theory*, p. 1.
15. Adorno, *Aesthetische Theorie*, p. 52; *Aesthetic Theory*, p. 44.
16. Dieter Wellershoff, *Die Auflösung des Kunstbegriffs* (Frankfurt am Main: Suhrkamp, 1976).
17. Peter Weiss, *Aesthetik des Widerstandes* (Frankfurt am Main: Suhrkamp, 1978) vol. 1, p. 54.

NANCY FRASER

WHAT'S CRITICAL ABOUT CRITICAL THEORY?

THE CASE OF HABERMAS AND GENDER

To my mind, no one has yet improved on Marx's 1843 definition of Critical Theory as "the self-clarification of the struggles and wishes of the age."[1] What is so appealing about this definition is its straightforwardly political character. It makes no claim to any special epistemological status but, rather, supposes that with respect to justification there is no philosophically interesting difference between a critical theory of society and an uncritical one. But there is, according to this definition, an important political difference. A critical social theory frames its research programme and its conceptual framework with an eye to the aims and activities of those oppositional social movements with which it has a partisan though not uncritical identification. The questions it asks and the models it designs are informed by that identification and interest. Thus, for example, if struggles contesting the subordination of women figured among the most significant of a given age, then a critical social theory for that time would aim, among other things, to shed light on the character and bases of such subordination. It would employ categories and explanatory models that revealed rather than occluded relations of male dominance and female subordination. And it would demystify as ideological rival approaches that obfuscated or rationalized those relations. In this situation, then, one of the standards for assessing a critical theory once it had been subjected to all the usual tests of empirical adequacy, would be: how well does it theorize the situation and prospects of the feminist movement? To what extent does it serve the self-clarification of the struggles and wishes of contemporary women?

In what follows,[2] I am going to presuppose the conception of critical theory that I have just outlined. In addition, I am going to take as the actual situation of our age the scenario I just sketched as hypothetical. On the basis of these presuppositions, I want to examine the critical social theory of Jürgen Habermas as elaborated in *The Theory of Communicative Action* and related recent writings.[3] I want to read this work from the standpoint of the following questions: in what proportions and in what respects does Habermas's critical theory clarify and/or mystify the bases of male dominance and female subordination in modern societies? In what proportions and in what respects does it challenge and/or replicate prevalent ideological rationalizations of such dominance and subordination? To what extent does it or can it be made to serve the self-clarification of the struggles and wishes of the contemporary women's movement? In short, with respect to gender, what is critical and what is not in Habermas's social theory?

This would be a fairly straightforward enterprise were it not for one thing. Apart from a brief discussion of feminism as a "new social movement" (a discussion I shall consider anon), Habermas says virtually nothing about gender in *The Theory of Communicative Action*. Now, according to my view of critical theory, this is a serious deficiency. But it need not stand in the way of the sort of inquiry I am proposing. It only necessitates that one read the work in question from the standpoint of an absence; that one extrapolate from things Habermas does say to things he does not; that one reconstruct how various matters of concern to feminists would appear from his perspective had they been thematized.

Thus, in part 1 of this chapter I examine some elements of Habermas's social-theoretical framework in order to see how it tends to cast childrearing and the male-headed, modern, restricted, nuclear family. In part 2, I look at his account of the relations between the public and private spheres of life in classical capitalist societies and try to reconstruct the unthematized gender subtext. And finally, in part 3 I consider Habermas's account of the dynamics, crisis tendencies and conflict potentials specific to contemporary, Western, welfare state capitalism, so as to see in what light it casts contemporary feminist struggles.[4]

1. THE SOCIAL-THEORETICAL FRAMEWORK: A FEMINIST INTERROGATION

Let me begin by considering two distinctions central to Habermas's social-theoretical categorial framework. The first of these is the distinction between the symbolic and the material reproduction of societies. On the one hand, claims Habermas, societies must reproduce themselves materially; they must successfully regulate the metabolic exchange of groups of biological individuals with a nonhuman, physical environment and with other social systems. On the other hand, societies must reproduce themselves symbolically; they must maintain and transmit to new members the linguistically elaborated norms and patterns of interpretation which are constitutive of social identities. Habermas claims that material reproduction comprises what he calls "social labor." Symbolic reproduction, on the other hand, comprises the socialization of the young, the cementing of group solidarity and the transmission and extension of cultural traditions.[5]

This distinction between symbolic and material reproduction is in the first instance a functional one. It distinguishes two different functions which must be fulfilled more or less successfully in order that a society survive. At the same time, however, the distinction is used by Habermas to classify actual social practices and activities. These are distinguished according to which of the two functions they are held to serve exclusively or primarily. Thus, according to Habermas, in capitalist societies, the activities and practices which make up the sphere of paid work count as material reproduction activities since, in his view, they are "social labor" and serve the function of material reproduction. On the other hand, the activities and practices which in our society are performed without pay by women in the domestic sphere—let us call them "women's unpaid childrearing work"—count as symbolic reproduction activities since, in Habermas's view, they serve socialization and the function of symbolic reproduction.[6]

It is worth noting, I think, that Habermas's distinction between symbolic and material reproduction is susceptible to two different interpretations. The first of these takes the two functions as two objectively distinct "natural kinds" to which both actual social practices and the actual organization of activities in any given society may correspond more or less faithfully. Thus, childrearing practices would in themselves be symbolic reproduction practices, while the practices that produce food and objects would in themselves be material reproduction practices. And modern capitalist social organization, unlike, say, that of archaic societies, would be a faithful mirror of the distinction between the two natural kinds, since it separates these practices institutionally. This "natural kinds" interpretation is at odds with another possible interpretation, which I shall call the "pragmatic-contextual" interpretation. It would not take childrearing practices to be in themselves symbolic reproduction practices but would allow for the possibility that, under certain circumstances and given certain purposes, it could be useful to consider them from the standpoint of symbolic reproduction—for example, if one wished to contest the dominant view, in a sexist political culture, according to which this traditionally female occupation is merely instinctual, natural and ahistorical.

Now I want to argue that the natural kinds interpretation is conceptually inadequate and potentially ideological. I claim that it is not the case that childrearing practices serve symbolic as opposed to material reproduction. Granted, they regulate children's interactions with other people, but also their interactions with physical nature (in the form, for example, of milk, germs, dirt, excrement, weather and animals). In short, not just the construction of children's social identities but also their biological survival is at stake. And so, therefore, is the biological survival of the societies they belong to. Thus, childrearing is not *per se* symbolic reproduction activity; it is equally and at the same time material reproduction activity. It is what we might call a "dual-aspect" activity.[7]

But the same is true of the activities institutionalized in modern capitalist paid work. Granted, the production of food and objects contributes to the biological survival of members of society. But it also and at the same time reproduces social identities. Not just nourishment and shelter *simpliciter* are produced, but culturally elaborated forms of nourishment and shelter which have symbolically mediated social meanings. Moreover, such production occurs via culturally elaborated social relations and symbolically mediated, norm-governed social practices. The contents of these practices as well as the results serve to form, maintain and modify the social identities of persons directly involved and indirectly affected. One need only think of an activity like computer programming for a wage in the US pharmaceutical industry to appreciate the thoroughly symbolic character of "social labor." Thus, such labor, like unpaid childrearing work, is a "dual-aspect" activity.[8]

Thus, the distinction between women's unpaid childrearing work and other forms of work from the standpoint of reproduction functions cannot be a distinction of natural kinds. If it is to be drawn at all, it must be drawn as a pragmatic-contextual distinction for the sake of focalizing what is in each case actually only one aspect of a dual-aspect phenomenon. And this, in turn, must find its warrant relative to specific purposes of analysis and description, purposes which are themselves susceptible of analysis and evaluation and which need, therefore, to be justified via argument.

But if this is so, then the natural kinds classification of childrearing as symbolic reproduction and of other work as material reproduction is potentially ideological. It could be used, for example, to legitimize the institutional separation of childrearing from paid work, a separation which many feminists, including myself, consider a mainstay of modern forms of women's subordination. It could be used, in combination with other assumptions, to legitimate the confinement of women to a "separate sphere." Whether Habermas so uses it will be considered shortly.

The second component of Habermas's categorial framework which I want to examine is his distinction between "socially integrated" and "system-integrated action contexts." Socially integrated action contexts are those in which different agents coordinate their actions with one another by reference to some form of explicit or implicit intersubjective consensus about norms, values and ends, consensus predicated on linguistic speech and interpretation. System-integrated action contexts, on the other hand, are those in which the actions of different agents are coordinated with one another by the functional interlacing of unintended consequences, while each individual action is determined by self-interested, utility-maximizing calculations typically entertained in the idioms, or as Habermas says, in the "media" of money and power.[9] Habermas considers the capitalist economic system to be the paradigm case of a system-integrated action context. By contrast, he takes the modern, restricted nuclear family to be a case of a socially integrated action context.[10]

Now this distinction is a rather complex one. It contains six, analytically distinct, conceptual elements: functionality, intentionality, linguisticality, consensuality, normativity and strategicality. However, I am going to set aside the elements of functionality, intentionality, and linguisticality. Following some arguments developed by Thomas McCarthy in another context, I assume that, in both capitalist workplace and modern, restricted, nuclear family, the consequences of actions may be functionally interlaced in ways unintended by agents; that, at the same time, in both contexts agents coordinate their actions with one another consciously and intentionally; and that, in both contexts, agents coordinate their actions with one another in and through language.[11] I assume, therefore, that Habermas's distinction effectively turns on the elements of consensuality, normativity and strategicality.

Once again, I think it useful to distinguish two possible interpretations of Habermas's position. The first takes the contrast between the two kinds of action contexts as registering an absolute difference. Thus, system-integrated contexts would involve absolutely no consensuality or reference to moral norms and values, while socially integrated contexts would involve absolutely no strategic calculations in the media of money and power. This "absolute differences" interpretation is at odds with a second possibility which takes the contrast rather as registering a difference in degree. According to this second interpretation, system-integrated contexts would involve some consensuality and reference to moral norms and values, but less than socially integrated contexts. In the same way, socially integrated contexts would involve some strategic calculations in the media of money and power, but less than system-integrated contexts.

Now I want to argue that the absolute differences interpretation is too extreme to be useful for social theory and that, in addition, it is potentially ideological. In few if any human action contexts are actions coordinated absolutely nonconsensually and absolutely nonnormatively. However morally dubious the consensus, and however problematic the content and status of the norms, virtually every human action context involves some form of both of them. In the capitalist marketplace, for example, strategic, utility-maximizing exchanges occur against a horizon of intersubjectively shared meanings and norms; agents normally subscribe at least tacitly to some commonly held notions of reciprocity and to some shared conceptions about the social meanings of objects, including about what sorts of things are exchangeable. Similarly, in the capitalist workplace, managers and subordinates, as well as co-workers, normally coordinate their actions to some extent consensually and with some explicit or implicit reference to normative assumptions, though the consensus be arrived at unfairly and the norms be incapable of withstanding critical scrutiny.[12] Thus, the capitalist economic system has a moral-cultural dimension.

Similarly, few if any human action contexts are wholly devoid of strategic calculation. Gift rituals in noncapitalist societies, for example, previously taken as veritable crucibles of solidarity, are now widely understood to have a significant stategic, calculative dimension, one enacted in the medium of power, if not in that of money.[13] And, as I shall argue in more detail later, the modern, restricted, nuclear family is not devoid of individual, self-interested, strategic calculations in either medium. These action contexts, then, while not officially counted as economic, have a strategic, economic dimension.

Thus, the absolute differences interpretation is not of much use in social theory. It fails to distinguish, for example, the capitalist economy—let us call it "the official economy"—from the modern, restricted, nuclear family. For both of these institutions are *mélanges* of consensuality, normativity and strategicality. If they are to be distinguished with respect to mode of action-integration, the distinction must be drawn as a difference of degree. It must turn on the place, proportions and interactions of the three elements within each.

But if this is so, then the absolute differences classification of the official economy as a system-integrated action context and of the modern family as a socially integrated action context is potentially ideological. It could be used, for example, to exaggerate the differences and occlude the similarities between the two institutions. It could be used to construct an ideological opposition which posits the family as the "negative," the complementary "other," of the (official) economic sphere, a "haven in a heartless world."

Now which of these possible interpretations of the two distinctions are the operative ones in Habermas's social theory? He asserts that he understands the reproduction distinction according to the pragmatic-contextual interpretation and not the natural kinds.[14] Likewise, he asserts that he takes the action-context distinction to mark a difference in degree, not an absolute difference.[15] However, I propose to bracket these assertions and to examine what Habermas actually does with these distinctions.

Habermas maps the distinction between action contexts onto the distinction between reproduction functions in order to arrive at a definition of societal modernization and at a picture of the institutional structure of modern societies. He holds that modern societies differ from premodern societies in that they split off some material reproduction functions from symbolic ones and hand over the former to two specialized institutions—the (official) economy and state—which are system-integrated. At the same time, modern societies situate these institutions in the larger social environment by developing two other ones which specialize in symbolic reproduction and are socially integrated. These are the modern, restricted, nuclear family or "private sphere" and the space of political participation, debate and opinion formation or "public sphere;" and together, they constitute what Habermas calls the two "institutional orders of the modern lifeworld." Thus, modern societies "uncouple" or separate what Habermas takes to be two distinct, but previously undifferentiated aspects of society: "system" and "lifeworld." And so, in his view, the institutional structure of modern societies is dualistic. On the one side stand the institutional orders of the modern lifeworld, the socially integrated domains specializing in symbolic reproduction, that is, in socialization, solidarity formation and cultural transmission. On the other side stand the systems, the system-integrated domains specializing in material reproduction. On the one side, the nuclear family and the public sphere. On the other side, the (official) capitalist economy and the modern administrative state.[16]

Now what are the critical insights and blind spots of this model? Let us attend first to the question of its empirical adequacy. And let us focus, for the time being, on the contrast between "the private sphere of the lifeworld" and the (official) economic system. Consider that this aspect of Habermas's categorial divide between system and lifeworld institutions faithfully mirrors the institutional separation of family and official economy, household and paid workplace, in male-dominated, capitalist societies. It thus has some *prima facie* purchase on empirical social reality. But consider, too, that the characterization of the family as a socially integrated, symbolic reproduction domain and of the paid workplace, on the other hand, as a system-integrated material reproduction domain tends to exaggerate the differences and occlude the similarities between them. For example, it directs attention away from the fact that the household, like the paid workplace, is a site of labor, albeit of unremunerated and often unrecognized labor. Likewise, it does not make visible the fact that in the paid workplace, as in the household, women are assigned to, indeed ghettoized in, distinctively feminine, service-oriented and often sexualized occupations. Finally, it fails to focalize the fact that in both spheres women are subordinated to men.

Moreover, this characterization presents the male-headed nuclear family, *qua* socially integrated institutional order of the modern lifeworld, as having only an extrinsic and incidental relation to money and power. These "media" are taken as definitive of interactions in the official economy and state administration but as only incidental to intrafamilial ones. But this assumption is counterfactual. Feminists have shown via empirical analyses of contemporary familial decision-making, handling of finances and wife-battering that families are thoroughly permeated with, in Habermas's terms, the media of money and power. They are sites of egocentric, strategic and instrumental calculation as well as sites of usually exploitative exchanges of services, labor, cash and sex, not to mention sites, frequently, of coercion and violence.[17] But Habermas's way of contrasting the modern family with the official capitalist economy tends to occlude all this. It overstates the differences between these institutions and blocks the possibility of analyzing families as economic systems, that is, as sites of labor, exchange, calculation, distribution and exploitation. Or, to the degree that Habermas would acknowledge that they can be seen that way too, his framework would suggest that this is due to the intrusion or invasion of alien forces; to the "colonization" of the family by the (official) economy and the state. This, too, however, is a dubious proposition. I shall discuss it in detail in part 3 below.

Thus Habermas's model has some empirical deficiencies. It is not easily able to focalize some dimensions of male dominance in modern societies. On the other hand, his framework does offer a conceptual resource suitable for understanding *other* aspects of modern male dominance. Consider that Habermas subdivides the category of socially integrated action-contexts into two subcategories. On the one hand, there are "normatively secured" forms of socially integrated action. These are actions coordinated on the basis of a conventional, prereflective, taken-for-granted consensus about values and ends, consensus rooted in the precritical internationalization of socialization and cultural tradition. On the other hand, there are "communicatively achieved" forms of socially integrated action. These involve actions coordinated on the basis of explicit, reflectively achieved consensus, consensus reached by unconstrained discussion under conditions of freedom, equality and fairness.[18] This distinction, which is a subdistinction within the category of socially integrated action, provides Habermas with some critical resources for analyzing the modern, restricted, male-headed nuclear family. Such families can be understood as normatively secured rather than communicatively achieved action contexts, that is, as contexts where actions are (sometimes) mediated by consensus and shared values, but where such consensus is suspect because prereflective or because achieved through dialogue vitiated by unfairness, coercion or inequality.

To what extent does the distinction between normatively secured and communicatively achieved action contexts succeed in overcoming the problems discussed earlier? Only partially, I think. On the one hand, this distinction is a morally significant and empirically useful one. The notion of a normatively secured action context fits nicely with recent research on patterns of communication between husbands and wives. This research shows that men tend to control conversations, determining what topics are pursued, while women do more "interaction work" like asking questions and providing verbal support.[19] Research also reveals differences in men's and women's uses of the bodily and gestural dimensions of speech, differences that confirm men's dominance and women's subordination.[20] Thus, Habermas's distinction enables us to capture something important about intrafamilial dynamics. What is insufficiently stressed, however, is that actions coordinated by normatively secured consensus in the male-headed, nuclear family are actions regulated by power. It seems to me a grave mistake to restrict the use of the term "power" to bureaucratic contexts. Habermas would be better to distinguish different kinds of power, for example, domestic-patriarchical power, on the one hand, and bureaucratic-patriarchical power on the other, not to mention various others kinds.

But even that distinction does not by itself suffice to make Habermas's framework fully adequate to all the empirical forms of male dominance in modern societies. For normative-domestic-patriarchical power is only one of the elements which enforce women's subordination in the domestic sphere. To capture the others would require a social-theoretical framework capable of analyzing families also as economic systems involving the appropriation of women's unpaid labor and interlocking in complex ways with other economic systems involving paid work. Because Habermas's framework draws the major categorial divide between system and lifeworld institutions, and hence between (among other things) official economy and family, it is not very well suited to that task.

Let me turn now from the question of the empirical adequacy of Habermas's model to the question of its normative political implications. What sorts of social arrangements and transformations does his modernization conception tend to legitimize? And what sorts does it tend to rule out? Here it will be necessary to reconstruct some implications of the model which are not explicitly thematized by Habermas.

Consider that the conception of modernization as the uncoupling of system and lifeworld institutions tends to legitimize the modern institutional separation of family and official economy, childrearing and paid work. For Habermas claims that there is an asymmetry between symbolic and material reproduction with respect to system integration. Symbolic reproduction activities, he claims, are unlike material reproduction activities, in that they cannot be turned over to specialized, system-integrated institutions set apart from the lifeworld. Their inherently symbolic character requires that they be socially integrated.[21] It follows that women's unpaid childrearing work could not be incorporated into the (official) economic system without "pathological" results. On the other hand, Habermas also holds that the differentiation of system-integrated institutions handling material reproduction functions is a mark of societal rationalization. The separation of a specialized (official) economic system enhances a society's capacity to deal with its natural and social environment. "System complexity," then, constitutes a "developmental advance."[22] It follows that the (official) economic system of paid work could not be dedifferentiated with respect to, say, childrearing, without societal "regression." But if childrearing could not be non-pathologically incorporated into the (official) economic system, and if the (official) economic system could not be nonregressively dedifferentiated, then the continued separation of childrearing from paid work would be required.

Now this amounts to a defense of one aspect of what feminists call "the separation of public and private," namely, the separation of the official economic sphere from the domestic sphere and the enclaving of childrearing from the rest of social labor. It amounts, that is, to a defense of an institutional arrangement which is widely held to be one, if not the, linchpin of modern women's subordination. And it should be noted that the fact that Habermas is a socialist does not alter the matter. For the (undeniably desirable) elimination of private ownership, profit-orientation and hierarchical command in paid work would not of itself affect the official-economic/domestic separation.

Now I want to challenge several premises of the reasoning I have just reconstructed. First, this reasoning assumes the natural kinds interpretation of the symbolic vs. material reproduction distinction. But since, as I have argued, childrearing is a dual-aspect activity, and since it is not categorially different in this respect from other work, there is no warrant for the claim of an asymmetry *vis-à-vis* system integration. That is, there is no warrant for assuming that the system-integrated organization of childrearing would be any more (or less) pathological than that of other work. Second, this reasoning assumes the absolute differences interpretation of the social vs. system-integration distinction. But since, as I have argued, the modern, male-headed, nuclear family is a *mélange* of (normatively secured) consensuality, normativity and strategicality, and since it is in this respect not categorially different from the paid workplace, then privatized childrearing is already, to a not insignificant extent, permeated by the media of money and power. Moreover, there is no empirical evidence that children raised in commercial day-care centers (even profit-based or corporate ones) turn out any more pathological than those raised, say, in suburban homes by full-time mothers. Third, the reasoning just sketched elevates system complexity to the status of an overriding consideration with effective veto-power over proposed social transformations aimed at overcoming women's subordination. But this is at odds with Habermas's professions that system complexity is only one measure of "progress" among others.[23] More importantly, it is at odds with any reasonable standard of justice.

What, then, should we conclude about the normative, political implications of Habermas's model? If the conception of modernization as the uncoupling of system and lifeworld institutions does indeed have the implications I have just drawn from it, then it is in important respects androcentric and ideological.

2. PUBLIC AND PRIVATE IN CLASSICAL CAPITALISM: THEMATIZING THE GENDER SUBTEXT

The foregoing difficulties notwithstanding, Habermas offers an account of the inter-institutional relations among various spheres of public and private life in classical capitalism which has some genuine critical potential. But in order to realize this potential fully, we need to reconstruct the unthematized gender subtext of his material.

Let me return to his conception of the way in which the (official) economic and state systems are situated with respect to the lifeworld. Habermas holds that with modernization, the (official) economic and state systems are not simply disengaged or detached from the lifeworld; they must also be related to and embedded in it. Concomitant with the beginnings of classical capitalism, then, is the development *within* the lifeworld of "institutional orders" that situate the systems in a context of everyday meanings and norms. The lifeworld, as we saw, gets differentiated into two spheres that provide appropriate complementary environments for the two systems. The "private sphere" or modern, restricted, nuclear family is linked to the (official) economic system. The "public sphere" or space of political participation, debate and opinion formation is linked to the state-administrative system. The family is linked to the (official) economy by means of a series of exchanges conducted in the medium of money; it supplies the (official) economy with appropriately socialized labor power in exchange for wages; and it provides appropriate, monetarily measured demand for commodified goods and services. Exchanges between family and (official) economy, then, are channeled through the "roles" of worker and consumer. Parallel exchange processes link the "public sphere" and the state system. These, however, are conducted chiefly in the medium of power. Loyalty, obedience and tax revenues are exchanged for "organizational results" and "political decisions." Exchanges between public sphere and state, then, are channeled through the "role" of citizen and, in late welfare capitalism, that of client.[24]

This account of interinstitutional relations in classical capitalism has a number of important advantages. First, it treats the modern, restricted, nuclear family as a historically emergent institution with its own positive, determinate features. And it specifies that this type of family emerges concomitantly with and in relation to the emerging capitalist economy, administrative state and (eventually) the political public sphere. Moreover, it charts some of the dynamics of exchange among these institutions. And it indicates some way in which they are fitted to the needs of one another so as to accommodate the exchanges among them.

Finally, Habermas's account offers an important corrective to the standard dualistic approaches to the separation of public and private in capitalist societies. He conceptualizes the problem as a relation among four terms: family, (official) economy, state and "public sphere." His view suggests that in classical capitalism there are actually two distinct but interrelated public-private separations. There is one public-private separation at the level of "systems," namely, the separation of the state or public system from the (official) capitalist economy or private system. There is another public-private separation at the level of the "lifeworld," namely, the separation of the family or private lifeworld sphere from the space of political opinion formation and participation or public lifeworld sphere. Moreover, each of these public-private separations is coordinated with the other. One axis of exchange runs between private system and private lifeworld sphere, that is, between (official) capitalist economy and modern, restricted, nuclear family. Another axis of exchange runs between public system and public lifeworld sphere or between state administration and the organs of public opinion and will formation. In both cases, the exchanges can occur because of the institutionalization of specific roles that connect the domains in question. Thus, the roles of worker and consumer link the (official) private economy and the private economy and the private family, while the roles of citizen and (later) client link the public state and the public opinion institutions.

Thus, Habermas provides an extremely sophisticated account of the relations between public and private institutions in classical capitalist societies. At the same time, however, his account has some weaknesses. Many of these stem from his failure to thematize the gender subtext of the relations and arrangements he describes.[25] Consider, first, the relations between (official) private economy and private family as mediated by the roles of worker and consumer. These roles, I submit, are gendered roles. And the links they forge between family and (official) economy are adumbrated as much in the medium of gender identity as in the medium of money.

Take the role of the worker.[26] In male-dominated, classical capitalist societies, this role is a masculine role and not just in the relatively superficial statistical sense. There is rather a very deep sense in which masculine identity in these societies is bound up with the breadwinner role. Masculinity is in large part a matter of leaving home each day for a place of paid work and returning with a wage that provides for one's dependents. It is this internal relation between being a man and being a provider which explains why in capitalist societies unemployment can be so psychologically, as well as economically, devastating for men. It also sheds light on the centrality of the struggle for a "family wage" in the history of the workers' and trade union movements of the nineteenth and twentieth centuries. This was a struggle for a wage conceived not as a payment to a genderless individual for the use of labor power, but rather as a payment to a man for the support of his economically dependent wife and children. A conception, of course, which legitimized the practice of paying women less for equal or comparable work.

The masculine subtext of the worker role is confirmed by the vexed and strained character of women's relation to paid work in male-dominated classical capitalism. As Carole Pateman puts it, it is not that women are absent from the paid workplace; it's rather that they are present differently[27]—for example, as feminized and sometimes sexualized "service" workers (secretaries, domestic workers, salespersons, prostitutes and more recently, flight attendants); as members of the "helping professions" utilizing mothering skills (nurses, social workers, childcare workers, primary school teachers); as targets of sexual harassment; as low-waged, low-skilled, low-status workers in sex-segregated occupations; as part-time workers; as workers who work a double shift (both unpaid domestic labor and paid labor); as "working wives" and "working mothers", i.e. as primarily wives and mothers who happen, secondarily, also to "go out to work"; as "supplemental earners." These differences in the quality of women's presence in the paid workplace testify to the conceptual dissonance between femininity and the worker role in classical capitalism. And this in turn confirms the masculine subtext of that role. It confirms that the role of the worker, which links the private (official) economy and the private family in male-dominated, capitalist societies, is a masculine role; and that, *pace* Habermas, the link it forges is elaborated as much in the medium of masculine gender identity as in the medium of gender-neutral money.

Conversely, the other role linking official economy and family in Habermas's scheme has a feminine subtext. The consumer, after all, is the worker's companion and helpmate in classical capitalism. For the sexual division of domestic labor assigns to women the work—and it is indeed work, though unpaid and usually unrecognized work—of purchasing and preparing goods and services for domestic consumption. You can confirm this even today by visiting any supermarket or department store. Or by looking at the history of consumer-goods advertising. Such advertising has nearly always interpellated its subject,[28] the consumer, as feminine. In fact, it has elaborated an entire phantasmatics of desire premised on the femininity of the subject of consumption. It is only relatively recently, and with some difficulty, that advertisers have devised ways of interpellating a masculine subject of consumption. The trick was to find means of positioning a male consumer which did not feminize, emasculate or sissify him. In *The Hearts of Men*, Barbara Ehrenreich quite shrewdly, I think, credits *Playboy* magazine with pioneering such means.[29] But the difficulty and lateness of the project confirm the gendered character of the consumer role in classical capitalism. Men occupy it with conceptual strain and cognitive dissonance, much as women occupy the role of worker. So the role of consumer linking official economy and family is a feminine role. *Pace* Habermas, it forges the link in the medium of feminine gender identity as much as in the apparently gender-neutral medium of money.

Moreover, Habermas's account of the roles linking family and (official) economy contains a significant omission. There is no mention in his schema of any childrearer role, although the material clearly requires one. For who else is performing the unpaid work of overseeing the production of the "appropriately socialized labor power" which the family exchanges for wages? Of course, the childrearer role in classical capitalism (or elsewhere) is patently a feminine role. Its omission here is a mark of androcentrism, and it has some significant consequences. A consideration of the childrearer role in this context might well have pointed to the central relevance of gender to the institutional structure of classical capitalism. And this in turn could have led to the disclosure of the gender subtext of the other roles and of the importance of gender identity as an "exchange medium."

What, then, of the other set of roles and linkages identified by Habermas? What of the citizen role which he claims connects the public system of the administrative state with the public lifeworld sphere of political opinion and will formation? This role, too, is a gendered role in classical capitalism, indeed, a masculine role.[30] And not simply in the sense that women did not win the vote in, for example, the US and Britain until the twentieth century. Rather, the lateness and difficulty of that victory are symptomatic of deeper strains. As Habermas understands it, the citizen is centrally a participant in political debate and public opinion formation. This means that citizenship, in his view, depends crucially on the capacities for consent and speech, the ability to participate on a par with others in dialogue. But these are capacities that are connected with masculinity in male-dominated, classical capitalism. They are capacities that are in myriad ways denied to women and deemed at odds with femininity. I have already cited studies about the effects of male dominance and female subordination on the dynamics of dialogue. Now consider that even today in most jurisdictions there is no such thing as marital rape. That is, a wife is legally subject to her husband; she is not an individual who can give or withhold consent to his demands for sexual access. Consider also that even outside of marriage the legal test of rape often boils down to whether a "reasonable man" would have assumed that the woman had consented. Consider what that means when both popular and legal opinion widely holds that when a woman says "no" she means "yes." It means, says Carole Pateman, that "women find their speech . . . persistently and systematically invalidated in the crucial matter of consent, a matter that is fundamental to democracy. [But] if women's words about consent are consistently reinterpreted, how can they participate in the debate among citizens?"[31]

Thus, there is conceptual dissonance between femininity and the dialogical capacities central to Habermas's conception of citizenship. And there is another aspect of citizenship not discussed by him that is even more obviously bound up with masculinity. I mean the soldiering aspect of citizenship, the conception of the citizen as the defender of the polity and protector of those—women, children, the elderly—who allegedly cannot protect themselves. As Judith Stiehm has argued, this division between male protectors and female protected introduces further dissonance into women's relation to citizenship.[32] It confirms the gender subtext of the citizen role.

And the view of women as in need of men's protection "underlies access not just to . . . the means of destruction, but also [to] the means of production—witness all the 'protective' legislation that has surrounded women's access to the workplace—and [to] the means of reproduction, [—witness] women's status as wives and sexual partners."[33]

Thus, the citizen role in male-dominated classical capitalism is a masculine role. It links the state and the public sphere, as Habermas claims. But it also links these to the official economy and the family. And in every case the links are forged in the medium of masculine gender identity rather than, as Habermas has it, in the medium of a gender-neutral power. Or, if the medium of exchange here is power, then the power in question is masculine power. It is power as the expression of masculinity.

Thus, there are some major lacunae in Habermas's otherwise powerful and sophisticated model of the relations between public and private institutions in classical capitalism. The gender blindness of the model occludes important features of the arrangements he wants to understand. By omitting any mention of the childrearer role, and by failing to thematize the gender subtext underlying the roles of worker and consumer, Habermas fails to understand precisely how the capitalist workplace is linked to the modern, restricted, male-headed, nuclear family. Similarly, by failing to thematize the masculine subtext of the citizen role, he misses the full meaning of the way the state is linked to the public sphere of political speech. Moreover, Habermas misses important cross-connections among the four elements of his two public-private schemata. He misses, for example, the way the masculine citizen-soldier-protector role links the state and public sphere not only to one another but also to the family and to the paid workplace, that is, the way the assumptions of man's capacity to protect and women's need of man's protection run through all of them. He misses, too, the way the masculine citizen-speaker role links the state and public sphere not only to one another but also to the family and official economy, that is, the way the assumptions of man's capacity to speak and consent and women's incapacity therein run through all of them. He misses, also, the way the masculine worker-breadwinner role links the family and official economy not only to one another but also to the state and the political public sphere, that is, the way the assumptions of man's provider status and of woman's dependent status run through all of them, so that even the coin in which classical capitalist wages and taxes are paid is not gender-neutral. And he misses, finally, the way the feminine childrearer role links all four institutions to one another by overseeing the construction of the masculine- and feminine-gendered subjects needed to fill *every* role in classical capitalism.

Once the gender-blindness of Habermas's model is overcome, however, all these connections come into view. It then becomes clear that feminine and masculine gender identity run like pink and blue threads through the areas of paid work, state administration and citizenship as well as through the domain of familial and sexual relations. This is to say that gender identity is lived out in all arenas of life. It is one (if not the) "medium of exchange" among all of them, a basic element of the social glue that binds them to one another.

Moreover, a gender-sensitive reading of these connection has some important theoretical and conceptual implications. It reveals that male dominance is intrinsic rather than accidental to classical capitalism. For the institutional structure of this social formation is actualized by means of gendered roles. It follows that the forms of male dominance at issue here are not properly understood as lingering forms of premodern status inequality. They are, rather, intrinsically modern in Habermas's sense, since they are premised on the separation of waged labor and the state from female childrearing and the household. It also follows that a critical social theory of capitalist societies needs gender-sensitive categories. The foregoing analysis shows that, contrary to the usual androcentric understanding, the relevant concepts of worker, consumer and wage are not, in fact, strictly economic concepts. Rather, they have an implicit gender subtext and thus are "gender-economic" concepts. Likewise, the relevant concept of citizenship is not strictly a political concept; it has an implicit gender subtext and so, rather, is a "gender-political" concept. Thus, this analysis reveals the inadequacy of those critical theories that treat gender as incidental to politics and political economy. It highlights the need for a critical-theoretical categorial framework in which gender, politics and political economy are internally integrated.[34]

In addition, a gender-sensitive reading of these arrangements reveals the thoroughly multidirectional character of social motion and causal influence in classical capitalism. It reveals, that is, the inadequacy of the orthodox Marxist assumption that all or most significant causal influence runs from the (official) economy to the family and not vice versa. It shows that gender identity structures paid work, state administration and political participation. Thus, it vindicates Habermas's claim that in classical capitalism the (official) economy is not all-powerful but is, rather, in some significant measure inscribed within and subject to the norms and meanings of everyday life. Of course, Habermas assumed that in making this claim he was saying something more or less positive. The norms and meanings he had in mind were not the ones I have been discussing. Still, the point is a valid one. It remains to be seen, though, whether it holds also for late welfare capitalism, as I believe; or whether it ceases to hold, as Habermas claims.

Finally, this reconstruction of the gender subtext of Habermas's model has normative political implications. It suggests that an emancipatory transformation of male-dominated capitalist societies, early and late, requires a transformation of these gendered roles and of the institutions they mediate. As long as the worker and childrearer roles are such as to be fundamentally incompatible with one another, it will not be possible to universalize either of them to include both genders. Thus, some form of dedifferentation of unpaid childrearing and waged work is required. Similarly, as long as the citizen role is defined to encompass death-dealing soldiering but not life-fostering childrearing, as long as it is tied to male-dominated modes of dialogue, then it, too, will remain incapable of including women, fully. Thus, changes in the very concepts of citizenship, childrearing and unpaid work are necessary, as are changes in the relationships among the domestic, official-economic, state and political-public spheres.

3. THE DYNAMICS OF WELFARE CAPITALISM: A FEMINIST CRITIQUE

Let me turn, then, to Habermas's account of late welfare capitalism. Unlike his account of classical capitalism, its critical potential cannot be released simply by reconstructing the unthematized gender subtext. Here, the problematical features of his social-theoretical framework tend to inflect the analysis as a whole and diminish its capacity to illuminate the struggles and wishes of contemporary women. In order to show how this is the case, I shall present Habermas's view in the form of six theses.

1. Welfare capitalism emerges as a result of and in response to instabilities of crisis tendencies inherent in classical capitalism. It realigns the relations between the (official) economy and state, that is, between the private and public systems. These become more deeply intertwined with one another as the state actively assumes the task of "crisis management." It tries to avert or manage economic crises by Keynesian "market-replacing" strategies which create a "public sector." And it tries to avert or manage social and political crises by "market-compensating" measures, including welfare concessions to trade unions and social movements. Thus welfare capitalism partially overcomes the separation of public and private at the level of systems.[35]

2. The realignment of (official) economy-state relations is accompanied by a change in the relations of those systems to the private and public spheres of the lifeworld. First, with respect to the private sphere, there is a major increase in the importance of the consumer role as paid work-related dissatisfactions are compensated by enhanced commodity consumption. Second, with respect to the public sphere, there is a major decline in the importance of the citizen role as journalism becomes mass media, political parties are bureaucratized and participation is reduced to occasional voting. Instead, the relation to the state is increasingly channeled through a new role, the social-welfare client.[36]

3. These developments are "ambivalent." On the one hand, there are gains in freedom with the institution of new social rights limiting the heretofore unrestrained power of capital in the (paid) workplace and of the paterfamilias in the bourgeois family; and social insurance programs represent a clear advance over the paternalism of poor relief. On the other hand, the means employed to realize these new social rights tend perversely to endanger freedom. These means are bureaucratic procedure and the money form. They structure the entitlements, benefits and social services of the welfare system. And in so doing, they disempower clients, rendering them dependent on bureaucracies and therapeutocracies, and preempting their capacities to interpret their own needs, experiences and life-problems.[37]

4. The most ambivalent welfare measures are those concerned with things like health care, care of the elderly, education and family law. For when bureaucratic and monetary media structure these things, they intrude upon "core domains" of the lifeworld. They turn over symbolic reproduction functions like socialization and

solidarity formation to system-integration mechanisms that position people as strategically-acting, self-interested monads. But given the inherently symbolic character of these functions, and given their internal relation to social integration, the results, necessarily, are "pathological." Thus, these measures are more ambivalent than, say, reforms of the paid workplace. The latter bear on a domain that is already system integrated via money and power and which serves material as opposed to symbolic reproduction functions. So paid workplace reforms, unlike, say, family law reforms, do not necessarily generate "pathological" side-effects.[38]

5. Welfare capitalism thus gives rise to an "inner colonization of the lifeworld." Money and power cease to be mere media of exchange *between* system and lifeworld. Instead, they tend increasingly to penetrate the lifeworld's *internal* dynamics. The private and public spheres cease to subordinate (official) economic and administrative systems to the norms, values and interpretations of everyday life. Rather, the latter are increasingly subordinated to the imperatives of the (official) economy and administration. The roles of worker and citizen cease to channel the influence of the lifeworld to the systems. Instead, the newly inflated roles of consumer and client channel the influence of the system to the lifeworld. Moreover, the intrusion of system-integration mechanisms into domains inherently requiring social integration gives rise to "reification phenomena." The affected domains are detached not merely from traditional, normatively secured consensus, but from "value-orientations *per se*." The result is the "dessication of communicative contexts" and the "depletion of the nonrenewable cultural resources" needed to maintain personal and collective identity. Thus, symbolic reproduction is destabilized, identities are threatened and social crisis tendencies develop.[39]

6. The colonization of the lifeworld sparks new forms of social conflict specific to welfare capitalism. "New social movements" emerge in a "new conflict zone" at the "seam of system and lifeworld." They respond to system-induced identity threats by contesting the roles that transmit these. They contest the instrumentalization of professional labor and the performatization of education transmitted via the worker role; the monetarization of relations and life-styles transmitted via the inflated consumer role; the bureaucratization of services and life-problems transmitted via the client role; and the rules and routines of interest politics transmitted via the impoverished citizen role. Thus, the conflicts at the cutting edge of developments in welfare capitalism differ both from class struggles and from bourgeois liberation struggles. They respond to crisis tendencies in symbolic as opposed to material reproduction; and they contest reification and "the grammar of forms of life" as opposed to distribution or status inequality.[40]

The various new social movements can be classified with respect to their emancipatory potential. The criterion is the extent to which they advance a genuinely emancipatory resolution of welfare capitalist crisis, namely, the "decolonization of the lifeworld." Decolonization encompasses three things: first, the removal of system-integration mechanisms from symbolic reproduction spheres; second, the replacement of (some) normatively secured contexts by communicatively achieved ones; and third, the development of new, democratic institutions capable of asserting lifeworld control over state and (official) economic systems. Thus, those movements like religious fundamentalism, which seek to defend traditional lifeworld norms against system intrusions, are not genuinely emancipatory; they actively oppose the second element of decolonization and do not take up the third. Movements like peace and ecology are better; they aim both to resist system intrusions and also to instate new, reformed, communicatively achieved zones of interaction. But even these are "ambiguous" inasmuch as they tend to "retreat" into alternative communities and "particularistic" identities, thereby effectively renouncing the third element of decolonization and leaving the (official) economic and state systems unchecked. In this respect, they are more symptomatic than emancipatory; they express the identity disturbances caused by colonization. The feminist movement, on the other hand, represents something of an anomaly. For it alone is "offensive," aiming to "conquer new territory"; and it alone retains links to historic liberation movements. In principle, then, feminism remains rooted in "universalist morality." Yet it is linked to resistance movements by an element of "particularism." And it tends, at times, to "retreat" into identities and communities organized around the natural category of biological sex.[41]

Now what are the critical insights and blind spots of this account of the dynamics of welfare capitalism? To what extent does it serve the self-clarification of the struggles and wishes of contemporary women? I shall take up the six theses one by one.

1. Habermas's first thesis is straightforward and unobjectionable. Clearly, the welfare state does engage in crisis-management and does partially overcome the separation of public and private at the level of systems.

2. Habermas's second thesis contains some important insights. Clearly, welfare capitalism does inflate the consumer role and deflate the citizen role, reducing the latter essentially to voting—and, we should add, also to soldiering. Moreover, the welfare state does indeed increasingly position its subjects as clients. On the other hand, Habermas again fails to see the gender subtext to these developments. He fails to see that the new client role has a gender, that it is a paradigmatically feminine role. He overlooks that it is overwhelmingly women who are the clients of the welfare state: especially older women, poor women, single women with children. He overlooks, in addition, that many welfare systems are internally dualized and gendered. They include two basic kinds of programs: "masculine" ones tied to primary labor-force participation and designed to benefit principal breadwinners; and "feminine" ones oriented to what are understood as domestic "failures," that is, to families without a male breadwinner. Not surprisingly, these two welfare subsystems are both separate and unequal. Clients of feminine programs, virtually exclusively women and their children, are positioned in a distinctive, feminizing fashion as the "negatives of

possessive individuals:" they are largely excluded from the market both as workers and as consumers and are familialized, that is, made to claim benefits not as individuals but as members of "defective" households. They are also stigmatized, denied rights, subjected to surveillance and administrative harassment and generally made into abject dependents of state bureaucracies.[42] But this means that the rise of the client role in welfare capitalism has a more complex meaning than Habermas allows. It is not only a change in the link between system and lifeworld institutions. It is also a change in the character of male dominance, a shift, in Carol Brown's phrase, "from private patriarchy to public patriarchy."[43]

3. This gives a rather different twist to the meaning of Habermas's third thesis. It suggests that he is right about the "ambivalence" of welfare capitalism, but not quite and not only in the way he thought. It suggests that welfare measures do have a positive side in so far as they reduce women's dependence on an individual male breadwinner. But they also have a negative side in so far as they substitute dependence on a patriarchal and androcentric state bureaucracy. The benefits provided are, as Habermas says, "system-conforming" ones. But the system they conform to is not adequately characterized as the system of the official, state-regulated capitalist economy. It is also the system of male dominance which extends even to the sociocultural lifeworld. In other words, the ambivalence here does not only stem, as Habermas implies, from the fact that the role of client carries effects of "reification." It stems also from the fact that this role, *qua* feminine role, perpetuates in a new, let us say "modernized" and "rationalized" form, women's subordination. Or so Habermas's third thesis might be rewritten in a feminist critical theory. Without, of course, abandoning his insights into the ways in which welfare bureaucracies and therapeutocracies disempower clients by preempting their capacities to interpret their own needs, experiences and life-problems.

4. Habermas's fourth thesis, by contrast, is not so easily rewritten. This thesis states that welfare reforms of, for example, the domestic sphere are more ambivalent than reforms of the paid workplace. This is true empirically in the sense I have just described. But it is due to the patriarchal character of welfare systems, not to the inherently symbolic character of lifeworld institutions, as Habermas claims. His claim depends on two assumptions I have already challenged. First, it depends on the natural kinds interpretation of the distinction between symbolic and material reproduction activities, i.e. on the false assumption that childrearing is inherently more symbolic and less material than other work. And second, it depends upon the absolute differences interpretation of the system vs. socially integrated context distinction, i.e. on the false assumption that money and power are not already entrenched in the internal dynamics of the family. But once we repudiate these assumptions, then there is no categorial, as opposed to empirical, basis for differentially evaluating the two kinds of reforms. If it is basically progressive that paid workers acquire the means to confront their employers strategically and match power against power, right against right, then it must be just as basically progressive *in principle* that women acquire

similar means to similar ends in the politics of familial and personal life. And if it is "pathological" that, in the course of achieving a better balance of power in familial and personal life, women become clients of state bureaucracies, then it must be just as "pathological" *in principle* that, in the course of achieving a similar end at paid work, paid workers, too, become clients, which does not alter the fact that *in actuality* they become two different sorts of client. But of course the real point is that the term "pathological" is misused here in so far as it supposes the untenable assumption of an asymmetry between childrearing and other work with respect to system integration.

5. This sheds new light as well on Habermas's fifth thesis. This thesis states that welfare capitalism inaugurates an inner colonization of the lifeworld by systems. It depends on three assumptions. The first two of these are the two just rejected, namely, the natural kinds interpretation of the distinction between symbolic and material reproduction activities and the assumed virginity of the domestic sphere with respect to money and power. The third assumption is that the basic vector of motion in late capitalist society is from state-regulated economy to lifeworld and not vice versa. But the feminine gender subtext of the client role contradicts this assumption. It suggests that even in late capitalism the norms and meanings of gender identity continue to channel the influence of the lifeworld onto systems. These norms continue to structure the state-regulated economy, as the persistence, indeed exacerbation, of labor-force segmentation according to sex shows.[44] And these norms also structure state administration, as the gender segmentation of US and European social welfare systems shows.[45] Thus, it is not the case that in late capitalism "system intrusions" detach life contexts from "value-orientations *per se*." On the contrary, welfare capitalism simply uses other means to uphold the familiar "normatively secured consensus" concerning male dominance and female subordination. But Habermas's theory overlooks this countermotion from lifeworld to system. Thus, it posits the evil of welfare capitalism as the evil of a general and indiscriminate reification. So it fails to account for that fact that it is disproportionately women who suffer the effects of bureaucratization and monetarization. And for the fact that, viewed structurally, bureaucratization and monetarization are, among other things, instruments of women's subordination.

6. This entails the revision, as well, of Habermas's sixth thesis. This thesis concerns the causes, character and emancipatory potential of social movements, including feminism, in welfare capitalist societies. Since these issues are so central to the concerns of this chapter, they warrant a more extended discussion.

Habermas explains the existence and character of new social movements, including feminism, in terms of colonization, that is, in terms of the intrusion of system-interpretation mechanisms in symbolic reproduction spheres and the consequent erosion and desiccation of contexts of interpretation and communication. But given the multidirectionality of causal influence in welfare capitalism, the terms "colonization," "intrusion," "erosion," and "desiccation" are too negative and one-sided to account for the identity shifts manifested in social movements. Let me attempt an alternative explanation, at least for women, by returning to Habermas's important insight that much contemporary contestation surrounds the institution-mediating roles of worker, consumer, citizen and client. Let me add to these the childrearer role and the fact that all of them are gendered roles. Now consider in this light the meaning of the experience of millions of women, especially married women and women with children, who have in the postwar period become paid workers and/or social/welfare clients. I have already indicated that this has been an experience of new, acute forms of domination. But it has also been an experience in which women could, often for the first time, taste the possibilities of a measure of relative economic independence, an identity outside the domestic sphere and expanded political participation. Above all, it has been an experience of conflict and contradiction as women try to do the impossible, namely, to juggle simultaneously the existing roles of childrearer and worker, client and citizen. The cross-pulls of these mutually incompatible roles have been painful and identity-threatening, but not simply negative.[46] Interpellated simultaneously in contradictory ways, women have become split subjects; and, as a result, the roles themselves, previously shielded in their separate spheres, have suddenly been opened to contestation. Should we, like Habermas, speak here of a "crisis in symbolic reproduction?" Surely not, if this means the desiccation of meaning and values wrought by the intrusion of money and organizational power into women's lives. Emphatically yes, if it means, rather, the emergence into visibility and contestability of problems and possibilities that cannot be solved or realized within the established framework of gendered roles and institutions.

If colonization is not an adequate explanation of contemporary feminism (and other new social movements), then decolonization cannot be an adequate conception of an emancipatory solution. From the perspective I have been sketching, the first element of decolonization, namely, the removal of system-integration mechanisms from symbolic reproduction spheres, is conceptually and empirically askew of the real issues. If the real point is the moral superiority of cooperative and egalitarian interactions over strategic and hierarchical ones, then it mystifies matters to single out lifeworld institutions—the point should hold for paid work and political administration as well as for domestic life. Similarly, the third element of decolonization, namely, the reversal of the direction of influence and control from system to lifeworld, needs modification. Since the social meanings of gender still structure late capitalist official economic and state systems, the question is not *whether* lifeworld norms will be decisive but, rather, *which* lifeworld norms will.

This implies that the key to an emancipatory outcome lies in the second element of Habermas's conception of decolonization, namely, the replacement of normatively secured contexts of interaction by communicatively achieved ones. The centrality of this element is evident when we consider that this process occurs simultaneously on two fronts. First, in the struggles of social movements with the state and official economic system institutions; these struggles are not waged over systems media above; they are also waged over the meanings and norms embedded and enacted in government and corporate policy. Second, this process occurs in a phenomenon not thematized by Habermas: in the struggles between opposing social movements with different interpretations of social needs. Both kinds of struggles involve confrontations between normatively secured and communicatively achieved action. Both involve contestation for hegemony over the sociocultural "means of interpretation and communication." For example, in many late capitalist societies, women's contradictory, self-dividing experience of trying to be both workers and mothers, clients and citizens, has given rise to not one but two women's movements, a feminist one and an antifeminist one. These movements, along with their respective allies and state and corporate institutions, are engaged in struggles over the social meanings of "woman" and "man," "femininity" and "masculinity;" over the interpretation of women's needs; over the interpretation and social construction of women's bodies; and over the gender norms that shape the major institution-mediating social roles. Of course, the means of interpretation and communication in terms of which the social meanings of these things are elaborated have always been controlled by men. Thus feminist women are struggling in effect to redistribute and democratize access to and control over the means of interpretation and communication. We are, therefore, struggling for women's autonomy in the following special sense: a measure of collective control over the means of interpretation and communication sufficient to permit us to participate on a par with men in all types of social interaction, including political deliberation and decision-making.[47]

The foregoing suggests that a caution is in order concerning the use of the terms "particularism" and "universalism." Recall that Habermas's sixth thesis emphasized feminism's links to historic liberation movements and its roots in universalist morality. Recall that he was critical of those tendencies within feminism, and in resistance movements in general, which try to resolve the identity problematic by recourse to particularism, that is, by retreating from arenas of political struggle into alternative communities delimited on the basis of natural categories like biological sex. Now I want to suggest that there are really three issues here and that they need to be disengaged from one another. One is the issue of political engagement vs. apolitical countercultural activity. In so far as Habermas's point is a criticism of cultural feminism it is well taken in principle, although it needs the following qualifications: cultural separatism, while inadequate as longterm political strategy, is in many cases a shorter-term necessity for women's physical, psychological and moral survival; and separatist communities have been the source of numerous reinterpretations of women's experience which have proved politically fruitful in contestation over the means of interpretation and communication. The second issue is the status of women's biology in the elaboration of new social identities. In so far as Habermas's point is a criticism of reductive biologism it is well taken. But this does not mean that one can ignore the fact that women's biology has nearly always been interpreted by men; and that women's struggle for autonomy necessarily and properly involves, among other things, the reinterpretation of the social meanings of our bodies. The third issue is the difficult and complex one of universalism vs. particularism. In so far as Habermas's endorsement of universalism pertains to the metalevel of access to and control over the means of interpretation and communication it is well taken. At this level, women's struggle for autonomy can be understood in terms of a universalist conception of distributive justice. But it does not follow that the substantive content which is the fruit of this struggle, namely, the new social meanings we give our needs and our bodies, our new social identities and conceptions of femininity, can be dismissed as particularistic lapses from universalism. For these are no more particular than the sexist and androcentric meanings and norms they are meant to replace. More generally, at the level of substantive content, as opposed to dialogical form, the contrast between universalism and particularism is out of place. Substantive social meanings and norms are always necessarily culturally and historically specific; they always express distinctive shared, but nonuniversal forms of life. Feminist meanings and norms will be no exception. But they will not, on that account, be particularistic in any pejorative sense. Let us simply say that they will be different.

I have been arguing that struggles of social movements over the means of interpretation and communication are central to an emancipatory resolution of crisis tendencies in welfare capitalism. Now let me clarify their relation to institutional change. Such struggles, I claim, are implicitly and explicitly raising the following sorts of questions. Should the roles of worker, childrearer, citizen and client be fully degendered? Can they be? Or do we, rather, require arrangements that permit women to be workers and citizens *as women*, just as men have always been workers and citizens *as men*? And what might that mean? In any case, does not an emancipatory outcome require a profound transformation of the current gender roles as the base of contemporary social organization? And does not this, in turn, require a fundamental transformation of the content, character, boundaries and relations of the spheres of life which these roles mediate? How should the character and position of paid work, childrearing and citizenship be defined *vis-à-vis* one another? Should democratic-socialist-feminist, self-managed, paid work encompass childrearing? Or should childrearing, rather, replace soldiering as a component of transformed, democratic-socialist-feminist, participatory citizenship? What other possibilities are conceivable?

Let me conclude this discussion of the six theses by restating the most important critical points. First, Habermas's account fails to theorize the patriarchal, norm-mediated character of late capitalist official-economic and administrative systems. Likewise, it fails to theorize the systemic, money- and power-mediated character of male dominance in the domestic sphere of the late capitalist lifeworld. Consequently, his colonization thesis fails to grasp that the channels of influence between system and lifeworld institutions are multidirectional. And it tends to replicate, rather than to problematize, a major institutional support of women's subordination in late capitalism, namely, the gender-based separation of the state-regulated economy of sex-segmented paid work and social welfare, and the masculine public sphere, from privatized female childrearing. Thus, while Habermas wants to be critical of male dominance, his diagnostic categories deflect attention elsewhere, to the allegedly overriding problem of gender-neutral reification. Consequently, his programmatic conception of decolonization bypasses key feminist questions; it fails to address the issue of how to restructure the relation of childrearing to paid work and citizenship. Finally, Habermas's categories tend to misrepresent the causes and underestimate the scope of the feminist challenge to welfare state capitalism. In short, the struggles and wishes of contemporary women are not adequately clarified by a theory that draws the basic battle line between system and lifeworld institutions. From a feminist perspective, there is a more basic battle line between the forms of male dominance linking "system" to "lifeworld" *and us*.

CONCLUSION

In general, then, the principal blind spots of Habermas's theory with respect to gender are traceable to his categorial opposition between system and lifeworld institutions. And to the two more elementary oppositions from which it is compounded, the reproduction one and the action-contexts one. Or rather, the blind spots are traceable to the way in which these oppositions, ideologically and androcentrically interpreted, tend to override and eclipse other, potentially more critical elements of Habermas's framework—elements like the distinction between normatively secured and communicatively achieved action contexts, and like the four-term model of public-private relations.

Habermas's blind spots are instructive, I think. They permit us to conclude something about what the categorial framework of a socialist-feminist critical theory of welfare capitalism should look like. One crucial requirement is that this framework not be such as to put the male-headed nuclear family and the state-regulated official economy on two opposite sides of the major categorial divide. We require, rather, a framework sensitive to the similarities between them, one which puts them on the same side of the line as institutions which, albeit in different ways, enforce women's subordination, since both family and official economy appropriate our labor, short-circuit our participation in the interpretation of our needs and shield normatively secured need interpretations from political contestation. A second crucial requirement is that this framework contains no a priori assumptions about the unidirectionality of social motion and causal influence, that it be sensitive to the ways in which allegedly disappearing institutions and norms persist in structuring social reality. A third crucial requirement, and the last I shall mention here, is that this framework not be such as to posit the evil of welfare capitalism exclusively or primarily as the evil of reification. It must, rather, be capable of foregrounding the evil of dominance and subordination.[48]

NOTES

1. Karl Marx, "Letter to A. Ruge, September 1843," in *Karl Marx: Early Writings*, tr. Rodney Livingstone and Gregor Benton (New York: Vintage Books, 1975), 209.
2. © Nancy Fraser 1986. This is a revised version of a paper that appeared in *New German Critique*, 35 (Spring/Summer 1985), 97–131. I am grateful to John Brenkman, Thomas McCarthy, Carole Pateman and Martin Schwab for helpful comments and criticism; to Dee Marquez for crackerjack word processing; and to the Stanford Humanities Center for financial support.
3. Jürgen Habermas, *The Theory of Communicative Action* (Boston: Beacon Press, 1984; Cambridge, UK: Polity Press, 19), vol. I: *Reason and the Rationalization of Society*, tr. Thomas McCarthy. Jürgen Habermas, *Theorie des kommunikativen Handelns*, 1981; Cambridge, UK: Polity Press, 19), (Frankfurt am Main: Surhkamp Verlag, vol. II: *Zur Kritik der funktionalistischen Vernunft*. I have consulted the following English translations of portions of *Theorie des kommunikativen Handelns*, vol. II: Habermas "New Social Movements" (excerpt from ch. VIII, section 3), tr. *Telos*, 49 (1981), 33–7; "Marx and the Thesis of Inner Colonization" (excerpt from ch. VIII, section 2, 522–47), tr. Christa Hildebrand and Barbara Correll, unpublished typescript; "Tendencies of Juridification" (excerpt from ch. VIII, section 2, 522ff), unpublished typescript.

   Other texts by Habermas: *Legitimation Crisis*, tr. (Boston: Beacon Press, 1975; Cambridge, UK: Polity Press, 19); "Introduction," in Jürgen Habermas, ed., *Observations on "The Spiritual Situation of the Age": Contemporary German Perspectives*, tr. Andrew Buchwalter (Cambridge, MA: MIT Press, 1984; Cambridge, UK: Polity Press, 19); "A Reply to my Critics," in David Held and John B. Thompson, eds, *Habermas: Critical Debates* (Cambridge, MA: MIT Press, 1982; Cambridge, UK: Polity Press, 19);

   I have also consulted two helpful overviews of this material in English: Thomas McCarthy, "Translator's Introduction," in Habermas, *Theory of Communicative Action*, vol. I, v–xxxvii; John B. Thompson, "Rationality and Social Rationalisation: An Assessment of Habermas's Theory of Communicative Action," *Sociology*, 17, 2 (1983), 278–94.
4. I shall not take up such widely debated issues as Habermas's theories of universal pragmatics and social evolution. For helpful discussions of these issues, see the essays in Held and Thompson, eds, *Habermas: Critical Debates*.
5. Habermas, *Theorie des kommunikativen Handelns*, vol. II, 214, 217, 348–9; *Legitimation Crisis*, 8–9; "A Reply to My Critics," 268, 278–9; McCarthy, "Translator's Introduction," xxv–xxvii; Thompson, "Rationality," 285.
6. Habermas, *Theorie des kommunikativen Handelns*, vol. II, 208; "A Reply to My Critics," 223–5; McCarthy, "Translator's Introduction," xxiv–xxv.
7. I am indebted to Martin Schwab for the expression "dual-aspect activity."
8. It might be argued that Habermas's categorial distinction between "social labor" and "socialization" helps overcome the androcentrism of orthodox Marxism. Orthodox Marxism allowed for only one kind of historically significant activity, namely, "production" or "social labor." Moreover, it understood that category androcentrically and thereby excluded women's unpaid childrearing activity from history. By contrast, Habermas allows for two kinds of historically significant activity, "social labor" and the "symbolic" activities which include, among other things, childrearing. Thus, he manages to include

women's unpaid activity in history. While this is an improvement, it does not suffice to remedy matters. At best, it leads to what has come to be known as "dual systems theory," an approach which posits two distinct "systems" of human activity and, correspondingly, two distinct "systems" of oppression: capitalism and male dominance. But this is misleading. These are not, in fact, two distinct systems but, rather, two thoroughly interfused dimensions of a single social formation. In order to understand that social formation, a critical theory requires a single set of categories and concepts which integrate *internally* both gender and political economy (perhaps also race). For a classic statement of dual systems theory, see Heidi Hartmann, "The Unhappy Marriage of Marxism and Feminism: Toward a More Progressive Union," in Lydia Sargent, ed., *Women and Revolution* (Boston: South End Press, 1981). For a critique of dual systems theory, see Iris Young, "Beyond the Unhappy Marriage: A Critique of Dual Systems Theory," in Sargent, ed., *Women and Revolution*: and "Socialist Feminism and the Limits of Dual Systems Theory," *Socialist Review*, 50–1 (1980) 169–80.

In parts 2 and 3 of this chapter, I am developing arguments and lines of analysis which rely on concepts and categories that internally integrate gender and political economy (see note 34 below). This might be considered a "single system" approach, in contrast to dual systems theory. However, I find that label misleading because I do not consider my approach primarily or exclusively a "systems" approach in the first place. Rather, like Habermas, I am trying to link structural (in the sense of objectivating) and interpretive approaches to the study of societies. Unlike him, however, I do not do this by dividing society into two components, "system" and "lifeworld." See this part below and especially note 16.

9. Habermas, *Theory of Communicative Action*, vol. I, 85, 87–8, 101, 342, 357–60; *Theorie des kommunikativen Handelns*, vol. II, 179; *Legitimation Crisis* 4–5; "A Reply to My Critics," 234, 237, 264–5; McCarthy, "Translator's Introduction," ix, xvix-xxx. In presenting the distinction between system-integrated and socially integrated action contexts, I am relying on the terminology of *Legitimation Crisis* and modifying the terminology of *Theory of Communicative Action*. Or, rather, I am selecting one of the several various usages deployed in the latter work. There, Habermas often speaks of what I have called "socially integrated action" as "communicative action." But this gives rise to confusion. For Habermas also uses this latter expression in another, stronger sense, namely, for actions in which coordination occurs by explicit, dialogically achieved consensus only (see below, this part). In order to avoid repeating Habermas's equivocation on "communicative action," I adopt the following terminology: I reserve the term "communicative achieved action" for actions coordinated by explicit, reflective, dialogically achieved consensus. I contrast such action, in the first instance, to "normatively secured action" or actions coordinated by tacit, prereflective, pregiven consensus (see below, this part). I take "communicatively achieved" and "normatively secured" actions, so defined, to be subspecies of what I here call "socially integrated action" or actions coordinated by any form of normed consensus whatever. This last category in turn contrasts with "system integrated action" or actions coordinated by the functional interlacing of unintended consequences, determined by egocentric calculations in the media of money and power, and involving little or no normed consensus of any sort. These terminological commitments do not so much represent a departure from Habermas's usage—he does in fact

frequently use these terms in the senses I have specified. They represent, rather, a stabilization or rendering consistent of his usage. See note 18 below.

10. Habermas, *Theory of Communicative Action*, vol. 1, 341, 357–9; *Theorie des kommunikativen Handelns*, vol. II, 256, 266; McCarthy, "Translator's Introduction," xxx.

11. In "Complexity and Democracy, or the Seducements of Systems Theory," *New German Critique*, 35 (Spring/Summer 1985), 27–55, McCarthy argues that state administrative bureaucracies cannot be distinguished from participatory democratic political associations on the basis of functionality, intentionality and linguisticality since all three of these features are found in both contexts. Thus, McCarthy argues that functionality, intentionality and linguisticality are not mutually exclusive. I find these arguments persuasive. I see no reason why they do not hold also for the capitalist workplace and the modern, restricted, nuclear family.

12. Here, again, I follow McCarthy, ibid. He argues that in modern, state administrative bureaucracies, managers must often deal consensually with their subordinates. This seems to be equally the case for corporate organizations.

13. I have in mind especially the brilliant and influential discussion of gifting by Pierre Bourdieu in *Outline of a Theory of Practice*, tr. Richard Nice (New York: Cambridge University Press, 1977). By recovering the dimension of time, Bourdieu substantially revises the classical account by Marcel Mauss in *The Gift: Forms and Functions of Exchange in Archaic Societies*, tr. Ian Cunnison (New York: W. W. Norton, 1967). For a discussion of some recent revisionist work in cultural-economic anthropology, see Arjun Appadurai, "Commodities and the Politics of Value," in Arjun Appadurai, ed., *The Social Life of Things: Commodities in Cultural Perspective* (New York: Cambridge University Press, 1986).

14. Habermas, *Theorie des kommunikativen Handelns*, vol. II, 348–9; McCarthy, "Translator's Introduction," xxvi–xxvii. The terms "pragmatic-contextual" and "natural kinds" are mine, not Habermas's.

15. Habermas, *Theory of Communicative Action*, vol. I, 94–5, 101; *Theorie des kommunikativen Handelns*, vol. II, 348–9; "A Reply to My Critics," 227, 237, 266–8; *Legitimation Crisis*, 10; McCarthy, "Translator's Introduction," xxvi–xxvii. The terms "absolute differences" and "difference of degree" are mine, not Habermas's.

16. Habermas, *Theory of Communicative Action*, vol. I, 72, 341–2, 359–60; *Theorie des kommunikativen Handelns*, vol. II, 179; "A Reply to My Critics," 268, 279–80; *Legitimation Crisis*, 20–1; McCarthy, "Translator's Introduction," xxviii–xxix; Thompson, "Rationality," 285, 287. It should be noted that in *Theory of Communicative Action* Habermas contrasts system and lifeworld in two distinct senses. On the one hand, he contrasts them as two different methodological perspectives on the study of societies. The system perspective is objectivating and "externalist," while the lifeworld perspective is hermeneutical and "internalist." In principle, either can be applied to the study of any given set of societal phenomena. Habermas argues that neither alone is adequate. So he seeks to develop a methodology that combines both. On the other hand, Habermas also contrasts system and lifeworld in another way, namely, as two different kinds of institutions. It is this second system-lifeworld contrast that I am concerned with here. I do not explicitly treat the first one in this chapter. I am sympathetic to Habermas's general methodological intention of combining or linking structural (in the sense of objectivating) and interpretive

approaches to the study of societies. I do not, however, believe that this can be done by assigning structural properties to one set of institutions (the official economy and the state) and interpretive ones to another set (the family and the "public sphere"). I maintain, rather, that all of these institutions have both structural and interpretive dimensions and that all should be studied both structurally and hermeneutically. I have tried to develop an approach that meets these desiderata in Nancy Fraser, "Feminism and the Social State," *Salmagundi* (forthcoming); in "Women, Welfare and the Politics of Need Interpretation," *Hypatia: A Journal of Feminist Philosophy*, 2, 1 (Winter 1987) 103–21; and in "Social Movements vs. Disciplinary Bureaucracies; The Discourses of Social Needs," CHS Occasional Papers, 8 (Center for Humanistic Studies, The University of Minnesota, 1987), 2–37. I have discussed the general methodological problem in "On the Political and the Symbolic: Against the Metaphysics of Textuality," *Boundary 2* (forthcoming).

17. See, for example, the essays in Barrie Thorne and Marilyn Yalom, eds, *Rethinking the Family: Some Feminist Questions* (New York and London: Longman, 1982). Also, Michele Barrett and Mary McIntosh, *The Anti-Social Family* (London: Verso, 1982).

18. Habermas, *Theory of Communicative Action*, vol. I, 85–6, 88–90, 101, 104–5; *Theorie des kommunikativen Handelns*, vol. II, 179; McCarthy, "Translator's Introduction," ix, xxx. In presenting the distinction between normatively secured and communicatively achieved action, I am again modifying, or rather stabilizing, the variable usage of *Theory of Communicative Action*. See note 9 above.

19. Pamela Fishman, "Interaction: The Work Women Do," *Social Problems* 25; 4, (1978), 397–406.

20. Nancy Henley, *Body Politics* (Englewood Cliffs, NJ: Prentice-Hall, 1977).

21. Habermas, *Theorie des kommunikativen Handelns*, vol. II, 523–4, 547; "Tendencies of Juridification," 3; "A Reply to My Critics," 237; Thompson, "Rationality," 288, 292.

22. McCarthy pursues some of the normative implications of this for the differentiation of the administrative state system from the public sphere in "Complexity and Democracy."

23. McCarthy makes this point with respect to the dedifferentiation of the state administrative system and the public sphere. Ibid.

24. Habermas, *Theory of Communicative Action*, vol. I, 341–2, 359–60; *Theorie des kommunikativen Handelns*, vol. II, 256, 473; "A Reply to My Critics," 280; McCarthy, "Translator's Introduction," xxxii; Thompson, "Rationality," 286–8.

25. I borrow the phrase "gender subtext" from Dorothy Smith, "The Gender Subtext of Power," unpublished typescript.

26. The following account of the masculine gender subtext of the worker role draws heavily on Carole Pateman, "The Personal and the Political: Can Citizenship be Democratic?" Lecture III of her "Women and Democratic Citizenship," The Jefferson Memorial Lectures, delivered at the University of California, Berkeley, February 1985, unpublished typescript.

27. Pateman, ibid., 5.

28. I am here adapting Althusser's notion of the interpellation of a subject to a context in which he, of course, never used it. For the general notion, see Louis Althusser, "Ideology and Ideological State Apparatuses (Notes toward an Investigation)," in his *Lenin and Philosophy and Other Essays*, tr. Ben Brewster (New York: Monthly Review Press, 1971).

29. Barbara Ehrenreich, *The Hearts of Men: American Dreams and the Flight from Commitment* (Garden City, NY: Anchor Books, 1984).

30. The following discussion of the masculine gender subtext of the citizen role draws heavily on Pateman, "The Personal and the Political."

31. Pateman, ibid., 8.

32. Judith Hicks Stiehm, "The Protected, the Protector, the Defender," in Judith Hicks Stiehm, ed., *Women and Men's Wars* (New York: Pergamon Press, 1983); and "Myths Necessary to the Pursuit of War," unpublished typescript. This is not to say, however, that I accept Stiehm's conclusions about the desirability of integrating women fully into the US military as presently structured and deployed.

33. Pateman, "The Personal and the Political," 10.

34. In so far as the foregoing analysis of the gender subtext of Habermas's role theory deploys categories in which gender and political economy are internally integrated, it represents a contribution to the overcoming of "dual systems theory" (see note 8 above). It is also a contribution to the development of a more satisfactory way of linking structural (in the sense of objectivating) and interpretive approaches to the study of societies than that proposed by Habermas. For I am suggesting here that the domestic sphere has a structural as well as an interpretive dimension and that the official economic and state spheres have an interpretive as well as a structural dimension.

35. Habermas, *Theorie des kommunikativen Handelns*, vol. II, 505ff.; *Legitimation Crisis*, 33–6, 53–5; McCarthy, "Translator's Introduction," xxxiii.

36. Habermas, *Theorie des kommunikativen Handelns*, vol. II, 522–4; "Marx," 1–2; "Tendencies of Juridification," 1–2; *Legitimation Crisis*, 36–7; McCarthy, "Translator's Introduction," xxxiii.

37. Habermas, *Theorie des kommunikativen Handelns*, vol. II, 530–40; "Marx," 9–20; "Tendencies of Juridification," 12–14; McCarthy, "Translator's Introduction," xxxiii-xxxiv.

38. Habermas, *Theorie des kommunikativen Handelns*, vol. II, 540–7; "Marx," 20–7; "Tendencies of Juridification," 15–25; McCarthy, "Translator's Introduction," xxxi.

39. Habermas, *Theorie des kommunikativen Handelns*, vol. II, 275–7, 452, 480, 522–4; "Marx," 2; "Tendencies of Juridification," 1–3; "A Reply to my Critics," 226, 280–1; *Observations*, 11–12, 16–20; McCarthy, "Translator's Introduction," xxxi-xxxii; Thompson, "Rationality," 286, 288.

40. Habermas, *Theorie des kommunikativen Handelns*, vol. II, 581–3, "New Social Movements," 33–7; *Observations*, 18–19, 27–8.

41. Habermas, *Theorie des kommunikativen Handelns*, vol. II, 581–3; "New Social Movements," 34–7; *Observations*, 16–17, 27–8.

42. For the US social welfare system, see the analysis of male vs. female participation rates, and the account of the gendered character of the two subsystems in Fraser, "Women, Welfare." Also, Barbara J. Nelson, "Women's Poverty and Women's Citizenship: Some Political Consequences of Economic Marginality," *Signs*, 10, 2 (1985); Steven P. Erie, Martin Rein and Barbara Wiget, "Women and the Reagan Revolution: Thermidor for the Social Welfare Economy," in Irene Diamond, ed., *Families, Politics and Public Policies: A Feminist Dialogue on Women and the State* (New York: Longman, 1983); Diana Pearce, "Women, Work and Welfare: The Feminization of Poverty," in Karen Wolk Fenstein, ed.,

Working Women and Families (Beverly Hills: Sage Publications, 1979); and "Toil and Trouble: Women Workers and Unemployment Compensation," *Signs: Journal of Women in Culture and Society*, 10, 3 (1985), 439–59; Barbara Ehrenreich and Frances Fox Piven, "The Feminization of Poverty," *Dissent* (Spring 1984), 162–70. For an analysis of the gendered character of the British social welfare system, see Hilary Land, "Who Cares for the Family?" *Journal of Social Policy*, 7, 3 (1978), 257–84. For Norway, see the essays in Harriet Holter, ed., *Patriarchy in a Welfare Society* (Oslo: Universitetsforlaget, 1984). See also two comparative studies: Mary Ruggie, *The State and Working Women: A Comparative Study of Britain and Sweden* (Princeton, NJ: Princeton University Press, 1984); and Birte Siim "Women and the Welfare State: Between Private and Public Dependence," (unpublished typescript).

43. Carol Brown, "Mothers, Fathers and Children: From Private to Public Patriarchy," in Sargent, ed., *Women and Revolution*. Actually, I believe Brown's formulation is theoretically inadequate, since it presupposes a simple, dualistic conception of public and private. Nonetheless, the phrase "from private to public patriarchy" evokes in a rough but suggestive way the phenomena a socialist-feminist critical theory of the welfare state would need to account for.

44. The most recent available data for the US indicate that sex segmentation in paid work is increasing, not decreasing. And this is so in spite of the entry of small but significant numbers of women into professions like law and medicine. Even when the gains won by those women are taken into account, there is no overall improvement in the aggregated comparative economic position of paid women workers *vis-à-vis* male workers. Women's wages remain less than 60% of men's wages. Which means, of course, that the mass of women are losing ground. Nor is there any overall improvement in occupational distribution by sex. The ghettoization of women in low-paying, low-status "pink collar" occupations is increasing. For example, in the US in 1973, women held 93% of all paid childcare jobs, 81% of all primary school teaching jobs, 72% of all health technician jobs, 98% of all Registered Nurse jobs, 83% of all librarian jobs, 99% of all secretarial jobs and 92% of all waitperson jobs. The figures for 1983 were, respectively, 97%, 83%, 84%, 96%, 87%, 99% and 88% (Bureau of Labor Statistics figures cited by Drew Christie, "Comparable Worth and Distributive Justice," paper read at meetings of the American Philosophical Association, Western Division, April 1985.) The US data are consistent with data for the Scandinavian countries and Britain. See Siim, "Women and the Welfare State."

45. See note 42.

46. This account draws on some elements of the analysis of Zillah Eisenstein in *The Radical Future of Liberal Feminism* (Boston: Northeastern University Press, 1981), ch. 9. What follows has some affinities with the perspective of Ernesto Laclau and Chantal Mouffe in *Hegemony and Socialist Strategy* (New York: Verso, 1985).

47. I develop this notion of the "socio-cultural means of interpretation and communication" and the associated conception of autonomy in "Toward a Discourse Ethic of Solidarity," *Praxis International*, 5, 4 (January 1986), 425–9. Both notions are extensions and modifications of Habermas's conception of "communicative ethics."

48. My own recent work attempts to construct a conceptual framework for a socialist-feminist critical theory of the welfare state which meets these requirements. See Fraser, "Women, Welfare;" "Feminism and the Social State;" "Toward a Discourse Ethic of Solidarity;"

and "Social Movements vs. Disciplinary Bureaucracies." Each of these essays draws heavily on those aspects of Habermas's thought which I take to be unambiguously positive and useful, especially his conception of the irreducibly socio-cultural, interpretive character of human needs, and his contrast between dialogical and monological processes of need interpretation. The present chapter, on the other hand, focuses mainly on those aspects of Habermas's thought which I find problematical or unhelpful, and so does not convey the full range either of his work or of my views about it. Readers are warned, therefore, against drawing the conclusion that Habermas has little or nothing positive to contribute to a socialist-feminist critical theory of the welfare state. They are urged, rather, to consult the essays cited above for the other side of the story.

SEYLA BENHABIB

THE UTOPIAN DIMENSION IN COMMUNICATIVE ETHICS

In his retrospective on Walter Benjamin, "On the Actuality of Walter Benjamin Consciousness-Raising or Rescuing Critique," Habermas discusses an issue which for many has seemed to point to a lacuna in his own understanding of moral progress and emancipation: "In the tradition that reaches back to Marx, Benjamin was one of the first to emphasize a *further* moment in the concepts of exploitation and progress: besides hunger and oppression, failure; besides prosperity and liberty happiness. Benjamin regarded the experience of happiness he named secular illumination as bound up with the rescuing of tradition. The claim to happiness can be made good only if the sources of that semantic potential we need for interpreting the world in the light of our needs are not exhausted."[1] In the semantic heritage of a cultural tradition are contained those images and anticipations of a fulfilled life-history and of a collective life-form in which justice does not exclude solidarity, and freedom is not realized at the expense of happiness. Certainly, Habermas continues, i is not possible to achieve freedom and to realize justice without unleashing (*entbinden*) the hidden potentials of culture. In that sense, the semantic unleashing of culture and the social overcoming of institutional repression are mutually supportive Yet the suspicion remains whether "an emancipation without happiness and lacking in fulfillment might not be just as possible as relative prosperity without the elimination of repression."[2]

Written a year before the *Legitimation Crisis* (1973) and four years before *The Reconstruction of Historical Materialism* (1976), this essay contained a programmatic anticipation of how Habermas proposed to argue not only against the tradition of counter-Enlightenment (Nietzsche, Spengler, Jünger and Heidegger) but against the messianic utopian strand of critical theory as well—Bloch and Benjamin in particular.[3] But these subsequent works have not dissipated the force of the suspicion which has been voiced. Increasingly in recent years, Habermas has pointed to the *limits* of a theory of practical discourse which focuses on freedom while excluding questions of the good life; which concerns the validity of normative sentences (*Sollsätze*) while ignoring the question of the integrity of values (*Werte*), which in short, concerns institutional justice but cannot say much about those qualities of individual life-histories and collective life-forms which make them fulfilling or unfulfilling.[4]

This questioning on Habermas' part is neither a coincidence nor of mere philological interest. It reveals the intimate relation between "transfiguration" and "fulfillment," between the poles of *utopia* and *norm* within which the discourse of a critical social theory unfolds. By "transfiguration" I mean that the future envisaged by a theory entails a radical rupture with the present, and that in such a rupture a new and imaginative constellation of the values and meanings of the present takes place. The concept of fulfillment, by contrast, refers to the fact that the society of the future executes and carries out the unfinished tasks of the present, without necessarily forging new, imaginative constellations out of this cultural heritage. These are concepts which I use to designate an essential tension in the project of critical theory and which can also be referred to as "utopia" and "norm" respectively.

Since Marx's early critique of civil society, the project of emancipation was viewed both as the fulfillment and transfiguration of the existing order. In developing an immanent critique of capitalism, critical Marxism held this social order to its own promises, and required that abundance, the betterment of human life, and an end to exploitation and misery be realized for all, and not only for some. This demand did not call into question the Enlightenment project of combining human freedom and happiness with the scientific-technologically based progress of productive forces. The course of European history after the beginning of the 20th century left little hope that the Enlightenment could fulfill its own *promesse du bonheur*. Critical theory lamented the dialectic of an Enlightenment condemned to leave its own promises unfulfilled. The project of emancipation was increasingly viewed not as the fulfillment, but as the transfiguration of the Enlightenment legacy. Their increasingly esoteric conception of emancipation forced the critical theory of Horkheimer, Adorno, and Marcuse into a series of aporias. More and more, emancipation ceased to be a public project and became a private experience of liberation achieved in the nondominating relation with nature and in moments of revolutionary eros.

Habermas has attempted to reestablish the link between Enlightenment and emancipation, and to bring the project of emancipation into the light of the public by going back to the Enlightenment legacy of practical reason. His project requires fulfilling the universalistic promise of social contract and consent theories which, since the 17th century, have always limited such universalism on the basis of sex, class, race and status distinctions.

Even when we concede that the realization of bourgeois universalism is a necessary condition for emancipation, it seems hardly sufficient. "Can we preclude," asks Habermas, "the possibility of a meaningless emancipation? In complex societies, emancipation means the participatory transformation of administrative decision structures."[5] If this were all that was meant by "emancipation," if indeed the goal of critique exhausted itself in the "joyless reformism" of a welfare-statist or social-democratic compromise, then indeed critical theory would have established the link between Enlightenment and emancipation by forsaking far too much of its utopian tradition. Let me ask, therefore, if the goal of realizing bourgeois universalism, of making good the unfulfilled promise of justice and freedom, must exhaust itself in a "joyless reformism," or whether, speaking with Benjamin, one cannot see a *Jetztzeit*, a moment of transfiguration, in this very process? I want to suggest that the seventh stage of moral development postulated by Habermas as a corrective and extension of the Kohlbergian scheme, that is, the stage of "universalized need interpretations," has an unmistakeable utopian content to it, and that it points to a transfigurative vision of bourgeois universalism.

I will begin with a brief outline of the central theses of Habermas' communicative ethics (II). I will then focus on the role of "need interpretations" in this theory (III). My thesis is that Habermas, following Mead, restricts moral autonomy to the standpoint of the "generalized other," and does not do justice to the utopian dimension in his own project.

II

The theory of communicative ethics has been named by Habermas also a "cognitivist ethics of language." The cognitivism of this theory rests with its assumption that normative statements like "Child molesting is wrong," cannot be translated into a statement like "I dislike child molesting," as the emotivists claim. The predicate "is wrong" in this statement is to be understood as a claim that there are good reasons to adopt the rule in our practices that children ought not be molested. To establish this meta-ethical premise Habermas develops the concepts of moral rightness and wrongness by means of a theory of practical argumentation. Basing himself on Stephen Toulmin's work in *The Uses of Argument*, he maintains that just as the truth of theoretical claims can only be established in light of an argument in which they are shown to be warranted with good grounds, so too the validity of normative claims can only be established via practical argumentations in which they are shown to be defensible with good grounds.

Arguments dealing with theoretical truth claims, with statements about what the case is, or with practical assertions, with statements about what ought to be done, are named "discourses." Discourses are described as special argumentation procedures in which both facts about what is the case and norms about what is right are challenged and no longer taken for granted. In discourses we "suspend belief" in the truth of propositions and the validity of normative claims that we ordinarily take for granted in our everyday transactions.[6]

The aim of discourses is to generate a "rationally motivated consensus" on controversial claims. The concept of the "ideal speech situation" is introduced in this context. The "ideal speech situation" specifies the formal properties that discursive argumentations would have to possess if the consensus thus attained were to be distinguished from a mere compromise or an agreement of convenience. The ideal speech situation is a "meta-norm" that applies to theoretical as well as to practical reason. It serves to delineate those aspects of an argumentation process which would lead to a "rationally motivated" as opposed to a false or apparent consensus.

The four conditions of the ideal speech situation are: first, each participant must have an equal chance to initiate and to continue communication; second, each must have an equal chance to make assertions, recommendations, explanations, and to challenge justifications. Together we can call these the "symmetry condition." Third, each must have equal chances as actors to express their wishes, feelings, and intentions; and fourth, the speakers must act *as if* in contexts of action there is an equal distribution of chances "to order and resist orders, to promise and to refuse, to be accountable for one's conduct and to demand accountability from others."[7] Let me call the latter two the "reciprocity condition." While the symmetry stipulation of the ideal speech situation refers to *speech acts* alone and to conditions governing their employment, the reciprocity condition refers to existing *social interactions* and requires a suspension of situations of untruthfulness and duplicity on the one hand, and of inequality and subordination on the other.

This "cognitivist ethics of language" is viewed by Habermas as a reinterpretation of Kantian universalism in moral theory in the light of the communicative foundations of human action. Indeed, one can illuminate some of the central theses of communicative ethics by briefly comparing it to Rawls's project in *A Theory of Justice*. There are two premises shared by Rawls and Habermas.[8] I will call the first the "consensus principle of legitimacy" and define it as follows: the principle of rational consensus provides the only criterion in light of which the legitimacy of norms and institutional arrangements can be justified. More significantly, Rawls and Habermas share the meta-theoretical premise: the idea of such rational consensus is to be defined *procedurally*. Rawls maintains that his theory of justice provides us with the only procedure of justification through which valid and binding norms of collective coexistence can be established. Habermas argues that the "ideal speech situation" defines the formal properties of discourses, by engaging in which alone we can attain a rational consensus. The fictive collective choice situation devised by Rawls and the "ideal speech situation" devised by Habermas are *normative justification procedures* serving to illustrate the consensus principle of legitimacy.

Despite these common assumptions, there are some fundamental differences between communicative ethics and the Rawlsian position which I would like to summarize around six points.

First, although the theory of communicative ethics also proceeds from a counterfactual called the "ideal speech situation," this construct is not to be interpreted as advocating a "veil of ignorance" but is to be understood as defining certain rules of discourse which we have *no good reasons* to want to deny.

Second, such argumentations as take place in discourses continue everyday moral dialogue with other means. What motivates the transition to discourse is not some abstract decision, but the fact that the self-explanatory character of our life-world often fails, and requires clarification and mutual reinterpretation. Discourses are continuous with the questioning, puzzling, explaining, and negotiating which form the matrix of everyday morality.

Third, since discourses are not hypothetical thought-experiments that can be carried out by isolated moral philosophers but are intended to be actual processes of moral dialogue among real actors, we do not need to predefine theoretically a concept of the person and the identity of moral actors. Such persons need not stand behind a veil of ignorance or be ignorant about the specific circumstances of their birth, ability, psychological make-up, status, and the like. Discourses only require from moral actors a reflexive attitude which enjoins them to settle normative controversies in a spirit of cooperative dialogue.

Fourth, it is not necessary to place any knowledge constraints upon such processes of moral reasoning and disputation, for the more knowledge is available to moral agents about the particulars of their society, its place in history, and its future, the more rational will be the outcome of their deliberations. Practical rationality entails epistemic rationality as well, and more knowledge rather than less leads to a more informed and rational judgment. To judge rationally is not to judge as if one did not know what one could know, as Rawls maintains, but to judge in the light of all available and relevant information.

Fifth, in such moral discourses agents can also change levels of reflexivity, that is to say, they can introduce meta-considerations about the very conditions and constraints under which dialogue takes place, and they can evaluate its fairness. There is no closure of reflexivity in this model as there is, for example, in the Rawlsian one, which enjoins agents to accept certain rules of bargaining before the choice of the principles of justice.

Sixth, if there are no knowledge restrictions upon such discourses, if the theory does not idealize the identity of moral agents, if reflexivity is encouraged rather than limited by the theory, then it also follows that there is *no privileged subject matter* of moral disputation. Moral agents are not only limited to reasoning about primary goods which they are assumed to want whatever else they want. Instead, both the goods they desire and their needs and desires can be legitimate topics of moral disputation. By focusing on the role of needs in communicative ethics, let me now analyze its radical departure from other neo-Kantian theories.

III

As early as the essay on "Theories of Truth," we encounter the claim that the appropriate language of morals "permits determinate groups and persons, in given circumstances, a truthful interpretation both of their own particular needs, and more importantly, of their common needs capable of consensus."[9] From the standpoint of universalistic ethical theories, whether it be Kant's or some contemporary version of it, like Rawls's or Gewirth's, such a requirement would transgress the *limits* of practical discourse. In Kant's case this would be so, simply because the requisite universality of morality can only be established by abstracting away from, indeed by repressing, those very needs, desires and inclinations which tempt moral agents away from duty. The disregard in contemporary deontological theory for "inner nature" is more complicated, but ultimately, it seems to me, it is based on the classical liberal doctrine that as long as the *public* actions of individuals do not interfere with each other, what they need and desire is their *business*. To want to draw this aspect of a person's life into public-moral discourse would interfere with their autonomy, i.e., with their right to define the good life as they please as long as this does not impinge on others' rights to do the same.[10]

Against this assumption of Kantian moral theories, Habermas draws upon an insight of Hegel's that has both empirical and normative relevance: this is the insight that the relation between self and other, I and thou, is *constitutive* for human self-consciousness. Empirically, this leads to a conception of the human personality as developing only in *interaction* with other selves.[11] Normatively, this conception of identity implies a model of autonomy according to which the relation between self and other is not external to the ego's striving for autonomy.

In requiring that need interpretations become the subject matter of practical discourses, Habermas is underscoring both points. From the standpoint of socialization theory, individual nature, while being "private," is not immutable; individual need-interpretations and motives carry with them the marks of societal processes by participating in which alone an individual learns to become an "I." The grammatical logic of the word "I" reveals the unique structure of ego identity: every subject who uses this concept in relation to himself or herself also learns that all other subjects are likewise "I's." In this respect the ego becomes an I only in a community of other selves who are also I's. Yet every act of self-reference expresses, at the same time, the uniqueness and difference of this I from all others. Discourses about needs and motives unfold in this space created by commonality and uniqueness, general societal processes, and the contingency of individual life-histories.

The requirement that a "truthful" interpretation of needs also be part of discursive argumentation means that ego autonomy cannot and should not be achieved at the expense of internal *repression*. Thus Habermas writes: "Internal nature is thereby moved in a utopian perspective; that is, at this stage internal nature may no longer be merely examined within an interpretive framework fixed by the cultural tradition in a nature-like way. . . . Inner nature is rendered communicatively fluid and transparent to the extent that needs can, through aesthetic forms of expression, be kept articulable or be released from their paleosymbolic prelinguisticality."[12] Ego autonomy is characterized by a twofold capacity: first, the individual's *reflexive* ability to question the interpretive framework fixed by the cultural tradition—to loosen, if you wish, those sedimented and frozen images of the good and happiness in the light of which we formulate needs and motives; second, such reflexive questioning is accompanied by an ability to *articulate* one's needs linguistically, by an ability to communicate with others about them. Whereas the first aspect requires us to assume a reflexive distance towards the content of our tradition, the second emphasizes our ability to become articulate about our own affective and emotional constitution.[13] In both instances, reflection is to be understood not as an abstracting away from a given content, but as an ability to communicate and to engage in dialogue. The linguistic access to inner nature is both a distancing and a coming closer. In that we can name what drives and motivates us, we are closer to freeing ourselves of its power over us; and in the very process of being able to say what we mean, we come one step closer to the harmony or friendship of the soul with itself.

If the highest stage of a universalistic ethical orientation is this open, reflexive communication about our needs and the cultural traditions in light of which they are interpreted, then a number of oppositions on which communicative ethics seemed to rest begin to lose their force: questions of justice merge with questions of the good life; practical-moral discourses flow into aesthetic-expressive ones; autonomy is not only *self-determination* in accordance with just norms but the capacity to assume the standpoint of the concrete other as well.

It should be emphasized how *different* this outcome is from that usually associated with universalistic ethical theories. As the definition of stage six in Kohlberg's moral theory reveals, the highest stage of moral orientation is the *public* discourse of rights and entitlements. Neither the needs which drive the actions through which rights are exercised, nor the concept of entitlement which the *ethos* of a right-bearing and invariable adult male implies, are called into question in such a moral theory. Thus, the insistence that "universalizable need interpretations" move into the center of moral discourse is not simply a further *evolution* of such a perspective; it entails a *utopian break* with it, or what I have named its "transfiguration." "Inner nature is moved into a utopian perspective," in the sense that its contents, our needs and affects, become communicatively accessible; in psychoanalytic terms, the threshold of repression is lowered. The utopia of society in which association (*Vergesell-schaftung*) is attained without domination, namely, justice, and socialization without superfluous repression, namely, happiness, moves to the fore. Conceptions of justice and of the good life flow into each other.

Discourses in which our needs and the cultural traditions shaping them are thematized; in which the semantic content of those interpretations defining happiness and the good life are brought to light, and what is fitting, pleasing, and fulfilling are debated, are named by Habermas "aesthetic-expressive" ones.[14] It is maintained that modernity institutionalizes not only the discursive evaluation of moral and political questions, but those of aesthetic and expressive subjectivity as well. Whereas practical discourses are oriented toward what is public and universalizable, aesthetic-expressive discourse is oriented toward what is semi-public, non-universalizable, and culturally specific. Expressive discourses cannot be abstracted from the hermeneutic and contingent horizon of shared interpretations and life forms.

This distinction between normative and aesthetic-expressive discourses does not do justice, however, to the significance of needs and their interpretations in the moral realm. In fact, by confining such debate concerning need interpretations to the expressive realm alone, Habermas is making an effort to preserve the purity of the normative realm which he has restricted to an analysis of the binding force of "normative ought sentences" (*Sollsätze*).[15] But the very fact that need interpretations also become thematized in moral discourses once more indicates that Habermas' construction of the model of communicative ethics is ambiguous. On the one hand, it shares with deontological theories like Rawls's the desire to separate the public discourse of justice from the more private discourse of needs; on the other hand, inasmuch as it is critical of theories of justice which do not extend to a critique of consumerist and possessive-individualist modes of life, it has to revert to the critique of needs, false socialization, and the like.

I want to suggest that Habermas does not thematize this utopian dimension adequately, for, following George Herbert Mead, he assumes the standpoint of the "generalized other," of rights and entitlements, to represent the moral point of view par excellence. Mead formulates the ideal of a community of communication as follows:

"In logical terms there is established a universe of discourse which transcends the specific order within which the members of the community, in a specific conflict, place themselves outside of the community order as it exists, and agree upon changed habits of action and a restatement of values. Rational procedure, therefore, sets up an order within which thought operates, that abstracts in varying degrees from the actual structure of society . . . It is a social order that includes any rational being who is or may be in any way implicated in the situation with which thought deals . . . It is evident that a man cannot act as a rational member of society, except as he constitutes himself a member of this wider commonwealth of rational beings."[16]

In this sociological reformulation of the Kantian Kingdom of Ends on Mead's part, Habermas sees two utopian projections: he names the first the perspective of *self-determination*, that is, of autonomous action oriented toward universalistic principles; the second perspective corresponds to that of *self-actualization*, the capacity to unfold one's individuality in its uniqueness.[17] "The ideal community of communication corresponds to an *ego identity* which allows self-actualization to unfold on the basis of autonomous action."[18] But whereas the perspective of autonomous action corresponds to the standpoint of the "generalized other," what, following Carol Gilligan, I would like to call the standpoint of the "concrete other," cannot be accommodated within the rather ego-centered notion of self-actualization.

The standpoint of the "generalized other" requires us to view each and every individual as a rational being entitled to the same rights and duties we would want to ascribe to ourselves. In assuming this perspective, we abstract from the individuality and concrete identity of the other. We assume that the other, like ourselves, is a being who has concrete needs, desires, and affects, but that what constitutes her moral dignity is not what differentiates us from each other, but rather what we, as speaking and acting rational agents, have in common. Our relation to the other is governed by the norm of *symmetrical reciprocity*: each is entitled to expect and to assume from us what we can expect and assume from her. The norms of our interactions are primarily public and institutional ones. If I have a right to "x," then you have the duty not to hinder me from enjoying "x," and conversely. In treating you in accordance with these norms, I confirm in your person the rights to humanity, and I have a legitimate claim to expect that you will do the same in relation to me. The moral categories that accompany such interactions are those of right, obligation, and entitlement; the corresponding moral feelings are those of respect, duty, worthiness, and dignity, and the vision of community is one of rights and entitlements.

The standpoint of the "concrete other," by contrast, requires us to view each and every rational being as an individual with a concrete history, identity, and affective-emotional constitution. In assuming this standpoint, we abstract from what constitutes our commonality and seek to understand the distinctiveness of the other. We seek to comprehend the needs of the other, their motivations, what they search for, and what they desire. Our relations to the other are governed by the norm of *complementary reciprocity*: each is entitled to expect and to assume from the other forms of behavior through which the other feels recognized and confirmed as a concrete, individual being with specific needs, talents, and capacities. Our differences in this case complement, rather than exclude one another. The norms of our interaction are usually private, non-institutional ones. They are the norms of solidarity, friendship, love, and care. Such relations require in various ways that I do, and that you expect me to do in the face of your needs, more than would be required of me as right-bearing person. In treating you in accordance with the norms of solidarity, friendship, love, and care, I confirm not only your *humanity* but your human *individuality*. The moral categories that accompany such interactions are those of responsibility, bonding, and sharing. The corresponding moral feelings are those of love, care, sympathy, and solidarity, and the vision of community is one of needs and solidarity.

These moral ideals and the corresponding moral emotions have been separated radically from each other in moral and political thought since Hobbes. The institutional distinction between the public and the private, between the public sphere of justice, the civic sphere of friendship, and the private sphere of intimacy, has also resulted in the incompatibility of an ethical vision of principles and an ethical vision of care and solidarity. The ideal of moral and political autonomy has been consistently restricted to the standpoint of the "generalized other." while the standpoint of the "concrete other" has been silenced, I want to suggest, even suppressed by this tradition.[19]

As is evidenced by Kantian moral theory, a public ethics of principles entails a repressive attitude towards, "inner nature." Our needs and affective nature are excluded from the realm of moral theory. This results in a corresponding inability to treat human needs, desires, and emotions in any other way than by abstracting away from them and by condemning them to silence. Institutional justice is thus seen as representing a higher stage of moral development than interpersonal responsibility, care, love, and solidarity; the respect for rights and duties is regarded as prior to care and concern about another's needs; moral cognition precedes moral affect; the mind, we may summarize, is the sovereign of the body, and reason the judge of inner nature.

By allowing need interpretations to move to the center of moral discourse and by insisting that "inner nature be placed in a utopian perspective," Habermas comes close to subverting this bias of traditional normative philosophy; but his insistence that the standpoint of the "generalized other" alone represents the moral point of view prevents this move. It is also inadequate to claim that aesthetic-expressive discourse can accommodate the perspective of the "concrete other," for relations of solidarity, friendship, and love are not aesthetic but profoundly moral ones. The recognition of the *human* dignity of the generalized other is just as essential as the acknowledgement of the *specificity* of the concrete other. Whereas the perspective of the generalized other promises justice, it is in the relation to the concrete other that those ephemeral moments of happiness and solidarity are recovered.

A communicative concept of autonomy attains utopian and motivating force insofar as it promises neither a merger nor a fusion, but the necessary interaction and confrontation of these two perspectives.[20] The ideal community of communication corresponds to an ego identity which allows the unfolding of the relation to the *concrete other* on the basis of *autonomous* action. Only then can we say that justice without solidarity is blind and empty.

As this discussion may indicate, while endorsing the necessity of the paradigm shift in critical theory which Habermas's work has initiated, I am less convinced by the abandonment of the utopian-anticipatory moments of critique. When communicative ethics, and the perspective of moral autonomy and community it entails, are presented as if they were the logical and inevitable outcome of a normal sequence of development, only carrying to its conclusion what is implicit in the process itself, one reverts back to the philosophy of the subject. One posits a fictional collective "we" that is not only the subject of evolution but the subject of history as well. Much like Hegel's *Phenomenology of Spirit*, the theorist then begins to speak in the name of a fictional collective "we" from whose standpoint the story of history is told. This fictive subject appears both as the subject of the past and of the future; it is empirical and normative at once. In Habermas's account, too, the empirical subjects as whose learning process the cultural evolution of modernity takes place, shift their status, and this process becomes a representative tale in which "we," the subjects of the present, are to discover ourselves.[21] What is objectionable in this procedure is twofold. First, who is the "we" in the present such that reconstructions present a process of development with which all can identify? Why is it assumed that one is already facing a collective singularity—mankind as such? This shift to the language of an anonymous species-subject preempts the experience of moral and political activity as a consequence of which alone a genuine "we" can emerge. A collectivity is not constituted theoretically but is formed out of the moral and political struggles of fighting actors.

In the second place, this shift to the language of a hypostatized subject has as a further consequence that the historical process is *naturalized*. History begins to appear as the semantic gloss on a structural process which proceeds with necessity and invariably from one sequence to the next. But we cannot naturalize the history of the species, for we have no models of development to compare it. At this point, a certain anticipatory utopia, a projection of the future as it could be, becomes necessary. Since the lines of development leading from present to future are fundamentally underdetermined, the theorist can no longer speak the language of evolution and necessity, but must conceive of herself as a participant in the formation of the future. By focusing on the seventh stage of moral development, which in Habermas's construction concerns universalizable need-interpretations, I have attempted to render this utopian moment visible.

NOTES

1. Habermas, "Walter Benjamin: Consciousness-Raising or Rescuing Critique," in *Philosophical-Political Profiles*, F. Lawrence, trans. (Cambridge, MA: MIT Press, 1983), p. 156. I have modified Lawrence's translation such as to render "Unterdrückung" in this context as "oppression" rather than "repression." Cf. "Bewusstmachende oder rettende Kritik—Die Aktualität Walter Benjamins" (1972), in: Habermas, *Kultur und Kritik* (Frankfurt: Suhrkamp, 1973), p. 340.
2. *Ibid.*
3. Joel Whitebook, "Saving the Subject: Modernity and the Problem of the Autonomous Individual," *Telos*, 50 (Winter 1981–82), 81–82.
4. Habermas, "A Reply to My Critics," in *Habermas: Critical Debates*, ed. by John B. Thompson and David Held (Cambridge, MA: MIT Press, 1982), pp. 166 and 262.
5. Habermas, "Walter Benjamin: Consciousness-Raising or Rescuing Critique," p. 158.
6. Habermas, "Introduction to the New Edition," *Theorie und Praxis* (Frankfurt: Suhrkamp, 1978), p. 25. English translation by John Viertel, *Theory and Practice* (Boston: Beacon Press, 1973).
7. J. Habermas, "Wahrheitstheorien," in *Wirklichkeit und Reflexion: Festschrift für Walter Schultz*, ed. by Helmut Fahrenbach (Pfullingen: Neske, 1973), p. 256. My translation, abbreviated in the following as *Wth*.
8. For a detailed discussion of this problem, cf. my article, "The Methodological Illusions of Modern Political Theory: The Case of Rawls and Habermas," in *Neue Hefte für Philosophie*, 21 (Spring 1982), 47–74.
9. Habermas, *Wth*, p. 252.
10. Rawls, *A Theory of Justice* (Cambridge, MA: Harvard University Press, 1972), pp. 24 and 513ff.
11. R. Döbert, J. Habermas, and G. Nunner-Winkler, "Introduction," *Entwicklung des Ichs* (Köln, 1977), p. 12.

12. Habermas, "Moral Development and Ego Identity," in *Communication and the Evolution of Society*, trans. by Thomas McCarthy (Boston: Beacon Press, 1979), p. 93.

13. Habermas, *Theory of Communicative Action*, Vol. I, trans. by Thomas McCarthy (Boston: Beacon Press, 1984), pp. 41ff. Abbreviated as *TCA* in the following.

14. J. Habermas, "A Reply to My Critics," in *Habermas: Critical Debates*, p. 262.

15. Habermas, *Moralbewusstsein und kommunikatives Handeln* (Frankfurt: Suhrkamp, 1983), and esp. the essay, "Diskursethik: Notizen zu einem Begründungsprogramm," pp. 53ff.

16. George Herbert Mead, *Selected Writings*, as quoted in J. Habermas, *Theorie des kommunikativen Handelns*, vol. 2 (Frankfurt: Suhrkamp, 1981), pp. 144–145.

17. *Ibid.*, p. 148.

18. *Ibid.*, p. 150.

19. Cf. Carol Gilligan, *In a Different Voice: Psychological Theory and Women's Development* (Cambridge, MA: Harvard University Press, 1982).

20. For a detailed account of the suppression of the "concrete other" in modern moral theory and a discussion of the relationship of these two perspectives, see my "The Generalized and the Concrete Other: The Kohlberg-Gilligan Controversy and Feminist Theory," forthcoming in *Praxis International*, special issue of Feminist Theory, S. Benhabib and Drucilla Cornell, guest editors.

21. "Moreover, evolution-theoretical statements on contemporary social formations have a direct practical relation insofar as they serve for the diagnosis of developmental problems. Thus the necessary restriction to retrospective explanation of the historical material is abandoned in favor of a *retrospective that is designed from action perspectives:* the diagnostician of our time takes the fictional standpoint of the evolution-theoretical explanation of a past lying in the future" ("History and Evolution," David J. Parent, trans. *Telos*, 44 (Spring 1979), 44). Only insofar as we can assume that empirical subjects in the present can discover themselves in this presentation of the past can we say that "theories of evolution and the explanation of epoch-making developmental leaps based on them can enter those 'discourses' in which competing identity-projections are 'subject to debate' " (*ibid*). My question is: whose identity? Of men or of women? Of Jews or of Gentiles? Of Westerners or of Africans? While it is not incumbent upon a social theorist engaged in explaining social evolution to necessarily offer an answer to these questions, it is nonetheless necessary to specify if these theoretical constructions succeed or fail when one attempts to mediate them with the formative history of specific groups. The problem will not go away by distinguishing between history and evolution, because the suspicion remains that this evolution is really the logic of the history of one group alone.

SELECTED BIBLIOGRAPHY

Theodor W. Adorno

Aesthetic Theory. Translated by Christian Lenhardt. London: Routledge & Kegan Paul, 1984.

Against Epistemology: A Metacritique. Translated by Willis Domingo. Cambridge, Mass.: MIT Press, 1982.

The Authoritarian Personality, with Else Frenkel-Brunswick, Daniel J. Levinson, and R. Nevitt Sanford. New York: Harper, 1950. Abridged version published by W. W. Norton, 1982.

Dialectic of Enlightenment, with Max Horkheimer. Translated by John Cumming. New York: Seabury, 1972.

In Search of Wagner. London: New Left Books, 1981.

Introduction to the Sociology of Music. New York: Seabury, 1976.

The Jargon of Authenticity. Translated by Knut Tarnowski and Frederic Will. Evanston, Ill.: Northwestern University Press, 1973.

Minima Moralia: Reflections from Damaged Life. London: New Left Books, 1974.

Negative Dialectics. New York: Seabury, 1973.

"On the Fetish Character of Music and the Regression of Listening," *The Essential Frankfurt School Reader*. Edited by Andrew Arato and Eike Gebhardt. New York: Continuum, 1982 (pp. 270–299).

Philosophy of Modern Music. Translated by Anne G. Mitchell and Wesley V. Blomster. New York: Seabury, 1973.

Prisms. Translated by Samuel and Shierry Weber. London: Neville Spearman, 1967.

"The Sociology of Knowledge and Its Consciousness," *The Essential Frankfurt School Reader*, pp. 452–465.

"Subject and Object," *The Essential Frankfurt School Reader*, pp. 497–511.

Jürgen Habermas

"The Analytical Theory of Science and Dialectics," *The Positivist Dispute in German Sociology*. Edited by T. W. Adorno et al. New York: Harper, 1976 (pp. 131–62).

"Civil Disobedience: Litmus Test for the Democratic Constitutional State." *Berkeley Journal of Sociology* 30 (1985): 96–116.

Communication and the Evolution of Society. Translated by T. McCarthy. Boston: Beacon, 1979.

"The Entwinement of Myth and Enlightenment." *New German Critique* 26 (1982): 13–30.

"Interpretative Social Science vs. Hermeneutics," *Social Science as Moral Inquiry*. Edited by N. Haan et al. New York: Columbia University Press, 1983 (pp. 251–67).

"Justice and Solidarity: On the Discussion Concerning 'Stage 6.' " *The Philosophical Forum* 21 (Fall/Winter 1989–1990): 32–52.

Knowledge and Human Interests. Translated by J. Shapiro. Boston: Beacon, 1971.

"Law and Morality: Two Lectures," *The Tanner Lectures On Human Values*. Edited by S. McMurrin. Salt Lake City: University of Utah, 1987 Vol. VIII (1987) (pp. 219–279).

Legitimation Crisis. Translated by T. McCarthy. Boston: Beacon, 1975.

Moral Consciousness and Communicative Action. Translated by Christian Lenhardt and Shierry Weber Nicholsen. Cambridge, Mass.: MIT Press, 1990.

"Neo-Conservative Cultural Critique in the United States and West Germany." *Telos* 56 (1983): 75–89.

"The New Obscurity: The Crisis of the Welfare State and the Exhaustion of Utopian Energies." *Philosophy and Social Criticism* 11 (1986): 1–17.

"On Social Identity." *Telos* 19 (1975): 91–103.

"On Systematically Distorted Communication." *Inquiry* 13 (1970): 205–218.

On the Logic of the Social Sciences. Translated by Shierry Weber Nicholsen and Jerry A. Stark. Cambridge, Mass.: MIT Press, 1989.

The Philosophical Discourse of Modernity: Twelve Lectures. Translated by F. Lawrence. Cambridge, Mass.: MIT Press, 1987.

Philosophical-Political Profiles. Translated by F. Lawrence. Cambridge, Mass.: MIT Press, 1984.

"A Positivistically Bisected Rationalism," *The Positivist Dispute in German Sociology*. Edited by T. W. Adorno et al. New York: Harper, 1976 (pp. 198–225).

"A Postscript to *Knowledge and Human Interests*." *Philosophy of the Social Sciences* 3 (1973): 157–189.

"Questions and Counter-Questions." *Praxis International* 4 (1984): 229–250.

"A Reply to My Critics," *Habermas: Critical Debates*. Edited by J. Thompson and D. Held. Cambridge, Mass.: MIT Press, 1982 (pp. 219–283).

"A Review of Gadamer's *Truth and Method*," in *Understanding and Social Inquiry*. Edited by F. Dallmayr and T. McCarthy. Notre Dame, Ind.: Notre Dame Press, 1981.

The Structural Transformation of the Public Sphere: An Inquiry into a Category of Bourgeois Society. Translated by T. Burger. Cambridge, Mass.: MIT Press, 1989.

The Theory of Communicative Action. Translated by T. McCarthy. 2 vols. Boston: Beacon, 1984, 1987.

Theory and Practice. Translated by J. Viertel. Boston: Beacon, 1973.

"Toward a Theory of Communicative Competence," *Patterns of Communicative Behavior*. Edited by H. Dreitzel. New York: Macmillan, 1970.

Toward a Rational Society: Student Protest, Science, and Politics. Translated by J. Shapiro. Boston: Beacon, 1970.

"Work and Weltanschauung." *Critical Inquiry* XV (Winter 1989), pp. 431–456.

Max Horkheimer

"The Authoritarian State," *The Essential Frankfurt School Reader*, pp. 95–117.

Critical Theory: Selected Essays. Translated by Matthew J. O'Connell et al. New York: Seabury, 1972.

Critique of Instrumental Reason. Translated by Matthew J. O'Connell et al. New York: Seabury, 1974.

Dawn and Decline. Translated by Michael Shaw. New York: Seabury, 1978.

Dialectic of Enlightenment, with T. W. Adorno. Translated by John Cumming. New York: Seabury, 1972.

Eclipse of Reason. New York: Seabury, 1974.

"The End of Reason," *The Essential Frankfurt School Reader*, pp. 26–48.

"The Lessons of Fascism," *Tensions That Cause Wars*. Edited by Hadley Cantril. Urbana: University of Illinois Press, 1950 (pp. 209–242).

"On the Concept of Freedom." *Diogenes* 53 (Spring 1964): 73–81.

"On the Problem of Truth," *The Essential Frankfurt School Reader*, pp. 407–443.

"The Relationship Between Psychology and Sociology in the Work of Wilhelm Dilthey." *Studies in Philosophy and Social Sciences* 8 (1940): 430–443.

"Schopenhauer Today," *The Critical Spirit: Essays in Honor of Herbert Marcuse*. Edited by Kurt H. Wolff and Barrington Moore, Jr. Boston: Beacon, 1967.

"Sociological Background of the Psychoanalytic Approach," *Antisemitism: A Social Disease*. Edited by Ernst Simmel. New York: International Universities Press, 1946.

Survey of the Social Sciences in Western Germany. Washington, D.C.: Library of Congress, Reference Department, European Affairs Division, 1952.

Herbert Marcuse

The Aesthetic Dimension: Toward a Critique of Marxist Aesthetics. Boston: Beacon, 1978.

"Contributions to a Phenomenology of Historical Materialism." *Telos* 4 (Fall 1969): 3–34.

Counterrevolution and Revolt. Boston: Beacon, 1972.

Eros and Civilization. Boston: Beacon, 1955.

"Eros and Culture." *The Cambridge Review* 1 (Spring 1955): 107–123.

An Essay on Liberation. Boston: Beacon, 1969.

"Ethics and Revolution," *Ethics and Society*. Edited by Richard T. DeGeorge. New York: Doubleday, 1966 (pp. 130–146).

"Existentialism: Remarks on Jean-Paul Sartre's *L'Être et le Néant*." *Journal of Philosophy and Phenomenological Research* 8 (March 1948): 309–336.

Five Lectures. Translated by Jeremy J. Shapiro and Shierry M. Weber. Boston: Beacon, 1970.

Hegel's Ontology. Translated by Seyla Benhabib. Cambridge, Mass.: MIT Press, 1987.

Negations: Essays in Critical Theory. Boston: Beacon, 1968.

"A Note on Dialectic," *The Essential Frankfurt School Reader*, pp. 444–451. Reprinted as the preface to the 1960 paperback edition of *Reason and Revolution*.

"On the Philosophical Foundation of the Concept of Labor in Economics." Translated by Douglas Kellner. *Telos* 16 (Summer 1973): 9–37.

"On Science and Phenomenology," in Vol. II of *Boston Studies in the Philosophy of Science*. Edited by Robert Cohen and Marx Wartofsky. New York: Humanities Press, 1965 (pp. 279–291).

One-Dimensional Man: Studies in the Ideology of Advanced Industrial Society. Boston: Beacon, 1964.

Reason and Revolution: Hegel and the Rise of Social Theory. Boston: Beacon, 1960.

"Re-examination of the Concept of Revolution." *New Left Review* 6 (July 1954): 515–525.

"Remarks on a Redefinition of Culture," *Science and Culture*. Edited by Gerald Holton. Boston: Beacon, 1967 (pp. 218–235).

"A Reply to Erich Fromm." *Dissent* 3 (Winter 1956): 79–81.

"Repressive Tolerance." *A Critique of Pure Tolerance* by H. Marcuse, Robert P. Wolff, and Barrington Moore, Jr. Boston: Beacon, 1965.

"Revolutionary Subject and Self-Government." *Praxis* (Zagreb) 1/2 (1969): 20–25.

"Some Social Implications on Freudian 'Revisionism.' " *Dissent* 2 (Summer 1955): 221–140. Reprinted as the epilogue to *Eros and Civilization*.

"Socialism in the Developed Countries." *International Socialist Journal* 2 (April 1965): 139–152.

"Socialist Humanism?" *Socialist Humanism*. Edited by Erich Fromm. New York: Doubleday, 1965 (pp. 96–106).

Soviet Marxism. New York: Vintage, 1961.

Studies in Critical Philosophy. Translated by Joris De Bres. London: New Left Books, 1972.

Works by Other Contributors

Benhabib, Seyla. *Critique, Norm, and Utopia: A Study of the Foundations of Critical Theory*. New York: Columbia University Press, 1986.

Foucault, Michel. *The Archaeology of Knowledge*. Translated by A. M. Sheridan Smith. New York: Pantheon, 1979.

―――. *Discipline and Punish: The Birth of the Prison*. Translated by A. Sheridan. New York: Pantheon, 1979.

―――. *The History of Human Sexuality*. Volume I: *An Introduction*. Translated by R. Hurley. New York: Pantheon, 1979.

―――. *Knowledge/Power: Selected Interviews and Other Writings by Michel Foucault, 1972–1977*. Edited by Colin Gordin. New York: Pantheon, 1980.

Fraser, Nancy. *Unruly Practices: Power, Discourse, and Gender in Contemporary Social Theory*. Minneapolis: University of Minnesota Press, 1989.

Lyotard, Jean-François. *The Postmodern Condition: A Report On Knowledge*. Translated by Geoff Bennington and Brian Massumi. Minneapolis: University of Minnesota Press, 1984.

Works of Related Interest

Alford, C. F. *Science and the Revenge of Nature: Marcuse and Habermas*. Gainesville: University of Florida Press, 1985.

Arato, Andrew, and Eike Gebhardt (eds.). *The Essential Frankfurt School Reader*. New York: Continuum, 1982.

Benhabib, Seyla, and Fred Dallmayr (eds.). *The Communicative Ethics Controversy*. Cambridge, Mass.: MIT Press, 1990.

Benhabib, Seyla and Drucilla Cornell (eds.). *Feminism as Critique: On the Politics of Gender*. Minneapolis: University of Minnesota Press, 1987.

Bernstein, Richard (ed.). *Habermas and Modernity*. Cambridge, Mass.: MIT Press, 1985.

Buck-Morss, Susan. *The Origin of Negative Dialectics: Theodor Adorno, Walter Benjamin, and the Frankfurt Institute*. New York: Harvester, 1977.

Connerton, Paul. *The Tragedy of Enlightenment: An Essay on the Frankfurt School*. Cambridge: Cambridge University Press, 1980.

Dews, Peter. *Logics of Disintegration: Poststructuralist Thought and the Claims of Critical Theory*. London: Verso, 1987.

————— (ed.). *Habermas: Autonomy and Solidarity: Interviews with Jürgen Habermas*. London: Verso, 1986.

Dubiel, Helmut. *Theory and Politics: Studies in the Development of Critical Theory*. Translated by Benjamin Gregg. Cambridge, Mass.: MIT Press, 1985.

Feenberg, Andrew. *Lukács, Marx, and the Sources of Critical Theory*. Totowa, N.J.: Rowman & Littlefield, 1981.

Geuss, Raymond. *The Idea of Critical Theory*. Cambridge: Cambridge University Press, 1981.

Görtzen, R., and F. van Gelder. "Jürgen Habermas: The Complete Oeuvre: A Bibliography of Primary Literature, Translations and Reviews," in *Human Studies* 2 (1979).

Gouldner, Alvin. *The Dialectic of Ideology and Technology*. New York: Seabury, 1976.

Held, David, and J. B. Thompson (eds.). *Habermas: Critical Debates*. Cambridge, Mass.: MIT Press, 1982.

―――. *Introduction to Critical Theory: Horkheimer to Habermas*. Berkeley: University of California Press, 1980.

Ingram, David. *Critical Theory and Philosophy*. New York: Paragon House, 1990.

―――. *Habermas and the Dialectic of Reason*. New Haven: Yale University Press, 1987.

Jay, Martin. *Adorno*. Cambridge, Mass.: Harvard University Press, 1986.

―――. *The Dialectical Imagination. A History of the Frankfurt School and the Institute for Social Research, 1923–1950*. Boston: Little, Brown, 1973.

Keat, John. *The Politics of Social Theory*. Chicago: University of Chicago Press, 1981.

Kellner, Douglas. *Herbert Marcuse and the Crisis of Marxism*. Berkeley: University of California Press, 1989.

Kortian, Garbis. *Metacritique*. Cambridge: Cambridge University Press, 1980.

McCarthy, Thomas. *The Critical Theory of Jürgen Habermas*. Cambridge, Mass.: MIT Press, 1979.

MacIntyre, Alasdair. *Marcuse: An Exposition and a Polemic*. New York: Viking, 1970.

O'Neill, John (ed.). *On Critical Theory*. New York: Seabury, 1976.

Roblin, Ronald (ed.). *The Aesthetics of the Critical Theorists: Studies on Benjamin, Adorno, Marcuse, and Habermas*. Lewiston, N.Y.: The Edwin Mellen Press, 1990.

Roderick, Rick. *Habermas and the Foundations of Critical Theory*. London: Macmillan, 1986.

Rose, Gillian. *The Melancholy Science: An Introduction to the Thought of Theodor W. Adorno*. New York: Columbia University Press, 1978.

Schoolman, Morton. *The Imaginary Witness: The Critical Theory of Herbert Marcuse*. New York: New York University Press, 1980.

Shroyer, Trent. *The Critique of Domination*. New York: Braziller, 1973.

Sensat, Julius. *Habermas and Marxism: An Appraisal*. Newbury Park, Calif.: Sage, 1979.

Tar, Zoltan. *The Frankfurt School: The Critical Theories of Max Horkheimer and Theodor W. Adorno*. New York: Schocken, 1977.

————, with Judith Marcus, co-editor. *Foundations of the Frankfurt School of Social Research*. London: Transaction Books, 1984.

Thompson, J. B. *Critical Hermeneutics: A Study in the Thought of Paul Ricoeur and Jürgen Habermas*. Cambridge: Cambridge University Press, 1981.

Wellmer, Albrecht. *Critical Theory of Society*. Translated by John Cumming. New York: Seabury, 1974.

White, Stephen K. *The Recent Work of Jürgen Habermas: Reason, Justice, and Modernity*. Cambridge: Cambridge University Press, 1988.